Royal Air Force
BOMBER COMM
LOSSES

Volume 8
Heavy Conversion Units & Miscellaneous Units
1939 - 1947

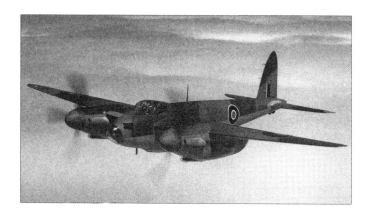

Royal Air Force
BOMBER COMMAND
LOSSES
Volume 8

Heavy Conversion Units
and Miscellaneous Units, 1939-1947

W R CHORLEY

**Royal Air Force Bomber Command Losses
Volume 8: Heavy Conversion Units
& Miscellaneous Units 1939–1947**

Copyright © 2003 W R Chorley
ISBN 1 85780 156 3

First published in 2003 by
Midland Publishing
4 Watling Drive, Hinckley, LE10 3EY, UK.
Tel: 01455 254490 Fax: 01455 254495
E-mail: midlandbooks@compuserve.com

Midland Publishing is an
imprint of Ian Allan Publishing Ltd.

Above: Three Short Stirling Mk.Is of
1651 CU, in 1942, with W7459 centre stage.
Photo: Kind permission of MG Rover Group,
Longbridge via John Reid, Stirling Acft
Photographic Research Library

On the Half-title page:
De Havilland Mosquito Mk.IV DZ594 on test.
Note the extended bomb bay.
Photo: Bruce Robertson collection

Printed in England by
Ian Allan Printing Ltd
Riverdene Business Park, Molesey Road
Hersham, Surrey, KT12 4RG.

The Royal Air Force Bomber Command
badge featured on the front cover
and title page is acknowledged as a
Crown copyright / RAF photograph.

Contents

Acknowledgements

Compilation of the eighth volume, in this tribute to the airmen and airwomen who gave their lives in the service of Bomber Command is complete. Similar to the previous volume, this book is concerned with the aircraft and their crews that came to grief during the training phase of their bomber service and, in many cases, details of the circumstances in which they crashed are not always forthcoming from unit records. I am, therefore, most appreciative of the help provided by Mike Hatch and the dedicated staff of the Air Historical Branch in guiding me towards records appropriate for me to trace the outcome of the hundreds of incidents dealt with in this volume.

I also acknowledge the help provided by The National Archives Public Record Office Kew, the Commonwealth War Graves Commission, and in particular to Peter Francis, the Royal Air Force Museum Hendon and the ever cheerful staff of the local studies research room at Salisbury library for allowing me to use the various fiche and microfilm readers. All, undoubtedly, have made a worthy contribution to the outcome of this book.

To Errol Martyn I am particularly indebted for allowing me free reign to use material from his invaluable reference books, commemorating the sacrifice made by New Zealand airmen from the earliest days of the First World War. Brian Mennell, whose history of Rufforth airfield, has saved me much time in my searches through records relating to 1663 Heavy Conversion Unit, while Bryce Gomersall and John Reid have been mines of information in respect of Stirling bombers lost from the training establishments.

Jock Whitehouse, too, an acknowledged expert in all matters pertaining to events at Stradishall, has given his help most freely.

Countless individuals have assisted me, either in respect of single incidents, or in verifying data from the huge selection of air reference books that have become available in recent years. Thus, my most grateful thanks is extended to Hedley Richards, Keith Whitfield, Eric Kaye, Brian Walker and Bill Baguley, the last two named being respected researchers in the Nottingham area. Robert Kirby and Harry Holmes have helped to answer questions regarding the Manchester and Lancaster respectively, while Don Bruce and Chris Pointon have, literally, at the drop of a hat, delved into matters mainly concerned with administration and awards.

Although not called upon so frequently, as with my earlier books, Oliver Clutton-Brock fully deserves his accolade in recognition for all things involving Allied air forces prisoners of war. Similarly, Rod Priddle and Bob Collis have helped me in respect of incidents in their regions of expertise, namely Wiltshire and East Anglia.

As always, in respect of Polish Air Force casualties, I am delighted to recognise the aid from Betty Clements and her many friends who continue to explore the rare fighting qualities synonymous with the Polish nation. Driven from their country by the events of 1939 and then, in so many cases, cruelly denied their return in 1945, the contribution made by the servicemen of this proud country is, indeed, legion.

It would be extremely remiss of me if I failed to mention the work of Hans de Haan of Almere in Holland. Over the years (and, I trust, for many yet to come) Hans has cast his eye over numerous pages of data and from his files has added much of key importance.

Others, whose contributions have been much appreciated, are acknowledged in the text.

Finally, I thank my family, and my publishers for their support throughout this ongoing series of books, proudly dedicated to those who flew with Bomber Command.

Bill Chorley,
Sixpenny Handley,
October 2003

Sources & Bibliography

Air Historical Branch:
Aircraft Accident Cards
Aircraft Movement Cards
Bomber Command Loss Cards

Australian War Museum:
Roll of Honour web site

Commonwealth War Graves Commission:
Cemetery & Memorial Registers, and web site

Gazettes-online:
Honours & Awards web site

The Canadian Virtual War Memorial

The National Archives Public Record Office Kew:
Allied Air Forces Prisoner of War File
Escape & Evasion Reports
Operations Record Books & Appendices

Air-Britain (Historians) Ltd:
Royal Air Force Aircraft K1000 to K9999, James J Halley
Royal Air Force Aircraft L1000 to N9999, James J Halley
Royal Air Force Aircraft P1000 to P9999, James J Halley
Royal Air Force Aircraft R1000 to R9999, James J Halley
Royal Air Force Aircraft T1000 to V9999, James J Halley
Royal Air Force Aircraft X1000 to Z9999, James J Halley
Royal Air Force Aircraft AA100 to AZ999, James J Halley
Royal Air Force Aircraft BA100 to BZ999, James J Halley
Royal Air Force Aircraft DA100 to DZ999, James J Halley
Royal Air Force Aircraft EA100 to EZ999, James J Halley
Royal Air Force Aircraft FA100 to FZ999, James J Halley
Royal Air Force Aircraft HA100 to HZ999, James J Halley
Royal Air Force Aircraft JA100 to JA999, James J Halley
Royal Air Force Aircraft KA100 to KZ999, James J Halley
Royal Air Force Aircraft LA100 to LZ999, James J Halley
Royal Air Force Aircraft MA100 to MZ999, James J Halley
Royal Air Force Aircraft NA100 to NZ999, James J Halley
Royal Air Force Aircraft PA100 to RZ999, James J Halley
Royal Air Force Aircraft SA100 to VZ999, James J Halley
Royal Air Force Flying Training and Support Units, Ray Sturtivant, John Hamlin and
    James J Halley
The Anson File, Ray Sturtivant
The Battle File, Sidney Shail
The Defiant File, Alec Brew
The Halifax File, R N Roberts
The Lancaster File, James J Halley
The Stirling File, Bryce B Gomersall
The Whitley File, R N Roberts

For Your Tomorrow, Volume One, Errol W Martyn, Volplane Press, 1998
For Your Tomorrow, Volume Two, Errol W Martyn, Volplane Press, 1999
Ksiega Lotnikow Polskich, Poleglych Zmarlych Izaginionych 1939-1946,
    Olgierd Cumft & Hubert Kazimierz Kujawa, Wydawnictwo Ministerstwa Obrony Narodowej, 1989
Royal Air Force Flying Training Losses in Yorkshire 1939-1947, David E Thompson, unpublished
They Shall Not Grow Old, A Book of Remembrance, Allison & Hayward, CATP Museum, 1992

Glossary of Terms

Adj	Adjutant	NJG	Nachtjagdgeschwader
AFC	Air Force Cross		
AFM	Air Force Medal	Oblt	Oberleutnant
ATA	Air Transport Auxiliary	OTU	Operational Training Unit
AC1	Aircraftman First Class		
AC2	Aircraftman Second Class	PAF	Polish Air Force
ACW2	Aircraftwoman Second Class	POW	Prisoner of War
		P/O	Pilot Officer
BQMS	Battery Quartermaster Sergeant		
		QGH	International Q-code Signal for
Capt	Captain		Controlled Descent through cloud
CBE	Commander of the Order of the		
	British Empire	RA	Royal Artillery
Cdt	Cadet	RAAF	Royal Australian Air Force
CFlt	Conversion Flight	RAF	Royal Air Force
CGM	Conspicuous Gallantry Medal	RCAF	Royal Canadian Air Force
Cmdt	Commandant	RCM	Radio Countermeasures
Cpl	Corporal	RN	Royal Navy
CSU	Constant Speed Unit	RNAF	Royal Norwegian Air Force
CU	Conversion Unit	RNZAF	Royal New Zealand Air Force
		RS	Radio School
DFC	Distinguished Flying Cross	RAF(VR)	Royal Air Force (Volunteer Reserve)
DFM	Distinguished Flying Medal		
DSO	Distinguished Service Order	SAAF	South African Air Force
		Sgt	Sergeant
FFAF	Free French Air Force	Sqn	Squadron
Flt	Flight	S/L	Squadron Leader
F/L	Flight Lieutenant	S/Lt	Sous-Lieutenant
F/O	Flying Officer		
F/S	Flight Sergeant	T/o	Take off
		T/S	Technical Sergeant
GCFlt	Group Communications Flight		
GTFlt	Group Training Flight	US	United States
GTTFlt	Group Target Towing Flight	USAAC	United States Army Air Corps
GSU	Ground Servicing Unit	USAAF	United States Army Air Force
G/C	Group Captain	U/t	Under training
HCFlt	Heavy Conversion Flight	WAAF	Women's Auxiliary Air Force
HCU	Heavy Conversion Unit	W/C	Wing Commander
HMS	His Majesty's Ship	W/O	Warrant Officer
Hptm	Hauptmann	WO1	Warrant Officer First Class
		WO2	Warrant Officer Second Class
Inj	Injured		
Int	Interned	+	Fatal casualty
LAC	Leading Aircraftman		
LACW	Leading Aircraftwoman		
LFS	Lancaster Finishing School		
LSgt	Lance Sergeant		
Lt	Lieutenant		
Lt-Col	Lieutenant Colonel		
MC	Military Cross		
MCU	Mosquito Conversion Unit		
MID	Mentioned in Despatches		
Misc	Miscellaneous		
MTU	Mosquito Training Unit		
MU	Maintenance Unit		

Bomber Command Aircraft

**A Representative Selection of the Aircraft Types used by the Heavy Conversion Units
and other Miscellaneous Units of Bomber Command, 1939-1947.**

The intention here is to provide a visual reminder of the majority of the different types of aircraft employed by
the Conversion Flights and the many other miscellaneous units controlled by Bomber Command during the
period covered by this volume, and at the same time offer some details about the aircraft concerned. All the types
featured will have suffered losses – the circumstances being described in the main chapters of the book.

This is a representative selection. Not every type of aircraft mentioned in the main body of text is featured; the
majority of those affected are the former civilian aircraft that were 'impressed' for military service and used in
very small numbers, often for communications duties.

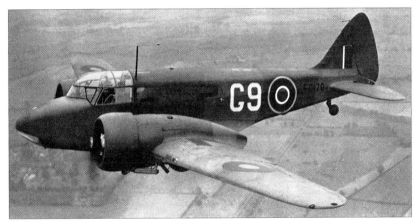

The Airspeed AS.10 Oxford served mainly in training roles during the war and until retirement in 1954. Over 8,500 were built.
ED170 of 6 PAFU is representative of the Armstrong Siddeley Cheetah-engined turretless Mk.IIs utilised by most of the Bomber
OTUs and several of the miscellaneous flights that came under Bomber Command control. P.H.T. Green collection

Once retired as a front-line bomber, the Armstrong Whitworth AW.38 Whitley served with distinction in Coastal Command, as a
glider tug for the airborne forces, with OTUs and numerous other units controlled by Bomber Command. Z6640 'Y', a Mk.V of
1484 Flight, shows signs of its former codes from its service with 78 Squadron. Z6640 survived the war. P.H.T. Green collection

The Avro 679 Manchester was a huge disappointment because of the unreliability of its Vulture engines, yet it served one OTU, ten Conversion Flights, five Heavy Conversion Units and ten Bomber Command front-line Squadrons. Re-born with new wings and four Merlin engines it found fame as the Lancaster. L7486, photographed in 1941, is a Mk.IA. P.H.T. Green collection

Arguably the best of the British 4-engined heavy bombers, at the height of its career the Avro 683 Lancaster was in service with 56 front-line squadrons. It also served with a multitude of miscellaneous training and support units. The Mk.IIs had Bristol Hercules engines but other versions were Merlin-powered, including this Mk.I, L7532 'C' of 1656 HCU. P.H.T. Green collection

Compromised as a day 'turret' fighter, the Merlin-powered Boulton Paul Defiant was redeployed in a variety of rôles. Of over 1,000 built, 290 had the turret removed and winch-gear installed, and as such were utilised by several Anti-Aircraft Co-operation Units, Air Armament Schools and Target-Towing Flights. This example, probably N1697, is a TT Mk.III. P.H.T. Green collection

Most of the RAF's Boeing Fortresses went to Coastal Command but the type also equipped two squadrons in Bomber Command's 100 Group. No.1699 Flight trained replacement crews for 214 Squadron, using Mks I, II and III. The Fortress II was equivalent to the USAAF B-17F Flying Fortress. FA706 above, was DBR in a ground collision in the Azores in 1944. Bruce Robertson collection

The Bristol 142 Blenheim light bomber outpaced the biplane fighters when introduced in 1937, but was superseded by the Mk.IV before war broke out. Some 200 acquired a ventral gun pack to become Mk.IF night-fighters. Four Bomber OTUs used the Mk.I, as did several other Flights. The above Mk.IF (K7159 ?) with AI Mk.III radar, served with 54 OTU. Bruce Robertson collection

The Bristol 156 Beaufighter, two-seat, four cannon long range fighter was a marked improvement on the Blenheim. Over 5,800 examples of this versatile workhorse were produced, spanning 10 major variants, and many more rôles. Some early marks had Merlin engines, most others had Bristol Hercules' as on this representative example, Mk.IF X7540. Bruce Robertson collection

Early production Consolidated Liberator Mk.Is reaching the UK went to Coastal Command, their very long range helping close 'the gap' in the middle of the Atlantic: AM917 served with 120 Squadron. The conversion of crews for Liberators for the Middle East Squadrons was entrusted to 1653 Conversion Unit, in 8 Group, using Mk.IIs, during 1942. Bruce Robertson collection

The RAF took over delivery of 140 Curtiss (P-40A) Tomahawk Mk.Is that had originally been ordered by France. These (and the later Mk.IIAs and 'Bs) served with front-line units at home and the Middle East, often before finding other employment. AH769 served with 268 Squadron then with 1686 Flight, one of six Bomber (Defence) Training units. Bruce Robertson collection

A small batch of Douglas Boston Mk.Is were used as trainers, the Mk.IIs were the night-fighter / night-intruder 'Havoc' variant, and the Boston (DB-7B) IIIs were light day bombers that replaced 2 Group's Blenheim IVs. The Mk.IIIs had 1,600hp Double Cyclone engines rather than the Mk.I/II's Twin Wasps. Boston III W8254 served with 1422 Flight. Bruce Robertson collection

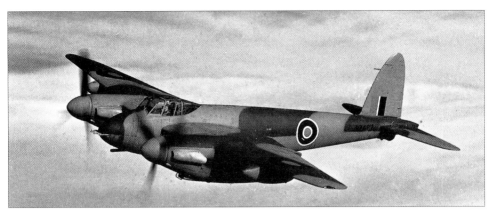

The superb de Havilland DH.98 Mosquito served the RAF as a PR platform, bomber, fighter and trainer. No less than ten variants were employed by units featured in this volume. The FB.VI (2,305 built) was a day and night fighter-bomber/intruder armed with four cannon, four machine-guns and bombs. PZ467 reportedly went to the French AF post-war. Bruce Robertson collection

The de Havilland Mosquito NF.XIX (280 built) was the fifth night-fighter variant to achieve production status. It was similar to the NF.XIII but with Merlin 25 engines and American SCR 720 (AI Mk.X) radar in a 'bull nose' fairing. The final night-fighter variant to see war service was the NF.30. After RAF use NF.XIX MM652 was sold to Sweden in 1948. Bruce Robertson collection

The Fairey Battle three-seat light bomber, obsolescent at the start of WWII, remained in front-line service until September 1940. It was then employed in a variety of secondary roles including training and target-towing Around 800 were shipped to Canada. K7558 was the very first production Mk.I and was involved in various tests until SoC in Sep 1940. Bruce Robertson collection

The Handley Page HP.57 Halifax was another fine British 4-engined front-line heavy bomber. It was also utilised by Bomber Command Conversion Flights and Heavy Conversion Units – the Mks I, II and V being Merlin-powered, the Mk.III having Hercules engines. The example illustrated is HR916, a Mk.II Series IA that served with 1659 and 1669 HCUs.   P.H.T. Green collection

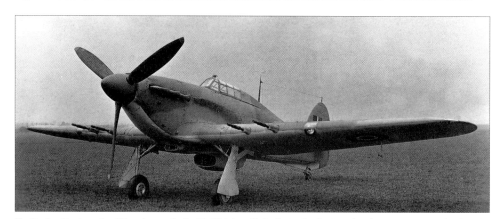

The Hawker Hurricane is still best known for its Mk.I fighting rôle in the Battle of Britain, but the cannon-equipped and Merlin XX powered Mk.II was a potent tank-buster. The Mk.IIC (here) and 'IID also served in several of Bomber Command's Heavy Conversion Units and Bomber (Defence) Training Flights. Hurricane production totalled over 10,000.   Bruce Robertson collection

The first Lockheed Hudsons were arriving for Coastal Command as war broke out. Later, some were delivered direct by air from Newfoundland. Rôles included anti-submarine and general reconnaissance, communications, transport, delivery of agents into France, and training (Ferry Training Flights etc). The Hudson Mk.III above is US No.41-23282.   Bruce Robertson collection

The Miles M.25 Martinet was designed for target towing, and powered by a Bristol Mercury engine. It served with Air Gunnery Schools and Anti-Aircraft Co-operation Units, and was employed by the Bomber OTUs and some of the Bombing Gunnery Flights. HN861, the first production Martinet Mk.I, was probably on test at A&AEE when this image was recorded. P.H.T. Green collection

The Short S.29 Stirling was the first of the RAF's Second World War 4-engined heavy bombers. Mk.I W7463 completed 11 ops with first-line units and after an undercarriage collapse went to 1657 HCU, in whose markings it is seen here. It ended its days following a belly-landing at Woodbridge, 5th July 1944. Roy Spear via John Reid (Stirling Aircraft Photographic Research Library)

The Short Stirling Mk.III had a new dorsal gun turret and the more powerful Bristol Hercules XVI engines. Mk.III EF465 flew a total of 27 operational sorties with 75 and 513 Squadrons before being allocated for training duties with 1651 HCU (seen here in that unit's markings) and 1657 HCU, until SoC in 1945. Fred Revell via John Reid (Stirling Aircraft Photographic Research Library)

This representative photograph of a Supermarine Spitfire shows a Mk.VB wearing the 'LO' code combination and lion insignia of 602 Squadron. Allegedly BM124, it also bears an inscription confirming that it was the gift of Queen Salote and the people of Tonga to Britain. Spitfire VBs and XVIs were issued to the Bomber Defence Training Flights.   Bruce Robertson collection

The Vickers Wellington was the standard night-bomber until the 4-engined 'heavies' came into service, after which they played an important part in the training role, being allocated to the majority of the Bomber OTUs as well as many of the miscellaneous units that came under the control of Bomber Command. This Mk.X is coded 'J' of 40 Squadron.   P.H.T. Green collection

The Westland Lysander is well known for its Army Co-operation work and SOE flights into occupied Europe, but it also served with distinction on Air Rescue duties and as a target tug. All the Bomber Command OTUs and Target Towing Flights appear to have had an allocation of Lysanders of various Mks for target towing and/or general support duties.   P.H.T. Green collection

Introduction

Before commencing the formal introduction to this volume, the eighth in the series, it is necessary for me to explain the criteria that justifies an entry in these books. It is, simply, an aircraft that to the best of my knowledge never flew beyond the date shown in the key line of the summary. I am, however, aware of one anomaly, namely a 617 Squadron Lancaster that having come to grief in Soviet Russia during September 1944 (see Bomber Command Losses, Volume 5, page 416) was repaired and saw service with the Soviet Air Force.

Ever since the publication of the first volume, over a decade ago, I have received many letters from readers asking why "their crash" has been omitted and, of course, the reply is, invariably, that "their aircraft" was repaired and continued to fly. As to why some aircraft were repaired, after seemingly sustaining major damage, and others with equal or lesser damage were written off, I am not qualified to give a definitive answer (frequently, little more than the collapse of the undercarriage unit could lead to a bomber being consigned to scrap or relegated for ground instructional duties).

Conversely, there are numerous examples of aircraft that were salvaged after sustaining major damage and taken for repairs in works, a procedure that, on occasions, took several months to complete.

A second observation, too, is worth noting (particularly in respect of the conversion flights and heavy conversion units) and this is to refute the misconceptions oft reported over the years that aircraft assigned to the training units were "clapped out" and, thus, were no longer fit for squadron use. Such allegations are very far from the truth for although aircraft were released into the training loop, the hours recorded on their airframes were, in many cases, surprisingly low. Furthermore, the number of operational sorties flown by the initial issues of four-engined types, prior to their being absorbed in the burgeoning conversion units, can often be measured in single figures and, certainly, no where near the number of operational flights implied in some reports.

Thus, the training formations were, in the main, equipped with aircraft that by wartime standards of servicing and build quality, reasonably sound.

Turning now to the formal introduction to this volume, its compilation has not been without its fair share of problems. Throughout the better part of 1942, (squadron) con-version flights and conversion units ran in parallel, though both formations were performing the same function, that being the conversion of crews from twin-engined types to the four-engined Halifaxes, Stirlings and Lancasters, then entering squadron service in ever increasing numbers. The majority of conversion flights came under the aegis of the parent squadron, though, as usual, there were exceptions to the rule. For example, Nos. 26 Conversion Flight and 28 Conversion Flight bore unit designators that came within the block of numbers reserved for Operational Training Units, while Nos. 10 Conversion Flight and 15 Conversion Flight, et al, fit well within the parentage of their respective squadrons. Confusion also arises when conversion flights were operating alongside conversion units, a situation which led to the "borrowing" of aircraft between units (this, too, was often the case between a conversion flight and its parent squadron). Where such matters are relevant to this book, I have drawn attention to the fact in the first line of summary.

As many readers of this series are aware, the movement of aircraft between units is recorded on Form Air Ministry 78. From a study of these forms, I can say that it is not unusual for an aircraft to be shown as written off under the authority of one unit, while on the reverse of the form a different formation is appended as the "striking off charge" authority. However, when referring to the bases for the two units in question, as often as not it will be realised that both were operating from the same airfield.

Furthermore, I have come across several examples of aircraft being identified in serial records as being written off from a conversion flight, long after the merging of the flight with a heavy conversion unit (the term "heavy" came into use with effect from 7 October 1942). In the majority of cases, the aircraft had been retained by the parent squadron, but this detail had not been noted on the movement form.

For clarity of reporting, the book is laid out in sections, each section being prefaced by a summary of explanation. Thus, the first part deals with the conversion flights and is followed by the conversion units, and so forth. Losses within each section appear in chronological order of date, unit, type, serial and, where known, the unit's code combination and the aircraft's letter.

In the majority of cases the duty will be described as "training" but from time to time, I will be able to clarify this further in the opening line of the summary.

In previous volumes, I have attempted to provide a reasonably accurate description of the crew functions and their order within the framework of names. With the conversion units and flights, this becomes extremely difficult for, all too frequently, training flights were undertaken with a duplication of trades. "Screened" instructors would often take more than one member of their respective trade on a training sortie and crew complements of ten (and sometimes more) were quite common. Therefore, it is not safe to assume the logical layout of trades, as shown in previous volumes (occasionally, the summary will give some clue as to the likely make up of a crew; for example, in a gunnery detail, where I have been able to identify the instructor, the names following his will be those of trainee air gunners).

In most cases, the location shown for a crash has been taken from official records and, therefore, the spelling may not always be accurate (particularly in respect of farm names). By consulting Ordnance Survey maps, I have been able to confirm, or amend, some of the data indicated and, usually, I have backed this up with a simple statement showing the distance and direction from a well known town. Where possible, too, I have included remarks pertaining to the cause of the accident, or the events that led up to the final crash.

Similar to the seventh volume, I have had to rely heavily on unit records and, from an historians perspective, these documents are either excellent or abysmal. Those that fall into the last category (and there are many) disregard completely the loss of an aircraft and its crew or merely confine their remarks to a single line entry.

Fortunately, there are other avenues that enable me to identify the aircraft in question and, thus, I am eternally grateful to James J Halley who, over close on three decades, has devoted much time and energy to a meticulous inspection of the Form AM 78 and, through the medium of Air-Britain (Historians), published his work in the aircraft serial registers. Without these registers to hand, it is unlikely that any of the books in this series would have seen the light of day.

Other sources of prime importance are the accident record cards (these allow me to, at least, discover the name of the pilot), the Commonwealth War Graves Commission cemetery registers and associated web site.

Similarly, the links with the Australian War Museum web site and The Canadian Virtual War Memorial, the latter site having been built and maintained by Veterans Affairs Canada, have proven most useful. Also, in respect of casualties suffered by the Royal Canadian Air Force, I find myself turning to Les Allison's and Harry Hayward's weighty tome, They Shall Grow Not Old, A Book of Remembrance dedicated to the thousands of Canadian airmen who lost their lives during near on six long years of war.

In similar vein, Errol W Martyn has produced a magnificent tribute to New Zealand's airmen who have perished in the pursuit and maintenance of freedom from 1915 to the turn of the Millennium. Also remembered are the warriors of the Polish Air Force who, having escaped the tyrannies of one aggressor saw, to their abhorrence, the recognition by the Allies of an equally hateful regime in the immediate aftermath of the war. For many who had survived there was never to be a triumphal return to the land of their birth, now (1945) in the iron grip of a Communist dictator. Commemorating their sacrifice is a fulsome work by Olgierd Cumft and Hubert Kazimierz Kujawa. Titled, Ksiega Lotnikow Polskich, Poleglych Zmarlych Izaginionych 1939 - 1946, I have referred to it on countless occasions and I am, indeed, grateful to Graham Warrener for his continued indulgence in permitting me its use.

On a lesser scale, but still nonetheless, important, I have drawn upon many privately published tributes and, where appropriate, I have given these excellent booklets, and their authors, due recognition.

Operational losses from the units about to be described were, in comparison to the OTUs featured in Volume 7, relatively few. Where such losses did occur, and airmen were taken into captivity, I have drawn upon AIR20/2336 (the Allied Air Forces Prisoner of War File) as well as taking council on such matters from an acknowledged expert, namely Oliver Clutton-Brock.

Appropriately, as this volume will be the last to report on losses of aircraft (the next will be a Bomber Command Roll of Honour and index to the series) some reflections on the purpose behind the series.

First, and foremost, I have attempted to set out a record of the awful attrition that quickly became the cross that Bomber Command was obliged to bear and to honour those who fell in their thousands. From the first mind numbing days of September 1939 and the so called "Phoney War" that followed, through the grim and unrewarding period between the fall of France and the arrival at High Wycombe of Sir Arthur Harris, on through the expansionist years of 1942 and 1943, when the terrible realisation of what lay ahead for Germany and her people entered the minds of the Axis camp, on through the winter of 1943-1944 when the Battle of Berlin resulted in the most horrendous casualties, onto and beyond the triumph of D-Day when the bombing campaign reached a pinnacle of awesome efficiency, this has been "their story" and most rightly so.

Admittedly, I have only been able to bring an all too brief summary of each loss to the readers attention, plus a general account of how Bomber Command reacted to the changing fortunes of war through the medium of a chapter lead-in. I trust, however, that these books will be viewed by generations to come of the debt, and honour, that we still owe to those all too young men of the 1930s and '40s who answered the clarion call for help when it was most sorely needed. It was their immediate and unselfish response that, ultimately, crushed the evil designs of one Adolf Hitler and his henchmen and restored a semblance of freedom to the greater part of a war ravaged western Europe.

Finally, it had been my intention (and, indeed, I so indicated as such on page 361 of Volume 7) to carry out a comprehensive review of all the losses in the series.

This, however, has had to be carried over to the next volume. Briefly, during a most exhaustive study of documents, principally at the Air Historical Branch, I have found evidence of further losses and, thus, an investigation of these is necessary before presenting a final table.

Section 1

Squadron Conversion Flights & Heavy Conversion Flights

As outlined in the introduction, this first section deals with the losses sustained by the conversion flights which, in the main, were parented by their respective squadrons. In total, thirty-two flights were formed (on paper at least), but not all received aircraft before being disbanded or merged with other formations. Also included within this section is a sub-section that reports on the seven Lancasters lost from the heavy conversion flights of which two are featured, namely 1678 Heavy Conversion Flight and 1679 Heavy Conversion Flight.

The purpose of a conversion flight was to convert crews from the twin-engined aircraft currently being used by their squadron, to the appropriate four-engined type arriving as their replacement.

In the main, it seems that squadron crews experienced few problems in the transition from flying medium bombers to becoming used to the complexities of operating "heavies", and, generally speaking, flying accidents were kept to an acceptable level. Thirty-two aircraft are summarised, of which five were lost under operational circumstances.

17 Dec	26 CFlt	Stirling I W7453 –G	Transit
1941	Sgt P J Lamason RNZAF		

T/o Waterbeach. Wrecked 1515 in a wheels up landing on the airfield, after Sgt Lamason RNZAF had reported that the undercarriage had jammed. Subsequently commissioned, he ended the war in captivity and when released had risen to the rank of squadron leader. Prior to becoming a prisoner, he had gained an immediate DFC (Gazetted 15 May 1942) for displaying great coolness during operations to Plzen on 25-26 April 1942; at the time he was flying with 218 Squadron and had completed over twenty operational sorties.

Note. In the aftermath of this accident, the Senior Engineering Officer submitted his findings as follows; "failed to go down (undercarriage) electrically due to dogs of magnetic clutch riding on dogs of gearbox clutch body, causing their edges to become worn. Commutators of motor was (sic) disintegrated by centrifugal force due to excessive speed of armature - caused by several movements of pilot operating lever with master switch ON. Failure to lower on hand device due to flight engineer (unnamed) turning on main undercarriage lowering before properly disengaging motor gears, sheering coupling pin connecting handle with gearbox." At the time of the incident, Sgt Lamason RNZAF had flown a total of 250 hours solo, of which five had been at the controls of Stirling bombers. Bryce Gomersall who, over many years has devoted much time to the investigation of Stirling operations, notes that eight days previous, Sgt W E Lucas (see next summary) was taxying W7453 when the tailplane damaged a car, parked on the side of the peritrack.

18 Dec	26 CFlt	Stirling I N6100 –A	Training
1941	Sgt W E Lucas		

T/o Waterbeach. Swung, while avoiding another aircraft, after landing at 1545. Due to the excessive thrust placed upon the unit, the undercarriage gave way. At this stage in his training, Sgt Lucas had flown the Stirling for ten hours, solo. Bryce Gomersall writes, "A Sgt Lucas was among the first three pilots to be trained on 15 Conversion Flight in January 1942, and he was posted back to the Operational Flights of 15 Squadron on 25 February 1942. In the squadron Operations Records Book, he is shown as "Sgt Lucas" and after twenty-four operations he was posted to 218 Conversion Flight on 1 August 1942 as P/O W E Lucas".

Note. 26 Conversion Flight was formed at Waterbeach on 5 October 1941, with eight Stirlings as its initial equipment and with its personnel drawn from 7 Squadron, based at Oakington. On 2 January 1942, the Flight was disbanded on the formation, at Waterbeach, of 1651 Conversion Unit. 15 Conversion Flight, mentioned in the summary, formed at Wyton on 21 January 1942, but operated from Alconbury until transferring to Waterbeach in early May 1942.

22 Dec	28 CFlt	Halifax I	L9522		Transit
1941	F/L R F Owen DFC		+	T/o 1025 Leconfield in extremely adverse	
	P/O R P W Barker RNZAF		+	weather, intending to fly to the Handley Page	
	P/O W S Beattie RNZAF		+	facility at Radlett. At approximately 1110,	
	Sgt L Merrifield		+	eyewitnesses on the ground saw the Halifax	
	F/O E A F Gibb DFM		+	flying through mist, close to the Leicestershire	
	Sgt S R Mayston DFM		+	and Lincolnshire border, and in the general area	
	Sgt J A Denning		+	of Barkston Woods. Not long afterwards, the	
	Cpl J A Hancock		+	bomber smashed into a ridge, known as Terrace	

Hills, close to the village of Knipton, some
ten miles or so NE of Melton Mowbray. F/L Owen, whose award was gained with
35 Squadron and Gazetted on 25 July 1941, was cremated at Golders Green. P/O
Barker RNZAF was taken to Grantham Cemetery (Errol Martyn reports that his
brother, who had joined the RAF, had been killed earlier in the year while
flying Hampdens with 83 Squadron (see Bomber Command Losses, Volume 2, page 21)
and that along with P/O Beattie RNZAF, he had been attached from 10 Squadron).
P/O Beattie's funeral was privately arranged, for he is buried in St. Mary
Church (St. Mary) churchyard, Torquay. Sgt Merrifield (his service number
indicates he was called up in July 1939 under the terms of the RAF(VR) Military
Training Act) rests at Horwich (Ridgmont) Cemetery; F/O Gibb lies in Edinburgh
(Warriston) Cemetery (his father was a Justice of the Peace) and like his
skipper he had served with 35 Squadron, his DFM having been published on
23 September 1941. Sgt Mayston was cremated at Croydon (Mitcham Road); he,
too, had flown with 35 Squadron and details of his award was promulgated on
the day following his untimely death. Both Sgt Denning and Cpl Hancock are
interred in Grantham Cemetery. During the enquiry into the tragedy, it emerged
that authorisation for the flight had been granted by 4 Group headquarters.
However, the Air Officer Commanding 4 Group, Air Vice-Marshal C R Carr, decreed
that, in future, the Station Commander at Marston Moor was best placed to make
such authorisations.

Note. This was the only flying accident, of note, reported from 28 Conversion
Flight, which had formed, with an establishment of eight Halifaxes, at Linton-
on-Ouse on 29 August 1941. On 2 January 1942, having moved across to Marston
Moor three days previous, the Flight disbanded upon the formation of 1652
Conversion Unit.

24 Dec	26 CFlt	Stirling I	N6066		Training
1941	Sgt V C Akes RAAF		inj	T/o Waterbeach for local flying, in the course	
	P/O H B Rowland RAAF		+	of which the Stirling flew into a tree and	
	Sgt E R Bowman		inj	crashed 1445 at West End Farm near Kempston	
	Sgt G H Savoy		+	on the SW fringes of Bedford. The injured, many	
	Sgt R J Clark		inj	of them dangerously so, were rushed to Bedford	
	Sgt E C Welsh		+	County Hospital where Sgt Akes RAAF, Sgt Bowman	
	Cpl S H Atkinson		inj	and Sgt Clark died. Those who were killed on	
	Cpl J W Dawson		inj	impact were removed to Cranfield Infirmary.	
	Cpl J Mainwaring		inj	Sgt Akes RAAF and Sgt Welsh (he hailed from	

Kingwilliamstown in the Cape Province) are
buried in Wyton (St. Margaret and All Saints) Churchyard, Houghton and Wyton.
P/O Rowland RAAF, a Queenslander like his skipper, was taken to Sussex and laid
to rest in Slinfold (St. Peter) Churchyard, his being the sole service burial
here from the Second World War, Sgt Bowman lies in Northern Ireland at Bangor
Cemetery. His brother, F/O Geoffrey Alexander Bowman was destined to be posted
missing in action while serving with 53 Squadron (Liberators) at St. Eval on 21
May 1944; he is commemorated on panel 204 of the Runnymede Memorial. Sgt Savoy
of Combust, Suffolk, is buried in Waterbeach Cemetery, while Sgt Clark's grave
is in Portland (St. George) Churchyard. Tragically, the three corporals who
survived (all were under training flight engineers) lost their lives in 1942,
whilst engaged on bombing operations and their names are perpetuated on the
Runnymede Memorial (see Bomber Command Losses, Volume 3, pages 218, 231 and
146 respectively). Again, Bryce Gomersall adds a postscript; "Cambridge
Observer Corps sent two messages to Waterbeach on Christmas Day. From Cpl
Mainwaring; 1. Request Sgt Dawson to hold my mail as I expect to be back
before going to Bristol and from Cpl Dawson; 2. Airmen in my room, Block 42,
may use my Christmas fare."

Note. This was the last serious flying accident sustained by the Flight
ahead of disbandment in early January 1942.

| 11 Feb | 149 CFlt | Stirling I | W7457 | | Training |
| 1942 | F/S H C Kimpton RNZAF | | | | T/o Lakenheath to practice circuits and landings. |

Landed 1530, with the undercarriage unlocked, despite a "green light" indicating the gear had lowered satisfactorily. Unbeknown to the crew, the undercarriage had failed to retract from the previous take off and, thus, they were mislead into believing the situation was normal. A broken knee joint on the starboard oleo was the primary cause of their misfortune.

24 Mar	97 CFlt	Lancaster I	L7531		Air Test
1942	S/L T H Boylan DFC				T/o 1445 Coningsby but the leading edge of the
	AC2 D O Jenkins		inj		port wing lifted, due to incorrect maintenance,

and became detached. At high speed, the bomber collided with a crane and crashed near the station's bomb dump. Amazingly, S/L Boylan was unscathed and AC2 Jenkins suffered only a slight head injury. This alarming incident is remarked upon in W/C Guy Gibson's wartime classic, "Enemy Coast Ahead" (Michael Joseph Limited, 1946), while an oblique reference appears on page 18 of Mike Garbett and Brian Goulding's, "Lancaster At War 2" (Ian Allan, 1979). Earlier in the war, S/L Boylan had flown Hampdens with 144 Squadron, gaining a Distinguished Flying Cross (Gazetted 13 September 1940).

16 Apr	35 CFlt	Halifax II	R9425		Training
1942	S/L E G Franklin DFC				T/o Linton-on-Ouse to practice three-engined
	P/O H R Astbury				overshoots. At around 1700, the Halifax climbed

away and commenced a circuit at 200 feet, only for the undercarriage and flaps failing to retract. Due to the low forward speed of the aircraft, S/L Franklin was unable to restart the fourth engine and, thus, he forced-landed, just off the airfield, at Newton-on-Ouse. It was subsequently recommended that the circuit height for all future exercises of this nature should be a minimum of 400 feet so that more time would be available to meet any such similar emergency. On 24 August 1941, the London Gazette had published details of S/L Franklin's award, gained in the service of 35 Squadron.

18 Apr	15 CFlt	Stirling I	N6090 LS-Z		Training
1942	F/S I L Charbonneau RCAF				T/o Alconbury for local flying practice. Upon
	Sgt W C Brodie				landing at 1350, the Stirling swung so violently

that the undercarriage collapsed. With a mere eighteen hours solo flying on type, the mishap was attributed to the pilot's inexperience. Sadly, within a month of this incident, F/S Charbonneau RCAF and his crew (including Sgt Brodie) were killed during operations to Warnemünde (see Bomber Command Losses, Volume 3, page 90). Bryce Gomersall reports in his revised edition of The Stirling File (Air-Britain Historians, 1987) that the Stirling, here summarised, had flown six operational sorties with 7 Squadron carrying the code combination MG-Y.

24 Apr	214 CFlt	Stirling I	N3646 BU-R		Training
1942	Sgt W W G Smith				T/o 1555 Waterbeach for local flying but as
	Sgt P Gray				the bomber attained flying speed, an engine
	Sgt H A Ward				cut. With its throttles fully open, the
	Sgt G K H Newman				Stirling swung rapidly to starboard and ran
	Sgt H F Farley				up against a sandbagged gun pit before hitting
	Sgt G N James				the Watch Office building. As the crew made
	P/O M Russell				their exit, the wreckage caught fire and it

was not until 1857 that the flames were finally extinguished. It is believed the crew were returned immediately to their parent Squadron at Stradishall (still operating Wellingtons) for Sgt Newman, sadly, was killed on operations a mere four days later (see Bomber Command Losses, Volume 3, page 83). Bryce Gomersall adds that the other escapees from the crash proceeded, on 30 April, to 161 Squadron. On 21-22 October 1942, Sgt (by then commissioned and awarded a DFC) Smith was killed when his Whitley crashed on return to Tempsford (see the same volume, page 244). Sgt Ward and Sgt Farley were also on board, but both escaped with their lives.

| 7 May | 35 CFLt | Halifax I | L9568 | | Ground |
| 1942 | | | | | At 0230 whilst parked 300 degrees off the |

flare path, secured and marked with red lights, damaged beyond repair after being struck by Halifax II W1051 TL-C (Sgt H A Brown) which was attempting to land, following operations to Stuttgart (see Bomber Command Losses, Volume 3, page 89).

8 May	78 CFlt	Halifax I	L9583	Training

8 May
1942
78 CFlt   Halifax I   L9583   Training
P/O C Mitchener
Sgt Stevens

T/o Croft in continuance of conversion training and first solo on type. At around midday, the Halifax was sighted on approach, though rather to the left of the runway´s centre line. Then, as it neared the threshold, right rudder was applied as if in an attempt to straighten out, but the bomber drifted and on landing a violent swing developed, leading to a total collapse of the undercarriage and fracture of the aircraft´s back.

11 May
1942
102 CFlt   Halifax II   V9982   Training
S/L P B Robinson DFC
F/S C C Harris RCAF

T/o 1420 Dalton for an exercise described on the accident form as, "one side flying, port motors feathered". At approximately 1630, the instructor decided to unfeather the engines as the weather had become marginal and his pupil was having difficulty in maintaining control. However, neither engine picked up and a forced-landing took place at Pickhill, 5 miles WNW of Thirsk, Yorkshire. No one was hurt, but within six months of the incident, both airmen had been lost from bombing operations. F/S Harris RCAF failed to return from the "1,000 plan" attack on Bremen in the June, while his instructor, having been posted to East Moor to command B Flight of 158 Squadron, was lost on 10-11 September 1942, while raiding Düsseldorf (see Bomber Command Losses, Volume 3, pages 136 and 212 respectively). The latter, who rests in Belgium at Oostende New Communal Cemetery, gained his award with 78 Squadron, details being published on 7 March 1941.

16 May
1942
78 CFlt   Halifax II   L9621   Training
F/S W E Lunan RCAF
Sgt W Dench

T/o Croft for night circuits and landings. Following five unsuccessful attempts by Sgt Dench to effect a landing, F/S Lunan RCAF assumed control. Touching down at around 0200, the Halifax veered sharply to starboard, whereupon the undercarriage gave way. F/S Lunan RCAF lost his life during operations to Mainz in August 1942 (see Bomber Command Losses, Volume 3, page 178).

30-31 May
1942
49 CFlt   Manchester I   L7429   Op: Köln
P/O J P Carter +
F/S D Block +
Sgt G C Haynes +
Sgt J C Ramsey +
Sgt L J Yeates +
Sgt A G Welch RAAF +
Sgt M S Ash +

T/o 2300 Scampton. Lost without trace. All are commemorated on the Runnymede Memorial.

21 Jun
1942
149 CFlt   Stirling I   N6122 OJ-Y East India 2   Training
S/L R I Alexander
P/O P K W Patrick

T/o 1550 Lakenheath. Landed 1720 but ran towards some rough ground and when the brakes were applied, the Stirling swung and lost its undercarriage. It is believed both officers survived the war, S/L Alexander gaining a DFC while serving with 101 Squadron (Gazetted 13 October 1944). A similar honour was awarded to P/O Patrick, who went on to fly twenty-seven sorties with 149 Squadron. He was serving as an instructor with 1651 HCU when details were promulgated in the London Gazette on 9 February 1943.

11 Jul
1942
102 CFlt   Halifax II   R9419   Training
F/O W J J Welch
Sgt R Mathews inj
Sgt J G Castle RCAF inj
Sgt J Burdon
AC2 Johnson

T/o Topcliffe to practice three-engined over-shoots. With Sgt Mathews at the controls, the bomber touched down at 1620 but ballooned back into the air. F/O Welch immediately took over and opened the throttles in an attempt to go round again. He also tried to restart the fourth engine, but without sufficient airspeed to rotate the airscrew, his efforts were unsuccessful. With the speed decaying, he decided to forced-land, heading for a nearby race course, but the Halifax´s tail clipped a roof top and seconds later the bomber crashed, heavily, onto a road. The two injured airmen were taken to Northallerton Hospital; Sgt Mathews was not too badly hurt but Sgt Castle RCAF had sustained quite severe head injuries. Both, however, recovered, only to fall in action as the war progressed (see Bomber Command Losses, Volumes 3 and 4, pages 231 and 282 respectively). The Halifax, here summarised, had accumulated 56.15 flying hours.

12 Jul 1942	**78 CFlt**	**Halifax II**	**L9624**	**Training**

P/O P Bunclark DFM   T/o Middleton St. George. Wrecked 1630 upon
F/O D A Kingston   landing with the port oleo still retracted.
F/O J M J A d'Ursel   Within a month of this incident, F/O Kingston
  Chevalier of the Order   and F/O d'Ursel had been lost from bombing
  Leopold, and Croixe de   operations (see Bomber Command Losses, Volume 3,
  Guerre (Belgium)   pages 179 and 175 respectively). P/O Bunclark,
whose DFM had been Gazetted on 23 December 1941
for meritorious service with 76 Squadron, was killed on operations to Berlin in
August 1943. At the time he was a Flight Commander with 78 Squadron (see the
same series, Volume 4, page 282). It will be noted that he was the captain of
the Halifax in which Sgt Castle RCAF (see the previous summary) was flying.

13 Jul 1942	**101 CFlt**	**Stirling I**	**N6075 SR-W3**	**Training**

Sgt R U Morrison   +   T/o Oakington for a cross-country, the crew
Sgt J E Williams   +   having been attached from 7 Squadron (Sgt
Sgt W A G Atkins   +   Dolphin was an electrician, whose parent unit
F/S J R Griffin RCAF   +   was No. 14 School of Technical Training at
F/S J F Hirst RCAF   +   Henlow; he was flying as a passenger). At
F/S T E Helgesen RCAF   +   1615, or thereabouts, while flying in poor
F/S L J Regimbal RCAF   +   visibility, the Stirling smashed into high
Sgt E Dolphin   +   ground at Merryton Low in the area of White
Peak and just over a mile E from Upper Holme,
three miles NNE of Leek, Staffordshire. The four RCAF members of crew were
taken to Buxton Cemetery in Derbyshire, the others being claimed by their next
of kin residing in England and in Scotland. When destroyed, their Stirling had
logged 94.40 flying hours.

Note. During the official enquiry, it emerged that Sgt Dolphin lived in a
detached stone cottage on the outskirts of nearby Biddulph (6 miles west of
Leek) and it was thought highly likely that the crew passed over his house
before heading in an ENE direction. Furthermore, as Bryce Gomersall reports,
Merryton Low was 200 feet above the height shown on the RAF charts. As the
summary notes, visibility was poor and the enquiry noted that The Roaches and
Merryton Low were both obscured at the time when the Stirling was sighted,
banking through a gap in the clouds above Meerbrook, a couple of miles or so
west-south-west of the impact point.

16 Jul 1942	**149 CFlt**	**Stirling I**	**R9299 OJ-Y**	**Training**

Sgt H P Johnson RNZAF   +   T/o Lakenheath to practice landings aided by
Sgt R A Hawkins   +   the Beam Approach system. At 1635, flying at
Sgt E Moores   +   1,500 feet some 2 miles SW of Newmarket a front
Sgt L E Pole RNZAF   +   crank pin on the outer starboard engine failed,
F/S J N Nicol RNZAF   +   allowing oil to spill over the hot exhaust ring.
Sgt M V Cato RNZAF   +   Within seconds the motor was alight and before
the crew could effectively react, the inner
engine, too, was burning fiercely. At about 300 feet, the starboard wing came
off and the bomber hurtled into the ground at Swaffham Bulbeck, 6 miles ENE of
Cambridge. The four New Zealanders were buried in Beck Row (St. John) churchyard while Sgt Hawkins and Sgt Moores were taken to their home towns of Tiverton
in Devon and Urmston, Lancashire respectively.

	158 CFlt	**Halifax II**	**BB203 NP-Z**	**Training**

P/O J W Craig   +   T/o East Moor for a training exercise involving
P/O J F Withy   +   three pilots and two flight engineers. On return
WO1 H W Williamson RCAF   +   to base, the pilot at the controls overshot his
Sgt E Place   +   turn that would have brought him onto finals and
Sgt A Dunn   +   on realising his mistake he made the fatal error
of increasing the bank in an attempt to come
into line with the runway. As the turn increased, the rudders stalled and
at 1137 the Halifax crashed at Manor Farm, Cornborough, near Sheriff Hutton,
ten miles NNE of York. P/O Craig and Sgt Dunn lie in Scotland at Ayr cemetery
and Beath Eastern cemetery respectively; P/O Withy and WO1 Williamson rest in
Newton-upon-Ouse (All Saints) churchyard, while Sgt Place is buried in Hartlepool
(Stranton) Cemetery.

Note. P/O Craig had arrived for instructional duties, from 1652 CU, on 22 June
and the two pupil pilots, P/O Withy and WO1 Williamson RCAF, had reported for
training six days later.

26-27 Jul	76 CFlt	Halifax II	R9485 MP-H	Op: Hamburg
1942	W/O E J Butt	pow		

26-27 Jul 1942 76 CFlt Halifax II R9485 MP-H Op: Hamburg

W/O E J Butt	pow
Sgt P Barr	+
P/O A S Hawkins	+
W/O R G W Woollard	pow
W/O C M Muir	pow
Sgt D L Osborne	+
Sgt E C Sudbury	pow

T/o 2303 Middleton St. George borrowed by the parent squadron. Hit by flak, while flying at 18,000 feet, and set on fire. Crash-landed, passing between a row of trees which smashed the mainplanes, at Heimbruch, 3 km S of Buxtehude. Those who died are buried in Becklingen War Cemetery. Their Halifax had flown 116.00 hours.

28-29 Jul 1942 101 CFlt Stirling I N6121 SR-W Op: Hamburg

F/O W R Butterfield	
Sgt R J Surfleet DFM	
P/O W Green	inj
P/O G R Wood	
Sgt Bond	
Sgt J Pollock	
Sgt Weston	

T/o 2311 Oakington but whilst gaining height collided at 2,300 feet with Wellington III X3668 of the parent squadron, which was climbing out from Bourn (for details of this aircraft, see Bomber Command Losses, Volume 3, page 165) and was sighted at the last moment beneath the Stirling's port bow. Desperately, F/O Butterfield pulled his aircraft up into a climbing turn to starboard, but to no avail and with a terrible rendering of metal, the Wellington carried away three parts of the Stirling's tailplane. Both bombers plunged to earth, circa 2330, between Rampton and Cottenham, 7 miles NNW from Cambridge. Sgt Surfleet had gained his DFM in the service of 7 Squadron, the London Gazette issue of 13 February 1942, carrying his details. He is thought to have survived the war. F/O Butterfield won a DFC with 75 Squadron, this being published on 22 September 1942 and he also received a mentioned in despatches before being posting missing in action on the eve of D-Day, 1944. At the time he was flying Mosquito VI PZ189 of 515 Squadron (see Bomber Command Losses, Volume 5, page 256). The Stirling had seen little active service, having sustained major battle damage during operation to Brest, with 7 Squadron, on 18 December 1941. Repairs took the better part of seven months to complete.

218 CFlt Stirling I N6129 HA-X Op: Hamburg

P/O C MacQ Farquharson	+
Sgt R K Helyer	+
Sgt H Windle	+
P/O R C Eldridge	+
Sgt N Jackson	+
Sgt R D Horder	+
Sgt R S Brandish	+

T/o 2327 Marham. Shot down by a night-fighter and crashed in the sea off Denmark's Romo island. Five bodies were eventually recovered and taken for burial in cemeteries located both in Denmark and in Germany. P/O Farquharson and Sgt Horder are commemorated on the Runnymede Memorial. Taken on charge by the parent squadron on 28 February 1942, the Stirling had amassed a grand total of 218.25 flying hours and had flown four operational sorties, all with the Conversion Flight.

30-31 Jul 1942 218 CFlt Stirling I R9332 HA-G Training

Sgt D W Thompson RNZAF	inj
Sgt T F Wilson	inj
F/S McPherson	
Sgt O E Amos RNZAF	inj
F/S Campbell	
F/S F Baker	
Sgt Strudwick	

T/o 2250 Marham for a night cross-country, returning to base to find visibility much reduced. Consequently, the crew failed to land from two approaches and at 0230 overshot their third attempt, and crashed heavily. A fire broke out, effectively destroying the bomber. Sgt Amos RNZAF was taken to RAF Hospital Ely, where he was placed on the dangerously ill list. Having made a good recovery, he was posted to 15 Squadron, only to be lost along with the rest of F/O W I Moffatt's crew while raiding Hamburg early in March 1943 (see Bomber Command Losses, Volume 4, page 58).

1 Aug 1942 103 CFLt Halifax II R9379 Training

Sgt W J Bagley	+
Sgt S Lightowler	+
Sgt J A Henson	+
Sgt A E Finney	+
Sgt J Munro	+
Sgt J W Keane RNZAF	+
Sgt O D Hancock	+
P/O A Simons	+
Sgt T L McDonald	+
Sgt L J Langan	+
Sgt T W Dinsdale	+
Sgt C H Morgan	+

T/o Elsham Wolds for general training, including a climb to high altitude. On return, and while downwind of the runway and turning to the left, the port outer engine commenced misfiring and from a mere 400 feet, the Halifax stalled and spun in a quarter-of-a-mile from the airfield. Five, including Sgt Keane RNZAF were taken to Brigg cemetery, while the others were buried in their home towns under private arrangements.

16 Aug 1942	**50 CFlt** F/S G K Dickenson Sgt R A Gotts RAAF Sgt Caverley Sgt Preseton Sgt H A Phillips RAAF Sgt Chapman LAC Owen	**Manchester I** inj	**L7475** T/o 1527 Talbenny but at 150 feet the starboard engine burst into flames. Three mintues later, F/S Dickensen put his crippled Manchester down in a field at Marloes, 4 miles SW of Talbenny, some 7 miles SW of Haverfordwest, Pembrokeshire. Three, F/S Dickenson and the two RAAF members of crew, were posted missing from operations to	**Training**

Wismar on 23-24 September 1942 (see Bomber
Losses, Volume 3, page 226).

18 Aug 1942	**102 CFLt** F/S J F W Towse RCAF	**Halifax II**	**BB197** T/o 0010 Pocklington for night solo practice, but on landing ten minutes later the Halifax	**Training**

swung to starboard, ground looped and lost its undercarriage.

23 Aug 1942	**78 CFlt** F/L R J Neal	**Halifax I**	**L9601** T/o 0007 Middleton St. George for night solo circuits and landings. Landed at 0017, where-	**Training**

upon the undercarriage collapsed. A technical investigation discovered that
the port tyre had deflated, due to "creep". Taken to a Handley Page facility
for further assessment, the bomber was declared beyond economical repair and
struck off charge on 12 September 1942. F/L Neal was destined to gain a DFC,
while serving with 78 Squadron, details being Gazetted on 13 August 1943.

19-20 Sep 1942	**149 CFlt** Sgt J Philp Sgt A J Ottoway Sgt L V Fossleitner Sgt I G Davies Sgt G K Reardon Sgt F H King Sgt R Spencer	**Stirling I** + inj inj +	**BF334 OJ-R** T/o Bourn. While returning to base, an engine failed and at around 0405, Sgt Philp ditched in the Channel off the Kent resort of Ramsgate. The impact was severe and the bomber broke into four section, several members of the crew being very badly injured. Bravely, Sgt Philp decided to swim for help and, assisted by Sgt Reardon, Sgt King was taken in tow. Four hours later,	**Op: München**

and close to exhaustion, they were sighted by a local fishing boat and dragged
from the water. Sadly, it was discovered that Sgt King had already succumbed
to his wounds. Meanwhile, an air-sea rescue launch had reached Sgt Fossleitner,
who was supporting a near unconscious Sgt Davies (it was later discovered that
his spine had been fractured) and took both men to safety. For their outstanding
devotion, Sgt Philp, Sgt Reardon and Sgt Fossleitner were decorated with the
British Empire Medal, Gazetted on 29 December 1942, by which time the cruel
fortunes of war had claimed the lives of Sgt Philp and Sgt Fossleitner (see
Bomber Command Losses, Volume 3, pages 273 and 260 respectively). The two
airmen, who died at the scene, are both commemorated on the Runnymede Memorial.

22 Sep 1942	**103 CFlt** W/O R J Fulbrook DFC F/S F W Hill WO2 N Hrehorak RCAF Sgt D R Evans F/S R L McCulloch RCAF	**Halifax II** + + + + +	**W1243 PM-B** T/o Elsham Wolds to practice overshooting on three-engines. While going round the circuit at 1215, the Halifax was seen to make a flat turn to starboard. The tail then dropped and as the starboard wing stalled, the bomber rolled onto its back and dived into the ground, bursting	**Training**

into flames on impact. Both Canadians rest in Brigg cemetery, while the others
were claimed by their next of kin. W/O Fulbrook was a Squadron veteran, whose
Distinguished Flying Cross had been published three months previous.

	460 CFlt F/O J W Purcivall DFC RNZAF F/L J A Falkiner RAAF Sgt L H Jones F/S R G Cox RAAF	**Halifax II** + + + +	**W1272** T/o Holme-on-Spalding Moor for a training exercise during which, it is believed, the instructor decided to demonstrate the effects of rudder stall, for at 1012, the Halifax spun in from a considerable height, bursting into	**Training**

flames on impact, a quarter-of-a-mile E of Middle Farm, Catterton, 2 miles NE
from Tadcaster, Yorkshire. F/O Purcivall RNZAF, a veteran of thirty-two
operational sorties with 103 Squadron and whose award had been Gazetted a
year previous, almost to the day, is buried near F/S Cox RAAF in Harrogate
(Stonefall) cemetery. Funeral services for F/L Falkiner RAAF, a Bachelor of
Arts graduate from Melbourne University, and Sgt Jones were arranged privately
at Wootton (St. Lawrence) churchyard and Adwick-le-Street cemetery respectively.

28 Oct	102 CFlt	Halifax I	L9510	Training

1942 Sgt Gurant T/o Pocklington. As the crew prepared to land, at around 1100, the top escape hatch in the roof of the cockpit blew open, the strong inrush of air undoubtedly distracting the pilot. Consequently, on touch down the bomber swung off the runway and lost its undercarriage. Accepted, ex-76 Squadron, on 2 July 1942, the Halifax had been involved in a minor accident ten days previous; it had flown 242.00 hours.

Section 1; sub-section

Only two heavy conversion flights were established in Bomber Command. Both came into existence on 18 May 1943; the first from a detachment of 1657 Heavy Conversion Unit, the new formation taking the number, "1678" while the second formed within its own right as 1679 Heavy Conversion Flight.

Another common factor was their equipment which was allocated in the shape of eight radial engined Lancaster IIs for 1678 Heavy Conversion Flight (at East Wretham in No. 3 Group) and four similar machines arriving at East Moor, a No. 6 (RCAF) Group station, for 1679 Heavy Conversion Flight.

The purpose of the former was to convert the Group's Wellington crews, while "1679" was charged with familiarising crews destined for the Group's Lancaster II squadrons.

1678 Heavy Conversion Flight had but a relatively brief existence, becoming a heavy conversion unit on 16 September 1943. Its Canadian counterpart soldiered on into the New Year, before being merged with 1666 Heavy Conversion Unit. At its peak, "1679" operated a dozen Lancaster IIs, but the establishment for "1678" remained at eight throughout its service as a heavy conversion flight.

2 Sep	1678 HCFlt	Lancaster II	DS608 SW-C	Training

1943 P/O G J Chequer RCAF
Lt Andrews

T/o 2120 Little Snoring for night dual, during which the crew experienced partial engine failure. An attempt was made at 2315 to land, but the brakes failed and P/O Chequer RCAF raised the undercarriage in order to stop within the confines of the airfield. A small fire broke out, but caused little damage. An investigation by the engineering officer concluded that both starboard engines lost both oil pressure, which gave rise to excessive temperatures, due to coring. Posted to 514 Squadron, P/O Chequer RCAF failed to return from Berlin on 30-31 January 1944 (see Bomber Command Losses, Volume 5, page 69). A photograph showing the remains of their heavy conversion flight Lancaster appears on page 55 of, "Lancaster At War 3" by Mike Garbett and Brian Goulding, Ian Allan 1984. It was probably taken following the loss of Lancaster II DS670, which is summarised on this page.

	1679 HCFlt	Lancaster II	DS635	Training

F/L J G McNeill DFC RCAF
F/O W B Stewart RCAF
F/O N M Bell

T/o 2100 East Moor for night training. While airborne, the port outer Hercules failed and the crew returned to base, but on touching down at 2125, the Lancaster swung from the runway and lost its undercarriage. Having slid to a stop, its fate was sealed when a fire broke out. The first two named both lost their lives, as the war progressed. On 12-13 June 1944, F/O (by then S/L and serving with 408 Squadron) Stewart failed to return from Cambrai, while two months later, F/L McNeill RCAF, now commanding 415 Squadron, died in a tragic midair collision over Yorkshire (see Bomber Command Losses, Volume 5, pages 279 and 390 respectively). W/C McNeill, as he then was, had gained his DFC with 426 Squadron, details appearing in the London Gazette on 13 August 1943.

6 Sep	1678 HCFLt	Lancaster II	DS670	Training

1943 F/S A A Greenwood RCAF

T/o 2045 Little Snoring but swung out of control and smashed into Lancaster II DS608, which had been damaged four evenings previous (see above for details).

Note. This was the last serious accident reported from 1678 Heavy Conversion Flight, which had moved to Little Snoring from East Wretham on 6 August 1943, and was destined to become a heavy conversion unit on 16 September 1943.

6 Nov	1679 HCFlt	Lancaster II	DS649	Training

6 Nov
1943

1679 HCFlt   Lancaster II   DS649   Training

F/O R A Davis RCAF	+
Sgt R C Mitchell	+
WO2 A H MacDonald RCAF	+
Sgt F W Hunt	+
F/S R L Green RCAF	+
Sgt L W Lehman RCAF	+

T/o 1655 East Moor for night training. About five minutes after clearing the runway, the Lancaster flew into trees and crashed near Rose Cottage Farm, Terrington, 8 miles WSW of Malton, Yorkshire. The four Canadians were taken to the regional cemetery at Harroagte (Stonefall), as was Glasgow born Sgt Mitchell. Sgt Hunt's funeral was arranged privately and he is buried in Leicestershire at Anstey cemetery. WO2 MacDonald RCAF had served previously with 420 Squadron and had been obliged to bale out from Wellington X HE422 in April 1943 (see Bomber Command Losses, Volume 4, page 102). F/O Davis RCAF is shown in the Harroagte cemetery register as being a member of 432 Squadron.

21 Dec
1943

1679 HCFlt   Lancaster II   DS615   Training

F/O J J McGavock DFC RCAF	+
F/O T E Major RCAF	+
Sgt K Forster	+
F/S R T J Welch RCAF	inj
Sgt J A Lawrenson	inj
Sgt W R Clapham	inj

T/o Wombleton (or Topcliffe) for night circuits and landings. At approximately 2110, the bomber was seen approaching the Topcliffe runway but, it seems, the pilot believed he was in danger of undershooting and, swiftly, opened the throttles. This rapid reaction, unfortunately, choked out both port engines and as his aircraft veered out of control it struck Halifax II DT548 a glancing blow before crashing with considerable force on the airfield. F/S Welch RCAF was critically injured, and he died forty-eight hours later. Along with his skipper and F/O Major RCAF, he is buried in Harrogate (Stonefall) cemetery. Sgt Forster rests in Stoke-on-Trent (Hartshill) cemetery. Remarkably, Sgt Lawrenson and Sgt Clapham escaped with only slight wounds, Sgt Clapham (and, probably, Sgt Lawrenson) being treated in station sick quarters. F/O McGavock RCAF had flown a tour of operations with 426 Squadron and his award had been promulgated on 15 June 1943. F/O Major RCAF is reported in the Harrogate register as belonging to 408 Squadron.

24 Dec
1943

1679 HCFlt   Lancaster II   DS624   Ground

| F/S J E Jean RCAF |

With all four engines idling, and while awaiting clearance to take off from Wombleton for a night exercise, the starboard inner caught alight. Prompt use of the fire extinguisher had no effect and after the crew made their exit at 1620, the Lancaster trundled onto the grass, where it continued to burn.

23 Jan
1944

1679 HCFlt   Lancaster II   DS839   Training

F/L R M Grove USAAC	+
Sgt L Thompson	+
F/S F W MacDonald RCAF	+
F/O R W Grosser RCAF	+
F/S J J Farrell RCAF	+
Sgt S A Carr RCAF	+
F/S L I Hogan RCAF	+

T/o 1400 Wombleton for a cross-country exercise. At around 2000, with all four engines running, the Lancaster came down in Seyanham Park, Ridgmont, 10 miles SSW of Bedford. Such was the destruction of the aircraft that accident investigators were at a loss as to the cause. F/L Grove USAAC hailed from New York and, it is likely, he was initially buried in Cambridge City cemetery where his five RCAF companions rest to this day. Sgt Thompson was taken home to Newcastle-under-Lyme in Staffordshire.

Note. While preparing the groundwork for this series, I recorded, from the aircraft serial registers, two serials of bombers purporting to belong to conversion flights but which, on perusal of their respective accident record cards, appear to have been written off under the authority of their parent squadrons. One concerns a Lancaster which I now believe to belong to 44 Squadron and the other a Stirling held by 218 Squadron. The former went unreported during the compilation of Volume 3 as I had assumed the entry placing it with 44 Conversion Flight to be correct, and as it crashed during a training sortie, it did not warrant inclusion. The Stirling, however, is shown on page 166, as it was lost during the course of operational flying, but I now suspect it belonged to the parent squadron and not with the conversion flight, as indicated. Although not included in the statistics reported in the appendices, I am showing their details in this section and I can only reiterate that it is examples of this nature that pose problems for any historian who is trying to present an accurate analysis of the Command's horrendous losses in World War II. Of course, I am mindful of the fact that evidence reported in one set of official documents may be refuted in another and this may be the case, here in question.

22 Apr	44 Sqn		Lancaster I	L7549 KM-Q	Training
1942	F/O G MacLagen	inj		T/o Waddington for a three-hour endurance test,
	P/O H J S Sturgess	inj		during which the port inner engine failed.
	P/O F W Belton	inj		Unable to maintain height, F/O MacLagen very
	Sgt R D Oliver			skillfully forced-landed in a field, roughly
	Sgt B L Nesbitt	inj		a mile NE of Ashwell, Rutland and within sight
	Sgt G W Hough	inj		of Cottesmore airfield. No one was seriously
	Sgt T D Moore	inj		hurt and all soon returned to duty. Very sadly,
	AC2 V G Edwards	inj		apart from AC2 Edwards (described as an under
				training wireless operator/air gunner) all (plus

Sgt W McD Crane) were reported missing from a visit to Warnemünde in May 1942 (see Bomber Command Losses, Volume 3, page 91). Subsequently, the squadron was notified that Sgt Moore had survived, albeit as a prisoner of war.

28-29 Jul	218 Sqn		Stirling I	W7464 HA-Z	Op: Hamburg
1942	Sgt J L Johnson	+		T/o 2343 Marham. Lost without trace. All are
	Sgt K Haworth	+		commemorated on the Runnymede Memorial.
	P/O F C Holloway	+		
	Sgt D E G Merritt	+		
	Sgt J T Davidson	+		
	Sgt J Cowen	+		
	Sgt D B Henshaw RCAF	+		

Section 2

Heavy Conversion Units

In parallel to the task of the conversion flights, described in the first section, was the work of the conversion units, the first of which were formed early in 1942. Similar to the flights, the conversion units came under the control of the established bomber groups and this continued to be the norm until early November 1944, when they were transferred to the authority of No. 7 Group. Late in 1945, by which time only three units were left in service, responsibility for their administration fell to No. 91 Group.

At the beginning, and for the greater part of 1942, the conversion units were but three in number; 1651 at Waterbeach in Cambridgeshire; 1652 at Marston Moor in Yorkshire and 1653 at Polebrook in Northamptonshire. The first served the needs of No. 3 Group, whose squadrons were equipped with the rather ungainly Stirling, while 1652 Conversion Unit, in No. 4 Group, was made responsible for Halifax training. The rôle of the Polebrook unit deserves a much broader explanation.

Reported in some sources as coming under the wing of No. 8 Group (which in January 1942 came, as far as I can be certain, outside of the recognised parameters of Bomber Command), "1653" was issued with Liberators and instructed to train crews earmarked for posting overseas in anticipation of the arrival in the Middle East and Far East theatres of 159 Squadron and 160 Squadron.

At the time, both units were in the embryo stages of their formation, "150" at Molesworth in Northamptonshire, and "160" across the border in Bedfordshire at Thurleigh.

In February 1942, the ground parties of both squadrons departed for their designated theatres of operations, though for reasons that are beyond the remit of this volume, 159 Squadron eventually served in India, while 160 Squadron ended up as a Middle East bomber formation, albeit only briefly.

Returning to "1653", it seems that within the terms of this series it was, at this stage, ineligible for inclusion, but having identified the serials of the three aircraft lost by the unit, prior to its disbandment on 31 October 1942, I discovered from the accident cards raised that the authority was shown as No. 3 Group, Bomber Command for the first two accidents, while No. 1 Group has been appended on the card raised in respect of Liberator Mk.II AL624.

Therefore, although the crews undergoing training were never intended for posting to Bomber Command, their administration, and casualty reporting procedures were being dealt with by a bona fide Bomber Command headquarters. Thus, their mention in this series is both proper and legitimate.

As recounted, for much of the year (1942) only three conversion units were in service (1654 Conversion Unit formed in the May with a mixed establishment of twin-engined Manchesters and four-engined Lancasters, and was assigned to No. 5 Group). Then, with the phasing out of the conversion flights, six more heavy conversion units were formed; 1656 in No. 1 Group, its two flights being equipped with Halifaxes and Lancasters; 1657 in No. 3 Group, receiving Stirlings; 1658 and 1659 in No. 4 Group (the last named would transfer to the control of No. 6(RCAF) Group on 1 January 1943), both with a sizeable complement of Halifaxes, while at Swinderby and Waddington respectively, 1660 and 1661 Heavy Conversion Units were formed within No. 5 Group, each formation having a liberal mixture of the unpopular Manchester, and the much favoured Lancaster.

A gradual expansion of heavy conversion units continued throughout 1943 ("1653" came back into the fold on 21 November, and being established within No. 3 Group was equipped with Stirlings) and, thus, by the end of the year, Bomber Command's heavy conversion formations stood at seventeen (1665 Heavy Conversion Unit, which had formed within No. 3 Group, at Mepal, in the April was given up to No. 38 Group on 1 December 1943).

From the expansionist viewpoint, 1944 saw very little change, but on 15 August, 1669 Heavy Conversion Unit came into existence at Langar in Nottinghamshire with an initial establishment of thirty-six Halifaxes.

This latest unit probably came under the protection of No. 5 Group but is reported to have joined No. 7 Group in October 1944, some four weeks ahead of the mass emigration of all heavy conversion units to the newly reformed bomber training group headquarters.

Basically, since the conception of the heavy conversion units, their equipment mirrored the type of aircraft currently in service with the operational squadrons of their respective groups. However, in 1943, as well as meeting the requirements of No. 3 Group, Stirlings were issued to three of the four heavy conversion units within No. 5 Group in order to release Lancasters back into front-line use. Over the years, the Stirling has been regarded as the "poor relation" of the "heavies" that became the backbone of Bomber Command, but as a heavy-bomber trainer, the Stirling proved to be an excellent workhorse with an accident rate that compared favourably with its stable companions. However, by the end of 1944, its days with Bomber Command were numbered and from thereon the units main equipment rested with Halifaxes and Lancasters, the latter having been brought back into the training loop. (Late in 1943, a number of Lancaster Finishing Schools were formed, remaining in existence for over a year. Their losses are dealt with in the next section).

Similar to the Operational Training Units, covered in the previous volume, the ending of hostilities signalled a rapid reduction of the training establishments and with the disbandment of No. 7 Group in December 1945, only three heavy conversion units were left for No. 91 Group to administer. Of these, 1668 Heavy Conversion Unit, now domicile at Cottesmore in Rutland, was the first to go, disbandment being announced on 7 March 1946. Then, on 11 November of that same year, 1660 Heavy Conversion Unit at Swinderby was absorbed by 1653 Heavy Conversion Unit. For another four months the Lancasters of "1653" at Lindholme continued to provide conversion to "heavies" for a Command which was, by the spring of 1947, a mere shadow of its former years of glory.

Appropriately, when "1653" laid up its number-plate, 230 Operational Conversion Unit was formed to take its place and, thus, for a few years longer the Lancaster would still be the aircraft upon which the budding bomber pilot would hone his skills.

As will be seen from the summaries that follow, the majority of accidents reported concern the various four-engined types that were the mainstay of these units.

However, unlike the conversion flights which used the type of bomber assigned to, or about to be received by their parent squadron, the heavy conversion units took on a host of supporting types. Thus, a glance at the aircraft issued to support 1653 Heavy Conversion Unit during its two periods of service show that, at least, one Blenheim IV was delivered to Polebrook, along with an Anson, a Ventura, a Tiger Moth and a Westland Lysander.

After re-forming in November 1943, support aircraft included Spitfires and Hurricanes, Beaufighters and Mosquitoes. Little, if anything is recorded in the unit's records, but it is probably safe to assume that the Spitfires and Hurricanes were used for fighter affiliation training exercises.

Indeed, this paucity of detail in respect of flying training is common throughout the record books kept by these formations. Sport often features, as does welfare, but flying records are frequently restricted to mundane statistics. Flying accidents, even when loss of life resulted, are either ignored or rate only a cursory mention. Of the many records examined in preparing this volume, the best, by far, are those compiled by the Canadians. Despite the grim wartime conditions of their temporary airfields, a splendid sense of fun is never far away. I am most grateful.

6 Jan 1942	1652 CU F/O P Johnston DFC	Halifax I L9519	Training

T/o Marston Moor for circuit training. At 1530, or thereabouts, the pilot under instruction realised he was going to overshoot his landing run and in order to avoid a deep trench, he tried to turn the Halifax onto the perimeter track. In doing so, the undercarriage collapsed, damaging the bomber beyond repair. F/O Johnson, the instructor, had recently completed a tour of duty with 35 Squadron, his award having been Gazetted a few weeks previous on 23 December. By the spring of 1943, and promoted to squadron leader, he had returned for a second tour with "35", now assigned to Pathfinder duties, losing his life during operations to Wuppertal in late May 1943 (see Bomber Command Losses, Volume 4, page 168).

8 Feb 1942	1651 CU Sgt K J C Richards	Stirling I N3642 −C	Training

T/o 1800 Waterbeach but a malfunction in the exactor controls caused the Stirling to swing violently off the runway, severely damaging the tail wheel unit. Down graded for instructional purposes as 3012M, the bomber was issued to No. 4 School of Technical Training at St. Athan. Subsequently, Sgt Richards went on to fly with 7 Squadron, becoming a prisoner of war in the wake of operations to St-Nazaire on 28-29 June 1942 (see Bomber Command Losses, Volume 3, page 142).

16 Feb 1942	1651 CU F/L J H Edwards	Stirling I N6023 −T	Training

T/o 1752 Newmarket for night training. At around 2130, F/L Edwards came in to land from a very steep angle of glide and on touch down, the undercarriage was totally smashed. The forward impetus carried the bomber for some distance and, when inspected in the cold light of day, was found to have sustained damage that was uneconomical to repair. Posted soon after to 7 Squadron, F/L Edwards was reported missing in action on 28-29 March 1942 (the night of Palm Sunday) when 234 bombers, including twenty-six Stirlings, raided the Baltic port of Lübeck (see Bomber Command Losses, Volume 3, page 55).

18 Feb
1942

1651 CU **Stirling I** **N3641** **-C**	**Training**

F/S H R Millichamp RCAF   T/o Waterbeach only to be damaged beyond repair in a heavy landing at 1600. Converted for instructional purposes, the airframe received the serial 3010M. Soon after this incident, F/S Millichamp RCAF joined 218 Squadron. On 25-26 April 1942, his Stirling failed to return from Plzen (see Bomber Command Losses, Volume 3, page 78). Along with his crew, he is buried in Rheinberg War Cemetery.

10 Mar
1942

1651 CU **Stirling I** **W7426** **-V**	**Training**

P/O W R B McCarthy   T/o Newmarket for solo circuits and landings in the course of which he landed, at 1530, with the undercarriage only partially lowered. On completion of his course, P/O McCarthy went to 218 Squadron, gaining a DFC (promulgated 27 July 1943) and was shot down over the North Sea in late August 1942 (see Bomber Command Losses, Volume 3, page 195). He is commemorated on the Runnymede Memorial.

13 Mar
1942

1652 CU **Halifax I** **L9513**	**Training**

W/C J B Tait DFC   T/o Marston Moor for dual circuits and landings.
S/L A J D Snow   Touched down 0800, whereupon a tyre burst and the undercarriage collapsed. W/C Tait ranks amongst the outstanding bomber pilots of the Second World War. In 1940, he had been a flight commander on 51 Squadron, surviving a serious crash on 7-8 September (see Bomber Command Losses, Volume 1, page 107), while in the summer of 1944, he was to succeed the much decorated W/C G L Cheshire as leader of 617 Squadron. Twixt September of that year and 12 November, he led "617" and 9 Squadron in three extremely difficult strikes against the Tirpitz, the last assault culminating in the battleship capsizing in Tromsö fiord. Sadly, long before this historic event his pupil, S/L Snow, had been killed on operations to Hamburg on 3-4 May 1942 (see Bomber Command Losses, Volume 3, page 85). At the time of his death, he was a flight commander on 78 Squadron.

14 Apr
1942

1652 CU **Halifax I** **L9576 GV-E**	**Training**

F/O F J Joshua   +   T/o Marston Moor for general flying practice.
F/S D R Cox RCAF   +   While flying on two engines, lost control and
Sgt A T Howell   +   crashed at 1938 to the N of Sandbeck Lane, a
Sgt J E Gurney   +   mile NE of Wetherby and some to 3 to 4 miles
Sgt E J Spencer   +   west-south-west of the airfield. F/S Cox RCAF
Sgt G Marks   +   and fellow pilot Sgt Howell were buried in
AC1 C G C Keighley   +   Harrogate (Stonefall) Cemetery; the others
AC1 T Mahady   +   rest in their home towns. The first four
AC2 F S Goodwin   +   named are identified as pilots.

16 Apr
1942

1652 CU **Halifax II** **R9431 GV-K**	**Training**

F/O K D Whisken DFC   T/o Marston Moor. Forced-landed 1400, at base, with an engine ablaze, caused by the failure of a big end cap. Earlier in his eventful day, F/O Whisken had crash-landed at around 1100 in Halifax I L9509, its undercarriage jammed. In late June 1942, and while still serving with 1652 CU, he was killed on operations to Bremen. Prior to his arrival at Marston Moor as an instructor, he had flown with 102 Squadron and details of his award had been Gazetted on 13 March 1942.

18 Apr
1942

1651 CU **Stirling I** **W7439** **-N**	**Training**

Sgt W G Bond   T/o Waterbeach for dual and solo night training.
Sgt C R Russell-Collins   During the detail, an outer engine failed and the pilot at the controls cut the switch of the faulty engine. As a consequence, he was unable to control the Stirling as it touched down at circa 0100 and in the ensuing swing the undercarriage gave way. In his report, the investigating officer concluded that had the pilot pulled out the carburettor cut control, he would have stopped both outer motors, thus negating the chance of swinging on landing. Both airmen went on to fly with 15 Squadron, neither to survive their tours of operations (see Bomber Command Losses, Volume 3, pages 98 and 223 respectively).

23 Apr
1942

1653 CU **Liberator II** **AL549**	**Ground**

F/O P D Short   At 2000, while taxying at Polebrook, lost brake pressure (due to the pilot failing to switch on the hydraulic booster pump) and wrecked after running into a ditch. Posted to the Middle East, F/O Short joined 70 Squadron (Wellingtons) and was reported missing on 24 September 1942. He is commemorated on panel 248 of the Alamein Memorial.

30–31 May	1652 CU	Halifax I	L9605 GV–Y	Op: Köln

30–31 May
1942

1652 CU   Halifax I   L9605 GV–Y   **Op: Köln**

F/L S G Wright   pow   T/o 2359 Marston Moor. Believed shot down by
W/O H P Lowman   pow   Oblt Reinhold Knacke, 3./NJG1, crashing near
F/L D G Cookson RNZAF   pow   Tegelen (Limburg), 4 km SSW from Venlo, Holland.
W/O R J Tavener   pow   Sgt Manley is buried in Jonkerbos War Cemetery;
Sgt K J A Manley   +   along with F/L Cookson RNZAF and W/O Tavener,
he had been attached from 158 Squadron. In the
last days of the war, W/O Lowman was one of the victims from a tragic attack by
Typhoons on a prisoner of war column near Gresse (see Bomber Command Losses,
Volume 6, page 210). He rests in Berlin 1939–1945 War Cemetery. With a crew
of five, the Halifax was being flown with the absolute minimum necessary for a
bombing operation. On 25 January 1942, whilst being flown by Sgt J W Stell
(destined to go to 76 Squadron and be killed raiding Bremen in early June 1942
(see the same series, Volume 3, page 116)), this Halifax had been damaged in a
landing mishap at Marston Moor.

1– 2 Jun
1942

1652 CU   Halifax II   R9372 GV–K   **Op: Essen**

F/L H A Williams   pow   T/o 0008 Marston Moor. Lost power from one
W/O H Jackson   pow   engine while over the target and, thereafter,
F/S F E Gostling   pow   was unable to maintain height. Shot down while
W/O C R Read   pow   nearing the Dutch coast, crashing on the dunes
W/O J Williams   pow   near Velsen (Noord Holland), just above IJmuiden.
WO2 H J W Daly RCAF   pow   W/Os Jackson, Read and Daly RCAF were attached
from 158 Squadron.

5 Jun
1942

1652 CU   Halifax II   L9610   –O   **Training**

Sgt T H Lane RCAF   inj   T/o 2215 Marston Moor but a tyre burst, causing
P/O Reynolds   the bomber to leave the runway and smash its
Sgt Gowing   undercarriage in the process. I much suspect
that Sgt Lane RCAF was commissioned and before
the cessation of hostilities was being held in captivity, this suspicion being
based on evidence reported in the Allied Air Forces Prisoner of War file.

16 Jun
1942

1651 CU C Flt   Stirling I   N6088 LS–X   **Training**

P/O M R Scansie RNZAF   +   T/o 1525 Waterbeach for a cross-country exercise.
Sgt E W Morris   +   At approximately 1610, the Stirling was seen, on
F/S J B Tomlinson   +   fire, and falling in a right hand spiral with
Sgt D B Robinson   +   flames streaming back from the port wing, which
Sgt J T Smith   +   broke away outboard of the outer engine. Now
Sgt R P Broadbridge   +   diving steeply, the bomber smashed onto the Great
F/S H L Johnson RCAF   +   North Road, in the area of Barnby Moor, some 2 to
Sgt R G Le Blanc   +   three miles NE of Retford, Nottinghamshire. Apart
from the observer, Sgt Robinson, who was taken
home to Lanark and laid to rest in Bedlay Cemetery, Calder, all were interred
in Finningley (St. Oswald) Churchyard extension. Sgt Le Blanc was the son of
Marcel Jean and Yvonne Alice Le Blanc of le Havre (Seine-Maritime), France.
When destroyed, the Stirling had flown 244.00 hours and had amassed twenty-two
operational sorties; a quite remarkable achievement. Bryce Gomersall reports
that a Coroner's Inquest was convened at 1500 hours on 18 June, at Finningley;
also, when the wreckage was recovered, the balloon cable cutters were still
attached to the portion of wing that came off.

24 Jun
1942

1652 CU   Halifax II   R9377   –N   **Air Test**

F/O K D Whisken DFC   T/o Marston Moor for a night flying test.
Landed at 1630, but swung and lost its under-
carriage. For further details concerning this officer, and his subsequent
fate, please refer to the previous page.

25–26 Jun
1942

1651 CU   Stirling I   W7442   –B   **Op: Bremen**

F/L W M Livingston   +   T/o 2358 Waterbeach. Shot down at 0039 by a
Sgt W Bennett   +   night-fighter and crashed in the Waddenzee.
P/O L A Booth   +   F/L Livingston, P/O Kenny (who hailed from
P/O F L Flynn RCAF   +   Athleague, Co. Roscommon in the Irish Republic)
P/O A J Kenny   +   and Sgt Coates are buried in Harlingen General
Sgt R Coates   +   Cemetery; the others are commemorated on the
P/O J Graham DFM   +   Runnymede Memorial. P/O Graham gained his award
with 7 Squadron, details having appeared in the
London Gazette on 4 July 1941. P/O Booth of Huby near Leeds had been capped for
England at Rugby Union International level.

25-26 Jun   **1652 CU**   **Halifax II**   **V9993 GV-U**   **Op: Bremen**
1942

F/O K D Whisken DFC	+	T/o 2358 Marston Moor. Shot down by a night-
WO2 H F Spratt RCAF	pow	fighter, possibly flown by Oblt Carstens of
F/S V A Martin	pow	III./NJG1 and crashed 0209 at Luttenberg in
F/O W H Andrews RCAF	pow	the Province of Overijssel, 6 km ENE from Raalte,
F/O D B E McKenzie RCAF	pow	Holland, where F/S Watson RCAF, an American from
WO2 R W Wagstaff RCAF	pow	Kansas City, is buried. His skipper, meanwhile,
F/S I R Watson RCAF	+	rests in Dalfsen General Cemetery, some fourteen

kilometres away to the north-north-west. During
his all too brief service with 1652 CU, F/O Whisken had been involved in two
very serious flying accidents and one minor incident (see pages 24 and 25).

6 Jul   **1654 CU**   **Manchester IA**   **L7496**   **Training**
1942

F/S G Lancey RCAF   T/o Wigsley. At approximately 1635, F/S Lancey
     attempted to overshoot the runway but as he
advanced the throttles the starboard engine cut and an emergency landing was
made, straight ahead. A fire broke out soon afterwards, but there are no
reports of injuries. F/S Lancey RCAF had been attached from 97 Squadron,
arriving at Wigsley two days previous.

13 Jul   **1654 CU**   **Oxford I**   **V3874**   **Training**
1942

Sgt L A J Dobie	+	T/o Wigsley. Flew into trees and crashed 1320
Sgt J R Warren	+	near Gunthorpe, 7 miles ENE from the centre of
Sgt R A von der Groeben RAAF	+	Nottingham. Sgt Dobie was taken to Bebington

Cemetery; Sgt Warren rests at Idridgehay (St.
James) Churchyard, while Sgt von der Groeben RAAF was buried in the churchyard
extension of Shelford (SS Peter and Paul); he had been attached from 50 Squadron
at Swinderby. This was the first fatal accident sustained by 1654 CU, which had
formed at Swinderby on 19 May 1942, prior to its move to Wigsley in mid-June.
Furthermore, it was the first loss from a Bomber Command conversion unit of a
support aircraft.

23 Jul   **1654 CU**   **Lancaster I**   **R5891**   **Training**
1942

Sgt F W Bottomer RAAF   T/o Wigsley for day training. On landing at
     around 1230, Sgt Bottomer RAAF overshot the
runway as he had failed to fully lower the flaps. Apart from pride, he was
unhurt but the Lancaster was beyond repair, despite being initially categorised
as worthy of salvage.

28-29 Jul   **1651 CU**   **Stirling I**   **N3655**   **-T**   **Op: Hamburg**
1942

P/O G C Bayley DFC	+	T/o 2330 Waterbeach. Crashed in the Oslebshausen
Sgt G W J Lovell	inj	district of Bremen, on the E bank of the Weser,
Sgt G Alder	+	and some 8 km NW of the city centre. All, in-
Sgt K S Spencer RNZAF	+	cluding Sgt Lovell who died from his wounds on
F/S E C Glenwright DFM	+	23 August 1942, are buried in Becklingen War
Sgt N R Kilpatrick RNZAF	+	Cemetery, having been exhumed from the Walner
Sgt C E Wells RNZAF	+	Friedhof. P/O Bayley had completed a tour of

operations with 75 Squadron during which he won
an immediate DFC (his navigator, F/O A G MacLeod, was honoured likewise) and
this was duly promulgated on 23 January 1942. A week following the operation,
which cost him his life, the London Gazette published details of F/S Glenwright's
award. Sgt Alder came from McLure in British Columbia. Errol Martyn notes that
Sgt George Wells RNZAF, brother to Sgt C E Wells RNZAF, served with 10 Squadron,
and was killed while raiding Hannover the previous July (see Bomber Command
Losses, Volume 2, page 103).

     1651 CU   **Stirling I**   **N6069**   **-G**   **Op: Hamburg**

P/O J D McGregor RNZAF	+	T/o 2325 Waterbeach. Lost without trace. All
F/O C S Ratcliffe RCAF	+	are commemorated on the Runnymede Memorial. It
Sgt C W Miles	+	is noted that P/O McGregor RNZAF had flown
Sgt A W Cushway	+	previously with 218 Squadron. For his parents,
P/O G F Love	+	notification that he was missing in action would
Sgt E M Innes	+	be followed a little over a year later with the
F/S H R Kedwell RCAF	+	news that their younger son, F/L Walter Young
Sgt A Rooney	+	McGregor RNZAF, a Beaufighter pilot with 227

Squadron, was missing from operations over the
Dodecanese Islands. Subsequently, they were informed that he had been buried
on the small island of Cos, but had been exhumed and taken for interment on
Rhodes. Sadly, of course, their first son has no known grave.

28-29 Jul	1651 CU	Stirling I	N6102	-B	Op: Hamburg
1942	F/L D A Parkins DFC	+			T/o 2307 Waterbeach. Lost without trace. All
	P/O L P Hancock RCAF	+			are commemorated on the Runnymede Memorial. All
	Sgt J Coy	+			F/L Parkins had recently completed an arduous
	Sgt P C Robson	+			tour of duty with 15 Squadron, gaining his DFC
	Sgt R F G Grant	+			(Gazetted 23 June 1942) in the wake of an attack
	Sgt P F O'Shea	+			on Essen, during which his Stirling had been
	P/O L B Thomas	+			extensively damaged by ground fire.
	Sgt AG Silvester	+			

	1651 CU	Stirling I	W7509	-Q	Op: Hamburg
	P/O V M Smith	+			T/o 2303 Waterbeach. Believed claimed by Oblt
	W/O J L Warren	pow			Von Hagenow, III./NJG1, crashing 0312 in the
	F/L D E Breed	pow			Dutch Province of Gelderland near Heelsum, some
	W/O R Morrow	pow			twelve kilometres west of Arnhem. The two air-
	W/O L Cox	pow			men who died are buried in Renkum (Oosterbeek)
	Sgt A Aldridge	+			General Cemetery.
	WO2 H V Dufour RCAF	pow			

30 Jul	1651 CU	Stirling I	N3676	-S	Air Test
	F/O M H Hardstaff				T/o 1445 Waterbeach and crashed just beyond the
	P/O C D Dobson RNZAF				airfield's boundary. In his report, F/O Hard-

staff stated that he had not been able to correct
a drift to starboard and having used up about three-quarters of the runway, he
decided to abort the flight. However, despite closing the throttles and applying
the brakes, he was unable to prevent the Stirling from running through a ditch
and across the main road leading from Cambridge to Ely, before finishing up in
a field. Within a month of this accident, P/O Dobson RNZAF had been killed on
operations with 149 Squadron (see Bomber Command Losses, Volume 3, page 199).
Errol Martyn believes it may have been his first sortie.

5 Aug	1653 CU	Liberator II	AL588		Training
1942	F/S B Williams	+			T/o 1714 Marston Moor but while banking east of
	Sgt A F Bell	+			the airfield, an elevator failed and the bomber
	Sgt W A Kup	+			crashed, totally out of control, into a field
	Sgt S Sampson	+			near Tockwith village. On impact the Liberator
	Sgt E Thorley	+			broke up. F/S Williams of Weybourne in Surrey
	P/O T H Jones	+			was cremated at Leeds (Lawn Woods) and military
	Sgt E A Smith	+			funerals were held at Harrogate (Stonefall)
	Sgt W H C Booth	+			Cemetery for Sgt Bell and Sgt Kup, the latter
	Sgt K Caselton	+			being a Bachelor of Arts (Oxford) graduate.
	Sgt D A Wood	+			For the remainder, their bodies were taken to
					their home towns under private arrangements.

Nineteen year old Sgt Caselton, one of the three trainee air gunners aboard,
is the sole service burial from the Second World War in Yalding (SS Peter and
Paul) New Churchyard; it is noted that this burial ground contains a single
grave from the First World War. It is believed the crew were either in the
process of commencing a fighter affiliation detail, or had done so and were
about to return to Polebrook. P/O Jones is described as a gunnery instructor
and Sgt Wood as a fitter armourer.

12 Aug	1651 CU	Stirling I	N6099	-P	Training
1942	P/O A Austin	inj			T/o 1500 Waterbeach from No. 2 runway and
	Sgt K Pudsey				collided with a Stirling taking off from No. 1
	Sgt H J Hudson				runway. The front of "P" struck the tail of
	Sgt R J Wicks				the other aircraft, causing it to turn over.
	Sgt E W E Jones	inj			P/O Austin's Stirling remained upright, though
	Sgt G A Pidgen				both machines were wrecked. Sgt Jones, the air
	Sgt K W Strange				bomber, was very seriously injured and was
					taken to RAF Hospital Ely; his skull, lower

jaw and right femur being fractured. Despite all care and medical attention,
he died at 1030 hours on 15 August. His grave is in Shrewsbury General Cemetery.
P/O Austin was only slightly hurt. Subsequently, he was decorated with the DFC,
details being published in the London Gazette on 16 February 1943. Sadly, he
was not destined to survive the war, his death occurring on 8 May 1944. He is
buried in Manchester Southern Cemetery.

12 Aug 1942	1651 CU	Stirling I	N6127	-V	Training

Sgt J E Ryan RCAF — inj
Sgt A S Milton — +
Sgt P S Williams — +
Sgt W M Jones — inj
Sgt D E Seeley RCAF

T/o 1500 Waterbeach from No. 1 runway and lost in the manner described at the bottom of the previous page. Sgt Milton, a regular airman and the son of Ordnance Lieutenant Sidney Harold Milton RN, is buried in Watford North Cemetery, while Sgt Williams was taken to King's Worthy (St. Mary) Churchyard. He was an honours graduate in the arts and his father was the Revd Claude St. Maur Williams of St. Mary Bourne in Hampshire. By an odd quirk of coincidence, Sgt W M Jones was an air bomber, similar to his namesake in the other Stirling involved. Sgt Ryan RCAF was not too seriously hurt. Subsequently, he converted to Halifaxes and was killed during operations to Hannover in October 1943 (see Bomber Command Losses, Volume 4, page 356). At the time of his death, he was serving with 431 Squadron.

16 Aug 1942	1652 CU	Halifax I	L9496		Training

Sgt W Beck

T/o Dalton. On conclusion of the sortie, the crew experienced problems with the undercarriage and while trying to land 1705 at Burn, the port oleo collapsed. An unconfirmed report indicates that the Halifax had been slightly damaged in an incident on 13 February 1942.

17 Aug 1942	1652 CU	Halifax II	L9609		Training

F/O J H Trethewy — inj
F/O B D G Gibson MID — inj
Sgt W A Lawson — +
P/O M K Brett — inj
Sgt S G Kitts — inj

T/o Dalton for night-flying practice. Crashed near Willow Grange at around 0210, a mile S of Thirsk, Yorkshire, while attempting to go round again following partial engine failure. It is thought that the excessive vibration may have caused the throttles to slip back. The four seriously injured airmen were taken to Northallerton Hospital, where the first two named died (F/O Gibson's demise was reported to his unit at 1345). Their funerals, and that of Sgt Lawson, a member of the pre-war auxiliary air force, were arranged by their families. The Halifax was the first production Mk. II and, initially, had been used by 76 Squadron, flying two operational sorties between 8 November 1941 and its transfer to Marston Moor on 14 February 1942. Having recovered from his injuries, P/O Brett went to 158 Squadron, only to be killed in late January 1943, while raiding the U-boat pens at Lorient (see Bomber Command Losses, Volume 4, page 29).

27 Aug 1942	1651 CU	Stirling I	BF331		Training

Sgt K Pudsey

T/o 1200 Waterbeach but swung out of control and came to a halt with a badly broken undercarriage. Delivered ex-works on the last day of July 1942, the Stirling had flown a mere 25.30 hours. Sgt Pudsey, it will be recalled, had emerged unscathed from the awful take off accident, at Waterbeach, on 12 August. His operational career flourished; with 115 Squadron he gained a DFM (Gazetted on 15 June 1943) and he was twice mentioned in despatches before being posted missing in action on 5 April 1945, when his 142 Squadron Mosquito failed to return from Magdeburg (see Bomber Command Losses, Volume 6, page 152).

28 Aug 1942	1651 CU	Tiger Moth II	N9326		Local Flying

F/S G A Mackie

T/o 1735 Waterbeach but ten minutes later, the pilot lost control and finished up in the River Cam, close to the airfield. At first it was mooted that the ailerons may have jammed during a climbing turn. This theory was, however, dispelled when the Accident Investigation Branch reported that the crash was consistent with loss of lateral control, followed by a stall. F/S Mackie was an experienced bomber pilot and had flown a tour of operations with 15 Squadron. On departing from Waterbeach in September 1943, he joined 214 Squadron and for over a year flew Stirlings, and later Fortresses, on bomber support duties. In his post-war civilian life, he resumed his educational studies and in 1947 gained a Diploma in Art and Design at Edinburgh College of Art. As a freelance designer, he was to enjoy a near forty year long collaboration with Archie Turnbull, both of whom were honoured by Edinburgh University Press with an exhibition of books in 1987. I am, indeed, most grateful to Bryce Gomersall for much of the background material, reported in this summary. Bryce also notes that the incident with the Tiger Moth is remarked upon in Murray Peden's book, A Thousand Shall Fall.

30 Aug
1942

1654 CU **Manchester I L7416** **Training**
P/O W J Pickin T/o Wigsley for flying practice, landing at around 1630 in a cross-wind. To his dismay, P/O Pickin discovered that he had no pressure left in the braking system and the wind was sufficiently strong enough to take the Manchester off the runway and into a nearby clump of trees. It had amassed a total of 82.25 flying hours. On 5-6 March 1943, F/L Pickin (as he then was) failed to return from the very successful raid on Essen, now recognised as the opening attack in The Battle of The Ruhr (see Bomber Command Losses, Volume 4, page 66).

1 Sep
1942

1654 CU **Manchester I L7298** **Training**
Sgt L G Knight RAAF T/o Wigsley for night flying practice, during which the fuel master cock was, inadvertently, partly closed. Starved of fuel, the engines failed and at approximately 2315 a wheels up landing was made, roughly a mile to the E of the airfield. Posted to 50 Squadron, Sgt Knight RAAF completed his tour of duty by March 1943, but returned to operational flying almost immediately with the formation at Scampton of 617 Squadron. Now commissioned, he participated in the historic operation to the Ruhr dams in May 1943, and is credited with breaching the Eder, under extremely difficult conditions caused by fog. Tragically, in mid-September 1943, his was one of five Lancasters that failed to return from a raid by "617" on the Dortmund-Ems canal (see Bomber Command Losses, Volume 4, page 322).

Note. The air bomber that flew with F/L Knight to the Eder, and who was with him for the fateful attack on the canal, was F/L Edward Cuthbert Johnson DFC, who died on 1 October 2002, aged 90, and whose obituary appeared in The Daily Telegraph on Monday the 7th. He had joined the Royal Air Force (Volunteer Reserve) in 1940 and was not, as I erroneously reported, a member of the Royal Australian Air Force.

2 Sep
1942

1651 CU **Stirling I N6103 –O East India 1** **Training**
P/O J Bell T/o 2030 Waterbeach and came to grief from an uncontrolled swing which deprived the Stirling of its undercarriage. It had logged a useful 199.05 flying hours.

3 Sep
1942

1652 CU **Halifax II W1163 GV–U** **Training**
Sgt J D Duffus + T/o Marston Moor for night circuit training.
Sgt R Gasken + It is believed the port outer engine failed as
Sgt J L Easter inj the Halifax approached the runway and while
Sgt R G Wraight + opening up in readiness to go round again, the pilot allowed the nose to rise rather steeply, and lost control. In the crash, that occurred at about 2220, the bomber burst into flames. Sgt Easter was admitted to York Military Hospital; those who died were buried under private arrangement. On 25 June 1942, while being flown by S/L R A Norman, the Halifax (then coded "O"), had lost its tail wheel in a landing accident.

5 Sep
1942

1654 CU **Manchester IA L7521** **Training**
S/L Carter T/o Wigsley for a demonstration in feathering procedures, during which the starboard airscrew jammed in the feathered position. S/L Carter headed for nearby Waddington, but his approach was baulked by an Oxford and while banking steeply, the Manchester stalled and crashed 1215 short of the runway. A photograph of the wreckage is on page 10 of "Lancaster At War 3" by Mike Garbett and Brian Goulding, published by Ian Allan in 1984. An aerial photograph, showing the Manchester in 61 Squadron markings, appears on the same page.

9 Sep
1942

1654 CU **Lancaster I R5852** **Training**
Sgt T Doolan T/o 1840 Wigsley for a night cross-country, in the course of which the navigator lost his way while trying to navigate by "dead reckoning". At approximately 2255, while circling a beacon, the crew saw searchlights shining towards (what turned out to be) the small Shropshire airfield of Condover. In his anxiety to get down, Sgt Doolan made a rather fast approach and when he realised he was going to overshoot the runway, he swung the Lancaster. Moments later, the undercarriage collapsed and on coming to a stop, the bomber caught fire. No one was hurt and not long afterwards Sgt Doolan joined 9 Squadron, going on to fly a successful tour of operations.

13–14 Sep **1651 CU** **Stirling I** **N3684 LS-O** **Op: Bremen**
1942
F/O T Ballauff	inj	T/o 0035 Waterbeach. Crash-landed at around
P/O G Turner RCAF	inj	0500 at Hockwoldchalkhole Farm near Feltwell
Sgt J McGhie		airfield in Norfolk, following loss of power
Sgt P H Conroy		from three engines. Prior to the forced-
Sgt I J Allen RNZAF	inj	landing, two members of the crew baled out.
Sgt J H Keeley RNZAF		The three injured airmen were taken to RAF
Sgt N A Young		Hospital Ely, suffering from slight concussion.
Sgt J F Bowman RNZAF		Subsequently, five from the crew, Sgts McGhie,

Conroy, Keeley RNZAF, Young and Bowman RNZAF,
were posted to 90 Squadron, the last four named failing to return from Hamburg
on 25-26 July 1943 (see Bomber Command Losses, Volume 4, page 242). Earlier,
on the last night of February 1943, Sgt McGhie had become a prisoner of war.
P/O Turner RCAF, meanwhile, went to 75 Squadron and had won a DFC before being
lost with his entire crew on a raid to Mannheim in late September 1943 (see the
same volume, pages 53 and 330 respectively). F/O Ballauff was honoured with a
Distinguished Flying Cross and two Bars; the first, gained with 149 Squadron,
was Gazetted on 27 October 1942, while the Bars were promulgated on 15 September
and 8 December 1944, by which time he had converted to Mosquitoes and served
with 139 Squadron.

1654 CU **Lancaster I** **W4108** **Op: Bremen**
P/O E F Dowdell	+	T/o 2330 Wigsley and briefed to bomb aiming
Sgt G A Walker	+	point "E". Shot down at 0222 by Oblt Ludwig
P/O P A Vivian RNZAF	+	Becker, II./NJG2, crashing onto farmland worked
F/S J J W Adams RCAF	+	by the Kleistra brothers at Buytenweg, Oudehorne
F/S R Robertson	+	(Friesland), 10 km E of Heerenveen, Holland. All
Sgt R L Moss	+	rest in Heerenveen (Nieuwehorne) Protestant
Sgt P K Jones	+	Cemetery. P/O Vivian RNZAF was flying his

thirty-second sortie, having recently completed
a tour with 83 Squadron. Apart from a single day, nominally on charge with
97 Squadron, the Lancaster had spent its entire service life at Wigsley and
when lost had flown a total of 102.45 hours.

14 Sep **1653 CU** **Liberator II** **AL624** **Training**
1942
P/O I H Betts	+	T/o Burn on a cross-country exercise, during
Sgt D E Warner	+	which the bomber flew into a hill, shrouded in
Sgt J C Freestone	+	cloud, near Millfore in Kirkcudbright. Five
Sgt G C Boar	+	were taken to the Royal Air Force plot in the
Sgt G D Calder RAAF	+	village of Kirkinner, nearly 3 miles S from
Sgt J E C A Steele-Nicholson	+	Wigtown, and laid to rest in the local cemetery.
Sgt V F Talley	+	The others were claimed by their next of kin.
Sgt J Bowrey	+	P/O Betts was the son of Commander Ernest

Edward Alexander Betts CBE RN.

16–17 Sep **1654 CU** **Lancaster I** **W4138** **–U** **Op: Essen**
1942
Sgt F H Huntley	+	T/o Wigsley. Shot down near Willich, some
Sgt R A Low	+	eight kilometres SSW from Krefeld, where all
F/S L E Bell RNZAF	+	were initially buried in the Krefeld-Bochum
F/S J N S King RCAF	+	Friedhof. Since 1945, their bodies have been
Sgt D R Gilchrist RAAF	+	exhumed and taken to the Reichswald Forest War
F/S S H Cowley RCAF	+	Cemetery. Sgt Huntley hailed from Salisbury
F/S M R Crocker RCAF	+	in Rhodesia and can be said to have headed a

very cosmopolitan crew.

22 Sep **1651 CU** **Stirling I** **N6003** **–K** **Training**
1942
Sgt B G Kemp   T/o 2200 Waterbeach and crashed almost straight
away after swinging out of control. Delivered
to 7 Squadron on 22 January 1941, serving operationally for the best part of a
year before being relegated to training, it had amassed 191.50 flying hours.

2 Oct **1651 CU** **Stirling I** **N3678** **–C** **Training**
1942
Sgt K H Becroft RNZAF   T/o 2210 Waterbeach with the intention of
carrying out a night exercise, but crashed
after developing a swing that could not be controlled. Following a successful
tour of operational duty, Sgt Becroft RNZAF returned to 1651 Heavy Conversion
Unit as an instructor. While so employed, he was involved in two serious
accidents (20 August and 27 October 1943 respectively) but escaped unharmed
on each occasion.

9 Oct **1658 HCU**   **Halifax I** **L9574**   **Training**
1942   P/O F Leach   + T/o Ricall for a training sortie, in the course
         Sgt G E Broughton   + of which, and while approaching the airfield
         Sgt A H Isaac   + from the direction of Thorganby (8 miles SE of
         Sgt G Buckland   + York), the Halifax shed a propeller. Unable to
                                        retain control, P/O Leach crashed 300 yards S
of Lodge Farm. Taken home to Birmingham, he was cremated at the Perry Bar
Crematorium. Sgt Broughton is buried in Norbury (St. Thomas) Churchyard;
Sgt Isaac rests in Exeter Higher Cemetery, while Sgt Buckland is interred
at East Grinstead (Mount Noddy) Cemetery. Formed two days previous from the
amalgamation of 76 and 78 Conversion Flights, this was the unit's first serious
accident. The term "Heavy" was adopted at the same time.

18 Oct **1651 HCU**   **Stirling I** **N3681**   **-A Bar**   **Training**
1942   P/O G J Ellis   T/o Waterbeach for a training exercise which
                                        culminated in the Stirling lying, on the air-
field, with its undercarriage collapsed, for on landing P/O Ellis had been
obliged to swing his aircraft in order to avoid overshooting the runway and
finishing up across a main road.

         1658 HCU   **Halifax II** **R9366**   **Training**
         Sgt D A Gold   T/o Riccall for night flying practice. Touched
         Sgt L J Cursley   down at 2020 but immediately ground looped as a
                                        tyre burst. Both pilots later joined 76 Squadron
and were killed quite early on in their tours; Sgt Gold failed to return on
17-18 January and Sgt Cursley was posted missing from operations on 29-30 March
1943; coincidentally, both raids were against Berlin (see Bomber Command Losses,
Volume 4, pages 22 and 84 respectively).

19 Oct **1656 HCU A Flt**   **Manchester I** **R5780**   **Training**
1942   F/O R D Horner   + T/o Breighton and set a course towards the
         F/O D M Murphy RAAF   + Midlands. While carrying out a "beat up" of
         F/O R W Wood RAAF   + a public house (which is believed to have been
         F/O L Forrester RAAF   + known to some members of the crew), flew into
         AC1 D W Hodges   + a tree and crashed 1245 some 2 miles ENE of
         AC2 S Dobell   + Fradley and 6 miles, or thereabouts, NE of
                                        Lichfield, Staffordshire. F/O Horner, the
son of Lieutenant Herbert John Horner, formerly of the Royal Engineers, and
his three Australian colleagues were buried in Fradley (St. Stephen) Churchyard, Alrewas. AC1 Hodges was taken to Wandsworth (Earlsfield) Cemetery, while
AC2 Dobell rests in Stoke-on-Trent (Hanley) Cemetery; he had lost his life
within about thirty miles of his home. It is believed the RAAF members of
crew had been posted, or were awaiting movement to 460 Squadron and, as
Christopher Pointon advises, they had recently completed their training
at 27 Operational Training Unit.

Note. Formed on 10 October 1942, at Lindholme, 1656 Heavy Conversion Unit
was the first such formation assigned to No. 1 Group (in 1943, the Group
would parent 1662 and 1667 Heavy Conversion Units).   Its nucleus of equipment came from 103 Conversion Flight and 460 Conversion Flight and, for the
first few weeks its aircraft continued to operate from the airfields used
by the now defunct Flights; Breighton in the case of 460 Conversion Flight
and Elsham Wold, home for 103 Conversion Flight.   The latter had operated
Halifaxes but at Breighton, a mixture of twin-engined Manchesters and four-
engined Halifaxes and Lancasters had graced the local scene. Thus, the
Flight at Breighton became A Flight, while B Flight used Elsham Wolds.

27 Oct **1657 HCU**   **Stirling I** **W7470**   **-H**   **Training**
1942   Sgt I T S Fulton   inj T/o Stradishall for a cross-country detail, by
         Sgt Dean   day. After losing power from the port inner
         F/S W D Topping   inj engine, the crew decided to curtail the flight
         Sgt W H Brazenall   + and return to base but at 1245, their Stirling
         Sgt Pullinger   came down at Catley Hill, Motty, in Co. Durham.
         Sgt Inerarity   Sgt Brazenall rests in Dudley Borough Cemetery,
         Sgt Bullock   while Sgt Pryke is buried at Newbury Old Cemetery.
         Sgt A W Pryke   + The injured were taken to Winterton Emergency
                                        Hospital at Sedgefield.   Sgt Fulton, an American
citizen, made a good recovery and was posted to 149 Squadron. On 29-30 March 1943
he failed to return from Berlin (see Bomber Command Losses, Volume 4, page 85).

28 Oct	1651 HCU	Stirling I	BF314	-Y		Training

1942
P/O J H Bomford RNZAF	inj	T/o Waterbeach for a night navigation exercise.
Sgt A E Mason	inj	Returned to base at 0147, landing on three
F/O A W McLean RNZAF	+	engines. Despite bouncing slightly on touch
F/O A F Koehn RCAF	+	down, the bomber continued along the runway
Sgt E H Turner RNZAF	+	for some distance before the pilot decided to
Sgt H Kenny	inj	go round again. Climbing steeply, the Stirling
F/S F S Dean RNZAF	+	stalled and spun in, bursting into flames on

impact. Four of the crew perished immediately,
the survivors, all grievously hurt, being rushed to RAF Hospital Ely where two
succumbed to their injuries before the day was out. F/O Koehn RCAF and the
four New Zealanders are buried in Cambridge City Cemetery, while nineteen year
old Sgt Mason, an ex-aircraft apprentice, was taken to Stockton-on-Tees (Durham
Road) Cemetery.

Note. Although I cannot be absolutely certain, I strongly believe this to be
the crash referred to in the obituary to Squadron Leader Charles Lofthouse and
published in The Daily Telegraph on 5 October 2002. The circumstances differ
slightly in that it suggests the pilot, while landing in fog, levelled out too
high, stalled and crashed, while the date quoted is given as "November 1942".
However, I have not been able to trace any incident in November 1942, that
would fit the general description of events reported in the Telegraph but the
accident, summarised above, certainly appears to be the one in which Charles
Lofthouse won an immediate Order of the British Empire (Military Division) for
his part in the rescue of the injured members of the crew. At the time, he
was acting as night duty pilot. In June 1943, Squadron Leader Lofthouse resumed operational flying when he was appointed to a flight commander position
with 7 Squadron, a Pathfinder Force unit at Oakington. On 23-24 August 1943,
his Lancaster was shot down while raiding Berlin (see Bomber Command Losses,
Volume 4, page 279).

29 Oct	1654 HCU	Lancaster I	R5660		Training

1942
| Sgt Smith | | T/o 2200 Wigsley for a night exercise. Not long |

after departing, Sgt Smith became convinced that
his port outer engine was failing and, possibly, on fire. He successfully shut
the Merlin down and feathered the propeller. Landing on three-engines, at 2240,
he overshot the runway and ran up against a gun post. In his report, the engineering officer stated he could find no evidence of a fire, as such, but he did
detect a loss of coolant.

	1660 HCU	Manchester I	L7417		Unknown

Declared as written off on this date, but the
circumstances are completely unknown. In his excellent analysis of the history
of the Avro Manchester (published in 1995 by Midland Publishing Limited), Dr.
Robert Kirby shows that it was taken on charge by 1660 Heavy Conversion Unit
on 20 October 1942 and written off nine days later, "cause unknown".

31 Oct	1652 HCU	Halifax I	L9491	GV-Q	Training

1942
Sgt W S Allard	inj	T/o Dalton. Crash-landed 1130, hitting a tree
LAC D P MacDonald	inj	in the process, at Chapel Farm, North Kilvington
SGT F B Ward	inj	some 2 miles N from Thirsk, Yorkshire. Shortly
Sgt J W Young		before the crash, the pilot reported that he was

trying to unfeather the starboard inner engine,
but, it seems, he inadvertently stopped the starboard outer. Sgt Allard and his
wireless operator, Sgt Ward, were quite badly injured and both were treated in
Northallerton Hospital. LAC MacDonald, the flight engineer, was taken to the
Lambert Memorial Hospital at Thirsk before being discharged to Station Sick
Quarters at Marston Moor. By the spring of 1943, Sgt Young was serving with
35 Squadron, a Pathfinder Force formation operating from Graveley. Outbound
to Plzen on 16-17 April 1943, his Halifax was shot down over France (see Bomber
Command Losses, Volume 4, page 109).

	1652 HCU	Halifax II	R9433	GV-R	Training

Sgt R Britcher	inj	T/o Marston Moor. Lost control, due to rudder
Sgt A Brannigan	inj	overbalance, and at 1720 flat spun to the ground
Sgt E J Taylor	inj	near Greets Farm, not far distant from Castle
Sgt P E Godfrey	inj	Howard School, 4 miles or so SW of Malton in
Sgt R M Eyles RAAF	inj	Yorkshire. Sgt Britcher was treated in Station
Sgt R G Boanas	inj	Sick Quarters; four went to Malton Hospital.

22 Nov　**1651 HCU**　　　　**Stirling I**　**BF333**　**–R**　　　　　　　**Training**
1942　　Sgt C K Easton RNZAF　　　　　T/o Waterbeach for a night cross-country, during
　　　　Sgt E Kirby　　　　　　　　　which the starboard inner failed. As the bomber
　　　　Sgt J B T Williams　　　inj　lost height, two of the crew baled out but their
　　　　Sgt J Banyer　　　　　　　　colleagues remained aboard and were not too
　　　　Sgt L H Pattison　　　　inj　seriously hurt in the ensuing crash-landing, at
　　　　Sgt W Jennings　　　　　inj　around 0140, a mile or so NNE of Portabello Farm
　　　　Sgt N R Hutchins RAAF　　inj　on the old Roman road one-and-a-half miles WSW
　　　　　　　　　　　　　　　　　　from Shipston-on-Stour, Warwickshire. Three,
Sgts Banyer, Pattison and Jennings went, eventually, to 15 Squadron where they
joined another RNZAF pilot, P/O J H Stowell. Sadly, all three died (as did their
skipper) on 4-5 May 1943 (see Bomber Command Losses, Volume 4, page 133).

27 Nov　**1661 HCU C Flt**　　**Lancaster I**　**R5908**　　　　　　　　　**Training**
1942　　Sgt R D Codlin　　　　　　　T/o 1925 Scampton for a night exercise. At
　　　　Sgt H Siddons　　　　　　　approximately 2015, Sgt Codlin made his approach
　　　　　　　　　　　　　　　　　　to land but failed to flatten out sufficiently
and, as a consequence, his arrival on the runway was heavy enough to break the
Lancaster's undercarriage. In his report, Sgt Codlin admitted to misjudging
his height, believing he was still 50 feet in the air when his aircraft arrived
on the ground. It is thought that both airmen survived the war.

Note. 1661 Heavy Conversion Flight had formed at Waddington on 9 November 1942,
having absorbed 9 Conversion Flight and 44 Conversion Flight. At Scampton, 49
Conversion Flight was included in the equation, becoming C Flight of the newly
established formation.

28 Nov　**1651 HCU**　　　　**Stirling I**　**BF374**　**–K**　　　　　　　**Training**
1942　　P/O J S Brydon RCAF　　　　T/o Waterbeach. Forced-landed at around 1700,
　　　　　　　　　　　　　　　　　　due to engine failure, at Smithy Fen Farm, two
miles N of Cottenham, a village near the airfield and lying some 6 miles N of
Cambridge. Today (2002), P/O Brydon RCAF is buried within ten miles of the
author's home at Sixpenny Handley, having lost his life in an operational crash
near Blandford Forum in February 1943 (Bomber Command Losses, Volume 4, page 43
refers). He hailed from Toronto in Ontario.

29 Nov　**1652 HCU**　　　　**Halifax I**　**L9608**　　　　　　　　　　**Training**
1942　　F/S J D W Stenhouse　　　　T/o 1200 Marston for circuits and landings but
　　　　　　　　　　　　　　　　　　swung violently to starboard. F/S Stenhouse was
unable to correct the situation, so he closed the throttles and applied the
brakes. At this point, the bomber wheeled about and its undercarriage gave way.
It was discovered that, inadvertently, the flight engineer had turned on the
wrong petrol cocks, this leading to engine failure as the Halifax approached
flying speed. In mitigation, the Court of Enquiry stated that the instructor,
who had left the aircraft after authorising F/S Stenhouse to continue circuit
practice, had failed to ensure that the petrol cocks had been correctly selected.
Posted to 51 Squadron, F/S Stenhouse was lost, with his crew, on 1-2 March 1943,
while raiding Berlin (see Bomber Command Losses, Volume 4, page 55).

1 Dec　**1661 HCU C Flt**　　**Manchester I**　**R5836**　　　　　　　　**Training**
1942　　P/O J M Desmond RAAF　　　T/o 1505 Scampton for day training. As dusk fell,
　　　　　　　　　　　　　　　　　　he approached the runway but was too high as his
aircraft passed over the threshold and from around fifteen feet, he stalled onto
the runway at 1710, damaging the Manchester beyond repair. Recently (24 November)
attached from 467 Squadron, P/O Desmond RAAF completed his training and returned
to his unit. On 27-28 May 1943, with the Battle of the Ruhr at its height, he
failed to make it home from Essen (see Bomber Command Losses, Volume 4, page 168).

2 Dec　**1652 HCU**　　　　**Halifax II**　**R9493**　　　　　　　　　**Training**
1942　　F/O A R Dawes　　　　　　　T/o 1920 Marston Moor and was at the point of
　　　　F/S N Garforth　　　　　　　becoming airborne when the cockpit lighting
　　　　　　　　　　　　　　　　　　failed. Without being ordered, F/S Garforth
closed the throttles and the Halifax careered off the runway and was wrecked.

3 Dec　**1659 HCU**　　　　**Halifax II**　**W1052**　　　　　　　　　**Training**
1942　　Sgt P K Chambers RCAF　　　T/o Leeming only to crash while trying to abort
　　　　Sgt Bell RCAF　　　　　　　the exercise. From Long Beach in California, he
　　　　　　　　　　　　　　　　　　failed to bring his 432 Squadron Wellington home
from Köln in early July 1943 (see Bomber Command Losses, Volume 4, page 222).

5 Dec	1658 HCU	Halifax II	R9531	Training

5 Dec
1942

1658 HCU   **Halifax II**   **R9531**   **Training**

F/S D C Cameron RCAF   +   T/o Riccall for a day cross-country (its crew
Sgt R J Marshall   +   was an unusual combination of air bomber, two
F/S J C Macaulay   +   wireless operator and three air gunners). At
Sgt C F Bonorino   +   roughly 1300, the Halifax was seen flying quite
Sgt J A Barrett-Lennard RAAF +   low when it banked steeply and spun in near the
Sgt H G Jenkins   +   North Lincolnshire steel town of Scunthorpe,
Sgt R F Pretty   inj   damaging some civilian property and injuring
a dozen people, either residing in the houses
or who were in the immediately vicinity at the time of the accident. Service
funerals for the two Commonwealth airmen, and Sgt Bonorino, formerly of the
Royal Artillery, were held at Brigg Cemetery, while the others who died were
claimed by their next of kin.

9 Dec
1942

1651 HCU   **Stirling I**   **N6101**   **-E**   **Training**

Sgt L J Dodd   T/o 2040 Waterbeach for a night exercise.
Crash-landed 2105, on the airfield, with both
port engines ablaze. Following salvage, the airframe became a training aid
with the serial 3495M applied. In a shade over a year of service, the Stirling
had flown 246.00 hours. Soon after this incident, Sgt Dodd left on posting to
218 Squadron, failing to return from Hamburg in early February 1943 (see Bomber
Command Losses, Volume 4, page 35).

11 Dec
1942

1654 HCU   **Lancaster I**   **W4255**   **Training**

Sgt B D C Cox   T/o Wigsley for night training. Due to a sudden
and unexpected deterioration in the weather, Sgt
Cox deemed it prudent to land as soon as possible. In the pouring rain, he had
great difficulty in keeping the Lancaster on the glide path and, thus, his
arrival on the runway at 2359 was extremely hard, causing the undercarriage
to collapse.

13 Dec
1942

1656 HCU   **Halifax II**   **W1011**   **Training**

W/O J Gibbs   T/o Lindholme for dual flying. Crashed, and
Sgt G A Austin   burnt out, at 1043, roughly a mile E of the
airfield.

1660 HCU   **Lancaster I**   **W4128**   **Training**

F/S D A Stewart RNZAF   T/o 1120 Swinderby for dual circuit training.
At 1200, the pupil pilot ballooned the bomber
as he landed and having opened the throttles to go round again, his instructor
raised the undercarriage. His actions were, unfortunately, premature and as
the Lancaster settled back, the port main wheel was ripped off. Control, was
retained and, subsequently, a wheels up landing was made at Scampton. After
being salvaged, the airframe became an instructional aid at No. 10 School of
Technical Training at Kirkham, the serial 3609M being applied. In a rider to
this incident, the Air Officer Commanding No. 5 Group, Air-Vice Marshal W A
Coryton, wrote, "This instructor (has) since developed into one of the best
and most conscientious in his unit".

29 Dec
1942

1652 HCU   **Halifax II**   **W7816 GV-E**   **Air Test**

W/C W S Hillary DFC DFM   inj   T/o 1450 Marston Moor with a full fuel load and
F/L S B Bailey   inj   new pattern exhaust shrouds, which were under-
Sgt J J Lomas   inj   going suitability tests. Within minutes of their
F/O E R Buckwell   inj   departure, the crew encountered heavy snow,
F/S G H Rogers   inj   accompanied by icing. Not surprisingly, the
F/L J W Hannant DFC   inj   engines were affected, the outer starboard in
Sgt W J Dowle   inj   particular. Having shut this unit down and
feathered the propeller, W/C Hillary headed
back towards the airfield, but as he approached from the east, the Halifax
became more and more difficult to control. His problems were heightened when
the flap mechanism jammed and, realising he was drifting towards the village
of Tockwith, an immediate forced-landing was made. Thus, at 1520, the bomber
skidded into a dyke, whereupon the fuselage broke up into several sections.
A pre-war regular airman, and a veteran of bombing operations with three
squadrons (he gained his DFM with 10 Squadron, this being published as early
as 30 July 1940), W/C Hillary's DFC had been Gazetted on 30 January 1942,
following service with 35 Squadron and 76 Squadron. F/L Hannant had flown
with 51 Squadron, his honour having been promulgated on 14 April 1942. F/L
Bailey was the unit's engineering officer.

29 Dec   **1657 HCU**   **Stirling I W7517   -I**   **Training**
1942   Sgt J C Ter Averst   T/o 0150 Stradishall but crashed almost straight
away due to lack of power from the starboard
inner motor. It transpired that during pre-take off engine running, Sgt Ter
Averst, whose birthplace was in Holland, had failed to notice a considerable
magneto drop on the failed unit. His Stirling had been delivered, ex-works,
to 15 Squadron on 28 March 1942, but this may have been a "paper issue" as it
was accepted the following day by 7 Squadron. On 22 June, it was slightly
damaged in a minor flying accident, returning to squadron charge on 18 July.
On 5 October, it was relegated to training duties with 1657 Heavy Conversion
Unit, and appears to have enjoyed trouble free service until the incident here
summarised (it was not officially struck off charge until 28 January 1943,
which suggests that repairs may have been contemplated), by which time it had
logged 260.35 flying hours.

Resumé. The training structure of Bomber Command was, by the end of 1942, more
or less complete. The operational training units, established in the spring
of 1940 and, at the time, deemed sufficient for the Command's needs, were
functioning well and would continue to play an important first step in the
development of a skilled and highly efficient bomber crew.

However, with the introduction of the "heavies", a further layer in the
training system was deemed necessary and, as outlined in the introduction,
for the best part of 1942, the requirements for heavy bomber conversion had
been satisfied via conversion flights which, principally, were offshoots of
their respective squadrons and the heavy conversion units, now coming to the
fore.

Again, as remarked upon in the introduction, scant information is available
in unit records but the task of the heavy conversion unit was not quite so exacting as the work done by the operational training unit. Courses, generally,
only lasted for a couple of weeks, time enough to familiarise the pilot with
the workings of a four-engined aircraft. For his crew, their training load was
not too burdensome, though, at this stage in their development, continuing to
practice the skills so recently learnt was extremely important. Furthermore,
it was at the heavy conversion unit that they were joined by a second air
gunner, as well as meeting their flight engineer for the first time.

The post of flight engineer was, at the beginning of 1942, still relatively
new and such was the shortage of suitably qualified personnel to fill the
vacancies that were opening up that volunteers from ground tradesmen were
actively sought. The most suitable airmen were those qualified as engine
fitters, and a perusal of the service numbers of airmen entering the trade
identifies large numbers coming from the ranks of ex-apprentices, the majority
being Halton trained. Ground instruction, in most cases, was provided at St.
Athan in South Wales and until his arrival at a heavy conversion unit, few had
had any experience whatsoever of flying.

Although called upon, from time to time, to support Main Force operations,
the heavy conversion units were not used to the same degree as the operational
training units, though in the latter stages of the war their aircraft did take
part in diversionary sweeps, designed to entice the Luftwaffe into the air and
use up their dwindling supplies of aviation fuel. This, however, was well into
the future and as 1942 drew to a close, the output of trained bomber crews
from the training formations was gathering a respectable pace.

| 2 Jan | 1658 HCU | Halifax II | R9388 | Training |

2 Jan 1943 **1658 HCU** **Halifax II R9388** **Training**

Sgt T D Watson	+	T/o 1000 Riccall for a day training detail,
Sgt W F Hewitt	+	the crew comprising of a flight engineer, air
Sgt J H Atkinson	+	bomber and an air gunner. Some fifteen minutes
Sgt G M Lipsett RCAF	+	later, the Halifax was seen nearing the runway

with one engine feathered. Instead of landing, however, power was increased and the bomber commenced climbing, very steeply. For a few minutes it continued on a westerly heading before it stalled and dived into the ground at Tile Bridge, less than a mile SSW of Cawood, 4 miles to the NW of Selby, Yorkshire. Those who died were buried under private arrangements; Sgt Watson in Lanark (St. Leonard's) Cemetery, Sgt Hewitt at Wellington Cemetery and Sgt Atkinson in London at Greenwich (Charlton) Cemetery. Very seriously injured, Sgt Lipsett RCAF was admitted to Selby Cottage Hospital, and then transferred to RAF Hospital Rauceby. He is believed to have made a good recovery and, it seems, to have survived the war.

1660 HCU **Manchester I L7482** **Transit**

F/O H C C Goodyear RCAF	inj	T/o Coleby Grange, having landed here in error
Sgt N P Tutt		following a flight from Swinderby, and set
P/O H Robertson		course for the intended airfield at Waddington.
P/O G J Gibbings	inj	Weather conditions were far from ideal and
Sgt W A Barker		while trying to climb above a snowstorm, the
Sgt W R Jakeway		flying controls iced up. Abandoned and left
P/O N Bird		to crash 1230 at Highfield Farm, not far from

Metheringham airfield. On 22-23 April 1944, F/O Goodyear RCAF, now serving with 61 Squadron, was killed during the course of a visit to Braunschweig (see Bomber Command Losses, Volume 5, page 178). The Manchester, here summarised, had seen no operational service; from late November 1941 to 7 June 1942, it had served with 25 Operational Training Unit and this was followed by a near six month stint with 97 Conversion Flight before being delivered to 1660 Heavy Conversion Unit on 20 October. Robert Kirby, an expert in Manchester matters, reports that it had flown 244.02 hours.

4 Jan 1943 **1658 HCU** **Halifax I L9569** **Training**

F/L D J B Hamilton	T/o 1445 Melbourne for circuits and landings but
Sgt M C Smith	before the exercise could be completed, the outer
	starboard engine failed. In the ensuing forced-

landing at 1500, on the airfield, the Halifax caught fire and was destroyed, though no one appears to have been hurt.

11 Jan 1943 **1661 HCU** **Lancaster I W4183** **Training**

Sgt A R B Airy RAAF   T/o 1907 Winthorpe to practice night circuits and landings but yawed to starboard and the tip of the starboard wing dug into the ground. Following an investigation, it was recommended that Sgt Airy RAAF be withdrawn from heavy bomber training and posted to a medium bomber unit. This duly took place and by the summer he was flying Wellingtons with 466 Squadron. Sadly, on 25-26 June 1943, while raiding Gelsenkirchen, he was shot down over the IJsselmeer (see Bomber Command Losses, Volume 4, page 212).

15 Jan 1943 **1651 HCU** **Stirling I N3769 -U** **Training**

Sgt G Stephens   T/o 2155 Waterbeach for night flying practice. Touched down at 2225 alongside No. 7 flare and swerved violently to port. On the wet grass, the brakes proved ineffective and moments later the bomber ran into a ditch. Not surprisingly, the undercarriage gave way and, soon afterwards, a fire broke out. On completing his course, Sgt Stephens proceeded to 90 Squadron and was posted missing from a trip to Hamburg (as a second pilot) on 3-4 February 1943 (see Bomber Command Losses, Volume 4, page 35).

1659 HCU **Halifax II R9369 -N** **Training**

F/O A A Stewart RNZAF	T/o 2130 Leeming for night circuit practice.
Sgt A S Green RCAF	Twenty minutes into the exercise, the Halifax
	came into land, with its undercarriage still

retracted. Despite the warning horn sounding, the crew failed to take the necessary overshoot action and, as a consequence, the bomber was damaged beyond repair in the crash that followed. On completion of his training, Sgt Green was posted to 419 Squadron, failing to return from Dortmund on 23-24 May 1943 (see Bomber Command Losses, Volume 4, page 159).

17–18 Jan	**1654 HCU**	**Lancaster I**	**R5843**	**–C**	**Op: Berlin**

17–18 Jan
1943

1654 HCU   **Lancaster I**   **R5843**   **–C**   **Op: Berlin**

P/O L Jenkinson   +   T/o 1647 Swinderby. Crashed at 2213 at Heis-
Sgt F Nuttall   +   felderfeld to the N of Leer. All were taken
Sgt F R Scargall   +   to Wittmund and interred on 30 January. Since
Sgt H R Wakley   +   then, their remains have been exhumed and laid
F/S W D Henderson RAAF   +   to rest in Sage War Cemetery. Prior to being
Sgt P J Newman   +   allotted "C", this Lancaster had carried the
Sgt B Hannaway   +   combination "UG" with "O" as its letter.

1654 HCU   **Lancaster I**   **W4772**   **–X**   **Op: Berlin**

P/O F A Read DFC   +   T/o 1627 Swinderby. Twice, at 2152 and again
F/O L E Stockwell   +   at 2220, the direction finding station at Heston
P/O B E Morgan   +   picked up faint transmissions from the Lancaster
F/O F R Leonard   +   and second class fixes indicated its position as
Sgt E C Webb   +   52.12N 05.28E and 52.32N 03.48E respectively.
Sgt D T Pitman DFM   +   All are commemorated on the Runnymede Memorial.
Sgt P H Pearce   +   P/O Read had recently completed a tour of duty
with 207 Squadron, while Sgt Pitman had either
finished his tour with 61 Squadron, or had been attached from this formation.
Their awards had been published on 6 November and 11 August 1942 respectively.
P/O Morgan was a Bachelor of Music (Oxford).

1656 HCU   **Lancaster I**   **ED316**   **Op: Berlin**

F/L S D L Hood MID RNZAF   +   T/o 1648 Lindholme. Lost without trace. All
Sgt H F Muller RAAF   +   are commemorated on the Runnymede Memorial.
F/O K B Walter RAAF   +   Errol Martyn has traced seventeen sorties flown
Sgt D J Lindsay RAAF   +   by F/L Hood while serving with 149 Squadron and
F/O K A C Weaving RAAF   +   one while instructing at 27 Operational Training
Sgt H Woodrow   +   Unit, where four of the five Australians had
F/S S E Logue RAAF   +   trained from the summer of 1942 onwards, the
exception being Sgt Muller RAAF.

18 Jan
1943

1658 HCU   **Halifax II**   **W1227**   **Training**

P/O H A Davies   T/o 1500 East Moor for a dual sortie but lost
power and crashed through some trees, before
ending up roughly 200 yards to the E of Low Carr Farr and not far from the
airfield's domestic site.

24 Jan
1943

1654 HCU   **Manchester I**   **L7457**   **Training**

F/S Taylor   T/o 1458 Wigsley for a combination of familiarisation, dual and circuit practice. Soon after
becoming airborne, the port engine burst into flames and at 1510, the Manchester
was forced-landed at West Bank, Saxilby, 6 miles NW from the centre of Lincoln.

26 Jan
1943

1661 HCU   **Manchester I**   **R5772**   **Training**

F/S Schnier RCAF   T/o 1037 Winthorpe for the pilot's first solo
on type but while in the circuit the port engine
cut. While trying to restart the motor, flames burst forth and a forced-landing
was made, in a field, a mile NE of the aerodrome. An investigation of the burnt
remains found that the No. 3 exhaust valve had broken.

28 Jan
1943

1659 HCU   **Halifax II**   **W1146**   **–H**   **Training**

P/O Y H Lefebre RCAF   inj   T/o Leeming for a cross-country. On return, and
Sgt H McGeach RCAF   inj   while letting down from the west through cloud,
Sgt R E Drago   +   crashed at 1228 in an area perhaps best described
F/S J H A Beliveau RCAF   +   as Thwaite Common near to Pickersett and lying
Sgt J D Stone   +   between two beacons some 3 miles SW of the hamlet
Sgt C L Pudney RCAF   inj   of Thwaite, 10 miles WSW from Reeth, Yorkshire.
F/S J R Askew RCAF   inj   Despite having sustained very serious injuries,
P/O Lefebre RCAF, assisted by Sgt Pudney RCAF,
himself bleeding profusely from wounds to his head and face, removed everyone
from the wreckage. Subsequently, those who had survived were taken to Catterick
Military Hospital, where F/S Askew RCAF died soon after admittance. Along with
F/S Beliveau RCAF and Sgt Drago of Bromley in Kent, he rests in Ripon Cemetery.
Sgt Stone was buried, privately, at Croydon (Mitcham Road) Cemetery. Very sadly,
having returned to active duty, Sgt Pudney RCAF was involved in another horrific
flying accident, this time involving a 405 Squadron Lancaster (see Bomber Command
Losses, Volume 4, page 187). From Belmar, New Jersey, he richly deserved his
award of the George Medal, which was Gazetted on 12 August 1943 (see Addendum).

28 Jan   **1661 HCU**   **Lancaster I**   **R5540**   **Training**
1943   Sgt G N Stephenson   T/o Winthorpe for night circuits and landings.
Approached to land at 2140, but over corrected
when a wing dropped and, as a consequence, the Lancaster touched down on one
wheel and ballooned back into the air. It then stalled and crashed, bursting
into flames soon afterwards. Posted to 44 Squadron and, later, commissioned,
Sgt Stephenson was killed during operations to Berlin in late August 1943 (see
Bomber Command Losses, Volume 4, page 300).

29 Jan   **1652 HCU**   **Halifax II**   **BB265**   **—S**   **Training**
1943   Sgt J L Downs   +   T/o Marston Moor for night circuit training.
         Sgt J R Burns   inj   In a statement, provided by the navigator,
         W/O F W Crawley   inj   W/O Crawley, it appears that the starboard
         Sgt E J Howell   inj   outer Merlin caught fire at 600 feet. The
         Sgt D R Raven   inj   petrol feed was turned off immediately, and
         Sgt L Rotheray   +   the flames went out. However, despite full
power being applied, the Halifax lost height
and crashed at 2050 a little over 3 miles SE of the airfield near Healaugh,
seven miles WSW from the centre of York. Those who died were claimed by their
next of kin. W/O Crawley's service number indicates he had joined the pre-war
volunteer reserve, possibly for pilot instruction.

1 Feb   **1659 HCU**   **Halifax II**   **BB275**   **—S**   **Training**
1943   WO2 J G Arsenault RCAF   +   T/o Leeming for a cross-country exercise which
         Sgt P Larsen RCAF   +   at some stage involved the crew flying over the
         F/S D C Carder RCAF   +   northern part of Wales and it was whilst the
         Sgt A B Wedderspoon   +   Halifax was over Anglesey that it dived into
         Sgt J B D George   +   the ground between Holyhead and Rhoscolyn on
         Sgt T H Clapham   +   the NW side of the island. WO2 Arsenault RCAF
         Sgt H F Gorrie RCAF   +   and both air gunners lie in Holyhead (St. Mary)
         F/S J L Boivin RCAF   +   Roman Catholic Cemetery; F/S Carder RCAF and
Sgt Larsen RCAF rest in Holyhead (Maeshyfryd)
Burial Board Cemetery, Holywood Rural. Sgt Wedderspoon was cremated at Golders
Green; Sgt George was taken to Oswestry General Cemetery, while Sgt Clapham's
grave is located in Flixton (St. Michael) Churchyard, Lancashire.

        1661 HCU   **Lancaster I**   **L7530**   **Training**
        Sgt B F Wilmot RAAF   inj   T/o 2205 Winthorpe for night circuit practice.
        Sgt A Macdonald   inj   At around 2225, Sgt Wilmot RAAF overshot the
        Sgt T W Hill   inj   runway and flew into rising ground at Main Road,
        P/O Pietsch   Beacon Hills, Newark-upon-Trent, Nottinghamshire.
        Sgt H H Lloyd RAAF   +   It is believed the pilot had become disorientated
        Sgt W J Fraser   inj   after being dazzled by floodlights. Sgt Lloyd
of Elwood, Victoria, lies in Newark-upon-Trent
Cemetery.

3 Feb   **1658 HCU**   **Halifax II**   **R9455**   **Training**
1943   Sgt J C Creswell   T/o 1030 Riccall. Crash-landed at around 1500 in
flood water on The Holmes, an area bordering the
north-west outskirts of Selby, Yorkshire. A combination of overheating engines
and a misunderstanding regarding the flaps and undercarriage were contributory
factors in this unfortunate accident.

        1658 HCU   **Halifax II**   **BB194**   **Training**
        Sgt J N Willoughby   inj   T/o 2145 Melbourne for night flying practice
        Sgt C G Street   inj   which ended fifteen minutes later with the bomber
        P/O Hellis   five hundred yards beyond the runway, and on fire
        Sgt Davies   having literally flown into the ground from a
        Sgt Cable   failed attempt to overshoot. Sgt Willoughby was
        Sgt Taylor   taken to York Military Hospital with a fractured
        Sgt S H Boulton   inj   skull (Sgt Boulton, too, was admitted to the
same hospital, though his injuries were less
serious), while Sgt Street was treated in the local Station Sick Quarters for
a sprained left ankle. All recovered from their wounds, but, subsequently,
Sgt Street and Sgt Boulton were reported as prisoners of war, the former in
the wake of an attack on Gelsenkirchen on 9-10 July 1943 (see Bomber Command
Losses, Volume 4, page 225) while flying with 51 Squadron. As it will be seen,
the circumstances surrounding his entry into captivity were, to say the least,
quite bizarre.

4 Feb 1943	1658 HCU D Flt	**Halifax II** R9373 25	**Training**

Sgt R J Hall
T/o 1450 Riccall. Wrecked following a landing, at base, with the wheels still retracted. The cause was attributed to a misunderstanding during the cockpit drill.

12 Feb 1943	1660 HCU	**Lancaster I** R5676	**Training**

F/O S R Jones +
Sgt W T Raeside +
F/O F M Krish +
F/O S Hoy +
Sgt J Westwood +
F/S G W Kennedy RCAF +
Sgt T H Jackson +
LAC E R Redfern +

T/o Swinderby. Broke up in flight, the starboard wing being first to fail, and crashed circa 1005 at Oldfields Farm, Sturton by Stow, 8 miles NW of Lincoln. F/S Kennedy RCAF, known to his family and friends as "Bunny", was buried in Thurlby (St. Germain) Churchyard, while the funerals for his seven colleagues were held under private arrangement. It is noted that F/O Hoy's younger brother had been killed in a flying accident a month previous (see Bomber Command Losses, Volume 7, page 190); both now lie in a joint grave at Hull Eastern Cemetery.

14 Feb 1943	1657 HCU	**Stirling I** W7451 -S	**Training**

Sgt R Watson
T/o 1050 Stradishall tasked for a load climb, but as the Stirling gained height, Sgt Watson found that he could not retract the undercarriage. Course was set for The Wash in order to jettison the bombs, but this intention was thwarted when the bomb doors refused to budge. Turning back towards the coast, his problems were further heightened when the crank case in the port outer engine fractured and soon after flames were seen emitting from the damaged motor. Despite being relatively inexperienced, Sgt Watson set his crippled aircraft down at 1120 in a small paddock, before eventually rolling to a stop in a ploughed field at Saddle Bow some 2 miles SSW of King's Lynn, Norfolk, the immediate area being surrounded by anti-invasion poles. Posted to 15 Squadron, he failed to return from Duisburg on 26-27 April 1943, though, happily, he was later reported as a prisoner of war (see Bomber Command Losses, Volume 4, page 123).

	1660 HCU	**Manchester I** L7286	**Training**

Sgt N C Keeffe RAAF
T/o 0916 Swinderby for continuation training. Flying at 1,000 feet, the flame traps to the "A" and "B" blocks on the starboard Vulture burned through, causing the unit to burst into flames. An immediate forced-landing followed, circa 1100, at Waddington with the wheels left retracted. Although little damaged, the airframe was struck off charge on 7 March, a total of 218.05 flying hours being recorded. A little over two months later, Sgt Keeffe RAAF was reported missing in action (see Bomber Command Losses, Volume 4, page 118).

19 Feb 1943	1661 HCU	**Lancaster I** R5850	**Training**

F/O G H Hartley inj
Sgt B F Wilmot RAAF inj
Sgt A Macdonald
Sgt T W Hill
P/O Pietsch
F/S M S Kahn RCAF +

T/o Winthorpe for a night exercise. At 2122, the Lancaster overshot the runway, flying into telephone wires as it came down close to the airfield. On impact, the bomber caught fire. F/S Kahn RCAF is buried in Nottingham (Wilford Hill) Jewish Cemetery. For the second time in less than three weeks, Sgt Wilmot RAAF had been injured in a serious flying accident and by a quirk of coincidence, the sole fatality on each occasion had been one of the aircraft's air gunners. Posted to 467 Squadron, he failed to return from Düsseldorf on 11-12 June 1943 (see Bomber Command Losses, Volume 4, page 180). With him on that fateful night was Sgts Macdonald, Hill and Fraser, the last named having been involved in the first of his two training accidents.

21 Feb 1943	1661 HCU	**Lancaster I** R5892	**Training**

Sgt E A Robbins
T/o Winthorpe for a cross-country exercise. While flying at 19,000 feet, an engine caught fire and before it could be quelled an explosion occurred which blew off the wing leading edge between the fuselage and the inner starboard Merlin. This was followed by loss of the unit's rear cowling. With commendable skill, Sgt Robbins flew his crippled machine out to sea and ditched, circa 1310, off St. Alban's Head on the Dorset coast, 5 miles WSW from Swanage. On impact, the rear fuselage fractured forward of the tail. Posted to 106 Squadron, he, along with the rest of his crew, went into captivity in late May 1943 (see Bomber Command Losses, Volume 4, page 166).

| 25 Feb 1943 | 1654 HCU | **Manchester I** | **L7400** | **Ground** |

Sgt J L Hendry RNZAF — At 1500, after being bombed up in readiness for an exercise, and while awaiting clearance for take off (from Wigsley), one of the practice bombs in bay 4 detonated. Badly damaged, the Manchester was officially struck off charge on 11 September. On completion of his conversion training, Sgt Hendry RNZAF joined 106 Squadron and was well established in his tour of operations when he was shot down, outbound to Berlin in late August 1943 (see Bomber Command Losses, Volume 4, page 302). For his parents, this was a double blow for two years previous their youngest son, Sgt William Nisbet Hendry RNZAF, had been reported missing from a "Circus" operation over northern France, his 485 Squadron Spitfire being last seen off Gravelines (see Fighter Command Losses, Volume 1, page 126).

| 26 Feb 1943 | 1652 HCU | **Halifax II** | **BB206** | **Ground** |

Sgt K A Toon RNZAF
Sgt N R Holledge — While having its tyres checked, reported at Rufforth, struck at 2235 by Halifax II BB307 from the same unit. The latter was repaired (though it was subsequently written off, still on the strength of 1652 HCU, on 10 January 1944), but Sgt Toon's aircraft was deemed as suitable only for salvage. Sadly, neither of the two pilots survived their operational tours; on 19 June 1943, Sgt Holledge's Halifax crashed soon after taking off from Elvington for a raid on le Creusot, while a month later Sgt Toon RNZAF died after being shot down over Belgium by a night-fighter (see Bomber Command Losses, Volume 4, pages 191 and 230 respectively).

| | 1658 HCU | **Halifax II** | **V9988** | **Training** |

Sgt T M L Dingwall   +
Sgt J I Drake RCAF   +
Sgt E J Wood   +
Sgt I D Williams   inj
Sgt R J Ball   inj

T/o 2208 Riccall for night flying practice but lost an engine soon after becoming airborne, crashing 2210 into trees at Manor Farm Orchard, Kelfield, a village some 3 miles NW of the airfield. Sgt Dingwall is buried in Scotland at Kirkcaldy Cemetery; Sgt Drake RCAF was interred in Selby Cemetery, while Sgt Wood was taken to Willesden New Cemetery. The two injured airmen were treated, initially, in Station Sick Quarters and both made a good recovery. Tragically, with only a few months of the war remaining, Sgt Ball lost his life during a Special Operations Executive mission over Denmark (see Bomber Command Losses, Volume 6, page 74).

| 27 Feb 1943 | 1656 HCU | **Halifax II** | **BB258** | **Training** |

P/O H F Snar RCAF — T/o 1000 Lindholme for general flying practice. Landed at midday, but drifted in the final seconds before touch down and, as a consequence, swung from the runway and lost its undercarriage. After salvage, the airframe (with the serial 4912M applied) was delivered to No. 12 Air Gunnery School at Bishops Court.

| 28 Feb 1943 | 1651 HCU | **Stirling I** | **R9304 —U** | **Training** |

P/O G K Bond
F/O I F Mackenzie — T/o 0030 Waterbeach for night dual instruction. On touch down, at 0200, the port main tyre burst, causing the Stirling to swing with such severity that the undercarriage collapsed. It was considered that channels cut into the runway were a contributory factor. Not long after this incident, F/O Mackenzie was posted to 90 Squadron; on 27 April 1943, he was posted missing in action (see Bomber Command Losses, Volume 4, page 123).

| | 1658 HCU | **Halifax II** | **BB222** | **Training** |

F/O W R Waite
Sgt T A MacQuarie — T/o Riccall but the undercarriage was prematurely retracted and, thus, on return to base thirty-five minutes later, the wheels would not lower fully. In the ensuing forced-landing, the Halifax was damaged beyond repair. Seven months previous, during operations to Düsseldorf with 76 Squadron F/O Waite and his crew had displayed outstanding determination after being very badly shot about over southern Holland by a night-fighter (see Bomber Command Losses, Volume 3, page 171 and To See The Dawn Breaking, pages 49 and 50).

| 2 Mar 1943 | 1652 HCU | **Halifax II** | **R9426** | **Training** |

Sgt E W Saywell RNZAF — T/o 2005 Marston Moor for solo flying practice. Landed rather heavily at 2035, whereupon the undercarriage collapsed. Sgt Saywell RNZAF was posted missing from Pathfinder duties on 13-14 July 1943 (see Bomber Command Losses, Volume 4, page 229).

2 Mar	1654 HCU	**Manchester I**	L7277	**Training**

2 Mar 1654 HCU   Manchester I L7277   Training
1943   F/L P J Stone DFC   inj T/o 1425 Wigsley to demonstrate feathering
       Sgt R F Lee   inj procedures to the trainee pilot. Shortly
       Sgt M W Hanley   inj before 1500, the port propeller failed to
       Sgt W C Brearley   inj disengage from its feathered position and
       Sgt M Y Smith   inj the exercise was terminated. On regaining
       Sgt F A John   inj Spilsby's circuit, F/L Stone could not get
       Sgt P Brook   + the undercarriage to lower and while trying
                                      to force -land, the Manchester struck a tree
and crashed, heavily, near North Scarle, 8 miles SW of Lincoln. Sgt Brook of
Hampstead is buried in Thorney (St. Helen) Churchyard. The injured were taken
to Newark's Emergency Hospital, where Sgt Brearley was placed on the dangerously
ill list. F/L Stone returned for a second tour of operations with 50 Squadron
and died when his Lancaster was shot down, by a night-fighter, over Holland in
June 1943 (see Bomber Command Losses, Volume 4, page 182); his DFC had been
Gazetted on 6 November 1942. Sgt Hanley, too, did not survive the war, being
killed in a flying accident whilst instructing at 1660 Heavy Conversion Unit
on 22 November 1944.

Note. When the circumstances of the accident summarised above were reported,
the serial was quoted as "L7577", and this has been entered on documents pertaining to the crew. In turn, this has led to the erroneous assumption that
Lancaster I L7577 was lost at North Scarle. Nothing could be further from the
truth, but several publications have, unfortunately, repeated this error.

5 Mar 1658 HCU   Halifax II   R9392   Training
1943   Sgt G E Sutton   T/o Melbourne for general flying practice.
                                       Touched down at 1643, port wheel first and
then bounced onto its starboard side, swung and smashed the undercarriage.
Interestingly, although the accident file has been raised by 1658 HCU, the
aircraft's movement card indicates it was still assigned to 10 Conversion
Flight, a formation that had been absorbed by "1658" on 23 November 1942.

10 Mar 1651 HCU   Stirling I   N6024   -R   Training
1943   Sgt R W Belshaw   T/o Waterbeach for night training. Swung
                                       on landing at 2100, and lost its undercarriage.
Posted to 214 Squadron, Sgt Belshaw, now commissioned, lost his life during the
opening raid in The Battle of Hamburg (see Bomber Command Losses, Volume 4,
page 239). A year later, on 28 July 1944 to be precise, the London Gazette
published details of his non-immediate award of the Distinguished Flying Cross.

       1659 HCU   Halifax II   W1241   Training
       F/O A B Shives RCAF   + T/o Leeming. While banking, in readiness to
       F/S A P M Aitkin RCAF   + land, went out of control and crashed 1410 on
       Sgt G E Clarke RCAF   + the SE side of the airfield, bursting into
       F/O W G McLaughlin RCAF   + flames as it impacted. All are buried in
       F/S L Taylor RCAF   + Ripon Cemetery. F/S Leckie RCAF was an American
       F/S R S Greengrass RCAF   + from Tifton, a town on the crossroads of US
       Sgt J H McGinn RCAF   + routes 41 and 82 in Georgia; Macon to its
       F/S A W Leckie RCAF   + north and Albany to the south. This was the
                                      first all RCAF crew to lose their lives at a
heavy conversion unit administered by Bomber Command. Their aircraft had been
damaged at Leeming on 19 November 1942, when F/L R T Langton, returning from a
weather reconnaissance, landed with the port wheel retracted.

11 Mar 1660 HCU   Halifax V   DK117   Training
1943   Sgt W J King   inj T/o 1150 Swinderby to practice three-engined
       Sgt K L Howard   inj flying. While flying at 2,000 feet, and trying
       Sgt C E Towill   inj to restart the port outer, lost control and
       P/O Bowden   crashed 1230 between the airfield at Cranwell
       Sgt R Stevens   inj and Leasingham, 2 miles NNW from Sleaford in
       Sgt N Jackson   inj Lincolnshire. P/O Bowden escaped unscathed,
       Sgt S J Proctor   inj but the rest were not so fortunate and after
                                      being admitted to RAF Hospital Rauceby, Sgt
Stevens died from his injuries. From Brighton in Sussex, he lies in Newark-
upon-Trent Cemetery. Subsequently, Sgts King, Towill and Jackson lost their
lives on operations (see Bomber Command Losses, Volumes 4 and 5, pages 311,
460 and 189 respectively).

12 Mar 1943	**1658 HCU**	**Halifax II**	**DT510**	**Training**

P/O D P Puddephatt   T/o Riccall for conversion to type training. Landed at 1537, but a tyre burst, sending the bomber off the runway, whereupon the undercarriage collapsed. P/O Puddephatt and his crew fell victim to a night-fighter, over Holland, in mid-May 1943 (see Bomber Command Losses, Volume 4, page 146).

1661 HCU	**Manchester I**	**R5838**	**Training**

W/O E Knight   T/o Winthorpe tasked to demonstrate feathering procedures, during which the port engine was shut down. Flying at 5,000 feet, the pilot attempted to re-start the motor, but the propeller jammed in fine pitch. Skillfully, W/O Knight crash-landed at 1255 on Wickenby airfield.

Note. Following a similar accident, ten days previous (see the first entry on the previous page), the Air Officer Commanding No. 5 Group (Air-Vice Marshal the Honourable R A Cochrane) issued instructions that exercises of this nature should be curtailed. It would appear that this order had not filtered through the chain of command to Winthorpe, or it had been recently rescinded.

1661 HCU	**Lancaster I**	**R5556**	**Training**

F/L J Cowan DFC RNZAF	+	T/o Winthorpe for general flying practice.
Sgt A R J Burgess	+	Came down at approximately 1745, following
Sgt D W Lovelady	+	an uncontrollable fire in the outer port engine,
F/S A E Hannay RCAF	+	at Cromwell, 4 miles NNW from Newark-upon-Trent,
Sgt E Hall	+	Nottinghamshire. Three, F/L Cowan RNZAF (he had
F/S H V Adams	+	recently completed a tour of at least twenty-
Sgt S C Johnson	+	seven operations with 9 Squadron), Sgt Burgess
Sgt A E Clark	+	of Oxford and F/S Hannay RCAF, were buried in
LAC K T Robson	+	Newark-upon-Trent Cemetery, while the others
AC1 L J Rogers	+	were claimed by their next of kin.

14 Mar 1943	**1651 HCU**	**Stirling I**	**N6086** **J MacRoberts Reply**	**Training**

Sgt W K Rendall RNZAF	inj	T/o Waterbeach for a night flying exercise,
Sgt D C Smith	+	during which an engine failed. While seeking
Sgt F Hall	inj	to make an emergency landing, the pilot lost
P/O N G Totty	inj	control and crashed, heavily, at 2100 into
Sgt W A Horsley	+	Oakington village, Cambridgeshire and not far
Sgt T R Davis	+	distant from the local airfield. The most
Sgt G C Sperden	inj	seriously injured were rushed to Addenbrooke's

Hospital, while Sgt Sperden was treated at Oakington's medical centre. Of those who perished, Sgt Horsley, a Freeman of Coventry, was buried in Cambridge City Cemetery; Sgt Smith, an ex-aircraft apprentice, rests in Mautby (SS Peter and Paul) Churchyard. His parents had already experienced the pain of losing another son, Air Fitter Trevor Paul Smith of the Fleet Air Arm who died in the Norwegian Sea on Sunday, 9 June 1940, when the aircraft carrier HMS Glorious was sunk by the German battle cruiser Scharnhorst. Along with many others from the ship's company, he is commemorated on the Lee-on-Solent Memorial. Sgt Davis's name, too, appears on a commemorative panel, namely the screen wall at Edmonton Cemetery. Having recovered well from his injuries, P/O Totty went, eventually, to 15 Squadron and was lost during operations to Berlin in February 1944 (see Bomber Command Losses, Volume 5, page 75).

15 Mar 1943	**1658 HCU**	**Halifax II**	**BB246**	**Training**

F/O D F Bertera   T/o 1340 Riccall for general flying practice. At 1540, the Halifax touched down from a fast approach and promptly swung off the runway and crashed. A little over a month later, F/O Bertera was busily evading capture having been shot down over France (see Bomber Command Losses, Volume 4, page 114 and In Brave Company, page 65).

18 Mar 1943	**1652 HCU**	**Halifax II**	**L9616 GV-D**	**Training**

P/O W C Richardson	T/o Marston Moor for a dual exercise. Crashed
F/S T M Moran RCAF	at around 1500, at Riccall, after arriving on the runway on one wheel and bouncing back into

the air. P/O Richardson had served previously with 76 Squadron, while his pupil went on to serve with 77 Squadron until his death in action on 13 May 1943 (see Bomber Command Losses, Volume 4, page 141).

19 Mar	1652 HCU	Halifax II	BB273	Training

1943   S/L J P M Haydon DFC RAAF   T/o 2015 Marston Moor from No. 6 runway but
Sgt R W F Munns   swung and damaged beyond repair after the port
main wheel dropped into a ditch. This Halifax
had been slightly damaged on 20 February 1943, when, with W/O F S Smith at the
controls, its tail wheel had collapsed while taxying. S/L Haydon RAAF had not
long served as an instructor, his recent tour of operations with 158 Squadron
having concluded in dramatic fashion with him having to evade capture (see
Bomber Command Losses, Volume 3, page 175 and In Brave Company, pages 27 and
49). His DFC was promulgated in the London Gazette on 5 February 1943. Sadly,
for Sgt Munns there was no happy conclusion to his tour (see Bomber Command
Losses, Volume 4, page 317).

24 Mar	1652 HCU	Halifax II	BB218 GV-F	Training

1943
Sgt F H Thomas   +   T/o 1450 Marston Moor for general training,
Sgt S J Tibbs RCAF   inj   but as the Halifax climbed away from the runway
Sgt R G A Platoni   +   flames were seen coming from the outer port
Sgt K W Peverley   +   engine. Sgt Thomas turned off the petrol but
Sgt J A Phillips   inj   had not feathered the propeller when the bomber
Sgt G S Worboys   inj   smashed into the ground on the south side of the
circuit near the village of Bickerton. Nineteen
year old Sgt Peverley from Dover was cremated at Harrogate Crematorium and a
similar service was held for Sgt Thomas at Northampton and Counties Crematorium,
Milton; Sgt Platoni rests in St. Pancras Cemetery. Although seriously injured,
the three survivors made good recoveries. Sadly, however, Sgt Phillips was
killed on operations with 178 Squadron on 8 May 1944. He is buried in Romania
at Bucharest War Cemetery.

	1660 HCU	Halifax V	DG362	Training

P/O J L Cooper DFC   T/o 1045 Swinderby but lost control in the
F/S W J Wilkinson   crosswind and came to a halt with both undercarriage legs ripped away. Subsequently, the
airframe was salvaged as a training aid, the serial 4454M being applied. This
was the first of three such incidents involving P/O Cooper, a recent addition
to the training staff, who had completed a tour of duty with 106 Squadron, his
Distinguished Flying Cross having being Gazetted on 12 January 1943.

	1661 HCU	Manchester I	L7453	Training

S/L R G W Oakley   T/o 1520 Swinderby only for the port Vulture to
Sgt G S Cole   burst into flames. Calmly, S/L Oakley flew
round the circuit and with the engine feathered,
he crash-landed at 1525, on the airfield, with the wheels retracted. Assigned
for repair in works, the Manchester was struck off charge on 1 May 1943, prior
to any serious work commencing. A photograph, purporting to show this aircraft,
appears on page 51 of "Lancaster At War 3" (compiled by Mike Garbett and Brian
Goulding, Ian Allan 1984), with the remarks that it was involved in a midair
collision with a Halifax in the Winthorpe circuit on 1 May 1943; I have not
been able to find any evidence to support this claim. Sgt Cole, the pilot
under instruction, was posted to 49 Squadron, failing to return from Ober-
hausen on 14-15 June 1943 (see Bomber Command Losses, Volume 4, page 185).

30 Mar	1658 HCU	Halifax II	BB189	Training

1943   F/O G A Sells   T/o 1220 Riccall for an air to sea firing
detail. On return to base at 1340, F/O Sells
experienced a strong crosswind and, as a consequence, he was unable to prevent
the Halifax from veering off the runway and losing its undercarriage. By the
autumn, he was commanding a flight on 78 Squadron but was killed in action on
22-23 October 1943 (see Bomber Command Losses, Volume 4, page 366).

2 Apr	1658 HCU	Halifax II	W1010	Training

1943
P/O F Williamson   T/o 0905 Riccall for dual circuit training.
P/O R Hoos   It would seem that prior to landing, at 0920,
a tyre either punctured or burst for on touch-
down the undercarriage gave way, causing very serious damage. Accepted by
10 Squadron on 13 February 1942, and remaining on charge (though it was shared
from time to time with the conversion flight) until absorbed by "1658", it was
initially deemed to be repairable, but was struck off charge before any work
was put in hand. P/O Hoos was posted to 35 Squadron and was killed in the May
(see Bomber Command Losses, Volume 4, page 168). He is buried in Belgium.

2 Apr	**1662 HCU A Flt**	**Lancaster III**	**ED729**	**Training**
1943	P/O E W Bennee			T/o 1330 Blyton for day training. Observed
	Sgt J S Stewart RAAF			nearing the runway with the starboard inner
				feathered and with the outer starboard mis-

firing. An attempt to re-start the inner motor came to nothing and with the Lancaster gradually losing height, P/O Bennee, aided by his flight engineer, changed the fuel supply and switched on the inversion pumps. When this had no effect, a forced-landing was made, at 1400, wheels up in a ploughed field some 4 miles N of Kirton-in-Lindsey, Lincolnshire. Just fifteen days later, twenty-two year old Sgt Stewart RAAF of Werneth in Victoria was dead, shot down, while flying as a second pilot, during operations to Plzen (see Bomber Command Losses, Volume 4, page 117).

3 Apr	**1652 HCU**	**Halifax I**	**L9509**	**Training**
1943	F/S A M Sargeant			T/o Marston Moor for circuits and landings.
				Landed at 1630, but the brakes failed and

the Halifax ended up, wrecked, in a ditch. Almost a year previous, the late F/O K D Whisken DFC had landed this aircraft with its undercarriage still partially retracted, while in an earlier incident, on 11 February 1942, a collision with a bank of frozen snow had removed the tail wheel. On that occasion, F/S P Bunclark had been at the controls.

4 Apr	**1652 HCU**	**Halifax II**	**R9441**	**─J**	**Training**
1943	Sgt H B Frisby RAAF				T/o 1815 Marston Moor but the starboard inner
	Sgt K A Myers RAAF				failed and, inadvertently, the starboard outer
					was feathered. Barely under control, a crash-

landing was inevitable and seconds later the bomber was on the ground twixt the Officers' Mess and Moor Side Farm on the western edge of the airfield. Soon after this frightening accident, the two pilots were posted; Sgt Frisby joining 158 Squadron, while his fellow countryman went to 76 Squadron. The former ended up in captivity (see Bomber Command Losses, Volume 4, page 285), but Sgt Myers RAAF participated in, at least, thirty sorties between the end of April and the end of September 1943 before being rested.

	1654 HCU	**Manchester I**	**L7291**	**Unknown**
				Reported as being destroyed by fire on this

date, but no accident card traced to confirm, or refute, this statement.

6 Apr	**1658 HCU**	**Halifax II**	**W7856**	**Training**
1943	Sgt A T Fraser RAAF		inj	T/o 1203 Burn only to lose an engine as the
	Sgt W Morse			aircraft lifted from the runway. A right hand
	Sgt R N Brand		inj	circuit was flown as the crew tried to control
	Sgt R F Glass RCAF			the runaway port outer. Then, whilst downwind
	Sgt H Edwards			an engine caught fire and Sgt Fraser RAAF very
				quickly put his crippled machine down, cross-

wind, smashing the undercarriage as he did so. All went to 102 Squadron and were reported missing on 10 July 1943 (see Bomber Command Losses, Volume 4, page 226). Subsequently, it was learnt that Sgt Brand and Sgt Edwards had survived and were in a prisoner of war camp.

	1658 HCU	**Halifax II**	**DT612**	**Training**
	Sgt W H Wyatt RCAF			T/o 1130 Riccall. Wrecked at 1500, following
				a collision with a motor transport vehicle

that drove onto the runway as the Halifax was committed to landing. Before the month was out, Sgt Wyatt RCAF had joined 158 Squadron but, sadly, his tour was all too tragically brief for on his seventh sortie he was shot down over Holland by a night-fighter (see Bomber Command Losses, Volume 4, page 166).

Note. To illustrate the frequency at which bomber crews operated in the spring and summer of 1943, as The Battle of The Ruhr reached its peak, Sgt Wyatt's all too brief contribution is hereby listed:

27 Apr	Halifax II	HR739	NP-Y	Gardening in Nectarine 1 area	
30 Apr	Halifax II	HR721	NP-S	Essen	Target bombed at 0304/20,000 feet
4 May	Halifax II	HR721	NP-S	Dortmund	Target bombed at 0133/19,000 feet
12 May	Halifax II	HR780	NP-D	Duisburg	Target bombed at 0230/18,000 feet
13 May	Halifax II	JB789	NP-X	Bochum	Target bombed at 0232/19,500 feet
25 May	Halifax II	HR775	NP-V	Düsseldorf	Target bombed at 0202/17,400 feet
27 May	Halifax II	HR775	NP-V	Essen	Failed to return

6 Apr	1663 HCU	Halifax V	DG413	–C	Training

1943

P/O S G Rawling DFC	+	T/o 1030 Rufforth for a fighter affiliation
Sgt R Brough MID RNZAF	+	detail, the crew comprising of an instructor,
Sgt R J Tarren	+	two trainee pilots, flight engineer, air bomber,
Sgt P A Tinch	+	wireless operator, five air gunners and a member
Sgt V C Burt	+	of the ground staff. Roughly twenty-five minutes
Sgt C P Sheppard	+	into the exercise, and while turning steeply at
Sgt D J Rees	+	6,000 feet, the starboard wing came off, outboard
Sgt T R Lawrence	+	of the inner engine. Totally out of control, the
Sgt H W O'Connor	+	Halifax dived into the ground at Hutton Cranswick
Sgt F H Warren	+	some 4 miles S of Great Driffield, Yorkshire.
P/O R E Jeffrey DFM	+	Four were taken to Driffield Cemetery, while the
AC2 D W Cresswell	+	rest were buried under private arrangements.

P/O Rawling's award was promulgated on 14 May
1943; he had served with 51 Squadron. Four days later, the London Gazette bore
notice of P/O Jeffrey's DFM. He, too, had flown with "51". Earl Martyn, meanwhile, notes that Sgt Brough RNZAF had flown an unknown number of operations with
the detachment of 10 Operational Training Unit at St. Eval, followed by a couple
of sorties with 10 Squadron. An air accident investigation into the cause of
their deaths reported that the wing attachment bolts had been torn out and it
was recommended that the mild steel fitments should be replaced by high tensile
steel. In conclusion, Brian Mennell records on page 53 of his excellent history
of Rufforth, published in 2002 under the title, "Wings Over York", this was the
unit's first and, as events would prove, greatest loss of life.

8 Apr	1654 HCU	Lancaster I	L7545 UG–S	Training

1943

Sgt J Wallace	+	T/o 1745 Wigsley for an evening training sortie,
P/O J H Wolton DFM	+	P/O Wolton being a screened flight engineer
Sgt G F M Walker	+	(while serving with 50 Squadron, and flying
Sgt L R Upperton	+	with S/L G H Everitt DSO, DFC, he had displayed
Sgt T Bailey	+	skill and airmanship of the highest order while
Sgt R F Davidson	+	over Germany in October 1942; for this he was
Sgt D G G Martin	+	awarded an immediate DFM, Gazetted on 6 November
Sgt B G Pilgrim	+	1942). Collided in the air, at 1815, over

Leicestershire, with an Oxford trainer, both
machines crashing at Burton Lazars, 2 miles SE of Melton Mowbray. Two, Sgt
Walker of Perth and Sgt Pilgrim from Pembury in Kent, were given service burials
in the extension to Cottesmore (St. Nicholas) Churchyard, while the others were
taken back to their home towns.

	14 PAFU	Oxford II	AB665	Training

Sgt J A Lemmerick RCAF	+	T/o Ossington and destroyed in the manner out-
Sgt A A Moors RCAF	+	lined above. Both are at rest in the extension

to Cottesmore (St. Nicholas) Churchyard.

10 Apr	1660 HCU	Lancaster I	R5848	Training

1943

F/L R O Calvert RNZAF	T/o 2307 Swinderby for night conversion to type.
F/O W N Lewis	While taking off for another circuit at 2332, a

swing developed and before it could be checked,
the Lancaster swerved from the runway and lost its undercarriage. Although experienced on type, F/L Calvert's instructional prowess was quite limited; in
fact, in respect of hours flown, his pupil's solo flying outstripped his by
nearly 2,000 hours! Happily, both survived the war.

	1661 HCU	Lancaster III	ED823	Training

F/S L W Lean RAAF	+	T/o Winthorpe for a night training exercise.
Sgt F Dunkin RAAF	+	Crashed at around 0125, after flying into
F/O E Lambert	+	high tension wires, off School Lane at the
Sgt H U Oxspring	+	village of Halam, 11 miles NE from the centre
Sgt W S L Graham	+	of Nottingham. Service funerals were held for
F/S R D Lewis RCAF	+	the three Commonwealth airmen at Newark-upon-
Sgt W G Stephenson	+	Trent Cemetery. F/O Lambert (at thirty-four

years of age he was older than most airmen
serving in Bomber Command) rests in Fleetwood Borough Cemetery; Sgt Oxspring
(he was twenty-seven) is buried at Hoyland Nether Cemetery; Sgt Graham's body
was conveyed to Glasgow and interred in the city's Western Necropolis, while
Sgt Stephenson lies in Leicester (Gilroes) Cemetery. Unusually, their flight
engineer was Australian.

11 Apr	1660 HCU	Manchester I	R5841	Training

11 Apr 1943

1660 HCU   **Manchester I**   R5841   **Training**

F/L J M Whitwell AFM	+	T/o Swinderby to practice circuits and landings
Sgt R Davies	+	during which, it is believed, an hydraulic pipe
Sgt H M Scott	inj	fitted forward of the bulkhead on the starboard
Sgt W J Robinson	inj	engine fractured. A fire broke out in the
Sgt B R Traves	inj	vicinity of the "B" block and F/L Whitwell,
Sgt A J Brooks	inj	a pre-war regular pilot commissioned from the
		ranks, had little choice but to crash-land.

This he accomplished, at 1850, alongside the River Brant at a place named on the accident card as "Navenby Lowfields". Three of the four survivors were taken to RAF Hospital Rauceby, where Sgt Brooks died from his injuries soon after being admitted. He was buried privately, as were his two companions. Sgt Scott went on to fly with 207 Squadron and was killed raiding Berlin in early January 1944 (see Bomber Command Losses, Volume 5, page 20). This was the last production Manchester and, as Robert Kirby notes, it had flown a total of 189.35 hours in fourteen months of service.

14 Apr 1943

1652 HCU   **Halifax I**   L9525   **Training**

Sgt H A Lander   T/o 1900 Marston Moor but swung out of control, struck a mound of earth and smashed its undercarriage. Salvaged, with a view to converting the airframe into a training aid (the serial 3642M was allotted), it is believed the scheme was abandoned. It is known that it had been flown by the late G/C G L Cheshire VC, for he was at the controls on 22 March 1942, when a hatch cover flew off and injured one of the crew.

15 Apr 1943

1654 HCU   **Manchester I**   L7294   **Training**

Sgt W H Eager RCAF	inj	T/o 1645 Wigsley. Whilst in flight, an engine
Sgt T D Viggers	inj	caught fire and Sgt Eager RCAF headed for base,
Sgt H T Petts	inj	but as he closed on the runway, at around 1850,
Sgt T H James	inj	the Manchester stalled and crashed. On impact
Sgt F R Stone	inj	it continued to burn. All are thought to have
Sgt G E Hunnington	inj	made good recoveries; Sgt Eager RCAF was later
Sgt A Jones	inj	commissioned but was killed, before the year
		was out, while instructing at Winthorpe. If,

as it is strongly suspected, Sgt Petts received a commission, then he died while serving with 463 Squadron in April 1944, while Sgt Stone is thought to have followed a similar path before being posted missing in the summer of 1944. Certainly, such a fate befell Sgt Jones and his name appears on the Runnymede Memorial (see Bomber Command Losses, Volumes 5 and 4, pages 178, 296 and 219 respectively).

16 Apr 1943

1657 HCU   **Lancaster II**   DS603   **Training**

F/L C R Barrett	+	T/o East Wretham crewed by an instructor, two
Sgt A C Lamond RAAF	+	pilots under instruction, a flight engineer and
Sgt S S Atkin	inj	a wireless operator, their brief being to carry
Sgt W S Humphreys	+	out three-engined flying practice. At 1131, the
Sgt S Dawson	+	Lancaster overshot the runway and after climbing
		to 300 feet went completely out of control and

crashed to the ground. Sgt Atkin was rushed to the West Suffolk General Hospital at Bury St. Edmunds. The first two named were buried in Beck Row (St. John) Churchyard at Mildenhall, while their two colleagues were claimed by their next of kin. After recovering, and completing his training, Sgt Atkin was posted to 115 Squadron. On 19-20 May 1944, his Lancaster was shot down near le Mans (see Bomber Command Losses, Volume 5, page 227).

1662 HCU B Flt   **Halifax V**   DK118   **Training**

S/L E I J Bell DFC		T/o 1302 Blyton for dual practice. On landing
Sgt Fry		at 1403, at Wickenby, a violent shimmy developed
		and before remedial action could be taken, the

bomber left the runway and ran into a ditch. Recovered for training purposes, the Halifax, now wearing the serial 4127M, was taken to No. 4 School of Technical Training at St. Athan. S/L Bell's war ended in captivity at Sagan.

Note. S/L E I J Bell had been appointed C Flight commander on 1 April 1943, at which date B Flight had been assigned to the command of F/L J K Douglas, while A Flight was in the hands of S/L J F Dilworth. It is believed that W/C E C Eaton DFC and ex-101 Squadron was their officer commanding.

18 Apr	1659 HCU	Halifax II	R9448	—L		Training

18 Apr
1943

1659 HCU		Halifax II	R9448	—L		**Training**
S/L H S Hill DFC RCAF				+		T/o Topcliffe the crew being an instructor,
WO2 R L Locker RCAF				+		two pilots under instruction, a couple of flight
F/S E W Pitt RCAF				+		engineers, a wireless operator, an air gunner
Sgt J L Gunn				+		and a pilot (F/O Davies) who had gone along for
Sgt F O Bonham				+		the ride. At 1008, two engines were deliberately
F/S E A Clyde				+		shut down, whereupon the aircraft spun out of
F/S H D E Messier RCAF				+		control and smashed onto Crockey Hill. Six were
F/O B T Davies				+		buried in Dishforth Cemetery, but Sgt Bonham was

taken back to Hampshire and laid to rest in
Hartfordbridge Cemetery (his being the sole Second World War grave), while
F/O Davies lies in Weston-super-Mare Cemetery. S/L Hill RCAF had recently
flown with 405 Squadron, his DFC having been Gazetted on the last day of
December 1942. Two months previous, he had learned that his brother, WO2 Raymond
Hepton Hill RCAF had been posted missing in action (see Bomber Command Losses,
Volume 4, page 36).

19 Apr
1943

1663 HCU		Halifax V	DG352			**Training**
F/O R P Wilkin						T/o Rufforth for dual training. Approaching the
Sgt R Sykes			inj			runway at 1005, the Halifax veered from its path

and flew into a tree. Sgt Sykes, the flight
engineer, is reported to have sustained slight chemical burns. On 23 October 1943,
he failed to return from Kassel (see Bomber Command Losses, Volume 4, page 367).
At the time he was flying with 102 Squadron.

20 Apr
1943

1651 HCU		Stirling I	N6096	—T		**Training**
P/O L F Smith DFC						T/o 1020 Stradishall but wrecked after swinging
Sgt K J Kinsella						off the runway and breaking its undercarriage.
Sgt R Blair						P/O Smith's award was Gazetted a few later on
P/O N B Blakey RNZAF						24 May and was in recognition of the twenty-
Sgt E M Ingpen						four sorties flown between October 1942 and
Sgt F Shepherd						March 1943, with 218 Squadron. During this
Sgt W J Hope						period, he had experienced one very close shave
Sgt W Heanny						(see Bomber Command Losses, Volume 3, page 269).

Sadly, he died from injuries received in a
flying accident on 7 September 1943. Bryce Gomersall adds, Sgt Kinsella flew
twenty-five missions with 90 Squadron between 8 May and 27 October 1943, after
which he returned to "1651" as a screened pilot.

1 May
1943

1652 HCU		Halifax II	BB198			**Training**
Sgt J W G Parker						T/o Marston Moor for non-operational training,

at night. Upon landing at 0220, the starboard
oleo collapsed, having failed to lock in the down position. Before the month
was over, Sgt Parker was missing in action while flying with 51 Squadron (see
Bomber Command Losses, Volume 4, page 155).

1660 HCU		Manchester I	L7468			**Training**
P/O J L Cooper DFC						T/o 1645 Swinderby for dual conversion to type.
Sgt T P Murphy						As the crew prepared to land, an engine caught

fire and the Manchester arrived on the runway
at 1730, well alight. Prompt action by the fire services ensured that damage
was slight and following salvage, the airframe was taken to No. 12 School of
Technical Training at Melksham in Wiltshire as 3732M. For P/O Cooper, this was
his second accident (see page 43) since arriving on the unit for instructional
duties. Sgt Murphy eventually departed to Woodhall Spa, where he joined 619
Squadron. On 29 June, his Lancaster fell victim to a night-fighter (see Bomber
Command Losses, Volume 4, page 217).

1663 HCU		Halifax V	DG408			**Training**
Sgt E F Williamson				+		T/o 1520 Rufforth for a cross-country exercise
Sgt C R L Thornton				+		which went terribly wrong and ended in tragedy
Sgt D C Butlin				+		circa 1925 in the sea off the French port of
Sgt W J Pelham				+		Brest. Seven now lie in cemeteries at Barnville-
Sgt D W Suffling				+		sur-Mer (Sgt Thornton), Siouville (Sgt Hunter,
Sgt A J Dunn				+		who hailed from Belfast) and Bayeux, the re-
Sgt H Hinett				+		maining five. On 3 June 1943, Sgt Butlin's
Sgt J Hunter				+		body came ashore on the Channel Island of Jersey

(near La Pulante) and he now rests at St. Helier
War Cemetery, his funeral being held with full military honours on 6 June.

| 2 May | 1651 HCU | Stirling I | BF388 | —F | Training |

2 May
1943

1651 HCU
Sgt E C Hughes

Stirling I BF388 —F

Training

T/o 1215 Waterbeach. During the flight, an exactor unit on one the starboard engines failed and the crew were obliged to return to base with the faulty motor shut down. At around 1245, the Stirling approached the runway, but due to his inexperience, Sgt Hughes misjudged the flare out and the ensuing heavy landing and swing broke the undercarriage. Until now, this Stirling had performed extremely well for since being accepted, ex-works, on 7 October 1942, it had logged 230.30 hours in the air. After salvage, it became a ground trainer with the serial 3766M.

2- 3 May
1943

1660 HCU
Sgt M M Cole

Lancaster I R5758

Training

T/o 2222 Swinderby for night conversion to type. At 0022, taking off for another circuit, an engine failed, causing the Lancaster to swing. Sgt Cole was able to correct the movement but before he could bring his aircraft to a halt, it ran into a drain. No blame was attached to the crew and, as the station commander remarked, it was an unfilled ditch that caused the Lancaster to be written off.

3 May
1943

1658 HCU
F/O J W H Harwood DFM
Sgt A W H Ayres

Halifax II DT649

Training

T/o 1150 Riccall to practice circuits and landings. For over two hours, the exercise proceeded without incident but at 1415, on touch down, the undercarriage folded and the bomber was damaged beyond repair. It is believed the arch on the starboard oleo had failed. F/O Harwood had joined 76 Squadron in the late autumn of 1941, and by the end of June 1942, he had flown sixteen sorties as captain; his DFM was Gazetted on 4 August of that year.

5 May
1943

1651 HCU

Stirling I BF393 —V

Ground

Wrecked at Waterbeach when a 97 Squadron Lancaster III ED880 OF-N, captained by Sgt A Reilly, diverted to Waterbeach on return from operations to Dortmund, overshot the runway and hit the Stirling (see Bomber Command Losses, Volume 4, page 135).

1661 HCU
Sgt R W Petty

Lancaster I W4775

Training

T/o 1815 Winthorpe to practice solo circuits and landings, an exercise which ended just ten minutes later with the Lancaster sideways on to the runway, its undercarriage broken. On completion of his course, Sgt Petty went to 49 Squadron and became a prisoner of war when his Lancaster was shot down near Berlin early in December 1943 (see Bomber Command Losses, Volume 4, page 409).

1663 HCU C Flt
Sgt V E Betterton
Sgt J Chisnall
Sgt F H Brown RNZAF
Sgt R Deacon
Sgt H Rowbottom
Sgt A W Oakley

Halifax V DG419 —H

+
+
+
+
+
+

Training

T/o 1900 Rufforth to practice feathering. While closing down the port outer Merlin, lost control and spiralled into the ground, at 1958, near Fridaythorpe, on the York to Bridlington road, some 9 miles WNW from Great Driffield. The pilot and his New Zealand born navigator were buried in Barmby-on-the-Moor (St. Catherine) Churchyard; the others were taken back to their home towns. Sgt Deacon's brother, Signalman Derrick Deacon, died on 24 August 1943, while serving with 4th Headquarters, Royal Corps of Signals. He is buried in Iraq at Baghdad (North Gate) War Cemetery. Sgt Oakley's service number indicates he had trained, initially, as a pre-war volunteer reserve pilot.

Note. Service burials ceased at Barmby-on-the-Moor in May 1943 (probably because of the selection of Harrogate (Stonefall) as a regional cemetery. Following the interment of Sgt Betterton and Sgt Brown RNZAF, the funeral took place in mid-May of an Australian pilot, F/O Thomas Archibald DFC of 77 Squadron (see Bomber Command Losses, Volume 4, page 141). His was the fifty-fourth, and last, service (all air force) funeral.

12 May
1943

1659 HCU
Sgt R G Freeman

Halifax II BB219 —A

Training

T/o Topcliffe. Landed at 1545, swung and lost its undercarriage. According to unit records, instructions advising the pilot not to land had been transmitted by wireless and as a last resort, the airfield controller ordered "red" Very cartridges to be discharged.

17 May
1943

| 1654 HCU | Manchester IA L7491 | Training |

P/O A Walters
Sgt C Firth

T/o 1015 Wigsley for circuit training. An hour and forty minutes later, the Manchester headed down the runway but as it accelerated a swing developed and while corrective action was being taken, the starboard undercarriage leg collapsed. It is thought that the brake on the starboard wheel seized, thus imposing excessive strain on the oleo.

18 May
1943

| 1660 HCU | Lancaster I R5917 | Training |

F/O W E D Bell

T/o 1107 Swinderby for day conversion to type. While preparing to land, F/O Bell discovered he was unable to better more than ten degrees of flap travel and, consequently, his arrival on the runway at 1142 was sufficiently fast enough to carry the Lancaster into the overshoot area, where the undercarriage fell into a ditch.

19 May
1943

| 1661 HCU | Manchester I L7297 | Training |

Sgt J Clifford

T/o 1045 Winthorpe for circuits and landings. Wrecked, at around 1215, after an engine fire and the deliberate raising of the undercarriage to prevent the aircraft from running off the airfield.

21 May
1943

| 1657 HCU | Stirling I R9301 | Training |

Sgt A E Maloney
Sgt S Knight   inj

T/o 1215 but swung out of control, whereupon the undercarriage collapsed. Sgt Knight, an air gunner, was treated in station sick quarters for minor abrasions and cuts over both eyes. Bryce Gomersall adds, Sgt Maloney (and Sgt Knight) was posted, initially, to 149 Squadron (3 June 1943) before proceeding to 620 Squadron on 17 June. In December 1943, 620 Squadron left Bomber Command for No. 38 Group and it was not until August 1944, by which time Sgt Maloney had flown thirty-two sorties, that he was deemed "tour expired". With his crew, less Sgt E A Taylor who was posted away when "620" changed rôles, he went to 1665 Heavy Conversion Unit at Tilstock.

22 May
1943

| 1652 HCU | Halifax II W7807 | Training |

F/S W F Pyle

T/o Marston Moor for non-operational training, at night. While attempting to land at 0320, the Halifax drifted off the centre line and collided with an obstruction. Posted to "Shiny Ten", F/S Pyle (and his crew) disappeared without trace during operations to the Peugeot motor factory at Montbéliard (see Bomber Command Losses, Volume 4, page 233).

| 1656 HCU | Lancaster I LM305 | Training |

Sgt E C Wright   +
Sgt N Potts   +
F/O D V Bishop   +
F/O R J Coomes   +
Sgt G H Potter   +
Sgt S Godfrey   +
Sgt A B Stevenson   +

T/o Lindholme for a cross-country. No signals received from the aircraft, after its departure. All are commemorated on the Runnymede Memorial. Sgt Wright had four hours solo flying on type, and 263 such hours in total.

23-24 May
1943

| 1654 HCU | Lancaster I W4303 UG-D | Training |

P/O G N J Bryde RAAF   +
Sgt C A Nelson RAAF   +
P/O J A Walker DFM   +
F/O F V P Turner   +
Sgt J H R Harper   +
Sgt W N McMullan   +
P/O L H Parker   +
Sgt D F Smith   +

T/o 2323 Wigsley for a night navigation detail, combined with fighter affiliation practice. At 0308 the Lancaster broke up, scattering debris over a wide area around Humbleton, roughly nine miles ENE of Hull, Yorkshire. P/O Bryde RAAF and his fellow Australian, Sgt Nelson RAAF, lie in Brandesburton Churchyard; funeral services for their six companions took place at various locations in England and Northern Ireland. P/O Walker's award, gained with 106 Squadron, was published three weeks later on 15 June 1943.

Note. The code combination, displayed with the above summary, has been taken from Jim Halley's magnificent compilation of Lancaster histories, and published by Air-Britain (Historians) in 1985. It is possible, however, that the markings, here depicted, had changed prior to the Lancaster's disappearance, as aircraft within the unit changed their codes from time to time; for example Lancaster III ED704 flew at various times as UG-D and UG-K.

25 May	1652 HCU	Halifax I	L9571 GV-H		Training

25 May
1943

1652 HCU   **Halifax I**   **L9571 GV-H**   **Training**

F/O A I T Moir DFC   +   T/o 0948 Marston Moor on a check dual flight but
F/S D E Veness RAAF   +   while in the circuit the port inner engine burst
Sgt F W Barns   +   into flames. F/O Moir, a most experienced pilot
Sgt T F King   inj   and who had recently completed an arduous tour
Sgt J Winchester   inj   of duty with 76 Squadron, tried to line up with
the runway, but crashed 0955, heavily, after
clipping the roof of Tockwith vicarage on the eastern side of the airfield.
One of the first to reach the terrible scene was G/C G L Cheshire VC, then
commanding Marston Moor, and he was later to recount, quite emphatically, that
he saw F/O Moir walking towards him, dishevelled but seemingly uninjured. He
was, therefore, shaken to the core when the station's medical officer told him
that Moir's body had been recovered from the wreckage of the cockpit. The son
of a Derbyshire doctor, he is buried in Harrogate (Stonefall) Cemetery (his DFC
had been published on 14 May 1943) alongside F/S Veness RAAF and their thirty-
four year old flight engineer, Sgt Barns of Sydenham, London.

1659 HCU   **Halifax II**   **W7704**   **Training**

Sgt L Chapman RCAF   T/o 0135 Topcliffe for a night training sortie.
WO2 J Sommerville RCAF   Wrecked on landing at 0250, the undercarriage
collapsing as the Halifax made contact with the
runway. No technical defect could be found, and it was mooted that a series of
heavy arrivals in the past had seriously weakened the unit but without leaving
any obvious signs of damage. Subsequently, Sgt Chapman RCAF became a prisoner
of war, and the sole survivor of his 419 Squadron Halifax, in the wake of a
trip to Essen on 25-26 July 1943 (see Bomber Command Losses, Volume 4, page 243).

1663 HCU   **Halifax V**   **DG356**   **Training**

P/O L J Hampton   T/o 1125 Rufforth for a dual exercise in three-
F/S H R W Whittle   engined flying. Landed, successfully, at 1145,
but having run normally for about 200 yards,
the Halifax veered off the runway and moments later the undercarriage folded.
By the end of June 1943, F/S Whittle was serving with 76 Squadron and he was
within weeks of being screened when he failed to return from Stuttgart in the
November (see Bomber Command Losses, Volume 4, page 402).

27 May
1943

1656 HCU   **Lancaster I**   **R5491**   **Training**

P/O S G Burton   T/o 2303 Lindholme for night circuit practice.
Sgt D B Davidson   Touched down ten minutes later and damaged
beyond repair as a consequence of the port
tyre bursting.

28 May
1943

1659 HCU   **Halifax II**   **W1273**   **Training**

P/O M O Frederick RCAF   T/o 2245 Topcliffe for night flying training
F/S F J Higgins DFM RCAF   but wrecked at 2305 in a landing mishap during
Sgt J D Hamilton RCAF   which the Halifax swung off the runway and lost
its undercarriage. The two pilots under in-
struction returned to 427 Squadron and both were lost on operations before the
end of June 1943 (see Bomber Command Losses, Volume 4, pages 212 and 202 respectively). F/S Higgins RCAF had gained an immediate DFM in the April and
details of this appeared in the London Gazette just three days previous to
the incident, here summarised. P/O Frederick RCAF survived the war.

29 May
1943

1657 HCU   **Stirling I**   **BF376**   **Training**

Sgt B H Church   T/o Stradishall for a night detail. Landed
at Lakenheath, touching down normally at 0155,
but when the brakes were applied, the port main wheel locked, causing the bomber
to swing sharply. Seconds later, the undercarriage gave way under the strain.

1 Jun
1943

1660 HCU   **Lancaster I**   **W4131**   **Training**

Sgt H C Warren RAAF   T/o 0029 Langar for night conversion training
and the exercise proceeded without hitch for
fifteen minutes. Then, while taking off for another circuit, the port outer
failed and Sgt Warren RAAF was unable to correct the resultant swing, which
led to the undercarriage collapsing.

Note. It is assumed that Langar was being used by 1660 Heavy Conversion Unit
on an occasional basis as, normally, the unit operated from Swinderby.

2 Jun 1943	**1663 HCU**	**Halifax V**	**DG300**	**Training**

S/L M W Renaut DFC   T/o Rufforth for a dual exercise, during which
Sgt G Sproat   the airfield at Pocklington was used. At 1128,
Sgt R O Chester   while approaching the runway, the Halifax
Sgt T Farnworth   inj   stalled and crash-landed at Spring House Farm,
     a little under a mile NW of Barmby Moor, the
village that nestles on the north-west edge of the airfield. Sgt Farnworth was
admitted to York Military Hospital, but his injuries were found to be not too
serious. On completion of his course, Sgt Sproat was posted to Pocklington,
where he joined 102 Squadron. Tasked for Nurnbërg in late August 1943, his
aircraft was shot down, over Belgium, by a night-fighter. Sgt Chester, meanwhile, went to 77 Squadron and he died a few nights later while raiding Berlin
(see Bomber Command Losses, Volume 4, pages 291 and 301 respectively). Their
instructor had reported to Rufforth on 25 April 1943, following a very involved
tour of operations which began in the United Kingdom with 76 Squadron and continued with the squadron's Middle East detachment before ending, still based
in North Africa, with 462 Squadron; S/L Renaut survived the war.

6 Jun 1943	**1652 HCU**	**Halifax II**	**W1234 GV-I**	**Training**

Sgt G R J Duthie RNZAF   T/o Marston Moor but dropped back onto the
     runway and damaged the main undercarriage unit
before climbing away. The wheels were then retracted, but on completion of
the flight, and on rejoining the circuit, Sgt Duthie RNZAF discovered that the
unit was firmly jammed. Thus, at 0215, he forced-landed and following a technical inspection the Halifax was written off. Posted to 158 Squadron, the young
New Zealander lost his life during operations to Aachen in July 1943 (see Bomber
Losses, Volume 4, page 231 and In Brave Company, pages 80 to 82).

	1658 HCU	**Halifax II**	**W7908**	**Training**

S/L P Dobson DFC AFC   T/o 1650 Riccall for dual training, landing
F/O J G Jenkins   heavily at 1750 on one wheel. As the Halifax
     ballooned back into the air, S/L Dobson took
control and having successfully overshot, he flew round the circuit before
bringing the aircraft down, safely, with its wheels retracted. A year later,
he took command of 158 Squadron, remaining at the helm for the next nine months.
On page 32 of "Halifax At War" by Brian Rapier (Ian Allan, 1987) there appears a
remarkable photograph of Halifax II R9430, belonging to "1658", being flown on
just the inner starboard. The pilot at the controls was Peter Dobson and he
was assessing the rate of height loss, should a pilot find himself reduced to a
single engine. His conclusion was that it was safer to bale out, rather than
attempt a landing!

11 Jun 1943	**1654 HCU**	**Lancaster III**	**ED833 UG-S**	**Training**

Sgt W Featherstone   +   T/o Wigsley to practice three-engined flying.
Sgt E Kirk   +   While turning at low altitude, with the star-
Sgt E R Broad   +   board inner feathered, a wing clipped a tele-
Sgt A M Milne   +   graph pole and the bomber crashed at 1722 onto
Sgt P R Farnell   +   houses on both sides of Highfield Avenue, West
Sgt R W E Peacock   +   Swanpool, destroying or badly damaging Nos.
Sgt C H Malkin   inj   22, 24, 25 and 27. As the Lancaster impacted,
     the rear turret broke off and landed, inverted,
Mrs L M Thacker   +   on a footpath to the rear of 18 Roydon Grove,
Mstr A Thacker   +   the injured occupant being pulled clear by a
Mr Whitby   inj   Mrs Hartley, aided by her son Dennis and his
Mstr L Whitby   inj   friend, Bernard Lake. Subsequently, Mr Harry
Miss M Marriott   +   Chester and Mr Edward Wing received gallantry
Mstr H Bishop   inj   awards for their part in trying to rescue those
Miss E Bishop   inj   trapped in the burning buildings. Sadly, though
     still alive when brought out from the remains
of what once had been 24 Highfield Avenue, Mr Whitby and his four year old son,
Lawrence, died. Anthony Thacker was aged three and Margaret Marriott, whose
home was at No. 25 Highfield Avenue, was twelve. Funeral services for the
six aircrew were held over the next few days, three being buried in the County
of Nottinghamshire; Sgt Farnell of Birmingham was laid to rest in Newark-
upon-Trent Cemetery, while Sgt Featherstone and Sgt Kirk lie in Sutton-in-
Ashfield Cemetery and Mansfield (Nottingham Road) Cemetery respectively.
Sgt Broad was taken to Baldock Cemetery; Sgt Milne to Dundee (Balgay) Cemetery
and Sgt Peacock to Bedford Cemetery. I am indebted to Mr Fred Hurt for the
details pertaining to the civilians caught up in this awful tragedy of war.

11 Jun 1943	1657 HCU	Stirling I	DJ976	–P	Training

Sgt L J Hopkins
Sgt E B Campion   inj
Sgt J McIlhinney
Sgt Otter

T/o Stradishall for flying practice. Upon landing at 0945, obliged to take evasive action in order to avoid running into an obstruction. By doing so, the undercarriage collapsed and the Stirling was damaged beyond worthwhile repair. In thirteen months of service, commencing with 218 Squadron, it had logged 325.40 flying hours. Although not too seriously hurt, Sgt Campion was admitted to RAF Hospital Ely; he is described as an air gunner.

16–17 Jun 1943	1656 HCU	Lancaster I	ED381		Training

Sgt M F Brown   +
Sgt E P Stewart   +
Sgt A M T D Temple-Murray +
Sgt M Gardner   +
Sgt J S Whitehead   +
Sgt M R J Arthurs   +
Sgt A J McKenzie   +

T/o 2145 Lindholme tasked for a night cross-country. At approximately 0140, collided in the air above Brize Norton with Wellington III BJ845 of 27 OTU at Lichfield (see Bomber Command Losses, Volume 7, page 228) and fell near Wicksted Farm, a mile ENE from the village of Highworth, 5 miles NE of Swindon, Wiltshire. Sgt Brown's funeral was arranged by Brize Norton while Little Rissington took similar steps in respect of Sgt Gardner; thus the two airmen now rest in Black Bourton (or Burton Abbots) (St. Mary) Churchyard and Little Rissington (St. Peter) Churchyard respectively. The bodies of their five companions were claimed by their next of kin. Sgt Gardner, it is observed, was the son of S/L G D Gardner.

Note. It is generally accepted that the surname "Arthurs" is not particularly common and, as far as I can tell, from a search of the Commonwealth War Graves Commission web site, only four airmen with this surname died during the course of the Second World War; three were members of the Royal Air Force and one was serving with the Royal Canadian Air Force. By the strangest quirk of chance, on the day that Sgt M R J Arthurs was killed, a Cpl C D Arthurs died in the Middle East (he is buried in Israel at Ramleh War Cemetery). It is not thought that they were related.

18 Jun 1943	1663 HCU	Halifax V	DG421		Training

Sgt A W James
Sgt A J Savage

T/o 0050 Pocklington for general training, at night. Landed at 0155, but swung violently and lost its undercarriage.

23 Jun 1943	1652 HCU	Halifax I	L9575	GV–H	Training

P/O H B Alcock RNZAF
Sgt D A Robinson

T/o Marston Moor to practice three-engined flying procedures, including landings. At around 0820 the Halifax was observed in the circuit with its port outer feathered but as it turned finals and began its approach, so the port inner cut. With commendable skill, P/O Alcock RNZAF force landed, at 0823, on the airfield having first managed to retract the undercarriage. Subsequently, Sgt Robinson was to put his flying skills to the finest test when, flying his seventeenth sortie as captain, he managed to fly his crippled 158 Squadron Halifax away from Berlin and successfully crash-land in northern Holland (see Bomber Command Losses, Volume 5, page 61 and In Brave Company, pages 122 to 124).

26 Jun 1943	1659 HCU	Halifax II	V9984		Training

F/L M S F Schneider RCAF
P/O J W Richardson RCAF

T/O Topcliffe but an engine failed and the Halifax was crash-landed at 1140 in a field some 250 yards N of Ray Banks Farm near the village of Brafferton, 3 miles NE from Boroughbridge, Yorkshire. As was so often the case, having walked away from what had been a very nasty accident, the two pilots lost their lives, in action, before the year was out. First to fall was P/O Richardson RCAF (see Bomber Command Losses, Volume 4, page 227), while his instructor died early in the October, while serving as a flight commander with 405 Squadron (see the same volume, page 356).

	1665 HCU	Stirling I	R9198	–F	Training

F/S A A Harlem RAAF

T/o 1408 Woolfox Lodge only to be caught in a particularly strong gust from the prevailing crosswind, which sent the Stirling crashing out of control. Although unscathed by the crash, F/S Harlem RAAF ended the day in station sick quarters, having been admitted with suspected appendicitis.

27 Jun	1664 HCU	Halifax V	DG341	Training

1943   Sgt J C Baldwin   T/o 1045 Croft for dual conversion but upon
        Sgt R G Freeman   landing, fifteen minutes later, the pupil
                                      pilot over corrected the swing and before
his mentor could intervene, the bomber had left the runway, its undercarriage collapsing beneath the imposed strain.

29 Jun	1659 HCU	Halifax II	DT553	Training

1943   F/L D J Corcoran RCAF   inj   T/o 1042 Topcliffe for a cross-country flight
       Sgt Venier   which ended, tragically in part, ten minutes
       P/O R E Nutter RCAF   +   later some 700 yards SW of Crosby Manor Farm
       P/O Webley   and practically astride the old Roman Road on
       Sgt R Crookes   +   the NE side of Thornton-le-Beans, 3 miles SE
       Sgt Holdsworth   from Northallerton, Yorkshire. The accident
       P/O D E Larlee RCAF   was attributed to engine failure. Of those who
                                      perished (unit records indicate they were
unable to get away from the nose of the Halifax before it crash-landed), P/O Nutter RCAF was taken to Dishforth Cemetery, while Sgt Crookes rests at Sheffield (Crookes) cemetery. F/L Corcoran RCAF was not badly hurt (and three got out without harm) and along with P/O Larlee RCAF was posted to 419 Squadron. Both became prisoners of war in the wake of a raid on Berlin at the end of August 1943 (see Bomber Command Losses, Volume 4, page 304).

Note. Although I cannot be 100 percent certain, I strongly believe that the air bomber, shown in unit records as "P/O Webley" without initials or service number, is the late F/O L C E Webley RCAF, killed on operations to Haine-St-Pierre on 8-9 May 1944 (see Bomber Command Losses, Volume 5, page 215), while flying with 431 Squadron.

4 Jul	1659 HCU	Halifax II	W1092	Training

1943   Sgt L P Pitt   T/o 0047 Topcliffe for a night exercise, but
        F/S R Stewart RCAF   while accelerating at high speed a tyre burst
                                      causing the bomber to ground loop and lose its undercarriage.

	1660 HCU	Manchester I	R5770	Training

       P/O J L Cooper DFC   T/o 1140 Swinderby for dual circuit training.
                                    Twenty minutes into the detail, and while in
the process of taking off, an engine lost power and P/O Cooper raised the undercarriage in order to prevent the Manchester from running off the airfield. A technical inspection of the failed Vulture revealed traces of a foreign matter in the carburettor. Struck off charge nine days later, the aircraft had flown a total of 213.05 hours. This was the third major incident featuring P/O Cooper (see pages 43 and 47 for his previous mishaps).

5 Jul	1665 HCU	Stirling I	BF339 -G	Training

1943   F/O L G Kennett   inj   T/o 0057 Woolfox Lodge for night solo circuits
       Sgt S L McGarrigle   inj   and landings but swung to starboard and, before
       P/O H T Ramsden   inj   being brought under control, ran into a vehicle
       Sgt G J Line   inj   before finishing up amongst some buildings. A
       Sgt N F Cook RCAF   inj   fire broke out, but prompt and efficient action
       P/O Cubby   on the part of the station's fire service, aided
       Sgt Sanders   by the National Fire Service appliance from
                                    Stamford, plus assistance from RAF Cottesmore,
greatly lessened what could have been very substantial damage to property. The first three named were treated for superficial injuries in station sick quarters but Sgt Line and Sgt Cook RCAF were both admitted to RAF Hospital Rauceby, the former with a fractured femur.

6 Jul	1660 HCU	Lancaster I	R5736	Training

1943   P/O E A Orchard   +   T/o Swinderby for a cross-country. While
       F/S B A Cook   +   flying in very marginal weather, smashed into
       Sgt C P Lucas   +   the side of a hill near Llangernyw, 12 miles
       Sgt R E Sadleir   +   west-north-west of Denbigh. P/O Orchard of
       Sgt R W A Dipple   +   Manor Park in Essex and Sgt Dipple of Peckham
       Sgt W C Williams   +   were provided with military funerals at Chester
                                    (Blacon) Cemetery. Their four companions were
buried under private arrangement. The time of the crash has been omitted from the accident card. In a year of   service, the Lancaster had flown 513.00 hours.

| 6- 7 Jul | 1659 HCU | Halifax II | DT676 | Training |
| 1943 | Sgt T Buchanan | | | |

T/o 2245 Topcliffe for a night exercise, in the course of which the fuel state ran perilously low and in turn this led to an emergency landing at 0345 on, or near, Dalton airfield the Halifax being wrecked in the process.

| | 1662 HCU A Flt | Lancaster III | DV169 | Training |
| | Sgt H H Adams | | | |

T/o 1955 Blyton for a night navigation detail. Returned to base at 0345, but overshot the runway and damaged beyond economical repair after running into an obstruction.

7 Jul	1657 HCU	Stirling I	N3722	Training
1943	F/O L F Smith DFC			
	Sgt Gry RNZAF			

T/o 2230 Stradishall for a night detail , during which the Stirling landed 2315, at Lakenheath.
As the bomber made contact with the runway, the port main tyre exploded and, thus, moments later it lay in a sorry state, damaged beyond repair. It will be recalled that F/O Smith had already survived two nasty crashes in his flying career (see page 47 for details).

| | 1662 HCU A Flt | Lancaster I | ED414 | Training |
| | Sgt D H Loop | | | |

T/o 0115 Blyton to practice circuits and landings at night. Twenty minutes passed without incident before a misunderstanding during cockpit drill led to the Lancaster overshooting the runway and colliding with an obstruction. Proceeding to 103 Squadron, Sgt Loop was killed operating to Hannover on 18-19 October 1943 (see Bomber Command Losses, Volume 4, page 359). His DFC was effective 18 October, though it was not formally Gazetted until 28 March 1944.

8 Jul	1652 HCU	Halifax II	BB308 -K	Training
1943	Sgt R Heuston			
	ACW2 J Scargill WAAF	+		

T/o Marston Moor for flying practice, which came to an abrupt, and tragic, conclusion when the Halifax overshot the runway and collided with a motor transport vehicle parked on one of the dispersal pans, the driver of which sustained fatal head injuries. Just twenty years of age, and married to Bombadier Jeffrey Scargill of the Royal Artillery, ACW2 Scargill (née Cowie) is buried in Kirkleatham (St. Cuthbert) Churchyard. The time of the accident is recorded as 1608.

9 Jul	1659 HCU	Halifax II	BB208	Air Test
1943	F/O F A Pope RCAF	inj		
	Sgt E Fahy	inj		
	P/O K G House RCAF	inj		
	P/O A H Durnin RCAF	inj		
	Sgt J D Clarke	inj		
	Sgt Schmidt			
	Sgt McLean			

T/o 1642 Topcliffe for an altitude test but crashed and caught fire at East Lodge Farm on the SW boundary of the airfield. An inspection of the wreckage revealed that the aileron locks had been left in place. Two, P/O Durnin RCAF and Sgt Clarke were classed as dangerously hurt and both were taken to Northallerton Hospital. All recovered from their injuries but three, including the two most seriously injured, were subsequently killed during 1944 on bomber operations; Sgt Fahy on 17 June, P/O Durnin RCAF on 29 July and Sgt Clarke, early in the year, on 3 January (see Bomber Command Losses, Volume 5, pages 286, 355 and 23 respectively).

| | 1661 HCU | Lancaster I | R5889 GP-M | Training |
| | Sgt A G A Barnet | inj | | |

T/o 0230 Winthorpe for night circuits and landings and was travelling at high speed when the starboard tyre burst. Sgt Barnet maintained control and succeeded in becoming airborne. For the next two hours and fifteen minutes he flew around the local area, waiting for daylight. Satisfied that he could see well enough for an emergency landing, he jettisoned part of the fuel load and made a good landing, on the runway, but as the Lancaster began to slow flames were seen streaming from the mainplanes and before the fire services could intervene, the bomber was well and truly ablaze. Later, the Chief Technical Officer reported that the starboard jettison trunk had broken off (possibly due to excessive airspeed) and this had allowed petrol to blow back and accumulate in parts of the wing; then, as the airspeed reduced, this fuel ran down the undercarriage struts and ignited as sparks flew up from the wheel rim. In retrospect, the station commander added, it might have been better to have landed on the grass and, perhaps, pilots should be advised not to jettison fuel in similar circumstances.

11–12 Jul	1656 HCU	Lancaster I	W4777	Training

1943	Sgt M G Eastlake	+	T/o 2145 Lindholme for a night cross-country.
	Sgt H A Lloyd	+	Crashed 0230 and totally destroyed at Mill Lane,
	F/O J H Tremear	+	Thorganby, 8 miles NE of Selby, Yorkshire. The
	Sgt W E L Harrison	+	two survivors were admitted to York Military
	Sgt P D Probert	inj	Hospital, Sgt Probert having sustained very
	Sgt R McLaughlan RCAF	inj	serious back injuries, while his Canadian
	Sgt G H Peck	+	colleague had fractured ribs and chest bones,
			plus serious contusions to the head. Both,

thankfully, recovered. Of those who died, two were buried locally in Selby Cemetery, namely F/O Tremear, a schoolmaster from Great Badslow, Essex, and the tail gunner, Sgt Peck, who hailed from Wallington in Surrey. The others were claimed by their next of kin.

12 Jul	1652 HCU	Halifax II	R9423	Training

1943	Sgt J Brooks		T/o 1517 Marston Moor. Swung out of control on
			landing at 1647 and came to a stop with the

undercarriage smashed. Following a similar incident on 31 December 1942, when W/O A S Younger had been at the controls, repairs had been deemed viable, but now the damage was assessed as being too severe to warrant similar action.

1663 HCU C Flt	Halifax V	DG404 OO-A	Training

F/O J S Barber	inj	T/o Rufforth for a night cross-country only to
Sgt W D Hall	inj	encounter atrocious weather conditions. Thus,
Sgt T H Woollard	+	at approximately 0200, the Halifax forced-
Sgt T Reid	+	landed, wheels down, on the eastern side of
Sgt J Godley	+	Heathfield Moor, some 2 miles NW from Pateley
P/O A J Walker	inj	Bridge, Yorkshire. Despite his injuries, Sgt
Sgt D H Batten RAAF	inj	Hall managed to summon help and as the night
		progressed, so the injured were brought to

Highfield Farm, then farmed by a Mr Simpson, where at least one died before the ambulance services could reach them. Sgt Woollard was buried in Harrogate (Stonefall) Cemetery, while Sgt Reid and Sgt Godley were taken back to Scotland and interred, respectively, at Glasgow (Eastwood) Cemetery and Cumbernauld Cemetery, Dunbartonshire. Over the next fifteen months, fate intervened to take the lives of the four survivors. First to fall was F/O Barber, lost with his 77 Squadron crew on operations to Kassel in late October 1943; next was the gallant Sgt Hall, posted to 10 Squadron and shot down while outbound to Berlin on 29–30 December 1943. A month later, Sgt Batten's 640 Squadron Halifax was lost without trace while raiding Magdeburg and, lastly, P/O Walker became a casualty on 14 October 1944, having successfully completed a tour of operations and becoming a recipient of the Distinguished Flying Cross. He is buried in Rugby (Whinfield) Cemetery. Apart from P/O Walker's demise, details for the others are contained in Bomber Command Losses, Volumes 4 and 5, pages 366, 439 and 51 respectively.

Note. During the day, following the crash, David Shuttleworth of Wath visited the scene and made a remarkable sketch of the wreck (which was substantially intact), an exercise which he repeated in 1964, when debris was still present in some quantities. In 1944, David Shuttleworth began his flying training in Canada, qualifying as a navigator. Although too late to participate in bombing operations, he served, briefly, with 170 Squadron, flying in Lancasters out of Hemswell. On his release from the service, he resumed his training as an architect, in time becoming senior partner in his own firm. Presently (2002), he resides in Pateley Bridge and is Honorary Secretary of the Cleveland and District Branch of the Aircrew Association.

17–18 Jul	1661 HCU	Lancaster I	W4947 GP-Z	Training

1943	Sgt R C Parkinson	+	T/o 2255 Winthorpe for a night navigation sortie
	Sgt T H Loftus	+	which involved the crew flying over the Irish
	Sgt C G Hirst	+	Sea. It is suspected that the Lancaster came
	P/O S C Dykes	+	down in the water at around 0240, possibly twixt
	Sgt E Saxon	+	Barrow-in-Furness, Lancashire and St. Bees Head,
	Sgt D G Leverton	+	south-south-west of Whitehaven on the Cumberland
	Sgt W L Haslam	+	coast. Two are commemorated on the Runnymede
			Memorial, but in due course of time the sea gave

up the rest of the crew and, following identification, three were claimed by their next of kin, while Sgt Loftus of Morden in Surrey and Sgt Leverton from Sherwood, Nottinghamshire, were buried in Chester (Blacon) Cemetery.

19 Jul 1943	**1663 HCU**	**Halifax V**	DG389		**Training**

P/O J R McCormack — T/o Rufforth for a night dual training exercise
P/O W J Williams — inj — only to lose power from the engines and crash-
Sgt L W Powis — inj — land, 2332, in a field on Moat Farm on the SE
side of Catterton, 7 miles SW from the centre
of York. A fire broke out as the Halifax broke up, on impact. The injuries
to P/O Williams and Sgt Powis were not serious.

20 Jul 1943	**1662 HCU A Flt**	**Lancaster I**	W4893		**Training**

F/S E E Norman RAAF — + — T/o Blyton for a day navigation exercise.
Sgt J G Lysaght — + — Lost without trace. All are commemorated
Sgt D H Head — + — on the Runnymede Memorial. F/S Norman RAAF,
Sgt R Raisbeck — + — his navigator, air bomber and wireless operator
Sgt J Haworth — + — had recently graduated from 27 Operational
Sgt G D McCulloch — + — Training Unit.
Sgt W E Pearce — +

22 Jul 1943	**1657 HCU**	**Stirling I**	R9296		**Training**

Sgt G Dalby — T/o 0155 Stradishall but lost its undercarriage,
Sgt Barlington — and wrecked as a consequence, after swinging out
Sgt Bennett — of control.
Sgt Dean

	1657 HCU	**Stirling I**	W7586	–C	**Training**

P/O L G Sellars RAAF — + — T/o Stradishall. Stalled and crashed 1746 while
Sgt J A Campbell — + — attempting to go round again from a three-
F/O R H Rutherford — + — engined approach. The three Commonwealth members
F/S R H Murdock RCAF — + — of crew rest locally in Haverhill Cemetery, the
Sgt R G Kings — + — others being claimed by their next of kin and
Sgt G F A Wix — + — conveyed to burial grounds (or as in the case
F/S E H B Saker RAAF — + — of Sgt Campbell, born in Fraserborough, cremated
at Golders Green) in Northern Ireland, Scotland
and England. As Tony Biles recalls, Sgt Kings ran the village carpenters shop
at Ettington in Warwickshire and is fondly remembered by the children, including
a then nine year old Tony Biles, for his skill in making arrows from scraps of
wood. At the time of his death, Sgt Kings had been married a mere six months,
his young widow Lucy being a nurse at Stratford-upon-Avon Emergency Hospital.

24 Jul 1943	**1652 HCU**	**Halifax II**	BB285 GV–Q		**Training**

Sgt E L Byrne — + — T/o Marston Moor. At 1322, the Halifax crashed
F/S C B Tingle — + — into the village sewerage works at Spofforth,
Sgt W G Richardson — + — midway between the Yorkshire towns of Harrogate
Sgt J A M Weir — + — and Wetherby. The cause of the crash was traced
Sgt C W Nowell — + — to a pin working loose in the mechanism control-
WO2 J J Duclos RCAF — + — ling the rudders, thus leading to a complete
Sgt R Roberts — inj — failure of the system. It is also reported that
the starboard outer engine was on fire, prior to
the crash and flames from the motor may have burned into the aileron controls.
Those who died are buried at various locations in England and Scotland; rather
surprisingly, WO2 Duclos RCAF was taken not to Harrogate, as may have been
expected, but to Lincoln (Newport) Cemetery. It is possible his funeral was
arranged by relatives of his family in Montreal. M H Brooke adds, since the
crash, the sewage treatment works have been re-sited, leaving just one building
on the old site, located in fields to the right hand side of the A661 leading
out of Spofforth village towards Harrogate.

	1665 HCU	**Stirling I**	BK621	–V	**Air Test**

P/O J Bailey RNZAF — T/o 1523 Woolfox Lodge on an acceptance test,
the Stirling having been given up from 1651 HCU,
but swung off the runway, whereupon the port oleo gave way.

25 Jul 1943	**1659 HCU**	**Halifax II**	R9420	–G	**Training**

F/O W J R Green RCAF — + — T/o Topcliffe. Spun in, from around 1,500 feet,
Sgt G W Stevenson — + — at 1345 and burst into flames about a mile E of
F/S W B Wheeler RCAF — + — Linton-on-Ouse airfield. Funerals for the five
F/S W B Kaiser RCAF — + — RCAF members of crew were held at Dishforth
Sgt J P H Ingle — + — Cemetery on 28 July, while their two companions
P/O S T Snead RCAF — + — were taken to Beath Eastern Cemetery in Fife,
P/O W D McKercher RCAF — + — and Skipton (Waltonwrays) Cemetery respectively.

| 25 Jul | 1665 HCU | Stirling I | EF354 | −C | Training |

25 Jul **1665 HCU** **Stirling I** **EF354** **−C** **Training**
1943   P/O P J Buck RNZAF   T/o 2237 Woolfox Lodge for a night sortie, but
        F/S E A Hill RAAF   not long after departing, the pilot called base
                                      to say he was experiencing problems with the
controls. Unfortunately, interference on the radio channel delayed the passing
of instructions, intended to assist the crew and, thus, at 2302 P/O Buck RNZAF
crossed the threshold, flaps down, at an estimated 140 miles per hour. All
might still have been well, but for another aircraft looming up in the path
of the fast travelling bomber. Harsh braking was applied and although a collision
was averted, the undercarriage collapsed and the Stirling, a survivor of fifteen
operational sorties with 15 Squadron, was wrecked. Six weeks later, F/S Hill
and his crew were lost during a sea mining operation off Denmark (see Bomber
Command Losses, Volume 4, page 307); their association with 15 Squadron had
been all too tragically brief.

25–26 Jul **1657 HCU** **Stirling I** **EF338** **Training**
1943   F/O A R Craddock   T/o 2344 Stradishall for dual circuits and
        F/S K G Whiting RAAF   landings, at night. Touched down at 0024, only
                                      for the starboard tyre to burst which, in turn,
                                      led to the loss of the undercarriage.

26 Jul **1651 HCU** **Stirling I** **W7583 BS–B** **Training**
1943   F/L L C Kingsbury   T/o Waterbeach for a night training exercise.
                                      Landed 0500, but swung out of control and ran
into Stirling I R9144. Damage to the latter was slight and, following local
repairs, it was returned to service by 5 August. On 30 November 1943, it was
given up to 1665 Heavy Conversion Unit, passing into storage with 6 Maintenance
Unit at Brize Norton on 26 March 1944, where it languished until struck off
charge on 14 January 1945.

27 Jul **1654 HCU** **Lancaster I** **ED591 UG–L** **Training**
1943   P/O N L Schofield RCAF   T/o 0015 Wigsley but the starboard tyre blew out
        F/L Brain   and moments later the Lancaster was irreparably
                                      damaged having come to rest amidst the remains
of some recently felled trees. As the unit commander wryly stated, "damage would
have been much less if the stumps had been removed", while the station commander
added, "concur - suggest substitute camouflage hedge"!

         1657 HCU **Stirling I** **EF344** **Training**
         F/S F E Langford RAAF   T/o 1710 Stradishall for circuit practice.
         Sgt R Cove   Suffered a fate similar to that reported for
         Sgt C Bevan   the unit's previous write off (see the second
                                      entry on this page), the accident occurring
at 1735. F/S Langford RAAF was posted to 90 Squadron and completed a tour
of operations, by which time he had been commissioned. On 23 May 1944, the
London Gazette published details of his Distinguished Flying Cross, this being
followed two days later by an announcement in the Commonwealth of Australia
Gazette. His accidental death was subsequently reported on 25 March 1947,
and he is buried in Townsville War Cemetery, Queensland.

28 Jul **1656 HCU** **Lancaster I** **W4200** **Training**
1943   Sgt I J Holmes   T/o 1140 Lindholme for day circuit training.
                                      At 1210, following several successful circuits,
commenced taking off but swung and ran over a flare, puncturing a tyre as it
did so. Moments later, the undercarriage collapsed and Sgt Holmes's second
solo flight was brought to an abrupt conclusion.

         1659 HCU **Halifax II** **DT500** **Training**
         Sgt R C Deegan RCAF   T/o 0234 Topcliffe for night dual, a detail
         Sgt J H Tovey RCAF   that commenced with circuits and landings and
                                      ended at 0244, when a tyre burst on touch down.
No one was hurt, but the resultant collapse of the undercarriage ensured that
the Halifax never flew again. On completing his course, Sgt Tovey RCAF joined
434 Squadron at Tholthorpe and was lost in action during the night of 6-7
September 1943 (see Bomber Command Losses, Volume 4, page 318).

29 Jul **1659 HCU** **Halifax II** **DT507** **Training**
1943   P/O L Haynes   T/o 1105 Topclife for circuits and landings and
        P/O H Brown RCAF   wrecked in a landing mishap twenty minutes later.

29 Jul   **1665 HCU**   **Stirling I** **EF337** **—J**   **Training**
1943   F/S E A Hill RAAF   T/o Woolfox Lodge to practice circuit flying.
Swung to port on landing, after which the
undercarriage collapsed. This was F/S Hill's second crash in four days (see
the previous page for details of this, and his subsequent fate).

2 Aug   **1656 HCU**   **Halifax II** **R9380**   **Training**
1943   P/O J E Gibbs   T/o 1407 Lindholme but as the Halifax lifted
       Sgt J Horsley   clear of the runway, a sharp report was heard,
suggesting a tyre had burst. This proved to be
the case and when, two hours later, the crew returned to base, their landing
was followed by the loss of their undercarriage.

2– 3 Aug **1656 HCU**   **Lancaster I** **W4781**   **Training**
1943   Sgt J D R Cromarty   T/o 2106 Lindholme for a night navigation detail.
On return to base at 0416, Sgt Cromarty landed on
the short runway, without any flap assistance and, not surprisingly, he overshot
and ended up with the Lancaster wrecked, minus its undercarriage. The technical
inspection that followed revealed that a split jack in the flap mechanism had
fractured, allowing the hydraulic fluid to escape. Despite his relative inexperience, Sgt Cromarty proceeded to Pathfinder duties and was commissioned
when posted missing from Berlin on 2-3 January 1944 (see Bomber Command Losses,
Volume 5, page 24).

4 Aug   **1651 HCU**   **Stirling I** **BF416** **—X**   **Training**
1943   Sgt J Griffiths   T/o 0345 Waterbeach for night training. Landed
thirty minutes later, but swung from the runway
and lost its undercarriage. In his report, Sgt Griffiths stated that he had
noticed a sharp rise in temperature on one of the engines and had decided to
land as soon as possible. Coupled with rather misty weather conditions, his
arrival at base was, perhaps, rather hasty and not fully controlled. Posted
to 196 Squadron, he became a prisoner of war in the aftermath of the Berlin raid
on the last night of August 1943 (see Bomber Command Losses, Volume 4, page 303).

        1658 HCU   **Halifax II** **W1093**   **Training**
       Sgt W A Burgum RAAF   T/o 1650 Riccall to practice circuits and
       F/O J G Jenkins   landings. Shortly before 1750, touched down
rather heavily, on one wheel, and bounced back
into the air. Control was maintained and another circuit flown, despite much
distraction from the warning horn sounding. On his next arrival, the undercarriage folded up, effectively damaging the aircraft beyond repair. Less
then three weeks later, Sgt Burgum RAAF failed to return from Berlin, while
flying with 158 Squadron (see Bomber Command Losses, Volume 4, page 286). In
the short space of time that he had been with "158", Sgt Burgum RAAF had flown
two complete sorties as captain, namely Peenemünde and Leverkusen.

        1659 HCU   **Halifax II** **JB916**   **Training**
       Sgt J Reynoldson RCAF   T/o Topcliffe for a night cross-country. While
cruising off the north Wales coast, the propeller
on the inner starboard engine broke away and this was followed by an explosion,
which prompted the crew to put their aircraft down in the sea off Trearddur Bay,
below Holyhead on Holy Island. The ditching was near copybook and, about an hour
later, all were saved as an Air Sea Rescue launch reached the scene.

        1665 HCU   **Stirling I** **BF446** **—C**   **Training**
       F/L B G Johnston RNZAF   T/o Woolfox Lodge. Swung on landing, the pilot
over correcting in an attempt to straighten out.
As a consequence, the Stirling ran onto soft at the edge of the runway, skidded
wildly and lost its undercarriage. During its time spent with 218 Squadron, it
flew, as Bryce Gomersall reports, thirty-three operational sorties.

10 Aug   **1657 HCU**   **Stirling I** **BF321**   **Training**
1943   F/S F P Lundon RNZAF   T/o Stradishall for night flying practice.
       Sgt W Thompson   Landed 0210, at Ridgewell, but veered off the
       F/S G M Pinker   runway and wrecked as a result of the under-
       F/S H Paraone   carriage collapsing. F/S Lundon RNZAF was killed
       Sgt A Houston   during a sortie, as second pilot, to Berlin with
       Sgt J Murphy   75 Squadron on 23-24 August 1943 (see Bomber
       Sgt H Howells   Command Losses, Volume 4, page 281).

10 Aug   **1659 HCU**   **Halifax II W1019**   **Training**
1943   Sgt I C R Bowden   T/o 0025 Topcliffe tasked for night circuit
      Sgt F Long   practice. As was so often the case, a tyre
blow out within ten minutes of the detail
commencing not only put paid to the exercise, but wrote the Halifax off at
the same time. Sgt Bowen went to 432 Squadron, and was posted missing in
action in late September 1943 (see Bomber Command Losses, Volume 4, page 339).

11 Aug   **1657 HCU**   **Stirling I N6080 –T**   **Training**
1943   Sgt W H Chappell   T/o 1625 Stradishall for circuit training.
      Sgt D Oxley   The dual effects of a burst tyre (on landing
      Sgt L J Crossman   inj   at 1655) and a collapsed undercarriage ended
      Sgt T J Higgins   inj   the flying service of this Stirling. It is
      Sgt A C Pool   not thought that those who sustained injury
      Sgt R G Knights   inj   were seriously hurt.
      Sgt R W Dunkley   inj

12 Aug   **1657 HCU**   **Stirling I N3700 XT–V**   **Training**
1943   F/L H Tilson RCAF   T/o Stradishall for a dual exercise, during
      P/O F Gribble   which the port undercarriage failed to lock
when the unit was selected "down". Diverted
to Newmarket, the Stilring was forced-landed at 0155, with its wheels safely
retracted. Following salvage, the airframe was allocated the serial 4669M
and by March 1944, was being used by the Parachute Regiment as a ground trainer.

13 Aug   **1658 HCU**   **Halifax II R9387**   **Training**
1943   Sgt R H Whittington RCAF   T/o 0109 Riccall for night circuits and landings
but the port tyre deflated and, consequently, on
landing at 0114, the undercarriage gave way. An examination of the damaged tyre
revealed an excessive amount of "creep". This Halifax had sustained a tail wheel
breakage on 25 March 1943, its pilot on that occasion being Sgt B S McCann, who
went soon afterwards to 76 Squadron and failed to return from Milano in mid-
August 1943 (see Bomber Command Losses, Volume 4, page 266).

17 Aug   **1658 HCU**   **Halifax II R9367**   **Training**
1943   Sgt J F A Bailey   T/o 1247 Riccall for circuits and landings, but
suffered a fate not too dissimilar to that re-
ported above, the difference being that Sgt Bailey stated that a tyre had burst
as he touched down at 1254. On completion of his course, he was posted to
Elvington and 77 Squadron and was lost during a raid to Kassel early in the
October (see Bomber Command Losses, Volume 4, page 346).

18 Aug   **1657 HCU**   **Stirling I R9300**   **Training**
1943   P/O F Gribble   T/o 1755 Stradishall but the starboard outer cut
and the resultant swing took the bomber off the
runway, its undercarriage giving way moments later. For the second time in less
than a week, P/O Gribble had been involved in a serious accident. Despite the
trauma of these events, he proved to be a competent heavy bomber pilot and by
the summer of 1944, he was flying Stirlings with 196 Squadron, a No. 38 Group
unit employed on airborne support duties, which included clandestine supply
drops to the French Resistance. On 5-6 June 1944, his Stirling IV LJ481 was
shot down at Cagny whilst engaged on Operation Tonga, a supply drop to a zone
identified as "N", east of the River Orne.

Note. I am, indeed, again indebted to Bryce Gomersall for the background notes
pertaining to P/O Gribble who, along with the majority of his crew, is buried in
Cagny Communal Cemetery.

19 Aug   **1656 HCU**   **Lancaster I R5667 –C**   **Training**
1943   Sgt D W H Butterfield   T/o Lindholme for a night exercise but a tyre
burst and upon landing at 0113, the Lancaster
swerved off the runway, losing its undercarriage, and taking light as it came
to a stop. No one was hurt, but the fire services were unable to prevent the
bomber from being destroyed. Sgt Butterfield, who was said to have taken all
precautions, went on the complete his course and by the autumn was stationed at
Wickenby and flying Lancasters with 12 Squadron. Sadly, his aircraft failed to
return from a sortie in early October 1943 (see Bomber Command Losses, Volume 4,
page 343). Prior to his death, he had applied for, and had been granted, a
commission and this was duly promulgated.

19 Aug
1943

| 1658 HCU | Halifax II | R9497 | | Training |

Sgt T C Ashley   +   T/o 1050 Riccall having being briefed for a
Sgt T R McMeekan   +   cross-country exercise. Some five minutes later,
Sgt A J Allan   +   and while climbing on a north-north-easterly
F/O R F Walker   +   heading, collided with a 1663 Heavy Conversion
Sgt J J O'Brien   +   Unit Halifax that was tracking south-east as
Sgt F Cosford   +   it climbed out from Rufforth. Both machines
Sgt D L H Wooster   +   plunged into fields at Manor Farm, just W of
the village of Copmanthorpe, a mere 4 miles SW
from the centre of York. All were claimed by their next of kin, Sgt O'Brien
being interred in the Irish Republic at Ballina (Templehollow) Graveyard, Co.
Tipperary (it is noted, however, that his parents were of Hacketstown, Co.
Carlow when CWGC prepared their Irish registers).

| 1663 HCU C Flt | Halifax V | DG420 | –H | Training |

Sgt D C Ravine   +   T/o 1054 Rufforth with a crew comprising of a
F/O M W Bonner RCAF   +   pupil pilot (at the controls), his instructor,
Sgt N J Hart   +   two flight engineers, a wireless operator and
Sgt J H Townsend   +   two air gunners. Destroyed in the circumstances
Sgt P C Parrott   +   described above. Crash and Rescue services from
Sgt F D Read   +   Rufforth and Marston Moor attended, the station
Sgt A E Gilverson RCAF   +   sick quarters from the latter unit being made
responsible for holding all fourteen bodies
Mr Atkinson   inj   while identification procedures were put in
Mstr J Dawson   inj   hand. Both Canadians, Sgt Ravine and Sgt Read
were buried under service arrangements at
Harrogate (Stonefall) Cemetery, while the others were taken to their home
towns. The two civilians caught up in this terrible accident were on a tractor
in a field where one of the Halifaxes fell (it is believed to have been the
Rufforth machine). Both, as Brian Mennell vividly reports in his book, "Wings
Over York", ran for their lives but were engulfed in blazing petrol. Thirteen
year old John Dawson sustained very severe burns to his legs and lost all his
hair but despite his appalling injuries, he found some sacking and did his ut-
most to beat out the flames that were all over the upper torso of his colleague,
Mr Atkinson. Both were admitted to York County Hospital, where John Dawson was
detained for three months (and Mr Atkinson for much longer). In August 1996,
the "York and North Yorkshire News" reported that Malcolm Bisley, who as a nine
year old schoolboy had witnessed the tragedy, headed an attempt to recover the
engines from the fields where they had lain, deep beneath the soil, for over
fifty years; their efforts proved unsuccessful.

20 Aug
1943

| 1651 HCU | Stirling I | BF395 | –Q | Training |

F/O K H Becroft RNZAF   T/o Waterbeach for night dual training. Forty-
Sgt A B Winstanley   five minutes later, wrecked after overshooting
the runway at Downham Market. News of the
crash was received in the Operations Room at Waterbeach at 2205. It will be
recalled that F/O Becroft RNZAF had passed through "1651" in the autumn of 1942
as an embryo bomber pilot and had been involved in a serious flying accident
(see page 30). His tour as a staff pilot would prove to be quite eventful!

21 Aug
1943

| 1658 HCU | Halifax II | DT697 | –C22 | Training |

F/S J A Mawson RCAF   +   T/o Riccall for a night navigation sortie.
Sgt L H W Green   +   When the two starboard engines failed, the
F/S C Rumble   inj   crew attempted to land at Bruntingthorpe, but
F/S B E Bell RCAF   +   hit a house near the boundary of the airfield
Sgt R S Moncreiff   +   and crashed 0055, heavily. F/S Rumble died
Sgt J Brown   inj   from his injuries on 22 August; he is buried
Sgt J L Ball   inj   in Edinburgh (Piershill) Cemetery. His fellow
Scot, Sgt Moncreiff, rests at Newburgh Cemetery
in Fife, while Sgt Green was taken to Thurrock (Chadwell St. Mary) Cemetery.
The two RCAF members of crew were interred at Oxford (Botley) Cemetery.

22 Aug
1943

| 1663 HCU | Halifax V | DK125 | –K | Training |

Sgt J Gordon-Davis   inj   T/o 2242 Rufforth but collided with the rear
F/S N McPhail RAAF   inj   of Halifax V EB195/O, which had burst a tyre
F/O N M Carruthers   inj   on landing and was stationary on the runway.
Amazingly, all appear to have escaped serious
injury and the other Halifax was repaired and returned to service (though it
would be written off early in 1944, while still on the strength of "1663").

23 Aug	1661 HCU	Lancaster I	W4190 GP-A	Training

1943   F/O B S Turner   T/o 1812 Winthorpe but swung violently to port and crashed. In his statement, F/O Turner indicated an engine had failed but the unit's engineering officer was unable to find any defect. However, it subsequently transpired that the carburettor of the port outer Merlin was faulty.

24 Aug	1652 HCU	Halifax II	W7806	-B	Training

1943

P/O S A Maslin	inj
F/O K A Petch RCAF	inj
Sgt R Cederbaum	inj
P/O T M Telford	inj
Sgt W H Curness	inj
P/O Napier	
P/O Potter	
Sgt Shirley	
Cdt Calvert ATC	inj
Cdt Gorman ATC	inj
Cdt Rushden ATC	inj

T/o Marston Moor for general flying practice, three Air Training Corps cadets being taken aloft for air experience. Shortly before 1215, the inner starboard engine shed its propeller and, as the bomber lost height, the order to bale out was given. Most complied, but one of the young cadets was unable to jump and the pilot, assisted by Sgt Cederbaum, forced-landed near Sherburn in Elmet airfield, coming to rest near the village church. Cdt Rushden, was very badly injured and, it is reported, his life was undoubtedly saved by the shock therapy administered by the station sick quarters at Eversley Park before his admittance to Northallerton Hospital.

	1661 HCU	Lancaster I	W4381 GP-B	Training

| F/O D Hamilton |
| Sgt D Warnes |
| Sgt C Oakley |

T/o 1550 Winthorpe for general training, during which a tyre burst in its bay, damaging the hydraulics. On regaining the airfield circuit, the crew used the emergency system to lower the undercarriage, but on touch down at 1645, the unit collapsed as the bomber swung off the runway.

	1663 HCU	Halifax V	DG394	-D	Training

| S/L D Carter |
| Sgt A C Dickenson |

T/o 1100 Rufforth but swung out of control and ground looped. This imposed such a strain on the undercarriage that it tore away from its mountings.

26 Aug	1659 HCU	Halifax II	DT629	Ground

1943   At 0320, while unoccupied, struck and set on fire by one of the unit's Halifaxes that had crashed, out of control, on landing.

	1659 HCU	Halifax II	DT802	Training

F/O R B Hermon RCAF	inj
Sgt W J Miller RCAF	+
F/O T E Beaman	inj
Sgt G Gold	inj
Sgt F A Cook	inj
Sgt V R Crane RCAF	inj
Sgt W E McDonald RCAF	+

T/o Topcliffe for a night exercise, at the conclusion of which the crew came into land at 0340 with the port inner motor feathered. The touch down was, unfortunately, at least twenty degrees off the runway's centre line and before the situation could be corrected, the bomber smashed into the Halifax described above. The injured were immediately rushed to Northallerton Hospital where, three days later, Sgt Cook died. He is buried in Derby (Nottingham Road) Cemetery; it is noted that his service number indicates that he underwent pilot training, before the war, with the volunteer reserve. Sgt Miller RCAF and Sgt McDonald RCAF both rest in Harrogate (Stonefall) Cemetery.

27 Aug	1663 HCU	Halifax V	DG412	-B	Training

1943

Sgt J P Williams	+
Sgt G R Wheatley	+
Sgt R F Stainsby	+
F/O W H Graham	+
Sgt J Taylor	+
Sgt H P Henry RAAF	+
F/S P C Bartle RAAF	+

T/o Rufforth on a Bullseye detail. Lost control while practising evasive flying and in the dive that followed, the Halifax came apart under the excessive loads imposed upon its airframe. It is almost certain that the crew were trapped by the centrifugal force and their bodies were recovered from the crash site at Langtree, 4 miles south-west of Great Torrington, Devon. Three, Sgt Williams of Haywards Heath in Sussex and his two Australian comrades, were buried in Heanton Punchardon (St. Augustine) Churchyard, a burial ground much used by RAF Chivenor, then a busy Coastal Command station on Devon's north coast near Barnstaple. The others were claimed by their next of kin.

31 Aug	**1651 HCU**	**Stirling I**	**N6005 -D2**	**Transit**

1943

F/O C W Woods DFM RAAF	+
F/S R G Cotton RNZAF	+
W/O R W Pratt	+
Sgt D Parsons	+
F/S I A Eliot RAAF	+
F/S J F B Wearne RAAF	+
F/S F Payne RNZAF	+
F/S G L Yensen RAAF	+
Sgt P Irwin	+

T/o 2130 Downham Market intending to return to
Waterbeach. Some ten minutes into the flight,
the Stirling banked steeply and spun into the
ground a mile N of Shippea Hill on the border
with Cambridgeshire and Suffolk and roughly
seven miles ENE from the cathedral city of Ely.
On 6 September, military funerals were held at
Cambridge City Cemetery for the six Commonwealth
and W/O Pratt, who hailed from Carlow in the
Irish Republic. Also from the Republic was
Sgt Irwin, but his body was taken back to Ireland and laid to rest in Glenlara
Old Graveyard in Co. Limerick. Sgt Parsons, whose father was Lt Roy Parsons MC,
was conveyed to Stockton-on-Tees (Oxbridge Road) Cemetery. F/O Woods RAAF had
flown a tour of operations with 214 Squadron and details of his DFM had been
Gazetted on 6 November 1942.

Note. Some years ago, I was sent an extract from the flying log book kept by
W/O W H Pengelley who, between September and October 1942, trained at "1651"
and flew in the above mentioned aircraft on a number of occasions. During
this time, it carried the letter "F". On completion of his training, W/O
Pengelley joined 15 Squadron and flew twenty-nine operational sorties.

	1654 HCU	**Lancaster I**	**W4260 UG-O**	**Training**

F/O R Burchett   T/o Wigsley for a night training sortie and
reported to have collided, near Ossington air-
field, at 0410 with Halifax II HR782 from 51 Squadron, which was returning from
a raid on Mönchengladbach. The Halifax landed safely and was little damaged,
but it was lost a few months later while raiding Leipzig (see Bomber Command
Losses, Volume 4, page 415).

Note. The details of the Halifax and the Lancaster have been entered on one
card and it is not absolutely clear as to who was flying which aircraft. It
is my belief that F/O Burchett was the captain of the Lancaster, but he might
well have been at the controls of the Halifax. F/S A B Simpson RAAF, too, is
mentioned in respect of this incident and, thus, he might well have been the
Lancaster pilot. What is not in doubt is the cause, this being attributed to
the high congestion of aircraft returning from bombing operations.

	1662 HCU	**Lancaster I**	**W4314**	**Training**

F/S L W Martin RAAF	+
F/S W Bradshaw	+
F/S J M Borthwick RAAF	+
F/S P R Good RAAF	+
F/S S A Grant RAAF	+
Sgt T Stearman	+
Sgt G Howard	+

T/o Blyton for a long night cross-country.
Flew into the ground, at 0325, near Laughton,
five miles NNE from Gainsborough, Lincolnshire.
The four Australian members of crew were buried
under military arrangement in Cambridge City
Cemetery, while their three colleagues were
taken to their home towns of Blackburn, Gates-
head and Blackpool respectively.

31- 1 Sep	**1654 HCU**	**Lancaster I**	**R5698 UG-P**	**Training**

1943

P/O J W M Macdonald	+
Sgt G R Joyce	+
F/O W S Jobling DFC	+
Sgt E N Jones	+
Sgt G H Tough	+
Sgt J H Hutchinson	+
F/S R W Rashbrook RAAF	+

T/o Wigsley for night training. At about 0330,
collided in the air with Lancaster III JB132 of
61 Squadron, which was homebound from Berlin,
and crashed near Southwell, some 6 miles W of
Newark-upon-Trent, Nottinghamshire. Neither
crew could have seen the navigation lights of
the other aircraft. F/O Jobling of Lincoln (he
had served with 50 Squadron, his DFC having
been promulgated on 17 August 1943) and F/S Rashbrook RAAF were buried in
Thorney (St. Helen) Churchyard, while the others were claimed by relatives;
Sgt Tough's body being taken home to Ireland and interred in Mount Jerome
Cemetery, Co. Dublin. For details of the 61 Squadron crew, please refer to
Bomber Command Losses, Volume 4, page 300.

3 Sep	**1659 HCU**	**Halifax II**	**W1240**	**Training**

1943

Sgt A M Nadeau RCAF   T/o Topcliffe for night flying practice, an
exercise which ended at 0245 when the Halifax
landed with its wheels still retracted. A technical inspection declared that
the damage was sufficiently severe to warrant write off action.

3 Sep	1661 HCU	Lancaster I	R5492 GP-N	Training

3 Sep
1943

1661 HCU   Lancaster I   R5492 GP-N   **Training**

P/O J F Curtis RAAF	+	T/o Winthorpe for a night navigation detail
Sgt L J Milton	+	which ended, tragically, with the Lancaster
F/S T D Phillips RAAF	+	diving into the ground at 2238, less than a
F/S L A Taylor RAAF	+	mile SW of Exeter airfield. P/O Curtis RAAF
Sgt D S Audley	+	and F/S Taylor RAAF were taken to Bath (Hay-
P/O S K Lowry RAAF	+	combe) Cemetery, but their two
F/S S A Gawler DFM	+	fellow Australians were buried locally in the
Sgt A Young	+	city's Higher Cemetery. Private burials were

held in respect of Sgt Milton, F/S Gawler (his
award had been announced in the London Gazette as recently as 17 August; he had
flown with 50 Squadron) and Sgt Young.

4 Sep
1943

1658 HCU   Halifax II   V9989   **Training**

F/S E T B Vicary RAAF   T/o 1335 Melbourne to practice circuit flying.
Overshot and crashed at 1410, the bomber being
wrecked after swinging out of control. On 25 May last, and with Sgt A C Woodley
in command, this Halifax had broken its tail wheel in a heavy landing.

5 Sep
1943

1661 HCU   Lancaster I   W4929 GP-R   **Training**

P/O N T Duxbury	+	T/o Winthorpe for a night cross-country. Flew
Sgt L Holding	+	into a heavy storm, over the Brecon Beacons,
F/O V R Folkersen RCAF	+	and crashed at 2320 near Trecastle, a village
Sgt R Wilson	+	on the main road twixt Llandovery and Brecon.
P/O T F E Johnson DFM	+	The two Commonwealth airmen were laid to rest
Sgt F W Pratt	+	in Hereford Cemetery, but Sgt Curran, who came
Sgt J G Curran	+	from Coldstream in Berwickshire, was interred
F/S E M Buckby RAAF	+	in Bath (Haycombe) Cemetery. P/O Duxbury and

his flight engineer, Sgt Holding, are buried
in Standish (St. Wilfrid) Churchyard (both were from Wigan); Sgt Wilson lies
in Clitheroe Cemetery; Sgt Pratt's grave is at Hemel Hempstead Cemetery, while
P/O Johnson was cremated at Woking (St. John's) Crematorium. He had recently
completed a tour of operations with 44 Squadron, the London Gazette carrying
details of his decoration in its edition of 13 July 1943.

1663 HCU   Halifax V   DG402 OO-G   **Training**

F/O J S Thomas	+	T/o 1500 Rufforth for a cross-country. Came
Sgt A C Dickinson	+	down at 1603 on high ground at Keys Beck on
Sgt F Johnson	+	Rudland Moor and near the isolated hamlet of
Sgt R W Woods	+	Low Mill, some 12 miles NW from Pickering,
Sgt A W Salt	+	Yorkshire. Debris from the Halifax was spread
Sgt E J Hitchcox	+	over a wide area of moorland, which made the
F/S R M Todd RCAF	+	recovery of bodies and wreckage an extremely
Sgt W J R Blakeley RCAF	+	difficult operation (carried out by 60 MU at

Skipton). As expected, Sgt Blakeley RCAF was
buried in Harrogate (Stonefall) Cemetery, but F/S Todd RCAF lies in Scotland
at Carluke (Wilton) Cemetery, Lanarkshire. This suggests his funeral was
organised by relatives of his family. The others, too, were laid to rest
under private arrangements. F/O Thomas was a Bachelor of Science graduate
from Birmingham University.

1665 HCU   Stirling I   BF318 OG-F   **Training**

P/O F J Wheeler   T/o Woolfox Lodge and upon its return to base
came into land with a quite severe crosswind
blowing. As a consequence, the Stirling touched down forty degrees off the
runway's centre line and promptly swung away to the left. Moments later, the
undercarriage folded and the bomber slid to a halt, damaged beyond repair.

Note. To the best of my knowledge, this was the last Stirling to be written
off from 1665 Heavy Conversion Unit, prior to the formation's departure from
Bomber Command to No. 38 Group on 1 December 1943. However, according to the
unit's Operations Record Book, Stirling BF341/X was classified category "E"
on 16 September 1943, the circumstances being summarised thus, took off from
Mildenhall to practice circuits and landings. Four successful circuits flown
but after the fifth take off, the port undercarriage dropped down as the aircraft climbed. Landed with the unit unlocked and the undercarriage collapsed.
The pilot at the controls is identified as F/O I W Renner RNZAF. Referring to
Bryce Gomersall's "Stirling File" (Air-Britain Historians, 1987), BF341 is
noted as "Struck off Charge" on 19 July 1945, "1665" being the last user.

7 Sep	1657 HCU	Stirling I	W7455	–U	Training

7 Sep
1943

1657 HCU	Stirling I	W7455	–U	Training
F/O L F Smith DFC		inj		T/o Stradishall for an evening exercise, during
F/S C G Gilkes RAAF		inj		which the Stirling was attacked by an enemy in-
Sgt Oulton		inj		truder (the unit being reported as V./KG2).
P/O N E Miles		inj		Unable to maintain height, the bomber was put
F/S D E L Reddy RAAF		inj		down at 2139 in a cornfield between Withers-
F/S G R Greaves RAAF		inj		field and Great Thurlow, 2 miles NE and 4 miles
Sgt J M Hadman RNZAF		inj		north-north-east respectively from Haverhill in
Sgt E V Cramp		inj		Suffolk. Soon, the Stirling was a mass of flames

watched by some very dazed survivors. It was at
this stage that F/S Reddy RAAF could not be accounted for. With total disregard
for his own well being, F/O Smith re-entered the fuselage and having found the
trapped air bomber, dragged him clear. In doing so, he sustained such terrible
burns that he died the next day. He is buried in Bletchley Cemetery. Very sadly,
F/S Reddy RAAF succumbed to his wounds on 27 September, and he now rests in
Cambridge City Cemetery. F/O Smith had already been involved in a number of
quite serious crashes (see pages 47 and 54 for details).

Note. Jock Whitehouse, who, over many years, has contributed so much to the
history of Stradishall and its units, advises that F/O Smith's son, Roger,
followed in his gallant father's footsteps, rising (at least) to squadron
leader rank and at one stage flew Jaguars with Coltishall based 41 Squadron.

1658 HCU	Halifax II	L9620	–M	Ground
Sgt A Berry				At 1705, while parked at Riccall, the under-

carriage gave way. Following a technical ex-
amination, the Halifax was reduced to spares and produce. On 9 January 1943,
following a taxying mishap, it had been damaged as it ran into a building.
On that occasion, S/L H H Drummond DFM, late of 76 Squadron, had been at the
controls. Sgt Berry, meanwhile, went to 78 Squadron and was shot down over
France while raiding Cannes in November 1943 (see Bomber Command Losses,
Volume 4, page 378).

1658 HCU	Halifax II	DT524	–C20	Training
F/O M M Caplan DFM		+		T/o Riccall for flying practice. Crashed at
F/O L G Dunlop RCAF		+		midday at Newsholme Plantation, a little less
P/O A W Bailey		+		than 3 miles NNW of Howden, Yorkshire and
Sgt A B G Williams		+		about 2 miles SSE from Breighton airfield.
Sgt F Reynolds		+		Service funerals were held for the three RCAF
F/S S R Parker RCAF		+		airmen at Harrogate (Stonefall) Cemetery, and
Sgt E L McCartie		+		it is possible that Sgt Gamble from the Eltham
Sgt A J Gamble		+		district of London was buried under military
F/S G Gibson		+		arrangements as he lies in Selby Cemetery.
F/O J Low RCAF		+		The others rest in cemeteries scattered far

and wide across the United Kingdom. Their
skipper had flown with 158 Squadron, and details of his DFM had been published
in the London Gazette on 20 April 1943. It is further noted that F/S Parker's
father, Lt-Col Samuel R Parker had won the Military Cross.

1663 HCU	Halifax V	DG415	OO-H	Training
Sgt A R Banks		+		T/o Rufforth for general flying training, and
Sgt G Slater		+		while so engaged lost the propeller and most of
Sgt T E Rae		+		the engine cowling from the starboard inner.
F/O R T Holloway		+		Eyewitnesses report seeing the Halifax in a
Sgt E Pennington		+		flat spin before it struck the ground, bursting
Sgt G W Midwinter		+		into flames, roughly 1,500 yards E of Bempton
Sgt W O Jones		+		and about 3 miles NNE from Bridlington on the

Yorkshire coast. All were claimed by their
next of kin; their average age was twenty.

7- 8 Sep
1943

1662 HCU B Flt	Lancaster I	W4773	Training
P/O G S Morgan			T/o 2210 Blyton for a night exercise. While

coming into land at 0255, the main wheels
clipped the roof of a house, and as a consequence of this the bomber touched
down on one wheel and was damaged beyond repair as the undercarriage folded.
From the statistics in respect of P/O Morgan's flying experience, it appears
he had flown a total of 257 hours, solo, of which thirteen had been at the
controls of Lancasters. His night flying on type was a mere two hours.

8 Sep	**1661 HCU**	**Lancaster I**	**R5547 GP-V**	**Training**
1943	F/S R A Erry RAAF			

T/o 1310 Winthorpe for non-operational flying. Landed 1510 at Balderton but swung to starboard after running along the runway. Braking proved ineffective and after the port undercarriage collapsed, flames were seen issuing from beneath the wing. These were soon quelled by the prompt arrival of the crash and rescue crew. However, it was decided that the damage was beyond worthwhile repair and the Lancaster was struck from charge.

	1664 HCU	**Halifax V**	**DG342**	**Training**
	Sgt W B Byers RCAF			
	Sgt G J Byers RCAF			

T/o 1605 Croft for a dual exercise in circuits and landings, the two pilots being identical twins. At first, all went well; then, some fifteen minutes into the detail, the Halifax swung as it touched down. Action to correct this was immediately taken, but the bomber swerved rather violently to port and, as a result, the undercarriage was so badly damaged that it was decided to reduce the airframe to scrap. Prior to re-mustering as pilots, the brothers had trained as engine fitters. Sgt W B Byers RCAF survived the war but his brother, sadly, did not and his name is now perpetuated on the Runnymede Memorial, having failed to return from Düsseldorf early in November 1943 (see Bomber Command Losses, Volume 4, page 375). At the time, he was serving with 429 Squadron and had already taken once to his parachute (see page 350 of the same volume).

Note. Formed at Croft on 11 May 1943, and assigned to No. 6(RCAF) Group, this Canadian sponsored formation took the name "Caribou" and, until the incident summarised above, had enjoyed relatively trouble free flying for four months, a non-fatal crash in late June (see page 53), being the only accident of note. In 1993, A A B Todd, produced an excellent account of the activities at Croft under the title, "Pilgrimages of Grace", and I am indeed fortunate to have a copy of this work to hand when commenting on the losses sustained by "1664" during its tenure at Croft.

9 Sep	**1657 HCU**	**Stirling I**	**N3767**	**-B**	**Training**
1943	F/S A J N Hockley RAAF		inj		
	Sgt W W Hallett				
	Sgt T D Glenn				
	Sgt R Y Gundy RNZAF				
	F/S R T Lyall RAAF		inj		
	Sgt R G V Simpson		inj		
	Sgt E Lovatt				

T/o 2050 Stradishall but a tyre burst and the bomber skidded to a stop, its undercarriage being little more than scrap metal in its wake. By the spring of 1944, all were flying on bomber support duties with 214 Squadron and had converted to the Boeing Fortress. On 24-25 May, their good fortune deserted them as they fell victim to a night-fighter. Five of the above named (and two who had joined them on the switch from Stirling to Fortress operations) survived to become prisoners of war, but F/S Hockley RAAF and Sgt Simpson died when their aircraft went down over the Oosterschelde (see Bomber Command Losses, Volume 5, page 244).

	1657 HCU	**Stirling I**	**R9315**	**Training**
	F/O L D Clay			
	Sgt C N William			
	Sgt W Fletcher			
	P/O A H Hall RCAF			
	Sgt T O W Purkiss			
	Sgt B M Slade			
	Sgt E J Bullock			

T/o Stradishall for flying practice. Swung on landing at 1258 and the undercarriage gave way, damaging the aircraft beyond repair. Posted to 199 Squadron, F/O Clay joined an experienced crew (captained by Sgt M A N Hodson) for a raid on Hannover, 27-28 September 1943. As was so often the case, his crew were left without a skipper. From Sgt Hodson's aircraft, only the air bomber survived (see Bomber Command Losses, Volume 4, page 337).

	1664 HCU	**Halifax V**	**DG339**	**Training**
	Sgt J O Smith			

T/o 2227 Croft and crashed almost immediately due to a sudden loss of power from the starboard outer engine. The cause of this alarming accident was traced to a faulty link in the propeller mechanism.

12 Sep	**1659 HCU**	**Halifax II**	**W7853**	**Training**
1943	Sgt R Reinelt			

T/o 1540 Topcliffe for circuit training, landing ten minutes later. As it did so, Sgt Reinelt braked, a little too severely, and lost his undercarriage, the Halifax coming to a stop with its bomb doors, nose section and under fuselage badly damaged.

13 Sep 1943	**1657 HCU**	**Stirling I**	**W7427**	**Training**

F/O R G Campbell RCAF
Sgt A Jameson
Sgt W C Pearce
Sgt C E Potten
Sgt N Bartlett
P/O N J Fairbairn
Sgt R S Moore
Sgt J Cochrane
Sgt A Maclean
Sgt E M Jones

T/o 0914 Stradishall for flying training. At 1124, and while approaching the runway, the main spar of the Stirling suddenly gave way and the crew crash-landed in a ploughed field, close to the airfield. All had a quite remarkable escape and, subsequently, the engineering officer was to remark that the failure of the spar was a legacy of many hours of training and some very rough landings. Of the ten aircrew, here named, six would lose their lives on 25 April 1944, while flying with 622 Squadron (see Bomber Command Losses, Volume 5, page 188), while Sgt Potten would write of his time in Bomber Command under the title, "7 x X x 90".

15 Sep 1943	**1659 HCU**	**Halifax II**	**BB210**	**Training**

F/O T C Kaye
F/S W F Burge RAAF
F/S R R Clegg RAAF   +
Sgt Pratt
Sgt Blake
Sgt Bechtold
Sgt Martin
P/O Lambert
Sgt Deane
Sgt Gilchrist
Sgt Addison
W/O McNamara

T/o Topcliffe for a fighter affiliation detail. Crashed 1215 into a ploughed field, a few hundred yards NW of Askham Richard village on the S side of Rufforth airfield, breaking up into three sections. Three days later, F/S Clegg RAAF was buried at Harrogate (Stonefall) Cemetery, the service being conducted by S/L Thrush RAAF. In attendance were S/L R T Langton (destined to lose his life while flying as a flight commander with 76 Squadron, see Bomber Command Losses, Volume 5, page 463) and F/L A J Scott. F/O Kaye was the aircraft's captain, but F/S Burge RAAF was at the controls during the forced-landing.

	1664 HCU	**Halifax V**	**EB198 ZU-O**	**Training**

F/O H A Poulter RAAF   +
Sgt Finlay
Sgt Way
P/O Christopher
Sgt S C Sharp   inj
Sgt Glass
Sgt Roninson

T/o Croft for flying practice, during which the pilot's escape hatch blew out, the slipstream whipping it against part of the tail with such force that the flying controls were effected. As the situation became worse, the order to bale was given. Six complied, after which F/O Poulter RAAF tried to forced-land. Sadly, his attempt failed and he died at 1235 as his aircraft came down on Mr Newton's farm between Stillington and Huby, some ten miles NNW from the centre of York. His funeral service at Harrogate (Stonefall) Cemetery on 21 September was conducted by the unit's chaplain, S/L Earl S Lautenslager RCAF (recently of 1659 HCU at Topcliffe). Four days previous, a Court of Inquiry into the accident had been convened with G/C H M Carscalleu appointed as president.

17 Sep 1943	**1654 HCU**	**Lancaster I**	**W4921 UG-O**	**Training**

Sgt D Matthews

T/o 1954 Wigsley for Exercise 21 and, almost immediately, crashed out of control, hitting the battle headquarters building with the port oleo and outer engine before finishing up, on fire, near the camp's 25-yard rifle range and facing in the opposite direction to its point of departure.

18 Sep 1943	**1651 HCU**	**Stirling I**	**R9141 -K**	**Training**

F/L M A Brogan
F/S P E Mason RNZAF

T/o 2038 Waterbeach but left the runway, having failed to correct a swing. Both instructor and pupil were killed as the war progressed, the former having risen to the rank of wing commander and being appointed to command 161 Squadron, his death in action being reported on 5 March 1945. F/S Mason, meanwhile, converted to Lancasters and was lost, with his entire crew, during the Braunschweig operation in mid-January 1945 (see Bomber Command Losses, Volumes 5 and 4, pages 106 and 34 respectively).

	1652 HCU	**Halifax II**	**DT547 -A**	**Training**

F/L J M Candlish RCAF

T/o Marston Moor for a training detail. At around 1505, the outer starboard engine fell from its frame and landed on Redhouse School, the Halifax being forced-landed near Moor Monkton, 7 miles NW from York. Two months later, F/L Candlish RCAF died on Pathfinder duties (see Bomber Command Losses, Volume 4, page 377).

18 Sep	1658 HCU	Halifax II	BB245	Training

```
18 Sep    1658 HCU          Halifax II   BB245                    Training
1943      Sgt E G Wilson            +   T/o Riccall for a night flying exercise, which
          Sgt T G Roberts          +   culminated in not only the deaths of six members
          Sgt J A Crudgington      +   of the crew, but in the taking of, at least,
          F/O D Beeley             +   four civilians (all from one family) and the
          Sgt E Cook               +   serious injury to four of their neighbours.
          Sgt T Clelland           +   It was just two minutes before midnight when
                                       the Halifax crashed into houses at Chapel Hill,
          Mr W Dean                +   Darrington, 2 miles SE from the centre of
          Mrs M Dean               +   Pontefract, Yorkshire. The height of the
          Mr H Dean                +   destruction was centred upon Womersley Road,
          Miss E M Dean            +   where three houses were either completely
          Mr M Pease             inj   destroyed or very seriously damaged. At
          Mrs H Pease           inj   "Glencoe", there were no survivors from the Dean
          Mr J Wardell          inj   family, but from "Hillcrest" and "Ashville", a
          Mrs A M Wardell       inj   total of four persons were brought out, alive.
                                       In the days that followed, those that had died
          in the tragedy were buried privately; the most likely cause of the accident
          being the break up, or loss, of a propeller blade.
```

```
          1658 HCU          Halifax II   BB304   -D23             Training
          F/S E T B Vicary RAAF  inj   T/o Riccall for flying practice. Lost power
          Sgt D A James         inj   from the outer starboard engine and forced-
          Sgt F Anderson        inj   landed, in a field, within sight of Lissett
          Sgt W C Wilson RNZAF  inj   airfield. Being so close, the injured were
          Sgt C Johns           inj   treated at the local station sick quarters.
          Sgt J Cahill          inj   By coincidence, having recovered and finished
                                       his training, Sgt Cahill found himself back at
          Lissett, then home to 158 Squadron. Sadly, his tenure was all too brief for
          he was killed during operations to Kassel in late October 1943 (see Bomber
          Command Losses, Volume 4, page 368).
```

```
          1658 HCU          Halifax II   JB905                    Training
          F/L R W W Frankish RAAF  +   T/o Riccall tasked for a night sortie. While
          Sgt A C Skinner       inj   cruising at 17,000 feet, both starboard motors
          Sgt J H Bulmer        inj   caught fire. Partially abandoned, the Halifax
          Sgt C J Ringer          +   crashed 2355 at Mount Pleasant Farm, Armthorpe
          Sgt A J Taylor          +   some 4 miles NE of Doncaster, Yorkshire and
                                       not far distant from Finningley airfield. Two
          of the three who died were claimed by their next of kin, a service funeral
          being held at Harrogate (Stonefall) Cemetery for their Australian skipper.
```

```
          1663 HCU          Halifax V    DG400                    Training
          Sgt W J Pasco                T/o Rufforth for general flying training, crash-
                                       landing 1320 on Holme-on-Spalding Moor airfield.
          Eyewitnesses report Sgt Pasco as making a heavy landing, and when the Halifax
          ballooned back into the air, he was not quite quick enough to open the throttles
          before the bomber stalled and fell back onto the runway. On 20 April 1943, this
          aircraft had been coded "D", and while being flown by P/O G Such (see Bomber
          Command Losses, Volume 4, page 238), the pilot's escape hatch had blown out,
          in flight, causing slight damage to the airframe.
```

```
21 Sep    1651 HCU          Stirling I   N3707   -D              Training
1943      F/S P F Mason RNZAF   inj   T/o 2310 Downham Market but swung out of control
          Sgt R F Laishley            and crashed into Stirling III EE966 (which was
          Sgt J S Gallagher RNZAF      unoccupied) belonging to 218 Squadron. The two
          F/O N J Depoe RCAF    inj   injured airmen were taken to RAF Hospital, Ely,
          Sgt L Kell RNZAF            F/O Depoe RCAF having fractured his left clavicle.
          Sgt J W Hennis             This painful blow, however, may well have saved
          Sgt H W Steggleo           his life as five of the crew, including his New
                                       Zealand pilot, went to 514 Squadron and were lost
          in action on 14-15 January 1944 (see Bomber Command Losses, Volume 5, page 34).
          The Stirling that they struck was repaired and survived until 11 May 1945, when
          it swung off the Gardermoen (Norway) runway and lost its undercarriage. At the
          time it was on the strength of 299 Squadron.
```

```
          1658 HCU          Halifax II   W7868                    Training
          Sgt E Render                 T/o 2137 Riccall but swung and crashed. Sgt
                                       Render, subsequently, became a prisoner of war.
```

23 Sep 1943	**1657 HCU**	**Stirling I**	**BF407**	**Air Test**

F/O J C Hornby
Sgt A F Challinor
Sgt N Bartlett
Sgt L C Casper
Sgt Toogood
P/O J B Colthurst
Sgt G Yardley
Sgt A Holt
Sgt G L Ward RCAF

T/o Stradishall for a night flying test, the additional members of crew being a second flight engineer and a second navigator. Landed 1430, rather heavily, and bounced back into the air, a loud report being heard as the port tyre burst. Before the pilot could open the throttles, in order to cushion its next arrival, the bomber thudded back onto the runway with such force that the undercarriage was completely smashed. Excluding Sgt Bartlett and Sgt Toodgood, the rest appear to have joined 115 Squadron, five of their number being killed in action during operations to Schweinfurt in February 1944 (see Bomber Command Losses, Volume 5, page 98 (Sgt Yardley was not flying with them at the time)), while Sgt Holt suffered a similar fate, in the April, when his aircraft failed to make it back from Karlsruhe (see the same volume, page 187). It is assumed that Sgt Yardley survived the war.

24 Sep 1943	**1657 HCU**	**Stirling I**	**R9142** **–H**	**Training**

Sgt E H Edwards
Sgt E Vamplough
P/O B Denness
Sgt P H Kilsby
Sgt D G Davies
Sgt D Meredith
Sgt H Porter   inj

T/o 2057 Stradishall but left the runway, out of control, and lost its undercarriage. The sole casualty was taken to station sick quarters. Posted to 218 Squadron, the crew were tasked for a special duties mission, from Tempsford, on 4-5 March 1944 (their ninth sortie). On return (to Tempsford) an engine failed as they were about to land and the Stirling crashed, heavily, killing the first five named, both air gunners being injured (see Bomber Command Losses, Volume 5, page 109 (Sgt D G Davies, as reported here, being confirmed correct)).

26 Sep 1943	**1658 HCU**	**Halifax II**	**BB190**	**Training**

P/O W E Elder RNZAF
F/S T A Wickham Jones

T/o 0445 Riccall for a dawn cross-country. On return to base at 1045, overshot from a three-engined approach and crash-landed on the N side of Riccall village. P/O Elder RNZAF had recently completed a tour of operations with 76 Squadron, during which he had survived too very close shaves, requiring hospital treatment following the second crash (see Bomber Command Losses, Volume 4, pages 245 and 281). He was screened from operations, soon afterwards and, in time, he returned to New Zealand.

	1660 HCU	**Lancaster I**	**W4937**	**Training**

P/O M P C Cuelenaere RCAF inj
Sgt G B Loney RCAF

T/o 2014 Swinderby for night conversion training. Swung on touch down at 2209, but Sgt Loney RCAF corrected the situation. However, just as he was centralising the rudders, his instructor's foot became jammed between the rudder pedals and almost immediately the Lancaster swerved off the runway, the main wheels buckling beneath the strain. Posted to 619 Squadron, Sgt Loney RCAF failed to return from Berlin in mid-December 1943 (see Bomber Command Losses, Volume 4, page 429). With his crew, he rests in Berlin 1939-1945 War Cemetery.

28 Sep 1943	**1664 HCU**	**Halifax V**	**EB181**	**Training**

F/O R H Highsted RCAF   +
Sgt J C Mitchell   +
Sgt F J Luckett   +
Sgt J J Timmins   +
Sgt C F West   inj
Sgt J Nelson   +
Sgt H P D Charlton   inj

T/o Croft for a night exercise. Crashed 0007 some 400 yards E of Limekiln House, on high ground, roughly 3 miles E of Kepwick and towards Hawnby, Yorkshire. The remains of the aircraft, along with two very badly injured airmen, were not located until 1430 hours. A mobile surgical unit from Friarage Hospital treated Sgt West and Sgt Charlton at the scene, before having them admitted to hospital. Sadly, Sgt Charlton's injuries were so grievous that he died on 9 October. F/O Highsted RCAF had reported to Croft from 24 Operational Training Unit on 4 September; he was buried at Harrogate (Stonefall) Cemetery four days after the crash, his funeral being attended by F/L N Smith RCAF and P/O E C Stewart RCAF. The others who died were either cremated, or buried under arrangements made by their next of kin. Sgt West made remarkable progress and having resumed flying duties, he completed his training and joined 425 Squadron. On 24 April 1944, the Halifax in which he was flying crashed with total loss of life near Topcliffe airfield (see Bomber Command Losses, Volume 5, page 186).

28 Sep | **1667 HCU** | **Lancaster I** | **W4904** | **Training**
1943

Sgt L R W Turley	+	T/o Lindholme for night navigation training.
Sgt M R Pearce	+	Emerged from cloud, diving steeply, and crashed
Sgt A Howell	+	at 0015 near Cockhill Farm, about a mile SE of
F/S A W Mullen RCAF	+	Old Edlington, a hamlet lying a similar distance
Sgt R P Weston	+	south-east from the outskirts of Conisbrough,
Sgt D R Brown RCAF	+	Yorkshire. The two RCAF airmen (F/S Mullen was
Sgt R E Butler	+	an American from Upper Darby, Pennsylvania) were
		taken to Harrogate (Stonefall) Cemetery, as was

Sgt Butler. Their four colleagues were claimed by their next of kin. This was the unit's first serious accident since its formation on 1 June 1943 (formal promulgation of this appeared three weeks later), though a taxying accident on 14 September had claimed the life of Sgt G H Uttley, an air gunner.

30 Sep | **1667 HCU** | **Lancaster I** | **R5685** | **Training**
1943

W/O R F Quarterman	inj	T/o 1142 Faldingworth for training but lost
Sgt C J Adair	inj	power from the port outer, and while trying
F/S T D Crossland RCAF	+	to land, crashed 1218 a mile to the E of the
Sgt H M Greene RCAF	inj	duty runway. F/S Crossland RCAF is buried in
Sgt T P Duffy RCAF	inj	Huddersfield (Edgerton) Cemetery; it is, there-
Sgt T H Kennedy	inj	fore, likely that his funeral was arranged by
Sgt Naney		relatives living in the United Kingdom.

1 Oct | **1660 HCU** | **Halifax V** | **DG275 -A** | **Training**
1943

F/L V Duxbury DFC	+	T/o Swinderby for general flying practice,
F/O J W Moore	+	the crew being made up of an instructor, two
Sgt H W F Russell	+	trainee pilots, three flight engineers, a
Sgt R H Bassett	+	navigator, an air bomber and Sgt Ellwood in
Sgt D R Pavitte	+	the wireless operator's compartment. Broke
Sgt G C Edwards	+	up, after failing to recover from a violent
Sgt J B Eastman	+	spin, the bulk of the debris falling near
F/S F H Roe RCAF	+	Bardney airfield in Lincolnshire. Four of
Sgt W E Ellwood	+	the nine airmen who died are buried in Thurlby
		(St. Germain) Churchyard, while the others

were claimed by their families. F/L Duxbury, of New Mills in Derbyshire, had served with 207 Squadron and details of his award had been published in the London Gazette on 6 November 1942.

3 Oct | **1657 HCU** | **Stirling I** | **N3683** | **Training**
1943

Sgt T C Elstub RAAF		T/o 2120 Earls Colne but swung out of control
Sgt D Dickson		and wrecked as the undercarriage gave way
Sgt J G McFarlane		beneath the forces imposed. Subsequently,
Sgt A H Hines RAAF		however, the airframe was salvaged and given
Sgt E J McMillan		the serial 4668M; as such, it was issued to
Sgt A J Smith		the 8th Parachute Battalion as a ground trainer,
Sgt S B Cribb RAAF		arriving circa March 1944. Sadly, the good
		fortune that had allowed the crew to escape

unharmed from this incident deserted them just nineteen days later and, apart from Sgt McFarlane, all lost their lives in another training accident.

5 Oct | **1658 HCU** | **Halifax II** | **W7920** | **Training**
1943

F/O H A Brown		T/o 1449 Riccall to practice three-engined
Sgt D M Pearson	inj	circuits and landings. With the pupil at the
		controls, the Halifax was seen nearing the

runway at 1455, but appeared to be sinking rather alarmingly. In his post accident statement, the instructor stated that when he realised they were almost certain to undershoot, he immediately opened the throttles in readiness to go round again, but as he did so the Halifax slipped into a near vertical bank and a wing tip dug into the ground, throwing the bomber out of control. Sgt Pearson was not seriously hurt and, not long after, was posted to 102 Squadron, only to be killed, along with his entire crew, during operations to Frankfurt in late November 1943 (see Bomber Command Losses, Volume 4, page 398).

	1662 HCU	**Halifax II**	**HR930**	**Unknown**

Reported in some papers as having been very badly damaged on this date, though initially assessed as worthy of repair. It is then indicated that the airframe was struck off charge, with effect from the same day (5 October). As yet, no accident card, or any indications as to what happened, traced.

11-12 Oct   **1659 HCU**   **Halifax II**   **JB893**   **Training**
1943   Sgt J J Maher RCAF   inj   T/o Topcliffe for a night cross-country and,
         Sgt B S Rowe RCAF   inj   according to all available evidence, abandoned
         Sgt G H Conran RCAF   inj   over the general vicinity of the borders twixt
                                                      south-east Warwickshire and north-west Oxford-
shire, the Halifax being found not far from Lower Brailes, a small village on
the Banbury to Shipston-on-Stour road. Amazingly, those searching the scene
came across a near senseless Sgt Conran RCAF who, after being admitted to a
hospital in Stratford-upon-Avon recounted that on hearing the order to bale
out, to his horror, found that he could not rotate his rear turret. As his
actions to escape became more desperate, he struck his head against a part of
the structure with such force that he was rendered unconscious, and was still
in a comatose state when the aircraft smashed into the ground, the entire
tail section being snapped off and hurled a considerable distance. And,
thus, he was found, bleeding from head wounds and with one arm fractured.
The pilot and Sgt Rowe RCAF were treated for minor injuries in station sick
quarters at Chipping Warden. Both, eventually, went to 431 Squadron and
were shot down whilst operating to Berlin in late January 1944. Sgt Maher
survived to become a prisoner of war; Sgt Rowe RCAF was not so fortunate
(see Bomber Command Losses, Volume 5, page 62).

14 Oct   **1659 HCU**   **Halifax II**   **JD419**   **Air Test**
1943   F/O J D Dickson DFM RCAF   inj   T/o Topcliffe for an oil consumption test but
         P/O P Shaw   inj   swung violently to port and hit an obstruction.
         F/L E Cook   inj   Despite being badly damaged, F/O Dickson RCAF
         F/S S W Dunn   inj   managed to drag the Halifax into the air, but
                                                   while struggling to gain height, clipped the
roof of a house in Kilvington Road, Thirsk. With his aircraft barely under
control, he crash-landed at around 1125 in a ploughed field, just off the
Stockton Road at South Kilvington. All were very badly hurt, P/O Shaw being
reported as losing his right foot, while F/L Cook, the unit's wireless leader,
sustained very severe facial burns. F/O Dickson had gained his DFM while
serving with 57 Squadron, details being announced in the London Gazette on 22 September
1942. Despite being very badly hurt, he recovered well and, in due course of
time, returned to Canada.

20 Oct   **1664 HCU**   **Halifax V**   **DG343**   **-L**   **Training**
1943   F/S W E Smillie RCAF   +   T/o Croft for a fighter affiliation exercise.
         Sgt G A Dixon   +   Crashed 1457, and burnt out, at Sadberge, some
         Sgt W G Bougourd   +   three miles ENE from the centre of Darlington,
         F/S H F Collins   +   Durham. The three RCAF airman, along with
         Sgt P H MacKintosh   +   F/S Collins, were taken to Harrogate (Stonefall)
         Sgt A McGurty RCAF   +   Cemetery, while the others were claimed by their
         F/S J K Fraser RCAF   +   next of kin.

21 Oct   **1657 HCU**   **Stirling I**   **N3760**   **Training**
1943   F/O J G Neilson DFC RNZAF   T/o Chedburgh for dual circuit training, landing
         Sgt P H Hamby   at 1945 with the wheels still in their bays.
         W/O R Shields   Assessed as suitable for further service as an
         Sgt J Stevens   instructional airframe, the Stirling was given
         P/O J S Ferrier RCAF   the maintenance serial 4670M and by March 1944,
         Sgt K G Francis   was being used by the 12th Parachute Battalion.
         Sgt T B Liddle   Apart from their instructor and W/O Shields, a
         Sgt F T Fuller   screened flight engineer, the rest were posted
                                                   to 7 Squadron. While flying as a second pilot,
Sgt Hamby was posted missing on 16 March 1944, while the others failed to return
from the infamous Nürnberg raid at the end of the same month (see Bomber Command
Losses, Volume 5, pages 111 and 144 respectively).

1664 HCU   **Halifax V**   **EB136 DH-K**   **Training**
    F/S D J Partridge RCAF   T/o 2040 Croft but swung to port and travelling
                                                   at high speed bore down towards Birch Springs
Farm, bordering the airfield. However, in its path lay a building in which was
stored various pyrotechnic devises and it was this building that arrested the
progress of the Halifax. As may well be imagined, the impact caused a quite
spectacular display with flames and rockets soaring into night sky. The crew,
meanwhile, scrambled from the remains of their aircraft with little more than
minor cuts and abrasions to show for their remarkable escape.

22 Oct	1654 HCU	Lancaster I	L7575 UG-Q	Training

1943

P/O E M Taylor RAAF	+
Sgt A Rooks	+
F/O E Williams	+
Sgt J F Thwaite	+
Sgt H T Green	+
F/S G B Davies RAAF	+
Sgt E P Stock	+

T/o 1855 Wigsley tasked for a command Bullseye.
It is suspected that the crew encountered very
severe turbulence and, possibly, icing which
led to structural failure of the outer wings
and tail. Thus, at 2012, debris literally
rained from the skies over Warren House Farm
at Colney Heath, 3 miles SE of St. Albans in
Hertfordshire. The two Australians were laid
to rest in Brookwood Military Cemetery, the bodies of their five companions
being entrusted to relatives for private burial.

1657 HCU	Stirling I	R9249	Training

W/O G A Harris RAAF	+
Sgt S F Cowcher	+
F/O J W Whitehouse	+
F/S K Riep RCAF	+
Sgt R A Gausden	inj
F/S G T Duane RAAF	inj
Sgt G P McCallum RAAF	inj

T/o Stradishall briefed for a special navigation
exercise. Crashed 2054 while attempting to land
on three engines at Chipping Warden. Weather
conditions in the area are described as poor and
it is thought the crew mistook the airfield's
perimeter track for the runway. In its final
seconds of flight, the Stirling hit a tree and
the roofs of two houses in the nearby village
of Aston le Walls before finishing up, irreparably damaged, on the north side
of the aerodrome. F/S Duane RAAF died the following day from his injuries and
he is buried in Oxford (Botley) Cemetery, as is his skipper, F/S Riep RCAF and
F/O Whitehouse (despite being very severely shocked, Sgt McCallum RAAF attended
their funerals). Thirty-four year old Sgt Cowcher was taken to Harrow (Weald-
stone) Cemetery, Middlesex.

1657 HCU	Stirling I	EF352 XT-U	Training

F/S T C Elstub RAAF	+
Sgt D Dickson	+
F/O J L Stalker	+
P/O V C Gerrard	+
P/O G P Hewson	+
F/S A H Hines RAAF	+
Sgt E J McMillan	+
Sgt A J Smith	+
Sgt S B Cribb RAAF	+

T/o Stradishall similarly tasked, the crew comprising of a flight engineer, three navigators,
an air bomber, wireless operator and two air
gunners. At approximately 2120, the Stirling
flew into the ground at Rosemaund Farm, Preston
Wynne, a shade over 6 miles NNNE from Hereford.
Five, including the three RAAF members of crew,
are buried in Bath (Haycombe) Cemetery, while
the others were laid to rest under private
arrangements. P/O Gerrard, a staff navigator
instructor, had completed a tour of operations with 90 Squadron. P/O Hewson
was the son of Commander Francis Thomas Hewson RN. It will be recalled that
most had been involved in a serious accident earlier in the month (see page 69).

Note. On 8 June 1987, at Holy Trinity Church, Preston Wynne, a Memorial Plaque
was unveiled by Mrs Doris Mintram, widow of the late Sgt McMillan. This moving
ceremony was organised by Sue Mintram-Mason in association with the "Malvern
Spitfire Team" and was attended by one hundred and fifty guests, some of whom
had travelled from Australia and the United States of America. Wreaths were
laid on behalf of the families, the Royal Air Force Association and the Bomber
Command Association. Services at the scene of the crash, and at Holy Trinity,
were conducted by the Revd Janet Gasper, Chaplain to 151 (Leominster) Squadron,
Air Training Corps and the Revd Charles Hill respectively.

1664 HCU	Halifax V	EB199 ZU-H	Training

F/S H R Simmons RCAF	+
Sgt R A Harris	+
F/O S H Martin RCAF	inj
Sgt A B White RCAF	+
Sgt K Irvin	+
Sgt J L Campbell RCAF	+

T/o Croft for a night flying detail. As the
crew prepared to land, the outer port engine
cut, causing the Halifax to roll steeply and
crash, 0135, into trees at Church House Farm,
Atley (or Attley) Hill, near the corner of the
Pepper Arden road end, South Cowton, Yorkshire.
Two local men, a Mr Clark and a Mr Severs, were
quickly upon the scene and between them they dragged F/O Martin RCAF from the
inferno that had engulfed the bomber. Rushed to Friarage Hospital, he lingered
for four days before slipping into death. Along with his three fellow Canadians,
he lies in Harrogate (Stonefall) Cemetery. Sgt Harris was taken to Coventry
(London Road) Cemetery, while Sgt Irvin was laid to rest in South Shields
(Harton) Cemetery. It is noted that Sgt Campbell's second Christian name
is reported as Louis in the CWGC register for Harrogate, but in "They Shall
Grow Not Old", it is shown as Lewis.

27 Oct	1651 HCU	Stirling I N3704	—E	Training

27 Oct
1943

1651 HCU   **Stirling I N3704**   **—E**   **Training**

F/O K H Becroft DFC RNZAF   T/o 1500 Waterbeach for dual instruction, the
F/S F R Burrows RAAF   weather conditions being described as "poor".
          At 1530, the Stirling crossed the threshold
and arrived on the runway with its wheels still retracted. It will be recalled
that F/O Becroft RNZAF had been involved in a night flying accident, at Downham
Market, on 20 August (see page 60), as well as emerging unscathed from a pre-
tour crash in October 1942 (see page 30). Confirmation of his DFC had appeared
in the London Gazette eight days previous. His pupil, meanwhile, converted to
Lancasters and died, with his crew, whilst attacking Laon in April 1944 (see
Bomber Command Losses, Volume 5, page 167). At the time of his death, he was
serving with 622 Squadron at Mildenhall.

1656 HCU   **Lancaster I W4776**   **Training**

Sgt T F Skipp   +   T/o 2150 Lindholme for night circuits and
Sgt G E Glass   +   landings. Ten minutes later, the Lancaster
F/S A W Turpin   +   was seen approaching the runway, though too
F/S V J Baker   +   high for a safe touchdown. This situation
Sgt T P Higgins   +   must have been recognised by the crew, for
Sgt F E Lovegrove   +   the engine note increased as the bomber began
Sgt J F Lea   +   to climb. Tragically, however, the flaps were
          raised (instead of the undercarriage) before
sufficient height had been gained and, as a consequence, the bomber plunged
into a field, belonging to Kilham Farm, 3 miles SSW from the airfield. All
were either buried or cremated under private arrangements.

31 Oct
1943

1651 HCU   **Stirling I DJ975 BS—W**   **Training**

F/S C E Light RAAF   T/o 2000 Waterbeach for night training. At
Sgt C A Myers   about 2155, a message was taken in the station's
          Operations Room stating that the bomber had been
wrecked in a landing accident at Witchford. Apparently, the Stirling had touched
down on the downward sloping runway, raced onto the overshoot area and finished
up in a field. This accident was traced to lack of brake pressure which, due to
a faulty instrument reading, would not have been realised by the pilot. Accepted
by 214 Squadron on 4 June 1942, and passed to "1651" on 7 October of that year,
the Stirling (a replacement for N3649, destroyed at Rochester on 15 August 1940,
by enemy bombing) had flown a respectable total of 542.30 hours.

6 Nov
1943

1657 HCU   **Stirling I R9192 AK—B**   **Training**

F/O D W Thomson DFC RNZAF   T/o 1842 Stradishall for a Bullseye sortie.
F/O V L Scantleton RAAF   At approximately 1905, collided in the air,
Sgt S T Nuttall   over Essex, with Wellington III X3637 out from
F/S J P Merritt RCAF   27 Operational Training Unit, Lichfield. The
F/O R E Forbes RNZAF   Wellington went down with fatal consequences
Sgt S Scott   inj its crew (see Bomber Command Losses, Volume 7,
F/S G S McDonald RAAF   page 260), but F/O Thomson RNZAF succeeded in
Sgt T M Taylor   getting his badly damaged machine back to base,
Sgt A Sloan   arriving in the circuit at 2045, and landing
BQMS I Colley RA   safely some twenty-five minutes later. A tour
LSgt W Millson RA   of operations with 218 Squadron had been rec-
          ognised with a DFC, details of which appeared
in the London Gazette on 14 May 1943. F/S Merritt RCAF was killed in action
with 622 Squadron on 31 March 1944 (see Bomber Command Losses, Volume 5,
page 158).

1659 HCU   **Halifax II W1251**   **Training**

F/S C A Turner RCAF   +   T/o Topcliffe for a cross-country exercise.
Sgt P E Krotz RCAF   +   While flying over the Isle of Man, a fire broke
F/O S M Flett RCAF   +   out and before the crew could make their escape,
F/S R F Mechin RCAF   +   the Halifax plunged from the sky, breaking apart
Sgt H J Ford   +   as it fell. Service funerals for the six RCAF
Sgt J E O'Grady RCAF   +   airmen were held at Jurby (St. Patrick) Church-
Sgt A B McVean RCAF   +   yard, while the body of their wireless operator
          was taken back across the water and laid to rest
          in Heywood Cemetery, Lancashire.

6- 7 Nov   **1663 HCU**   **Halifax V**   **DJ983 OO-M**   **Training**
1943   Sgt F W Huckerby   T/o 2140 Rufforth for a night map reading
                                    exercise. On return to base, the crew were
unable to "persuade" the undercarriage to lower and in the ensuing forced-
landing, their aircraft was wrecked. On 9 June 1944, now commissioned and
serving with 76 Squadron, P/O Huckerby, and his crew, had the narrowest of
escapes during a low-level attack on Laval airfield in France, struggling home
with their Halifax III MZ693 MP-F holed by bomb splinters thrown up in the wake
of their bombing run which was made at 600 feet! At his debriefing, P/O Huckerby
remarked that they saw the hangars, quite clearly.

7 Nov   **1663 HCU**   **Halifax V**   **DG312 OO-N**   **Training**
1943   F/O R G Spicer   T/o 1400 Rufforth for flying practice, an
                                    exercise which was terminated forty-five minutes
later when an uncontrolled swing on landing was followed by the total collapse
of the main undercarriage. Having completed his course, F/O Spicer proceeded
to Elvington and 77 Squadron, being killed in action in mid-March 1944 (see
Bomber Command Losses, Volume 5, page 117).

     1663 HCU   **Halifax V**   **EB134**   **-L**   **Training**
F/S A S Johnston RAAF   +   T/o Rufforth for an exercise, at the completion
Sgt E W Camp   +   of which the crew were instructed to proceed to
Sgt R M Clark   +   Marston Moor, and land. This order was ack-
F/S G H Sansome RAAF   +   nowledged but, for reasons that are a mystery,
F/S A J Gallagher RAAF   +   they never arrived. However, at 2243, the
Sgt L H Wildman   +   look out post at Flat Head, Co. Cork, in the
WO1 N W Gardner RCAF   +   Irish Republic heard the Halifax and, sub-
                                    sequently, its passage northwards was observed
from various points. Then, at around 2350, the flight ended in a ball of fire
near Lavally, Barnaderg some 6 miles NE from Tuam in Co. Galway. All seven
bodies were recovered and handed over to the authorities in Northern Ireland,
where the four Commonwealth members of crew lie in Co. Fermanagh; F/S Gallagher
at Irvinestown (Sacred Heart) Roman Catholic Churchyard and the others nearby
in Irvinestown Church of Ireland Churchyard. Funerals for the three British
airmen were arranged by their next of kin.

Note. I am indebted to Martin Gleeson of Dooradoyle in Co. Limerick for many
of the details summarised above.

     1664 HCU   **Halifax V**   **EB187**   **Transit**
P/O A H Woolverton RCAF   T/o 2010 Fulbeck (Station 488 of the United
                                    States Ninth Army Air Force) intending to return
to Croft, but the port outer cut and the Halifax crashed out of control. Earlier,
the Halifax had landed here after running low on petrol. P/O Woolverton RCAF had
reported for training on 30 September 1943, on completion of his Operational
Training Unit course at Kinloss. In the early hours of 20 February 1944, his
428 Squadron Halifax crashed into the IJsselmeer, just one of the many bombers
reported missing from Leipzig (see Bomber Command Losses, Volume 5, page 90).

10 Nov   **1660 HCU**   **Lancaster III**   **ED812**   **Training**
1943   P/O S G Scutt   +   T/o 1853 Swinderby for a Bullseye detail.
Sgt C W H Baughen   +   Dived steeply, from a considerable height,
Sgt I C Brough   +   the mainplanes failing before it smashed into
F/O J K Paterson   +   the ground at around 2145. From what could be
Sgt F D Grant   +   determined amongst the debris collected from
Sgt W Halliwell   +   the fields near Dunholme Lodge airfield, it
Sgt E W Plowman   +   appears most likely that the crew were faced
AC1 N Wade   +   with an in-flight fire but as to whether or not
                                    this led to the loss of control could not be
ascertained. Following formal identification, the bodies were released for
private burials.

11 Nov   **1656 HCU**   **Lancaster I**   **W4924**   **Training**
1943   F/S J M Booth RAAF   T/o 1058 Lindholme but the right rudder pedal
                                    slipped fully forward and before the pilot
could react, the Lancaster veered from the runway and lost its undercarriage.
Within a few weeks of this incident, F/S Booth RAAF had become one of the
earliest casualties in the "Battle of Berlin" (see Bomber Command Losses,
Volume 4, page 413).

11–12 Nov	1654 HCU	Lancaster I	W4902 UG–Q	Training

1943

P/O R L Barton-Smith	+
Sgt F J Snedker	inj
Sgt H D Ryder	+
Sgt C W Wilkes	inj
Sgt R J Huish	+
Sgt W B Crawford RAAF	inj

T/o 1730 Wigsley for a night exercise. While flying in limited visibility, was obliged to take quick evasive action in order to avoid a midair collision (the aircraft's type is not reported) and in doing so went out of control and crashed 2245 at Hackthorn, 7 miles NNW of Lincoln. P/O Barton-Smith rests in Greenwich (Charlton) Cemetery, Sgt Ryder lies in Adel Friends Burial Ground, Yorkshire, his being the sole Second World War service grave in this quaintly named graveyard, while Sgt Huish was taken to Worle (St. Martin) Churchyard.

12 Nov	1659 HCU	Halifax II	BB326	Transit

1943

P/O G K Patman RCAF	+
Sgt D Sharp	+
F/S F N S Fearneley RCAF	+
F/O D M Blair	+
Sgt G P Fuller	+
Sgt R T Gibson	+
F/S K D Ross RCAF	+
P/O T M Murdock RCAF	inj

T/o 1315 Halfpenny Green only to crash minutes later at Bobbington, a Staffordshire village five miles ESE from Bridgnorth, Shropshire. The service authorities at Halfpenny Green were requested to make the necessary funeral arrangements and, in due course, two of the Canadians were interred in Chester (Blacon) Cemetery, but F/S Fearnley RCAF was taken to Pendlebury (St. John) Churchyard for a private burial. The others who perished rest in cemeteries located across England, Scotland and Northern Ireland. P/O Murdock RCAF, it is reported, was thrown out on impact, but though very seriously injured, he appears to have made a good recovery and returned home.

14 Nov	1652 HCU	Halifax II	DG230	Air Test

1943

F/O T McKinley DFC RNZAF	+
S/L P J Emerton	+
P/O N N Beale	+
AC1 G H Harrison	+
AC2 T D McCormack	inj

T/o 1608 Marston Moor but as the bomber climbed away on a northerly heading, so both engines on the starboard side spluttered and died. Out of control, the Halifax fell into a pond at the rear of the Green Hammerton Hotel at Kirk Hammerton, nine miles WNW from York. The test had lasted for a mere three minutes. Amazingly, AC2 McCormack was found to have sustained relatively minor injuries and he was admitted to station sick quarters. Those who were not so fortunate rest in various graveyards, F/O McKinley RNZAF, as may be expected, being laid to rest in Harrogate (Stonefall) Cemetery. Details of his award had been published on 17 August 1943, following a successful tour of operations with 102 Squadron. He had, according to Errol Martyn, logged a total of 818 flying hours.

20 Nov	1663 HCU	Halifax V	DG234	Training

1943

| F/S F Lovatt | |

T/o Rufforth for night flying, during which an attempt to land at Holme-on-Spalding Moor was executed at 0018, but the visibility was so poor that instead of coming down on the runway, F/S Lovatt arrived, in pouring rain, near the dispersal pans and before he could take any evasive action, he ran into Halifax V DK205 MP-P Bar belonging to 76 Squadron (see Bomber Command Losses, Volume 4, page 388), both aircraft being totally wrecked. Having survived this very nasty incident, and completed his training, F/S Lovatt was killed in late March 1944, while serving with 78 Squadron (see the same series, Volume 5, page 142).

22 Nov	1664 HCU	Halifax V	EB150 DH–O	Training

1943

F/O J V Williamson	+
F/S J H Millroy RCAF	inj
Sgt M N G Swindle	+
F/S S T Litynesky RCAF	+
WO2 S R Doney RCAF	+
Sgt R B Sellars	+
Sgt N J Collins RCAF	+

T/o 1916 Croft for night circuits and landings only to crash, out of control, at Blue Anchor Farm, near Scotch Corner (the well known junction leading off the Great North Road to the A66 main road that runs across the North Yorkshire Moors to the Lake District). Of those who died, four were given military funerals at Harrogate (Stonefall) Cemetery, while the bodies of Sgt Swindle and Sgt Sellars were conveyed to Keswick (St. John) Churchyard in Cumberland and Glasgow (Cardonald) Cemetery respectively.

Note. It is believed that F/S Millroy RCAF made a complete recovery. Unit documents report his initials as "J H" (as given above), while another set of records indicates "J N".

23 Nov 1943	**1658 HCU**	**Halifax II**	**DT578**	**Training**

Sgt S Chadwick   +   T/o 2327 Riccall for a night cross-country.
Sgt F J Robinson   +   Shortly before midnight, the Halifax flew into
Sgt F W Robson   +   the west face of Great Whernside at Longcliffe
Sgt N Martin   +   Edge, above the isolated village of Kettlewell,
Sgt D P Aitken   +   some 25 miles NW from Harrogate, Yorkshire. The
Sgt E Stabler   +   most likely cause of this accident was reported
Sgt K Vincent   +   as severe icing. For the remainder of November
and throughout December and on into the New
Year, a recovery team from 60 Maintenance Unit, based at Skipton, worked on
the site which is described in their records as being 2,600 feet above sea
level and very difficult to access. Eventually, all bodies were conveyed to
their next of kin. On 16 May 1943, the Halifax, here summarised, was damaged
when the starboard inner airscrew broke up, fragments piercing the fuselage,
as it prepared for take off. At the controls was S/L P Dobson DFC AFC.

23-24 Nov 1943	**1658 HCU**	**Halifax II**	**DT541**	**Training**

Sgt C Elton   T/o 2315 Riccall for three-engined flying
practice. Swung on landing, 0128, crashed
and caught fire. In his report, Sgt Elton was of the opinion that his air
speed indicator was at fault.

	1658 HCU	**Halifax II**	**JB926 ZB-A**	**Training**

Sgt R E C Bacon   +   T/o Riccall tasked similarly to Sgt Chadwick's
Sgt J Titterington +   crew and lost, most probably, through the same
Sgt G H Manley   +   reasons as those suggested above, the time of
F/O H McCarthy   +   the crash being quoted as 0115. Clearance
F/S J J MacGillivray RCAF +   operations duly took place near Slipstone Crags
Sgt B F Taylor   +   on Agra Moor to the west of Healey, 10 miles NW
Sgt A J Winton   +   of Ripon, Yorkshire. Sgt Bacon of Thorpe End,
Sgt D E Phillips   +   Norwich, Sgt Manley from Chidwall, Liverpool and
F/S MacGillivray their Canadian air bomber, were
buried in Harrogate (Stonefall) Cemetery, while funeral services for the others
were held at churches in England, Wales, Scotland and Northern Ireland.

Note. This particular crash has been well documented, though the records
for 60 Maintenance Unit erroneously refer to the Halifax as a "Lancaster"
but, similar to their experiences with the other Riccall based aircraft,
the crash site was extremely isolated. Fortunately, the army were able to
provide a Bren carrier, and this was used to take much of the wreckage to
the unit's own transport, parked some three miles distant.

24 Nov 1943	**1656 HCU**	**Lancaster I**	**W4953**	**Training**

P/O F A Dines   +   T/o 0130 Lindholme for night circuit practice.
Sgt H Ganly   +   Crashed five minutes later roughly 3 miles E of
P/O Charles   the airfield at a place described as Roe Carr in
Sgt R D Jack   inj   one set of records and West Hale near Sandtoft
Sgt Jones   in another. At the time of the accident, the
P/O E S Atkinson   +   Lancaster was flying on the crosswind leg and
Sgt King   is believed to have stalled. Sgt Ganly from
Shepherd's Bush rests in Harrogate (Stonefall)
Cemetery, while the others who died were taken to their home towns. Sgt Jack
was admitted to Lindholme's station sick quarters, his injuries being reported
as "slight". Having made a good recovery, he resumed flying and by the spring
of 1944, was continuing his training with 1667 Heavy Conversion Unit, based at
Sandtoft. Then, on 27 April, he was involved in another crash which, sadly,
cost him his life.

25 Nov 1943	**1678 HCU**	**Lancaster II**	**DS653 SW-S**	**Training**

Sgt J Batterham RAAF   +   T/o Foulsham for a high-level cross-country,
Sgt L Slater   +   the crew drawn from the far corners of the
WO2 E G Johnston RCAF +   Commonwealth. Exploded in flight at 1149,
F/S O A Burton RNZAF   +   casting debris over a wide area around the
Sgt R E Harris   +   community of Sturminster Newton, 8 miles SW
Sgt G A Bennett   +   of Shaftesbury, Dorset (most was recovered
F/S M S Beyer RAAF   +   from behind the Red Lion Inn in Tures Yard,
but a good deal was found in woods bordering
the Blandford Forum to Sherborne road and west of Sturminster Newton). All
were taken for burial in Bath (Haycombe) Cemetery at Englishcombe.

| 26 Nov 1943 | **1651 HCU** | **Stirling I** | **BF332 −Q** | | **Training** |

F/S G L Webster RAAF — inj
Sgt C H Bridges — inj
F/S J L Henry RAAF — inj
Sgt J G Waple — inj
Sgt S C Longhurst — inj

T/o 1106 Wratting Common for conversion training but almost immediately lost power from one motor and in consequence of this, the crew decided to land at Downham Market. However, at a critical stage during their approach, the pilot lost control and spun in from about seventy feet, crashing at 1126. From all accounts, the crew emerged from the wreck, shaken, but not too badly hurt. It was the unit's first serious incident since moving to Wratting Common six days previous.

| | **1658 HCU** | **Halifax II** | **DT490** | | **Training** |

Sgt T E Jones — +
Sgt L Lee — +
Sgt R Ginsberg — +
Sgt R Fletcher — +
Sgt L S Jenkins — +
Sgt J F Megranahan — +
Sgt F S Quine — +

T/o Riccall for night flying practice. Crashed at around 1955, bursting into flames on impact, just N of Whythe Sike Farm, south of the road leading to Marton and a mere mile-and-a-half west of Pickering, Yorkshire. All were taken to their home towns for burial under private arrangements. It is noted that Sgt Megranahan adopted a shortened form of his surname and, thus, served as "Megran".

| | **1663 HCU C Flt** | **Halifax V** | **EB183 OO−G** | | **Training** |

Sgt C Walker — inj
Sgt F Hughes
Sgt J Sutherland RCAF
Sgt A Abrahams
Sgt P C Gizzi
Sgt K C Southward
Sgt G A Shield — inj

T/o 2000 Rufforth only to swing violently and and crash against a large pile of contractors rubble, which smashed the undercarriage. The two injured airmen were treated in their local station sick quarters, both being soon released. Posted to 76 Squadron, all were reported missing in the wake of the Magdeburg raid in January 1944 (see Bomber Command Losses, Volume 5, page 44).

| 28 Nov 1943 | **1651 HCU** | **Stirling I** | **R9159 YZ−O** | | **Training** |

Sgt D A Duncliffe
Sgt C K Guy
Sgt G F Lewis
Sgt H J Bourne — inj
Sgt S Hollis
Sgt W Saxon

T/o 2230 Wratting Common briefed for night circuit training. Thirty minutes into the detail, and while preparing to land, an engine failed; on touch down the Stirling skidded out of control and ran into a building, near the Watch Office.

| 29 Nov 1943 | **1658 HCU** | **Halifax II** | **DT776** | | **Training** |

Sgt E R Anderson

T/o 2301 Riccall to carry out night circuit practice and wrecked five minutes later.

| 30 Nov 1943 | **1658 HCU** | **Halifax II** | **DG221** | | **Training** |

S/L S J R Hamilton
Sgt L Melling

T/o Riccall for dual conversion training only to be wrecked, at 1115, in a landing mishap. A technical inspection revealed serious weakening of the lug attachment on the outer radius rod.

| 1 Dec 1943 | **1652 HCU** | **Halifax II** | **BB241 GV−W** | | **Unknown** |

Reported as damaged beyond repair in a taxing mishap at Snaith. However, no accident card has been located to support this claim.

| 2 Dec 1943 | **1664 HCU** | **Halifax V** | **DG282** | | **Training** |

F/S P R Gray RCAF — +
Sgt S Fletcher
Sgt J H Catto RCAF — +
Sgt G A Chilvers — +
F/O J A Foulston RCAF — +
Sgt H B Bellew RCAF — +
Sgt C H Hills RCAF — inj

T/o Croft to practice circuits and landings. At 2131, the Halifax was sighted coming in low and very fast and before any warning could be given, the bomber flew into a corn stack. This barely impeded its progress and seconds later it thudded into the branches of an ash tree, standing one hundred yards from the officers' mess. Slewing sharply, it crashed to the ground between the administrative centre and No. 4 Technical Site. Miraculously, Sgt Fletcher walked away, unharmed and Sgt Hills RCAF escaped with a broken collar bone. Of the five who died, four now rest in Harrogate (Stonefall) Cemetery while Sgt Chilvers lies in Great Yarmouth Roman Catholic Cemetery. It is thought that smoke from a passing train may have distracted the pilot's attention.

2 Dec 1943	1664 HCU	Halifax V	DJ982	Training

F/O W J Taylor RCAF   +   T/o Croft for a fighter affiliation exercise.
Sgt W J Morgan   +   At 1500, or thereabouts, the Halifax went out
F/S J M Beatty RCAF   +   of control from 6,700 feet and spiralled into
F/O D C Walker RCAF   +   Springwell Lane on the western side of North-
Sgt T J Skyrme   +   allerton, Yorkshire. On impact, the aircraft
Sgt J O Winters   +   exploded into a ball of flame and a nearby
F/S J Wallace RCAF   +   cottage, too, was destroyed (no civilians are
reported as casualties, so it is assumed that
the property was either empty, or its occupants were able to make good their
exit). The four RCAF airmen rest in Harrogate (Stonefall) Cemetery; the body of
Sgt Winters was conveyed to Northern Ireland and interred in Belfast (Dundonald)
Cemetery, while Sgt Morgan and Sgt Skyrme were taken home to Wales and laid to
rest at Mountain Ash, the former in Maesyrarian Cemetery and the latter at
the town's Ynysybwl Cemetery.

9 Dec 1943	1652 HCU	Halifax II	W7815 GV-K	Training

F/L D R Fisher DFC DFM   inj   T/o Marston Moor for dual training. Following
Sgt S T Wells   inj   problems with the engines, the crew were obliged
Sgt J R Weaver   to forced-land at 1024 in a built up area near
Sgt R H Brown   Basingstoke Farm, Greasbrough, a sizable village
W/O Allen   in Yorkshire and situated NE of Sheffield and
W/O Hughes   north-north-west of Rotherham. F/L Fisher, the
F/S Gray   instructor, had flown two tours of operations,
both with 77 Squadron. During his first tour,
he displayed such exceptional determination during an attack on Rostock (in the
April of 1942) that he was awarded an immediate DFM (Gazetted 15 May 1942), while
his second spell of operations was rewarded by a DFC, published on 11 June 1943.
By the summer of 1944, he was serving as a flight commander with 102 Squadron
and, as remarked upon on page 285 of Bomber Command Losses, Volume 5, was, at
the time, one of the youngest officers to hold such a post in Bomber Command.
Sadly, as the 1944 caption reveals, his Halifax was lost without trace from a
raid on Sterkrade. It is likely that the crew he was instructing survived one
tour of operational duty, for Sgt Wells was commissioned and was awarded the
American Air Medal. He, along with Sgt Weaver and Sgt Brown, is commemorated
on the Runnymede Memorial after failing to return from operations on 3 March
1945, at which time the trio were flying Halifaxes with 644 Squadron, then
based at Tarrant Rushton in Dorset.

1658 HCU	Halifax II	R9429	Training

F/S E D S Tennant RAAF   T/o 1935 Riccall for a night exercise, but
swung off the runway and ran into one of the
airfield's gun emplacements. No one was hurt, but the Halifax was damaged
beyond repair. Thirteen months previous, on 11 November 1942, Sgt A F Dilling
had swung on landing this same Halifax, colliding with an obstruction as he
departed from the runway. On completing his training, F/S Tennant RAAF was
posted to Italy, joining 624 Squadron at Brindisi. From here he failed to
return on 1 February 1944, from operations over the Balkans. He is buried
in Albania at Tirana Park Memorial Cemetery.

1660 HCU	Lancaster III	ED811	Training

F/S E E Franke RAAF   inj   T/o Swinderby for a navigation detail. Flew
Sgt P Entwistle   inj   into the ground, at roughly 1745, at Glebe Farm
Sgt J Mellor   inj   on Blankney Fen, some 10 miles N from Sleaford,
WO2 K R Schiller RCAF   +   Lincolnshire. At the time of the accident, the
F/S Knight   crew were searching for Spilsby, having received
Sgt W M Hall   inj   instructions to land here due to adverse weather
conditions at base. WO2 Schiller RCAF was buried
in Thurlby (St. Germain) Churchyard. It is believed the injured were first taken
to the station sick quarters at Metheringham, from where Sgt Hall was transferred
to RAF Hospital Rauceby. Sgt Mellor was killed in action on 10 May 1944, while
serving with 467 Squadron (see Bomber Command Losses, Volume 5, page 219).

11 Dec 1943	1663 HCU	Halifax V	DK128 OO-A	Transit

P/O M G Brown RAAF   T/o 1625 from an unidentified airfield and
set course for Rufforth. On his arrival, he
landed at 1725, heavily, and smashed the undercarriage to such an extent that
repairs were deemed to be not worth the cost.

12 Dec	1652 HCU	Halifax II	BB240 GV-H	Training

F/O J H Williams DFC   T/o 1658 Marston Moor but as the Halifax began
F/S A H Welch   to lift, a loud report signalled the bursting
of one of its tyres. F/O Williams immediately
assumed command and, having flown a short circuit, landed two minutes later with
the wheels retracted. Details of his award had appeared in the London Gazette
on 13 August 1943.

13 Dec	1651 HCU	Stirling I	W7619	Training

F/O D A McInnes   T/o 1712 Wratting Common only to swing out of
F/S H H Bruhns RNZAF   control as a tyre exploded. The Stirling's
Sgt J Williams   momentum carried it a further half-a-mile before
Sgt V C Cornish   it halted, damaged beyond repair. F/S Bruhns
Sgt H Everleigh   and the last five named were posted soon after
Sgt E A Wilkes   to 75 Squadron, failing to return from their
F/S L L Butler RNZAF   ninth sortie, a minelaying mission over Kiel Bay
Sgt W J Summers   (see Bomber Command Losses, Volume 5, page 102).
Sgt R E Hall
F/S A H Sawtell RAAF

16 Dec	1661 HCU	Lancaster I	LM307 GP-T	Training

F/O W H Eager DFC RCAF   + T/o 2014 Winthorpe for night circuit training
P/O K C Hampson   + but within two minutes of their departure, six
Sgt L B Lawrance   + were dead and a seventh was lying mortally
Sgt W S Austin   + injured in the wreckage, a mile E of South
F/S R W Baldwin RCAF   + Muskham and just a couple of miles NNW from
Sgt R H Woolcock   + Newark-upon-Trent, Nottinghamshire. The sorely
Sgt P Dillon   inj wounded airman, Sgt Dillon, died in the early
Sgt F W East   inj hours of the next day, while being treated in
Newark Hospital. He rests at Oxford (Botley)
Cemetery, close to where his two Canadian colleagues are buried. The others
who perished were claimed by their next of kin. F/O Eager RCAF had recently
completed an operational tour of duty with 61 Squadron and confirmation of
his Distinguished Flying Cross had been promulgated a month earlier. A bad
pre-tour training crash, involving this officer, is summarised on page 46.

	1662 HCU A Flt	Halifax II	DT669	Training

F/S G M Vautier RAAF   + T/o Blyton for a long navigation exercise, at
Sgt R E C Bottle   + night. Crashed, 2335, while preparing to land,
F/S J E Findley RAAF   + coming down at Corringham, 3 miles ENE from
F/S E Hoskings RAAF   + Gainsborough in Lincolnshire. The five RAAF
F/S N R B Toy RAAF   + airmen were buried with full military honours
Sgt E J Strawbridge RAAF + in Cambridge City Cemetery, while their flight
engineer, Sgt Bottle, was buried by his next
of kin at Havant and Waterloo (Waterlooville) Cemetery, Hampshire. It seems
that the aircraft was operating with a crew of six.

	1663 HCU	Halifax V	EB208 OO-R	Training

F/O W G Driscoll   inj T/o Rufforth for local night flying practice,
Sgt E Hurst   inj a detail which ended at 2250 with the Halifax
F/O L Fletcher   + lying, wrecked, in a ploughed field near Whixley
Sgt J A MacTavish RCAF inj Lodge on the main A59 road, York to Knaresborough
Sgt B Standing   inj and a little under 3 miles NNW from Marston Moor
F/O F M Parks RCAF   inj airfield. Moments before the crash, F/O Driscoll
Sgt N Soulsby   inj had emerged from cloud and, it is suggested, he
became disorientated while looking for the Drem
lights. F/O Fletcher was taken the short distance to his home in Worsborough
Dale and buried in Barnsley (Ardsley) Cemetery. Having recovered from this very
serious incident, at least three proceeded to North Africa and while operating
out of Blida (Algeria) with 624 Squadron, failed to return from operations on
14 August 1944. Thus, F/O Driscoll, Sgt Hurst (who enlisted on 11 February
1936) and Sgt Soulsby are commemorated on the Malta Memorial, panels 13 and
15 on column 1, and panel 15 on column 3 respectively.

Note. The Halifax, summarised above, was part of a batch of one hundred Mk.V
aircraft, manufactured by Rootes Securities, Speke and delivered between April
and July 1943. Accepted by 1663 Heavy Conversion Unit on 26 August, it had
logged 210.30 flying hours in total, apparently free from incident.

16 Dec 1943	1667 HCU	Halifax V	EB185	Training

Sgt R T Stoneman   +   T/o Faldingworth for a night exercise. Crashed
Sgt H Poole   +   at 2325, roughly 2 miles NE of the airfield.
F/S H M Tait RCAF   +   Two of the three Commonwealth airmen were taken
Sgt J Pennington   +   to Cambridge City Cemetery, but F/O Cameron was
F/S K F Wightman RAAF   +   cremated at Nottingham Crematorium; he had wed
Sgt R L Cox   +   Nora Blanche Cameron of Buenos Aires. Their four
F/O A R Cameron RCAF   +   British compatriots rest in their home towns.

20 Dec 1943	1657 HCU	Stirling I	BF324	Training

F/O G Kewley   T/o 0123 Stradishall but an engine on the
starboard side cut and during the resultant
swing the undercarriage folded, damaging the Stirling to such an extent that
its future use was restricted to ground instruction. As such, it was allotted
the maintenance serial 4531M.

21 Dec 1943	1659 HCU	Halifax II	BB251 RV-V	Training

Sgt C L Howland USAAC   T/o Topcliffe for night flying training. Landed
at Croft, touching down at 2313 in conditions of
driving rain, which seriously reduced visibility. Thus, it was only at the last
moment that Sgt Howland USAAC sighted Halifax V LK991 SE-U, belonging to the
resident 431 Squadron, looming up from the gloom, too late to avoid a collision.
The impact wrecked the "1659" machine, but "431's" Halifax was repaired.

23 Dec 1943	1663 HCU	Halifax V	DK151	Training

Sgt L Slade   T/o 0955 Rufforth for non-operational training.
Overshot and crash-landed 1140, wrecking the
main undercarriage and sustaining heavy damage to the nose area. Posted to
Holme-on-Spalding Moor, where he joined 76 Squadron, Sgt Slade flew, at least,
thirty-four sorties (the majority in Halifax III MZ516 MP-V "Vera the Virgin",
a unit "veteran" which completed seventy-seven missions before coming to grief
in February 1945 - see Bomber Command Losses, Volume 6, page 57), by which time
he had been commissioned. By coincidence, the Halifax, here summarised, had
been received from 76 Squadron on 10 November 1943, having flown sixteen
operations in a little over five months of service.

	1664 HCU	Halifax V	EB191 ZU-C	Training

F/S M L John RCAF   +   T/o Dishforth for a night cross-country. Got
Sgt J Quinn   +   into difficulties and partially abandoned before
F/S R H Mitchell RCAF   inj   crashing 2338 at 57 Kent Street, Harrogate (close
P/O G L Crowe RCAF   inj   to a power station). P/O Crowe RCAF was admitted
Sgt Harvey   to the town's General Hospital, while on his
WO2 Marsden   return to Dishforth, F/S Mitchell RCAF received
Sgt C R Choma RCAF   +   attention in station sick quarters. The two
Canadians were buried in Harrogate (Stonefall)
Cemetery, while Sgt Quinn was buried, privately, at Dewsbury Cemetery. It was
the unit's first major accident since arriving at Dishforth from Croft.

27 Dec 1943	1652 HCU	Halifax II	JB788	Training

F/S T E Scotland RAAF   inj   T/o Marston Moor for fighter affiliation practice
Sgt R Lewis   and it was while awaiting the arrival of the
Sgt D Hopper   fighters that the propeller on the port inner
Sgt E Riley   engine sheered off. F/S Scotland RAAF promptly
Sgt W Weekes   ordered his to crew to bale out; then, having
Sgt W Smith   satisfied himself that all had complied, he
Sgt W Butler   forced-landed at 1615 in a field off Drub Lane,
Hunsworth near Cleckheaton, Yorkshire. For his
coolness in the face of a very difficult situation, he, subsequently, received
a Commanding Officers' Commendation.

29 Dec 1943	1663 HCU C Flt	Halifax V	DG245 OO-H	Training

Sgt D Joseph   T/o 2120 Rufforth but swung out of control and
the port wheel made sharp contact with a large
block of concrete. This, effectively, concluded the flying days of this aircraft which, in fourteen months of service, had logged 301.50 hours (prior to
its arrival at Rufforth, it had flown with 408 Squadron). Sgt Joseph, meanwhile,
went to 76 Squadron and failed to return from Frankfurt in mid-March 1944 (see
Bomber Command Losses, Volume 5, page 119). In due course of time, news was
received that he was a prisoner of war.

Resumé. 1943 was the year, at the end of which, the Allies could sense, with a degree of confidence, that the war in Europe was turning inexorably in their favour. In the late spring, all Axis forces had been expelled from North Africa, thus concluding three years of desert warfare that had seen the battle sway in favour first of one of the combatants and then the other. This welcome success was soon followed by the invasion of Sicily and the first tentative steps in the long haul along the spine of the Italian mainland. By the summer, Mussolini had been ousted from office and the partnership was in such disarray that, by early September, Italy had signed an armistice (though months of exhausting fighting remained as the Allies inched northwards in the face of resolute resistance from the Wehrmacht. Field-Marshal Albrecht Kesselring had no intention of allowing the Allied armies an easy passage.

Earlier in the year, at Stalingrad, a battle begun in the high summer of 1942, and fought with scant quarter between the Soviet armies, commanded by Marshal Grigori Zhukov and Field-Marshal Friedrich Paulus's 6th Army reached its bloody climax with the enemy suffering in the region of 147,000 casualties, while Friedrich Paulus and the 91,000 survivors from the "6th" and 4th Panzar Army marched away through the Russian snow and into captivity, many never to see their homeland again.

The implications of this crushing defeat would not have been lost on their comrades in North Africa, squeezed from two sides with the Mediterranean on one flank and the barren wastes of the desert on the other. By the end of the year, Hitler's generals knew that an Allied invasion of occupied Europe was no longer a distant possibility but a cast iron certainty.

A key factor in the these reverses of fortune for the enemy, particularly in North Africa, had been the Allies supremacy in the air. Across northern Europe, the Luftwaffe was very much on the defensive as Bomber Command maintained an almost nightly presence over Germany and the Americans sent their Fortresses and Liberators, heavily escorted, out by day to bomb strategic targets across the breadth of those countries still under Nazi domination as well as penetrating deep into the Third Reich itself. The crisscross of condensation trails were becoming a very familiar, and heartwarming, sight to the millions living under the heel of their oppressors.

Of late, it has become all too fashionable for revisionist historians to heap scorn on the achievements of the Allied bombing offensive (and to vilify their commanders) but it is an indisputable fact that from the time our land forces were embarked from the beaches around Dunkerque, the aggressiveness of the bombing campaign (first by the Royal Air Force, and later joined by the Americans) succeeded in forcing the German High Command to tie down much needed front-line resources in defence of the country's industrial base; the weight of the attacks was, at last, beginning to tell.

Throughout the spring and summer, the industrial towns of the Ruhr were bombed with much vigour while four night raids on Hamburg in late July and early August resulted in destruction on a scale hitherto unknown in the annals of modern aerial warfare. Now, in the dying embers of 1943, Berlin was becoming the focal point for Bomber Command (the Americans were not drawn in, much as Sir Arthur Harris wished) and this far distant target would continue to occupy the minds of the High Wycombe staff well into the New Year.

Not surprisingly, as the bombs rained down, both by night and by day, the Luftwaffe rose to meet the challenge, inflicting the severest of losses on the Allied air forces. But no matter how severe, or wounding their actions might seem, both air forces were able to absorb the punishment handed out. In respect of Bomber Command, heavy bomber production was outstripping losses, while any gaps in the front line squadrons could be met from the outpouring of fresh crews from the training establishments.

Victory was yet to be assured, but the spectre of defeat was ebbing fast as the Command moved towards its fifth year of night bombing.

For those units charged with schooling embryo bomber crews for the task ahead, the year had been extremely busy and there could be no slackening of effort for the foreseeable future. However, before summarising the losses for 1944, it is observed that towards the end of 1943, heavy conversion units equipped with the Lancaster (except for "1678" using the radial-engine Lancaster II) had the type replaced by a mixture of Stirlings and Halifaxes. Thus, as the Lancasters were withdrawn, some were released to operational squadrons, while others formed the initial establishment of the Lancaster Finishing Schools, the first of these being formed in the September. As to why it was thought appropriate to add yet another layer to the training scheme, I am not able to comment but from late 1943 onwards, hundreds of aircrew would pass out from the heavy conversion units and then embark on a Lancaster conversion course before commencing operations.

1 Jan　**1659 HCU**　　　　**Halifax II　W1095**　　　　　　　　　　**Training**
1944　　W/O S J Pearce　　　　　　T/o 1105 Topcliffe for dual circuits and landings
　　　　F/S E A Vigor RCAF　　　　combined with three-engined flying practice, with
　　　　　　　　　　　　　　　a crew of eight. Fifteen minutes later, undershot
from a three-engined approach, in order to avoid a contractors working party,
hitting several large piles of sand and gravel. A gusting wind was a contributory
factor in this first heavy conversion write off of the New Year. F/S Vigor RCAF,
sadly, did not live to see another for he was killed during the course of a raid
on the marshalling yards at Montzen on 27-28 April 1944 (see Bomber Command
Losses, Volume 5, page 201); at the time he was flying with 434 Squadron.

3- 4 Jan　**1658 HCU**　　　　**Halifax II　DT626**　　　　　　　　　　**Training**
1944　　P/O A H Fotheringham RAAF　+　T/o Riccall for a night cross-country, the
　　　　Sgt W Pinder　　　　　　+　culmination of which would have seen the crew
　　　　F/O J G Macleod RCAF　　　+　posted to an operational squadron. At roughly
　　　　F/S W C Thompson RCAF　　+　0045, the Halifax crashed with great force
　　　　Sgt L Dowse　　　　　　　+　(having partially broken up in the air) a mile
　　　　Sgt P Rogerson　　　　　+　south-west of Pentrefoelas onto land near Gwern
　　　　Sgt R H Wright　　　　　+　Hywel Uchaf, the village (Pentrefoelas) being
　　　　　　　　　　　　　　　fifteen miles SW of Denbigh and just about on
the border with Merioneth, above Ysbyty Ifan. The three Commonwealth members
of crew were taken to Chester (Blacon) Cemetery, their four companions being
claimed by their relatives. The circumstances of the crash, and the backgrounds
of the seven airmen who died, has been extensively researched and reported upon
by Terry R Hill in his remarkable tribute, "Tragedy at Pentrefoelas". A placque
commemorating the crew was unveiled during a service of dedication, held in the
local church, on 3 September 2000. I am indebted to Hedley Richards of Oswestry
for advising me of this, and for other similar incidents in Wales. The parents
of Sergeant Leonard Dowse had already suffered the loss of another of their sons,
namely Lance Corporal Wilfred Lawrence Dowse of the 5th Battalion Green Howards,
killed in Libya on 31 May 1942. He rests in Knightsbridge War Cemetery, Libya.

　　　　1667 HCU　　　　**Halifax V　EB193　-G**　　　　　　　　　**Training**
　　　　Sgt V B Temple　　　　　　T/o 2012 Faldingworth briefed for a night
　　　　　　　　　　　　　　　navigation exercise. During the flight, the
crew experienced quite severe engine problems; the oil pressure gauge for the
starboard outer fluctuated alarmingly and an early return was deemed prudent.
However, while preparing to land, oil pressure on the port outer suddenly
dropped to zero and the motor cut, flames being seen soon afterwards. Unable
to reach the runway, the Halifax was crash-landed at 0047, in a field, quite
close to base. In his summing up, Sgt Temple's commanding officer stated that
he (Sgt Temple) had done all that was possible in the circumstances. A technical
examination of the wreck revealed a bearing failure in the outer starboard while
a leak from port outer's oil cooler had been the precursor of the unit's failure.

4 Jan　**1657 HCU**　　　　**Stirling I　N3675　-W**　　　　　　　　**Training**
1944　　F/S K C Seagrave　　　　+　T/o Stradishall but a tyre burst as the bomber
　　　　Sgt T R Thompson　　　　+　climbed away. On return to base, at 2120, the
　　　　WO2 W J Kilpatrick RCAF　+　Stirling was observed closing on the runway, but
　　　　F/S H T McDonald RCAF　　+　flying quite slowly and, as it drew nearer, it
　　　　Sgt A McConnell　　　inj　stalled and dived into Lord's Wood, 5 miles NE
　　　　Sgt J F Phillips　　　+　of Haverhill, Suffolk. The two Canadians were
　　　　Sgt F V Nolan　　　inj　buried in Cambridge City Cemetery, while the
　　　　Sgt W C Warman　　　inj　others who lost their lives were taken to their
　　　　　　　　　　　　　　　home towns. Sgt Warman was a flight engineer,
but is reported to have joined the crew as a passenger; along with Sgt McConnell
he was taken to RAF Hospital Ely, and both were placed on the "dangerously ill"
list. Sgt Nolan was less seriously hurt and he was treated in station sick
quarters. Sgt Thompson's service number indicates he had transferred from
the army, possibly prior to September 1939.

5 Jan　**1656 HCU**　　　　**Halifax II　W7772**　　　　　　　　　　**Training**
1944　　P/O W M Addison DFC　　　T/o 1125 Lindholme for general flying practice,
　　　　P/O A J Jenkins　　　　　during which the instructor stopped and feathered
　　　　　　　　　　　　　　　the starboard engines, but due to low accumulator
voltage, he was unable to reverse the procedure. Lowering the wheels, he forced-
landed at 1215 in a field at Oatland Farm, Gringley on the Hill, some 7 miles NNE
of Redtford, Nottinghamshire. As the Halifax rolled, the pupil pilot applied the
brakes, whereupon the aircraft tipped onto its nose.

7 Jan   **1662 HCU**   **Halifax V**   **DG290**   **Training**
1944   P/O D G Edwards DFC   T/o 1550 Blyton for circuit practice, the crew
totalling eight. Upon landing, with the pupil
pilot (he is not named on the accident card) at the controls, the Halifax swung
to starboard. Despite the best efforts of the instructor and his pupil to bring
the situation under control, the undercarriage collapsed. P/O Edwards had flown
with 100 Squadron, details of his award being Gazetted on 10 December 1943.

1663 HCU   **Halifax V**   **DG417**   **–D**   **Training**
Sgt H H Wastell   T/o Rufforth for the pilot's first night solo
on type. Landed 1930, at Pocklington, rather
heavily and, as a consequence, it ballooned back into the air. On its next
arrival, the Halifax ran off the runway and finished up, wrecked, amidst a large
heap of root crops.

7– 8 Jan   **1667 HCU**   **Halifax V**   **DG287**   **Training**
1944   Sgt F B Peaker   T/o 1850 Faldingworth for a night cross-country,
with a crew complement of six. As the evening
wore on, the weather deteriorated and orders to divert to another airfield were
transmitted. However, by midnight the conditions were such that the crew could
not pinpoint their position and, at approximately 0125, with the petrol gauges
registering near empty, Sgt Peaker climbed to a safe height and all baled out,
safely, leaving the Halifax to fall at Swallow, 8 miles WSW of Cleethorpes in
Lincolnshire.

10 Jan   **1652 HCU**   **Halifax II**   **BB307**   **Training**
1944   F/O J R Fisher   T/o 1510 Marston Moor for a combined exercise
in bombing and air-to-sea gunnery. However, as
the Halifax gathered speed it began to veer to port, followed by a loud report
as the starboard tyre burst. Seconds later, the crew emerged from the wreckage
of their aircraft, which was now minus its undercarriage. With only four hours
of solo flying, on type, combined with a slight crosswind, F/O Fisher had been
confronted with a situation that was not experienced enough to deal with. It
will be recalled that on 26 February 1943, this Halifax had been involved in a
a serious accident at Marston Moor (see page 40 for details).

1652 HCU   **Halifax II**   **HR664**   **–J**   **Training**
F/O J H Williams DFC   +   T/o 0944 Marston Moor for a check dual flight
Sgt H B Annan   +   only to crash two minutes later, inverted, in
P/O A L Langworthy DFM   +   the River Ouse near Fairfield Sanatorium below
Sgt W R Windsor   +   Skelton, 4 miles NW from the centre of York.
F/S M J Trenaman   +   The body of F/O Williams was never recovered
F/S H A Perriam RAAF   +   and his name is perpetuated on the Runnymede
Sgt R G E Sandy   +   Memorial. F/S Perriam RAAF was buried under
service arrangements at Harrogate (Stonefall)
Cemetery, while the others were taken to their home towns. F/O Williams had
only recently escaped unscathed from a serious incident (see page 78); his
flight engineer was an ex-Halton apprentice who had completed a tour of duty
with 10 Squadron, notification of his award appearing in the London Gazette
on 15 June 1943. F/S Perriam's first Christian name is reported by the CWGC
as "Howard", but the Royal Australian War Museum Roll of Honour database shows
him as "Harold". Various theories were put forward as to what might have
caused this accident, but nothing conclusive was ever proven.

13 Jan   **1651 HCU**   **Stirling I**   **W7468**   **–T**   **Training**
1944   F/O F R Pugh   T/o 1030 Wratting Common with a complement of
F/O E V Sage RNZAF   nine, probably to practice circuits and landings.
Sgt E G R Pepper   At around 1050, landed with the undercarriage
only partially locked and, as a result, the
airframe was damaged beyond repair. Later, the Stirling served as a ground
instruction trainer, the serial 4532M being applied. In total, it had flown
four hundred and fifty-four hours in a quite eventful service life, during which
it had been categorised as beyond repair (10 June 1942), only to be reinstated a
week later. F/O Pugh had served previously with 90 Squadron and, as Bryce
Gomersall reports, following his stint as an instructor, flew Stirlings on
army support and transport operations with "295" and 242 Squadrons. F/O Sage
eventually converted to Lancasters and joined 550 Squadron. On 9-10 May 1944,
he was posted missing (as was Sgt Pepper) from a raid on a coastal battery (see
Bomber Command Losses, Volume 5, page 217).

13–14 Jan 1944	1656 HCU	Halifax II	DT781	–D2	Training

F/S W R Wilson RCAF   +   T/o 2149 Lindholme for a night navigation detail.
Sgt R H Dolden   +   While cruising at 20,000 feet, caught fire and
F/O F J Hjartarson RCAF   +   broke up following a fire in the port outer and
F/S J J Clearly RAAF   +   a subsequent loss of control. The bulk of the
Sgt R C Bradbury   +   wreckage, which fell at around 0140, was found
Sgt R Burgess   +   to the east of Holsworthy, Devon. The trio of
Commonwealth airmen were taken to Bath (Haycombe)
Cemetery, while the others were buried under private arrangements, Sgt Bradbury
having to be conveyed to the south of the county and laid to rest in Plymouth
(Weston Mill) Cemetery.

Note. Air Accident Investigation Branch staff were becoming extremely skilled
in determining the cause of flying accidents and the sequence in which various
parts of the airframe failed; thus, in their report for the Halifax summarised
above it was noted that as the bomber plunged, the outer starboard mainplane
failed in an upwards direction.

14 Jan 1944	1652 HCU	Halifax II	BB191		Training

Sgt R F E Duckworth   T/o Marston Moor for night circuit flying,
carrying a crew of five. At 2256, upon touch
down, the wheels folded and the bomber was damaged beyond repair. In his statement, Sgt Duckworth was quite emphatic that the "green" lights had come on, and
it is thus assumed the unit failed to lock.

	1653 HCU	Stirling III	BF525	–A	Training

Sgt D S J Richards   +   T/o Chedburgh (crew No. 15) in the company of
F/S M C Barnard   +   Stirling "D", Sgt A Merricks, crew No. 16 and
Sgt G G G Rann   +   Stirling "G", Sgt B Green RNZAF, crew No. 18,
Sgt R Hunt   +   all tasked to fly base - Bodmin - Land's End -
F/O A Nova RCAF   +   St. David's Head - Fishguard - 5133N 0510W -
Sgt N E Pratt   +   Aberystwyth - Church Honeybourne - base. Last
Sgt W C Freeborn   +   seen near Land's End; all are commemorated on
Sgt B W Matheson RCAF   +   the Runnymede Memorial. Generally, the crew were
older in years than average; three were twenty-
eight and Sgt Freeborn was thirty-four. It was the unit's first major incident
since reforming as a heavy conversion unit (previously "1653" had, in 1942,
trained Liberator crews, destined for the Middle East and Far East theatres)
on 21 November last. It was also the first loss of Mk.III Stirling engaged in
crew conversion training.

18 Jan 1944	1659 HCU	Halifax II	R9386	–J	Training

F/O F H Baker RCAF   inj   T/o Topcliffe to practice circuit flying, during
Sgt S R Hill   inj   which the port outer lost power, either through
Sgt Hynes   failure of a gear wheel or the breakup of the
WO2 J H Sharpe RCAF   inj   impeller shaft. Thus, while trying to get down
Sgt J S Bradley   inj   on three engines, F/O Baker RCAF drifted away
Sgt Johnson   from the centre line and elected to overshoot.
F/S L L Petry RCAF   inj   However, with full flap selected down, the
bomber was reluctant to climb and at 1012 it
flew into a tree and crashed hear Halfway House on the Thirsk to Topcliffe road
and less than a mile SE of the runway. The impact was severe and of those taken
to Northallerton Hospital, WO2 Sharpe RCAF and F/S Petry RCAF died soon after
admittance. Both are buried in Harrogate (Stonefall) Cemetery. Soon after
being declared medically fit to resume flying, Sgt Bradley joined 405 Squadron
and was killed in action on 28 April 1944 (see Bomber Command Losses, Volume 5,
page 199). With those who died alongside him, he is buried in Belgium.

	1659 HCU	Halifax II	LW334	–T	Training

F/O J P Lavallee RCAF   +   T/o Topcliffe for a day cross-country, only to
Sgt R G Kimball RCAF   +   fly into high ground, 1,100 feet above sea level
F/O W L Boisvert RCAF   +   at around 1030, in the region of the Black
F/O W Phillips RCAF   +   Hambleton hills some 2 miles SE of Osmotherley
WO1 G E Giff RCAF   +   and 10 miles NNE from Thirsk, Yorkshire. It is
Sgt G H Hivon RCAF   +   reported that fog and mist were prevalent in
the area of the crash. All were taken to the
regional cemetery at Harrogate (Stonefall) and buried with full military honours.
As David Thompson so advises, a cross bearing their names was dedicated to the
crew at a special service conducted on 18 January 1994, by the Revd Stuart East.

20 Jan	1653 HCU	Stirling III	LJ455 H4–C	Training

1944

P/O S G Johnson DFC RNZAF	+	T/o Chedburgh (crew No. 9) for a night cross-
F/S J P Bartington	inj	country, base - Land´s End - Dulverton - Reading
Sgt R Hallam	+	and thence to Goole before returning to base. On
Sgt R J Teague	+	regaining Chedburgh, the crew acknowledged their
WO2 R D Poe RCAF	+	landing instructions but at 2326 the Stirling
F/S J K Callow RAAF	+	ploughed into trees 400 yards SSW of Hargrave
Sgt W H Spibey	inj	Rectory, a few miles NW from the airfield. It is
Sgt A J Wood	+	believed the pupil pilot was at the controls, and
Sgt F Tempan	+	he may have become disorientated by the airfield´s

lighting system. The two injured airmen died soon
after the crash. Five are buried in Cambridge City Cemetery, while the others
were claimed by their relatives. P/O Johnson RNZAF, whose DFC had been Gazetted
on 19 October 1943, had flown with 218 Squadron and, in total, he had logged
just over six hundred flying hours.

	1657 HCU	Stirling I	W7571	Training

F/L J G Neilson DFC RNZAF	+	T/o 1745 Stradishall for night flying practice,
F/S T J Hogan RAAF	+	having been delayed for nearly a quarter of an
Sgt J V Powell	+	hour due to the presence on the runway of the
Sgt A C Parker	+	flare path lorry. Eyewitness reports indicate
Sgt S F Wise	+	an erratic take off and when, eventually, the
Sgt R J Fuller	+	Stirling became airborne it had veered off the
Sgt L H Robinson	+	runway and was quite close to the perimeter
Sgt C W K Clisby	inj	track. Agonisingly, it climbed to about one

hundred feet, before side-slipping into the
far north-west corner of the bomb dump, where it struck a building used to
store incendiaries. On impact, the rear fuselage broke away (this, undoubtedly
saved Sgt Clisby´s life) and moments later the rest of the aircraft erupted in
a sheet of flame. Both Commonwealth airmen, and Sgt Parker, were taken to
Cambridge City Cemetery, while the others who died were buried privately.
Similar to his fellow countryman and pilot, described in the summary above,
F/L Neilson RNZAF had served on 218 Squadron, his award having been published
on 14 May 1943 (he had been a compatriot of F/O Thomson RNZAF - see page 72).
An investigative board concluded that the starboard outer engine had failed.

21 Jan	1661 HCU	Stirling III	EF151	Training

1944

Sgt E Docherty	inj	T/o 0300 Winthorpe for general training. Lost
Sgt W G A Venables	inj	power from the port outer, which was feathered,
WO2 G C Munro RCAF	+	and on return to base the wheels only partially
F/S F C Biddle RCAF	inj	lowered. Sgt Docherty also experienced problems
Sgt A F Cooper	+	with the trimmers and, subsequently, the bomber
Sgt A S Humphreys RAAF	inj	crashed at 0630 after flying into trees at
Sgt R Southey	inj	Glebe Farm, Brough, a village on the Lincoln-

shire/Nottinghamshire border and some 2 miles
north-east from the airfield. Two were taken to Newark-on-Trent General Hospital
where, not long after being admitted, Sgt Venables died; he is buried in Wales
at Brymbo (St. Mary) Churchyard. WO2 Munro RCAF lies in Oxford (Botley) Cemetery,
while Sgt Cooper rests at Plaistow in the East London Cemetery. Less than two
months later, Sgt Humphreys RAAF perished in an horrific midair collision,
involving two Lancasters from "463" and 625 Squadrons respectively (see Bomber
Command Losses, Volume 5, pages 115 and 116 respectively).

	1667 HCU	Halifax V	EB152 —J	Training

F/O L F Brewer	+	T/o Faldingworth for a Bullseye sortie. It is
Sgt D L Mansfield	+	believed the Halifax entered the London Defensive
P/O F W Newson	+	Zone, after which all contact was lost, All are
Sgt H S Harrison	+	commemorated on the Runnymede Memorial. In the
Sgt K Butler	+	absence of any wreckage, but with the knowledge
Sgt A Blanksby	+	that enemy air activity occurred shortly after
Sgt E Weatherley	+	the Halifax was due to leave the area, the

investigating panel summarised their report as
follows; probably (1) enemy action, (2) friendly anti-aircraft fire, (3) icing
that may have rendered the aircraft´s altimeter inoperable.

22 Jan	1658 HCU	Halifax II	DT619	Training

1944

F/O B W T Parker	T/o 1225 Riccall for a cross-country, during
	which the port outer failed. While circling

Wigtown airfield, another motor failed and the crew forced-landed at 1450.

22 Jan 1944	**1662 HCU**	**Halifax II**	**DT693**		**Training**

F/S E J Rayner   +   T/o 2214 Blyton with the intention of carrying
Sgt A E Chaffe   +   out circuits and landings. However, within a
F/S K A Hill RNZAF   +   few minutes a message was received to say that
Sgt G Brand   inj   the bomber was down 2 miles beyond the runway,
Sgt A M Griffiths   inj   at Scroggs Farm near Corringham. Two badly
injured airmen were brought into station sick
quarters and Sgt Brand died before he could be transferred, with Sgt Griffiths,
to the War Memorial Hospital at Scunthorpe. F/S Hill RNZAF rests in Cambridge
City Cemetery, while F/S Rayner, Sgt Chaffe and Sgt Brand lie in burial grounds
located in England, Wales and Scotland respectively.

23 Jan 1944	**1667 HCU**	**Halifax V**	**DG358**	**-J**	**Training**

F/S P K E Bennett   +   T/o Faldingworth for a high-level cross-country.
Sgt E R Gawler   +   At a little before 1440, flying at 20,000 feet,
Sgt J W Gibb   +   the starboard outer engine failed and the
Sgt D Ramsay   +   Halifax lost height, soon being swallowed up in
F/S J S Spriggs   +   thick storm clouds. Icing built up and within
Sgt N Fisher   +   seconds the bomber was plunging out of control,
Sgt W H Wareham   +   its starboard wing being wrenched off as it
Sgt A A Clark   +   fell and smashed into the starboard tail section.
Sgt W G Wyatt   +   No one was able to parachute before the remnants
of the aircraft hurtled into fields near Cwm Farm
scattering debris and bodies over the meadows and along the banks of the Nant-
rhyd-ros-lan at Bryn-y-groes, about a mile SSW of Bwlch-y-ffridd. F/S Spriggs,
the son of Dr. Neville Ivens Spriggs and Emily Jane Spriggs of Leicester, was
taken to Chester (Blacon) Cemetery, while his eight companions were conveyed
to their home towns. On 7 November 1998, a service of dedication was conducted
at Aberhafesp church and for this auspicious occasion, Brian Poole, a church-
warden at Aberhafesp, prepared a detailed account of the tragedy which is well
documented in his excellent booklet, "Down in Aberhafesp". The results of his
exhaustive research ranks amongst the best of its kind and is a wonderful
tribute, not only to the crew who died, but to the many local inhabitants
who were witness to this awful crash.

26 Jan 1944	**1663 HCU**	**Halifax V**	**EB133**	**-M**	**Training**

F/O J K Mountney   T/o 1125 Rufforth for general flying practice.
Sgt E M Fox   Twenty minutes later, attempted to land but
overshot the runway and crashed heavily.

26-27 Jan 1944	**1660 HCU**	**Stirling III**	**EH933**		**Training**

Sgt R A Partridge   +   T/o Swinderby for a night cross-country, with
Sgt A Thursby   +   two flight engineers included in the crew of
Sgt H Hewitt   +   eight. While flying at high altitude, just
Sgt C V Tomkinson   +   inland from the south coast of Devon, a sudden
Sgt T H Jones   +   and terrible disaster overtook the crew and
Sgt B Ackroyd   +   their aircraft dropped from the sky, breaking
Sgt J Kerry   +   apart as it fell. Thus, at 0004, the fuselage
Sgt R Street   +   and most of the mainplanes crashed onto a hillside at Coppleham Cross, N of Exton and a mere
six miles SSE from the city of Exeter. Eventually, debris was recovered from
along a path stretching three-and-a-half miles eastwards from the main impact
point and Air Investigation Branch specialists later determined that the rear
fuselage had detached at around 14,000 feet, followed at circa 10,000 - 11,000
feet by the elevators and rear turret. Following identification, the eight
airmen were buried, under private arrangements, by their next of kin.

27 Jan 1944	**1652 HCU**	**Halifax II**	**W1091 JA-E**		**Training**

F/S J C Bond RAAF   T/o 2058 Burn for night flying, heading away
F/S J N Keys RAAF   from the airfield on a south-easterly course,
but failed to maintain height and crash-landed
on the banks of the River Aire (becoming partially submerged) near Beal, just
over 2 miles NE of Knottingley, Yorkshire. A technical inspection could not
find any evidence of mechanical failure and it seems likely that in raising
the flaps, the pilot pushed the lever past "neutral" and in to the "down"
position. This caused the nose to rise and though his airspeed did not decay,
he was unable to arrest the loss in altitude. Very sadly, after being posted
to 466 Squadron, both airmen were lost during operations on 10-11 April 1944
(see Bomber Command Losses, Volume 5, page 169).

28 Jan
1944

1657 HCU	**Stirling I**	**BK601 XT- East India V**	**Training**

Sgt R Lemoine
Sgt H Watson
Sgt R C Dean   inj
Sgt C Fallis RCAF
Sgt D Guard
Sgt R B Hodgins RCAF   inj
Sgt E Oliver RCAF

T/o 2140 Bury St Edmunds using the east - west runway, but before becoming airborne the bomber ran onto rough ground and the undercarriage gave way. The two injured airmen were treated at the West Suffolk General Hospital. Sgt Hodgins RCAF went on to fly with 625 Squadron and was killed in action shortly after "D-Day" (see Bomber Command Losses, Volume 5, page 271). Bryce Gomersall advises that a photograph taken at the scene of the crash clearly shows the code combination "XT" and what appears to be "East India V", but the aircraft's individual letter is too indistinct to read.

29 Jan
1944

1660 HCU	**Stirling III**	**EF246 -C**	**Training**

F/O J M Greig DFC   +
P/O V F Dickinson   +
Sgt A Spence   +
Sgt G J Williams   +
F/O E P Neary   +
Sgt S Walker   +
Sgt D L Helsby   +
F/S J P Hayden RAAF   +

T/o Swinderby briefed for a combined Bullseye and searchlight cooperation exercise. At around 2200 the Stirling dived into the Humber, not far from North Killingholme on the Lincolnshire bank of the river. It is suggested that the pilot may have been dazzled by the searchlights, whereupon he took violent evasive action and, in so doing, lost control. Four, including the staff pilot instructor (F/O Greig had flown with 57 Squadron and details of his award had been published on 13 August 1943) have no known graves and four were taken to their home towns for interment. In 1975, Bryce Gomersall writes, part of a flap measuring eleven feet by six feet was found about a thousand yards distant from the main crash area.

30 Jan
1944

1664 HCU	**Halifax V**	**DG308**	**Training**

F/L J M Bissett DFM RCAF

T/o 1910 Dishforth for night training. Some fifteen minutes into the detail, the crew came into land but the trainee pilot (he is not named on the accident card) inadvertently lowered the bomb doors instead of the flaps. A fast landing followed and when braking proved ineffective, F/L Bissett RCAF swung the Halifax, the main wheels folding under the high stress loads. Soon after this incident, he was posted to 427 Squadron to take over a flight commander's post, only to lose his life during the infamous Nürnberg raid at the end of March 1944 (see Bomber Command Losses, Volume 5, page 154). His DFM had been gained with 78 Squadron, notification having appeared in the London Gazette on 19 May 1943.

31 Jan
1944

1660 HCU	**Stirling III**	**EF232 -J**	**Training**

F/O J H Mason DFC RCAF   inj
F/S S E Martin   inj
Sgt R H Appleton   +
Sgt G B Lamb   inj
W/O J B McKnight   +
F/O H G Trueman RCAF   +
Sgt R E Duke   +
Sgt H Nelson   +

T/o Swinderby for a night exercise, the crew including a pupil pilot and two flight engineers. At 2132, soon after departing, the Stirling came down at Carlton-le-Moorland, 9 miles SSW from Lincoln. The three injured airmen succumbed to their wounds on 1 February and together with those who perished in the crash they are buried in various parts of the United Kingdom. It is likely that F/O Mason's funeral was arranged by relatives as he rests in Scotland at Aberdeen (Springbank) Cemetery. His DFC, gained with 50 Squadron, had been promulgated on 10 December 1943.

1664 HCU	**Halifax V**	**DJ988**	**Training**

F/O J S Sugden
F/O N G McLeod RCAF

T/o Dishforth for dual circuits and landings. Landed at 1420 in a quite strong crosswind and while manipulating the throttles and brakes in an effort to maintain a straight course, the undercarriage collapsed. No one was hurt but the Halifax was damaged beyond worthwhile repair.

1664 HCU	**Halifax V**	**DK185**	**Training**

P/O D G McLeod RCAF   +
WO2 L Riggs RCAF   +
Sgt R H Rahn RCAF   +
WO1 W G King RCAF   +
Sgt G Martin RCAF   +
Sgt A L Mullen RCAF   +

T/o Dishforth for a night navigation sortie. Drifted some 40 miles S of track and at circa 1720/1730 flew into high ground on the south side of the Yorkshire town of Ilkley. All are buried in Harrogate (Stonefall) Cemetery.

2 Feb
1944

1658 HCU   **Halifax II**   **W1168**   **Training**

P/O T J Bishop   T/o 1440 Riccall for dual circuits and landings.
Sgt D Johnson   Touched down at 1500, but the trainee misjudged
his height and instead of flaring out into a
neat three point landing, the main wheels struck the runway, the force being
sufficient to balloon the bomber back into the air. The instructor immediately
took over control and attempted to go round again, calling to his pupil to take
off some of the flap. However, before he could do so, the Halifax careered into
an obstruction near the boundary and crashed.

3 Feb
1944

1652 HCU   **Halifax II**   **W1102**   **Transit**

F/O G F Turner   T/o 1555 Burn with the intention of returning
to Marston Moor. Initially, all was normal,
but as the speed increased and the tail rose, F/O Turner sensed he had no
elevator control. Promptly, he closed the throttles but was unable to halt
his aircraft before it ran into the overshoot area. At the time, a strong to
gale force wind was blowing across the airfield and this was thought to have
contributed to the pilot's problems.

5 Feb
1944

1653 HCU   **Stirling I**   **EF396 A3–G**   **Training**

F/O R Waugh   T/o 2004 Chedburgh for night dual circuits and
Sgt J W Nicholls   inj   landings, during which the throttle control for
Sgt B C F Dean   the outer starboard engine failed. Landed at
F/S J B Grady RCAF   2046 but swung sharply to port and wrecked
Sgt G E Rhead   after running into Stirling I BK594, belonging
Sgt A A Rivers   to the same unit. Damage to the other aircraft
Sgt Challoner   was less severe, and repairs were authorised.
Sgt E Markson   By the high summer, Sgt Nicholls and his crew
were engaged on Specials Operations Executive
missions with 161 Squadron. On 8-9 August, Sgt C G Bragg having replaced Sgt
Challoner, they failed to return from a sortie over France (see Bomber Command
Losses, Volume 5, page 375).

1658 HCU   **Halifax II**   **DT740**   **–P**   **Training**

F/O W E Elder RNZAF   T/o Riccall to practice three-engined landings.
Sgt C G Grubb   Forced-landed, circa 1000, following a failed
attempt to go round again from a poor approach,
coming down SW of the runway near the hamlet of Wistow Lordship. For F/O Elder,
this was his second mishap, as an instructor (see page 68 for the earlier
incident). His pupil, sadly, did not live to see the end of the war. Posted
to the Middle East, he died on 8 January 1945, and is now buried in Israel at
Khayat Beach War Cemetery, located some 5 km SW from Haifa.

1662 HCU   **Halifax II**   **W7781**   **Training**

Sgt G G Hingley   T/o 2135 Blyton for night circuit practice,
with a five-man crew, but swung violently
and ground looped as a consequence, losing the undercarriage.

7 Feb
1944

1656 HCU   **Halifax II**   **BB320**   **–A2**   **Training**

F/O E C D Richards   +   T/o 1740 Lindholme for a night navigation
Sgt A J Denny   +   detail. At approximately 1830, the Halifax
Sgt K Murray   +   emerged from the cloud cover, spinning, and
F/O H L Kerr RCAF   +   crashed in Blakeley Lane, Leek Road on Kingsley
Sgt W D Joshua   +   Moor near Cheadle, Staffordshire. F/O Kerr RCAF
Sgt H J Couling   +   and his skipper and tail gunner were laid to
rest in Chester (Blacon) Cemetery; their three
companions were conveyed to their home towns.

1662 HCU   **Halifax II**   **V9983**   **Training**

F/S W H A Daly RAAF   +   T/o 2013 Blyton for night circuits and landings
Sgt T R Davison   +   but crashed, with fatal consequences, within
Sgt L N Singer   +   five minutes of commencing the exercise. At
Sgt J E G Nowlan   +   the inquest into the accident, which occurred
Sgt R J Payne   +   just off the East Lound to Graizelound road,
Sgt H R Freeman   +   near Haxey, Lincolnshire, concluded that the
pilot had been obliged to take evasive action
in order to avoid a midair collision, and in doing so he lost control and spun
to the ground. F/S Daly RAAF was given a service burial at Cambridge City
Cemetery; his crew were laid to rest under private arrangements.

7 Feb 1944	**1663 HCU**	**Halifax V**	DK192	**Training**

F/L A J S Hodson DFC   +   T/o Rufforth for a day cross-country in rather
F/S S Bright   +   misty weather. At 1014, the Halifax struck the
Sgt J F Nelson   +   top of Garrowby Hill between Cot Nab Farm and
F/O J K Meyler   +   South Wold Farm, skidding across the main York
Sgt K Smith   +   to Great Driffield road, carrying with it a
Sgt P G McDonald   +   passing milk lorry which had been picking up
Sgt S J Booker   +   churns from farms in the area. Within seconds
                               of the impact, the bomber was a blazing inferno
Mr A W Kirkby   +   from which there was no escape. Six of the crew
                               were claimed by their relatives, but their
instructor, F/L Hodson, was buried in Harrogate (Stonefall) Cemetery. In the
June of 1943, at the height of "The Battle of the Ruhr", he had commenced a
tour of operations with 76 Squadron, and when "screened" he had participated
in at least twenty-seven sorties as captain. It is observed that he was one
of a relatively select group of bomber pilots who took part in all four attacks
on Hamburg and then went on to flying in the Peenemünde raid. His richly
deserved award was Gazetted on 7 January 1944.

Note. On 8 May 1996, a granite memorial to the memory of the crew, and the
thirty-nine year old driver of the milk lorry, was unveiled on Garrowby Hill.
The principal instigator behind this project was Alun Emlyn-Jones, the crew's
air bomber who missed the flight after being admitted to hospital suffering
from appendicitis. In the years since the tragedy, members of the York Gliding
Club have laid wreaths at the crash site. During the service of dedication,
which was conducted by the Revd Alastair Davies, two Tucano twin-seat trainers
from Linton-on-Ouse passed overhead in aerial salute. To David Thompson of
Eaglescliffe and to Brian Mennell, author of "Wings Over York", I am indebted
for much of the details here imparted.

1663 HCU	**Halifax V**	EB195	**Training**

F/O J R McCormack RNZAF   T/o Rufforth to practice three-engined circuits
F/S B D Bancroft RAAF   and landings, the crew complement comprising of
                               nine. However, one landing was made at Lissett
and soon after taking off, with the outer starboard feathered, the starboard
inner cut and the bomber was forced-landed at 1206 in a field at Harpham Farm,
close to the airfield. By coincidence, F/S Bancroft RAAF was posted to Lissett
and flew a successful tour of operations, gaining an immediate DFC for his outstanding airmanship during a visit to the Trappes marshalling yards, just prior
to "D-Day" (see Bomber Command Losses, Volume 5, page 252 and In Brave Company,
pages 149 and 150).

Note. On 22 August 1943, the Halifax summarised above had been damaged in an
incident at Rufforth (see page 60) at which time it carried the letter "O".

8 Feb 1944	**1663 HCU**	**Halifax V**	DG401 −K	**Training**

P/O J K Mountney   T/o 1005 Rufforth for general training, eight
Sgt E M Fox   airmen making up the crew. Wrecked fifteen
                               minutes later after swinging from the runway
                               following a three-engined landing.

1664 HCU	**Halifax V**	DG247	**Training**

F/S W V Studnick   T/o Dishforth for the pilot's first solo on
                               type. Touched down at 1145, swung and ground
looped with sufficient severity to break the undercarriage.

11 Feb 1944	**1657 HCU**	**Stirling I**	R9277	**Training**

F/O J Lawson   T/o 1115 Stradishall for a flying training
                               exercise but the pilot immediately detected
that his ailerons were not responding. On closing the throttles, the bomber
dropped back onto the runway and with the brakes failing to take effect, it
ran onto a bank of earth, whereupon the port undercarriage collapsed.

1659 HCU	**Halifax II**	W1173	**Training**

F/S H W Barr RCAF   T/o 2303 Topcliffe for night circuit practice.
                               While taxying at 2333, turned rather too sharply
and the aircraft's speed was sufficient to send the Halifax into a ground loop.
Before the situation could be remedied, the wheels folded and the aircraft was
damaged beyond repair.

11–12 Feb	1659 HCU		Halifax V	DK129		Training

11–12 Feb 1944 **1659 HCU** **Halifax V** **DK129** **Training**

P/O E Fairhead RCAF	+
Sgt E G R Gates	inj
F/S J B Fox RCAF	+
Sgt R E Iggulden RCAF	inj
Sgt A E Jennings	+
Sgt A T Tasker	inj
Sgt E T Bennett	inj

T/o 1855 Topcliffe intent on flying a night navigation sortie. Shortly after midnight, the Halifax was reported to be nearing the runway when, at 0007, it suddenly swung through ninety degrees to starboard and crashed 700 yards NW of Rush Farm on the north-north-west side of Maunby, 5 miles south-south-west from Northallerton, Yorkshire.

Apart from Sgt Tasker, who was treated in station sick quarters at Leeming, the injured were admitted to Northallerton Hospital, Sgt Iggulden RCAF and the tail gunner being placed on the "dangerously ill" list. Of the three who perished, both Canadians were interred in Harrogate (Stonefall) Cemetery, Sgt Jennings being taken to Rochdale Cemetery for a private funeral.

12 Feb 1944 **1658 HCU** **Halifax II** **DT585 TT–D** **Training**

W/O J C Kemp	
Sgt W G Lawrie	
Sgt Moore	
Sgt C Carr	+
Sgt L A Lewis	
Sgt H Dale	
Sgt D C Rhodes	

T/o 1857 Riccall tasked for a night cross-country. At 2308, W/O Kemp called "finals" and moments later his aircraft swung to the right and flew into the airfield's windsock. On the ground, the port outer caught fire and the Halifax commenced turning in circles, the fire continuing to take a hold. Unable to cut the engine switches, the pilot ordered his crew to get out but only six were able to do so, the air bomber having become trapped. From the Govan district of Glasgow, thirty-two year old Sgt Carr was buried with full military honours at Harrogate (Stonefall) Cemetery (his service number indicates previous service with the army, certainly prior to 1939). Posted to 35 Squadron, W/O Kemp, along with five of those named above, was posted missing in action during a raid on marshalling yards in France, early in May 1944 (see Bomber Command Losses, Volume 5, page 214).

13 Feb 1944 **1651 HCU** **Stirling I** **BK622 BS–S** **Training**

F/S D S McKenzie RAAF	

T/o 1844 Wratting Common for dual training. Landed 1904 at Downham Market, only to run into an obstruction which smashed the starboard oleo and damaged the bomber beyond worthwhile repair.

14 Feb 1944 **1652 HCU** **Halifax II** **W1005** **Training**

F/O A Hagues	
Sgt J A Griffin	inj
Sgt R E Nash	inj
Sgt E A Elleston	inj
Sgt Norrish	

T/o Marston Moor for a day exercise. At around 1730, with the weather beginning to deteriorate, the Halifax came over the threshold and landed, travelling at high speed. Almost immediately, the bomber veered to port and before F/O Hagues could correct the situation his aircraft lay wrecked after running into a ditch that had been dug a mere ten to fifteen yards from the side of the runway. The injured were treated locally in station sick quarters. An interesting comment has been added to the official accident form, noting that the ditch had been the scene of at least four accidents and, as yet, there had been no response to an application made two years previous to have this foreseen hazard filled in.

15 Feb 1944 **1658 HCU** **Halifax II** **JB919** **Ground**

F/S D C Crawford	

At 1859, while stationary on the runway (at Riccall), struck by a Mosquito XIII which came in, inadvertently, onto the wrong airfield! In the last moments before the accident, the tail gunner of the Halifax (which was preparing for night circuit practice) saw the approaching fighter and warned his pilot over the intercom. In turn, F/S Crawford alerted the control tower, but it was too late to avoid a collision.

264 Sqn **Mosquito XIII** **HK474 PS–** **Training**

F/L A J Baker	inj

T/o Church Fenton for an exercise which, upon nearing its completion, the pilot called over the radio to request lighting assistance for his landing. This was acknowledged but, probably due to poor visibility, he mistook Riccall's lights for those of Church Fenton. In the aftermath of the crash, the Mosquito caught fire and was totally destroyed.

16 Feb
1944

1659 HCU   **Halifax II** **JB929**   **Training**
F/O N J Blake RCAF   T/o 1541 Topcliffe for practice flying, carrying
                                  a standard crew of seven. Landed 1656 but left
the runway and, after running onto soft ground, ground looped. The side forces
imposed were sufficient to cause the undercarriage to collapse.

1663 HCU   **Halifax V**   **EB245**   **Training**
F/S R W Surman   + T/o Rufforth for a cross-country flight but lost
Sgt F C Sheppard   inj power from the port outer. Having feathered the
Sgt Borowski   engine, F/S Surman elected to continue with the
F/S D Fraser RAAF   inj exercise. However, for reasons that are not
Sgt Bennett   entirely clear, he decided to restart the motor,
Sgt Taylor   but was unable to release the propeller from its
Sgt Eastman   feathered position as all the oil had drained
                                  out from the mechanism. With the bomber steadily
losing height, he made for Woolsington airfield (now the site of Newcastle Air-
port) but overshot his approach and crashed at 1320 on land belonging to High
Luddick Farm (some documents quote Low Luddick), Ponteland, 4 miles NNW from
Longbenton, Northumberland. Brought home to Wiltshire, F/S Surman rests in
Wilton Cemetery. Not many years previous, he had attended Bishop Wordsworth
Grammar School, in the shadow of Salisbury Cathedral. In recent years, Bamburgh
Castle Aviation Artefacts Museum has been presented with fragments from this air-
craft, including a propeller blade with a small plaque attached.

19 Feb
1944

1664 HCU   **Halifax V**   **DG385 ZU-D**   **Training**
F/S J J Halterman RCAF   T/o Dishforth for a night cross-country. Came
                                  into land at 2013, flying on three-engines, but
just before touching down the Halifax swung off the centre line and arrived on
the grass. As the bomber skidded along the ground, its undercarriage shattered,
a fire broke out and the crew owe their escape to the smart and efficient work
of the crash and rescue team.

1667 HCU   **Halifax V**   **DG314**   **Training**
Sgt L Hint   T/o 2215 Sandtoft for night flying practice.
                                  At 2245 the Halifax accelerated along the runway
for another circuit of the airfield, when the port tyre exploded. Sgt Hint cut
the throttles and braked hard, by which time his aircraft was on the grass, less
its undercarriage. With only five hours solo on type, two of these being flown
at night, the young pilot was faced with a situation that, within the limits of
his flying experience, he was not equipped to deal with.

22 Feb
1944

1652 HCU   **Halifax II** **V9994**   **Training**
Sgt C Shackleton   T/o 1137 Marston Moor for circuits and landings,
                                  seven crew being aboard. Landed at 1145, but
began to swing; this was checked, only for a second swing to develop and this
time Sgt Shackleton realised he was heading towards a lorry. Immediately, he
closed the throttles but the Halifax continued to turn sharply and seconds later
there was an ominous rendering of metal as the undercarriage gave way. Posted
soon afterwards to 51 Squadron, he failed to return from operations over France
in the April (see Bomber Command Losses, Volume 5, page 173).

1652 HCU   **Halifax II** **JN907**   **Training**
Sgt T G Harrison   T/o 1010 Marston Moor for a bombing exercise.
                                  On return to base at 1205, the Halifax arrived
on the runway with such force that it ballooned back into the air. Before the
pilot could react with the throttles, a gust of wind caught the aircraft and
its port wing tip dug into the ground, resulting in a violent ground loop which
collapsed the wheels. Posted to 578 Squadron, Sgt Harrison was commissioned
(Supplement to the London Gazette, 18 July 1944, with seniority back-dated to
1 June 1944) before being posted missing from Bottrop on 20-21 July 1944 (see
Bomber Command Losses, Volume 5, page 341).

1653 HCU   **Stirling I** **W7570** **-T**   **Training**
Sgt A W Rycroft   T/o 1055 Chedburgh for solo flying, mixed with
                                  circuits and landings, but as the Stirling rose
from the runway, its port tyre burst. Sgt Ryecroft remained airborne for over
ninety minutes before making a wheels up landing, at base, without hurt to
himself or his crew.

22 Feb **1662 HCU** **Halifax II** **BB213** **Training**
1944 P/O N J Fisher T/o 1430 Blyton for a training detail, using
"Gee". Returned to base at 1605, but bounced
quite badly and despite a reasonably good second arrival, the starboard oleo
gave way, damaging the Halifax beyond repair. After converting to Lancasters,
P/O Fisher joined 626 Squadron but failed to return from air operations early
in May (see Bomber Command Losses, Volume 5, page 210). For his parents, the
news came as a double blow to their lives for on 7 July 1940, their other son,
Pte Kenneth George Fisher, died while serving with the Royal Army Medical Corps.
He is buried in Hertfordshire at New Southgate Cemetery.

Note. Allotted to 158 Squadron on 9 August 1942, this Halifax was passed, the
same day, to 1658 Heavy Conversion Unit and survived a serious flying accident
on 27 January 1943. It had been on "1662" strength since 26 November 1943.

23 Feb **1658 HCU** **Halifax II** **R9370** **Training**
1944 P/O J Jenkinson T/o 1105 Riccall for a day training flight,
F/S G R French carrying a crew of nine. Landed safely, but
at 1350, while taxying over a grassed area,
the starboard wheel dropped into a hole and the undercarriage collapsed. It
transpired that the hole had been dug, quite recently, as an aid for drainage,
but for some inexplicable reason it had not been marked as a hazard (though,
apparently, Flying Control staff were aware of its position on the airfield).
F/S French went on to serve with 51 Squadron and was killed on operations in
the early part of May 1944 (see Bomber Command Losses, Volume 5, page 203).

1664 HCU **Halifax V** **DG278 DH-N** **Training**
F/S J V Irvine RCAF T/o Dishforth for day flying, combined with
practice bombing. During the exercise, the
starboard inner suffered a coolant leak and the unit had to be shut down; then,
just before 1105, the starboard outer cut and being unable to maintain height,
F/S Irvine RCAF forced-landed, wheels retracted, in a field at Gale House Farm
on the east side of Newton upon Derwent, 7 miles ESE from centre of York.

24 Feb **1662 HCU** **Halifax II** **BB365** **Training**
1944 Sgt L V Honor T/o 1725 Blyton for a cross-country exercise,
at night. Problems with the inner port engine
obliged the crew to return to base, approaching the runway with the motor in
coarse pitch but before reaching the airfield, the starboard inner failed and
a wheels up landing was skilfully executed at 2245. Sgt Honor's commanding
officer considered the young non-commissioned officer pilot made the correct
decision for, in his opinion, had he tried to go round again, with the wheels
down, fatalities might well have been the consequence.

1664 HCU **Halifax V** **DK146 DH-N** **Training**
F/L J G Broder RCAF + T/o 2108 Dishforth but after climbing steeply
P/O J G Stewart RCAF + to approximately 400 feet, and heading in a
Sgt A P Reid + northerly direction, dived steeply and smashed
Sgt C W Gugins RCAF + into the ground near Rainton, 5 miles NE from
Sgt R W Cottrell + Ripon, Yorkshire. The four Canadians were laid
P/O A I Sinclair RCAF + to rest in Harrogate (Stonefall) Cemetery,
while Sgt Reid lies in Edinburgh (Newington)
Cemetery and Sgt Cottrell is buried at Bristol (Arnos Vale) Cemetery. Their
final flight had lasted for roughly sixty seconds.

25 Feb **1661 HCU** **Stirling III** **LJ529** **Training**
1944 P/O M Sharp + T/o 1850 Winthorpe for a night cross-country.
Sgt A C Brown + While over Scotland, one of the propeller's
F/S P A Lucha + began to windmill. Three attempts were made
WO2 W P Hamilton RCAF + to set the Stirling down on Port Ellen airfield
Sgt K W Radford inj and while making their fourth approach, the
Sgt M H Widdows + bomber crashed at 2137 near the Watch Office.
Sgt G Hamilton inj Initially treated at station sick quarters,
the badly injured tail gunner was transferred
to Hairmyres Hospital at East Kilbride suffering from several fractured ribs.
His compatriot, Sgt Radford was too ill to be moved and he succumbed to his
injuries the next day. WO2 Hamilton RCAF is buried on the Isle of Islay at
Kilarrow New Parish Churchyard. The others who perished were taken to their
home towns.

25 Feb 1944	**1662 HCU**	**Halifax II**	**W7866**	**Training**

Sgt K Walmsley   +   T/o 2144 Blyton for his first night solo, and
Sgt M A Bowles   +   authorised to carry out circuits and landings.
Sgt C T James   +   Eyewitnesses report that the Halifax appeared
Sgt F N Bower   +   to climb quite normally to about 500 feet at
which point it dived steeply and crashed into
a wheat stack, bursting into flames, near Laughton village. All were buried
by private arrangements at their home towns. A careful investigation of the
wreckage could not find any technical defects.

25-26 Feb 1944	**1661 HCU**	**Stirling III**	**EF127**	**Training**

F/S W V Manuel RAAF   +   T/o 1830 Winthorpe for a night cross-country.
Sgt G Davison   +   It would seem likely that the aircraft ran short
F/S C D Bird RAAF   +   of petrol and, shortly before the crash at 0130,
F/S G Macoun RAAF   +   a "Mayday" call was picked up but despite a clear
F/S S E Christie RAAF   +   broadcast response, no acknowledgement was forth-
F/S R J Plath RAAF   inj   coming. Subsequently, the Stirling was found
F/S W I Taylor RAAF   inj   near the village of Edwinstowe at the northern
end of the Sherwood Forest. F/S Plath RAAF was
admitted to Mansfield Hospital, while F/S Taylor RAAF was treated for relatively
minor wounds in Winthorpe's station sick quarters. Sadly, having survived this
major accident, he failed to return from Braunschweig in May 1944 and with the
rest of his 630 Squadron crew, he is commemorated on the Runnymede Memorial
(see Bomber Command Losses, Volume 5, page 235). Of those who perished in the
crash, four lie in Oxford (Botley) Cemetery, while Sgt Davison is buried at
Tanfield (St. Margaret) Churchyard Extension, Stanley in Co. Durham.

28 Feb 1944	**1657 HCU**	**Stirling I**	**W7460**	**Training**

P/O H G Wilkie RNZAF   T/o Stradishall for dual circuit training. At
Sgt W H Mayo   around 1215, with Sgt Mayo at the controls, the
Stirling touched down, whereupon the port under-
carriage indicator light went out and the warning horn sounded. Assuming command,
P/O Wilkie RNZAF elected to overshoot but as the wheels left the ground, the port
light came on, so he cut the throttles and landed further up the runway. While
taxiing towards its dispersal, the wheels suddenly folded. Salvaged, and later
issued to the 8th Parachute Battalion with the serial 4777M applied.

29 Feb 1944	**1664 HCU**	**Halifax V**	**LK643**	**Training**

F/O R F Smith RCAF   T/o Dishforth for a cross-country, with a crew
F/O W G Wright RCAF   complement of eight. While cruising above the
Welsh mountains, the port inner failed and the
crew were unable to feather the propeller. Thus, with their height rapidly
decaying, an emergency landing was made at the nearby airfield of Aberporth,
which was reached at about 1440. Unfortunately, their approach speed was on
the high side and the bomber finished up, wrecked, astride a banked hedge.

	1666 HCU	**Halifax II**	**JD386 -T**	**Training**

P/O J Sigurdson RCAF   +   T/o 1230 Wombleton for a day navigation detail.
Sgt R T G Loughrin   +   It is suggested that, while flying at high
F/O G L Muskett RCAF   +   altitude, the pilot lost control (possibly
F/O J B Eaton RCAF   +   due to rudder stall) for eyewitnesses on the
WO1 J M Healey RCAF   +   ground state that he seemed to be trying to
Sgt F E Wilts RCAF   +   bring the aircraft under control by using the
Sgt P Zayets RCAF   +   throttles. At around 800 feet, however, the
bomber went into a spiral dive from which it
did not recover before hitting the ground, at 1710, near Bridge Farm, Broughton,
some 4 miles ESE from the centre of Scunthorpe, Lincolnshire. All, including
Sgt Loughrin who hailed from Cookstown, Co. Tyrone, in Northern Ireland, were
buried with full military honours in Harrogate (Stonefall) Cemetery. It is
noted that WO1 Healey RCAF came from Greenwich, Connecticut, a town NE of New
York and looking out across Long Island Sound.

Note. Formed way back in the early part of June 1943, 1666 Heavy Conversion
Unit had operated for eight months without any serious mishap. Originally established at Dalton, "1666" moved to Wombleton on 21 October 1943, by which time
it had been titled "Mohawk", this being in keeping with all Royal Canadian Air
Force units; 1664 Heavy Conversion Unit, which began life at Croft ahead of
moving to Dishforth, being "Caribou" (the one exception, however, was "1659"
which did not take a title on joining the Canadians from No. 4 Group).

1 Mar	1661 HCU	Stirling III	EF518 GP-E	Air Test

S/L M Crocker DFC & Bar — T/o 1207 Winthorpe but as the throttles were
W/C B R Hallows — advanced the Stirling veered sharply to port
and ran into a bank of frozen snow, losing its
undercarriage. According to the statistics, entered on the accident card,
neither pilot was overly experienced on type; S/L Crocker is shown as having
fourteen hours behind him, while W/C Hallows, who was occupying the right-hand
seat, is shown as "2,000 hours solo, nil on type". Considering he was the unit's
Chief Flying Instructor, this could well be a misprint. S/L Crocker, meanwhile,
rose to wing commander rank and was killed on operations with 49 Squadron (see
Bomber Command Losses, Volume 5, page 291). His awards had been Gazetted on
15 October 1943 and 18 January 1944 respectively, the former for his devotion
to duty with 57 Squadron and the latter for similar work with 630 Squadron,
which had formed from B Flight of 57 Squadron, at East Kirkby, on 15 November
1943. From his first entry, I deduce he was a flight commander.

3 Mar 1944	1658 HCU	Halifax II	JB797	Training

F/L W G W Warren — T/o 1950 Riccall for night dual circuits and
F/O R A Slater — landings. Ten minutes later, following a very
heavy landing, the exercise was terminated and,
following a technical inspection, it was reported that the starboard mainplane
was fractured to such an extent that repairs would be not be economically viable.

	1659 HCU	Halifax II	R9382 –F	Training

F/O S J Joplin RCAF — T/o Topcliffe for day circuit practice. Upon
crossing the threshold at 1306, with a fairly
strong crosswind blowing at ten degrees off the centreline, the port wing dipped
and the Halifax touched down on one wheel. Before F/O Joplin RCAF could take any
corrective measures, his aircraft was on the grass and damaged beyond repair. On
19 July 1944, now serving with 420 Squadron, he was detailed for a fighter
affiliation exercise, only to crash within minutes of take off (see Bomber
Command Losses, Volume 5, page 339).

	1666 HCU	Lancaster II	DS650 –P	Training

P/O R G Calder RCAF + T/o 1845 Wombleton tasked for a night cross-
Sgt R Bell + country. Presumed to have lost control, in
WO2 W W Campbell RCAF + cloud, and broke up as it plunged earthwards
Sgt J Simms RCAF + at 2200. Search and recovery teams located
WO1 F J Leech RCAF + the wreckage in The Cheviots, a mile-and-a-half
Sgt J Speight + east of the Catcleugh Reservoir which borders
Sgt R C Gibbs + the bleak A68 road snaking through Redesdale
Forest and on towards the Scottish borders.
Three of the four RCAF airmen were brought to Harrogate (Stonefall) Cemetery
but their skipper, who came from Kenora in Ontario, had married Elizabeth
McGregor Fraser Calder of Edinburgh and he rests in this city at Morningside
Cemetery. The others who died were claimed by their next of kin. This was
the unit's first Lancaster loss since absorbing 1679 Heavy Conversion Flight.

4 Mar 1944	1663 HCU	Halifax V	DK179 OO-L	Training

P/O L G J King — T/o 1335 Rufforth for general training, during
Sgt Hammond — which the Halifax flew into a very heavy snow
P/O J W Symington inj shower. Thus, at 1720, having descended to a
P/O Watson — thousand feet, the port outer began to spew out
Sgt J Stewart inj clouds of smoke, tinged with flames. Feathered,
Sgt J G Ormiston inj the fire went out but by this time P/O King was
Sgt Grenfell — experiencing severe handling problems and his
situation was not improved when, upon regaining
the airfield circuit, similar symptoms prevailed from the inner port. Although
downwind, the crew decided to land as quickly as possible, the undercarriage
being promptly lowered. However, as the bomber turned towards the runway,
both starboard engines commenced smoking and the port wing dropped. With
the control column to starboard and pulled hard back, the Halifax thumped
into a field on the perimeter of Rufforth. Sgt Stewart was admitted to Mayburn
Military Hospital, while his two less seriously hurt companions were treated in
station sick quarters. An examination of the badly buckled aircraft revealed
snow blocking the air intakes of the inner port and outer starboard motors,
while the port outer had lost most of its coolant. In the circumstances, the
crew (and P/O King in particular) had performed extremely well in getting the
bomber down without any fatalities.

7 Mar	1662 HCU	Halifax II	HR657	Training

7 Mar
1944

1662 HCU   **Halifax II** **HR657**   **Training**

F/O Z Ingling PAF   +   T/o 1800 Blyton for a night navigation detail,
Sgt B Kot PAF   +   the crew having being attached from 300 Squadron
F/O K Lenartowicz PAF   +   of the Polish Air Force. Collided over the
F/O H J Jarnicki PAF   +   Mission bombing range, at 2350, with another
Sgt G Liskiewicz PAF   +   Halifax (see the next summary for details),
Sgt A Loksza PAF   +   both machines crashing between Graizelound and
Sgt B Machulak PAF   +   Haxey, 11 miles SW of Scunthorpe, Lincolnshire.
                                F/O Ingling PAF was taken to Solihull in
Warwickshire but his six fellow countrymen lie in Newark-upon-Trent Cemetery.

1667 HCU   **Halifax V** **EB184 GG-D**   **Training**

Sgt P A Street   +   T/o 1835 Sandtoft for night flying and lost in
Sgt H Russon   +   the circumstances described above. F/O Bayer of
Sgt A Fox   +   the Royal Canadian Air Force was buried with
F/O E G Bayer RCAF   +   full military honours at Harrogate (Stonefall)
Sgt H W Green   +   Cemetery, while the others were taken to their
Sgt L F Woods   +   home towns (in the case of Sgt Henderson, this
Sgt J W Henderson   +   entailed a road, rail and sea journey to Walls
Sgt W N Farrell   +   Parish Churchyard, Zetland in the Shetlands).

8 Mar
1944

1653 HCU   **Stirling I** **W7532**   **Training**

F/S A L Dickison RNZAF   T/o Chedburgh (crew No. 53, course No. 12) for
P/O J A Lees   for a mixture of dual and solo flying. Crash-
Sgt R Heslop   landed 1325 at Newmarket with a defective under-
W/O L F J Wyeth   carriage (it had failed to lock in the "down"
P/O T N Wilkes   position). A little over a week later, all
Sgt Wooley   would be involved in a similar mishap.
Sgt J R Lee RCAF

9 Mar
1944

1667 HCU   **Halifax V** **DJ998 GG-E**   **Training**

F/O S Burton DFC   +   T/o 1330 Sandtoft for dual circuits and landings
P/O E J Patterson RNZAF   +   but only five minutes had elapsed when the
Sgt G R Marshall   +   Halifax spun in from 700 feet, bursting into
Sgt R G Williams   +   flames as it impacted at Belton, roughly 7 miles
Sgt J MacMillan-Clark   +   west-south-west from Scunthorpe, Lincolnshire.
Sgt D St. Clair   +   Four were buried under military arrangements at
Sgt D R W Hall   +   Harrogate (Stonefall) Cemetery, while the others
Sgt A Forsyth   +   were conveyed to their home towns. F/O Burton
                                had flown a tour of operations with 625 Squadron
and promulgation of his DFC had appeared in the London Gazette on 21 January 1944

10 Mar
1944

1659 HCU   **Halifax II** **BB303**   **Training**

P/O J Y J Cote RCAF   inj   T/o Topcliffe for practice in three-engined
F/S J L Asselin RCAF   inj   flying, the crew comprising of pilot, wireless
Sgt J P E Leduc RCAF   inj   operator, three air gunners and one (Sgt Germain)
Sgt K E Jenkins   inj   whose aircrew category is not known. With the
Sgt S G B Lavoie RCAF   inj   inner starboard feathered, the Halifax overshot
Sgt Germain   at 1800, after which P/O Cote RCAF decided to
                                 restart the motor. While attempting to do so,
a wing dropped and the bomber crash-landed, in a field, some 400 yards W from
Hunter's Hill Farm and a mile W of Danby Wiske, 4 miles NNW of Northallerton,
Yorkshire. A fire broke out soon afterwards and the aircraft was destroyed.

12 Mar
1944

1651 HCU   **Stirling III** **LK520**   **Ground**

                                Caught fire at 1245, while being refuelled,
at Wratting Common. Before the flames could be brought under control, a certain
amount of motor transport equipment had been lost.

12-13 Mar
1944

1660 HCU   **Stirling III** **EF463 TV-D Bar**   **Training**

F/O B K Purdie RAAF   T/o 2235 Swinderby for conversion training, at
F/O Hornsby   night. Returned to base with the port outer
Sgt Frost   engine unserviceable, landing heavily on its
F/S Hind   starboard wheel at 0200. Immediately, the
F/O Papworth   aircraft lurched back into the air, swung to
W/O Needham   the left and hit the ground for a second time,
F/S Schmerl   the force being sufficient to collapse the
Sgt Beaver   wheels.

| 14 Mar 1944 | **1652 HCU** | **Halifax II** | **W1276 GV-F** | **Training** |

F/S D O Thomas RCAF — T/o 2230 Marston Moor for night flying, but swung off the runway, the undercarriage being raised in order to prevent the Halifax from running beyond the perimeter fence. Posted to 640 Squadron, F/S Thomas RCAF failed to make it back from Hasselt in mid-May 1944 (see Bomber Command Losses, Volume 5, page 224).

| | **1652 HCU** | **Halifax II** | **JN887** | **Air Test** |

F/O F Williams DFM — inj
F/S K V Browne RAAF — inj
P/O J C Harris-Ward DFC — inj
F/S Patterson

T/o Marston Moor with a crew of four, combining the air test with local flying. While cruising at 2,000 feet the inner starboard shed its propeller and struck the fuselage, severely injuring P/O Harris-Ward. Moments later, the starboard outer cut, leaving F/O Williams no option but to forced-land. This was achieved at 1015, the bomber being put down in Haverah Park, Beckwithshaw, three miles SW from the centre of Harrogate, Yorkshire. The two pilots were admitted to Harrogate and District General Hospital, both having sustained second degree burns, while their flight engineer was taken to Northallerton Hospital. F/O Williams had gained his award with 78 Squadron, details being Gazetted on 10 September 1943. On making a good recovery, he joined 640 Squadron and was killed in action in late May 1944 (see Bomber Command Losses, Volume 5, page 247). His Australian pupil went to 158 Squadron and distinguished himself during a pre "D-Day" visit to the Trappes marshalling yards. Subsequently, the London Gazette for 7 November 1944, published details of a DFC awarded to this gallant Australian and nine days later, the Australia Gazette also carried the news of his decoration.

Note. It is indicated that P/O J C Harris-Ward was decorated with a Distinguished Flying Cross, his service number being 53998. Such a number suggests he had been commissioned from the ranks of the regular air force and, indeed, the Supplement to the London Gazette, published on 9 November 1943, shows a W/O Joseph Clifford Harris-Ward (566800) being commissioned in the General Duties Branch as a "Pilot Officer on probation" with seniority back-dated to 24 August 1943; his service number changing to 158284. However, his non-commissioned service number, 566800, indicates that he joined the service, pre-war, as an aircraft apprentice and I would have expected his commissioned number to have been five digits, similar to that shown in the second line of this footnote. On 15 February 1944, the London Gazette has an entry for P/O Joseph Clifford Harris-Ward (158284) being decorated with a Distinguished Flying Cross, his unit being annotated as 51 Squadron. Then, the Supplement issued on 14 March 1944, shows a J C Harris-Ward (53998) as being promoted from pilot officer to flying officer with effect from 25 February 1944, but no award has been appended against his name. However, the Supplement issued on 7 December 1945, identifies a J C Harris-Ward DFC (53998) being promoted from flying officer to flight lieutenant rank, effective 25 August 1945. Although I cannot be one hundred percent certain, I very much suspect that John Clifford Harris-Ward (158284) and J C Harris-Ward (53998) are one and the same person.

| | **1660 HCU** | **Stirling III** | **EF120** | **Training** |

F/S L L Pemberton RAAF
Sgt L Peace
Sgt J Orr
Sgt L W Bryan
F/O A Clarkson
Sgt J H Morrison
Sgt L Hilder
Sgt I Bowley

T/o 1315 Swinderby for conversion training. Descended from 11,000 feet, with the starboard outer feathered, but overshot the base runway and crash-landed 1615 near Norton Disney, 9 miles south-west from Lincoln. After converting to Lancasters, most went to 106 Squadron and were killed in action on 29 July 1944 (see Bomber Command Losses, Volume 5, page 361).

| | **1662 HCU** | **Halifax II** | **W7711** | **Training** |

P/O F J Kelly RAAF
P/O F W Baker

T/o 1903 Blyton for dual flying practice, at night. Landed 2123, at Wittering, with a burst starboard tyre and wrecked as the aircraft swung off the runway.

| 15 Mar 1944 | **1662 HCU** | **Halifax II** | **W1212** | **Training** |

Sgt D C Barton — T/o 2025 Blyton for a night exercise but swung slightly and as the wheel slipped off the runway, so it fell into a drain and was promptly torn off, damaging the Halifax beyond reasonable repair. First operated by 103 Squadron and later by 51 Squadron and, prior to "1662", 1654 and 1668 HCUs, this aircraft had flown 240.10 hours.

16 Mar	1664 HCU	Halifax V	DG295	Training

16 Mar
1944

| 1664 HCU | | Halifax V | DG295 | Training |

P/O F R Dionne RCAF   +   T/o 0942 Dishforth for local flying and an
Sgt J A Lang   +   exercise in low-level bombing over the Strenshall
F/S R A Pelletier RCAF   +   ranges. At 1012, the aircraft emerged from cloud
F/O R A Walld RCAF   +   and flew into the ground 800 yards E of Black
WO1 A J P Normandeau RCAF   +   Averham Farm near Flaxton, 8 miles NE of York.
Sgt J L P D Carrier RCAF   +   The six RCAF members of crew were laid to rest
Sgt J J O Cournoyer RCAF   +   in Harrogate (Stonefall) Cemetery, while their
flight engineer, Sgt Lang, was taken to Scotland
and interred in Dumbarton Cemetery. Sgt Carrier RCAF had been quite badly hurt
in December 1943, while training at 23 Operational Training Unit (see Bomber
Command Losses, Volume 7, page 266). WO1 Normandeau´s brother, Sgt Paul Emery
Normandeau RCAF, died from injuries sustained on 20 August 1944, when he fell
through a skylight at the Knights of Columbus Club in Leinster Terrace, London.
At the time of this most unfortunate accident, he was undergoing training at
22 Operational Training Unit; he is buried in Brookwood Military Cemetery.

| 1664 HCU | Halifax V | EB206 | Training |

Sgt H R Collver RCAF   T/o 0946 Dishforth for general training, the
crew of seven escaping unhurt when the Halifax
swung on landing at 1014, smashing its undercarriage as a result.

17 Mar
1944

| 1653 HCU | Stirling I | BK613 | -T | Training |

F/S A L Dickison RNZAF   T/o Chedburgh (crew No. 53, course No. 12) for
P/O J A Lees   night circuit practice, possibly being briefed
Sgt R Heslop   to use Stradishall for it was here that the
W/O L F J Wyeth   Stirling landed, at 2100, only to swing off
P/O T N Wilkes   the runway and lose its undercarriage. It will
Sgt Wooley   be recalled that F/S Dickinson RNZAF had been
Sgt J R Lee RCAF   involved in a similar mishap nine days previous
(see page 94) and following this latest accident
he was posted for other flying duties. By the onset of winter, Sgt Lee RCAF was
serving with 424 Squadron, losing his life during operations to Osnabrück early
in December (see Bomber Command Losses, Volume 5, page 505).

18 Mar
1944

| 1657 HCU | Stirling I | W7633 | -Z | Training |

F/O J E Heywood   +   T/o Stradishall for dual night circuit practice.
Sgt P Sears   +   Seven circuits were successfully flown and it
Sgt S Greig   +   was during the eighth that the Stirling came
F/S A H Lister RNZAF   +   down, at 2246, near the village of Little Thurlow.
Sgt F E R Evans   +   A local lady, Enid Gridley, managed to drag a
Sgt K Stubbs   +   terribly injured Sgt Dacre away from the remains
Sgt J H Dacre   inj   of his rear turret but, sadly, he died from his
wounds on 4 April; he was nineteen years of age.
Apart from F/S Lister RNZAF who was taken to Cambridge City Cemetery, all were
buried under private arrangements at their home towns.

| 1662 HCU | Halifax II | DT485 | Training |

Sgt A E Slade   T/o 1130 Blyton for a training detail that
involved eight members of crew. For several
hours, all went well but shortly after 1405, the Halifax overshot the runway
and the flight engineer reported he was unable to get the main wheels to retract. With full flap on, the bomber sank rapidly and a forced-landing was
made near Blyton village. It is thought a lock formed in the hydraulic lines,
rendering the system unserviceable. On completion of his training, Sgt Slade
reported for duty with 576 Squadron and had been commissioned by the time he
was reported missing in mid-May 1944 (see Bomber Command Losses, Volume 5,
page 226).

| 1662 HCU | Halifax V | DG270 | Training |

F/O R J Bunter   T/o 2048 Blyton for dual circuits and landings,
F/O D A Josey   at night. With the trainee pilot at the controls
the Halifax touched down at 2055 but as he had
misjudged his rate of descent, the aircraft ballooned back into the air. At
this point, his instructor took over the controls but as he went to open the
throttles, so the flying speed decayed and the bomber stalled onto the runway,
bursting the port tyre. Moments later, the crew were clambering from the
wreckage of their Halifax, now lying forlorn and without an undercarriage.

18–19 Mar	1667 HCU	Halifax V	EB149 GG–C	Training

1944

P/O J Hetherington	inj	T/o 1949 Sandtoft for a night cross-country.
Sgt D C Orme	inj	While in flight, the starboard outer overheated
F/O W B Handy RCAF	+	and was shut down. On regaining Sandtoft, and
Sgt R C A Rollo RCAF	+	shortly before 0024, the pilot called "funnels"
Sgt D A Edwards	+	and was observed making a normal approach,
Sgt E Crossthwaite	+	albeit with the troublesome engine feathered.
Sgt E R H Hynes	inj	Then, to the dismay of those watching from the
		ground, the Halifax flew into some pylons and

crashed, heavily, near Crowle, about 9 miles WNW from Scunthorpe, Lincolnshire.
Rescue services were quickly on the scene and the injured were taken, without
delay, to Scunthorpe War Memorial Hospital. Of those who died, the two RCAF
airmen were taken to Harrogate (Stonefall) Cemetery, while Sgt Edwards and
Sgt Crossthwaite lie in Tywyn Cemetery and Preston (New Hall Lane) Cemetery
respectively. On regaining his fitness, P/O Hetherington was posted to nearby
Lindholme and 1656 Heavy Conversion Unit; tragically, he was killed (along with
his entire crew) towards the end of May in another night flying accident. His
flight engineer, Sgt Orme, eventually joined 166 Squadron and died in action
in mid-November 1944 (see Bomber Command Losses, Volume 5, page 486).

21 Mar	1661 HCU	Stirling III	LJ533	Training

1944

P/O L N Simpkin	T/o 1409 Winthorpe for day training, only for
	the port outer engine to fail. Despite their

best efforts, the crew could not feather the propeller and, thus, forced-landed
near the airfield, at 1524, striking a tree in the process. Not long after
joining 49 Squadron, P/O Simpkin's Lancaster was one of the thirty-eight that
were lost from the Wesseling raid on 21–22 June 1944 (see Bomber Command Losses,
Volume 5, pages 290 to 296).

21–22 Mar	1664 HCU	Halifax V	LK930	Training

1944

Sgt H R Collver RCAF	inj	T/o 1905 Dishforth for a night navigation detail
Sgt R I Pym	inj	in the course of which the port inner failed and
F/O Pilkington		resisted all attempts to feather. Partially
Sgt Peel		abandoned before crash-landing at 0050 astride
W/O Loucus		the Scarcliffe to Polterton road in Derbyshire.
Sgt W A R Andrew RCAF	+	The injured were removed to Mansfield General
Sgt A C Starnes RCAF	+	Hospital and station sick quarters at Worksop
		respectively. The two air gunners are buried

in Harrogate (Stonefall) Cemetery. It was Sgt Collver's second accident in
less than a week (see page 96).

22 Mar	1653 HCU	Stirling I	R9280 A3–Z	Training

1944

Sgt N J J Dobson	T/o 2140 Chedburgh (crew No. 57, course No. 13)
Sgt D B Sheehan	for the pilot's first night solo on type, but
Sgt A Walker	as the bomber picked up speed, the port inner
Sgt L E Amos	started to misfire. Sgt Dobson closed the
Sgt D E Ray	throttles but could not prevent the Stirling
Sgt W Connors	from leaving the runway, whereupon the port
Sgt J D Glaister RCAF	undercarriage was torn from its mountings.
	Apart from Sgt Connors and Sgt Glaister RCAF

(but see Addendum) all were lost during operations to Laon with 90 Squadron
on 22–23 April 1944 (see Bomber Command Losses, Volume 5, page 183).

	1658 HCU	Halifax II	W7865	Training

P/O P T Bath RCAF	+	T/o Riccall for general training. Crashed
Sgt A S Heaton	inj	at 1757 near Cattal Station, just beyond the
Sgt W H W Husband RCAF	inj	village of Kirk Hammerton on the York to
F/O F E Ireland RCAF	inj	Knaresborough railway line and little over
P/O T N W Bissett	inj	two miles NNE from Marston Moor airfield.
Sgt J A Poling RCAF	inj	At least two of the injured were treated at
Sgt R Thorpe	inj	Rufforth's station sick quarters and three
F/O A J Cogbill	inj	were taken to Naburn Military Hospital where
		F/O Cogbill, a member of the flying control

staff, died on arrival. Meanwhile, Sgt Thorpe succumbed to his injuries at
Rufforth; both were claimed by their next of kin, Sgt Thorpe being buried in
Richmond Cemetery, while F/O Cogbill rests at Honington (All Saints) Church-
yard, Warwickshire. P/O Bath RCAF, as expected, was taken to Harrogate
(Stonefall) Cemetery.

22 Mar
1944

1659 HCU **Halifax II R9368** **Training**
P/O J L Webb RCAF T/o 1730 Topcliffe for circuits and landings, the exercise progressing satisfactorily until the port tyre burst as the Halifax accelerated along the runway. P/O Webb RCAF managed to get his aircraft into the air and around the circuit, but on his next arrival at 1743, he was unable to prevent the bomber from swinging quite sharply which in turn led to the undercarriage collapsing.

24 Mar
1944

1656 HCU **Halifax II W1009** **Training**
P/O W C H Munsch T/o 0800 Lindholme for fighter affiliation
P/O D R Tait practice, the crew complement totalling nine.
F/S McLoughlin RAAF Shortly after beginning the detail, P/O Munsch carried out a series of evasive manoeuvres and while doing so took the Halifax into cloud. Momentarily disorientated, he stalled the bomber in a tight turn and upon regaining control, returned to base and landed at around 0900. As a consequence of the stresses and strains imposed upon the airframe, the Halifax was declared a write off. A month later, having being posted to 166 Squadron, P/O Tait was killed on operations (see Bomber Command Losses, Volume 5, page 187).

1656 HCU **Halifax II DT482** **Training**
F/L J E Sanderson DFC + T/o 2047 Lindholme for night circuits and
F/O R H Gardner + landings. At 2112, the Halifax crashed, and
Sgt B J Brawn + burst into flames, at Woodgate Farm near the
Sgt P D Newman + village of Auckley, 6 miles ESE from the centre
Sgt J H Gilbertson RCAF + of Doncaster, Yorkshire. At the Court of Inquiry convened to investigate this awful accident, it was supposed that the most likely cause was a premature raising of the flaps, following an overshoot of the runway. Hamilton born Sgt Gilbertson RCAF, along with F/O Gardner of Leeds and Sgt Newman from Fulham, was buried in Harrogate (Stonefall) Cemetery, while F/L Sanderson and Sgt Brawn rest in their home towns. Between January and September 1943, F/L Sanderson flew at least twenty-six operational sorties with 76 Squadron before being posted at the end of the month to 18 Operational Training Unit. On 25 February 1943, he had survived a very serious crash, shortly after becoming airborne and bound for Nürnberg (see Bomber Command Losses, Volume 4, page 48).

1659 HCU **Halifax II BB305** **Training**
F/O R C Penrose RCAF T/o 1930 Topcliffe briefed for a Bullseye detail but soon after setting forth, both starboard engines failed and at 1935, the Halifax was forced-landed, in a ploughed field, just to the S of Little Ouseburn, Yorkshire.

1659 HCU **Halifax II JD317** **Training**
F/O M S Little RCAF + T/o 1920 Topcliffe similarly tasked. Shortly
F/O J S Beresford RCAF inj before 2330, the Halifax entered the London
Sgt J H MacKenzie RCAF inj Defensive Zone and was hit by anti-aircraft
Sgt N E J Cowan RCAF inj fire. Having ordered his crew to bale out, F/O Little RCAF bravely tried to save his aircraft but crashed at Lodge Farm, Lodge Lane, near Little Chalfont, a couple of miles ESE from Amersham, Buckinghamshire. He is buried in Brookwood Military Cemetery. It was subsequently discovered that the bomber had strayed off course and at the time it was being shot at, it should have been in the vicinity of Bristol.

24-25 Mar
1944

1667 HCU **Halifax V DG293 GG-M** **Training**
Sgt R J B Cann T/o 1945 Sandtoft for a night exercise, during which the port outer failed. Returned to base at 0105 but having touched down safely, ran beyond the flare path and in order to avoid a hangar (that loomed up through the darkness) was swung from its course. Seconds later, it collided with another Halifax, unoccupied and parked on its dispersal pan. Later commissioned, Sgt Cann was nearing the end of his operational tour with 166 Squadron, when his Lancaster was shot down in late July 1944, during a visit to Stuttgart. However, the entire crew got out unscathed, evaded capture and returned home (see Bomber Command Losses, Volume 5, page 352 and 546 for the file identities of their evasion reports).

25 Mar
1944

1667 HCU **Halifax V EB144 -A** **Ground**
Destroyed in the circumstances, shown above.

26 Mar **1651 HCU**   **Stirling I**   **BF385 BS-H**   **Transit**
1944   Sgt W Holmes   T/o 2305 Shipdham intent on returning to
                                     Wratting Common, but swung badly and ran
up against a large block of concrete. Active as a military airfield from
the mid-summer of 1942 until June 1945, Shipdham was used, principally, by
the 44th Bomb Group of the United States Army Air Force, being equipped all
the while with B-24 Liberators.

1662 HCU   **Halifax II**   **W1246**   **Training**
F/L W G Cole   T/o 1645 Blyton for dusk and night training.
P/O W J D Charles RCAF   Six hours later, and while accelerating down
                                     the runway, the port tyre burst and before
either pilot could react the impetus took the Halifax off the runway, whereupon
the undercarriage folded and the bomber was damaged beyond repair. Posted to
103 Squadron, P/O Charles RCAF was shot down over Germany by a night-fighter
and together with his crew he is buried in the Reichswald Forest War Cemetery
(see Bomber Command Losses, Volume 5, page 237).

27 Mar **1659 HCU**   **Halifax II**   **W1112**   **Training**
1944   P/O G B Ellis   T/o 1003 Topcliffe for circuits and landings
       P/O G A Wolstencroft RCAF   but both port engines cut and the Halifax ran
                                     onto soft ground, losing its undercarriage
in the process. Tasked to bomb railway yards at Villeneuve, a month after
"D-Day", P/O Wolstencroft's 433 Squadron Halifax was shot down; happily, he
survived, albeit as a prisoner of war (see Bomber Command Losses, Volume 5,
page 317).

1667 HCU   **Halifax V**   **DG305 GG-D**   **Training**
Sgt D R Harkin   T/o 0023 Sandtoft for night circuit practice
                                   but swung from the runway, the undercarriage
                                   collapsing as a result.

28 Mar **1651 HCU**   **Stirling I**   **EF388 QQ-G**   **Training**
1944   Sgt J Thornton   T/o 1930 Wratting Common for a night cross-
       Sgt Brayley   country. Returned to base at 2330, only to
       Sgt Killen   swing on touch down and run into a hut, sited
       Sgt Rose   near the bomb dump. The hut was demolished
       Sgt Wilcox   and the Stirling was damaged sufficiently to
       Sgt Peters   warrant its write off.
       Sgt Thomas

29 Mar **1652 HCU**   **Halifax II**   **DT736**   **Training**
1944   F/S K J Caladine RAAF   +   T/o 1958 Marston Moor for a Bullseye sortie.
       Sgt W H Hickson   +   While over Scotland, a blade broke away from
       F/S E L Reay RAAF   +   the outer starboard engine and, out of control,
       F/S G A Gooderham RAAF   +   the bomber came down at 2218 to crash near
       F/S P Sinclair RAAF   +   Dundonald, 5 miles WSW from Kilmarnock in
       F/S R A Grosvenor RAAF   +   Ayrshire. The bodies of the six Australians
       F/S R C Walker RAAF   +   were recovered to Harrogate (Stonefall) Cemetery
                                     and that of Sgt Hickson to Southend-on-Sea
                                   (Sutton Road) Cemetery.

30 Mar **1662 HCU**   **Halifax II**   **W7846**   **-B2**   **Ground**
1944   P/O G J R Clark   While taxiing at Blyton, at 0029, the aircraft's
                                     Aldis Lamp failed and moments later the Halifax
lay wrecked after running off the perimeter track and into a ditch. Not long
after this unfortunate incident, P/O Clark departed on posting to 166 Squadron
and was killed in action on 12 May 1944 (see Bomber Command Losses, Volume 5,
page 222).

1664 HCU   **Halifax V**   **DK127**   **Training**
Sgt E J Davies   T/o 1900 Dishforth for a long cross-country,
                                   at night, combined with bombing practice. While
flying at 18,000 feet, both engines on the port wing failed and though Sgt Davies
was able to reach Wrexham airfield, he could not get the main wheels down before
being obliged to forced-land, at 2145. No one was hurt, but following a technical
evaluation of the airframe, it was decided that no repairs would be sanctioned.

30 Mar	1664 HCU	Halifax V	DK268	Training

30 Mar 1944 — **1664 HCU** — **Halifax V** DK268 — **Training**
F/O W W MacKeracher RCAF inj — T/o 0955 Dishforth for a combined air-to-air
Sgt R Sharrock inj — firing detail and bombing practice. Not long
Sgt J D Reid RCAF inj — after becoming airborne, an engine failed and
F/O L S Cruikshank RCAF inj — the crew headed for home. At 1045, having
F/S J J Woodstock RCAF — misjudged his approach, F/O MacKeracher RCAF
Sgt F J McLeod RCAF inj — attempted to go round again but flew into a
Sgt E F Graham RCAF inj — tree on the airfield's SW boundary and crashed
at Marton-le-Moor.

31 Mar 1944 — **1656 HCU** — **Halifax II** R9435 — **Training**
P/O R H Jopling RAAF — T/o 0443 Lindholme for night conversion training
and written off fifteen minutes later after
swinging through one hundred and eighty degrees on touch down.

1657 HCU — **Stirling I** N6104 –B — **Training**
F/O C G Washer RNZAF — T/o 2030 Stradishall for night circuit training
Sgt H Medlor — during which the weather deteriorated and before
Sgt J Andrew — the crew could get down, icing caused the port
Sgt K Burmester — inner to fail. Abandoned, and left to crash at
Sgt J Casey — 2115 about a mile N of Cavendish, 12 miles SSW
Sgt D Cooper — from Bury St. Edmunds, Suffolk.
Sgt J Mercier

1667 HCU — **Halifax V** DG307 — **Training**
Sgt D R Harkin — T/o 2248 Sandtoft for solo night flying, five
crew being aboard. Five successful circuits
were accomplished but after arriving on the runway for the sixth time, the
Halifax swung violently and ended up on the grass with a broken undercarriage
(see the previous page for an earlier accident involving Sgt Harkin, who came
from Irish Republic).

1 Apr 1944 — **1656 HCU** — **Halifax II** JP190 — **Training**
F/O R E Ross MBE MM + — T/o 2015 Lindholme for a night navigation
Sgt C Farthing + — exercise, two flight engineers being carried.
Sgt B A Bell + — At approximately 2330, the Halifax flew into
F/S P Burchell + — high ground in the vicinity of Muckle Knowe in
F/O J Birkett + — Roxburghshire, Scotland. As the bomber struck
Sgt H W Simpson + — the hillside the night sky was illuminated by
Sgt H Smith + — flames as debris was scattered over a wide
Sgt J G Hinder + — area. All now rest in various cemeteries across
the English counties. As a warrant officer,
F/O Ross had been appointed an MBE (Military Division) in the New Year's Honours
List published in the London Gazette on 1 January 1941. On 1 September 1943, his
appointment to a commission was promulgated, seniority being back-dated to
22 July 1943. F/O Birkett was the son of the Revd Alvan Birkett and Mabel
Emily Birkett, residing at Chesham Bois Rectory in Buckinghamshire circa 1961.

1667 HCU — **Halifax V** DG355 –G — **Training**
F/O B A Templeman-Rourke — T/o 1804 Sandtoft but swung off the runway,
P/O G R Davies — the port main undercarriage being broken as
a consequence of the pilot's over correction.

6- 7 Apr 1944 — **1666 HCU** — **Lancaster II** DS607 — **Training**
P/O McIntyre RCAF — T/o 1935 Wombleton for a night cross-country,
in moonlight conditions, seven crew aboard.
Late in the exercise, the hydraulic system failed and the emergency system was
employed to lower the undercarriage and flaps, though in respect of the latter,
only ten degrees could be attained. Thus, at 0130, P/O McIntyre RCAF tried to
land at Topcliffe, but being dissatisfied with his approach he elected to go
round again. However, the Lancaster was barely above the ground when its
port wheel clattered against a disused gun-pit (sited about 150 yards from
the end of the runway) tearing off the oleo. Completing the circuit, his
next arrival, not surprisingly, resulted in a violent ground loop which inflicted substantial damage on the mainplanes. It was, however, a very favoured
bomber and, in the words of its maintenance crew, "they have other aircraft far
better suited for the scrap heap than the one lost". Principally equipped with
Halifaxes, this, plus one lost early in March (see page 93), were the only
examples of this Mark written off by "1666" during 1944.

8 Apr	1667 HCU	Halifax V	DG386	Training

8 Apr 1944 — **1667 HCU** — **Halifax V** **DG386** — **Training**

P/O D W Lee RNZAF   inj T/o 0120 Sandtoft for the pilot's first night solo on type, all proceeding well for the first fifteen minutes of the exercise. Then, at 0135, having taken off and climbed to 600 feet, a tappet in the outer port engine fractured and, momentarily, the Halifax teetered out of control, this being regained by stopping the starboard outer. The bomber then turned, slowly, to port and forced-landed in a field, at Epworth, 8 miles SW of Scunthorpe, Lincolnshire.

9 Apr 1944 — **1658 HCU** — **Halifax II** **W7927 TT-R** — **Training**

Sgt C G Grubb   T/o Riccall for a solo cross-country, at night, with a crew complement of eight. While cruising at 17,000 feet, the starboard outer failed and was feathered, height being lost to around 15,000 feet. Not long afterwards, the oil temperature reading for the outer port engine rose and this motor, too, was stopped and feathered. Unable to maintain height, Sgt Grubb headed for Fairwood Common airfield, Glamorgan, but in the final moments of his approach, another aircraft flew into his path. With the undercarriage down and his speed decaying alarmingly, he managed to restart the outer port but the engine ran so roughly that it was doubtful if he was gaining any significant amount of power. As he warned his crew to brace themselves for a crash-landing, so his aircraft flew into a building (near the airfield); miraculously, no one was too badly hurt (see page 87 for details of a previous accident involving Sgt Grubb and for notes on his subsequent fate).

10 Apr 1944 — **1653 HCU** — **Stirling I** **BF397 -K** — **Training**

F/L A M F Alexander RNZAF   T/o Chedburgh (crew No. 80, course No. 17) for
F/O S G W Stokes   circuits and landings. Bounced on landing at
Sgt R A Partridge   circa 1450, with the trainee pilot at the
F/O W A Airey   controls, and promptly began to swing in the
F/O A M Rattray RCAF   prevailing crosswind. F/L Alexander RNZAF took
Sgt E R Bradbury   over but was unable to check the swing before
Sgt J F Wilson RCAF   making contact with the runway for a second time,
Sgt E G Cooper   whereupon the wheels folded. Over the next three hours, salvage workers concentrated on clearing the runway of the wreck.

11 Apr 1944 — **1661 HCU** — **Stirling III** **LK456 GP-T** — **Training**

P/O J D'A Langlois RCAF + T/o 1624 Winthorpe for practice bombing, but
Sgt T Dunn + crashed five minutes later, on the airfield,
Sgt L Frisby + following an engine fire. The two RCAF officers
Sgt W J C Lowin + were taken to Harrogate (Stonefall) Cemetery,
F/O G A Charlesworth RCAF + while Sgt Robertson and Sgt Nicholl, both from
Sgt E W Buckley + Glasgow, plus Sgt Thomson, were interred at
Sgt J M Robertson + Oxford (Botley) Cemetery. The others were
Sgt R Nicholl + claimed by their next of kin.
Sgt W B Thomson +

12 Apr 1944 — **1651 HCU B Flt** — **Stirling I** **N3766 -Z** — **Training**

Sgt T Wilson   T/o 1145 Wratting Common for day training, seven crew aboard. Touched down at 1512, bounced and landed firmly, running on for about 500 yards before suddenly swerving off the runway and ending up amongst trees bordering the airfield. At the time of the mishap, in which no one was hurt, the wind was approximately twenty-five degrees across the duty runway but was quite light; five to eight miles per hour.

1654 HCU — **Stirling III** **LJ450 UG-F** — **Training**

F/S J J G Nicholson + T/o Wigsley for a long night cross-country,
Sgt Durham   combined with bombing practice over the ranges
Sgt J E Lowe + at Bassingham, south of Lincoln. While in the
Sgt G J Lewis + range area, intercepted and shot down at 0125 by
Sgt Howell   an enemy intruder, thought to have been a Bf 410
Sgt Rowland   from II./KG51. F/S Nicholson, who is buried in
Sgt Hamilton   Thorney (St. Helen) Churchyard, had married Joan
Sgt K L MacFarlane + Nicholson of Witbank in the Transvaal. His rear gunner, who rests at Cambridge City Cemetery, came from Chisamba in Northern Rhodesia. Private funerals were arranged for Sgt Lowe and Sgt Lewis at Wellingborough (Finedon) Cemetery and Rhondda (Ferndale) Cemetery respectively. The survivors escaped by parachute. This was the unit's first major incident since 11 November 1943 (see page 74).

13 Apr 1944	**1663 HCU**	**Halifax V**	**DG353 OO–J**	**Training**

F/S P S Wade RAAF — T/o 1451 Rufforth for day flying practice. Landed at 1701 but while slowing down, drifted slightly to port. F/S Wade RAAF attempted to correct the situation but over compensated and the Halifax swung sixty degrees to starboard and lost its main undercarriage. Posted to 76 Squadron, he was killed during the Aachen raid on 24-25 May 1944 (see Bomber Command Losses, Volume 5, page 240).

	1663 HCU	**Halifax V**	**EB204 OO–G**	**Training**
	F/O R S Ewart RCAF	+		
	Sgt J Illingworth	+		
	F/O R C P Medhurst RCAF	+		
	Sgt S Oates	+		
	Sgt F C Pinfold	+		
	F/S H F Owen	inj		

T/o 0049 Rufforth for a night exercise only to crash within a minute, amongst trees, and broke up on land belonging to Mr A Timms near Healaugh on the SW side of the airfield and in line with the duty runway. The two Canadians were buried in Harrogate (Stonefall) Cemetery, while the others who perished were taken to their home towns. At least four had been attached to "1663" from 158 Squadron. Eye-witnesses report that the Halifax appeared to have sufficient flying speed and the most likely reason for the crash lay in premature retraction of the flaps, causing a sudden loss of the all important height.

	1667 HCU	**Halifax V**	**DG351**	**–U**	**Training**

P/O C D McIvor RCAF — T/o Sandtoft for a general training detail, the crew being nine in total. While in flight, the port outer failed and the engine was feathered and on return to base, P/O McIvor had great difficulty in aligning his aircraft with the runway. Consequently, a series of overshoots were made and while going round for a third time, he was unable to maintain height and a forced-landing followed at 1726, straight ahead, without hurt to his crew.

15 Apr 1944	**1664 HCU**	**Halifax V**	**EB203**	**Training**
	T/S P Watkins USAAC	+		
	Sgt K D Holden	+		
	F/O H A Wallace RCAF	+		
	F/S H L Muisiner RCAF	+		
	WO1 J Huddleston RCAF	+		
	Sgt L J Cull RCAF	+		
	Sgt C E Lovett RCAF	+		

T/o 2010 Dishforth for an evening cross-country. On return to base, the crew encountered failing visibility and while attempting to land, crashed at 2325 setting fire to an old haystack on the west-north-west side of Bishop Monkton and near the road leading from the village to Ripon, some three miles distant. The land on which the aircraft came down belonged to Hungate Farm, farmed by the Lowther family who left the area in the late 1940s. It is likely that Top Sergeant Watkins USAAC was buried with the five RCAF members of his crew in Harrogate (Stonefall) Cemetery. Twenty year old Sgt Holden was taken to Tyldesley Cemetery. It is further noted that WO1 Huddleston RCAF and the navigator, F/S Muisiner RCAF, were Americans, hailing from Granta Pass, Oregon and Kane, Pennsylvania respectively. Both air gunners were aged eighteen.

	1664 HCU	**Halifax V**	**EB205**	**Training**
	F/O D R Holloway RCAF	inj		
	Sgt H G C Powell	+		
	F/O S H J Pearce RCAF	inj		
	F/O S W Jobson RCAF	+		
	F/O J H Smith RCAF	inj		
	Sgt J W Tynski RCAF	inj		
	Sgt K French RCAF	+		
	Mr A G Stone	+		
	Mrs C Stone	+		
	Mr J McNulty	+		

T/o Dishforth similarly tasked, returning to base circa 2300 when the local weather conditions were deteriorating fast. F/O Holloway RCAF over-shot his approach and while climbing out for a second attempt, he caught sight of the lights for nearby Topcliffe. He was, it seems, having trouble with the port engines and had ordered his crew to take up their crash positions, Thus, he decided to try and land at Topcliffe, rather than fly round the local circuit. Sadly, his decision ended in tragic failure for at 2305 he overshot the Topcliffe runway and smashed into a railway bridge and cottages bordering the main London North Eastern rail line. A fierce fire developed and the four badly injured survivors were dragged from the flames by some local farmers, Alfred Rooke and Tom and Cecil Starr. Two died almost immediately, while Sgt Tynski RCAF never flew again. F/O Pearce RCAF did, only to be killed on operations with 434 Squadron in the December (see Bomber Command Losses, Volume 5, page 512). The Canadians who died rest in Harrogate (Stonefall) Cemetery, while Sgt Powell lies in Wandsworth (Streatham) Cemetery. Mr McNulty was an Irish labourer from Curradraish Foxford in Co. Mayo. It is assumed he was taking a short cut from the local inn back to his lodgings when fate overtook him (see the following page for a footnote).

Note. Before continuing with the summaries, I wish to acknowledge the kind assistance provided by Keith E Whitfield in respect of the last two aircraft summarised. Concerning the first summary, several publications refer to the farm as "Lowther Farm", whereas it was "Hungate Farm" that happened to be in the ownership of the Lowther family and it is this point that Keith has been able to clarify. I am also indebted to Isabel Merston of Victoria, British Colombia, for her helpful comments regarding the first incident.

17 Apr	1658 HCU	Halifax II	BB427		Training

1944   F/S J A Phillips   T/o Riccall to practice three-engined landings.
F/O W J van Stockum   inj   From a poor approach, at 1415, the Halifax bounced on touch down, swung and failed to gain height when the crew tried to go round again. Travelling at high speed, the bomber ran beyond the runway, crossed the A19 main road and finished up close to the railway twixt Selby and York. The son of Colonel A J van Stockum of the Royal Netherland Navy and a graduate from the universities of Dublin and Toronto, F/O van Stockum was killed shortly after "D Day" whilst flying with 10 Squadron (see Bomber Command Losses, Volume 5, page 270).

18 Apr	1657 HCU B Flt	Stirling III	EJ108	—W	Training

1944
F/L H C Wilkie DFC RNZAF   +   T/o 2235 Grafton Underwood but, tragically, hit
F/S C G Nairne RNZAF   some American servicemen cycling on the runway.
Sgt F T G Atkins   +   The Stirling became airborne and the crew were
W/O W A Watson DFM   +   advised to land at Woodbridge but shortly before
F/S L C Perry RNZAF   reaching their destination, they were startled
P/O F G Rickard RNZAF   by an explosion from within the aircraft, which
Sgt S A G Woodford   immediately adopted a steep nose up attitude.
Sgt A R Stannard   Partially abandoned before crashing 2330 at
F/S P Falkiner RNZAF   Moat Farm near Little Glemham, 7 miles NE of
     Woodbridge town, Suffolk. F/L Wilkie RNZAF,
Sgt D K Ollre USAAC   +   whose DFC was Gazetted on 27 July 1943 following
Cpl J A Moore USAAC   +   service with 15 Squadron, was taken to Cambridge
Cpl T B Potocki USAAC   +   City Cemetery; W/O Watson, the "screened" flight
     engineer, rests in Auchtergaven Parish Church-
Mr W Carter   yard (his award had been gained with 90 Squadron
Miss Carter   and its details promulgated on 15 June 1943),
     while Sgt Atkins is buried in Hammersmith New
Cemetery. He, too, bailed out but had failed to secure his parachute harness securely and, consequently, he slipped through the webbing and plunged to his death. Apart from P/O Rickard RNZAF, the survivors went to 75 Squadron and were posted missing from operations on 30 July 1944 (see Bomber Command Losses, Volume 5, page 364). The two civilians have been identified by Bryce Gomersall as a brother and sister whose thatched cottage was hit by part of the Stirling; both are believed to have emerged unscathed.

19 Apr	1660 HCU	Stirling III	LJ534		Training

1944   F/S M J Roe RAAF   T/o Swinderby but the port tyre burst and the crew were ordered to head for Woodbridge. On their arrival at 1230, the undercarriage folded as the bomber touched down.

20 Apr	1657 HCU	Stirling I	R9353	—X	Training

1944
F/S J Gold RNZAF   +   T/o 0112 Stradishall for a night flying detail.
Sgt J Cooper   +   Landed 0312 only to bounce back into the air,
F/S W M Aitken RNZAF   +   the throttles being opened in order to go round
F/S G R Weston RNZAF   +   again. But, as the bomber gained height, its
F/S D H De Laney RNZAF   +   port wing dipped and moments later it dived into
F/S F P Hudson RNZAF   inj   the ground. Of those who died, three were taken
Sgt H Frew RNZAF   inj   to Cambridge City Cemetery, but F/S Westpn RNZAF
     was buried alongside his brother, S/L George
Ernest Weston DFC (see Bomber Command Losses, Volume 3, page 230) in a family plot at Hemblington (All Saints) Churchyard. Sgt Cooper's funeral was held at Islington Cemetery, Finchley. Of the two survivors, Sgt Frew RNZAF was treated for shock and minor abrasions in station sick quarters, but F/S Hudson RNZAF was transferred to RAF Hospital Ely.

Note. In his second volume, devoted to the air casualties sustained by the New Zealanders since 1915, Errol Martyn shows that the hours flown by the deceased totalled 222, 270, 264 and 265 hours respectively.

20 Apr
1944

1662 HCU **Halifax II** **L9613** **Training**

F/S F Rembecki PAF T/o 1356 Blyton but after climbing to 200 feet, both outer engines failed (the port motor caught fire) and a forced-landing was made. Posted to 300 Squadron, F/S Rembecki PAF was killed, along with his entire crew, during operations to Gelsenkirchen in mid-June 1944 (see Bomber Command Losses, Volume 5, page 275).

21-22 Apr
1944

1654 HCU **Stirling III** **EH926** **-T** **Training**

P/O G R Jeans + T/o 2103 Wigsley for a night navigation sortie.
Sgt R V Searle + While preparing to land, and circling at the
Sgt J G Case + time, collided at 0358 with another Stirling,
Sgt J W Willies + both machines plunging to earth near Eagle,
Sgt A J G King + seven miles SW from the centre of Lincoln.
Sgt L Allen + All were buried under private arrangements.
Sgt A D Short + Sgt Short's elder brother, Corporal Albert Edward Short died in the service of the Durham
Light Infantry on 26 July 1940. He is commemorated on the Brookwood Memorial.

1660 HCU **Stirling III** **EF498** **-P** **Training**

P/O A M Lees + T/o 2203 Swinderby similarly tasked and lost
Sgt T Mitchell + in the manner described above. The two RCAF
Sgt J E Rowley + members of crew were taken north to Harrogate
F/O M P O'Keefe + (Stonefall) Cemetery, while Sgt Mitchell of
Sgt P B Illingworth + Campbeltown, Argyllshire, was laid to rest in
Sgt L Burman + Thurlby (St. Germain) Churchyard. The others
Sgt N H B Garrity RCAF + lie in cemeteries in England, Wales and Scot-
Sgt A L Stoneham RCAF + land.

22 Apr
1944

1651 HCU A Flt **Stirling I** **N3671** **-C** **Transit**

F/O J C Blair T/o 1045 Wratting Common with a complement of
F/S R S Wisker RNZAF eleven, only to experience a jammed under-
F/O C K Curtis carriage. Ordered to land at Woodbridge, the crew duly complied and at 1055, the Stirling was written off as it crash-landed on the emergency strip. F/O Curtis, the "screened" flight engineer, had flown a tour of operations with 149 Squadron; he later served at the Central Flying School before returning to operations, first with 138 Squadron (see Bomber Command Losses, Volume 5, page 439) and then with 161 Squadron.

1662 HCU **Halifax II** **HR668** **Training**

F/O Kelly RAAF T/o 2220 Blyton for night circuits and landings.
F/S Israel RAAF Landed at 2230, but with the wheels still in their bays. Both pilots emphatically state that all indications pointed to the undercarriage being down and they were supported by the flight engineer.

1667 HCU **Halifax V** **DK186** **-A2** **Ground**

P/O R G Watts RAAF Taxying 0310 at Sandtoft, swung from the runway and ran into a deep ditch, whereupon the wheels folded. Posted to 460 Squadron, P/O Watts RAAF gained a DFC (details appearing in the London Gazette on 19 January 1945 and the Australia Gazette six days later). "Screened" to 29 Operational Training Unit, he was killed in a flying accident on 2 April 1945 (see Bomber Command Losses, Volume 7, page 337).

23 Apr
1944

1659 HCU **Halifax II** **R9384** **-G** **Training**

P/O H M R Herbert RCAF + T/o 1434 Topcliffe but was immediately in trouble
Sgt T Ellams + and crashed near The Grange at Baldersby St.
Sgt A L Lunan RCAF + James, a couple of miles WSW from the airfield.
Sgt F R Dawson RCAF + Four are buried in Harrogate (Stonefall) Cemetery
Sgt J T McGovern RCAF + while Sgt Ellams (he enlisted in the Auxiliary Air Force on 2 May 1939) rests at Ashton-under-
Lyne and Dunkinfield Joint Cemetery. This Halifax had been involved in a minor incident on 17 November 1942, when P/O C W Higgins had been at the controls.

24-25 Apr
1944

1654 HCU **Stirling III** **LK552 JF-C** **Training**

P/O G Lee T/o 2120 Wigsley for a night navigation detail. While in flight, at 11,000 feet, the port inner engine failed but, inadvertently, the outer port motor was stopped. Abandoned and crashed 0105 near Cheese House on the Trent, Nottinghamshire.

25 Apr 1944	**1651 HCU**	**Stirling I**	**W7577**	**Training**

F/O A W Lowe RNZAF
F/S G W Patterson RNZAF

T/o Wratting Common for night training, with nine crew in total. Made a reasonably good landing, 2230, at Newmarket but swung to port and as the pilot was bringing the Stirling back towards the flare path, it bounced causing the port oleo to collapse. On coming to a stop, an engine caught fire. Although initially classified as repairable in works, the age and general condition of the aircraft deemed such a course of action as un-economical and with 530.00 flying hours to its credit, the bomber was struck off charge on 16 May 1944.

1656 HCU	**Halifax II**	**BB264**	**Training**

P/O J MacDonald — inj
Sgt R E Sharp — inj
Sgt Pym
Sgt Thompson
Sgt Tell
Sgt McDonald
Sgt Grant
Sgt Parton

T/o 1110 Lindholme for day training, nine crew being aboard. Landed 1515, but ballooned back into the air and upon its second arrival, the main undercarriage and tail wheel were ripped off. P/O MacDonald stated that he had been reluctant to overshoot, due to a faulty air speed indicator.

1658 HCU	**Halifax II**	**W7821**	**Training**

F/S W H Rumney

T/o 2340 Riccall for night flying practice and written off six minutes later in a landing mishap, the port undercarriage breaking under the strain of an uncorrected swing. Tragically, three nights after this incident, F/S Rumney and his crew failed to return from a night exercise after being involved in a midair collision.

1662 HCU	**Halifax II**	**BB383**	**Air Test**

P/O R J Bunten DFC — inj
Sgt Burton
Cpl D Eyre — inj
Cpl White
AC2 Malia
LACW Scadden WAAF

T/o 1825 Blyton but an engine failed and the Halifax crash-landed about a mile from the runway, hitting a tree in its last seconds of flight. The two injured airmen were treated in their local station sick quarters, neither were seriously hurt. P/O Bunten (his promotion to F/O became effective eight days later) had flown Lancasters with 103 Squadron and details of his award had been Gazetted on 16 November 1943.

26 Apr 1944	**1666 HCU**	**Halifax II**	**W7804**	**Ground**

F/O J A Weir RCAF

At 1915, while taxying along the perimeter track, the starboard wheel "slipped" from the tarmacadam and dropped into soft ground. Immediately, the tyre burst and the wheel hub dug in deeply, the consequence being a ground loop which fractured the struts and as the oleo folded, so severe damage was inflicted upon the starboard mainplane and undersurfaces of the fuselage.

Note. Twenty-four hours later, "1666" reported another taxying accident, involving Halifax II JB859 (F/O W R J Wells RCAF) and Halifax II JD106 (F/O W R Chalcroft RCAF) and which resulted in the tragic death of the tail gunner aboard JD106, namely Sgt W T Falan RCAF.

26-27 Apr 1944	**1667 HCU**	**Halifax V**	**EB146**	**-B**	**Training**

F/O C D McIvor RCAF — +
Sgt G A F Hearn — inj
Sgt J A Tarrant — inj
Sgt R D Jack — +
Sgt J Irons — +
F/S D J Mackie RNZAF — inj
Sgt A H King — inj

T/o 2156 Sandtoft for a night cross-country. While cruising at 20,000 feet, the outer port engine commenced vibrating and as the situation became steadily worse, the order to bale out was given. Four did so before the bomber came down, at 0036, near Marshfield, 12 miles E from the centre of Bristol. F/O McIvor RCAF, who had been involved in a crash on 13 April (see page 102) is buried in Bath (Haycombe) Cemetery, while Sgt Jack was taken to Tealing Cemetery and Sgt Irons to Dundee's Eastern Necropolis, both burial grounds being in Angus, Scotland. Sgt Jack had but recently returned to flying following a terrible crash on 24 November 1943 (see page 75), at which time he was training with 1656 Heavy Conversion Unit at Lindholme. Those who survived the accident, here summarised, were treated at Colerne's station sick quarters, though F/S Mackie RNZAF was later transferred to the Royal Air Force Hospital at Melksham, having sustained multiple abrasions.

28 Apr	1652 HCU	Halifax II	HR847	Training

1944   F/O W F Rabbitt RAAF   T/o 1028 Marston Moor for a cross-country, a standard crew of seven being carried. During the sortie, and while flying at 18,000 feet, F/O Rabbitt RAAF was obliged to feather the port inner Merlin and when, some twenty minutes later, the inner starboard lost power, he attempted to land at Lichfield. His approach was good but he touched down, at 1223, rather fast and as the Halifax was about to run into the overshoot area, he raised the undercarriage.

	1667 HCU	Halifax V	DG317 UG-J	Ground

P/O W R Ireland   While taxying at 0056, at Sandtoft, in readiness for night circuit training, collided with another of the unit's aircraft, both machines being damaged beyond repair.

	1667 HCU	Halifax V	DG347 UG-O	Ground

P/O K A Wells   Wrecked in the manner described above. In his report, P/O Wells said that he had stopped near the marshalling point in order to have his tyres checked. No injuries reported.

28-29 Apr	1658 HCU	Halifax II	BB374	Training

1944
F/S W H Rumney   +   T/o Riccall for a Bullseye exercise which took
Sgt E J Hurr   +   the crew out over the Irish Sea and it was while
Sgt C A James   +   in position 52.47N 04.41W that a collision took
Sgt N MacBeth   +   place, at 0020, with another Halifax. Out of
Sgt R D P Barrett   +   control, F/S Rumney's machine dived into the
Sgt J Morgan   +   water. In time, the body of Sgt Rimmer was
Sgt C A Howson   +   recovered and he lies in Whiston (St. Nicholas)
Sgt H Rimmer   +   Churchyard. The Runnymede Memorial perpetuates the names of his seven companions (see the previous page for an earlier mishap involving F/S Rumney).

	1663 HCU	Halifax V	DG297 -D	Training

Sgt P Bailey   T/o 2035 Rufforth similarly tasked and at 0020 struck by the Halifax, described above. Although his aircraft was seriously damaged, Sgt Bailey maintained control and he was able to crash-land, wheels up, at Broadwell airfield in Oxfordshire. An examination of the wrecked bomber revealed extensive buckling to the undersurfaces and, subsequently, his flying-log received a "green" endorsement for his skilled handling of the very dangerous situation in which he found himself.

29 Apr	1656 HCU	Halifax II	R9437	Training

1944   F/O W G Shearer USAAC   inj   T/o 1710 Lindholme for solo circuit training. While accelerating to take off at 1725, and just as the wheels eased from the runway, the starboard outer failed. With the undercarriage and flaps down, the bomber veered through ninety degrees and crashed 300 yards off the runway, close to a dispersal pan.

30 Apr	1666 HCU	Halifax II	DT737	Training

1944
S/L H Gowan RCAF   T/o 1725 Wombleton for initial dual on type.
Sgt S Huston RCAF   Landed at 1735 with a burst port tyre, this having occurred during the previous take off. It is remarked that S/L Gowan RCAF made an excellent attempt to save his aircraft and for a while managed to run the Halifax on its good wheel. He could not, however, prevent the bomber from leaving the runway and as it ran onto soft ground, the hub of the broken wheel dug in and two violent ground loops followed, resulting in the fuselage breaking just aft of the rear entrance door. No injuries reported.

2 May	1659 HCU	Halifax II	BB247	Training

1944
F/O J L McKinnon RCAF   +   T/o 1420 Topcliffe but climbed very steeply
Sgt D W M Giles   +   before stalling and diving into the ground,
F/O W A Pope RCAF   +   a minute later, some 200 yards NE of East
F/O M T Seabrook RCAF   +   Lodge Farm. The six Canadians were interred
Sgt E J Donnelly RCAF   +   at Harrogate (Stonefall) Cemetery, while Sgt
Sgt H R Davies RCAF   +   Giles was buried in Trowbridge Cemetery.
Sgt H Astrand RCAF   +   Initially accepted by 77 Squadron on 15 October 1942, this Halifax was passed to 78 Squadron eleven days later and was then given up, on 30 January 1943, to "1659". It appears to have enjoyed a trouble free life until the accident, here reported.

3 May	1656 HCU	Halifax II	HR913	Training

1944   F/S H D Murray   T/o 2200 Lindholme for conversion training, at
night. At 12,000 feet, the oil pressure reading
for the port outer dropped quite dramatically and the engine was shut down. On
landing at 2300, the aircraft swung to starboard and left the runway and upon
entering a ditch near the perimeter, the undercarriage folded.

3- 4 May	1662 HCU	Halifax II	BB316	Training

1944   Sgt J N Robertson   +   T/o 2155 Blyton tasked for a Bullseye detail.
Sgt H J Street   +   Returned to base at around midnight and while
F/O S J Chaplin   +   approaching the circuit, with the starboard
F/O R V Spencer   +   outer feathered, the Halifax was observed to
Sgt W M Harvey   +   make a steep turn to the right, lose height
Sgt S Bird   +   and crash, at 0005, near Kirton in Lindsey
Sgt L G Garrod   inj   village. On impact, the bomber burst into
flames. Sgt Robertson of Bath was taken to
Cambridge City Cemetery, while the others who perished were claimed by their
next of kin. Sgt Garrod was admitted to Scunthorpe War Memorial Hospital.
Such was the severity of the crash, its cause could not be fully determined
but it is thought that the inner starboard may have cut, due to running out
of fuel.

4 May	1664 HCU	Halifax V	DG232	Training

1944   P/O M E Gray RCAF   T/o 1110 Dishforth for dual circuit practice.
Sgt W J Taylor RCAF   Landed, heavily, at 1130 following a low speed
approach, by Sgt Taylor RCAF, which P/O Gray,
the instructor, tried to rectify, but without success. Moments after touching
down, the starboard oleo broke.

6 May	1653 HCU	Stirling I	N3702 –J	Training

1944   F/S V A Adolph RNZAF   T/o 1145 Chedburgh (crew No. 103, course No. 21).
Sgt G R Jones   Landed fifteen minutes later, at Waterbeach, port
F/S R Phillip RNZAF   wheel first and bounced. On its next arrival,
F/O R J Hodgson RNZAF   the starboard wing dug in and the ensuing crash
Sgt L Sampson   damaged the Stirling beyond repair.
Sgt J P Swale
F/S C M White RNZAF

	1660 HCU	Stirling III	EF449 TV–X	Training

Sgt N J Evans   T/o 0057 Swinderby for a night navigation detail.
Lost power from the starboard inner at 15,000
feet. With the propeller feathered, the crew headed for Exeter, only to overshoot their approach and crash, 0308, beyond the runway. The London Gazette
for 4 July 1944, shows details of the commission granted to Sgt Evans, his
seniority being back-dated to 11 May 1944.

	1663 HCU	Halifax V	DK138	Training

Capt Leclere FFAF   T/o 1401 Rufforth for a training exercise,
S/Lt A L Chourgnoz FFAF during which the starboard inner failed and
followed soon after by the outer starboard.
Both motors were feathered, but the Halifax lost height very rapidly and the
crew crash-landed at 1641, wheels retracted, at or near Hawarden airfield.

Note. This was the unit's first report of an accident involving airmen from
the Free French Air Force and, it seems, that the majority (if not all) of
their personnel attended the courses run by 1663 Heavy Conversion Unit. Ten
days after the incident, summarised, 346 Squadron formed at Elvington, this
being the first of two Halifax-equipped heavy bomber squadrons assigned to
No. 4 Group, Bomber Command.

8 May	1667 HCU	Halifax V	LL391 –O	Training

1944   P/O R T J Holmes   T/o 2159 Sandtoft for a night cross-country,
six members of crew aboard, but as the aircraft
gathered speed it swung to starboard and then, as a result of over correction,
it swerved violently to port. P/O Holmes closed the throttles but was too late
to prevent the Halifax from skidding out of control. With a rendering of metal
the undercarriage collapsed and soon after flames were seen issuing from the
outer starboard engine.

9 May   **1657 HCU**   **Stirling I**   **R9273**   **-M**   **Training**
1944   Sgt D O Bonner   inj   T/o Stradishall for night circuits and landings.
        Sgt M N Beachan   inj   While flying at 250 feet, in the landing pattern,
        Sgt N Derham   inj   the port wing dropped and seconds later, at 2354,
        Sgt C J Brooker   inj   the bomber hit the ground close to the playing
        WO2 S M Oakes RCAF   inj   fields. Five were treated in the local station
        Sgt C P Anspach   inj   sick quarters, but WO2 Oakes RCAF, the air bomber
        Sgt E J Aldridge   inj   and Sgt Aldridge, the tail gunner, were admitted
                                         to RAF Hospital Ely, the former with a suspected
fracture to his spine. Subsequently, Sgt Derham went on to fly Lancasters with
514 Squadron and lost his life during operations to Homberg on 20-21 July 1944
(see Bomber Command Losses, Volume 5, page 344).

        1657 HCU   **Stirling I**   **BF342**   **-L**   **Training**
        P/O W A C Yates   T/o Stradishall for a training detail which
        Sgt S Sterry   terminated at 1400, with the Stirling lying
        Sgt N Nicholson   just off to the right of the runway with its
        Sgt J Carter   undercarriage broken. Sadly, none of those
        Sgt G Wood   involved would live to see the end of their
        Sgt T R Farley   course.
        Sgt J W Grainger

9-10 May   **1651 HCU**   **Stirling I**   **R9244 BS-L**   **Training**
1944   F/O J W Stratton   T/o 2230 Wratting Common for a night training
                                         sortie. Wrecked 0230 when the starboard oleo
collapsed on landing. It his statement, F/O Stratton said he had experienced
problems in getting the unit to lower.

10 May   **1658 HCU**   **Halifax II**   **JB789**   **Training**
1944   F/S T R Laver RAAF   +   T/o Riccall for a night exercise which ended
        Sgt D McDermott   +   at 0102 in the most awful circumstances with
        Sgt P H Rockingham   +   the Halifax flying into the spire of St. James's
        F/S B K Storer RAAF   +   church, Selby, Yorkshire. Within seconds the
        F/S N J Knight RAAF   +   bomber had demolished, or seriously damaged,
        F/S J Roper RAAF   +   four properties, Nos. 30, 32, 34 and 36 Port-
        F/O J R Dixon RAAF   +   holme Drive, plus another building identified
                                         as Portholme Mill. As the aircraft smashed
        Mr H W Osbourn   +   its way through this residential area, at least
        Mrs D Osbourn   +   fourteen civilians were either killed or very
        Mstr B Osbourn   +   seriously injured; at least four bodies and one
        Miss J Osbourn   inj   survivor being pulled from the remains of what
        Miss P Osbourn   +   once had been No. 30 Portholme Drive. Of the
        Mrs E Clavert   +   seven airmen, recovered from the scene, five
        Miss J Clavert   +   were laid to rest in Harrogate (Stonefall)
        Mr J Mather   +   Cemetery, while Sgt McDermott of Wakefield
        Mr J Saynor   inj   and Sgt Rockingham of Birkenhead were buried
        Mr A Robinson   inj   in Selby Cemetery. It is reported that Mr Saynor
        Mrs Robinson   inj   died from his injuries. Mstr Coote is believed
        Miss Robinson   inj   to have been just seventeen months old.
        Mrs M Coote   inj
        Mstr D Coote   inj

        1667 HCU   **Halifax V**   **DG309**   **Training**
        WO1 J K Murray RCAF   T/o Sandtoft for his first solo on type, making
                                         four good circuits before swinging out of control
as he gained speed for a fifth at 2044. Despite closing the throttles and braking
hard, WO1 Murray RCAF finished up, off the runway, with the undercarriage of his
aircraft broken.

11 May   **1653 HCU**   **Stirling I**   **EF363**   **-S**   **Training**
1944   S/L R R Megginson DFC   T/o Chedburgh (crew No. 105, course No. 21) for
        F/O J K Aitken RNZAF   a night sortie, damaging both tyres while in the
        Sgt R T Taylor   process of becoming airborne. On return to base
        F/O D W Hodgson RNZAF   at 0140, the port oleo folded as the wheels made
        F/O R D Mayhill RNZAF   contact. Posted to 75 Squadron, Sgt Taylor was
        Sgt G Grindlay   killed in late November 1944 (see Bomber Command
        Sgt W A Monk   Losses, Volume 5, page 497). Bryce Gomersall
        Sgt A H Monk   writes, "the Monk's were twins, hailing from
                                         Brazil and both were later commissioned".

11 May	1654 HCU	Stirling III	LJ524	–H		Training

11 May 1944

1654 HCU   Stirling III   LJ524   –H   Training

P/O R W Dunn RAAF	+
Sgt E J Wild	inj
Sgt E A Wilmshurst	+
W/O H E Hughes RAAF	+
F/S W J Lea RAAF	+
F/S R W Ely RAAF	+
F/S G R Whimpey RAAF	inj
F/S G E Dowling RAAF	inj

T/o Wigsley for a long night cross-country. Crashed 0253, near the airfield, while trying to go round again from a three-engined approach. As the bomber broke up, F/S Whimpey RAAF was thrown clear but despite being badly shocked he was one of the first to enter the burning fuselage and begin the task of pulling bodies from the wreckage; sadly, five were already beyond medical aid. For his courage, he was awarded the British Empire Medal but by the time this honour was Gazetted, on 22 August 1944, this brave Australian had perished in action (see Bomber Command Losses, Volume 5, page 316) with 463 Squadron, along with F/S Dowling RAAF. His bravery was noted in the Australia Gazette on 31 August 1944. Of those who died at Wigsley, four were taken to Oxford (Botley) Cemetery, while Sgt Wilmshurst is buried at Bottesford (St. Peter Ad Vincula) Churchyard in Lincolnshire.

1657 HCU   Stirling I   N6089 XT–G   Training

F/O P W Bickford RCAF	
Sgt P L Dooley	
F/O A N Johnston RCAF	
F/O W G Scanlan RCAF	
Sgt U B Butters	
Sgt D Dawson RCAF	
Sgt D G Flood RCAF	

T/o 0555 Stradishall but swung out of control and lost its undercarriage. After converting to Lancasters, the crew joined 115 Squadron at Witchford and were lost on operations in mid-September (see Bomber Command Losses, Volume 5, page 428). F/O Bickford was an American from Pennsylvania; F/O Johnston RCAF hailed from Quebec while the rest of the Canadians came from Ontario.

13 May 1944

1658 HCU   Halifax II   JB927 TT–P   Training

F/O J G Jenkins DFC	inj
F/S T H Sinclair RNZAF	
Sgt T V Murphy	
Sgt T H Hill RNZAF	
F/S N K Brabent RNZAF	
F/S T A R Sharpe RAAF	inj
Sgt H J Draper	
Sgt F McAuliffe RAAF	
Sgt Clarke	

T/o Riccall to practice three-engined flying, combined with circuit practice. On approach, at 500 feet and with full flap selected, the pupil pilot (F/S Sinclair RNZAF) was unable to correct the aircraft's drift away from the runway's centre line. F/O Jenkins, in his capacity of instructor, took over and tried to set the Halifax down on the grass, bordering the runway, but when he realised he was likely to fly into a hut, he opened the throttles in an attempt to go round again. Unfortunately, he was unable to gain sufficient height before hitting some trees, at 1403, on Skipworth Common, an area of land on the NE side of the airfield. F/S Sinclair RNZAF (and the next six named) arrived at Lissett on 31 May 1944, going to fly a successful tour of operations with 158 Squadron. F/O Jenkins had already played his part in the bombing campaign, gaining an immediate DFC (Gazetted 24 August 1943) while operating with 10 Squadron to Hamburg on 2-3 August 1943.

1667 HCU   Halifax V   LK991   Training

F/O A Carey RNZAF	
P/O W G Parsons RAAF	inj
Sgt Thomas	
P/O Hatfield	
F/O Honeyman	
F/S Lyons	
F/S Lindoref	
F/S J Lister RAAF	inj

T/o 1709 Sandtoft for circuits and landings. Approaching the runway, at 1724, the instructor warned his pupil that he was a shade too high, but when P/O Parsons RAAF flared out, without sufficient throttle to cushion his arrival, the instructor was too late in opening up to go round again and as a consequence the Halifax stalled and crashed heavily. The two injured airmen were admitted to station sick quarters.

14 May 1944

1653 HCU   Stirling I   R9195   –M   Training

F/L A M F Alexander RNZAF	inj
F/O M L Hore RNZAF	
Sgt J S Hortop	
P/O A F Bessener	
P/O J S Harris RNZAF	
Sgt L E Hargreaves	
Sgt K W Hailey	
F/S D K Blake RNZAF	

T/o Chedburgh (crew No. 112, course No. 22) for dual instruction, but as the bomber climbed out so a tyre burst and the wheel broke off from its axle. F/L Alexander RNZAF, the instructor, made for Woodbridge, landing here at 1500. On inspection it was decided to write the Stirling off; it will be recalled that F/L Alexander had been involved in a serious crash a month previous (see page 101).

14 May 1944	1667 HCU	Halifax V	DG284	-F2		Training

F/O W H Aldrich — inj
Sgt H G Hewitt — inj
Sgt E Martindale — inj
F/O J E McGowan RCAF — inj
Sgt M G Hudson — inj
Sgt B H Cave — inj
F/S C C Evans — inj

T/o Sandtoft for circuits and landings. Flying at a thousand feet, the starboard outer cut and was feathered. Unable to regain their base, the crew forced-landed at 1553 on Wedge Hall Moor, near Thorne, Yorkshire. F/O McGowan RCAF was taken to Scunthorpe War Memorial Hospital, while his less seriously hurt colleagues were treated in Sandtoft's station sick quarters.

15 May 1944	1653 HCU	Stirling III	EE958	-T		Transit

F/L R H Cochrane DFC RCAF — inj
F/O C B Noble RAAF — inj
P/O G J H Hughes — +
Sgt F E Hunt — inj
P/O T J McQuaid RCAF — inj
P/O C A Bender RAAF — inj
F/S M L Woodland RAAF — inj
Sgt L V James RAAF — inj
F/S W B Burton RAAF — +

T/o 2215 Chedburgh (crew No. 113, course No. 22) with the intention of flying to Tuddenham for circuit practice. Encountered very severe icing which in turn led to a serious reduction in power from the starboard engines. Thus, fifteen minutes after their departure, the crew crash-landed in a wooded area at Banstead Manor, Cheveley, a Cambridgeshire village 3 miles SE of the Suffolk town of Newmarket. The two airmen who died were buried in Whitchurch (St. Mary) Churchyard and Cambridge City Cemetery respectively. Sgt Hunt, as Bryce Gomersall advises me, had replaced Sgt A E Funnell, the crews' regular flight engineer.

	1659 HCU	Halifax II	BB248			Training

F/O R N Wilson RCAF

T/o 1627 Topcliffe for fighter affiliation, a crew complement of five being aboard. As the Halifax became airborne, F/O Wilson RCAF retracted the wheels, but his actions were somewhat premature and the undercarriage was damaged as a consequence. On return to base, at 1727, he found it impossible to lower the damaged unit and the ensuing forced-landing damaged the aircraft beyond repair. On completing his course, F/O Wilson RCAF proceeded to 419 Squadron and was posted missing from operations over France on 12-13 June 1944 (see Bomber Command Losses, Volume 5, page 279).

16 May 1944	1659 HCU	Halifax II	BB274			Training

F/S L H McDonald RCAF

T/o 1710 Topcliffe for circuit practice. At approximately 1835, F/S McDonald RCAF landed with such force that the tail wheel hold down bolts sheered. Although not too seriously damaged, repairs were not sanctioned and the bomber was struck off charge.

17 May 1944	1661 HCU	Stirling III	EE956			Training

P/O F G Murray RCAF — +
Sgt W Hoffie — +
Sgt K Foster — +
F/S A P Hebbes — +
F/S J M Wolowiec RCAF — +
F/S W H England RCAF — +
Sgt N Bingham — +
Sgt C R Roe — +
Sgt A W Huppe RCAF — +

T/o 2334 Winthorpe tasked for a night navigation exercise. Encountered icing of such severity that control was lost and as the bomber spiralled it broke up, the bulk of the debris falling into an ironstone quarry, at 2353, a mile north-west of Rothwell in Northamptonshire. The four RCAF members of crew were buried at Brookwood Military Cemetery, while Sgt Foster of Leeds was taken to Oxford (Botley) Cemetery. The remainder were claimed by their next of kin.

	1666 HCU	Halifax II	DT551			Training

F/O G L Heron RCAF
F/O L Stewart RCAF

T/o 1005 Wombleton for initial dual practice. Landed normally at 1130, but while travelling at speed the port oleo collapsed, causing the aircraft to ground loop. An investigation revealed the main casting had been badly cracked, a fault that had gone unnoticed during a recent inspection.

17-18 May 1944	1664 HCU	Halifax V	EB200 ZU-A			Training

F/O N E Streight RCAF
Sgt D S Smith — +
F/O W H Potts RCAF — inj
F/O S B Duern RCAF — inj
P/O Collins
Sgt Reed
Sgt R B Hamilton RCAF — inj

T/o 2135 Dishforth for a night cross-country. Shortly before 0155, the starboard inner cut and the bomber came down, barely under control, and crashed 0155 about a mile S of Norton le Clay and 5 miles E of Ripon, Yorkshire. The sole fatality, Sgt Smith, rests in Gillingham (Woodlands) Cemetery, Kent.

19 May	1661 HCU	**Stirling III**	**LK546**	**–N Bar**	**Training**

19 May　**1661 HCU**　　　**Stirling III**　**LK546**　**–N Bar**　　　　　**Training**
1944　F/S P J Eason　　　　　　　　T/o Winthorpe tasked for a day cross-country.
　　　　　　　　　　　　　　　　　While over the West Country, both port engines
and the starboard outer gave trouble and the crew attempted to land at Culmhead,
a relatively small airfield situated in the Blackdown Hills south of Taunton.
Thus, at 1403, the Stirling overshot its approach and came to rest amongst
the many trees that lay beyond the runway.

19–20 May　**1663 HCU**　　　　**Halifax V**　**DG231**　　　　　　　　**Training**
1944　S/Lt A L Chourgnoz FFAF　　+　T/o 2255 Rufforth on a night cross-country,
　　Lt J J Beason FFAF　　　inj　climbing to 20,000 feet. At around 0130, and
　　Sgt P Marchi FFAF　　　　+　now over South Wales, an engine caught fire
　　Lt J J Y Cam FFAF　　　inj　and the flames spread rapidly into the wing
　　Adj P C Weber FFAF　　　inj　structure. Realising that he was not going
　　Sgt M Y Retore FFAF　　inj　to be able to retain control, S/Lt Chourgnoz
　　Adj C Vignolles FFAF　　+　ordered his crew to bale out, but only five
　　Sgt M Lemouser FFAF　　+　were able to do so before the Halifax dived
　　　　　　　　　　　　　　　　　into the ground at Fention Farm to the W of
Haverfordwest, Pembrokeshire. Tragically, one of the five who managed to
escape from the doomed aircraft opened his parachute prematurely and the canopy
became engulfed in flames. Those who died were initially laid to rest in
Haverfordwest (City Road) Cemetery, but since the end of the war their bodies
have been exhumed and taken home to France. It will be recalled that the
pilot had been involved in an accident earlier in the month (see page 107).

20 May　**1659 HCU**　　　　**Halifax V**　**LK684**　　　　　　　　**Training**
1944　Sgt R B Maxwell RCAF　　　　T/o 1845 Topcliffe for circuits and landings.
　　Sgt J G K Feasby RCAF　　inj　Landed fifteen minutes later, but swung sharply
　　　　　　　　　　　　　　　　　to port and before corrective action could be
taken, the Halifax ground looped and lost its undercarriage. Sgt Feasby RCAF,
the wireless operator, required attention from the station sick quarters staff.

21 May　**1662 HCU**　　　　**Halifax II**　**W7811**　　　　　　　**Training**
1944　P/O J B Fleming RAAF　　+　T/o 1130 Blyton for a day cross-country, during
　　Sgt Gault　　　　　　　　　which the starboard inner failed and then burst
　　Sgt Place　　　　　　　　　into flames. The order to abandon was given and
　　F/O J D Stent　　　　inj　apart from P/O Fleming RAAF all were able to
　　Sgt J B Fischer RAAF　inj　comply before the bomber smashed to earth, at
　　Sgt Barden　　　　　　　　around 1425, near the village of Altarnun on the
　　Sgt Kite　　　　　　　　　eastern side of Bodmin Moor, some 7 miles WSW
　　Sgt I C Wheatland　　inj　from Launceston, Cornwall. The three who were
　　　　　　　　　　　　　　　　　hurt were conveyed to station sick quarters at
Davidstow Moor which enjoyed the dubious distinction of being the highest op-
erational airfield in the United Kingdom. P/O Fleming RAAF was taken for a
full military burial service at Oxford (Botley) Cemetery.

23 May　**1658 HCU**　　　　**Halifax II**　**JD299**　　　　　　　**Training**
1944　F/O P A Tuck RAAF　　　inj　T/o 2240 Riccall for a night cross-country but
　　Sgt R G Middleton　　inj　soon after departing, the starboard outer became
　　F/O H H Hackney RAAF　inj　unserviceable and problems arose when the crew
　　F/O M Hall RAAF　　　　+　tried to feather the unit. Height was lost and
　　Sgt C R Mudee RAAF　　inj　the situation worsened considerable when the
　　Sgt M P H Macdonnell　inj　port outer failed. Thus, at 2330, the Halifax
　　Sgt S J Kirk　　　　　inj　crash-landed in Duke´s Wood, Eakring, 9 miles
　　　　　　　　　　　　　　　　　east of Mansfield, Nottinghamshire. The injured
were taken to station sick quarters at Ossington, F/O Hackney RAAF succumbing to
his wounds at 1255 hours on 27 May. Along with fellow Australian, F/O Hall, he
is buried in Harrogate (Stonefall) Cemetery, both being shown on the Australian
War Museum Roll of Honour as belonging to 82 Operational Training Unit which, at
the time of the crash, was domicile at Ossington.

　　1666 HCU　　　　**Halifax II**　**JB969**　**–X**　　　　　**Training**
　　F/O G L Heron RCAF　　　　　T/o 1110 Wombleton for a combined exercise in
　　　　　　　　　　　　　　　　　air-to-air firing and practice bombing. At
around 1235, flying at 1,500 feet just off the coast, the revolutions from the
port outer began to fluctuate and the engine temperature rose alarmingly. Soon
after, the motor caught fire and F/O Heron RCAF carried out a very skillful
ditching, a mere 500 yards off Saltwick Nab near Whitby, Yorkshire. All were
rescued, unscathed after observing their Halifax float for thirty minutes.

24 May　**1651 HCU A Flt**　　**Stirling I N6044　-E**　　　　　　**Training**
1944　　　P/O Smith RNZAF　　　　　　T/o 2325 Wratting Common for night circuit
　　　　P/O Andrews RNZAF　　　　　　practice, an exercise that proceeded well for
　　　　　　　　　　　　　　　　　thirty minutes at which stage the starboard
main tyre burst on touch down, sending the bomber skidding out of control.
Coming to a halt 100 yards off the runway, the crew were not a little sur-
prised to find the unit still intact, but the stress to the airframe was such
that repairs were deemed uneconomical and the bomber was duly written off.

　　　　1667 HCU　　　　　　**Halifax V DG403**　　　　　　　**Training**
　　　　P/O E P Burke RAAF　　　　inj　T/o 2217 Sandtoft for a night navigation detail
　　　　Sgt R P Fowler　　　　　　inj　but when black smoke was seen issuing forth from
　　　　Sgt R A Bell　　　　　　　inj　the starboard outer, it was decided to terminate
　　　　Sgt G K E John　　　　　　inj　the sortie and return to base. With the engine
　　　　F/S J M Meggitt RAAF　　　inj　feathered, this was accomplished but while on
　　　　F/S J E Bateup RAAF　　　　inj　the downwind leg, the inner starboard failed.
　　　　Sgt T R Wood　　　　　　　inj　Finding it impossible to turn to the left,
　　　　　　　　　　　　　　　　　P/O Burke RAAF had little option but to forced-
land straight ahead, doing so at 2312, finishing up in a field at Map Reference
290262. An examination of the starboard motors revealed a stuck exhaust valve
in the inner unit, while No. 2 con-rod had broken up in the outer engine. On
16 January 1945, P/O Burke RAAF lost his life while operating with 166 Squadron
to Zeitz. He was accompanied by Sgt John, F/S Meggitt RAAF and Sgt Wood, all
of whom survived as prisoners of war. F/S Bateup RAAF, meanwhile, had joined
153 Squadron and he perished, in action, a week later (see Bomber Command
Losses, Volume 6, pages 49 and 54 respectively).

24-25 May　**1663 HCU**　　　　　**Halifax V DG416　-Q**　　　　　**Training**
1944　　　Cmdt G C Ostre FFAF　　　　T/o 2158 Rufforth for night flying. Landed
　　　　　　　　　　　　　　　　　at 0238, only to swing off the runway and come
to a stop with a broken undercarriage. Like so many of the Free French Air
Force pilots, Cmdt Ostre was very experienced and, at the time of the crash,
he had logged at least 4,330 hours of solo flying (sixteen of these on Halifax
bombers). Sadly, he died when his Halifax crashed on return from Hagen in mid-
March 1945 (see Bomber Command Losses, Volume 6, page 129). At the time of his
death, he was commanding 347 Squadron at Elvington.

Note. Further information pertaining to Cmdt Ostre's last mission can be
obtained from "Night Flight", admirably researched and written by Geoffrey
Jones and published by William Kimber in 1981.

25 May　**1651 HCU**　　　　　　**Stirling I EF385 BS-H**　　　　　**Training**
1944　　　F/O W H Cheek　　　　　　T/o Wratting Common for dual night circuits and
　　　　Sgt N R Modeland RCAF　　　landings. It is reported that after fifteen
　　　　Sgt J D Jordan　　　　　　minutes of flying, a heavy landing ensued and
　　　　Sgt J F Hartford RCAF　　　the Stirling ended up, beyond the runway, with
　　　　P/O D G McKenzie RCAF　　　its mainplanes irreparably damaged. Within a
　　　　Sgt B Coward　　　　　　　matter of weeks of this incident, Sgt Modeland
　　　　WO1 H Davies RCAF　　　　　was to distinguish himself during operations to
　　　　WO1 R S Dollard RCAF　　　Caen (with 90 Squadron). Subsequently, he was
　　　　　　　　　　　　　　　　　awarded a DFM, details of which were published
　　　　　　　　　　　　　　　　　in the London Gazette on 1 September 1944.

26 May　**1653 HCU**　　　　　　**Stirling I W7625　-H**　　　　　**Training**
1944　　　F/S G M P Moore RNZAF　　　T/o Chedburgh (crew No. 116, course No. 22) but
　　　　Sgt Huckstepp　　　　　　a tyre burst, though F/S Moore RNZAF succeeded
　　　　F/S W R Morris RNZAF　　　in becoming airborne. Diverted to Woodbridge,
　　　　F/S J L P Sherriff RNZAF　the Stirling was written off here in a wheels up
　　　　Sgt G Taylor　　　　　　　landing at 1655.
　　　　Sgt J W Glendenning
　　　　F/S R R Chatfield RNZAF

　　　　1661 HCU　　　　**Stirling III LJ558**　　　　　　　**Training**
　　　　Sgt J S Laws　　　　　　　T/o 1809 Winthorpe for general flying practice.
　　　　　　　　　　　　　　　　　Two hours later, at 2009, the Stirling touched
down, but swung out of control and clipped Stirling III BK766 (repaired) before
crashing into a workshop. There are no reports of casualties.

26-27 May	1654 HCU	Stirling III	LK502 JF-M	Training

1944

F/O G N Leach	+	T/o 2210 Wigsley briefed for a night cross-
Sgt F T J Nicholls	inj	country. All went well for about four hours
Sgt A C Brett	inj	but then problems with the starboard engines
Sgt G N Wise	inj	necessitated both units being shut down. It
Sgt D C Watson	inj	is then believed that rudder control was lost
F/S B D Fine RAAF	+	and at 0245 the Stirling crashed at Cliffe
Sgt C D Howes	+	Park, Rudyard, a little less than 3 miles WNW
Sgt H Ward	+	from Leek, Staffordshire. At least three of
		the injured were treated at a hospital in

Leek, while those who died were taken to various cemeteries within the United Kingdom. Following their recovery and return to duty, three were destined to lose their lives on bombing operations. First to fall was Sgt Wise, who died whilst flying with 50 Squadron; next came Sgt Brett, serving with 57 Squadron and last, Sgt Nicholls who failed to return from Karlsruhe on 2-3 February 1945, while operating with 189 Squadron (see Volumes 5 and 6 of Bomber Command Losses, pages 414, 484 and 62 respectively).

	1656 HCU	Halifax II	DG219	Training
P/O J Hetherington		+	T/o 2135 Lindholme for a night navigation
Sgt P Kindlen		+	sortie. At around 0240, radio contact with
F/O W S Garland RCAF		+	the Halifax was established and having joined
Sgt D R Persse		+	the circuit at 4,000 feet, P/O Hetherington
Sgt E G J Bridgeman		+	was instructed to descend to a thousand feet
W/O H L Walters DFM		+	and call again. Nothing further was heard
Sgt G Long RCAF		+	and it was later established that the bomber
			had crashed at 0247 near Broadway Stainforth,

six miles NNE of Doncaster, Yorkshire. Four, both Canadians, Sgt Persse and Sgt Bridgeman were buried in Harrogate (Stonefall) Cemetery, while the others were claimed by their relatives. P/O Hetherington had but recently returned to active duty following a very serious crash while under training with 1667 Heavy Conversion Unit (see page 97). W/O Walters had completed a tour of duty with 49 Squadron, details of his award having been Gazetted on 18 May 1943, and less than a year later, the parents of Sgt Long RCAF would be notified on the death of his brother, F/O Richard Hartley Long RCAF, who died on 16 March 1945, while air testing Mosquito XIII HK382 of 409 Squadron.

27 May	1659 HCU	Halifax V	LL286 RV-R	Training

1944

P/O J R Bradley RCAF	+	T/o Topcliffe for a high-level cross-country,
Sgt D A P Pickering	+	at night, carrying a crew of eight. Despite
Sgt J Newlands	+	an extensive search, no trace of the aircraft
Sgt T F Scott RCAF	+	was ever found but two bodies were recovered
F/O R P Gagnebin RCAF	+	from the sea and it seems likely that the
WO2 W Blair RCAF	+	pilot had attempted to ditch. WO2 Blair RCAF
Sgt G H Nelson RCAF	+	rests in Wigtownshire at Stoneykirk Cemetery,
Sgt F C Stevens RCAF	+	while Sgt Pickering lies in Moulton Cemetery.
		The others are commemorated on the Runnymede
		Memorial.

	1662 HCU	Halifax II	LW336	Training
P/O Veitch RAAF			T/o 1415 Blyton for a cross-country but not
			long after departure the outer starboard had

to be feathered and the crew turned back for base but undershot the runway and crashed, 1440, at Mount Pleasant Farm. No one seems to have been hurt.

	1666 HCU	Halifax II	HR834	-B	Training
WO2 P H Poirier RCAF		inj	T/o 1029 Wombleton for an exercise in bombing
Sgt G F Kinnear RCAF		inj	and air-to-air firing but as the aircraft began
F/O Kallall			to gain height, the starboard outer engine cut.
Sgt Harnish			Within seconds, the bomber had yawed sharply to
Sgt Park			starboard and smashed through the tops of four
Sgt Hayward			trees and finished up in the adjoining field,
P/O K Franklin		inj	where it broke up. An investigation into the
Sgt J Atherton RCAF		inj	cause of the failure reported that a valve
Sgt G J Arksey RCAF		inj	spring had broken, which led to the mixture in
			the inlet manifold exploding before reaching the

cylinders. The Merlin in question, it was said, was brand new and since its installation had run for a total of fourteen hours.

28 May 1944	**1657 HCU**	**Stirling III**	**BK689**	**-X**	**Training**

F/S R J Hoggard RAAF
Sgt W Hunter
F/O I Law RCAF
Sgt D Garber RCAF
F/S O F Meredith RAAF
Sgt N Richardson
Sgt L Jeffrey RAAF

T/o 1130 Shepherds Grove but swung off the runway and ran into Stirling III EF454 belonging to the same unit. A fire broke out but, subsequently, the airframe of the stationary Stirling was repaired, being given a new serial, TS261. However, as such, it saw no unit service and was eventually struck off charge on 21 June 1947. F/S Hoggard RAAF, meanwhile, converted to Lancasters and joined 15 Squadron. On 2 November 1944, he had the terrible misfortune to collide, over Holland, with another Lancaster. Four others died with him, but Sgt Garber RCAF and Sgt Jeffrey RAAF are presumed to have parachuted safely; Sgt Richardson had been replaced by a Sgt J C Millar (see Bomber Command Losses, Volume 5, page 468).

	1659 HCU	**Halifax V**	**LL288**	**RV-R**	**Training**

F/S E J Henn RCAF
Sgt J J Berch RCAF   inj

T/o 1605 Topcliffe tasked for circuit training but the Halifax swung to port and F/S Henn RCAF called to his flight engineer to close the throttles. At that moment, the aircraft ran onto soft ground and as the port wheel sank into soft earth, the oleo was wrenched off. Initially declared as repairable at unit level, no work was undertaken and the airframe was struck off charge on 9 June 1944.

28-29 May 1944	**1667 HCU**	**Halifax V**	**DG236**		**Training**

F/S W T Ramsden   inj
Sgt Chestnut
Sgt Howard
F/O R P Simpson   inj
Sgt Crompton
Sgt Stubbing
Sgt R D Macdonald   inj

T/o 2315 Sandtoft for general night flying practice, during which the oil pressure reading for the port inner Merlin dropped considerably. Having successfully feathered the motor, the crew continued with their detail but when the remaining engines failed, at 10,000 feet, the order to bale out was given, leaving the bomber to crash at 0325 near Holton, 2 miles NW from Wragby in Lincolnshire. F/S Ramsden was treated in Sandtoft station sick quarters for an ankle injury and F/O Simpson was taken to Lincoln Military Hospital, similarly afflicted. For eight hours after the crash, nothing could be found of Sgt Macdonald until his unconscious form was spotted, trapped in the remains of the rear turret. Admitted to RAF Hospital Rauceby where his head wounds received attention.

29 May 1944	**1657 HCU**	**Stirling I**	**R9283**	**XT-H**	**Enemy Action**

Damaged beyond repair, while in a hangar at Shepherds Grove, as a consequence of the incident summarised below.

	1657 HCU	**Stirling I**	**R9298**	**-O**	**Enemy Action**

F/O W A C Yates   +
Sgt S Sterry   +
Sgt N Nicholson   +
Sgt J Carter   +
Sgt G Wood   +
Sgt T R Farley   +
Sgt J W Grainger   +

T/o Shepherds Grove for night circuit practice. On approach to land, shot down from 1,000 feet at 0239 by an enemy intruder from II./KG51 and crashed onto a hangar, wrecking the Stirling summarised above and Mk.III LK506. Debris from the stricken aircraft also fell onto the night-flying equipment store. Sgt Grainger was buried in Cambridge City Cemetery, the others were conveyed to their home towns. It will be recalled that F/O Yates and his crew had been involved in a serious accident on 9 May (see page 108).

	1657 HCU	**Stirling I**	**BF404**	**-Y**	**Training**

S/L W N Crebbin DFC
F/S W P Moffat RNZAF
Sgt A H R Williams
Sgt D Bailey
Sgt P Bellingham
Sgt W Ashcroft
Sgt R Apps
Sgt J Stansell

T/o 0033 Shepherds Grove intending to carry out night circuit training but a tyre burst and the crew were directed to land at Woodbridge. This was duly accomplished, at 0103, with the wheels retracted. S/L Crebbin had been amongst the first to fly the Stirling, gaining his DFC, which was Gazetted on 16 January 1942, with 7 Squadron.

	1657 HCU	**Stirling III**	**LK506**	**AK-S**	**Enemy Action**

Wrecked as a result of the incident described above (Stirling I R9298).

29 May
1944

1663 HCU **Halifax V DG276 OO-A** Training

P/O R E C Hogg RNZAF T/o 0123 Rufforth for night circuits. Made a low approach and the pilot elected to overshoot. Having done so, the controls became extremely sluggish and on touch down at 0138 the Halifax veered from the runway and lost its undercarriage. On coming to a stop, a fire broke out but there are no reports of anyone being hurt.

31 May
1944

1654 HCU **Stirling III LK517** Training

P/O S R Wilson + T/o 1400 Wigsley for a cross-country detail.
Sgt D W Curtis + Broke up in cloud and crashed 1650 at West
Sgt N H Crawford + Thickley Farm between Midridge and Shildon,
F/O J McC Brooks + two miles W of Aycliffe, Durham. It was con-
Sgt F Bates + sidered that the tail assembly had been put
Sgt T Parr + under excessive strain and this led to the
Sgt W J Lawton + eventual structural failure. All were buried,
or cremated, in cemeteries around the United Kingdom, the last four named all being taken to Lancashire. David Thompson reports that a commemorative bench and plaque naming the crew has been placed on the boundary of Shildon Cricket Field.

31-1 Jun
1944

1667 HCU **Halifax V LL414** Training

P/O L L Williams RCAF + T/o 2219 Sandtoft for a night cross-country,
Sgt S W Doughty + that eventually carried the crew towards eastern
Sgt J A Treby + Scotland. At approximately 0200, the Halifax
F/O W Campbell RCAF + went into a spiral dive, broke up and plunged
F/S R T Dean RCAF + into Park Shielin, Caenlochan Forest, Glenisla,
WO1 J S MacDonald RCAF + Angus (Map Reference QO 6999). Six of the crew
Sgt T Goldie RCAF + were buried under service arrangement at Montrose
Sgt V T Sherven RCAF + (Sleepyhillock) Cemetery. Sgt Doughty was brought south for a private interment at Barking (Ripple-side) Cemetery, while it seems likely that the body of F/O Campbell RCAF was claimed by relatives as he rests in Uphall Cemetery in West Lothian. Air accident investigation branch staff were unable to determine the cause of the crash, but it was thought that engine failure and the prevailing weather conditions were strong possibilities.

3 Jun
1944

1666 HCU **Halifax II W1235 -F** Training

F/O J W How RCAF T/o 1500 Wombleton for circuits and landings. Arrived on the runway at 1522, bounced twice and finished up in a field bordering the airfield. F/O How RCAF (he had 1,137 solo flying hours to his credit, but only 1.40 on type) stated that he tried to go round again, but the Halifax seemed to lose its flying speed.

4 Jun
1944

1656 HCU **Halifax II BB271** Training

F/S F E Elliot RCAF T/o 1040 Lindholme for a cross-country. On return to base, the crew were unable to lower the undercarriage, despite using the emergency system. Ordered to fly to the emergency strip at Carnaby, the crew complied and crash-landed there at 1845, their Halifax being declared a write off.

5 Jun
1944

1658 HCU **Halifax II JD462** Training

P/O R L Giles RAAF + T/o Riccall tasked for an air-to-sea firing
Sgt H W Stow + exercise. It is believed the crew made contact
Sgt H W Fricker + with base at around 1240, after which nothing
Sgt A Thomson + further was heard. All are Commemorated on
F/S E A Durrant + the Runnymede Memorial.
Sgt M R Bonser +
Sgt F W B Norris +
Sgt J T H Johnstone +

6 Jun
1944

69 Sqn **Wellington X JA619** Training

S/L A G Dawson + T/o Northolt for a night exercise, during which
F/O A S Smith inj the starboard engine lost power. An emergency
F/L H Wigley inj landing was attempted at Wratting Common but,
F/S C J Gubbins + tragically, the Wellington ploughed into a
W/O Willis RAAF Stirling that had burst a tyre on landing and was awaiting movement from the runway. Three scrambled from the flames that engulfed the two bombers, but it was not until the fire was brought under control that the bodies of the deceased were found.

6 Jun   **1651 HCU A Flt**   **Stirling III BF473   –C**   **Ground**
1944   Landed at Wratting Common at 0050 but the port
tyre burst and after coming to a stop, on the runway, the crew disembarked and
arrangements were put in hand to tow the damaged aircraft clear. However,
before this could be accomplished, a Wellington from 69 Squadron (see the
previous summary) arrived over the threshold at 0105 and crashed into the
Stirling. Within seconds a fierce fire had broken out and it would be two
hours before the combined efforts of Wratting Common's fire appliance and
the National Fire Service brigades from Haverhill and Balsham were able to
bring the blaze under control.

           1667 HCU   **Halifax V DG345**   **Training**
           F/O F H Tritton   T/o 0046 Sandtoft for night dual circuits and
           F/O C D Thieme   landings. Swung on landing, at 0101, running
                                               into a parked Halifax before coming to a stop
with a broken undercarriage. It was found that the throttles controlling the
port engines had jammed, thus preventing the pilot from reducing power evenly.

           1667 HCU   **Halifax V EB194 GG–N**   **Ground**
                                               Damaged beyond worthwhile repair in the
                                               incident summarised above.

6– 7 Jun **1667 HCU**   **Halifax V LL231   –G**   **Training**
1944   P/O C H Henry RNZAF   T/o 2356 Sandtoft for a night sortie. Several
                                               hours later, the coolant leaked from the port
inner and the motor was shut down. An attempt was made to get into Gamston and
the colours of the night were fired as the crew approached the runway. Touched
down at 0334, only to run into Wellington X LN535 belonging to the resident
Operational Training Unit (see Bomber Command Losses, Volume 7, page 298).

7 Jun   **1652 HCU**   **Halifax II DT554 GV–P**   **Training**
1944   F/O W H Dixon   inj T/o 1045 Marston Moor for fighter affiliation
           Sgt J R Dodsworth   inj training. At approximately 1220, the Halifax
           F/O W T Harding   crashed between Mickley and West Tansfield, two
           P/O I D H Clarson   small villages 5 and 6 miles respectively NW of
           P/O M P Moreton   Ripon, Yorkshire. Sgt McGoldrick's injuries
           Sgt D R Brown   inj proved fatal and he died at 1920 hours while
           Sgt J McGoldrick   inj undergoing treatment in York Military Hospital;
                                        he rests in Byer Moor Roman Catholic Cemetery.
Four, F/O Harding, P/O Clarson, P/O Moreton and Sgt Brown re-crewed with
W/O G H Stratford of 76 Squadron and all perished during a raid against a
flying-bomb facility at Acquet on 18-19 July 1944 (see Bomber Command Losses,
Volume 5, page 335).

           1654 HCU   **Stirling III LK594**   **Training**
           S/L J Swyers   +   T/o 0300 Wigsley for night training and crashed
           Sgt L T Cordon   +   three hours later near Saltby airfield. It is
           F/O F D Collinge RCAF   +   thought that S/L Swyers, who came from Newfound-
           F/O A E Lindenfield RCAF +   land to join the Royal Air Force on a short
           Sgt G V Bowden   +   service commission, may have lost control while
           Sgt M Hough   +   descending through cloud. He had 1,215 solo
           Sgt A J Davies   +   flying hours behind him, but only twenty-three
                                        on Stirlings (ten of these at night). His
funeral took place at Lincoln (Newport) Cemetery, but the two RCAF officers
were taken to Harrogate (Stonefall) Cemetery, while the others were claimed
by their next of kin.

7– 8 Jun **1654 HCU**   **Stirling III LK515**   **Training**
1944   P/O D C Gundry RAAF   T/o 2218 Wigsley for a Bullseye mission, seven
           F/S V J Scheldt RAAF   crew aboard. While cruising at 15,000 feet,
           F/S E Burke RAAF   the port inner failed and the crew headed for
                                         Crosby-on-Eden where, on touch down at 0118,
the inner starboard cut and moments later the Stirling ran into an irrigation
ditch. The sudden drop was sufficient to smash the undercarriage. After converting to Lancasters, the crew joined 463 Squadron, failing to return from
an attack on St-Cyr airfield on 24-25 July 1944 (see Bomber Command Losses,
Volume 5, page 351).

7- 8 Jun	1666 HCU	Halifax II	LW279 QY-A	Training

1944

P/O A T Gill RCAF	+
Sgt R R Norman RCAF	+
F/O W B Hawkins RCAF	+
Sgt W W Astles RCAF	+
WO1 W J Banner RCAF	+
F/O T H Wilson RCAF	+
P/O R F Warne RCAF	+

T/o 2214 Wombleton for a Bullseye. At 0359, the bomber flew into the ground roughly 500 yards SW of Cawton, 14 miles ESE from Thirsk, Yorkshire and burst into flames. A sudden deterioration in visibility was a contributory factor. All are buried in Harrogate (Stonefall) Cemetery. It is noted that Sgt Astles came from London, Ontario. No next of kin details have been appended, but the entry above his name in "They Shall Grow Not Old" is for a F/O John James Astles RCAF, also of London, Ontario, who was killed during operations to Leipzig in February 1944 (see Bomber Command Losses, Volume 5, page 89).

	1667 HCU	Halifax V	LL459	Training

P/O R L Francis RAAF	+
Sgt F W Reed	+
F/S W R R Porter RAAF	+
F/O W E L Moody RAAF	+
F/S G F Brown RAAF	+
F/S K W Hennessy RAAF	+

T/o 2140 Sandtoft for a night cross-country. Dived, out of control, circa 0210 onto the banks of the Humber, at a place known locally as Howden Dyke Island, just to the S of Hook and more or less directly E of Goole, Yorkshire. It is believed the Halifax stalled. The five RAAF airmen were buried in Harrogate (Stonefall) Cemetery, while Sgt Reed was cremated at Charing (Kent County) Crematorium.

8 Jun	1663 HCU B Flt	Halifax II	HX153 OO-U	Training

1944

Sgt I Rebick RCAF	

T/o 1303 Rufforth for the pilot's first solo on type. Twenty minutes later, and while flying at 1,000 feet, the port outer Merlin began to shower sparks into the slipstream. With the engine feathered, the crew headed for home but before they could land, the port inner lost power and had to be stopped. Losing height, the tail wheel slammed into the roof of the station's sick quarters and seconds later the bomber was on the ground and burning near the domestic site. Amazingly, the crew emerged from the wreckage, shaken but otherwise unharmed.

9 Jun	1652 HCU	Halifax II	LW295 GV-R	Training

1944

F/O S R Bolter	+
Sgt R H Kilner	+
P/O J Hoar RAAF	inj
F/O J I T Irwin	+
F/S J W H Cruse RAAF	inj
P/O R W H Charles	inj
F/O A F Tidmarsh DFC	+

T/o 0037 Marston Moor for a night exercise but failed to gain height before flying through the upper branches of some eighty foot high trees and crashed, heavily. Of those who lost their lives, three were buried privately, while their skipper was interred in Harrogate (Stonefall) Cemetery. F/O Tidmarsh had previously flown with 51 Squadron and details of his award had appeared in the London Gazette on 19 October 1943. At the time of the accident, slight rain was blowing across the airfield.

	1662 HCU	Halifax II	W1187	Training

F/S R H Williams RNZAF	

T/o 1832 Blyton for circuits and landings, a total of three persons being aboard. A mere six minutes later, the Halifax swerved sharply on landing and the undercarriage folded under the strain.

10 Jun	1659 HCU	Halifax V	DK235 RV-V	Training

1944

F/O R G Goddard	
P/O D D McNeil RCAF	inj
F/O J F Harris RCAF	

T/o 0119 Topcliffe for dual in night circuit practice, the crew comprising of an instructor, two pupil pilots and four others. At 0124, possibly with P/O McNeil RCAF at the controls, the Halifax landed but ballooned back into the air, swung to the right and before F/O Goddard could intervene, the aircraft was on the ground, its undercarriage smashed and a fire developing in the outer port engine. Having been posted to 431 Squadron, F/O Harris RCAF failed to return from Hamburg in late July 1944 (see Bomber Command Losses, Volume 5, page 358).

2 Jun	1652 HCU	Halifax II	LW299	Training

944

Sgt M S Bruce	

T/o Marston Moor to practice circuits and landings. Landed at 1237, normally, only for the port undercarriage leg to snap.

16 Jun   **1651 HCU B Flt**   **Stirling I**   **BK623 BS-V**   **Air Test**
1944   F/O H J Dalzell DFM RNZAF   T/o 1135 Wratting Common, four being aboard.
Cruising at 700 feet, the port outer cut and
the crew tried to land at Stradishall. Their approach, however, was unsatisfactory but while trying to go round again, the Stirling was reluctant to
climb and a crash-landing ensued at 1210. Posted to "1651" on 26 June 1943,
F/O Dalzell RNZAF had gained an immediate DFM during a visit to Rostock in
the April. Serving at the time with 75 Squadron, his award was Gazetted
on 25 May 1943.

17 Jun   **1660 HCU**   **Stirling III**   **EF209 TV-H**   **Training**
1944   F/O M F Smith DFC RAAF   +   T/o Swinderby to practice three-engined landings.
F/S F A Martin   +   Crashed 0345 near Stapleford, 10 miles SW from
Sgt J Stabler   +   Lincoln, after taking violent evasive action to
Sgt J Totten   inj   avoid a midair collision. Those who survived
F/S R H Turrell DFM   +   were taken to various hospitals, Sgt Totten and
Sgt R L Wade   inj   Sgt Wade dying within hours of being admitted to
F/S H W R Tufts RCAF   +   Newark General Hospital. F/O Smith RAAF, whose
Sgt E E Allen   inj   award had been won with 467 Squadron (Gazetted
Sgt D F Cook   inj   30 June 1944) was laid to rest in Cambridge City
Sgt D G Smith   inj   Cemetery, but F/S Tufts RCAF was taken north to
Harrogate (Stonefall) Cemetery. The others who
died were conveyed to their home towns for burial. F/S Turrell had recently
completed a tour with 44 Squadron and the London Gazette carried details of his
award thirteen days after his untimely death. Sgt Cook eventually returned to
active duty and was killed whilst flying with 189 Squadron in early March 1945
(see Bomber Command Losses, Volume 6, page 103).

18 Jun   **1663 HCU**   **Halifax V**   **DK194**   **-J**   **Training**
1944   Sgt J D R Jackson   +   T/o 1022 Church Fenton to practice circuits
Sgt D Pritchard   +   and landings, combined with procedures for over-
F/O R W Crutcher   +   shooting and it was while carrying out such an
Sgt H G Smith   +   action that eyewitnesses saw thick black smoke
Sgt G Brazier   +   pouring from the outer port engine. Flying
Sgt B G H Small   +   Control then heard a brief call from the pilot,
indicating he was losing control and almost
immediately the bomber smashed into a field on the NE side of the airfield,
near the hamlet of Ryther, and burst into flames. F/O Crutcher of Rainham in
Eseex was buried at Harrogate (Stonefall) Cemetery, the others being claimed
by their next of kin.

19 Jun   **1656 HCU**   **Halifax II**   **BB272**   **Training**
1944   P/O F G Ferriday RAAF   T/o 0055 Sandtoft for night circuit practice.
Landed at 0115, but swung to port. P/O Ferriday
attempted to bring the Halifax back into line, but over corrected and as the
swerve to starboard increased, the port oleo folded.

19-20 Jun   **1663 HCU**   **Halifax V**   **LK725**   **Training**
1944   F/O C A Kirkham DFM   T/o 2357 Lindholme for dual in night flying,
Capt Brohou FFAF   at least three of the complement of eight
being Free French Air Force. With Capt Brohou
at the controls, the Halifax accelerated for take off at 0107 but swung with
such violence that before F/O Kirkham could take over the bomber was sliding
sideways, minus its wheels. Posted to "1663" on 14 February 1944, following
an eventful tour of operations with 76 Squadron, during the course of which
he had been wounded (see Bomber Command Losses, Volume 4, page 296), the
London Gazette of 15 October 1943, carried the citation for F/O Kirkham's
immediate award of the Distinguished Flying Medal.

21 Jun   **1658 HCU**   **Halifax II**   **LW289 TT-S**   **Training**
1944   F/L C C Kane   T/o 1007 Riccall to practice three-engined
F/S T S Coram RAAF   landings. Nearly an hour later, at 1102, the
Sgt L Blundell   inj   pilot under instruction allowed his approach
Sgt Callingham   speed to fall to a critical level and despite
Sgt Indge   opening the throttles to go round again, the
Sgt Ridley   Halifax crash-landed in a field bordering the
Sgt Risc   airfield. Sgt Blundell was treated for minor
injuries in station sick quarters.

21 Jun	1661 HCU	Stirling III	EH940		Training

1944

F/O F S Bradbury	+	T/o Winthorpe for his first solo on type and
Sgt F Dauble	inj	while flying at 1,800 feet, flames suddenly
Sgt T W Farrell	inj	appeared from one of the engines. Immediately,
P/O W R Clayton	+	the bomber dived and then banked to starboard
F/O G W Rankin	+	before crashing 1738 at Park Farm, Kettlethorpe,
Sgt A M McCune	inj	nine miles WNW from the centre of Lincoln. In
Sgt J A Micallef	+	the blaze that followed, considerable damage was
Sgt W H Miller	+	done to a barn and farm machinery. Three were

given service burials at Oxford (Botley) Cemetery
while P/O Clayton and F/O Rankin were laid to rest at Ashton-under-Lyne (Hurst)
Cemetery and Cathcart Cemetery respectively. Their skipper came from Lomas De
Zamora, Argentina.

1663 HCU	Halifax V	LL488	-A		Training

F/O L Falgate DFC	T/o 0900 Holme-on-Spalding Moor with seven
Lt Lau FFAF	Free French Air Force crew aboard for a demon-
	stration in three-engined flying. Ten minutes

later, while taking overshoot action, the pilot at the controls lowered the
nose in order to increase speed but failed to notice that he was dangerously
close to trees bordering the airfield. Thus, the port wing struck some branches
and jammed the aileron, necessitating an immediate forced-landing. Similar to
F/O Kirkham (see page 118), F/O Falgate had completed a tour of operations with
76 Squadron, participating during 1943 in all four attacks on Hamburg and then
taking part in the crucial raid on Peenemünde. Sadly, his death was reported
on 9 April 1946, and he is buried in Stanley New Cemetery, Co. Durham.

22 Jun	1652 HCU	Halifax II	R9494 GV-O	Training

1944

F/S J P Prouting RAAF	T/o Marston Moor for circuit practice, five
	crew, in total, being carried. Landed 1031,

but swung to the left and lost the starboard undercarriage, due to harsh braking.

22-23 Jun	1666 HCU	Halifax II	JD106 ND-T		Training

1944

F/O A P Haacke RCAF	+	T/o 2125 Wombleton for a night navigation detail,
Sgt P R Davis	+	during which the weather deteriorated to the
F/O M A Foy RCAF	+	extent that the crew became totally lost. Thus,
F/O H W Garwood RCAF	+	at approximately 0105, and while descending
WO1 J M C Plante RCAF	+	through the overcast, the Halifax flew into
P/O L B Lemon RCAF	inj	high ground at Rudland Rigg near Three Houses
P/O L A Scutt RCAF	+	on the ESE side of Cockayne, some 10 miles NNE
Sgt R W L Lucas	inj	of Helmsley, Yorkshire. Remarkably, P/O Lemon
		was not too seriously hurt, but Sgt Lucas was

very seriously injured. Of those who died, five rest in Harrogate (Stonefall)
Cemetery, while Sgt Davis, a Londoner, lies in Abney Park Cemetery. A footnote
pertaining to a taxying accident, involving this Halifax, appears on page 105.

Note. I am indebted to David Thompson for details concerning the crash location
which he visited in November 2001. At the time, a few small fragments of metal
could be seen, including a hand held Graviner fire extinguisher.

24 Jun	1653 HCU	Stirling I	EF334	-F		Training

1944

P/O R D Jennings RAAF	inj	T/o 1415 Chedburgh (crew No. 166, course No. 27)
Sgt J A Biddell		but obliged to swerve in order to avoid running
Sgt J K Fawcett		into a parked aircraft. This rapid change in
P/O J H Watts		direction caused the undercarriage to collapse.
F/S G W Johnson RAAF		
F/O G H Tregoning RAAF		
F/S R R Banks RAAF		

1656 HCU	Halifax II	LW345		Training

F/O L J C Remy	T/o 2212 Lindholme for night dual, the Halifax
	being crewed by just the two pilots. While in

flight, at 2,000 feet, the oil pressure gauge for the port outer displayed a
very low reading and the motor was shut down. F/O Remy made a good approach
and touched down at 2232, but almost immediately the bomber swung viciously,
ground looped and came to a stop with its undercarriage broken. Soon after,
the port outer caught fire and before the fire services could bring the flames
under control, the airframe was little more than a charred wreck. It is noted
that F/O Remy came from Belgium.

24 Jun	1662 HCU	Halifax II	JD267	—G2	Training

24 Jun 1944

1662 HCU   Halifax II   JD267   —G2   **Training**

P/O W H O'Callaghan RAAF   inj   T/o 1435 Blyton for circuit training but, in-
Sgt A Slack   +   advertently, the aileron locking bar had not
Sgt J C Waddell   +   been removed from the right hand control column.
F/S A S Kidman RAAF   +   In his post-crash statement, the pilot said he
W/O H R Molony RAAF   +   managed to climb to 500 feet but could not raise
F/S T N I Jones RAAF   +   the undercarriage. The Halifax then adopted a
moderately steep bank, which he was unable to
correct and not long afterwards the aircraft came down some 9 miles east of
Blyton. The three Australians who died were taken to Cambridge City Cemetery,
while Sgt Slack was laid to rest in Streatham Park Cemetery. His fellow flight
engineer, Sgt Waddell, lies in Cadder Cemetery, Lanarkshire. At the time, his
elder brother, Lt James Watson Waddell was in Italy with the 6th Battalion
Gordon Highlanders. On 29 September 1944, he fell in battle, probably during
the fighting for the Catarelo Ridge. He is buried in Faenza War Cemetery.

Note. For details regarding the death of Lt Waddell, I visited first the
Commonwealth War Graves Commission web site and then, after instigating a
search using Google.Com, located an excellent web page devoted to the 6th
Battalion Gordon Highlanders.

1662 HCU   Halifax V   LL366   —M2   **Training**

Sgt A Abrams RCAF   T/o 1015 Blyton for solo circuits and landings
but swung to the left. Sgt Abrams RCAF checked
the movement, but, again, the Halifax veered to port and this time he was unable
to control the situation. As he throttled back, the aircraft changed direction,
swerving to starboard and before coming to a halt, the undercarriage folded.

26 Jun 1944

1667 HCU   Halifax V   DG395   **Training**

F/O G N C Smyth   +   T/o 0036 Sandtoft for an exercise in night
Sgt J S Cherry   +   bombing, combined with circuit practice. Ten
Sgt B H Yates   +   minutes later, the authorities were notified
F/O E C Splane   +   that the Halifax had crashed in open country,
Sgt E Smallbone   +   some 2 miles E of Thorne, Yorkshire. It is
F/S R G Lugton RAAF   +   believed that the crew had collided with a
line of high-tension cables. F/S Lugton RAAF
and Sgt Yates were afforded service funerals; the former at Harrogate (Stone-
fall) Cemetery and the latter at nearby Hatfield (Woodhouse) Cemetery. Their
four companions were buried by private arrangements.

28 Jun 1944

1659 HCU   Halifax II   HR801 RV-D   **Training**

F/L D Boyle RCAF   T/o 2135 Topcliffe for a radar assisted cross-
country. Not long after their departure, the
port outer failed and the sortie was abandoned. Approaching Dalton airfield
at 2250, the Halifax overshot the runway and hit a Nissen hut. This wrecked
both the building and the aircraft, but there are no reports of injury.

1661 HCU   Stirling III   BK654   **Training**

F/O C B White   T/o Winthorpe for a night cross-country. Lost
power from two engines, first the starboard outer
and then the outer port. Unable to maintain height, a forced-landing took place
at 0740 near Gosberton, 10 miles SW of Boston, Lincolnshire.

30 Jun 1944

1653 HCU   Stirling I   R9269   **Training**

F/S R H Thompson RAAF   T/o Chedburgh (crew No. 174, course No. 28) for
Sgt J K Boulton   circuits and landings. Bounced twice on touch
F/S W S Ward RAAF   down but managed to go round again. Arriving on
F/S R J Dilley RAAF   the runway for the second time, at 1035, the
F/S R W Bland RAAF   starboard oleo gave way. On completion of their
Sgt D E Smith   training, the crew reported to 622 Squadron and
Sgt P S Withers   it was during the early part of their tour that
Sgt Withers, an ex-Air Training Corps cadet,
sustained wounds that proved fatal (the target was Kiel on 26-27 August 1944).
He is buried in Beck Row (St. John) Churchyard.

Note. An appreciation of the life of this eighteen year old air gunner
appears on page 35 of P and M Wilson's fine tribute to the airmen lying
in this Suffolk churchyard (The Airmen of St. John's- Beck Row).

30 Jun 1944	**1654 HCU**	**Stirling III**	**BK803**	**Training**

F/O W G F Filby   T/o Wigsley for a night navigation exercise.
During the flight, one of the port engines
became unmanageable and though the crew, eventually, stopped the engine they
were unable to feather the propeller. Their problems were further exacerbated
when the unit caught fire and at 2300, or thereabouts, all took to their parachutes and left the Stirling to crash near Rufford Colliery, Ollerton, on the
north-east side of Clipstone Forest, Nottinghamshire. After converting to
Lancasters, F/O Filby reported to East Kirkby and while flying as a second
pilot to F/L A G Henriquez of 630 Squadron, failed to return from operations
to Stettin in mid-August 1944 (see Bomber Command Losses, Volume 5, page 387).

1658 HCU	**Halifax II**	**DT549**	**Training**

Sgt P J McBrinn RCAF   T/o 0911 Riccall for a fighter affiliation
exercise, which was safely accomplished and
an uneventful landing made at 1121. However, while taxying towards its dispersal pan, the brakes failed and Sgt McBrinn RCAF was unable to prevent the
Halifax from rolling into a tree. By the winter of 1944-1945, he was based
at Holme-on-Spalding Moor, flying Halifaxes with 76 Squadron. During the
late evening of 1 February, his aircraft crashed in Norfolk while returning
from a raid on Mainz, killing five members of its crew, including F/S McBrinn
(see Bomber Command Losses, Volume 6, page 57).

1667 HCU	**Halifax V**	**DG338**	**Training**

F/O G S Baker RCAF   T/o 1837 Sandtoft briefed for circuit practice
but as the bomber gathered speed, the port tyre
burst. Out of control, the Halifax left the runway and moments later the oleo
on the starboard side collapsed. This was the aircraft's third, and final take
off accident; in March 1943, while on the strength of 1660 Heavy Conversion Unit
and with Sgt J R Saxton at the controls, it had been damaged at Swinderby, while
on 1 February 1944, and now at Sandtoft, P/O B A Templeman-Rooke had experienced
a similar mishap.

1- 2 Jul 1944	**1667 HCU**	**Halifax V**	**LL497**	**Training**

F/O G F Hutchinson RCAF   +   T/o 2212 Sandtoft for a night cross-country,
Sgt A Orrick   +   and last made contact at around midnight, at
F/O D J Evans RCAF   +   which time it was thought the bomber was in the
F/S G F Murphy RCAF   +   general vicinity of Shrewsbury. The entire crew
Sgt R M Pitts RCAF   +   are commemorated on the Runnymede Memorial.
Sgt A J M F Bailey   +
Sgt E Clayden   +
Sgt C B Norman   +

2 Jul 1944	**1654 HCU**	**Stirling III**	**EE899 JF-B**	**Training**

P/O J McKearn RAAF   T/o Wigsley for practice bombing. Landed 1201
F/O A M Harrison RAAF   inj   at Winthorpe, on three engines, but ballooned
Sgt K J N Williams RAAF   inj   back into the air, stalled and crashed, injuring
both air gunners. It is not thought, however,
that they were seriously hurt but damage to the Stirling was such that repairs
were considered to be impracticable.

1664 HCU	**Halifax V**	**EB156**	**Training**

P/O M F Troy RCAF   T/o 0920 Marston Moor for circuit training but
F/O D L Buchanan RCAF   after twenty minutes of normal flying, the
pilot made an approach and landed on the wrong
runway. Caught by the cross-wind, the bomber swung and lost its undercarriage.
Poor visibility, coupled with unfamiliarity of the airfield ("1664" was based
at Dishforth), were mitigating factors in this unfortunate incident.

4 Jul 1944	**1657 HCU**	**Stirling III**	**LK507 -L**	**Training**

F/S W E Richards RAAF   T/o Shepherds Grove for general training. Came
Sgt R Martin   in to land, on three engines, at 1840 and after
F/S R Kidd   touching down was deliberately swung in order
F/O W Mildren   to avoid running onto rough ground. Not sur-
Sgt J Doyle   prisingly, this action imposed an impossible
Sgt H Papps   load on the undercarriage which gave way,
Sgt K Nicholson   damaging the airframe beyond economical repair.

5 Jul	**1651 HCU**	**Stirling I**	**R9193 BS-B**	**Training**

5 Jul
1944

1651 HCU   **Stirling I**   **R9193 BS-B**   **Training**

P/O Zapalowski PAF   T/o 1545 Wratting Common carrying a standard crew complement of seven, tasked for general day flying training. On return to base at 1600, touched down on one wheel, bounced and before the pilot could open the throttles to cushion his next arrival, the Stirling thudded down and its tail wheel banged into a sodium flare. On inspection, it was decided that the damage was sufficient to write the airframe off charge. To the best of my knowledge, this was the only occasion at a Bomber Command heavy conversion unit, equipped with Stirlings and involving a Polish Air Force pilot that was deemed serious enough to declare the aircraft beyond repair.

1653 HCU   **Stirling III**   **LK458**   **-A**   **Training**

F/L A M F Alexander RNZAF   T/o 1300 Chedburgh (crew No. 181, course No. 29)
F/S A V Simmons   but while travelling at high speed, the starboard
Sgt K C Richards   main tyre exploded and this caused the under-
Sgt R W M Fulford   carriage to fold. For F/L Alexander RNZAF, this
F/O A Martin   was his third serious accident in three months of
Sgt R H Finlayson   instructing (see pages 101 and 109). The trainee
Sgt F G Owen   crew went to 90 Squadron and all were killed in
Sgt H E Newman   action in late August 1944 (see Bomber Command
                                 Losses, Volume 5, page 393).

1657 HCU   **Stirling I**   **W7463**   **-X**   **Training**

F/S E N Devine RAAF   T/o Shepherds Grove for circuit training, by
Sgt R C M Meyer   day. Diverted to Woodbridge and written off
Sgt J B Bell   here at 1415, while trying to land with its
Sgt M B Blaubaum RAAF   starboard undercarriage jammed. On completion
F/S G R Ferguson RAAF   of their training, and now flying Lancasters,
Sgt J J Coyle   all disappeared without trace while operating
Sgt R Burton   with 622 Squadron on 11-12 September 1944 (see
                                 Bomber Command Losses, Volume 5, page 415).

1662 HCU   **Halifax II**   **DG229**   **Air Test**

F/O E J Sharpe RAAF   T/o 1440 Blyton but damaged the undercarriage
                           (due to premature retraction) and having climbed away, could not get the unit to lock. Diverted to Carnaby and written off in the ensuing emergency landing, at 1625, when the unserviceable unit collapsed.

1667 HCU   **Halifax V**   **DG414**   **Training**

F/L B E McLaughlin DFC   +   T/o 1250 Sandtoft for dual instruction, the
P/O E Barley   +   crew comprising of an instructor, pupil pilot,
Sgt P Morrissey DFM   inj   four flight engineers, navigator, air bomber and
Sgt T E Carr   inj   a wireless operator air gunner. Lost control, at
Sgt I H Simmonds   inj   two hundred feet, while flying on three engines,
Sgt G Beedle   +   and crashed 1315 at Alkborough on the south bank
F/S J N Bond RAAF   +   of the Humber, 7 miles NNW from Scunthorpe,
Sgt H Fryer   +   Lincolnshire. Within thirty minutes of the
F/S R A Wixted RAAF   +   crash, F/L Brown, the unit's Medical Officer,
                               and an ambulance were at the scene. Of the three survivors, Sgt Carr was taken to station sick quarters at Elsham Wolds, while his two fellow flight engineers were admitted to Scunthorpe War Memorial Hospital where, soon after his arrival, Sgt Simmonds succumbed to his wounds. Those who died rest in various burial grounds, the two Australians being taken to Harrogate (Stonefall) Cemetery. F/L McLaughlin had flown a tour with 12 Squadron and detail of his award had been Gazetted on 12 November 1943. Sgt Morrissey's DFM had been gained with 101 Squadron and would be published on 19 September 1944. Tragically, having made an excellent recovery, Sgt Carr was killed on operations in mid-January 1945, while flying with 166 Squadron (see Bomber Command Losses, Volume 6, page 49).

6 Jul
1944

1651 HCU D Flt   **Stirling III**   **EF490**   **-E**   **Training**

F/O J W Davidson RCAF   T/o 0905 Wratting Common for bombing practice
                           over the Elmdon ranges. While flying at 6,500 feet, collided with Stirling III EF189 (which landed safely). F/O Davidson RCAF maintained control of his badly damaged aircraft but on return to base, overshot the runway and crashed at 1325. After converting to Lancasters, he proceeded to 115 Squadron, only to die during operations to Dortmund on 15 November 1944 (see Bomber Command Losses, Volume 5, page 486).

10–11 Jul	1666 HCU	Halifax II	HX147	Training

10–11 Jul 1944   **1666 HCU**   **Halifax II**   **HX147**   **Training**

F/L J D Best RCAF	+
Sgt B A Barker	+
F/O V Zoratti RCAF	+
F/O W A Corley RCAF	+
F/O J P Kolomic RCAF	+
WO1 R K Moore RCAF	+
Sgt N J Kidney RCAF	+
Sgt R F Simmons RCAF	+

T/o 2210 Wombleton for a night cross-country. According to a statement in, "They Shall Grow Not Old", the Halifax collided with a Wellington (its unit and serial are not identified), coming down at 0325 and bursting into flames on a road, a mile N of York, leading to Sutton-in-the-Forest. The seven Canadians were interred at Harrogate (Stonefall) Cemetery, while their flight engineer, Sgt Barker of Norbury, Surrey, was buried in Fulford Cemetery.

11 Jul 1944   **1653 HCU**   **Stirling III**   **LK450 H4-R**   **Training**

P/O I J Bittner RCAF	
Sgt J Templeton	
Sgt D G Ursel RCAF	
Sgt J W Minshall RCAF	
Sgt M C Murphy	
Sgt E A Mason	
Sgt G M Durant RCAF	

T/o 0400 Chedburgh (crew No. 115, course No. 26) tasked for a Bullseye. However, before lifting off, the pilot realised the air speed indicator was not functioning and he tried to abort the mission. Unfortunately, he had insufficient runway remaining and moments later the bomber sped into the overshoot area, where the wheels folded beneath him.

1657 HCU   **Stirling III**   **EH953**   **Air Test**

F/O A N Ward RNZAF	
Sgt F Samuel	
F/O R Zillwood	

T/o Shepherds Grove, carrying a crew of three. Overshot and crashed 1705, hitting an obstruction which snapped off the port oleo. Having come to a stop, straddling a ditch on either side of the road, the port inner caught fire and when the fire tender arrived, the position of the Stirling presented the firemen with great difficulty in getting their hoses near the seat of the flames.

12–13 Jul 1944   **1662 HCU**   **Halifax II**   **W7778**   **Training**

P/O A R Harris	+
Sgt R H Brooks	+
Sgt J J H Smith	+
Sgt A J Allen	+
F/S F W Filmer	+
Sgt J A Malcolm	+
Sgt V B Myers	+
Sgt A R Rogers	+

T/o 2305 Blyton for a Bullseye sortie. At 0320 the Halifax flew into the ground, three hundred feet above sea level and half-a-mile SW from Sotby, 7 miles NNW of Horncastle, Lincolnshire. The force of the impact reduced the aircraft to a collection of scattered bits and pieces and accident investigators were unable to determine the precise cause of the crash. In their report, it was stated that the evidence pointed to the Halifax hitting the ground at an angle of forty-five degrees, nose down, and at the time weather conditions were far from ideal; heavy drizzle with visibility varying between 2,000 and 4,000 yards though the cloud base was 2,000 feet. All were buried under private arrangements.

1652 HCU   **Halifax II**   **HR748 JA-J**   **Training**

Sgt R J P Barrell	inj
Sgt J G Grist	inj
Sgt H Osbourn	inj
Sgt D Park	+
Sgt H C Finch	+
F/S Ambrose	
Sgt H B Tennant	inj
Sgt G F Terry	inj

T/o Marston Moor, similarly tasked. While letting down through cloud and trying to home on the airfield, the starboard outer commenced rough running and was closed down; at the time, the crew were uncertain of their position. Subsequently, the Halifax crashed at 0505 between Huggate and North Dalton, roughly eight miles WSW of Great Driffield, Yorkshire. Sgt Park is buried in Scotland at Linlithgow Cemetery, while Sgt Finch lies in Parr (St. Peter) Churchyard, Lancashire. Of the survivors, Sgt Barrell and Sgt Terry were destined to spend the last few months of the war in captivity, while Sgt Osbourn and Sgt Tennant died when their 76 Squadron Halifax crashed in the Mainz area in late February 1945 (see Bomber Command Losses, Volume 6, page 98).

14 Jul 1944   **1662 HCU**   **Halifax V**   **DG424**   **Training**

P/O T Batley	

T/o 0155 Blyton for his fourth solo on type. Landed at 0205, but swung off the runway and damaged beyond repair when the port undercarriage folded. Just under a year later, on 3 July 1945, P/O Batley was killed, in Canada, while serving with No. 5 Operational Training Unit; he is buried in British Columbia at Matsqui (Hazlewood) Cemetery.

14–15 Jul 1944	1651 HCU D Flt	Stirling III	LK565 QQ-R	Training

F/S D H Wilson RAAF   +   T/o 2245 Wratting Common having being tasked to
Sgt J B Fairservice   +   carry out a Bullseye sortie. While banking at
F/O P Davie   +   3,000 feet, lost control and spun in, circa 0330,
Sgt W J Morgan   +   at Wendens Ambo near Saffron Walden, Essex. Both
F/S H W Evans RAAF   +   Australians were buried under military arrange-
Sgt S Houston   +   ments, while their six companions were claimed
Sgt H L Williams   +   by their next of kin. F/O Davie had accompanied
Sgt M Wilkinson   +   in his capacity as a "screened" navigator.

16 Jul 1944	1654 HCU	Stirling III	LK489	Training

F/L A Sandison   T/o Wigsley for night circuit training, a detail
F/L R A Hinkley   that concluded with the all too familiar sight
of the Stirling lying forlorn with its under-
carriage broken and the airframe stressed beyond repair. On this occasion, the
port tyre had blown out as the bomber touched down at 2340.

16–17 Jul 1944	1666 HCU	Halifax II	JD212 QY-H	Training

F/O J D Walace RCAF   T/o 2225 Wombleton for a night cross-country.
Landed at 0355, but swung violently to starboard
and damaged beyond repair. In his report, F/O Walace (sic) stated that he had
experienced great difficulty throughout the flight in keeping the Halifax trimmed
Subsequently, it was discovered that three starboard front centre spar braces had
been badly buckled.

17 Jul 1944	1658 HCU	Halifax II	JD202	Training

F/L A D Andrew   T/o 1041 Riccall to practice circuits on three-
P/O J H Bridgett RAAF   engines. Whilst carrying out the exercise, the
starboard inner propeller came off and as it
fell away, so it damaged two of the remaining three engines. With commendable
skill, F/L Andrew forced-landed at 1047 near Wistow Lordship, a hamlet somewhat
less than 2 miles N of Selby, Yorkshire. For his cool handling of a potentially
very dangerous situation, he received a "green" endorsement in his flying log.

17–18 Jul 1944	1653 HCU	Stirling III	LK521 H4-M	Training

P/O W B Martin RAAF   T/o 2150 Chedburgh (crew No. 170, course No. 27)
Sgt R G Brind   for a night cross-country, base – Oxford –
F/S R F Bush   Bristol – Tiverton – Barnstaple – St. Mary's –
F/O J Hordley   St. David's – Fishguard – Seagull Island –
Sgt N R Bainbridge   Aberystwyth – Granborough – Luton – base. At
Sgt W F Johnston   approximately 0200 the outer starboard failed
Sgt J Morris   and the bomber could not maintain its cruising
altitude. Despite these problems, the crew
managed to get back to base, but having run the remaining engines on a rich
mixture, fuel supplies were critical and at 0350 a forced-landing was made,
wheels up, on the south side of the airfield, in the vicinity of the bomb dump.
In the last moments of flight, the port outer engine had cut – starved of petrol.

18 Jul 1944	1654 HCU	Stirling III	EJ114	Training

F/O J S Ludford   T/o 1025 Wigsley to practice overshooting, on
F/S R A Jones RAAF   three-engines. Having done so at 1120, the
Stirling failed to climb and the crew forced-
landed, without hurt, at Girton, 8 miles NNE of Newark-upon-Trent, Nottingham.
Not long after his arrival at 463 Squadron, F/S Jones RAAF failed to return
from a raid on Calais (see Bomber Command Losses, Volume 5, page 436).

	1659 HCU	Halifax V	LL142 FD-L	Training

F/O O D Graham RCAF   T/o 0002 Topcliffe to practice night circuits
F/O J J Bell RCAF   inj   and landings, the crew of eight including an
F/O J W Lowe RCAF   inj   instructor and two pupil pilots. Having taken
off and climbed to 300 feet, the starboard
outer began to misfire. The pilot at the controls stopped the engine and,
having feathered the propeller, tried to land back on the airfield but misjudged his approach, opening the throttles in an attempt to go round again.
While doing so, the starboard inner cut and at 0015 a successful forced-landing
was accomplished, midway between Topcliffe and Skipton-on-Swale. An inspection
of the starboard engines revealed a broken inlet valve in the outer, which led
to the flames traps being burnt through, and a major coolant leakage from the
inner. Neither of the two pupil pilots were badly injured.

18 Jul   **1663 HCU**   **Halifax V** **DK178 OO-S**   **Training**
1944   Lt E E Deleyze FFAF   T/o 1451 Rufforth for fighter affiliation, an
exercise that proceeded to plan until the crew
made ready to land. Nearing Rufforth, they discovered that the undercarriage
was firmly stuck in its up position and, subsequently, they were advised to
divert to the emergency landing strip at Carnaby. This they did, forced-landing
at 1807 without injury.

19 Jul   **1654 HCU**   **Stirling III** **LJ539**   **Training**
1944   F/S C Bausch   T/o Wigsley but on climb out and upon applying
the brakes, prior to selecting the undercarriage
up, the Stirling began to vibrate quite alarmingly. F/S Bausch promptly turned
back and landed at 1310, but overran the runway and finished up in the overshoot
area with the wheels folded.

         1658 HCU   **Halifax II** **JB844**   **Training**
         P/O A F Forrest   T/o 1549 Riccall for fighter affiliation and
air-to-sea firing. While flying in cloud, both
starboard engines failed and a crash-landing ensued at 1609 roughly one hundred
yards N of Mount Pleasant Farm on the Farlington road, W of Sheriff Hutton and
about 10 miles NNE from the centre of York.

19-20 Jul **1654 HCU**   **Stirling III** **EH951**   **Training**
1944   F/S L Peart RAAF   T/o 2245 Wigsley for a long night navigation
sortie. Cruising at 11,000 feet, the port
inner engine caught fire and all attempts to feather the unit were unsuccessful.
Lost height to around 8,000 feet, at which stage the starboard inner stopped.
Wisely, the crew decided to take to their parachutes and at 0145 the Stirling
fell to earth at Glebe Farm, Clipstone, 5 miles NE from Mansfield, Nottingham.

20 Jul   **1661 HCU**   **Stirling III** **EF444 GP-F**   **Training**
1944   Sgt S Bowden   inj T/o Winthorpe for general training, during which
         Sgt A K Moncur   + problems were experienced with all four engines.
         Sgt L W Nagley   The order to bale out was given and seven were
         Sgt S C Alldis   able to do so before the bomber crashed at 1030
         P/O Bray   at Dawson's Corner, Farsley on the Leeds to
         Sgt Hughes   Bradford road. It is presumed Sgt Moncur failed
         Sgt Hammett   to leave the stricken aircraft and he is buried
         Sgt S C Green   in Scotland at Dundee Eastern Necropolis. By
                                the autumn, most of the crew were flying with
57 Squadron, their tour being brought to a premature close on Armistice Day when
they failed to return from Harburg (see Bomber Command Losses, Volume 5, page 484).

         1664 HCU   **Halifax V** **DG348**   **Training**
         F/O H W Elder RCAF   T/o 0141 Dishforth for circuit practice, at night.
Landed ten minutes later, but swung to starboard,
ground looped (in order to avoid parked aircraft) and came to rest minus its
undercarriage.

21 Jul   **1654 HCU**   **Stirling III** **LJ628**   **Training**
1944   F/O J O'Leary   T/o 1005 Wigsley to practice both two and three-
         P/O L Gardiner   engined flying. On two engines, the Stirling
         Sgt Ludlow   would not hold its height and before remedial
         Sgt McDonald   action could be taken, the aircraft emerged from
         Sgt T Burroughs   inj the cloud base and flew into the ground, circa
          Sgt Coulson   1045, on Upper Commons, between Margery Hills
         Sgt Walsh   and Bradfield in the Peak District. The tail
         Sgt L S Van Nierkerk   inj gunner came from Shabani in Southern Rhodesia.

23-24 Jul **1666 HCU**   **Halifax II** **JD372 ND-V**   **Training**
1944   P/O A D Moffat RCAF   + T/o 2145 Wombleton for a Command Bullseye.
         Sgt I Livingstone   + Spun from 7,000 feet and crashed 0355 following
         F/O G A Lewthwaite RCAF   + an uncontrollable fire in the starboard outer,
         F/S D F Dittmer RCAF   + coming down roughly 2 miles SE from Slingsby,
         P/O F H Green RCAF   + eight miles SW of Pickering, Yorkshire. Five
         Sgt A C Reynolds RCAF   + of the Canadians rest in Harrogate (Stonefall)
         Sgt J C Ludlow RCAF   + Cemetery, while P/O Green RCAF, who had married
                                Nellie Green of Parkstone, lies in St. Pancras
Cemetery at Finchley. Sgt Livingstone is buried in Oban (Pennyfuir) Cemetery.

24 Jul	1660 HCU	Stirling III	EH978		Training

24 Jul 1944 1660 HCU Stirling III EH978 Training

F/O J B Josling DFC	+
F/L A L Ray RNZAF	+
Sgt A S A Johnson	+
Sgt N Fox	+
Sgt G W Holford	+
F/O H J Bennett	+
Sgt H S Buckley	+
Sgt J Mitchison	+
Sgt R W Parker	+

T/o 0040 Swinderby for a night exercise but hit an oak tree and lost the port tail plane and elevator. With the Stirling perilously unstable, F/O Josling made a desperate effort to land straight ahead at nearby Winthorpe, only to be baulked at the last moment by an aircraft on the runway. Seconds later, he lost the last remaining vestiges of control and crashed near the airfield. Three are buried in Cambridge City Cemetery, one being Sgt Johnson, a Nigerian from Bluite Metta, Lagos. He had enlisted on 4 August 1943. The others were claimed by their next of kin. F/O Josling had served previously with 57 Squadron and details of his award had been Gazetted on 21 January 1944. Errol Martyn, in his remarkable tribute the New Zealanders who fell while flying, observes that F/L Ray's elder brother (by a year), F/S Dudley Thomas Ray RNZAF, a wireless operator with 14 Squadron, was killed when his Marauder IA FK375 crashed into the sea off Serifos during the course of a shipping strike. His memory is perpetuated by the Alamein Memorial.

24-25 Jul 1944 1661 HCU Stirling III LK591 Training

P/O A E Bullock RAAF	inj
Sgt J A Edmonds	+
Sgt F C White	+
F/O B C Roderick RAAF	+
F/O H E A Brown RAAF	inj
F/S J J Ferguson RAAF	inj
F/S C R Neilson RAAF	inj
Sgt K G Judd RAAF	inj

T/o 2342 Winthorpe for a Command Bullseye. While operating at 15,500 feet, the oxygen supply failed and the crew had descended to 9,500 feet when the port outer cut. No sooner had this motor been feathered, when the inner port caught fire. Heading for Gaydon, the instructor (P/O Bullock RAAF) restarted the port outer but as the Stirling was by now very low he called off his first approach and tried to go round again, opening the throttles accordingly. However, the crippled aircraft refused to climb and at 0236 the flight ended with a severe crash, just short of Gaydon's runway. Those who survived the impact were admitted to Wellesbourne Mountford's station sick quarters. F/O Roderick is buried in Oxford (Botley) Cemetery; Sgt Edmonds rests in Stoneleigh (St. Mary) Churchyard, while Sgt White was taken to Streatham Park Cemetery. Both were flight engineers.

1664 HCU Halifax V LK694 ZU–J Training

F/O A P Hulhala RCAF

T/o 2306 Dishforth similarly tasked. After three hours flying, the starboard outer was feathered, following problems with the constant speed unit. Thus, on return to base, F/O Hulhala RCAF was obliged to land on three engines, doing so at 0406, only to swing off the runway and come to a stop with a broken under-carriage.

25 Jul 1944 1667 HCU Halifax V EB190 GG–H Training

P/O S M Laird	+
Sgt D G E Wilkins	inj
Sgt J G McLeod	+
Sgt A M Salter	+
P/O B W H Stalvies	+
F/S A L Cheatle RAAF	inj
Sgt J M Wishart	inj
Sgt E G Woodward	inj

T/o 0145 Sandtoft for night circuit practice. Two minutes later, the Halifax dived from a height of 400 feet, failed to recover, and crashed just inside the border with Yorkshire and about 5 miles NE from Doncaster, where the survivors were rushed by ambulance. Soon after their arrival at the Royal Infirmary, two, Sgt Wilkins and F/S Cheatle RAAF, died from their injuries. The latter, along with P/O Stalvies of Nottingham and Surrey born Sgt Salter, rests in Harrogate (Stonefall) Cemetery, while the others who perished were conveyed to their home towns. Sgt Woodward made a good recovery and by the autumn had resumed his training. Then, on 10 October, his Halifax crashed during a night exercise and on this occasion he did not survive the outcome.

26 Jul 1944 1651 HCU Stirling I BK600 YZ–R Training

F/S A S Woodbridge

T/o 0855 Wratting Common for day practice in circuit procedures. For the next fifty minutes the sortie proceeded, as planned, but then a slightly misjudged landing resulted in the undercarriage being ripped from its mountings. A little over three weeks later, F/S Woodbridge crashed while still in the throes of training and lost his life.

| 26 Jul
1944 | 1657 HCU | Stirling III | EF252 —C | Training |

F/S K A M Palmer RAAF + T/o 2245 Shepherds Grove but the outer starboard
Sgt K J Abraham + engine cut and before F/S Palmer RAAF could take
Sgt F Bowers + steps to correct the situation, his aircraft had
Sgt D J Whiffin + slammed into the Watch Office killing him and
Sgt S T Collis + most of his crew. Along with Sgt Whiffin, he
Sgt F Barber inj was buried in Cambridge City Cemetery, while the
Sgt P L Capon inj others were taken to their home towns. Of the
two survivors, Sgt Barber was admitted to RAF
Hospital Ely, while Sgt Capon was treated for shock in station sick quarters.

| | 1660 HCU | Stirling III | LK483 —V | Training |

F/O T Bain T/o 0930 Swinderby but commenced to swing. The
Sgt D W Dunthorpe inj throttles were closed but with the boundary hedge
Sgt Cryer looming ever closer, F/O Bain raised the wheels
Sgt R J Harris inj and, thus, effectively reduced his aircraft to
Sgt C J Western inj a ground training aid. As such, it took the
Sgt Melody serial 4860M.
Sgt Hardy
Sgt Oberneck

| 26–27 Jul
1944 | 1656 HCU | Halifax II | BB221 | Training |

F/O R Crowther RCAF T/o 2205 Lindholme for a night cross-country,
at high-level. Indeed, it was while flying at
twenty thousand feet that the starboard outer failed, followed almost immediately
by the port inner, which caught fire. This was quelled by prompt use of the
Graviner and both engines were feathered. F/O Crowther RCAF then contacted
Wrexham, by radio, and was given permission to land. Unfortunately, the duty
runway was relatively short (a length of 1,100 yards is quoted) and at 0120
the Halifax ran into its overshoot area, carried over a bank and caught fire.

| 27–28 Jul
1944 | 1651 HCU | Stirling III | LJ451 QQ–C | Training |

P/O J W Hocking RAAF inj T/o 2337 Wratting Common for a night cross-
Sgt D E Johnson inj country. According to No. 31 Base report, flames
Sgt McFarlane were seen streaming from the starboard inner as
Sgt B Thorgrimson RCAF the bomber flew at 7,500 feet over East Anglia.
F/S S R Tebutt RAAF Within seconds, the remaining engines appeared
Sgt H V Brooker inj to fail and at 0002 the bomber crashed near a
Sgt H W Benson inj Royal Observer Corps post at Benick, not far
from March, Cambridgeshire. It seems likely
that all, or most, of the crew baled out as the injuries reported are mainly
described as slight, Sgt Johnson and Sgt Brooker sustaining sprained ankles.
P/O Hocking RAAF, however, was grievously hurt and succumbed to his wounds soon
after; from Nambour in Queensland he is buried in Cambridge City Cemetery.

| 28 Jul
1944 | 1657 HCU | Stirling III | LJ506 | Training |

P/O V Davis T/o 1330 Shepherds Grove with the pitot tube
Sgt J Shewen cover still in place. With no indication of
Sgt J Furness air speed, the take off was abandoned and the
F/S J Lowe Stirling ran into a ditch, whereupon its main
F/S Skilbeck wheels folded.
Sgt S Taylor
Sgt P Wilson

| 29 Jul
1944 | 1654 HCU | Stirling III | LJ585 | Training |

F/S P A Jacobs + T/o 1605 Wigsley for what is described as a
Sgt S A Findlater + short cross-country, combined with practice
F/S J Jones + bombing. Those who survived (having baled out)
P/O N H B Lucas DFC + state that a violent engine vibration was felt
Sgt Harding throughout the aircraft and was followed by
F/S Mackenzie complete failure of the unit. Subsequently,
Sgt Morgan the Stirling went down, on fire, to crash at
Sgt Sasey approximately 1840 near Normanton-on-Trent,
Sgt Hodgkins ten miles N of Newark-upon-Trent, Nottingham.
F/S Jacobs was laid to rest in Croydon (Mitcham
Road) Cemetery, Sgt Findlater was taken back to Edinburgh and interred in the
city's Easter Cemetery, F/S Jones was buried in Leicester (Belgrave) Cemetery
and P/O Lucas, a staff navigator, was cremated in Hull Crematorium. His DFC,
gained during a recent tour with 9 Squadron, was published on 17 October 1944.

30 Jul	1656 HCU	Halifax II	BB261		Training

30 Jul 1944 — **1656 HCU** — **Halifax II** — **BB261** — **Training**

P/O G E Collins +
Sgt R J Neeson +
Sgt H Jones +
Sgt N L Skidmore +
Sgt T W Lowes inj
Sgt G F P McCarthy +
Sgt L Marshall inj

T/o 0224 Lindholme for night circuit practice. At 0228, following the aircraft's second take off, the bomber flew into a swirl of mist and crashed near Hatfield Woodhouse, 7 miles NE from Doncaster, Yorkshire. Sgt McCarthy of York was buried in Hatfield (Woodhouse) Cemetery but the others who died were claimed by relatives.

1 Aug 1944 — **1661 HCU** — **Stirling III** — **LK494** — **Training**

F/O L A Coxhill
F/S W Riddel

T/o 1608 Winthorpe but a tyre burst and the undercarriage gave way, damaging the aircraft beyond repair. None of the ten airmen aboard were hurt.

3 Aug 1944 — **1661 HCU** — **Stirling III** — **EE967 GP-Q** — **Training**

F/O M W Bell

T/o 1558 Winthorpe but began to swing. This was partially corrected, only for the pilot to realise he was heading toward another aircraft and while taking avoiding action the already stressed undercarriage gave up the ghost and collapsed. Converting to Lancasters, F/O Bell was nearing the end of his operational tour when he failed to return from Lutzkendorf in mid-March 1945 (see Bomber Command Losses, Volume 6, page 127). At the time, he was flying with 227 Squadron.

1666 HCU — **Halifax II** — **JD274** — **Training**

P/O J W R G Sicotte RCAF

T/o 1345 Wombleton for bombing practice. During the sortie, it became necessary to feather the outer starboard Merlin, after which the Halifax gradually lost height until the altimeter was reading 1,100 feet. At this point, the inner engine began to show signs of failure and, as a precaution, P/O Sicotte RCAF attempted to restart the outer motor. Unfortunately, he was not successful and the effect of a windmilling propeller induced so much drag that he was obliged to forced-land, at 1725, near Holtby Grange on the Great North Road, a little over 2 miles NNW from Leeming Bar in Yorkshire.

5 Aug 1944 — **1663 HCU** — **Halifax V** — **DG411 OO-S** — **Training**

Capt D Hellen SAAF

T/o Rufforth to practice circuits and landings. At this stage in his training, Capt Hellen SAAF had 249 hours of solo flying in his log book, but only two of these on type and was, therefore, relatively inexperienced. Thus, when he touched down at 1454, and swung to starboard he was unable to rectify the situation. Furthermore, his situation was not helped by the sight of a Halifax, parked on its dispersal pan, and in order to avoid a collision, he increased the turn and thereby imposed such a strain on the oleos that the wheels promptly folded.

6 Aug 1944 — **1651 HCU** — **Stirling I** — **R9243 QQ-K** — **Training**

F/O R T Gausden

T/o 2345 Waterbeach for night circuit practice but after fifteen minutes of the exercise, he lost control while accelerating to take off and when, eventually, the aircraft came to a stop it was damaged beyond repair.

7 Aug 1944 — **1664 HCU** — **Halifax V** — **DG363 DH-U** — **Training**

F/O L A Green RCAF +
Sgt G Morgan RCAF +
F/O A S McTavish RCAF +
F/O A T Gorman RCAF +
Sgt J W Ellis RCAF +
F/S V E Clark RCAF +
Sgt W L Southwick RCAF +

T/o 1420 Dishforth for air-to-air firing, the pilot having been briefed to keep his speed to 140 - 145 knots, relevant to that of the drogue towing aircraft. This instruction was adhered to, but, as the drogue towing crew later reported, F/O Green RCAF appeared to lose control while banking in a formation turn. With only 1,500 feet in hand, he was unable to recover before the Halifax plunged into the sea, less than a mile off the Yorkshire resort of Scarborough. In the aftermath of this tragedy, fresh orders were issued with 160 knots being advised as the recommended speed. Six bodies were never recovered and their names are perpetuated by the Runnymede Memorial but F/O McTavish RCAF, a Bachelor of Education, was given up by the sea and he now lies in Harrogate (Stonefall) Cemetery. It is also noted that F/O Green RCAF was an American from Montgomery, Alabama while with Gwynfryn as his Christian name, Sgt Morgan RCAF may have been of Welsh extraction, though no next of kin details appear in the Runnymede register to support this theory.

8 Aug	1666 HCU	Halifax II	HR855	Training

8 Aug 1944 — **1666 HCU** — **Halifax II** — **HR855** — **Training**

F/O W Osborne RCAF — T/o 1805 Wombleton with the intention of flying a practice bombing exercise, but the Halifax swung violently to the left, raced on for a further three hundred yards before the undercarriage was retracted in order to avoid a collision with aircraft parked near the airfield's boundary. The post accident inspection noted a high degree of buckling to the forward fuselage, suspected warping of the main spar, severe damage to the engine mountings for the outer starboard motor, plus other airframe damage that made repairs totally uneconomical.

9 Aug 1944 — **1663 HCU** — **Halifax V** — **LK700 OO-A** — **Training**

P/O L G L Mabile FFAF — T/o 2244 Rufforth tasked for fighter affiliation training, at night. As the Halifax cleared the runway, its port outer cut and a minute later an emergency forced-landing was made on the south side of the airfield, near Askham Richard. A fire broke out and before this could be quelled, the practice bombs began to explode in the heat. There are no reports of anyone being seriously hurt.

1666 HCU — **Halifax II** — **HR780** — **Training**

F/O W Harris RCAF — T/o 1208 Wombleton for bombing practice, combined with air-to-air firing. During the detail, the starboard outer failed and F/O Harris RCAF contacted Middleton St. George but was denied landing permission, due to an aircraft blocking the duty runway. However, the situation had become so fraught, that he was obliged to forced-land, at 1228, less than a mile NW of Sadberge, some 4 miles ENE from the centre of Darlington, Durham. Subsequently, an inspection of the damaged engine revealed traces of burnt glycol.

10 Aug 1944 — **1653 HCU** — **Stirling III** — **BK695 -B** — **Training**

F/O R T Hussey
Sgt J Bland
F/O R L Simpson RAAF
F/S G C Dalton RAAF
Sgt R May
Sgt C T O'Connor
Sgt G H Potter

T/o 0130 Chedburgh (crew No. 225, course No. 33) for night circuit practice. For the next fifty minutes all went smoothly but at 0220, as the Stirling was gathering speed, the port tyre deflated and this was followed by the main undercarriage collapsing.

1663 HCU — **Halifax V** — **DG360** — **Training**

Adj R A Hannendouche FFAF — T/o 0410 Rufforth for general training, a crew complement of eight being aboard, only to swing out of control. The pilot attempted to correct the situation by braking, but was too severe in his actions and the main wheels folded as a consequence.

1663 HCU — **Halifax V** — **DK204 -T** — **Training**

F/O E Lancaster — T/o 0100 Pocklington (having been detached here for night circuit training) but swerved, while landing, a mere five minutes later. Heading, at speed, down a disused runway, the port tyre ran over a number of sharp flints and was punctured. Within the next few seconds, the bomber was off the runway with its undercarriage broken.

11 Aug 1944 — **1654 HCU** — **Stirling III** — **EF510** — **Training**

F/O R G Lewis — T/o Wigsley for a short cross-country. While flying at 2,000 feet, both outer engines lost power. Unable to maintain altitude, the crew forced-landed at 1550, wheels up, at Willow Farm near Metheringham airfield in Lincolnshire.

12 Aug 1944 — **1653 HCU** — **Stirling III** — **EF192** — **Training**

W/O J Baines RNZAF
Sgt J Aldridge
Sgt P A Holt RNZAF
F/S J K Clements RAAF
Sgt J Brown
Sgt R Creasey
Sgt E A Bates

T/o 1410 Chedburgh (crew No. 231, course No. 34) for circuits and landings. But, before becoming airborne, a vicious swing developed and before corrective measures took effect, the main wheels had parted company with the rest of the aircraft.

Note. This particular Stirling had performed well on operations. Initially used by 199 Squadron as EX-J, it flew nineteen sorties and then, in the hands of 149 Squadron it mustered a further sixteen before being given up for training duties. With "149" it had carried the code combinations OJ-S and OJ-F.

12 Aug 1944	**1667 HCU**	**Halifax V**	**EB192**	**Training**

P/O W Wells   + T/o 0133 Sandtoft for a night bombing exercise.
Sgt E Heath   + While banking to starboard, in cloud, lost
F/S W Thompson RAAF + control and crashed 0153, onto high ground
F/S A B Talbot RAAF + at Winston Park, North Bawtry, on the border
F/S K K Abrams RAAF + between Nottinghamshire and Yorkshire (the
Sgt A S Watt   + aircraft's accident record card indicates the
Sgt A G Monnington + site as Map Reference 153/180090). Two of the
three Australians aboard, along with the tail
gunner, Sgt Monnington of Radford, Coventry, were taken to Harrogate (Stonefall)
Cemetery, but F/S Talbot RAAF had married Mary Talbot of Upton, Pontefract and
he was interred in Moorthorpe Cemetery. The others, too, were claimed by their
next of kin.

13 Aug 1944	**1653 HCU**	**Stirling I**	**R9254**	**-F**	**Training**

F/O W A Kirk RAAF T/o 1510 Chedburgh (crew No. 227, course No. 34)
F/O N G Flaxman   for circuits and landings only to come to grief
Sgt N R Allen   in circumstances not dissimilar to those reported
F/O M G Stewart   on the previous page (see W/O Baines RNZAF).
F/O J Adamson
F/O G R Soderberg
Sgt K F Thurman
Sgt W J Sadler

	1658 HCU	**Halifax II**	**DT743**	**Training**

F/S J A Phillips   T/o 1220 Riccall for circuit practice with the
P/O H F Robinson   trainee pilot, P/O Robinson, at the controls.
As the Halifax accelerated, F/S Phillips felt
the bomber drop suddenly to the right (its starboard tyre had burst) but before
he could react, the aircraft swung to port and lost its undercarriage. As the
official report concluded, "the undercarriage arch casting fractured, due to
side loads encountered in the swing, accentuated by the burst tyre; no evidence
of previous defects."

	1659 HCU	**Halifax V**	**LL171 FD-F**	**Training**

P/O J G Locke RCAF   T/o 2210 Topcliffe for a Bullseye sortie, eight
crew being aboard. Within minutes, however, the
oil pressure and temperature readings for the port outer rose above their safe
limits and the engine was feathered. On returning to base, and no doubt anxious
about having to land on three-engines, P/O Locke RCAF failed to notice that his
main wheels had failed to lock in the down position and, as a consequence, the
touch down at 2225 was followed immediately by a total collapse of the unit.

14 Aug 1944	**1654 HCU**	**Stirling III**	**EE914**	**Training**

F/O G C Lavigne RCAF T/o Wigsley for an air-to-sea firing detail,
over the North Sea. Flying at 1,000 feet, off
the Lincolnshire coast, the outer starboard failed and at around 1530, the bomber
was set down in the sea, some thirteen miles from the shore and twixt the towns
of Mablethorpe and Skegness. The outcome of this ditching is best described by
Bryce Gomersall; "a message was received by the Air Sea Rescue Marine Craft Unit
at Grimsby, at 1600, that an aircraft had ditched at 5314N 0030E and it was believed the crew had been rescued by two merchant vessels in the vicinity. Thus,
HSL 2573 left Grimsby at 1605 and at 1725 made contact with the "SS Daniel M",
which confirmed having picked up the entire crew of a Stirling from Wigsley at
1540 hours and having transferred the seven men, all uninjured, to the "SS WH
Daniels" bound for the Humber. The "SS WH Daniels" was met at 1745, ten miles
south of the Humber light vessel and the airmen were transferred to HSL 2573,
which returned to Grimsby at 1915 hours. A Warwick (P/254 Squadron, captained
by F/O Care) had seen the ditching, while on local flying, and provided the first
report. The Stirling floated for about thirteen minutes, and then sank."

	1666 HCU	**Halifax II**	**DT584 ND-J**	**Training**

P/O W A Egan RCAF   T/o 0040 Wombleton for a session of night
circuits and landings. At 0050, the Halifax
arrived over the threshold, touched down and swung to starboard. While trying
to bring his aircraft back onto the centreline, P/O Egan RCAF over corrected
and the ensuing swerve to the left was sufficient to remove the undercarriage
and cause substantial damage to the nose, starboard mainplane, flaps, rudder
and stabilisers.

14–15 Aug   **1663 HCU A Flt**   **Halifax V**   **DG277 OO–F**   **Training**
1944

F/O T G Smith RNZAF	inj	T/o 2333 Rufforth for an exercise in night
F/S J S Piper	+	navigation. At 0258, in conditions of poor
F/O D Gordon RNZAF	inj	visibility, the Halifax flew into rising ground
F/S A C M Ackrill	inj	on the SW side of Long Marston, a village to the
Sgt J C Finn	inj	west of the home airfield and 7 miles WSW from
F/O E H Ewin	inj	the centre of York. F/S Piper was buried,
F/O W D Waller	inj	privately, in Coulsdon (St. John) Churchyard,

Coulsdon and Purley. He was thirty-five years
of age. It seems likely that the survivors were quite seriously injured for
it is known that both air gunners died in an air accident on 5 March 1945,
while undergoing training at 1658 Heavy Conversion Unit, Riccall, this indicating they had not long since resumed active flying.

15 Aug   **1660 HCU**   **Stirling III**   **EE975**   **Training**
1944

P/O D McF Bowe RAAF	+	T/o Swinderby for a night exercise, in the
Sgt L R Frazer		course of which both outer engines failed.
Sgt S Nelson		As the bomber lost height, the crew were told
F/S R J Douglas RAAF	+	to bale out. Five left the doomed Stirling
F/S C O'Neill RAAF		in good order but by the time the pilot and
F/S G Maloney RAAF		navigator made their exit, the bomber had
Sgt C M Davis	inj	dropped below the safety margin for their

parachutes to fully deploy. Both were found
on Firth Fell and, subsequently, were buried with full military honours in
Harrogate (Stonefall) Cemetery. In due course of time, the wreckage of their
aircraft was cleared from Old Cote Farm near Arncliffe, an isolated village
on the bleak North Yorkshire moors, some 13 miles NNW from Skipton.

16 Aug   **1657 HCU**   **Stirling III**   **BF527**   **–Q**   **Training**
1944

F/O R J C Higgins	T/o 0050 Shepherds Grove but the undercarriage
Sgt D Walker	gave way as a consequence of the port tyre
F/O J Peyton	bursting.
F/S F Austerberry	
Sgt M McAteer	
Sgt D Denby	
Sgt R O'Connor	

17–18 Aug   **1651 HCU D Flt**   **Stirling III**   **LK519 QQ–O**   **Training**
1944

F/S A Woodbridge	+	T/o 2157 Wratting Common for night training.
Sgt F C Reeve	inj	At 0206 the crew were given permission to land
F/S I B Yorkston RAAF	inj	but reported they were having problems with the
Sgt W H Ford	inj	undercarriage. For the next forty minutes a
F/S D C McLellan RAAF	inj	series of exchanges took place, by radio, twixt
Sgt J Thompson	inj	the Stirling and Flying Control. Then, at 0257,
Sgt E S Campbell	inj	as Flying Control were responding to the crew's

latest message, two words were heard, "crash
land", and almost immediately the Stirling was sighted, flying at tree top
height, heading towards No. 4 runway where it smashed into a Stirling that
had been immobilised with a burst tyre. F/S Woodbridge was taken to Up Nately
(St. Stephen) Churchyard in Hampshire. It will be recalled that he had been
involved in a serious flying accident on 26 July (see page 126). Of the six
survivors, Sgt Campbell was dangerously injured and he was taken to station
sick quarters with severe bruising, head injuries and fractures to his right
clavicle and radius.

18 Aug   **1651 HCU A Flt**   **Stirling III**   **EF514**   **–K**   **Ground**
1944   Destroyed in the circumstances described in
the previous summary. Arrangements had been made to have the bomber towed
clear, but these had not been implemented before the accident occurred.

21 Aug   **1652 HCU**   **Halifax II**   **JD373 JA–A**   **Training**
1944

F/L F J L Wyatt	T/o 1621 Marston Moor for dual circuit training
F/S Williams	only for problems to manifest with the under-
	carriage. For several hours, the crew tried

all manner of ways to get the unit to fully retract and then, having been
diverted to the emergency strip at Carnaby, discovered that the wheels would
not lock down. Thus, at 1826, the Halifax was damaged beyond repair in the
crash-landing.

23 Aug **1944**	**1657 HCU**	**Stirling III**	**LK446 AK-D**	**Training**

P/O N Hesketh   +   T/o 2210 Shepherds Grove for a night navigation
Sgt E Pook   +   sortie. Lost without trace. All are commemorated
Sgt G J Baldwin   +   on the Runnymede Memorial. Both air gunners were
Sgt G C Hinves   +   nineteen years of age, as was Sgt Pook.
Sgt J McA Hutchens   +
Sgt H J Hutchinson   +
Sgt K P R Motley   +

24 Aug **1944**	**1652 HCU**	**Halifax II**	**DG226**	**Training**

Sgt C R Osborne RCAF   +   T/o 1429 Marston Moor but as the Halifax gained
F/S J E Robinson   +   altitude, the outer port burst into flames.
F/S E G Barrie RCAF   +   Those watching from the ground saw the bomber
F/O G D W Burnie RCAF   +   roll onto its back and dive onto Wetherby golf
F/O H Jones DFM   +   course, sited midway between the railway and the
F/S J D Morrison RCAF   +   River Wharfe. On impact, a huge cloud of black
smoke rose skywards. Four, the RCAF members of
the crew, are buried in Harrogate (Stonefall) Cemetery, while F/S Robinson and
F/O Jones rest in Altrincham, Bowden and Hale Cemetery and Hawarden Cemetery
respectively. The last named gained his DFM, Gazetted on 18 January 1944,
while serving with 76 Squadron. Immediately after the crash, the port outer
Merlin was recovered and subjected to a technical inspection. This revealed
a broken con-rod on No. 3 cylinder and the piston missing. In the opinion of
the specialist officer, overseeing the investigation, Sgt Osborne RCAF would
not have been able to feather the propeller. During 1978, two more engines
were excavated, one of these being restored and placed on display at the
Yorkshire Air Museum at Elvington.

	1653 HCU	**Stirling III**	**LJ445 -E**	**Training**

P/O B J Crocker RAAF   T/o 1210 Chedburgh (crew No. 211, course No. 32)
Sgt S L Miller   with the battery leads still attached. Despite
F/S A Segnit RAAF   some damage to the tail section, the crew climbed
Sgt P J Farmer   away but on return to base, at 1345, the under-
F/S W A Johnston RAAF   carriage collapsed, due in part to a rather
Sgt A D Smithson   heavy arrival.
Sgt A L Thompson

	1666 HCU	**Halifax II**	**LW325 QY-J**	**Training**

Lt P B Franklin SAAF   +   T/o 2102 Wombleton for a night cross-country
Sgt J B Iles   +   during which the propeller blades broke up on
F/S C B Schuller RAAF   +   the starboard outer. This, it was subsequently
F/O J V Hudson   +   assessed, would have set in train a violent
F/S J P Mansell RAAF   +   vibration and as Lt Franklin SAAF lost control
Sgt J D Greensmith   +   the elevators overbalanced and the tailplane
Sgt E W A Dunford   +   detached. Debris was spread over a wide area
some four miles S of Defford airfield. Five
were buried in Bath (Haycombe) Cemetery, while two, F/O Hudson and Sgt Dunford,
were claimed by their relatives. Lt Franklin SAAF had reported for training on
21 July, along with a fellow South African, Capt I F Watson and two New Zealand
crews, the unit diarist noting them as being the first to be accepted by this
Wombleton based conversion unit.

25 Aug **1944**	**1658 HCU**	**Halifax II**	**JD421**	**Training**

F/O G B Pope   T/o 1309 Riccall for fighter affiliation practice
F/O C J Butler   but had only just cleared the runway when the
starboard outer cut. Neither of the two pilots
were particularly experienced; F/O Pope had fifteen hours on type and F/O Butler
is credited with twenty-two, their solo flying being noted as 257 and 240 hours
respectively. Nevertheless, they pulled off an excellent forced-landing, at 1310,
in a field at Osgodby, a village in line with the runway and a mere 2 miles NE
from Selby, Yorkshire. Not long after this incident, F/O Pope proceeded to
Lissett and 158 Squadron, flying his first operational sortie as captain on
10 September (Le Havre).

25 Aug **1944**	**1664 HCU**	**Halifax II**	**JP130 ZU-Z**	**Training**

F/O J E Cox RCAF   T/o 2157 Dishforth for a Bullseye detail but
at 550 feet, the starboard outer failed and
the crew made an emergency landing, at 2204, just short of the runway, coming
to rest astride the Great North Road; a fire breaking out soon after.

26–27 Aug	1661 HCU	Stirling III	LK616 GP–G	Training

1944

P/O H G Round RNZAF	+
Sgt F Beeby	+
F/S W C Brown RCAF	+
F/S D J McAllister RCAF	+
F/S L Hanford	+
Sgt E Sanderson	inj
Sgt D Solly	inj

T/o 2100 Winthorpe for a night navigation detail which appears to have been completed without un- due incident. At approximately 0140, the crew returned to base and received instructions to join the circuit and land. Eyewitnesses saw the Stirling pass overhead, flying at around a thousand feet, but apart from a routine call advising its position, nothing further was heard. Some fifteen minutes elapsed before Flying Control was informed that the bomber had crashed, and burnt out, 4 miles SW of the airfield and close to the anti-aircraft batteries at Hawton. The two air gunners were admitted to RAF Hospital Rauceby where Sgt Sanderson died at 1230 hours on 31 August. He was cremated at Nottingham Crematorium. Of the others who died, Sgt Beeby and F/S Hanford received private funerals, while P/O Round RNZAF was laid to rest in Oxford (Botley) Cemetery, his Canadian colleagues being taken north to Harrogate (Stonefall) Cemetery. Errol Martyn reports that P/O Round's elder brother, F/O Arthur Kavhan Round, had been killed in a Fairey Battle crash, in Iceland, on 26 May 1941, involving P2330 of 98 Squadron. Although a salvage team reached the site in 1941, it has only been in recent years that the bodies of the crew, buried on site, have been recovered.

27 Aug	1657 HCU	Stirling III	BK772 AK–U	Training

1944

P/O J Marsland	+
Sgt W Hughes	+
Sgt W J Smith	inj
Sgt D Hamer	+
Sgt A L Corlett	+
Sgt G Morgan	+
Sgt W Webb	inj

T/o 1855 Shepherds Grove for an exercise that would combine cross-country flying using H2S as an aid. Within the hour, however, the crew had returned to base, the sortie having been term- inated due to engine trouble. Then, while trying to land the starboard outer cut and at 1955, the Stirling smashed into the heart of an oak tree on Tothill Farm, near Haughley, three miles from Stowmarket, Suffolk. The two injured airmen were taken to the East Suffolk and Ipswich Hospital. Those who perished were laid to rest in their home towns, P/O Marsland and his air bomber, Sgt Hamer, both being buried in Cheshire at Hyde Borough Cemetery. It is further noted that in the church- yard of St. George's, Ticknall, where Sgt Hughes lies, the three service graves all relate to Bomber Command, all losing their lives at training establishments, supporting the Command. Sgt Morgan was an ex-Air Training Corps cadet.

29 Aug	1659 HCU	Halifax II	DT546 RV–V	Training

1944

P/O A J Martell RCAF

T/o 1315 Topcliffe for his first solo on type but swung out of control and ended up, wrecked, in soft ground bordering the runway.

30 Aug	1660 HCU	Stirling III	EF200	Training

1944

P/O J L Bairstow RAAF	+
Sgt F J Ward	+
F/S E Smith	+
F/S I H Jones RAAF	+
F/S A D O'Hara RAAF	inj
F/S W D Fawcett RAAF	+
Sgt W Toole	inj
Sgt W P Mills	inj

T/o Swinderby for a cross-country. While cruising at 12,000 feet, the outer port failed and the crew turned back for base. Their first approach was unsatisfactory but while going round again, P/O Bairstow RAAF lost control and crashed, at 1532, slightly N of Hardwick Grange between the village of Hardwick and the Blythe to Ollerton road, Nottinghamshire. The three Australians who died were buried in Oxford (Botley) Cemetery, while Sgt Ward was taken to Ilford Cemetery and F/S Smith, his fellow flight engineer, to Halifax (Stoney Road) Cemetery.

30–31 Aug	1664 HCU	Halifax V	LL283	Training

1944

F/L M K McGuire RCAF	+
Sgt A W Pack	+
Sgt Vabson	
F/O Bucke	
Sgt Swan	
P/O C J Hogan RCAF	inj
Sgt J F Morris RCAF	inj
F/S R S Lowe RCAF	inj

T/o 2050 Dishforth for a night navigation detail. While in flight, over North Wales, an engine caught fire and the flames spread rapidly along the wing. F/L McGuire RCAF gave the order to abandon but only six had done so before the bomber crashed, at 0140, near Llanystumdwy on the south side of the Lleyn Peninsula, 16 miles SSW of Caernarfon. The body of the pilot was conveyed to Chester (Blacon) Cemetery, while his flight engineer rests in Enfield (Hertford Road) Cemetery, Middlesex.

31 Aug	**1654 HCU**	**Stirling III**	**LJ630**		**Training**

31 Aug
1944

1654 HCU   **Stirling III**   **LJ630**   **Training**

P/O B G Wilkinson RAAF   +   T/o 2325 Wigsley for what is described as a
F/S W E J Cox   +   long cross-country. Crashed twenty-five minutes
Sgt J Lambell   +   later with, according to eyewitness reports,
Sgt R G Alexander   +   one of the starboard engines ablaze, at Stanton
Sgt A Hughes   +   by Dale, 6 miles WSW from Nottingham. The two
F/S P D Arthur RAAF   +   RAAF members of crew rest in Oxford (Botley)
Sgt T H Westhead   +   Cemetery, while the others, less Sgt Westhead,
                                                   were buried in Thorney (St. Helen) Churchyard,
a burial ground that was used on at least six occasions by Wigsley 'twixt March
1943 and January 1945. Sgt Hughes had been attached from 25 (Pilots) Elementary
Flying Training School.

1659 HCU   **Halifax V**   **LL168 FD-L**   **Training**

F/O E R Millbank RCAF   inj   T/o 2319 Topcliffe for night circuits and
P/O J T W C Anderson RCAF   inj   landings but lost power, almost immediately,
Sgt E J Perry   inj   and crashed with some force about a thousand
Sgt D Robinson   inj   yards WSW of the airfield on land belonging
F/O H G Crossley RCAF   inj   to Sowerby House Farm. P/O Brown RCAF, an
P/O J Brown RCAF   inj   American from Wichita in Kansas, was critically
Sgt C R Knight RCAF   inj   injured and he died the next day; his grave now
Sgt E M Hooker RCAF   inj   being in Harrogate (Stonefall) Cemetery. After
                                                   completing his training, Sgt Hooker RCAF went
to 429 Squadron and was killed during air operations on 31 March 1945 (see
Bomber Command Losses, Volume 6, page 150).

1660 HCU   **Stirling III**   **LJ637**   **-H Bar**   **Training**

F/O W A Verrals   T/o 0001 Swinderby for night conversion training
                                                 carrying a crew of eight. While turning to star-
board, with the outer starboard motor stopped and the wheels extended, the bomber
touched down on the runway at 0215, swung violently and crashed. No injuries are
reported, but the bomber was declared a write off.

1 Sep   **1659 HCU**   **Halifax V**   **EB275**   **Training**
1944

F/O A F Scheeler RCAF   T/o 2209 Topcliffe for night circuit practice
                                                 but on its first circuit the port outer Merlin
caught fire. P/O Scheeler RCAF succeeded in feathering the unit and landed
at 2215, swinging to port as he touched down. While attempting to correct
the situation, the Halifax veered to the right and lost its undercarriage.

2 Sep   **1656 HCU**   **Halifax II**   **LW344**   **Training**
1944

P/O D J Black RAAF   +   T/o 1100 Lindholme for day training, with
P/O H Garthwaite   +   P/O Black RAAF as the instructor. Ran into
Sgt D S Thompson   +   a violent thunderstorm and within seconds the
Sgt E C Alsop   +   controls had iced over and the Halifax was
F/S H A A Bodin   +   falling, out of control, to crash at 1250 near
F/S S G Jacobs RAAF   +   Little Casterton, 10 miles E of Oakham. Three,
Sgt W Campbell   +   the two Australians and Sgt Trimby of Bourne-
Sgt A F M Trimby   +   mouth, were buried in Cambridge City Cemetery
                                                   while their five companions were taken to
churchyards in England and Scotland. F/S Bodin was the son of the Revd William
Bodin and Elizabeth Patterson Marr Bodin of Lochee.

1662 HCU   **Halifax II**   **DT643**   **Training**

F/L J E Holland   T/o 1120 Blyton to practice circuit flying,
                                                 a reconnaissance of the local area and training
in "Gee" procedures. Flying at 900 feet, the starboard outer cut and the crew
were unable to feather the engine. Their difficulties increased when the unit
suddenly burst into flames and F/L Holland did exceptionally well in getting
down in a field, at 1235 wheels up, near Camby Corner.

1662 HCU   **Halifax V**   **LL362**   **Air Test**

F/O J Esdale   +   T/o 1020 Blyton but was soon in trouble, the
F/L L Cumberworth   +   pilot remarking that his ailerons "had gone".
F/S E A Brown   inj   It then seems that the port outer began to
                                                 overheat, after which it became impossible
to maintain height. Thus, at 1045, the bomber went through the tops of some
trees and crashed, 1045, at Swanland, 6 miles WSW from Hull, Yorkshire. The
two pilots rest in their home towns; F/S Brown was taken to Hull Royal Infirmary.

2 Sep 1944	**1663 HCU B Flt** P/O R E Goulden	**Halifax V**	**DG407 SV-S**	**Training**

T/o 0117 Rufforth for night flying only to swing out of control and crash. After sliding to a halt, a fire broke out but the crew made good their exit without hurt.

3 Sep 1944	**1656 HCU** P/O L G Walker RAAF Sgt F R Jones F/O M Cox RAAF W/O J A White RAAF F/S K Panwick RAAF F/S R Walmsley RAAF	**Halifax II**	**JD417**	**Training**

+ T/o 1130 Lindholme for a day navigation detail.
+ Entered cloud and crashed at 1500 on Yr Eifl
+ near Trevor on the north side of the Lleyn
+ Peninsula, 12 miles SW of Caernarfon. The
+ five Australians were laid to rest in Chester
+ (Blacon) Cemetery, while Sgt Jones was buried privately at Barwick-in-Elmet (All Saints) Churchyard, Yorkshire.

6 Sep 1944	**1658 HCU** P/O W D Friend RAAF	**Halifax II**	**JD120**	**Training**

T/o 1455 Riccall for general training. Came down at 1930 near Full Sutton airfield. The enquiry that followed reported that one of the port engines had failed, due to impeller failure, while a severe glycol leak had caused one of the starboard Merlins to overheat. In addition, loss of the hydraulics had prevented the pilot from lowering the undercarriage. Initially deemed repairable, the Halifax was categorised nine days later as suitable only for salvage, though it was March 1945, before the airframe was finally struck off charge.

	1667 HCU F/O J R Pound RCAF Sgt R Hughes F/O M E Vandekinder RCAF F/O W F Woolgar RCAF Sgt J A Coughtrey Sgt B G Kitchen RCAF Sgt K A Watson RCAF	**Halifax V**	**DK133**	**Training**

+ T/o 2246 Sandtoft for night circuit practice
+ and crashed three minutes later at Crowle,
+ seven miles WNW from Scunthorpe, Lincolnshire.
+ Eyewitnesses report seeing the bomber, in a
+ right hand bank, no higher than 200 feet before
+ it dived into the ground. It is believed that
+ F/O Pound RCAF lost control while concentrating on his instruments as he had been briefed not to attempt a turn until he had reached 700 feet. The five Canadians were taken to Harrogate (Stonefall) Cemetery, while Sgt Hughes and Sgt Coughtrey are buried at Newcastle-upon-Tyne (St. John's Westgate) Cemetery and Hadleigh (St. James The Less) Churchyard respectively.

8 Sep 1944	**1663 HCU** Adj A Vidal FFAF	**Halifax V**	**DK132 OO-C**	**Training**

T/o 1714 Rufforth only for the port inner and starboard outer engines to fail. Forced-landed one minute later, wheels retracted, at Colton, 6 miles from the centre of York.

9 Sep 1944	**1663 HCU** F/O L K Fennell Lt C A Nottelle FFAF	**Halifax V**	**DJ987 OO-Y**	**Training**

T/o Rufforth to practice circuit flying, nine crew aboard. Landed safely at 1340, but as the aircraft turned off the runway onto the perimeter track, the flight engineer inadvertently raised the undercarriage. This Halifax, and its sister machine summarised above, had been on C Flight during the spring of 1943, the latter carrying the individual letter "F" until it was replaced by Halifax V DG360 (see page 129 for details of its demise).

12 Sep 1944	**1653 HCU** F/O N H MacDonald RCAF Sgt T W Hunter F/O S K McGuigan RCAF F/O R W Murphy Sgt G J Canham Sgt L W Bowd Sgt G F Bennett	**Stirling III**	**LK499 -K**	**Training**

+ T/o Chedburgh (crew No. 255, course No. 36) for
+ a cross-country, base - Rugby - Bristol -
+ Plymouth - Bude - St. David's - Fishguard -
+ Seagull Island - Aberystwyth - Granborough -
+ Luton - base. Nearing Plymouth, something
+ quite catastrophic overtook the crew and at
+ 2225 debris and bodies were scattered over the south-west fringes of Dartmoor in the vicinity of Cadover Bridge, Lee Moor, 9 miles from the city's railway station. Such was the force of the impact that two of the crew were either never found, or could not be identified. Thus, F/O McGuigan RCAF and F/O Murphy are commemorated on the Runnymede Memorial. Their skipper was taken to Brookwood Military Cemetery but the others were buried under private arrangements. Sgt Hunter's second Christian name was Wyper.

| 12 Sep
1944 | **1663 HCU D Flt**
W/O R W C Poley
W/O Cohen
F/S Johnson
Sgt Maxwell
Sgt Tidd
Sgt Meredith
Sgt Ebdon
Sgt E T Wiston | **Halifax II** | **HX188 OO–S**

inj | **Training**
T/o 2038 Rufforth for a Group Bullseye, eight
crew in total being aboard. During the flight,
W/O Poley suspected that the port outer had
failed (his engine instruments indicated the
propeller was over speeding) and as a precaution
he closed the unit down. Diverting to Carnaby,
the port inner cut as the Halifax approached the
runway and a forced-landing took place, at 2238,
on farmland, a mile south of the emergency strip. |

Soon after, the bomber caught fire. Sgt Wiston was not too seriously hurt, but he was admitted to a hospital at Driffield.

| 12–13 Sep
1944 | **1658 HCU**
F/L R D McLeod RCAF
Sgt M N Jones
F/O A G Mathews RCAF
F/S G H Noble RCAF
Sgt V Sobeski RCAF
Sgt V W Clarke
Sgt G S Perry RCAF | **Halifax II** | **JD380**
+
+
+
+
+
+
+ | **Op: Diversion**
T/o Riccall tasked to carry out a sweep over the
North Sea, the purpose being to induce the Luft-
waffe night-fighters to respond and thereby use
up their dwindling supplies of aviation fuel. In
total, 138 aircraft were drawn from the training
establishments and F/L McLeod's aircraft was the
loss. All are commemorated on the Runnymede
Memorial. |

| 14 Sep
1944 | **1666 HCU** | **Halifax II** | **DT548 ND–X** | **Unknown**
Reported as being involved in an incident on |

this date, but, as yet, no details have been unearthed, though an instructional airframe serial 4863M was allotted and the Halifax issued to Dalton.

| 16 Sep
1944 | **1666 HCU** | **Halifax II** | **W1231** | **Unknown**
Reported as sustaining severe damage to its |

rear fuselage following a heavy landing, at Wombleton, at 1235. However, no accident card can be found to verify this statement.

| 17 Sep
1944 | **1652 HCU**
F/O E F H Haly DFC
F/L A A Bacon
Sgt D E Ell
Sgt J R McCarthy
F/O D G Clough
F/O J L Fox
F/S M B Waugh RAAF
Sgt W Goodbrand
Sgt J D Forbes | **Halifax II** | **BB360 GV–B**
+
+
+
+
+
+
+
+
+ | **Training**
T/o Marston Moor heading ESE to practice three-
engined circuits. On approach at 1,000 feet,
with its wheels down, the Halifax dived into the
ground at 1512, bursting into flames near the
hamlet of Angram, 5 miles WSW from the centre
of York. Accident investigators, sent to the
scene, found a pin with a ferrile which, they
concluded, had shorn off from an elevator control
joint. F/O Haly of British Guiana (he had wed
Daphne Pauline Haly of Wokingham), F/O Clough |

from Upper Norwood and F/S Waugh RAAF were buried in Harrogate (Stonefall) Cemetery. Both air gunners were taken back to Scotland, while the others rest in cemeteries in the south of England.

| 17–18 Sep
1944 | **1652 HCU**
F/O G J Hodgson
F/O Crane
F/S Ord
Sgt Duffell
Sgt McKnight
F/S Keris | **Halifax II** | **BB372 JA–O** | **Op: Diversion**
T/o Marston Moor to join a force of 241 aircraft
ordered to make two diversionary sweeps in
support of "Market Garden", one element to
turn for home, after reaching the Dutch coast,
while the second force pressed on into Holland.
It is not known as to which of the elements the
crew were assigned, but while returning to base |

both port engines became troublesome and at 2206 the Halifax landed at Halesworth in Suffolk, base for the 489th Bomb Group USAAF. During the landing roll, the brakes failed and as the bomber ran off the runway, so it clipped, and slightly damaged one of the resident B.24 Liberators before finishing up in a field on Andrews Farm, Holton St. Peter, where it caught fire.

Note. The ever efficient local police were soon at the scene and a full report of the incident was submitted by Sergeant Cedric W Spall of the East Suffolk Police, based at Halesworth Station. Subsequently, I am indebted to Richard Pymar for sending me a copy of Sergeant Spall's report. Some publications show the airfield as Molesworth and, I can only assume, this error has come about due to poor writing on the accident form.

17 Sep
1944

1661 HCU	**Stirling III**	**LJ523 —E Bar**	**Training**

P/O J S Hunter RAAF   T/o 1915 Winthorpe for a night cross-country.
Sgt C E Dunlop   inj   On return, and in poor weather conditions, the
                                       crew were unable to raise Winthorpe, or the
briefed diversionary airfield. Thus, at 2330, the Stirling landed at Harlaxton, a small grass airfield in Lincolnshire. Unable to stop within the confines of the field, the bomber ended up, wrecked, near one of the defence posts. The sole "casualty", the aircraft's tail gunner, was treated locally.

18 Sep
1944

1654 HCU   **Stirling III**   **BF481**   **Training**

F/O J G Barker   T/o Wigsley for night circuit training, eight
F/O E R Newland RCAF   crew in total. Wrecked at 2105, after swinging
                                         to starboard on landing and losing part of its
undercarriage. Progressing to Lancasters, F/O Newland RCAF joined 61 Squadron but failed to return from München in December 1944 (see Bomber Command Losses, Volume 5, page 513).

1663 HCU D Flt   **Halifax II**   **HR873 OO-R**   **Training**

F/O C A Rogers   T/o 1031 Rufforth for a cross-country but swung
                                         badly. Nevertheless, F/O Rogers pulled the
aircraft off the runway and moments later he flew into a barn on the edge of the airfield. Miraculously, no one was hurt and not long after this incident, he joined 158 Squadron. On returning from Kamen, on 3-4 March 1945, he found his home base under attack from Luftwaffe intruders and he was ordered not to land. Moments later, his Halifax was shot down, falling at Sledmere Grange (see Bomber Command Losses, Volume 6, page 102 and Appendix 12 for details of Unternehmen Gisela).

20 Sep
1944

1654 HCU   **Stirling III**   **EF115**   **Training**

F/O J S Ludford DFC   inj   T/o Wigsley for three-engined landing practice.
F/S J K Waring RAAF   Landed at 1645, swung and having departed the
Sgt H W Parkins   inj   runway, ran across a tree trunk which smashed
Sgt J Smith   one of the oleos. Within weeks of arriving on
F/S J L Brosnan RAAF   463 Squadron, F/S Waring RAAF crashed in France
F/S G C Groves RAAF   while returning from Heilbronn on 4-5 December.
F/S R M Howell RAAF   With him was Sgt Smith and the five Australians
Sgt R P Templeton RAAF   here named, of which only Sgt Cheeseman survived
Sgt L H J Cheeseman RAAF   (see Bomber Command Losses, Volume 5, page 501).

23 Sep
1944

1664 HCU   **Halifax V**   **DK143**   **Training**

F/O E A Robitaille RCAF   +   T/o 2218 Dishforth to carry out night circuit
Sgt S Darlington   +   training, this being the pilot's second night
F/S J A C Duhamel RCAF   +   solo on type. Observers on the ground watched
Sgt C P J Dessertine RCAF   +   the Halifax climb steadily to 700 feet, level
Sgt J P A Vigneault RCAF   +   off and then, for some inexplicable reason, nose
                                         over and dive to the ground. Despite a very
careful sifting of the burnt remains, sited at Skelton Boroughbridge, 2 miles south-east of Ripon, Yorkshire, the accident investigators were unable to find a plausible reason for the crash, though with some eyewitnesses stating that the bomber made a sharp right turn as it dived, it is possible the starboard outer failed. It is further noted that the port outer's reduction gear could not be located. Four rest in Harrogate (Stonefall) Cemetery, while Sgt Darlington was interred at St. Peter-in-Thanet Churchyard, Kent.

25 Sep
1944

1661 HCU   **Stirling III**   **LK561 GP-A**   **Training**

P/O S A Hill   +   T/o 0045 Winthorpe for a night navigation detail.
F/L H V Gavin RAAF   While flying in the vicinity of Bradwell Bay, the
P/O A G Buxton   port outer overheated and then, having defied all
Sgt W M White   to close the unit down, the propeller sheered off.
Sgt Brown   As the bomber lost height, the port inner stopped
Sgt Beighton   and feathered automatically. P/O Hill managed to
F/O Burrows   reverse the situation, only for the engine to fail
F/O Sainsbury   completely. At 0300, eight of the crew took to
F/O Redden   their parachutes but the body of P/O Hill was
                                         recovered from the wreckage, lying at Point Clear,
St. Osyth, 3 miles WNW from Clacton-on-Sea, Essex. Claimed by his next of kin, he is buried in Heston and Isleworth (Iselworth) Cemetery, Middlesex.

26 Sep 1944	1663 HCU	Halifax V	DG422 OO-A	Training

F/L J B Robinson   T/o 2342 Rufforth for night training, nine crew
Capt Martin FFAF   aboard. Ten minutes into the exercise, and with
                          Capt Martin FFAF at the controls, the Halifax
neared the threshold but he allowed his speed to decay and before F/L Robinson
could take over, the port main wheel caught the lip of a ditch and the bomber
slid across the ground, the left oleo breaking off. Weather conditions are
described as moonlight, but with a strong wind.

26-27 Sep 1944	1654 HCU	Stirling III	LK453	Training

P/O J R Townley   +   T/o 2230 Wigsley for night bombing practice.
Sgt T W Lightley   +   On return to base, visibility had worsened to
Sgt A T Collins   +   the extent that the crew were advised to circle
Sgt G P Barber   +   and await an improvement in the weather. While
Sgt N E Mead   +   doing so, the Stirling went out of control and
Sgt S C Howard   +   crashed 0110 about a mile N of the airfield.
Sgt K Clayton   +   All were taken to their home towns for burial.

27-28 Sep 1944	1658 HCU	Halifax II	JP129	Training

F/O R Fender   inj   T/o 1912 Riccall for a night cross-country.
Sgt R D Campbell   On return, and while in the circuit, the port
Sgt W B Morton   inj   outer and starboard inner Merlins failed and
Sgt Donaldson   at 0107 the bomber was forced-landed on the
Sgt C P T Brown   inj   north side of the airfield, just inside the
Sgt Ward   boundary. Those who were hurt were treated
Sgt R O Walton   inj   in station sick quarters.

Note. Graham Sacker of Cheltenham has kindly drawn my attention to the fact
that the above Halifax had served operationally with 78 Squadron, displaying
the code combination EY-A. Whilst returning from Magdeburg on 21-22 January
1944, and captained by F/L R N Shard DFM, it had forced-landed at Foulsham,
F/L Shard gaining an immediate Distinguished Flying Cross for his airmanship
on that occasion. Sadly, he was killed the following month during operations
to Berlin (see Bomber Command Losses, Volume 5, page 76).

28 Sep 1944	1660 HCU	Stirling III	LJ474 TV-Q	Training

F/S N S Culpan RNZAF   T/o 0001 Swinderby for high-level bombing.
                              Returned to base with both outer engines stopped
and its wheels firmly stuck in their bays. Crash-landed at 0150 and wrecked as a
consequence. Posted to 57 Squadron, F/S Culpan RNZAF died while flying as second
pilot to F/O A V Donkin during a raid on München on 17-18 December 1944 (see
Bomber Command Losses, Volume 5, page 513).

30 Sep 1944	1651 HCU	Stirling III	LK501 QQ-L	Training

P/O L H Biesiot RAAF   +   T/o 1940 Wratting Common tasked for a Flashlight
Sgt A S Titchener   +   sortie but within a few minutes flames streamed
Sgt S F Davies   +   from the outer port engine, spreading quickly
F/S B T F Johnson RAAF   inj   towards the fuselage. By now out of control,
Sgt G Crozier   inj   the Stirling crashed at 1945 at Horse Heath,
Sgt J Dare   +   Streetly End, Cambridgeshire. Amazingly, two
Sgt H Stephenson   +   survived the impact but Sgt Crozier died in the
                              hour before midnight, while being treated in
station sick quarters. F/S Johnson RAAF, meanwhile, was transferred to RAF
Hospital Ely, his injuries consisting of a dislocated right elbow, burns to
his left hand and forearm, plus abrasions to the head. P/O Biesiot RAAF and
Sgt Titchener received service funerals at Cambridge City Cemetery, while the
others who lost their lives were taken to their home towns.

	1653 HCU	Stirling III	EF466	Training

F/O R M Herapath RAAF   T/o 2140 Chedburgh (crew No. 295, course No. 40)
Sgt R C Starkey   for a night solo but began to fishtail to star-
Sgt D J Job   board. All attempts to check the situation failed
Sgt W H A Horton   and F/O Herapath RAAF closed the throttles. His
Sgt W T Hartland   actions were, however, too late to prevent the
Sgt G Creaser   wheels from folding up as the bomber ran onto
Sgt D MacKinnon   the grass. On 12 December 1944, the first six
                              named, now with 195 Squadron, failed to return
from Witten (see Bomber Command Losses, Volume 5, page 508), Sgt Horton sur-
viving to see out the remainder of the war in captivity.

1- 2 Oct 1944	**1664 HCU**	**Halifax II**	**JP204 ZU-O**	**Training**

F/O M J Hamblin RCAF   +   T/o 2000 Dishforth for a night navigation task.
Sgt G F Cumming RCAF   +   Flew into the ground, at 0115, at high speed and
F/S R Smith RCAF   +   with the port outer on fire, less than a mile
P/O C J Hogan RCAF   +   west of Galphay, 4 miles WNW of Ripon, Yorkshire.
F/S E W Reid RCAF   +   No doubt realising the seriousness of the situation, three managed to bale out and though injured, survived; their names are not recorded. Those who died are buried in Harrogate (Stonefall) Cemetery.

3 Oct 1944	**1656 HCU**	**Halifax II**	**HR927**	**Training**

Sgt C A Paton RCAF   T/o 1128 Lindholme for a cross-country, carrying a crew of eight. On return, and having descended in the circuit to one hundred feet, the starboard inner failed and caught fire, followed almost immediately by loss of power from the inner port. Realising he was not going to make it to the runway, Sgt Paton RCAF aimed his aircraft towards a small field and moments later the starboard wing struck the ground. The impact sent the Halifax flying into a cartwheel, whereupon it broke up and began to burn but the crew, it appears, escaped relatively unscathed.

4- 5 Oct 1944	**1666 HCU**	**Halifax II**	**JN886 QY-N**	**Training**

F/O M J G Cooke RCAF   +   T/o 1900 Wombleton for a night cross-country and
Sgt C G Ayres   +   practice bombing. Quite early on in the flight,
Sgt J S Turnbull RCAF   inj   the starboard inner failed but the crew decided
F/S H A Wintermute RCAF   +   to continue with the detail. Some two-and-a-half
Sgt J A Murden RCAF   inj   hours later, and while flying at 1,500 feet, the
Sgt K G Rose RCAF   inj   starboard outer cut, probably due to lack of fuel
Sgt J A Craig RCAF   inj   (the aircraft had been in the air for close on five hours). F/O Cooke RCAF ordered his crew to bale out but only three had left the Halifax before it crashed at 0005 into a field behind Crab Lane, Blackley, in the northern suburbs of Manchester. Both Canadians were taken to Chester (Blacon) Cemetery, while Sgt Ayres was buried at Mansfield (Nottingham Road) Cemetery. As Harry Holmes writes, "Sgt Craig RCAF was still in the aircraft, when it crashed, and staggered from the wreckage very badly injured. He recovered and, eventually, returned to Canada. Each year, on the date of the accident, members of Blackley British Legion hold a brief service of remembrance."

5 Oct 1944	**1653 HCU**	**Stirling III**	**BK763 H4-T**	**Training**

P/O F H Mason   T/o 1325 Chedburgh (crew No. 291, course No. 39)
Sgt A R Heasley   tasked for a day navigation exercise. On return
Sgt H F Coleman   to base the port oleo failed to lower and still
Sgt E Collins   remained stuck, even after all emergency lowering
Sgt W S Bubb   methods had been tried. Then, as the crew were
Sgt W E Jones   contemplating what next to try, the troublesome
Sgt W F Upton RCAF   unit dropped of its own accord, and at the same time the dinghy sprang from its housing. Diverting to Woodbridge, the Stirling was landed at 1735, but on touch down the wheels folded and the aircraft was damaged beyond repair.

Note. Air-Britain (Historians) Stirling File, compiled by Bryce Gomersall, indicates that this Stirling served with 214 Squadron, carrying the letters BU-F and, later, BU-A. In total, it flew twenty operational sorties before being relegated to training duties.

	1660 HCU	**Stirling III**	**LJ624 TV-C**	**Training**

F/O H R Hayward RCAF   T/o 0303 Swinderby for conversion training, at night. Landed 0423, in poor visibility, touching down just off the runway and colliding with Stirling III LK389. Damage to the latter was slight and, following repairs, it was returned to service.

8 Oct 1944	**1667 HCU**	**Halifax V**	**LK642 -O**	**Training**

F/O G G Smith   inj   T/o 2040 Sandtoft for dual circuit training.
P/O C R Applewhite   inj   Landed 2059 rather awkwardly and F/O Smith took
Sgt F W J Crouch   inj   command and initiated overshoot action. The
Sgt C Wilson   inj   Halifax, however, failed to gain sufficient
Sgt H G A Allan   inj   height before it struck a cottage and crashed
Sgt A W J Enstone   inj   a mile from the airfield, near Belton village.

10 Oct 1944	**1658 HCU**	**Halifax III**	**MZ634**		**Training**

F/O A Humphreys
P/O R J Hampshire
Sgt K D Barracatt   inj
Sgt T F Morrison
Sgt D R C Glossop
Sgt E Dixon
Sgt J W Kenny   inj
Sgt A Ainsley

T/o 1414 Riccall to practise circuits using three-engines. Upon landing at 1420, bounced with such severity that the bomber went out of control and finished up in a wood. This was the first Mk. III Halifax to be written off at a heavy conversion unit operating under Bomber Command authority. Not long after this frightening incident, the crew, less their instructor F/O Humphreys, departed to Lissett and 158 Squadron and it was while outbound to Worms on 21 February 1945, that they were involved in an horrendous crash near Leiston, Suffolk, in which four, Sgt Morrison, Sgt Dixon, Sgt Kenny and Sgt Ainsley perished (see Bomber Command Losses, Volume 6, page 87). It is noted that Sgt Barracatt came from Black River, Jamaica.

	1661 HCU	**Stirling III**	**LK617 GP-V**	**Training**

F/O C G Fiset RCAF

T/o Winthorpe for a night sortie but was unable to retract the main wheels. To add to their problems, the dinghy stowage hatch flew off. So, with the exercise aborted, the crew headed for Woodbridge, landing here at 2025, whereupon the faulty undercarriage collapsed.

	1667 HCU	**Halifax V**	**LL501**		**Training**

Sgt R W Christie RCAF   inj
Sgt E F Gazley   +
F/O L E Cameron RCAF   +
Sgt C B Greer RCAF   +
Sgt H R Latham RCAF   +
Sgt E G Woodward   +

T/o 1805 Sandtoft for a night cross-country. At approximately 2330, while descending to ascertain his position, Sgt Christie RCAF had the awful misfortune to fly full tilt into the side of a river bank. Of those who died, two of the three Canadians were taken to Harrogate (Stonefall) Cemetery, Sgt Gazley is buried in Romford Cemetery, while both air gunners are commemorated on the Runnymede Memorial. Sgt Woodward's death was particularly poignant as he had already survived one terrible accident, which claimed the lives of six of his companions (see page 126 for details).

12 Oct 1944	**1657 HCU**	**Stirling III**	**LK465 AK-B**		**Training**

F/O A R Hall RCAF   inj
Sgt R P Richardson   inj
F/S B L White RCAF   +
Sgt J J Donnachie   +
F/L A B Snelling   inj
F/S C C Stewardson RCAF   inj
Sgt R Christie RCAF

T/o Stradishall for a night cross-country. Attempted to land at Chedburgh, on three-engines, but lost control and crashed 2040 near the camp cinema. The first two named died from their injuries the next day, as did F/S Stewardson RCAF. Thus, F/O Hall RCAF and F/S White RCAF were taken to Brookwood Military Cemetery, but F/S Stewardson RCAF, who had married Evelyn Stewardson of Elgin rests at Elgin New Cemetery. Sgt Richardson, a nineteen year old ex-Air Training Corps cadet, is buried in Ipswich Cemetery, while Sgt Donnachie lies in Chester General Cemetery. Of the two who survived, F/L Snelling spent many weeks recovering in RAF Hospital Ely. He had sustained fractures to both legs, as well as suffering from multiple burns. Sgt Christie RCAF is reported to have emerged from the debris of his aircraft, virtually unscathed.

14 Oct 1944	**1658 HCU**	**Halifax II**	**JB784**	**Training**

F/S M Roberts

T/o 2040 Riccall for night circuit practice but the starboard outer cut causing the bomber to swing from the runway and end up, its undercarriage collapsed, amongst some bushes, where it caught fire.

14-15 Oct 1944	**1664 HCU**	**Halifax II**	**HR802**		**Op: Diversion**

P/O A H MacLeod RCAF   +
Sgt L A Howser   +
F/S W R Wickham RCAF   +
F/S B J Becker RCAF   +
P/O G A F Whinfield RCAF   +
Sgt H W McKay RCAF   +
Sgt B T Taylor RCAF   +

T/o Dishforth tasked, along with 141 crews drawn from the Command's training units, to sweep in the direction of Heligoland. Observed to dive, on fire, into the sea. All are commemorated on the Runnymede Memorial. At nineteen years of age, F/S Wickham RCAF was amongst the youngest Canadian navigators to die on operational duties during the Second World War.

15 Oct 1944	1667 HCU	Halifax V	DK116 GG-Z		Training

P/O H G Haddrell	+	T/o 1745 Sandtoft for a night cross-country.
Sgt J Nielson	+	While flying at 12,000 feet, the port inner
F/S J Mahoney	inj	caught fire and the crew were unable to quell,
Sgt Reid		or control, the flames as they spread towards
Sgt Hammond		the fuselage. Three managed to bale out from
W/O M F James	+	the stricken Halifax before it smashed into the
W/O G Symonds	+	heavily wooded Copreston Fell on Glendhu Hill in
		Kielder Forest (official records show the site as

Sheet 3 067086 55.10N 02.40W and the time of the crash as 2230). Those who died were buried under private arrangements. F/S Mahoney's injuries were relatively slight and he later joined 170 Squadron. On 7-8 March 1945, his Lancaster failed to return from Dessau (see Bomber Command Losses, Volume 6, page 118). It is further noted that the Bomber Command Association newsletter for April 2000 carries a report of a commemorative service, organised by "Handley Page 57 Rescue" at the Kielder site where, to this day, substantial debris exists.

17 Oct 1944	1664 HCU	Halifax II	JP197 ZU-Y		Training

F/O R E Hutcheon RCAF		T/o 2239 Dishforth tasked for a night navigation
Sgt A Bell RCAF	inj	detail but having climbed to three hundred feet,
		the bomb doors were opened in mistake for raising

the flaps. Consequently, the aircraft began to sink towards the ground, at which stage the pilot compounded the error by lowering full flap. Thus, at 2242, the Halifax mushed into the ground some two miles west of the airfield. Sgt Bell RCAF, the aircraft's wireless operator was admitted to Northallerton Hospital, but his injuries were not too serious.

	1664 HCU	Halifax V	LL240 ZU-K		Training

F/O G J Strickland RCAF	+	T/o 2344 Dishforth similarly briefed but crashed
Sgt J S Matsuyama	+	two minutes later at Green Lane, Melmerby on the
F/O J F Landsky RCAF	+	north-west side of the airfield. The six RCAF
F/O W J Lee RCAF	+	members of crew were buried in Harrogate (Stone-
Sgt J L Powell RCAF	+	fall) Cemetery, while Sgt Matsuyama was taken to
Sgt E J Neumann RCAF	+	Streatham Park Cemetery.
Sgt G L Spencer RCAF	+	

18 Oct 1944	1666 HCU	Halifax II	JB917		Training

F/S W Zoethout		T/o 1602 Wombleton for circuits and landings.
		Touched down at 1617, ran to the end of the

runway whereupon the pilot raised the undercarriage instead of the flaps.

18-19 Oct 1944	1651 HCU C Flt	Stirling III	LK488 QQ-E		Training

F/S P D Young RNZAF	+	T/o 2305 Wratting Common on a low-level cross-
Sgt B G Davis	+	country. As the sortie progressed, visibility
F/S N C Burgess RNZAF	+	became increasingly hazy and when, at 0315, the
F/S J M Stack RNZAF	+	Stirling ploughed into the summit of a mist-
F/S R P Furey RNZAF	+	covered Mickle Fell (2,591 feet above sea level)
F/S G Child RNZAF	+	the crew had drifted roughly thirty-five miles
W/O A G Small RNZAF	inj	from their briefed track. Despite being badly
		injured, W/O Small RNZAF managed to crawl down

to Birkdale Farm and raise the alarm. In 1970, he returned to the scene of the tragedy that had claimed six lives, at which time very substantial remains of the Stirling were still lying in situ. Seven years later, approximately five tons of wreckage was recovered during the months of August and September and deposited with the Royal Air Force Museum. Thus, for the six crew, now resting in Harrogate (Stonefall) Cemetery, something other than their headstones exists as a reminder of the sacrifice they made on a cold autumn night in 1944.

	1658 HCU	Halifax III	MZ697		Training

F/L O C Mundin	T/o 2137 Riccall for a night navigation sortie.
	While flying on autopilot, the Halifax dropped

out of control and rolled over. The order to abandon was given, and despite the understandable confusion as the bomber wallowed, the navigator managed to release the forward escape hatch and bale out. As he departed, F/L Mundin regained some semblance of control and at 0347 he force-landed at Pershore. In his report, he stated that shortly before the autopilot failed, he had changed tanks and was feeling rather fatigued, due to having to constantly monitor the gyro horizon indicator, which was showing signs of becoming unserviceable.

19 Oct 1944	1656 HCU	Halifax II	BB266	Training

P/O J A Seargroatt — T/o Lindholme for night solo circuit practice. Landed at 2200, swung and before corrective action could be taken, the wheels folded. No one was hurt, but the Halifax was deemed to have been damaged beyond economical repair.

20 Oct 1944	1666 HCU	Halifax II	LW235	Training

F/O J H MacLean RCAF	inj	T/o 0110 Wombleton for a bombing exercise which
Sgt H Vance	+	was successfully completed. However, on return
F/O L E Sherwood RCAF	inj	to Wombleton, and while flying downwind, the
F/O E L Somerville RCAF	inj	Halifax smashed into trees, the force of the
Sgt G N Pollock RCAF	inj	impact removing the mainplanes. Moments later,
Sgt F W Thomas RCAF	inj	at 0255, the aircraft was on the ground and on
Sgt J Wakefield RCAF	+	fire north of Nunnington, 14 miles ESE from

Thirsk, Yorkshire. Sgt Vance was taken home to Northern Ireland and buried in Belfast City Cemetery, while eighteen year old Sgt Wakefield RCAF was interred at Harrogate (Stonefall) Cemetery. The five survivors were all treated in Northallerton Hospital. At the time of the crash, visibility is described as being extremely poor.

22 Oct 1944	1659 HCU	Halifax V	LL505 -S	Training

F/O J A Johnston RCAF	+	T/o 1249 Topcliffe for a cross-country which
Sgt H E Pyche RCAF	+	ended at 1907 in a terrible crash on Great Carrs
Sgt W B Ferguson	+	in the Lake District, roughly 3 miles NW of the
P/O F A Bell RCAF	+	village of Coniston on the north side of the
F/O R N Whitley RCAF	+	lake that shares its name. Service funerals
Sgt C G Whittingstall RCAF	+	for the seven Canadians were held at Chester
Sgt G Riddoch RCAF	+	(Blacon) Cemetery, while Sgt Ferguson, a flight
Sgt D F Titt RCAF	+	engineer, was laid to rest in Lanarkshire at

New Monkland (Landward) Cemetery. On page 84 of Brian Rapier's "White Rose Base", there is a photograph, taken in 1971 on Great Carrs, showing huge chunks of this Halifax.

23 Oct 1944	1656 HCU	Halifax II	BB284	Training

P/O T A Ellison	+	T/o 1200 Lindholme for a cross-country, during
Sgt J F C Wheeler	+	which the outer starboard caught fire. Unable
Sgt Brownhill		to bring the blaze under control, P/O Ellison,
Sgt A E Parker	inj	regular officer recently commissioned from the
Sgt T P Roberts	inj	ranks, ordered his crew to bale out, after
Sgt Robinson		which the Halifax crashed at 1515 at Upper
Sgt Pointer		Whittingslow Farm, between Little Stretton

and Marshbrook, 15 miles SSW from Shrewsbury. P/O Ellison is buried in Chester (Blacon) Cemetery, while Sgt Wheeler, his co-pilot, was taken to Bridgwater (Quantock Road) Cemetery. Neither had left the aircraft. The injured were treated at RAF Hospital Cosford.

24 Oct 1944	1659 HCU	Halifax V	LL232	Training

F/O R M Gould RCAF	T/o 1941 Topcliffe for dual circuit training.
F/L T Coughlan RCAF	Soon after take off, Flying Control received a

message stating that the constant speed unit on the port inner had failed and the engine was feathered. Due to low cloud, the instructor was advised not to exceed a thousand feet in the circuit but almost immediately, the port outer failed and at 1951 the Halifax forced-landed, under control, on Catton Moor, less than a mile W of the airfield. As the bomber slid to a halt, it came up against some trees and, soon after, a fire developed on the starboard side of the aircraft. All nine crew emerged unscathed.

27 Oct 1944	1666 HCU	Halifax II	HR723	Training

F/L H B O'Neill RCAF		T/o 1945 Wombleton for a cross-country flight
P/O H W Ferris RCAF	+	in the course of which the crew encountered very

severe icing at 15,000 feet. Unable to maintain height, or control, the order to abandon was signalled and as the bomber slipped below 5,000 feet, so the last of the crew made his exit. Unfortunately, for the wireless operator, P/O Ferris RCAF, he had failed to secure the leg straps on his harness and he plunged to his death. Twenty years of age, and from Toronto, he was taken to Chester (Blacon) Cemetery. The rest of the crew landed safely, the time being roughly 2330, and in due course the wreckage of their aircraft was cleared from the fields around Pydew near Llandudno Junction, a few miles below the North Wales resort of Llandudno, Caernarfon.

28 Oct
1944

1661 HCU	Stirling III	EE907	–K	Training

F/L S H Martin — inj
F/O R J Fairhead — inj
F/O J Robertson DFC — +
Sgt J J Glasgow — +
F/O A W Gayford — inj
Sgt R Reed — +
Sgt J E Buckminster — inj
Sgt A W Coombes — inj

T/o 1950 Winthorpe for a night exercise, during which it became necessary to shut one engine down. On return to base, Flying Control ordered the crew to divert to nearby Swinderby, due to inclement weather conditions at the home air- field. Thus, while making their approach to Swinderby the remaining motors lost power, provoking a violent yaw to starboard which, despite the Herculean efforts from F/L Martin and his air bomber, F/O Gayford (who was occupying the second pilot's seat), could not be corrected. Now out of control, having swung through 180 degrees, the bomber crashed 2320 into Horsham Wood near Norton Disney, a village SSE of Swinderby and 7 miles SSW from the centre of Lincoln. F/O Gayford and his skipper were thrown from the Stirling, the former dying from his injuries on 31 October. He was buried under private arrangements (as were the others who lost their lives) in Thurrock (Grays) New Cemetery. F/O Robertson had served previously with 467 Squadron, details of his award having appeared in the London Gazette on 21 April 1944.

Note. F/L Martin had served his first tour of duty, 1940 - 1941, as a wireless operator, completing thirty-three sorties with 83 Squadron. He was next posted to 14 Operational Training Unit, as an instructor, until re-mustering and train- ing as a pilot, in Canada. Having recovered from his injuries, he remained in the air force, retiring as a wing commander, decorated with an OBE, in 1968. I am indebted to him for describing the circumstances of this terrible accident.

1661 HCU	Stirling III	LJ586 GP–Y	Training

P/O A K R Steele — inj
Sgt A E Baggaley — inj
F/S N S Harbor RCAF — +
Sgt T N C Johnston — +
Sgt D W Lee — inj
Sgt J W Ford — +
Sgt E H Bailey — inj

T/o 1405 Winthorpe for a high-level cross- country. Cruising at 17,500 feet, the crew experienced very severe icing, which forced the bomber lower and lower until it broke free of the clouds at 3,000 feet. Still the aircraft would not respond effectively and at 2205 it crashed in a field at Home Farm near Iwerne Minster, 5 miles NNW of Blandford Forum in Dorset and burst into flames. The injured were rushed to Shaftesbury Hospital, where Sgt Bailey died; he is buried in Burnley Cemetery. F/S Harbor RCAF was taken to Brookwood Military Cemetery, while Sgt Johnston and Sgt Ford rest in Newcastle-upon-Tyne (St. John's Westgate) Cemetery and Lennel Old Churchyard respectively. It will be recalled that on 13 June 1940, a 16 Operational Training Unit Hampden came to grief at Iwerne Minster (see Bomber Command Losses, Volume 7, page 19).

29 Oct
1944

1664 HCU	Halifax V	DK115 DH–G	Training

P/O M W Robolash RAAF

T/o 2050 Dishforth for circuit practice but on landing ten minutes later, the Halifax swung badly and moments later, as the pilot tried to correct the situation, the port oleo gave way, damaging the airframe beyond repair.

30 Oct
1944

1660 HCU	Stirling III	EF212 TV–U	Training

F/O K Johnston

T/o 2030 Swinderby for night conversion training. Landed 2355, only to be confronted by another aircraft on the runway and while taking avoiding action, the undercarriage gave way, effectively wrecking the Stirling.

1661 HCU	Stirling III	EF177 GP–S	Training

F/S P G De Saville RAAF — inj
Sgt James
Sgt McCause
Sgt Howson
F/S A L Barr RAAF — inj
Sgt L J Curtis — inj

T/o 1950 Winthorpe for a night cross-country, a crew complement of six being carried. While in flight, problems arose with the port outer which defied all efforts to feather, and it was not long before the windmilling airscrew sheered off and crashed up against the inner engine. Abandoned at 2250, and left to crash at Alveston some 10 miles SW from Dursley, Gloucestershire. F/S Barr RAAF landed awkwardly and broke one of his legs; he was admitted to Bristol Royal Infirmary. His skipper, along with Sgt Curtis, was treated for minor injuries in Filton's station sick quarters.

30 Oct 1944	**1664 HCU**	**Halifax V**	**LL151**		**Training**

F/O R H Jenkins RCAF — T/o 1505 Dishforth for a combined exercise in air-to-air firing, plus bombing. Both details were completed satisfactorily, but soon after touch down at 1750, the inner starboard burst into flames and despite prompt use of the Graviner, the air-craft was damaged beyond repair.

	1667 HCU	**Halifax V**	**LL226**		**Training**

P/O L W Linklater RAAF +
Sgt Hill
F/S H J Kyle RAAF inj
Sgt Drummond
F/S J E Brown RAAF inj
F/S Wright
F/S Whitty

LAC T S Nixon +

Mr H Wraith +
Mrs A Wraith (nee Waite) +

T/o 1856 Sandtoft tasked for a night cross-country but problems with the port engines prompted the crew to turn back early. The approach to land came from the downwind direction and when the Halifax overshot the runway, it had the awful misfortune to crash into a bungalow, killing the occupants. A passing cyclist also died. P/O Linklater RAAF is buried in Harrogate (Stonefall) Cemetery; LAC Nixon, aged thirty-nine was taken to Carlisle (Stanwix) Cemetery. It is not clear if he was the "passing cyclist" or a passenger in the aircraft.

3 Nov 1944	**1653 HCU**	**Stirling III**	**LJ444**	**—H**	**Training**

F/O J R Hannah RCAF inj
Sgt D F Payne inj
F/O J Deminick RCAF inj
F/O J A Douglas RCAF inj
Sgt J J Moloney inj
Sgt E Parkinson RCAF inj
Sgt L E Eddie RCAF +

T/o 2050 Chedburgh (crew No. 312, course No. 42) for special radar training, at night, but almost immediately both port engines cut. F/O Hannah managed to feather the inner unit but at 2110, the Stirling crashed heavily between Chedburgh and Stradishall. Eyewitnesses state that the bomber was heading for a row of cottages, but the pilot turned in time, but by doing so he could not avoid a line of trees that lay in his path. Sgt Eddie RCAF is buried in Brookwood Military Cemetery. Those who survived were admitted to Chedburgh's station sick quarters. On 1 February 1946, Sgt Payne died while serving with 115 Squadron. He rests in Leicestershire at Stockerston (St. Peter) Churchyard.

4 Nov 1944	**1659 HCU**	**Halifax II**	**JD199**		**Unknown**

Reported to have crashed while making a three-engined approach into Topcliffe, but no evidence found to support this assertion.

	1661 HCU	**Stirling III**	**EF266**	**—M Bar**	**Training**

F/L J C W Weller DFC inj
F/L W A W Strachan inj
F/S Powell
Sgt J H Harrison inj
F/O A A Chappell inj
F/S Newby
F/S R T M Fuller RAAF inj
P/O W L Lund inj

T/o 0820 Winthorpe for three-engined landings. Approaching to land, at around 0925, it seemed that the aircraft was in grave danger of under-shooting the runway. Then the engine note in-creased but as it did so, the bomber yawed and crashed at Collingham, 5 miles NNE from Newark-upon-Trent, where the instructor, F/O Chappell and P/O Lund were admitted to the local hospital for treatment. F/S Strachan, Sgt Harrison and F/S Fuller RAAF were taken to Winthorpe's station sick quarters. F/L Weller had served with 630 Squadron and details of his DFC had been Gazetted on 11 April 1944. A pre-war non-commissioned officer, his commission had been announced a year previous (27 April 1943) with seniority backdated to 20 February 1943.

5 Nov 1944	**1660 HCU**	**Stirling III**	**EH977**	**—Z**	**Training**

F/S R J Chambers RAAF +
Sgt M A Rand +
Sgt S F Weedon +
F/O N U Bibb +
F/S K J Gerathy RAAF +
Sgt W F Whalley +
Sgt W B Telford +

T/o Swinderby for night conversion training. Crashed at around 0240, while banking to the right, on Bassingham Fen, 8 miles SSW of Lincoln. Eyewitnesses to the crash report the Stirling as experiencing engine trouble and, subsequently, the findings of the accident investigation branch suggest that an engine had, indeed, failed but feathering action had been applied to one of functioning motors. Both Australians, and F/O Bibb of Birmingham, were laid to rest in Cambridge City Cemetery. However, Sgt Whalley, who hailed from Rochdale, was interred at Thurlby (St. Germain) Churchyard, a burial ground that contains thirty air force graves of which a third belong to airmen who died while undergoing training with 1660 Heavy Conversion Unit. The others were conveyed to their next of kin.

| 8 Nov 1944 | 1663 HCU | | Halifax V | DK149 00-F | | Training |

Sgt A P Maroux FFAF   +   T/o 1454 Rufforth for a fighter affiliation
Lt R Vial FFAF   +   exercise, working with a Hurricane IID from
Adj J Toiron FFAF   +   1689 Flight. At 1529, both machines collided
Sgt M Crolas FFAF   +   and spun down, out of control, the Hurricane
Sgt E Didier-Laurent FFAF   +   pilot managing to parachute, but the Halifax
Sgt P Delpech FFAF   +   crew had no such good fortune and their bodies
Sgt J J A Tournon FFAF   +   were recovered from Warrendale Plantation,
Sgt J B Noyez FFAF   +   near Londsborough, 11 miles WNW of Beverley,
Sgt L Pinelli FFAF   +   Yorkshire. Sgt Maroux FFAF was taken south
to Brookwood Military Cemetery but the rest
of the crew were laid to rest in Harrogate (Stonefall) Cemetery. Since the
end of the war (it is presumed) their bodies have been exhumed and conveyed
to France. As a group, they had enjoyed a training run of good fortune and
this crew were the first FFAF fatalities since 20 May 1944 (see page 111).
Further details, regarding the Hurricane, will appear in the section devoted
to losses from the flights.

| 1664 HCU | | Halifax V | LK703 ZU-T | | Training |

Sgt C B Raucot RCAF   T/o 2224 Dishforth for night circuits and
landings but, inadvertently, seventy degrees
of flap was selected and, as a consequence, the bomber was reluctant to climb
and two minutes after "staggering" into the air, came down on a hillside near
High Barn, Skelton on Ure, 3 miles ESE from Ripon, Yorkshire.

| 1666 HCU | | Halifax II | DT803 | | Transit |

F/O N A McHolm RCAF   inj   T/o 1915 Peterhead from whence it had landed
in order to attend to an escape hatch that
had partially opened, with the intention of returning to Wombleton. But, as
the bomber picked up speed, it swung violently to port and ran into a ditch.
F/O McHolm RCAF sustained a very painful compound fracture to his nose, and
was admitted to the Royal Naval Hospital at Kingseat, Aberdeen.

| 1667 HCU | | Halifax V | LK901 | | Training |

P/O W A Edmonds RAAF   +   T/o 2045 Sandtoft for a night cross-country.
F/S W C Picton   +   At approximately 2355, the Halifax disintegrated
F/O A W S Maggs RAAF   +   after the pilot lost control in cu nimbus cloud.
F/S A W Cooke RAAF   +   Accident branch investigator, sent to the scene
F/S J J Grieve RAAF   +   near Glenshee Post Office, near Perth (the map
F/S K E Jeffery RAAF   +   reference quoted being QO 5795 56.48N 03.27W)
F/S C B Mackay RAAF   +   could find no evidence to suggest technical
failure and it was concluded that the Halifax
had iced up and the up load forces imposed on the airframe, as it fell, led to
structural failure. Six were buried in Montrose (Sleepyhillock) Cemetery, while
F/S Picton, who held a Diploma in Engineering, was buried, privately, at Enfield
(Hertford Road) Cemetery. His elder brother, Sgt Horace Sydney Picton, an air
gunner serving on 550 Squadron, had been killed in action a few months previous
on air operations over France (see Bomber Command Losses, Volume 5, page 400).

| 8- 9 Nov 1944 | 1656 HCU | | Halifax II | JP192 | | Training |

P/O S G Folkes   T/o 2055 Lindholme for a night cross-country.
Landed at 0130, whereupon the undercarriage
collapsed. No one was hurt, but the Halifax was declared to be a write off.

| 9 Nov 1944 | 1656 HCU | | Halifax II | HR796 | | Training |

F/L B L Eva   inj   T/o 1830 Lindholme for a night cross-country.
Sgt J Bromley   inj   Cruising nicely at 19,000 feet, F/L Eva was
Sgt B E Skinner   inj   obliged to take evasive action and before he
Sgt E W Meyer   inj   could resume level flight, the Halifax yawed
Sgt C R Tervit   inj   through twenty degrees to starboard, before
Sgt N Woollard   inj   reversing direction and diving away to port.
Sgt K E Sandercock   inj   With the airspeed indicator registering 180
knots, and with the bank angle now at thirty
degrees, he was unable to bring his aircraft under control. With very little
option left open to him, he ordered his crew to take to their parachutes and
as the bomber dived below 6,000 feet, he made good his own exit. Thus at 2100,
or thereabouts, the Halifax crashed at Horsewood Chailey, near East Chiltington
some 4 miles NW of Lewis, Suffolk, bursting into flames as it impacted. F/L Eva
had flown 1,695 hours, solo, but only twenty-seven had been logged on type.

10 Nov 1944	**1661 HCU**	**Stirling III**	**EF122 GP-Q**	**Training**

F/S J M Burns RAAF — T/o 1002 Winthorpe for a cross-country, in the course of which the port inner failed. Ordered to Carnaby, the Stirling landed there at 1447 but ran beyond the runway and collided with a lorry.

11 Nov 1944	**1662 HCU**	**Halifax II**	**JN967**	**Training**

Sgt L Milewski PAF + T/o 1752 Blyton for a night navigation detail,
Sgt S Manek PAF + combined with practice bombing. Eight minutes
Sgt S Babiacki PAF + later, after climbing to 3,000 feet, the bomber
P/O M E Wisniewski PAF + crashed in flames at East Ferry, 8 miles SW of
Sgt F Piwoda PAF + Scunthorpe, Lincolnshire. It was ascertained
Sgt M Kozlowski PAF + that one of the starboard engines had caught
Sgt J Rzetelny PAF + fire and, it is thought, the Graviner system
was operated before the propeller had been
fully feathered. Such was the destruction of the Halifax, that the cause of
the blaze could not be determined. All rest in Newark-upon-Trent Cemetery.

12 Nov 1944	**1656 HCU**	**Halifax II**	**BB362**	**Training**

P/O M F A Ryan RCAF — T/o 1110 Lindholme for a cross-country. Late in the sortie, when the port inner commenced emitting black smoke and displaying symptoms of rough running, the propeller was feathered and the crew ordered to divert to Carnaby. While preparing to land on the emergency strip, the port outer burst into flames. P/O Ryan RCAF quelled the flames and managed to restart the inner motor, but on touch down at 1700, the Halifax swung off the runway and ran into some trees.

1666 HCU	**Halifax II**	**W1046 ND-M**	**Training**

T/o Wombleton to carry out circuits and landings and, at 1300, was damaged in a heavy landing, the tail oleo attachments being fractured. This aircraft (for which the accident card has been mislaid) was, according to unit records, "a circuits and landings aircraft and had over 690 flying hours". Subsequently, the airframe was struck off charge, without any repairs taking place.

1667 HCU	**Halifax V**	**LL389**	**Training**

F/O P H O'Neill RCAF — T/o Sandtoft for a cross-country. On return to base at 1615, landed heavily, bounced and on its next arrival on the runway, the port tyre burst. This resulted in the bomber veering to the left and, as it did so, the oleo snapped. In his report, the pilot said he had made a steeper than normal approach, due to poor visibility.

15 Nov 1944	**1652 HCU**	**Halifax II**	**HX170 GV-W**	**Training**

P/O A W Pitt — T/o 2200 Marston Moor with the intention of carrying out a night training detail, but when the Halifax swung to starboard, in the prevailing crosswind, the undercarriage collapsed before P/O Pitt could take remedial action.

1656 HCU	**Halifax II**	**W7771**	**Training**

S/L K R Butler — T/o 1615 Lindholme briefed for a night cross-country. Overshot and crashed 2210, at Squires Gate, a relatively small airfield near Blackpool, best known as a test facility for the locally produced Wellington bombers. A report into the incident noted that both inner engines had to be feathered, after failing at 2,000 feet (though it also states that problems with the constant speed unit on the inner starboard prevented this motor from being feathered). It was also noted that the flight had been made in extremely cold conditions, a temperature of -40 degrees centigrade being mentioned. Although having 1,531 hours of solo flying recorded in his log, S/L Butler had only recently been introduced to the Halifax and at the time of the accident had accumulated twenty-two hours on type.

1657 HCU	**Stirling III**	**LK437**	**-R**	**Training**

F/L E S Henderson RCAF — T/o 1840 Stradishall for local flying, during
Sgt D Homer — which the starboard outer failed. Following
Sgt C Eagley — three unsuccessful attempts to land at base,
F/O M Modlinsky — and while trying to reach Ridgewell the remainin
Sgt C Bingham — engines lost power, necessitating a forced-landi
Sgt N Lacey — at 1935 near Tilbury-juxta-Clare, Suffolk.
Sgt J Killingbeck

15 Nov
1944

1663 HCU	Halifax III	MZ648	–B		Training

F/L R V Hazelhurst	inj
P/O J W Furniss RNZAF	inj
Sgt J W Stewart	inj
Sgt G M Hirst	inj
Sgt N Lewis RAAF	inj
Sgt W Melton	inj
Sgt C Oliver	inj

T/o 1137 Rufforth to practise three-engined circuits. At 1144, the throttles were opened in order to go round again, but control was lost and the Halifax came down at Askham Bryan on the south-south-east side of the airfield. At least three of the injured had to be taken to York's Military Hospital. After making a complete recovery, P/O Furniss RNZAF and his crew joined 158 Squadron, making their first operational sortie together on Chemnitz, 5-6 March 1945 and by the end of the war their names had appeared on the "Battle Order" on at least twelve occasions.

1664 HCU	Halifax V	LL137 ZU–L		Training

F/L R L Garvie RCAF	+
Sgt G F Higgins RCAF	+
Sgt J E Armstrong RCAF	+
F/O N H Boss RCAF	+
F/O G L O Berg RCAF	+
Sgt N J Anderson RCAF	+
Sgt J Gamborski RCAF	+
Sgt E J Pridham RCAF	+

T/o 1650 Dishforth for a night cross-country. While flying at 18,000 feet, over Devon, collided with a Halifax from 1666 HCU. Both machines fell at 2130 in the general vicinity of Bow, 14 miles NE of Exeter, and roughly 5 miles SE from the airfield at Winkleigh. All were taken to Brookwood Military Cemetery. F/L Garvie RCAF, it is noted, was an American from Detroit, Michigan, while his navigator, F/O Boss, was a Bachelor of Science graduate from the University of British Columbia.

1666 HCU	Halifax II	JP201 QY–X		Training

P/O K H Pugh RAAF	
Sgt A E Ackcral	+
Sgt J E L Sherwin	+
Sgt B E Saunders	+
F/S I O´Connor RAAF	+
Sgt P Straiton	+

T/o 1650 Wombleton similarly tasked and lost in the manner described above, P/O Pugh RAAF being the sole survivor after being thrown clear as his aircraft went down. Sgt Sherwin of Coundon in Warwickshire and F/S O´Connor RAAF were laid to rest in Bath (Haycombe) Cemetery, while the others who died rest in burial grounds in Yorkshire, Surrey and Perthshire respectively. It is reported that the bulk of this aircraft was found at Crookstock Farm. It is believed that the vision of both pilots had been restricted, due to ice forming on their windscreens.

16 Nov
1944

1663 HCU	Halifax II	JP128	–P		Training

F/L W J Matthews	+
Sgt F G Smith	+
F/O J T Lewis	+
F/O L B Stone	+
Sgt E A J Raymer	+
Sgt R L Felce	inj
Sgt E N Genno	+
Mr G R Hildreth	+
Mrs M J Hildreth	+
Mr K R Hildreth	+
Mr N M Hildreth	
Miss B Hildreth	inj
Mr W Masterman	inj

T/o 1748 Rufforth for a night cross-country. On their return to base, the crew were confronted with patches of swirling fog. Three unsuccessful landing attempts were made, but at 2218, the aircraft appeared to be perfectly in line with runway 06 only to stray at the very last moment away from the centre line. Moments later, the Halifax smashed through the roof and upper floors of Grasslands Farmhouse in Bradley Lane on the western edge of the airfield. From here, the stricken bomber careered into one of several dispersed Halifaxes before crashing into a hangar where it burst into flames, the inferno consuming another Halifax that had been undergoing maintenance. Crash and Rescue:

LAC Bannister	
LAC Fox	
Mr L Steele	
Mr S Smith	
PC R Hutchinson	

Not only was the hangar burning furiously, but petrol spilling from ruptured tanks had ignited and set light to farm outbuildings, trapping many animals, most of which perished before the brave actions of the three civilians, here identified, could free them from their stalls. Subsequently, Mr Steele and Mr Smith were decorated for their bravery. Those who died, both in the aircraft and at the farmhouse, were buried under private arrangements. For a full account of this terrible tragedy, I can only recommend that you read Brian Mennell's excellent tribute to Rufforth, "Wings Over York", published in 2002. It is observed that F/O Stone is buried at Croydon (Mitcham Road) Cemetery in a joint grave with his brother, Sgt John Dennis Stone, who died when his 1659 Heavy Conversion Unit Halifax crashed on 28 January 1943 (see page 37).

16 Nov 1944	**1663 HCU**	**Halifax V**	**LK910**	**Ground**

This was the Halifax undergoing servicing in the hangar and destroyed in the circumstances summarised on the previous page.

	1663 HCU	**Halifax V**	**LL133**	**Ground**

This was the Halifax parked at a dispersal and damaged beyond repair in the accident, previously described.

18 Nov 1944	**1664 HCU**	**Halifax V**	**EB220 DH-D**	**Training**

F/O R C King RCAF   T/o 1545 Dishforth for bombing practice. At around 1615, and while flying at 1,800 feet, the two port engines failed. Unable to maintain altitude, the crew forced-landed their aircraft in Sessay Park on the south side of Sessay, 4 miles SSE from Thirsk, Yorkshire and a mere couple of miles ESE from Dalton airfield.

19 Nov 1944	**1666 HCU**	**Halifax II**	**DT735**	**Training**

F/O T R Bailey DFC RCAF   +   T/o 1530 Wombleton to carry out a detail that
F/O J N O'Donnell RCAF   +   included two and three-engined flying mixed
Sgt E V Norris   +   with circuit practice. Nothing further was
F/O J E Osborn RCAF   +   seen, or heard, of the Halifax after it flew
F/O E A Hine RCAF   +   off into the gloom of an early winter evening
WO1 J F Emery RCAF   +   and all are now commemorated on the Runnymede
Sgt R S Gray RCAF   +   Memorial. At the court of inquiry, it was
Sgt C N Flette RCAF   +   learnt that three months and three weeks had
elapsed since the aircraft's compass had been swung. F/O Bailey RCAF had recently completed a tour of duty with 408 Squadron and notification of his award had been Gazetted a month previous on 17 October.

20 Nov 1944	**1652 HCU**	**Halifax V**	**LL238**	**Training**

P/O M C Cranfield   T/o 2000 Marston Moor for a night cross-country but swung out of control, at high speed, and ran into another Halifax. In mitigation, the court of inquiry was told that although the pilot had over corrected, his circumstances were not helped by a fairly strong crosswind that was blowing across the airfield at twenty-five degrees off his port bow.

	1652 HCU	**Halifax V**	**LL508**	**Ground**

Wrecked at Marston Moor in the manner outlined above. These were the first Mark V Halifaxes written off from "1652".

	1656 HCU	**Halifax II**	**W7875**	**Training**

F/O J D A East RCAF   +   T/o 2158 Lindholme tasked for a night navigation
Sgt K Stodden   +   exercise and almost immediately crashed through
F/O C Currie RCAF   +   some trees at Lings Farm, near the village of
F/O L E Pike RCAF   +   Dunsville, 6 miles NE from Doncaster, Yorkshire.
Sgt N R Rusher   +   On impact, the bomber went up in flames. It is
Sgt N R Stubbs RCAF   +   believed the flaps were raised in mistake for
the wheels. The four Canadians were taken to Harrogate (Stonefall) Cemetery, Sgt Stodden was interred at Falmouth Cemetery, while Sgt Rusher is buried in Burnham (St. Peter) Churchyard, Buckinghamshire.

	1656 HCU	**Halifax II**	**BB254**	**Training**

F/O M A Gleason RCAF   +   T/o 2051 Lindholme similarly tasked but failed
Sgt D A Dilley   +   to climb and struck the gable end of a house in
F/O D J Povey   +   Coppice Avenue, Hatfield and then dived into a
F/O P D R Senn   inj   poultry farm (possibly Dalepit Farm) on the
Sgt R Thompson   +   opposite side of the road. A mere two minutes
Sgt A Blanchard   inj   had elapsed since the Halifax cleared the west
Sgt H S Emery   +   runway. F/O Gleason RCAF was laid to rest with
his fellow countrymen, identified above, while F/O Povey of York was buried locally in Hatfield (Woodhouse) Cemetery. Of the others who perished, Sgt Dilley lies in Braunstone (St. Peter) Churchyard, Sgt Thompson is interred at Watford North Cemetery, while Sgt Emery was conveyed to Durham for burial in South Hetton (Holy Trinity) Churchyard. Miraculously, F/O Senn was freed from the wreckage with only slight injuries to show for his horrifying experience, but Sgt Blanchard was dangerously hurt and was admitted to Doncaster's Royal Infirmary. Again, it is thought the flaps were raised in error for the undercarriage.

20 Nov 1944	1656 HCU	Halifax II	HR794	Training

F/O G L Halsall RCAF — inj
Sgt R L Morgan — inj
F/O R S Mattison RCAF — inj
F/S F N Drummond — inj
Sgt J C Conolly — inj
Sgt G J Birtwistle RCAF — inj

T/o 2105 Lindholme briefed in similar fashion to the two crews previously summarised and came to grief 1,500 yards beyond the runway on farmland known as Hale Hill. A fire broke out, and the Halifax was destroyed. An investigation of the remains revealed that the aircraft's bomb doors had been opened, thus imposing an adverse effect on its ability to climb. Five were treated in station sick quarters but Sgt Birtwistle RCAF joined Sgt Blanchard (see previous page) in Doncaster Royal Infirmary. On 20-21 February 1945, while flying as second pilot to S/L Warner of 101 Squadron, F/O Halsall RCAF died when their aircraft was shot down over Germany (see Bomber Command Losses, Volume 6, page 81).

Note. I am particularly grateful to David Maughan of Doncaster for his input regarding the aircraft lost from 1656 Heavy Conversion Unit, especially in regard to the locations quoted. David also adds that two young girls were asleep in the house at Coppice Avenue and were rudely awakened when tiles, and debris came crashing down into their bedroom. Thankfully, they were not too seriously hurt.

21 Nov 1944	1652 HCU	Halifax V	LL494	Training

F/S F Mitchell RAAF

T/o Marston Moor for his first night solo, instructed to carry out circuits and landings. His first landing, at 2055, was rather heavy and as a result an undercarriage radius rod snapped. Thus, upon his second arrival on the runway, the wheels folded and the Halifax was damaged beyond repair.

	1662 HCU	Halifax V	LL126	–G	Training

F/O J S Kisielewicz PAF — +
F/S W W Rucinski PAF — +
P/O J Malkowski PAF — +
Sgt J S Radonski PAF — +
Sgt F Kruszczak PAF — +
Sgt S Jurka PAF — +
Sgt S Jaguszczak PAF — +

T/o 1755 Blyton for night cross-country flying and practice bombing. At approximately 1930, eyewitnesses observed the aircraft at a height estimated between 10,000 and 12,000 feet turning onto a reciprocal heading before diving steeply, and crashing 200 yards from the village church at Long Ashton near Bristol. The cause of the accident remains obscure, but in memory of the crew, the Severnside Aviation Society, in September 1984, fixed a plaque bearing their names to the wall of the church. Their graves, maintained in perpetuity, are at Newark-upon-Trent Cemetery.

	1663 HCU	Halifax V	EB155	–Q	Training

F/O L D Jones
F/L S J Holliman

T/o 1057 Rufforth for dual circuit training. Landed, heavily, at 1102 and as a consequence the starboard tyre burst, followed soon after by a violent swing and loss of the undercarriage.

22 Nov 1944	1660 HCU	Stirling III	EF201	Training

F/O L W H Craig — +
Sgt D J Waller — inj
F/S M W Hanley — +
Sgt A J Wallace — +
F/S W J Dickie RCAF — +
P/O L F Todgell
Sgt E T H Williams — inj
Sgt P L Edwards — inj
Sgt A J Brown — +

T/o 1015 Swinderby for a cross-country, an exercise that soon became dogged with engine problems. Initially, the difficulties were confined to the port outer, which was feathered but soon after the inner port began to over speed and F/O Craig attempted to restart the outer motor. Unfortunately, due to a fuel cock being left off, he was unsuccessful and the windmilling blades created such a drag that he lost control. Thus, at 1120, the Stirling came down near Northleach airfield in Gloucestershire. Two, Sgt Waller and Sgt Edwards were taken to RAF Hospital Innsworth, while a critically injured Sgt Williams was rushed to an American hospital at Cirencester where, despite immediate attention, he soon succumbed to his wounds. His grave is in Port Talbot (Holy Cross) Churchyard. Of the others who died, two received service burials and three were laid to rest under private arrangements.

Note. Volume 6 of the acclaimed "Action Stations" series, published in the 1980s by Patrick Stephens, describes Northleach as a reserve landing ground, sited 10 miles NE of Cirencester which, by late 1944, was hardly used due to 3 Glider Training School abandoning Stoke Orchard in favour of Zeals.

24 Nov 1944	**1657 HCU**	**Stirling III**	**LJ505 —M**	**Training**

F/O R Webb
Sgt G Grais
P/O R Rutherford
Sgt E Oxborough
Sgt J Corley
Sgt D Poll
Sgt Simmons

T/o 1920 Stradishall for night circuit practice and almost straight away it became necessary to feather the port outer. Then the electrical system failed and with the undercarriage stuck in the down position, F/O Webb just could not maintain height. From 800 feet, the aircraft sank until it was forced-landed at 1925 near the church at Hundon, some 5 miles NE from Haverhill, Suffolk. The crew, it seems, escaped unharmed but the Stirling was deemed to be beyond repair.

1669 HCU	**Halifax V**	**LL132**	**Training**

F/O G C G Davies
Sgt K Szynaski PAF

T/o 1145 Langar for initial dual instruction on type. Ten minutes later, the Halifax bounced on touch down, swung and with a likelihood of running onto a dispersal looming, the starboard engines were opened up. This led to the bomber crashing into an engine stand. In the concluding report, attention was drawn to the language difficulties between instructor and pupil whose grasp of English was said to be poor. This was the unit's first major accident since forming on 15 August 1944.

25 Nov 1944	**1669 HCU**	**Halifax II**	**DT519**	**Training**

F/S N O Dunsford RNZAF

T/o 1740 Langar for a night exercise in cross-country flying. Shortly before 2240, the crew experienced engine problems, one of the motors having to be shut down. While trying to land at Bottesford, F/S Dunsford RNZAF lost control and collided with some trees and a Nissen hut before coming to a stop, his aircraft wrecked. Considerable radio frequency interference was a contributory factor.

26 Nov 1944	**1656 HCU**	**Halifax II**	**W7808**	**Training**

F/S R E Moore

T/o 1145 Lindholme for a day training sortie. While in low-level flight (800 feet) the outer engines failed and could not be feathered. Sighting an airfield, F/S Moore made a direct approach, lowering his undercarriage but after touching down, at 1530, he overran the runway and ended up amongst some trees standing in what is described as "boggy ground". No one was hurt and it was left to the Skellingthorpe authorities to remove the broken Halifax from its surroundings. Sadly, in late March 1945, F/S Moore was killed in action while serving with 166 Squadron (see Bomber Command Losses, Volume 6, page 144).

27 Nov 1944	**1659 HCU**	**Halifax III**	**LK828 RV-P**	**Training**

F/O O D Graham RCAF

T/o 0758 Topcliffe for circuits and landings. Landed at 1013 from a three-engined approach, but the Bowden cable on the pilot's brake lever snapped and he was unable to prevent the Halifax from running into a ditch. Described as a diligent instructor, F/O Graham RCAF had been involved in a serious accident the previous July (see page 124 for details).

1666 HCU	**Halifax V**	**LL131**	**Training**

F/O R J Grisdale RCAF

T/o 1253 Wombleton for a cross-country. On returning to base in the murk of a late November day, F/O Grisdale RCAF made a low approach and as a consequence he landed, 1823, well off the runway and outside of the perimeter track. Thus, when the starboard tyre came up against the lip of the track, the impact collapsed the oleo and sent the Halifax sideways onto a vacant dispersal pan. An inspection of the airframe revealed serious damage to the starboard wing and its outer Merlin, plus buckling of the centre section and tail area. On completion of their course, the crew joined 433 Squadron, only to fall in battle on 10 April 1945 (see Bomber Command Losses, Volume 6, page 159). Their graves are in the Berlin 1939-1945 War Cemetery.

29 Nov 1944	**1666 HCU**	**Halifax V**	**LL536**	**Ground**

F/O W Mennie RCAF

At 0915, while running up prior to departing for a practice bombing detail, F/O Mennie RCAF quite inadvertently raised the undercarriage. The result was a cloud of dust and debris as the propellers bit in, while the forward section of the fuselage thumped to the ground and was very badly damaged.

3– 4 Dec	1663 HCU	Halifax II	HR879	–T	Training

1944   F/L W E J Morgan

T/o 1838 Rufforth for a night cross-country. Late on in the detail, the port outer failed as did the propeller's constant speed unit. Soon afterwards, the motor caught fire, but despite these difficulties, the crew managed to regain their base, coming into land at 0008. In the last moments, however, F/L Morgan sensed he was going to undershoot and as he increased power, the Halifax clipped a tree and two huts before finishing up, wrecked, on the airfield.

4 Dec	1652 HCU	Halifax II	LW278	Training

1944
P/O G E McGrath RAAF — +
Sgt P H Reynolds — +
Sgt W R Edwards — inj
Sgt J F Cromarty — +
F/S D M Lee RAAF — +
Sgt R Bosley — inj
Sgt N Wilson — inj

T/o 2225 Marston Moor for night bombing practice which ended at 2310 with the Halifax flying into a hillside near Southwood Hall, Thirlby, 5 miles east-north-east of Thirsk, Yorkshire. The three survivors were taken to Northallerton Hospital, where their injuries were described as serious. P/O McGrath RAAF, his fellow countryman F/S Lee and Sgt Reynolds of Stoke Newington were buried in Harrogate (Stonefall) Cemetery, while Sgt Cromarty was taken to Edinburgh (Rosebank) Cemetery; he held a Bachelor of Science degree in agriculture. Four days after the crash, Sgt Edwards lost his fight to live and he, too, rests in Scotland, at Inverness Cemetery. Accident investigators were able to determine that the aircraft had first struck high ground, 1,050 feet above sea level, at a shallow angle of attack before turning to starboard and crashing half-a-mile distant from the initial impact point.

	1661 HCU	Stirling III	EF186 GP–V	Training

F/O G R Campbell RAAF — +
F/S D J Standring — +
Sgt L G Diggins — +
Sgt W L Howarth — +
Sgt E W Heaton — +
Sgt A L Terry — +
Sgt A Winn — +
Sgt B Stowe — +
Sgt K C Glinz RCAF — +

T/o 2030 Winthorpe to practice recovering from unusual attitudes of flight, an exercise that demanded high levels of concentration on the part of the pilot, especially at night. At approximately 2055, the Stirling entered a bank of cu nimbus cloud and is presumed to have iced up almost immediately. Out of control, the bomber crashed onto Breeder Hills, 4 miles due W from Grantham, Lincolnshire. Five of the crew rest in Oxford (Botley) Cemetery, but Sgt Glinz RCAF was taken to Harrogate (Stonefall) Cemetery. Sgt Diggins (one of the two flight engineers aboard), Sgt Heaton and Sgt Terry were buried under arrangements made by their next of kin. In recent years, as reported in the February/March 2001 newsletter put out under the title "Flight Recorder" by the aviation archive collectors, it is noted that a memorial has been dedicated at the Drove Lane site of the Newark Air Museum. In the form of a cairn, the memorial supports a propeller hub, recovered from the crash site. Bryce Gomersall adds that a Grantham based historian suggests the area around Breeder Hills may have been used for sheep breeding in centuries past.

	1669 HCU	Halifax V	LL172 6F–Q	Training

W/O K Artymuik PAF
Sgt W Pa Wlowicz PAF

T/o 2210 Langar for initial night circuit dual, the pupil pilot having logged two hours of day solo flying, on type. Landed at 2218, but bounced, swung and flew into Halifax II JN917 which was parked, on its pan, eighty yards off the runway. A fire broke out, but this was quickly extinguished and at first it was thought both aircraft were suitable candidates for repair. In the event, only one was returned to service, the bomber here summarised being struck off charge.

7 Dec	1651 HCU	Lancaster I	PB749	Training

1944
F/S J Hall — +
Sgt M Carty — +
Sgt D J Taylor — +
Sgt P E Costin — +
Sgt F R Smith — +
P/O A Yoxon — +
Sgt D G Mackenzie — +

T/o 1150 Woolfox Lodge for local flying and practice bombing. Weather conditions are described as being generally misty but the cloud base was high (12,000 feet) with visibility up to four miles. At 1214, the Lancaster, the first of its type to be lost from "1651", broke up and crashed near Langtoft. Five were taken to their home towns for burial, in the case of Sgt Mackenzie all the way to Berriedale Parish Churchyard, Caithness, while Sgt Costin of Harrow and Sgt Smith from Hunnington in Worcestershire were buried in Cambridge City Cemetery.

7 Dec 1944	1667 HCU	Halifax V	LK952		Training

P/O W J Havell   T/o 1745 Sandtoft for a high-level night cross-country. Cruising at 20,000 feet, all went well until the port inner Merlin failed. Despite his best efforts, P/O Havell could not feather the engine and neither could he arrest the bomber's rapid decline in height. Then, the starboard inner began to misfire and as the crippled aircraft slid below 10,000 feet he, very wisely, ordered his crew to bale out. All did so, safely, and at 2045 the Halifax spread itself across Keep Hill near High Wycombe in Buckinghamshire.

9 Dec 1944	1661 HCU	Stirling III	EF208		Training

F/S B A C Beer RAAF   T/o 0935 Winthorpe with a complement of nine intent on carrying out practice bombing. At around midday, the Stirling forced-landed ESE of King's Lynn, Norfolk, after losing power from two engines. Metal filings were, subsequently, located in the oil filter of the port inner, but the starboard outer is deemed to have failed through the mishandling of the fuel cocks.

	1662 HCU	Halifax V	LL498	-D	Training

Sgt P Kalinowski PAF
F/S J S M Percival   T/o 1040 Blyton for bombing practice. Returned to the circuit but as the crew prepared to land, a fuel warning light for the inner starboard flickered and the Halifax dropped to around 700 feet. Sgt Kalinoswki PAF increased power but was obliged to crash-land, wheels up, on the airfield, his arrival being timed at 1245 hours.

10 Dec 1944	1658 HCU	Halifax III	HX323		Unknown

Reported as damaged in a flying accident on this date, initially being categorised as "repairable". Seven days later, struck off charge. Initially delivered to 35 Squadron on 19 December 1943, this Halifax had been damaged in action on 25 February 1944, and on completion of the repairs it passed immediately into the hands of 10 Squadron, effective from 16 March. On 5 October 1944, it was given up to "1658" as a trainer.

11 Dec 1944	1651 HCU	Lancaster I	NG270		Training

F/O C L Makewell +
F/S J O Edwards +
F/O T M Watson +
F/O E R Turvey +
Sgt A P T Henry +
Sgt J W Salmon +
Sgt E H Winzar +   T/o 1852 Woolfox Lodge for a night navigation sortie, the weather being overcast with continuous slight rain and visibility down to four thousand yards. At 1910, the bomber fell from the sky and crashed at, or near, Upton in Northamptonshire. All were buried under private arrangements, Sgt Edwards being taken home to the Irish Republic and Co. Mayo, where his grave is in Aughaval Cemetery. Evidence from the crash site suggests the crew fell victim to very severe icing.

12 Dec 1944	1659 HCU	Halifax III	MZ517		Ground

Reported to have been destroyed in a hangar fire at Topcliffe. It had been on unit strength since 2 October 1944.

Note. Although I have no reason to suspect the authenticity of this report, I have not been able to find the relevant accident card. However, the aircraft's movement records confirm its issue to 1659 Heavy Conversion Unit.

	1662 HCU	Lancaster I	W4859		Training

F/L R K Eames +
Sgt N G Millar +
F/L G R Gill +
Sgt P Murphy +
Sgt E Booth +   T/o 2133 Blyton for night circuit practice, the crew comprising of a pilot, pilot/flight engineer, navigator, wireless operator and an air gunner. At 2141, the Lancaster bounced, staggered back into the air and crashed, from fifty feet, a minute later near Blyton railway station, where it caught fire. It is believed the flaps were retracted far too quickly. F/L Gill was taken to Cambridge City Cemetery, his skipper rests in Appledram (St. Mary) Churchyard (he had gained a Diploma from the South-Eastern Agricultural College), two, Sgt Millar and Sgt Murphy received cremation and funeral services respectively in Edinburgh while Sgt Booth is buried in Glossop Cemetery, Derbyshire.

12 Dec 1944	1664 HCU	Halifax V	LL541		Training

P/O G L Lister RCAF   +   T/o 1013 Dishforth briefed for a cross-country
Sgt F Willmer RCAF   +   and carrying two flight engineers amongst its
Sgt A F McMurtry RCAF   +   complement of eight. While flying over North
F/O E H Brautigam RCAF   +   Wales, disintegrated and crashed 1303 some
F/S D Levine RCAF   +   two-and-a-half miles WNW from Rhayader, Radnor.
F/S J H Preece RCAF   +   All were buried with full military honours in
Sgt G G Goehring RCAF   +   Chester (Blacon) Cemetery. Their average age
Sgt J S Overland RCAF   +   was twenty-one, nineteen being the youngest
and twenty-three the eldest.

	1666 HCU	Halifax II	JN969		Training

P/O J Kinniburgh RCAF   T/o 1630 Wombleton for a night cross-country,
returning to base at 2325, but only to land
heavily and wreck the port undercarriage. Extensive damage was also inflicted
on the centre section and main spar.

	1668 HCU	Lancaster III	JA908		Training

F/O L J Richer RCAF   inj   T/o 1014 Bottesford for a training detail, eight
Sgt B C Terry   inj   crew aboard. During the sortie, the flames traps
P/O L G Gillard   inj   on the port outer burnt through and, now reduced
Sgt J E Cable   inj   to three engines, the crew were instructed to
Sgt V Lenney   inj   divert to East Kirkby. On their arrival, they
P/O R W Miller RCAF   inj   were confronted with rather poor visibility and
F/O E J May RCAF   inj   on touch down the Lancaster bounced back into
F/O Kissack   the air, losing its starboard main wheel as it
did so. While trying to overshoot the bomber
was so reluctant to climb that F/O Richer RCAF had no option but to forced-land
at 1309, in the circuit. As the aircraft skidded to a halt, a fire broke out.
This was the unit's first serious mishap since reforming on 28 July last as a
formation concerned with Lancaster training.

15 Dec 1944	1669 HCU	Hurricane IIC	LF393		Training

WO1 W J Morrison RCAF   inj   T/o Langar for fighter affiliation training
but became lost in failing weather. After
finding the airfield at Saltby, approached from downwind and landed at 1210.
The aircraft's momentum took it beyond the runway, and through a hedge
before flipping over onto its back. WO1 Morrison RCAF was quite badly hurt
and he was admitted to an American hospital, identified as Station 346. At
the time of his accident, he had logged 370 solo flying hours, 227 of these
on Hurricane fighters.

16 Dec 1944	1669 HCU	Halifax II	HR691		Training

F/O L J Morgan   inj   T/o 2131 Langar for initial night dual in-
F/S A J Evans   inj   struction. At 2140, shortly after taking off
P/O J Smith   inj   for another circuit, the port outer began to
F/S G Hopkins   inj   over speed and F/O Morgan was unable to bring
W/O E H Clegg   inj   the engine under control. With high ground
P/O E N Bickley DFM   inj   ahead, he made a left turn and crash-landed.
F/S F B J Burton   inj   No one was too badly injured and the resources
of the station's sick quarters proved adequate
for their treatment. P/O Bickley's award had been Gazetted on 27 June 1944,
his tour of operations being completed with 101 Squadron.

17 Dec 1944	1666 HCU	Halifax V	LL285		Training

F/O J A Crane RCAF   T/o 1820 Wombleton for a Bullseye sortie but
F/O A L Fieldhouse RCAF   inj   the engines failed to give full power and at
1823 the Halifax flew into a telegraph pole
near Caulkleys Bank Top, about a mile S of Nunnington, Yorkshire, slightly
injuring the navigator, F/O Fieldhouse RCAF.

	1666 HCU	Lancaster I	PB841		Transit

F/O S J Peirce   T/o Wombleton with a crew of two but was obliged
to forced-land ten minutes later near Skipton-
on-Swale airfield after three engines failed; both outer Merlins first, followed
by the starboard inner. The destination aerodrome, in respect of the transit,
is not identified.

Resumé. As recounted in my summing up of the achievements for 1943, the tide
had turned in favour of the Allies and with the Normandy landings taking place
in June 1944, the end of Nazi domination over Europe was in sight.

Although attention would now focus on the land battles ahead, the successful
outcome of the breakout from France would depend, in part, on continued Allied
domination in the air. Thus, Bomber Command still had an extremely important
part to play and to this end, as the operational commitment increased, there
could be no relaxing of effort from the training establishments.   Throughout
the year, the heavy conversion units were often hard pressed to maintain the
flow of trained crews to replace the still heavy losses being sustained by the
front line squadrons.

For the greater part of 1944, the seventeen heavy conversion unit formations
operated with a mixture of Halifax and Stirling types, Lancaster conversion
being entrusted to the Lancaster Finishing Schools. However, towards the end
of the year came a seed change. The faithful Stirling was cast aside to be replaced with Lancasters, while the Halifax establishments commenced equipping
with the much improved radial-engined Mk.III.

At the beginning of 1944, the heavy conversion units were still administered
by their respective group authorities; within No. 1 Group, the airfields at
Lindholme, Blyton and Sandtoft, all came under its protective umbrella, but in
early November, No. 7 Group headquarters reformed at Grantham and for the next
thirteen months, this group would be responsible for the Command's heavy conversion units.

As will be observed from the summaries, flying accidents tailed off towards
the end of the year and there were no major incidents after 17 December. The
signs, therefore, were encouraging for the start of the New Year.

2 Jan	1666 HCU	Halifax II	BB390		Training

1945

P/O R A Reith RCAF
Sgt T H Lightly RCAF
Sgt J R D Baker RCAF
P/O T N Boehk RCAF
Sgt R C Wilkes RCAF
Sgt L D Johnson RCAF
Sgt J Sklar RCAF

T/o 2330 Wombleton for night bombing practice over the Pickering ranges but after climbing to two thousand feet, the port outer failed and the sortie was aborted. Then, as P/O Reith RCAF turned for base, his starboard outer cut and unable to maintain height he forced-landed near Trowbridge Farm, just a mile SE from the airfield. No one was hurt and only a mere five minutes had elapsed since making good their departure and their now unexpected return.

3 Jan	1662 HCU	Lancaster I	W4376		Training

1945

F/L W A Rainey DFC   inj
P/O Adamowski PAF
Sgt Kurman PAF
Sgt Notyka PAF
Sgt Turek PAF

T/o 1047 Blyton for dual circuits and landings and for fifteen minutes or so the detail went according to plan. But, at 1103, while going through pre-take off checks, the undercarriage folded, without warning, damaging the aircraft beyond worthwhile repair. F/L Rainey was not too badly hurt and his injuries were treated in Blyton's station sick quarters. He gained his DFC with 576 Squadron, details being published on 8 December 1944.

	1667 HCU	Halifax V	LL456		Transit

F/O J Mortimer

T/o 1115 Sandtoft and set course for Hawarden, arriving here at 1245. Touched down in a strong crosswind (assessed as gusting up to thirty-five miles per hour and blowing at ninety degrees to the duty runway) the port wheel making contact. As it did so, the Halifax lurched back into the air and as the port wing lifted, the starboard mainplane struck the ground and the Halifax finished up damaged beyond repair.

4 Jan	1652 HCU	Halifax III	NR276		Training

1945

F/S R E Herbert   +
Sgt I D B Danks   +
F/S R A Young RNZAF +
Sgt D Morrison   +
Sgt C B Herridge   +
F/S L E H Blay   +
Sgt H J King   +

T/o Marston Moor for a combined exercise in fighter affiliation and air-to-air firing. The crew successfully completed the first part of their task, and then flew out over the North Sea to carry out the next phase of the detail. Nothing further was heard. Subsequently, all are commemorated on the Runnymede Memorial. At the enquiry into the aircraft's loss, it was stated that weather conditions in the range area were poor, with a high risk of snow showers. Thus, it is likely the Halifax fell victim to sudden and very severe icing.

6 Jan	1668 HCU	Lancaster II	LL636		Training

1945

F/O G D George RAAF
P/O J K Watts RAAF

T/o 1010 Bottesford for day training. Landed safely, but while taxying at 1126 flames were seen coming from one of the starboard motors. Prompt action was taken and the flames soon died away and little damage was caused. However, repairs were not put in hand and the aircraft was struck off charge. A close inspection as to the cause of the blaze revealed that the fuel pressure warning light transmitter retaining nut had been incorrectly locked, allowing the transmitter to rotate about its piston, thereby causing fuel to leak into a magneto, where it ignited.

12 Jan	1656 HCU	Lancaster I	W4889		Ground

1945

At 1539, while undergoing a minor inspection in No. 4 hangar, at Lindholme, an airman had the misfortune to drop his chisel, which sparked on contact with the metal surfaces of the wing, igniting vapour from No. 3 petrol tank. Within seconds, a fierce fire was raging and it was not until 1745 that the fire section were satisfied that the area was safe, by which time parts of the hangar roof had been burnt through.

13 Jan	1664 HCU	Halifax III	MZ587 ZU-G		Training

1945

F/O J Howard RCAF

T/o 2022 Dishforth for night circuit practice. Landed eight minutes later, but with such force that the undercarriage promptly folded and as the bomber skidded to a halt, so a fire developed in the region of the port outer engine.

14 Jan 1945	**1654 HCU**	**Stirling III**	**EF204**		**Training**

P/O R W Holditch   inj   T/o Wigsley for a Bullseye exercise and it was
Sgt N Thompson   +   in the closing stages of the detail that the
Sgt C H Gilbert   +   crew encountered very severe weather conditions.
F/O G D Wright   +   Thick banks of cloud shielded the earth and it
Sgt J W Humphrey   +   was while letting down through the murk that
Sgt G R Best   +   the Stirling flew into the ground, at 2325,
Sgt O M Aldrich   inj   near Barnby in the Willows, 4 miles ESE from
                                Newark-on-Trent, Nottinghamshire. Sgt Aldrich,
who had served since September 1939, was not too badly hurt, but his skipper died
from his injuries on 17 January, while being treated at RAF Hospital Rauceby.
Identified by the Commonwealth War Graves Commission as being of New Zealand,
and the son of Robert Reginald Holditch and Hilda Edith Holditch (neé Holmes)
of Sutton Coldfield, he rests alongside his air bomber, Sgt Humphrey of Penge,
Kent, in Thorney (St. Helen) Churchyard. The others who died were claimed by
their next of kin.

	1661 HCU	**Stirling III**	**EH988**		**Transit**

S/L S L Cockbain DFC   +   T/o 1000 Winthorpe, the crew comprising a
F/S T A Balls   +   pilot, flight engineer, navigator, wireless
F/S E C Barton   +   operator and an air gunner. Fifteen minutes
Sgt J Littlemore   +   later, their lives ended in a terrible smash
Sgt K Harris   +   at Home Farm, Annesley Park, Hucknall on the
                                south-west side of Nottingham. Eyewitnesses
report flames streaming from one of the starboard engines as it plunged towards
the ground. S/L Cockbain, whose DFC had been won in the service of 44 Squadron
and promulgated on 9 June 1944, was taken to Oxford (Botley) Cemetery. Described
as a pilot/instructor, he came from Verwood in Dorset. His crew, meanwhile, were
buried under private arrangements.

14–15 Jan 1945	**1666 HCU**	**Lancaster I**	**HK756**		**Op: Diversion**

F/O V R Adams RCAF   +   T/o Wombleton as part of a force of one hundred
Sgt L F B Goodwin RCAF   +   and twenty-six aircraft, drawn from the training
F/O J Klatman RCAF   +   units, ordered to sweep across the North Sea in
F/O W A Booth RCAF   +   the hope of luring the Luftwaffe into the air.
F/S W A Wegenast RCAF   +   Lost without trace; all are commemorated on the
Sgt M La V Long RCAF   +   Runnymede Memorial. At nineteen years of age,
Sgt W H G Field RCAF   +   F/O Adams RCAF was amongst the youngest bomber
                                pilots to lose his life in the Second World War.
Sgt Goodwin RCAF is believed to have been born in London but his parents are
shown as living in Peterborough; he is thought to have volunteered his services
in Canada.

15 Jan 1945	**1656 HCU**	**Lancaster III**	**ND757**		**Training**

F/S R E Plante RAAF   T/o 1135 Lindholme with a crew complement of
                                nine, tasked for a cross-country. Touched down
at 1625, at base, but travelling at too high a speed and as a consequence the
Lancaster ran into the overshoot area, where its undercarriage collapsed. At
the court of inquiry, it was reported that F/S Plante RAAF had only six hours
of type experience and, therefore, it was concluded he should not, at this
stage, have been sent on such a demanding exercise. Very sadly, he would not
live to complete his course.

	1659 HCU	**Halifax III**	**LK871**		**Training**

F/O F W Mooney RCAF   T/o 1850 Topcliffe with a crew complement of
F/S G Walton   nine, briefed to carry out circuits and landings
                                but before becoming airborne, the Halifax swung
to starboard and ground looped, being damaged beyond repair as a result.

	1659 HCU	**Halifax III**	**LK878**		**Training**

F/O F W Mooney RCAF   +   T/o 2055 Topcliffe just two hours and five
F/S G Walton   +   minutes after being involved in the crash,
Sgt A R Robson RCAF   +   summarised above, tasked, once again, to carry
F/O J A McCrea RCAF   +   out night circuits and landings. Within three
F/O D P McGregor RCAF   +   minutes all had perished as their aircraft flew
Sgt J A Savy RCAF   +   into high ground at Catecliffe Wood near Felix-
Sgt M O'Sullivan   +   kirk, 4 miles NE of Thirsk, Yorkshire. The
Sgt L C Stavenow RCAF   +   seven Canadians rest in Harrogate (Stonefall)
Sgt A J MacDonnell RCAF   +   Cemetery, the others being claimed by relatives.

15 Jan 1945	1664 HCU	Halifax III	NA632		Training

F/O R K Blythe RCAF — T/o 1915 Dishforth for night bombing practice. Wrecked 2030, at Rufforth, after landing too fast and running beyond the runway and colliding with a totem pole. The accident followed five unsuccessful attempts to get down.

	1668 HCU	Lancaster III	LM619		Training

F/O I V L Thompson RAAF	+
F/S J Rawlinson	+
Sgt J G Hazelden	+
Sgt C R C Mann	+
F/S A B Thomas RAAF	+
Sgt D G Brun	+
Sgt G F Ashby	inj

T/o 1820 Bottesford for night bombing practice. Crashed, after reportedly overshooting, at 2030, coming down at Westborough, Lincolnshire (the official report shows map reference S55 1 inch 312641). Those who perished rest in various cemeteries within the United Kingdom, both Australians being taken to Oxford (Botley) Cemetery at North Hinksey.

16 Jan 1945	1653 HCU	Lancaster III	DV161		Training

F/S N D Pattinson RAAF	+
F/O S W Goodman DFM	+
Sgt N Pasquill	+
Sgt J P King	+
P/O W A Marritt	+
Sgt W R Mallory	+
Sgt W F Porter	+
Sgt G L Maycock	inj
Sgt G L Longman	inj

T/o 2303 North Luffenham to practice circuit flying but crashed two minutes later while turning onto the crosswind leg, coming down at Morcott, 7 miles SE from Oakham. The two survivors were taken to RAF Hospital Ely where, it is reported, both responded well to treatment. Their less fortunate colleagues lie in various churchyards across the country, the two pilots and Sgt King being interred in Cambridge City Cemetery. F/O Goodman had gained his award while serving with 218 Squadron, details being Gazetted on 17 August 1943. His flight engineer, at the time, Sgt J Parkinson, was also mentioned in the citation which pays tribute to their skill and courage during operations to Essen the previous month.

19 Jan 1945	1667 HCU	Lancaster I	W4154		Training

P/O W A Taylor — T/o 2055 Sandtoft for a combination of circuits and practice bombing. At 2110, the Lancaster bounced heavily on completion of a circuit and then touched down on the grass. While trying to bring his aircraft back onto the runway, and with some eighty yards to go, the starboard wheel dropped into a ditch, whereupon the oleo gave way. Although no one was hurt, the bomber was declared to be beyond repair.

	1669 HCU	Halifax II	BB367		Training

WO1 E R Peterson RCAF — T/o 1230 Langar for day operational training. Landed 1455 at Cheddington, from a normal three-engined approach, but on making contact with the runway the port oleo collapsed. An examination of the undercarriage led to the conclusion that the breakage may well have been caused by structural failure.

27 Jan 1945	1651 HCU	Lancaster III	ED413		Training

F/O T H Symmons	
F/O W L MacDougall	
Sgt W P A Smith	inj
F/S Hall	
F/S Angus	
F/O Catte	
P/O Elvins	
Sgt J W Roberts	inj
Sgt A W A King	inj

T/o 1440 Woolfox Lodge with a crew complement of nine. Having climbed to a safe altitude, the instructor feathered three of the four engines, but as the Lancaster descended, under control, he was unable to restart any of the motors. At 1530, he forced-landed at Castle (or Castel) Farm, near Barnwell, a little under 2 miles SSE from Oundle, Northamptonshire. Sgt Smith was seriously injured and he was admitted to an American service hospital, identified as the 49th Station Hospital. The two air gunners, meanwhile, were taken to Lillford Hall Hospital, near Thrapston. Subsequently, Sgt Roberts joined 1654 Heavy Conversion Unit and was killed during a training exercise on 19 July 1945.

28 Jan 1945	1659 HCU	Halifax III	LW645		Training

P/O A T Wilkinson RCAF — T/o 1809 Topcliffe for a night cross-country, but swung from the runway and still travelling at high speed, crashed up against a bank of frozen snow. As the wheels made contact, the starboard undercarriage radius rods sheared and the Halifax slid to a stop, damaged beyond repair.

| 28 Jan | 1660 HCU | Stirling III | LK400 | Training |
| 1945 | | | | |

F/S F G M Khan RAAF   T/o 1605 Swinderby for conversion training. Shortly before 1730, both inner engines failed at 1,400 feet and this led to a forced-landing, with the wheels retracted, in a field near Norton Disney, 9 miles SSW from Lincoln. This was the last serious incident involving a Stirling at a Bomber Command heavy conversion unit, though the type would continue to provide conversion training for crews destined for transport duties.

| | 1664 HCU | Halifax III | LL576 | Training |
| | | | | |

F/O W Hustwitt RCAF   inj   T/o 1830 Dishforth for an exercise in night
Sgt F G Wright RCAF   inj   navigation but soon after setting forth, the
Sgt E M Bowman RCAF   +   starboard outer engine failed. After feathering
F/S K I Gove RCAF   +   the airscrew, the crew decided to turn back, but
F/O M F Stevens RCAF   +   while trying to establish their position, the
F/S W C Watts RCAF   +   aircraft's H2S set failed. The navigator next
Sgt G T Watson RCAF   inj   tried his Gee equipment, but on breaking through
Sgt R A McIntyre RCAF   inj   the overcast, the bomber flew into high ground near Greenhow Hill, a small settlement 3 miles west-south-west of Pateley Bridge, Yorkshire. As the bomber impacted, a fierce blaze broke out. The crew had been airborne for forty-five minutes. Those who died were buried with full military honours in Harrogate (Stonefall) Cemetery. It is thought that F/S Gove RCAF had either just finished a tour, or was awaiting posting to 424 Squadron.

| 1 Feb | 1659 HCU | Halifax III | LW368 | Training |
| 1945 | | | | |

P/O C W Berg RCAF   T/o Topcliffe for a day cross-country. During the sortie, and while operating at 1,400 feet, it became necessary to feather the port inner and in this condition the crew returned to base. P/O Berg RCAF made a good approach, but at the last moment levelled off a shade too high and as a result the port wing dropped. While trying to correct the situation, he lost control and the Halifax swung and finished up in a ditch with its port undercarriage leg broken.

| 5 Feb | 1654 HCU | Lancaster I | ME440 | Training |
| 1945 | | | | |

F/S D R Keast RAAF   +   T/o Wigsley for a cross-country detail. Lost
Sgt W Burns   +   without trace. All are commemorated on the
Sgt M Moore   +   Runnymede Memorial. Sgt Bulger of Tramore,
Sgt F G A Shaboe   +   Co. Waterford in the Irish Republic, had en-
Sgt C Glatt   +   listed on 3 December 1942.
Sgt A P Bulger   +
Sgt W A A Clark   +

| | 1669 HCU | Lancaster III | PB570 | Training |
| | | | | |

F/S I A West RAAF   +   T/o 2245 Langar for a night navigation detail.
Sgt G F A Clapton   +   Lost without trace. All are perpetuated by the
Sgt R Holmes   +   Runnymede Memorial. Sgt Keeling, occupying the
Sgt H W N Drawbridge   +   mid-upper position was thirty-nine years of age;
Sgt L M Tannen   +   his compatriot in the tail turret, ex-ATC cadet
Sgt E D Keeling   +   Sgt Voller was twenty years his junior. Both
Sgt P H Voller   +   had unusual second Christian names, Durham and Hadrian respectively.

| 6 Feb | 1653 HCU | Lancaster III | NE132 | Training |
| 1945 | | | | |

P/O D H R Evans RAAF   +   T/o North Luffenham tasked for a cross-country.
Sgt G E W Hodge   +   Entered cu-nimbus cloud, iced up rapidly, and
F/O M W Moon RAAF   +   dived out of control, coming apart as it fell.
Sgt C W Souden   +   Debris was scattered over a wide area, with a
Sgt A E Oliff   +   considerable concentration being found near the
Sgt A D Gash   +   summit ridge of Rhinog Fawr above the Afon Artro
Sgt H Nielsen   +   valley in Snowdonia. Two, P/O Evans RAAF and Sgt Gash, are commemorated on panels 283 and 274 of the Runnymede Memorial; F/O Moon RAAF and Sgt Nielsen of Vina del Mar in Chile are buried in Chester (Blacon) Cemetery, while the others who were identified were claimed by their next of kin.

Note. In his well researched book, "No Landing Place, A Guide to Aircraft Crashes in Snowdonia", (Midland Counties Publications, 1985), Edward Doyle-rush quotes, "in Rhinogs" with the map reference 124/632285.

6 Feb
1945

| 1656 HCU | Lancaster I | LM175 | Training |

F/S R E Plante RAAF + T/o Lindholme for a night cross-country. Last
Sgt E Smails + heard from when flying in the general vicinity
F/S L C Barrett RAAF + of Shrewsbury, the transmission being timed at
Sgt J Mackie + 0051. All are commemorated on the Runnymede
Sgt J E Ralph + Memorial. F/S Plante RAAF, it will be recalled,
Sgt A G R Macfarlane + had been involved in a serious accident in mid-
Sgt R H H Side + January (see page 156). At the time of his
disappearance, he had logged twenty-two hours
solo on Lancasters, ten of these at night. Sgt Macfarlane's father, Frederick
Macfarlane, was a serving officer in the Royal Air Force.

7 Feb
1945

| 1651 HCU | Lancaster III | ME325 BS-P | Training |

P/O J B Bird RAAF T/o 1125 Woolfox Lodge for a cross-country.
On return to base, and while on approach at
approximately 1720, P/O Bird RAAF realised he was heading for the wrong runway.
Then, as he opened up to go round again, his cockpit suddenly filled with smoke
and without further ado, he forced-landed in a nearby field. It transpired that
a practice bomb had dropped onto the bomb bay doors, due to a fault in the bomb
release mechanism. There are no reports of injuries.

| 1652 HCU | Halifax III | NA506 | Training |

P/O J L Gibby RAAF T/o 2320 Marston Moor for night circuit practice.
Landed at 2330, but swung out of control and ran
onto soft ground, whereupon the undercarriage collapsed.

| 1668 HCU | Lancaster III | JA684 | Training |

F/O J L Walker DFC inj T/o 2158 Bottesford for night dual in circuits
F/O F G Wilkinson RCAF inj and landings, the screened pilot giving in-
Sgt C M L Thomson inj struction in three-engined overshoots. While
Sgt Mullen doing so, the pupil pilot inadvertently took
F/S McLean up the flaps before gaining sufficient height
Sgt Roper and at 2208 the bomber hit the ground, beyond
Sgt Munro the runway, and caught fire. F/O Wilkinson RCAF
was very seriously injured and he was taken to
RAF Hospital Rauceby. F/O Walker, whose DFC had been Gazetted on 17 October 1944,
and had served with 622 Squadron, was treated in station sick quarters, as was
the flight engineer, Sgt Thomson.

10 Feb
1945

| 1666 HCU | Lancaster I | ME750 QY-T | Training |

F/O E D Tait RCAF + T/o 1049 Wombleton for a navigation exercise.
Sgt D G MacKenzie + From eyewitness reports, it seems that at
F/O H G Christie RCAF + roughly 1500, the aircraft emerged from cloud,
F/O K M Pridham RCAF + in a spin and with flames streaming in its
F/L A J Snetsinger RCAF + wake. Unchecked, it hurtled into the ground
Sgt A W Heard RCAF + approximately half-a-mile SW of South Cerney
F/O W H Matheson RCAF + airfield in Gloucestershire. The six RCAF
members of crew were taken to Brookwood Military
Cemetery, while Sgt MacKenzie was interred in his native Scotland at Kilmarnock
Cemetery. In Les Allison and Harry Hayward's tribute to fallen Canadians,
"They Shall Grow Not Old", F/O Christie is shown as holding a Distinguished
Flying Cross and First Bar; these honours are not appended in the Brookwood
cemetery register. Accident investigation branch officials, who scoured the
scene of the crash, formed the opinion that icing was the most likely cause
but were at a loss as to why all four engines had been feathered.

| 1667 HCU | Lancaster I | W4890 | Training |

F/L G A Liversidge + T/o 1225 Lindholme similarly tasked and lost,
F/O C D Callum + at 1455, in circumstances not dissimilar to
Sgt C Woodhead + that summarised above, the main debris falling
F/O H S J King + into "The Great Deeps" near Thorney Island air-
Sgt H Metzger + field, Hampshire. Two bodies were never found
Sgt P B Kellegher + and the Runnymede Memorial perpetuates the names
Sgt C B Darby + of Sgt Woodhead and F/O King.

13 Feb	1659 HCU	Halifax III	LW414	Ground

LAC V G Mattson RCAF + Six days previous, this Halifax had landed at base with its undercarriage retracted. Placed on jacks to await a technical inspection, nothing untoward happened until, without warning, the supports collapsed, pivoting the aircraft on its axis and striking the unfortunate LAC Mattson RCAF, who was working nearby. Just twenty years of age, and from Medicine Hat, Alberta, he is buried in Harrogate (Stonefall) Cemetery.

19 Feb	1669 HCU	Lancaster III	NE179	Training

1945
F/O A D Denard inj T/o 1120 Langar for a cross-country, the flight
Sgt S G Hodges inj to be conducted at high-level. Thus, while in
Sgt H J H Beaumont inj the process of changing tanks, at 21,000 feet,
P/O H M Carr RAAF inj the Lancaster dived out of control, performing
F/O D R Gould inj a series of involuntary aerobatics as it fell.
F/S R P Wipani RNZAF inj With what must have been great difficulty at
Sgt J Waters + least six, and possibly the entire crew, managed
to bale out, two leaving the doomed bomber from less than 500 feet, just seconds before it went into a field at 1315 south of Fenton Tower, Kingston, East Lothian. Sadly, in addition to Sgt Waters, two died from their injuries; Sgt Hodges now rests in Chester (Blacon) Cemetery, F/O Gould is buried in Kettering (London Road) Cemetery while Sgt Waters, who may have been trapped in his rear turret, lies in Oldham (Hollinwood) Cemetery.

20 Feb	1658 HCU	Halifax III	NR281	Training

1945
F/O H D Melville T/o 1946 Riccall for night training. Ten
F/S L Corrigan RAAF minutes later, while carrying out an overshoot, the port inner lost power. F/O Melville, the instructor, immediately throttled back and managed to land on the runway. He could not, however, prevent the Halifax from running onto soft ground, where it nosed over. No one was hurt, but the aircraft was declared a write off.

	1669 HCU	Lancaster I	HK729	Training

F/S A N H Davis RAAF inj T/o 1858 Langar for a night cross-country.
Sgt F L Dean inj At 2133, while approaching the runway and down
F/S W Jakubowski RCAF inj to 750 feet, a flash bomb broke free and slid
Sgt A T Dunn inj along the bomb bay. On making contact with the
Sgt R F Luck + front bulkhead, it exploded and set light to
Sgt A Hawkes inj the fuselage. At the same time, both starboard
Sgt D Llewelyn inj engines stopped and the Lancaster crash-landed
half-a-mile SE of Barnstone Railway Station. Two of the injured, Sgt Dean and Sgt Hawkes, were admitted to RAF Hospital Rauceby. Sgt Luck is buried in Northampton (Kingsthorpe) Cemetery.

22 Feb	1658 HCU	Halifax III	LL611	Training

1945
P/O J A Phillips T/o 1520 Riccall for day circuit training.
Sgt A E Gamble RCAF Crossed the threshold ten minutes later, but floated and when eventually making contact with the runway, the pilot had insufficient distance in which to stop or to safely take off again. Moments later, the Halifax ran onto soft ground, where its undercarriage collapsed.

	1663 HCU	Halifax III	NA530	Training

Capt R L Rouguette FFAF T/o 0929 Rufforth for practice bombing. On completion of the detail, and returning to base, the crew were unable to get the port wheel to lower. Instructed to divert to Carnaby, the Halifax landed here at 1304, touching down with the starboard oleo extended. No one was hurt, but the aircraft was wrecked.

24 Feb	1663 HCU	Halifax III	PN366	Training

1945
S/Lt J A Grimaud FFAF + T/o Rufforth on exercise "Sweet Potato", during
Lt J L A Dedieu FFAF + which the port outer cut. Inadvertently, it is
Asp G Roque FFAF + thought, the crew feathered the inner port and
Sgt F L Rougier FFAF + this sent the Halifax into a very steep bank,
Sgt M Laurent FFAF + structural failure following as a consequence.
S/C R Blassieaux FFAF + The bulk of the debris, along with the bodies
S/C R Arrachequesne FFAF + of the crew, were recovered near Edmonthorpe,
seven miles ESE from Melton Mowbray, Leicester. All now rest in France, having been exhumed from Cambridge City Cemetery.

25 Feb	1660 HCU	Lancaster I	ME490		Training

25 Feb 1945   **1660 HCU**   **Lancaster I**   **ME490**   **Training**

F/O J E Gibberd DFC RAAF   +   T/o 1505 Swinderby to demonstrate three-engined
S/L J B Sayers AFC MID   +   landings. Only a mere ten minutes had elapsed
F/S H Hayes   +   before the Lancaster crashed from 300 feet, its
F/S D W Dunthorpe   +   port outer feathered. From witness reports, it
W/O H B Jones   +   was evident that the pilot had stalled while
W/O H W Bennett   +   trying to lift a wing at too low an air speed.
F/S T V W Rigby   inj   F/S Rigby, a prewar regular airman, was treated
at RAF Hospital Rauceby. In general, the crew
were very experienced; F/O Gibberd RAAF, who had gained his award while flying
with 61 Squadron (London Gazette, 22 September 1944 and Australia Gazette six
days later) had accumulated 262 hours on type, while his pupil, who joined the
volunteer reserve before the war, had logged 1,224 hours solo but had no prior
experience on Lancasters; he is buried in Sedgefield New Cemetery. F/O Gibberd
was, as expected, taken to Cambridge City Cemetery, while the others who died
rest in churchyards in Yorkshire, Essex, Carmarthen and Yorkshire respectively.

1669 HCU   **Lancaster I**   **NG382**   **Training**

F/S D F E White RAAF   T/o 1900 Langar but swung to port and when the
pilot over compensated, the Lancaster veered
sharply to starboard and ran into a building used by the motor transport section.
Soon afterwards, a fire broke out. It was assessed that the throttles had been
advanced too quickly and this error was compounded by over tightening of the
friction nuts, thus preventing a smooth retarding. This was the last serious
incident reported by the unit ahead of disbanding on 16 March 1945. During
the seven months that the unit had been operational, it had suffered ten major
flying accident.

26 Feb 1945   **1668 HCU**   **Lancaster II**   **DS838**   **Ground**

F/O K J MacKenzie RCAF   Taxying 1420, at Bottesford, in readiness to take
off for his first solo on type, F/O MacKenzie
over used the aircraft's brakes and when he realised he was about to overshoot
his turn from the perimeter track onto the runway, his attempts to stop failed
completely and the Lancaster sank into soft ground, major damage being caused
to the propellers as he tried to power his way onto a firmer surface.

1 Mar 1945   **1658 HCU**   **Halifax III**   **LW445**   **Training**

P/O W H Scott RAAF   T/o 2110 Riccall for night solo flying but
P/O Scott RAAF became distracted by the beam
shining from another aircraft's Aldis lamp and, consequently, this lack of
total concentration resulted in his aircraft drifting to starboard. As he
tried to correct the situation, his glove snagged the throttle friction nut,
momentarily locking the port outer throttle in a fully open position. This
sudden surge of power increased the swing and as the bomber left the runway,
its wheels folded.

2- 3 Mar 1945   **1651 HCU**   **Lancaster I**   **ME781**   **Op: Diversion**

F/O D F Law   +   T/o 1903 Woolfox Lodge as part of a force of
Sgt R Leigh   +   sixty-nine aircraft ordered to support minor
F/O P N Young   +   operations over Germany and minelaying off the
F/O W J Trice   +   Norwegian coast. At 0048, the Lancaster was
Sgt H Vaudrey   +   sighted making what appeared to be a normal
Sgt S J Webb   +   three-engined approach. As it drew near to
Sgt W G Kneen   inj   the runway, its speed decayed to what Flying
Control estimated was about eighty miles per
hour and, as a consequence, the bomber began to sink rapidly. Sensing he was
in grave danger of undershooting, F/O Law increased power but as his engines
picked up, so he seemed to lose all directional control, yawing violently to
port before crashing near the airfield. Miraculously, Sgt Kneen was pulled
clear with only minor injuries and he was treated in station sick quarters.
The others were less fortunate and all now lie in cemeteries scattered across
the United Kingdom.

3 Mar 1945   **1660 HCU**   **Lancaster I**   **NN809**   **Training**

F/S S Goodall RNZAF   T/o 0015 Swinderby for night conversion training
but upon landing fifteen minutes later, the air-
craft's starboard tyre burst and in the ensuing swing, the Lancaster left the
runway and lost its undercarriage.

3- 4 Mar   **1651 HCU**   **Lancaster III**   **JB699 BS-F**   **Op: Diversion**
1945

F/L D J Baum	+	T/o Woolfox Lodge as part of a diversionary
Sgt J A W Smith	+	force of ninety-five aircraft supporting main
F/O D C Davies	+	force operations. Shot down by an intruder at
F/S R Warne	+	0135, diving almost vertically to crash near
F/S C E Gardener RNZAF	+	Cottesmore airfield (though some reports in-
F/O K R Brook DFC RAAF	+	dicate the Lancaster fell 450 yards from the
Sgt T Platt	+	Control Tower at Woolfox Lodge). F/O Davies,

F/S Warne and F/S Gardener RNZAF were buried
in Cambridge City Cemetery; F/L Baum was taken to Edinburgh (Piershill) Cemetery,
Sgt Smith lies in Longbenton (Benton) Cemetery, F/O Brook RAAF received a private
funeral, arranged by his wife, at Bradford (North Bierley) Cemetery (his DFC had
been Gazetted on 6 June 1944, following a tour with 578 Squadron), while ex-ATC
cadet, Sgt Platt, was interred in Golborne (St. Thomas) Churchyard.

1651 HCU   **Lancaster III**   **ND387 BS-K**   **Op: Diversion**

F/S A Howard	+	T/o Woolfox Lodge similarly tasked and destroyed
Sgt A W Darling	+	in the manner described above, falling thirty
Sgt W J Pullan	+	minutes earlier some 3 miles N of its home air-
F/O K C Millar	+	field (the combat is reported to have taken place
F/S R B Wilson RNZAF	+	at 4,000 feet). Of the six who died, three rest
Sgt A W Taylor	+	in Cambridge City Cemetery, while F/S Howard,
Sgt J Thompson	inj	Sgt Darling and Sgt Taylor are buried in Marlow,

Barking (Rippleside) and Alyth cemeteries re-
spectively. Sgt Thompson was treated in station sick quarters after, it is
presumed, making good his escape by parachute.

1654 HCU   **Lancaster III**   **LM748 UG-H**   **Op: Diversion**

P/O A E Lutz RAAF	+	T/o Wigsley similarly tasked and shot down by
F/S H F Cox	+	an intruder at 0105, coming down approximately
F/O J A C Chapman	+	two hundred-and-fifty yards E of Stapleford,
Sgt S Shaw	+	ten miles SSW of Lincoln. Such was the force
Sgt A F Warbey	+	of impact that three bodies were either never
Sgt H Frost	+	found, or could not be positively identified.
Sgt A C Davy	+	Therefore, the names of F/O Chapman, Sgt Shaw

and Sgt Davy are inscribed on the panels of the
Runnymede Memorial. P/O Lutz RAAF was taken to Oxford (Botley) Cemetery, while
F/S Cox, Sgt Warbey and Sgt Frost were buried under private arrangements.

Note. The above entry corrects the summary published in Bomber Command Losses,
Volume 6, page 212, and I am indebted to E B Peck of Stapleford, Nottingham, an
ex-flight engineer who served on 622 Squadron, for alerting me of my error.

1654 HCU   **Lancaster III**   **PB118 UG-Q**   **Op: Diversion**

F/S R H Pinkstone	inj	T/o Wigsley similarly tasked. Partially abandoned
F/S H Evans	inj	after being shot about by an intruder, falling at
Sgt C G Rouse	inj	0057 near Church Warsop, 8 miles SSW of Worksop,
Sgt J Pringle	inj	Nottinghamshire. F/S Pinkstone and Sgt Morgan
Sgt R Campbell	+	were taken to Wigsley's station sick quarters,
Sgt J S Morgan	inj	while Mansfield Hospital received F/S Evans,

Sgt Rouse and Sgt Pringle. Sgt Campbell, aged
nineteen, is buried in Scotland at Gamerig Cemetery, Kirkmichael.

1664 HCU   **Halifax III**   **NA612**   **-S**   **Op: Diversion**

P/O K W Griffey RCAF	+	T/o Dishforth similarly tasked and suffered the
Sgt S Forster	+	same fate as the four previous aircraft. This,
WO2 J W Buttrey RCAF	+	the only training establishment Halifax to fall,
F/O G H Lloyd RCAF	+	was dispatched at 0144 and crashed at Brafferton
WO2 L T Chevrier RCAF	+	some 8 miles S of Thirsk, Yorkshire. Five of the
Sgt L Boardman RCAF	+	six Canadians were buried in Harrogate (Stone-
F/S J E Fielder RCAF	+	fall) Cemetery, but WO2 Buttrey RCAF was taken

to Pulverbatch (St. Edith) Churchyard. It is
almost certain that his funeral was arranged by his United Kingdom relatives,
his registry entry indicating that he had married Florence Evelyn Buttrey of
Saskatoon. Sgt Forster rests in Newcastle-upon-Tyne (St. Nicholas) Cemetery.

Note. For further details concerning the Command's losses on this night, please
refer to Bomber Command Losses, Volume 6, pages 101 to 106 and Appendix 12; the
summaries, here reported, now reflect amendments to the original information.

4 Mar	1653 HCU	Lancaster I	PD431 H4-V		Training

4 Mar 1945 — **1653 HCU** — **Lancaster I** — **PD431 H4-V** — **Training**

F/O B W Drake	+
F/S T G Truskett RAAF	+
Sgt D W Gilbert	+
F/S I B Yorkston RAAF	+
F/S W H Ford	+
W/O D C McLellan RAAF	+
Sgt J Thompson	+
Sgt W G Radcliffe	inj

T/o 1130 North Luffenham for a cross-country. Returned to base circa 1600 but bounced quite badly as it landed. Power was increased, and the crew prepared to go round again, but as the Lancaster climbed away, its undercarriage hit an obstruction and seconds later the aircraft ploughed into the tops of nearby trees and crashed near the village of Edith Weston, four miles SE from Oakham. Sgt Radcliffe was rushed to RAF Hospital Rauceby. The three Australians, along with the air bomber, F/S Ford of Droylsden in Lancashire, were buried under military arrangements at Cambridge City Cemetery, while the others were conveyed to their home towns. It will be recalled that F/S Yorkston RAAF, F/S Ford, W/O McLellan RAAF and Sgt Thompson had been badly hurt in a crash while training at 1651 Heavy Conversion Unit the previous August (see page 131).

1663 HCU — **Halifax III** — **MZ561** — **Ground**

F/L R A V Hazelhurst DFC	
S/Lt I P Doussett FFAF	inj
Sgt Pagnier FFAF	
Lt Chidone FFAF	
Lt R Ponsetti FFAF	inj
Sgt I A Boyer FFAF	
Sgt L Boyer FFAF	
Sgt R Laquille FFAF	inj

At 2000, while on the duty runway at Rufforth and awaiting clearance for take off, struck by another of the unit's aircraft which was, erroneously, taking off from the wrong runway. The injured were admitted to York Military Hospital. F/L Hazelhurst had flown a tour of operations with 102 Squadron and details of his DFC had been Gazetted on 14 November 1944.

1663 HCU — **Halifax III** — **NR278** — **Training**

P/O T J C M Varkevisser	inj
Sgt Oxlade	
Sgt Long	
Sgt Gray	
Sgt Ramsay	
Sgt Fletcher	
Sgt Dawson	
Sgt Purvey	

T/o 2000 Rufforth but from the wrong runway and collided with the bomber summarised above. P/O Varkevisser was taken to York Military Hospital.

4-5 Mar 1945 — **1658 HCU** — **Halifax III** — **LL544** — **Training**

F/L F C Neville	inj
Sgt D R Goodman	inj
F/O J Hooper	+
F/O V E Phillips	inj
Sgt W G Mowbray	+
F/O E H Ewin	+
F/O W D Waller	+

T/o 1955 Riccall for night cross-country flying. Returned to base at approximately 0020 but over-shot its approach. Power was applied, but while banking steeply the pilot lost control and came down about a mile N of Skipwith on the NE side the airfield. The three survivors were taken to Northallerton Hospital. Two, F/O Hooper of Richmond, Surrey and F/O Ewin of Didsbury, were buried in Selby Cemetery, while Sgt Mowbray and F/O Waller rest in cemeteries at Carlisle (Upperby) and Sketty in Glamorgan respectively. The two commissioned air gunners had already survived one very serious air accident (see page 131).

5 Mar 1945 — **1658 HCU** — **Halifax III** — **NA566** — **Training**

| F/S F Whitehurst | |

T/o 1920 Riccall with a crew complement of seven to practice night flying. During the sortie, the starboard outer failed and F/S Whitehurst was ordered to land at Carnaby. His approach to the emergency strip was not helped by a quite strong crosswind and on touch down, at 2221, the undercarriage gave way and on coming to a stop an engine caught fire, the flames spreading quickly to engulf the entire aircraft. Fortunately, the crew had, by this time, made their escape.

1662 HCU — **Lancaster I** — **PD437** — **Training**

F/S A Wilson RAAF	+
Sgt P E W Moore	+
Sgt A Bligh	+
Sgt R H Page	+
Sgt F W Ward	+
Sgt H A Warman	+
F/S J H Skinner RCAF	+

T/o 1851 Blyton tasked for a night navigation detail. At 2341, the Lancaster's starboard wing sliced into a twenty-five foot high tree, before crashing into a field near Woodbeck, five miles SE from Retford, Nottingham. Three lie in Cambridge City Cemetery, F/S Skinner RCAF was taken to Harrogate (Stonefall) Cemetery, and three were claimed by their next of kin.

10 Mar 1945	1652 HCU	Halifax III	LK786		Ground

Caught fire at 0052, after being struck by the Halifax described in the next summary.

	1652 HCU	Halifax III	NR282		Training
	F/S G Downton		inj		
	Sgt E A Westall		inj		
	Sgt G R Sexton		inj		
	Sgt A L W Pitt		inj		
	Sgt R Matthewson		inj		
	Sgt T D Denholm				
	Sgt A Usher				

T/o 0052 Marston Moor for night circuits and landings but swung off the runway and struck the Halifax, identified in the last summary. The impact caused an immediate fire and three, Sgts Sexton, Pitt and Matthewson sustained second degree burns and had to be admitted to York Military Hospital. Although not classified as injured, both air gunners are reported as being badly shocked.

	1668 HCU	Lancaster III	JB228		Training
	F/S J P Paddison				
	Sgt H L D´arcy		inj		
	Sgt Cowley				
	Sgt L A Mitchell		inj		
	F/O Smith				
	Sgt Moore				
	F/S Trowbridge				
	Sgt Bradley				

T/o 1115 Bottesford for a cross-country sortie, but soon after setting course, the port outer failed. F/S Paddison managed to feather the propeller but was unable to trim out the tendency for the Lancaster to turn to the left. Thus, at around 1150 he landed at Fiskerton, whereupon the aircraft promptly swung off the runway and slid to a stop with its wheels folded. Sgt Mitchell and Sgt D´arcy were quite badly hurt and both required treatment at RAF Hospital Rauceby.

14 Mar 1945	1663 HCU	Halifax III	NA521		Training
	S/Lt J Hiebel FFAF				

T/o Rufforth for day training, during which all four engines overheated. Curtailing the exercise, S/Lt Hiebel FFAF returned to Rufforth and landed at 1325, but was obliged to swing the Halifax in order to avoid running through the boundary fence. By doing so, the stresses imposed on the oleos were such that both units collapsed.

15 Mar 1945	1664 HCU	Halifax III	MZ481		Training
	F/L F E Connors RCAF		+		
	Sgt K J Parrish		+		
	F/O J C Pearson RCAF		+		
	F/L J M Fowlie RCAF		+		
	F/S A H Jones RCAF		+		
	F/S J Graham RCAF		+		
	F/S J H J Grahame RCAF		+		

T/o Dishforth for a cross-country and failed to return at its appointed time. Despite an intensive search, no trace of this aircraft, or its crew, was found. All are commemorated on the Runnymede Memorial. On 6 April 1945, slightly less than two years from its formation, the unit disbanded.

16 Mar 1945	1662 HCU	Lancaster I	HK749		Training
	F/O A C Blackie		inj		
	F/S R J Scott RNZAF		inj		
	F/S L A Potter		inj		
	F/O L V Scott		inj		
	Sgt T B Browne RNZAF		inj		
	Sgt I E Peate		inj		
	Sgt J Ellarby		+		

T/o 1615 Blyton for dual circuit training. At 1650, the instructor attempted to demonstrate a three-engined overshoot but, inadvertently, selected full flap instead of forty degrees. This resulted in the aircraft climbing very sluggishly to 100 feet, at which point it veered through 180 degrees, crashed and caught fire. Sgt Ellarby is buried in Yorkshire at Elland Cemetery. This was the last major accident reported from "1662", which, like "1664", disbanded on 6 April 1945.

18-19 Mar 1945	1663 HCU	Halifax III	NP974		Op: Diversion
	P/O R W Aldridge				

T/o 2230 Rufforth tasked to fly in the direction of France, a force of seventy bombers, drawn from the training establishments being employed. During the flight, and presumably on the return leg, the crew experienced difficulties with the undercarriage and then became uncertain of their position. Subsequently, after running low on petrol, everyone baled out at 1610, landing in the general area of Scunthorpe in North Lincolnshire. Meanwhile, the Halifax continued on its northerly heading before falling to earth near Duggleby, 11 miles NW from Great Driffield, Yorkshire. The aircraft's accident card indicates that two members of crew were injured but their names, so far, have not been identified.

20 Mar | **1653 HCU** | **Spitfire VB AR395** | **Training**
1945 · F/O L W Marshall DFC RAAF + T/o North Luffenham for a fighter affiliation duty. At 1107, after breaking away from an attack on a Lancaster, collided at 5,000 feet with a Dominie trainer, out from No. 1 Radio School, Cranwell. Both machines fell out of control and are thought to have crashed in the vicinity of Witham on the Hill, 4 miles SW of Bourne in Lincolnshire. F/O Marshall RAAF had recently completed a tour of operations with 15 Squadron and details of his DFC duly appeared in the London Gazette on 13 April 1945, repeated thirteen days later in the Australia Gazette. His was the first Spitfire to be destroyed at a heavy conversion unit; he rests in Cambridge City Cemetery.

1 RS | **Dominie I NF889** | **Training**
F/S C S Jones + T/o Cranwell for a training exercise, its crew
W/O W E Durber + comprising of a pilot, wireless instructor and
AC2 H Price + four trainees. Lost in the circumstances
AC2 C J Russell + described above. All were taken to their home
AC2 F Salkead + towns for burial. Four months previous, on
AC2 G H Sargent + 4 December 1944, AC2 Russell's elder brother, Sgt Peter Geoffrey Russell, had died while serving with the Royal Air Force in India. He is buried in Rawalpindi War Cemetery (now Pakistan). At the Court of Inquiry into the tragedy, it was concluded that the Dominie's pilot was totally unaware of other training activities in his area of operation.

22 Mar | **1663 HCU** | **Halifax III MZ535 OO-C** | **Training**
1945 · P/O D N Jones RCAF · T/o 1704 Rufforth but swung to starboard and ran into an obstruction, which put paid to the undercarriage. This had been the pilot's first attempt to solo on type.

23-24 Mar | **1666 HCU** | **Lancaster III ND656** | **Ground**
1945 · P/O F W Cash RCAF · T/o 1835 Wombleton for a night training sortie, which was safely accomplished. However, while going through the closing down checks, at 0145, the flight engineer's parachute harness snagged on the undercarriage lever and seconds later the wheels folded as the lever was pulled into the "up" position. Although "1666" did not disband for another five months (3 August 1945), this was the last serious incident reported from the unit.

24 Mar | **1651 HCU** | **Lancaster I PB871** | **Training**
1945 · P/O J H Wilson · T/o 2012 Woolfox Lodge for a night cross-country but the port outer cut, causing the aircraft to swing. P/O Wilson attempted to retrieve the situation but over corrected and when he realised the Lancaster was now veering off to starboard, he over corrected, yet again, and this time the undercarriage gave under the strain as the bomber departed the runway on the left hand side.

1661 HCU | **Lancaster I HK738 KB-D** | **Training**
F/O J J Sett · T/o 2010 Winthorpe for an instrument flying
F/O T M Rae · exercise, mixed with three-engined procedures, this forming the initial part of the night's training. Following several approaches, on three-engines, and overshooting successfully on each occasion, the crew were obliged to forced-land at 2024, when the flaps jammed in the "down" position, at Langford, some 3 miles NNE from Newark-upon-Trent, Nottinghamshire. It was the unit's first serious mishap since disposing of their Stirlings.

25 Mar | **1656 HCU** | **Lancaster I NN815** | **Training**
1945 · F/O W F McElwain DFC RNZAF inj · T/o 1533 Lindholme to practice three-engined
P/O G M Henderson RNZAF · landings and crashed ten minutes later, after
Sgt McCall · receiving a "red" from the airfield controller.
F/O Payne · F/O McElwain RNZAF was not vastly experienced as
F/O V Pilkington inj · an instructor and due to the position of the sun
F/S Baxendall · entering the cockpit, it is thought he failed to
F/S Wilson · see the "red" until the last moment, therefore
F/O Harrison · becoming hurried in trying to go round again. Two days after this incident, the London Gazette carried the news of his Distinguished Flying Cross, gained during the course of an operational tour of duty with 166 Squadron.

2 Apr 1945	**1651 HCU**	**Lancaster I**	**HK655 BS-F**		**Training**

2 Apr
1945

1651 HCU　　　　　**Lancaster I**　**HK655 BS-F**　　　　　　　　**Training**

F/L F E Sheppard DFC　　　+　T/o 0850 Woolfox Lodge for familiarisation
F/O B J Walls　　　　　　+　flying. Stalled from 50 feet and crashed at
Sgt W G Cooley　　　　　+　approximately 0920, hitting a building, on
F/S G A Flindall　　　　+　approach to Fiskerton. It seems that all
Sgt H G Allan　　　　　　¦　four motors had failed. Sgt Lunt was slightly
F/O G A Outterson　　　+　hurt and he was treated in RAF Hospital Rauceby.
F/S R L T Knight　　　　+　Those who perished lie in various cemeteries,
Sgt H A Johnson　　　　　+　three, F/O Walls, F/S Flindall and F/S Knight
Sgt H A Lunt　　　　inj　being interred in Cambridge City Cemetery.
　　　　　　　　　　　　　It is also observed that Sgt Johnson rests
in a joint grave with his father, Pte Arthur Henry Johnson, aged 53, of the
30th Battalion, Middlesex Regiment, in Edmonton Cemetery. He, his father, had
died on 20 October 1943. F/L Sheppard had flown Stirlings with 90 Squadron
and his award had been promulgated on 15 October 1943.

2- 3 Apr　**1656 HCU**　　　　　**Lancaster I**　**NG227**　　　　　　　**Training**
1945
W/O S F Rayner　　　　　　　T/o 2025 Lindholme for a night cross-country.
　　　　　　　　　　　　　　Landed at 0120, only to balloon into the air
and on making contact with the runway for a second time, the starboard oleo
snapped. Although initially declared worthy of repair, no work was undertaken
and the Lancaster was struck off charge.

4 Apr　　**1663 HCU**　　　　**Halifax III**　**NA622**　　　　　　　**Training**
1945
S/Lt R C M Veyre FFAF　　　　T/o 0036 Rufforth for solo night circuits and
　　　　　　　　　　　　　　landings. Touched down at 0050, but bounced
and before the situation could be checked, the port wing tip hit the ground,
causing the Halifax to ground loop and lose its undercarriage.

4- 5 Apr　**1652 HCU**　　　　**Halifax III**　**NA193**　　　　　　　**Training**
1945
P/O N W N Tanner RAAF　　　+　T/o 2225 Marston Moor and set a northerly
Sgt L A Cooke　　　　　　+　course towards its briefed Bullseye target
F/S R W Faulks RAAF　　+　of the huge fleet anchorage at Scapa Flow.
Sgt A Card　　　　　　　+　Crashed, after midnight, in the Moray Firth
F/S J C Hughes RAAF　　+　due to reasons that have never been determined.
F/S J N Donald RAAF　　+　Six are commemorated on the Runnymede Memorial,
F/S C F Ford RAAF　　　+　while the air-sea rescue services recovered two
Sgt W J R Semple　　　　+　bodies from the water; Sgt Cooke now rests in
　　　　　　　　　　　　　Romford Cemetery, while F/S Faulks RAAF was
buried in Wick Cemetery. The last four named were all aged twenty.

　　　　　　1667 HCU　　　**Lancaster III**　**ND639**　　　　　　**Training**
P/O J E Grayson RAAF　　+　T/o 2200 Sandtoft for a Bullseye detail. Presumed
Sgt S J Crawhall　　　　+　to have lost control, crashing 0258 near Crowle,
F/S M B Kilsby RAAF　　+　a village roughly 4 miles NNE from the airfield
W/O E J Castor RAAF　　+　and about 7 miles WNW from Scunthorpe, Lincoln.
F/S W S Bennett RAAF　　+　Four of the six Australians rest in Harrogate
F/S T Evans RAAF　　　　+　(Stonefall) Cemetery, but the names of F/S Evans
F/S D L Hayes RAAF　　　+　and F/S Hayes RAAF are perpetuated on the panels
　　　　　　　　　　　　　of the Runnymede Memorial. Sgt Crawhall, who is
identified as a pilot, lies in Newcastle-upon-Tyne (St. Andrew's and Jesmond)
Cemetery. It is presumed he was carrying out the duties of flight engineer.

5 Apr　　**1658 HCU**　　　　**Halifax III**　**LW480**　　　　　　　**Training**
1945
F/O H D Melville　　　　　　T/o 1345 Riccall but as the bomber lifted clear
F/O M Morse RCAF　　　　　　of the runway, the starboard inner engine caught
　　　　　　　　　　　　　　fire, followed just moments later by the outer
starboard. It was impossible to feather the two units and with his wheels still
down, F/O Melville very calmly put his crippled machine down in a field near
Hemingbrough, 3 miles ESE from Selby, Yorkshire. The flight had lasted a mere
five minutes and, as the Court of Enquiry subsequently reported, F/O Melville
had acted most creditably throughout the difficult circumstances in which he
found himself. It will be recalled that he had been involved in a serious
incident in the February (see page 160).

7 Apr　　**1658 HCU**　　　　**Halifax III**　**MZ704 ZB-R**　　　　**Training**
1945
F/S A H Monk　　　　　　　　T/o 1115 Riccall for a cross-country which ended
　　　　　　　　　　　　　　at 1330, in a Wiltshire field having overshot an
attempt to land on a small grass airstrip with its port inner windmilling.

8 Apr	1653 HCU	Lancaster III	ND647 H4-P		Training

1945

F/O N E Cook	+	T/o North Luffenham for fighter affiliation.
Sgt J Winterbottom	+	Lost control and crashed at 1515 near Scraptoft
F/O T Neale	+	on the eastern outskirts of Leicester. F/O Cook
W/O R C Wingrove	+	of Birmingham and W/O Wingrove from Bedford
Sgt G Gore	+	Park in Middlesex, were taken to Oxford (Botley)
Sgt J F J Stanley	+	Cemetery, while the others were claimed by their
		next of kin.

1659 HCU	Halifax III	HX292		Training

F/O R F Pellen RCAF	T/o 0950 Topcliffe for a day cross-country.
F/O D A Cowman RCAF	Not long after setting out, an engine caught
	fire and with the flames threatening to spread

throughout the airframe, F/O Pellen RCAF wisely, and without further ado, put
his aircraft down at 1018 on the Rufforth runway. No one was hurt and an inspection of the burnt remains concluded that petrol had leaked from a poorly
tightened fuel line connector.

1659 HCU	Halifax III	LV935		Training

P/O J G L R Sicotte RCAF	+	T/o Topcliffe for a radar demonstration, failing
Sgt J Stevenson RCAF	+	to return. All are commemorated on the Runnymede
F/O J A R G Heroux RCAF	+	Memorial. The memorial's register, published by
F/O J E Stillings RCAF	+	the Commonwealth War Graves Commission, indicates
F/O J L P Routhier RCAF	+	F/O Stillings RCAF was an American, but his home
WO1 J A L Potvin RCAF	+	address in "They Shall Grow Not Old" is reported
F/S J C Valiquette RCAF	+	as Crossfield, Alberta. His first Christian name
F/S J C P A Laferriere RCAF	+	was John, sharing this with the flight engineer,
		Sgt Stevenson RCAF. For the remainder of the
		crew, their first Christian name was Joseph.

9 Apr	1667 HCU	Lancaster III	DV165		Training

1945

| S/L M D Wood | T/o 1535 Sandtoft briefed for a cross-country |
| | but swung to port and in order to avoid a hedge, |

S/L Wood tried to increase the turn. As he did so, the undercarriage folded and
on coming to a stop a fire developed. Although reported as accumulating 1,034
solo flying hours, his experience on Lancasters was limited to just two.

12 Apr	1654 HCU	Lancaster I	NG222		Training

1945

F/S C W F Wedd RAAF	+	T/o 1125 Wigsley for air-to-sea firing over
F/S F A Baker	+	The Wash. Reported to have flown into the sea
F/S A Darby DFM	+	some 27 miles N of Spurn Head. Later, a dinghy
P/O I Hardman MID	+	and some wreckage was sighted in position
F/O B P Smith RAAF	+	5533N 0048E. Eight are commemorated on the
F/O A G Rolston RAAF	+	Runnymede Memorial, while F/S Darby is buried
F/O J W Sharp RAAF	+	in Newcaster-under-Lyne Cemetery. A regular
Sgt D W Hope	+	airman (he had enlisted on 11 May 1939), his
Sgt K Chapman	+	award had been Gazetted on 17 October 1944,
		following service with 50 Squadron. His

younger brother, Sgt William Darby, also a flight engineer, flew with 50
Squadron and was killed on operations in early November 1944 (see Bomber
Command Losses, Volume 5, page 479).

14-15 Apr	1661 HCU	Lancaster III	PB213		Training

1945

F/S F E Hearn	inj	T/o 2020 Winthorpe for a night navigation
Sgt G A Martin	inj	sortie. Flew into the ground at 0025, near
Sgt P J Froggatt	+	Hall Farm, Oxton, 8 miles NE from the centre
F/S E A Crutchfield	+	of Nottingham. Sgt Martin succumbed to his
Sgt P L Doggett	+	injuries on 28 April and he was taken back
Sgt E D Dash	inj	to Northern Ireland and buried in Belfast
Sgt S C Boiling	inj	City Cemetery. Sgt Froggatt of Sheffield
		rests in Oxford (Botley) Cemetery, while

Sgt Crutchfield and Sgt Doggett lie at Walthamstow (Queen's Road) Cemetery
and Wymering (St. Peter and Paul) Churchyard respectively.

Note. During the enquiry as to the likely cause of this accident, it was
learnt that the pilot (and probably his crew, as well) had flown a quite
demanding exercise shortly before the night detail and, thus, it was felt
general fatigue may have had a bearing on the tragic outcome.

15 Apr	1667 HCU	Lancaster III	PB565	Training

15 Apr 1945 — **1667 HCU** — **Lancaster III PB565** — **Training**

P/O H P Speed +
F/S R Ollerton +
F/S J W Hamilton RAAF +
F/O B A Savage +
F/O E D Carss +
Sgt S J Kingdon +
Sgt R B R Cook +
Sgt E H J Martin +

T/o 1455 Sandtoft for a cross-country. Thirty minutes later, the Lancaster was sighted flying at 3,000 feet, when it suddenly nosed over and as the angle of dive increased, it broke up before impacting near Owston Ferry, 8 miles south-west of Scunthorpe, Lincolnshire (the official map reference is given as sheet 38 265185). Three, F/S Hamilton RAAF, F/O Savage and Sgt Martin, were taken to Harrogate (Stonefall) Cemetery, while funeral services for the rest were arranged privately.

17 Apr 1945 — **1663 HCU** — **Halifax III LV922 SV-W** — **Training**

Capt G C Sirmet FFAF

T/o 0050 Rufforth for a night exercise but the starboard outer cut before the Halifax was airborne. Capt Sirmet FFAF immediately reduced power, but was little too quick in his actions and moments later the aircraft was off the runway, its undercarriage broken and with the port outer on fire.

20 Apr 1945 — **1660 HCU** — **Lancaster I HK598** — **Training**

P/O J B Kram RCAF inj
Sgt C E Brenton RCAF inj
F/S F T Thompson RCAF inj
F/S R T Bridger RCAF +
WO1 R C Fleming RCAF inj
F/S F C M Robitaille RCAF +
F/S G P Charlebois RCAF +

T/o 1515 Swinderby for night bombing practice. Crashed 1650 at Claypole, 4 miles SE of Newark-upon-Trent, Nottinghamshire. The four survivors were taken to RAF Hospital Rauceby; those who died being interred at Harrogate (Stonefall) Cemetery. Apparently, an engine had failed and P/O Kram RCAF had not been able to feather the propeller.

27-28 Apr 1945 — **1660 HCU** — **Lancaster III DV166** — **Training**

F/S W C Newman

T/o 2102 Swinderby for night flying practice at high altitude. When the oxygen supplies ran low, the pilot was obliged to descend and while doing so his engines were subjected to severe icing. Consequently, he crash-landed, wheels up, at 0312 on, or close to, Hemswell airfield.

28 Apr 1945 — **1652 HCU** — **Halifax III LW470** — **Training**

F/O J A Henderson

T/o 0228 Marston Moor for night circuits and landings, with a standard crew complement of seven. Overshot at 0243 and finished up across a road on the eastern side of the airfield, close to Tockwith village.

1653 HCU — **Lancaster III LM719 H4-M** — **Training**

F/L N W Guy RCAF +
Sgt H W Jones +
F/O R K Ourom RCAF +
F/S D R Wilson RCAF +
F/O J D Travis RCAF +
Sgt V E Cline RCAF +
Sgt J R Williams RCAF +

T/o North Luffenham for a cross-country, during which the crew ran into a violent snowstorm, raging above the Oxfordshire countryside. Out of control, the Lancaster plunged down at 0320 and crashed at South Stoke, 4 miles SSW from Wallingford. The RCAF members of crew were buried in Brookwood Military Cemetery, while Sgt Jones, one of a growing number of pilots now seconded to flight engineer duties, was laid to rest in Romford Cemetery. Sgt Cline RCAF was a twenty-one year old Californian from Willows, a small town in the Sacramento Valley some 40 miles or so NW of Yuba City.

30 Apr 1945 — **1667 HCU** — **Hurricane IIC LF567** — **Training**

W/O W A H Chambers

T/o 2200 Sandtoft for night fighter affiliation training but half-an-hour later, W/O Chambers forced-landed some two hundred yards short of the Lindholme runway after running out of fuel. An investigation revealed that he had taken off using the reserve tank and when his engine cut, he failed to realise that his main tanks still contained a plentiful supply of petrol.

1 May 1945 — **1658 HCU** — **Halifax III LW193 ZB-B** — **Unknown**

Reported to have forced-landed near Cambrai in the Department of Nord, France, during the course of a cross-country flight but, so far, no accident card has been traced. However, the aircraft's movement form indicates the Halifax was reported as category "E" on this date and was struck off charge on 26 May 1945.

1 May	1659 HCU	Halifax III	MZ585		Training

1 May 1945 1659 HCU Halifax III MZ585 **Training**
F/O W G Wilson RCAF T/o 1327 Topcliffe briefed to exercise his crew in fighter affiliation tactics. Landed at 1419 but swung to starboard and once on the grass, the Halifax skidded out of control, smashing the undercarriage. A strong crosswind, blowing at eighty-five degrees off the runway was a contributory factor.

2 May 1945 1652 HCU Spitfire VB AB198 **Training**
W/O J Moss inj T/o 1111 Marston Moor for fighter affiliation duties, heading north-north-west. But, as the Spitfire climbed away, its Merlin cut and W/O Moss crash-landed, wheels up, a mile or so distant near the village of Cattal. Of his 446 solo flying hours, thirty-two had been logged on type.

1661 HCU Lancaster III PB733 **Training**
F/O F D Hubbard inj T/o 2258 Winthorpe for night circuit practice.
F/S A J Kelns RAAF Came in to land at 2308 but the pilot at the controls misjudged his height and levelled off too high. As a consequence, the bomber thudded onto the runway with such force that the oleos were completely smashed.

3 May 1945 1659 HCU Halifax III MZ600 **Training**
F/L L E Krope RCAF inj T/o Topcliffe for dual circuits and landings.
F/O S R Daviss RCAF At 0054, while taxying towards the take off position, F/L Krope RCAF had to make an emergency turn in order to avoid an aircraft that was overshooting. Moments later, he felt a severe jolt and, immediately, the wheels collapsed and the Halifax dropped onto its nose. In the dark, he had failed to see the arrester gear and the aircraft's speed had been sufficient to break the undercarriage.

4 May 1945 1654 HCU Lancaster III ME309 **Training**
F/O J Vasey T/o 2235 Wigsley for night circuits and landings.
F/O J R Leadon Twenty minutes into the exercise, the Lancaster touched down, swung to port and its starboard oleo collapsed. Although not too severely damaged, no repairs were put in hand and the airframe was reduced to spares and produce.

Note. Earlier in the day, on a still chilly Lüneburg Heath in Germany, Field Marshal Bernard Law Montgomery and his staff of 21st Army Group Tactical Headquarters met with representatives of the German High Command, the meeting concluding with Admiral Hans von Friedeburg signing the document providing for the surrender of all German forces in North West Germany. The war in Europe was to all intents and purposes over.

6- 7 May 1945 1667 HCU Lancaster I HK751 **Training**
F/S J D Kirby inj T/o 2155 Sandtoft for a night navigation sortie. Landed at 0150 but bounced back into the air. F/S Kirby attempted to go round again, but his flight engineer misunderstood his skipper's shout to take his hands away from the throttles and the Lancaster hit the runway for a second time, this time the force being sufficient to break the undercarriage. Radio static within the intercom system had been a factor in the mixup between pilot and flight engineer.

10 May 1945 1651 HCU Lancaster I ED631 **Training**
F/O L Boyer inj T/o 2320 Woolfox Lodge to practice three-engined
F/O J T Whitby inj landings. Soon after commencing the drills, the
F/S T H Cotterill inj propellers on the starboard side automatically
F/S A R Gunn inj feathered, probably due to defective electrics.
Sgt S F Trapp inj Out of control, the Lancaster crash-landed on the
F/O H C Mansfield inj runway at 2335, but bounced and went through the
F/O A Broadbent inj hedge bordering the airfield. F/S Cotterill, one
Sgt J W Hunter inj of the pilots under instruction, was critically
Sgt J B Lambert + injured and he died in the early hours of 12 May while being treated at RAF Hospital Rauceby. He is buried in Cropredy (St. Mary) Churchyard; Sgt Lambert, who was killed outright, rests in Bradford (North Bierley) Cemetery. This was the first serious accident involving a Bomber Command heavy conversion unit crew since the long awaited peace in Europe.

| 10 May 1945 | 1663 HCU | Halifax III | LK785 SV-A | Ground |

Wrecked 2340, at its dispersal, when another of the unit's aircraft went out of control on take off (see below for details).

| | 1663 HCU | Halifax III | NA621 SV-S | Training |

F/S E G Seekings

T/o 2340 Rufforth for night circuit practice but swung to starboard and, despite throttling back, F/S Seekings could not prevent his aircraft from ground looping and running into the Halifax summarised above. These were the last serious incidents reported by Rufforth ahead of the unit disbanding on 28 May 1945.

| 13 May 1945 | 1668 HCU | Lancaster III | LM724 | Training |

F/O J B Allen

T/o 1525 Bottesford for circuit training, five crew aboard. As the Lancaster lifted from the runway, its port tyre burst and Flying Control immediately ordered F/O Allen to divert to Carnaby. Landed here at 1610, but swung sharply and the undercarriage folded, causing severe damage to the airframe.

| 14-15 May 1945 | 1659 HCU | Halifax III | NR140 | Training |

W/O J Thomas

T/o 2200 Topcliffe and set course for France. During the flight, serious engine problems arose and while still over the French countryside, all eight members of crew took safely to their parachutes, leaving the Halifax to crash at 0030 at map reference VT 8007.

| 16 May 1945 | 1659 HCU | Halifax III | MZ590 | Training |

F/O J M C Wade RCAF
P/O W Edwards

T/o 1120 Topcliffe for day training. Landed at 1210 following the loss of part of flaps, a quite large section becoming detached. The post landing inspection revealed that four of the nipples and spokes from the inboard flap hinge had sheered. Although very little damaged, the Halifax was written off charge.

| 17 May 1945 | 1659 HCU | Halifax III | HX268 FD-V | Training |

F/O O R Gillette RCAF	+
Sgt E R Lynn	+
Sgt A R Armstrong RCAF	+
F/S B Trymbulak RCAF	+
F/O H A Jones RCAF	+
F/O W J Long RCAF	+
F/S T A Vincent RCAF	+
F/S A F W Torbett RCAF	+

T/o 2105 Topcliffe for a dusk cross-country. At 2235, the Halifax was seen spinning into the sea with its starboard engines feathered. As the bomber hit the water a sheet of flame and smoke shot skywards. The position of the crash is reported as 070 degrees, 10 miles Fifeness, 5621N 0158W. Two bodies were later brought ashore; those of F/O Jones RCAF and F/S Vincent RCAF. Following identification they were buried in Montrose (Sleepyhillock) Cemetery. Their six companions are commemorated on the Runnymede Memorial.

Note. Following three serious incidents in less than a week, 1659 Heavy Conversion Unit continued in existence for another four months without any serious mishaps before disbanding on 10 September 1945.

| 18 May 1945 | 1668 HCU | Lancaster I | HK739 J9-K | Training |

F/O G S Sanders
P/O H H Pickett

T/o 1054 Bottesford but failed to become airborne and wrecked having swung off the runway and crashed through the hedge bordering the airfield; no injuries reported.

| 25 May 1945 | 1661 HCU | Lancaster III | PB227 | Training |

S/L J V Comans RAAF
F/S T E Stubbs

T/o 2240 Winthorpe for night dual instruction. Landed at 2353 only to swing to port, with such violence, that its undercarriage collapsed. It is noted that S/L Comans RAAF was considerably experienced in Lancaster flying, having logged 519 hours solo on type, 325 of these at night. His pupil had flown thirty-one hours, solo, on type, nine being at night.

Note. Three months later, on 24 August, 1661 Heavy Conversion Unit disbanded. The accident, summarised above, was the last involving the total write off of one of its aircraft. Notification of disbandment had been signalled a month previous, and, it is believed, all effective flying training ceased fourteen days before the official date of the unit closing down.

31 May	1660 HCU	Lancaster I	PB864	Training

31 May 1945 — **1660 HCU** — **Lancaster I PB864** — **Training**

F/L N Birtwistle	+
P/O R F Double	+
F/O G Summers	+
F/L V G Eden	+
F/O A O Pearson DFC	+
F/O C Davies	+
W/O J S Elwood RAAF	+
F/O A I Tweedie	inj

T/o Swinderby setting course for France and a night exercise in navigation. While flying by the aid of "George", went out of control and crashed 2310 at St-Pierre Eglise (Manche), the Lancaster breaking up as it fell. Six of those who died were buried in Bayeux Cemetery but W/O Elwood RAAF was taken to Ryes British Cemetery. F/O Tweedie was thrown out and he landed safely by parachute, his injuries being not too serious. F/L Eden was a Bachelor of Science (Economics), while the air bomber, F/O Pearson, came from Liguanea, Jamaica. He had been commissioned since 22 August 1944, with seniority backdated to 21 June 1944. F/L Birtwistle had logged at least 1,062 hours of solo flying, but his Lancaster experience was limited to nineteen of these solo hours.

8 Jun 1945 — **1654 HCU** — **Hurricane IIC PG605** — **Training**

F/O J R Hendry	

T/o 1200 Swinderby for a fighter affiliation sortie, but on reaching 300 feet on climb out, the engine cut. F/O Hendry turned downwind and crash-landed, wheels up, on the airfield with plumes of white smoke gushing from the exhausts.

9 Jun 1945 — **1656 HCU** — **Lancaster I PD443** — **Ground**

LAC C Hardcastle	inj

At 0515, at Lindholme, during the process of disarming, a flash-bomb fell to the ground and exploded, setting light to the Lancaster. LAC Hardcastle was admitted to Doncaster Royal Infirmary.

13 Jun 1945 — **1652 HCU** — **Halifax III LW573 GV-B** — **Training**

P/O J H Britten	

T/o 0005 Marston Moor for night circuits and landings but swung with sufficient force to persuade P/O Britten to close the throttles and apply the brakes. He could not, however, prevent his aircraft from running towards the overshoot area and in order to stay within the confines of the airfield, he raised the wheels. No one was hurt, but the Halifax, the last of its type to be written off in Bomber Command service, was wrecked. Twelve days later, "1652" disbanded.

19 Jun 1945 — **1667 HCU** — **Lancaster III JB306 LR-E** — **Training**

F/L E M Beattie	
F/S J G H Pearce	

T/o Sandtoft for a cross-country. At 1709, the Lancaster was sighted in the circuit with both port engines stopped. However, in trying to line up with the runway, F/L Beattie attempted to restart the port outer but with no power forthcoming, he was obliged to forced-land a quarter-of-a-mile to the north of the airfield, retracting the wheels as he did so. This was the last serious accident reported from "1667" which continued to train bomber crews for another five months before disbanding on 9 November 1945.

20 Jun 1945 — **1656 HCU** — **Lancaster I LL811** — **Training**

F/S D G Gilbert	

T/o 2340 Lindholme for his first night solo on type but as the Lancaster accelerated so it began to swing and before F/S Gilbert could take corrective action, the bomber had left the runway and lost its undercarriage.

1660 HCU — **Lancaster I NN808** — **Training**

S/L H R Pooley DFC	+
F/L T Clay	+
Sgt K E Terry	+
F/L L Green	+
F/O H Signey	+
F/O G M Eden	+
Sgt J B R Brazier	inj
F/O B W Alford	inj
Sgt E Such	inj

T/o 1411 Swinderby for conversion training, a complement of nine being aboard. Three hours later, while approaching the runway with its port outer feathered, the inner port suddenly feathered of its own accord and from a height of no more than fifty feet, the bomber dived into the ground and burst into flames. Of the three survivors, Sgt Brazier died soon after his admittance to Lincoln Military Hospital. F/O Alford, described as an instructor, along with Sgt Such, was taken to RAF Hospital Rauceby, neither, it seems, being too badly hurt. S/L Pooley had served previously with 9 Squadron, details of his award being Gazetted on 16 February 1945. He is buried in Cambridge City Cemetery, while the others who died were claimed by their relatives. Variable winds on the approach leg may have played a part in this unfortunate accident.

22 Jun
1945

1668 HCU   **Beaufighter VIF MM883**   **Air Test**
F/O D F Gillman   inj T/o 1525 Bottesford for a night flying test.
On return to base at 1542, the starboard tyre
blew out on landing, causing the Beaufighter to swing violently and smash its
undercarriage. It is believed this was the only Beaufighter to be written off
at one of the Command's heavy conversion units.

13 Jul
1945

1656 HCU   **Lancaster III W4994**   **Ground**
F/O K Moore   T/o 1115 Lindholme for circuits and landings.
W/O N M Trendall   Landed at 1245 but while taxying the pilot at
the controls turned off the runway and onto the
grass. A turn through one hundred-and-eighty degrees followed and after the
Lancaster had straightened out and commenced moving forward, its undercarriage
folded. Although very little damaged, no repairs were sanctioned and the aircraft was eventually struck off charge on 28 December 1945.

19 Jul
1945

1654 HCU   **Lancaster I HK746**   **Training**
F/L G A May   inj T/o 0024 Wigsley for a night training exercise,
F/S T Howe   inj for the pilot this being his third night solo.
Sgt A W McMaster   inj Climbed to 150 feet, then turned to port with its
Sgt W B Smart   inj left wing down and before any recovery action was
Sgt J H Dawson   inj taken, it swung through one hundred-and-eighty
Sgt A E Driver   inj degrees and dived into the station's bomb dump.
Sgt J W Roberts   +   On impact, the aircraft caught fire. Sgt Smart
was treated in station sick quarters, but five
were admitted to Lincoln Military Hospital. Sgt Roberts, sadly, was beyond all
human aid and he now lies in Newcastle-upon-Tyne (St. John's Westgate) Cemetery.
It will be recalled that he had already survived one very serious crash while
undergoing training with 1651 Heavy Conversion Unit (see page 157). Accident
investigators later concluded that the port inner had stopped due to failure of
supercharger bearings which were of the Hoffmann type, now superseded by Lister
type bearings. This was the unit's last major accident ahead of disbanding on
1 September 1945.

20 Aug
1945

1656 HCU   **Lancaster III ED905**   **Training**
F/S E A McMillan RNZAF   T/o Lindholme for his first solo on type and
briefed to carry out circuits and landings.
Touched down at 1145, swung to the right and while trying to bring his aircraft
back onto the centre line, he over corrected and as the Lancaster veered towards
the left hand side of the runway, the starboard oleo snapped.

Note. This was the last serious flying accident reported from a Bomber Command
heavy conversion unit prior to the end of the war in the Far East.

18 Sep
1945

1653 HCU   **Lancaster I HK703**   **Training**
F/L F G H Meadows   T/o 1345 North Luffenham for circuit practice.
F/L J F Bower   Forced-landed at 1415, wheels retracted and with
W/O Thompson   the Merlins on the port wing stopped, in a field
P/O Isaacs   near the airfield. In his report, F/L Meadows
Sgt Lauther   stated that he had feathered the port outer and
Sgt Mullins   while trying to restart the engine, the
Sgt Edwards   inner motor suddenly cut. This led to a rapid loss
Sgt Cox   of height and the subsequent emergency landing.
Sgt G W Isaacson   inj   The injured air gunner was admitted to station
sick quarters.

3 Oct
1945

1668 HCU   **Lancaster I NG274**   **Training**
F/L D G Baker   + T/o 2150 Cottesmore for the pilot's first night
F/O J Davey   + solo, on type. All went well for nearly an hour
F/O B J McOwan DFM   + until, at approximately 2230, he overshot the
F/O T Bell   + runway with his port inner feathered. To those
F/O K White   + watching from the ground, it was immediately
Sgt O O Williams   + apparent that the Lancaster's speed was decaying
fast and just moments later it stalled and dived
into the ground near Burnley (or Burley) Bushes, the map reference being quoted
as 64 357299. F/O McOwan was buried in the local cemetery extension of St.
Nicholas; his immediate award had been Gazetted on 17 December 1943, while
serving in the Middle East with 178 Squadron. The others were laid to rest
under private arrangements.

9 Oct
1945

1656 HCU	Lancaster I	PB857		**Training**

P/O H Reid
P/O Griffin
Sgt Kettle
Sgt Harman
Sgt E N Wallace   inj
Sgt F W Wookey   inj

T/o 1225 Lindholme for general flying training. After experiencing problems with the port outer engine the crew returned to base with the air-screw windmilling. Approaching the runway at 1336, P/O Reid was unable to maintain control and he forced-landed three quarters-of-a-mile south-south-west of Lindholme Lake. Sgt Wallace was admitted to station sick quarters, but Sgt Wookey, an ex-Air Training Corps cadet, needed to be taken to RAF Hospital Rauceby. A month later, "1656" was disbanded without any further serious incidents being reported.

25 Oct
1945

1653 HCU	Lancaster I	NG118	**Training**

W/C J H Irvin

T/o 1905 North Luffenham for night circuit training, a crew of seven aboard. At 2005 the Lancaster arrived on the runway with its wheels still in their bays, the pilot having been distracted by what seemed to be unserviceable flaps.

30 Oct
1945

1653 HCU	Lancaster I	NN813		**Training**

F/O K F Sidwell DFC   +
P/O J C Prince   +
Sgt G A Boddy   +
F/O W S Lees   +
Sgt J O E Ogden   +
Sgt R J Trebble   +
Sgt P Cumberworth   +

T/o North Luffenham for familiarisation on type, P/O Prince being the pupil pilot. Lost without trace. All are commemorated on the Runnymede Memorial. F/O Sidwell had flown a tour of operations with 550 Squadron, his Distinguished Flying Cross being promulgated in the London Gazette on 20 July 1945. The crew composition was unusual; instructor, pupil pilot, two flight engineers, a wireless operator and two air gunners.

30 Nov
1945

1660 HCU	Lancaster I	NN814	**Training**

F/L G Gregory

T/o 0925 Swinderby for circuits and landings. Landed, normally, at 1050 and ran straight ahead. Then, the starboard tyre deflated and the Lancaster veered to the right, but not too violently. However, before coming to a stop, the port wheel and axle sheered, leaving the aircraft damaged beyond repair.

17 Jan
1946

1653 HCU	Hurricane IIC	LF632	**Training**

F/L V J Tyler

T/o North Luffenham for fighter affiliation, at night. Forced-landed, wheels up, on the airfield at 2035. Although having 1,125 hours of solo flying to his credit, F/L Tyler was relatively inexperienced on Hurricanes, having logged a mere nine hours on type. His misfortune was traced to a serious loss of hydraulic fluid, the cylinder of the flap operating jack having split.

28 Feb
1946

1660 HCU	Lancaster I	PB900	**Training**

W/C K P MacKenzie

T/o 1835 Swinderby for bombing practice, a crew complement of seven being aboard. At around 2025, the aircraft landed but as it decelerated a violent tail wheel shimmy commenced. W/C MacKenzie, who had twenty-three hours of Lancaster flying behind him, tried to correct the situation but was unable to do so and before coming to a stop, the bomber had swung to starboard, its tail wheel assembly broken.

18 Mar
1946

1653 HCU	Lancaster I	NG437		**Training**

W/O R T Nutting   +
F/S F K Dexter   +
Sgt A F B Blaikley   +
F/S A J Rossiter   +
F/S A A W Thomas   +
Sgt A Bone   +
Sgt T E Valler   +

T/o 1420 North Luffenham for the pilot's first solo on type, climbing steeply to three hundred feet. At this stage in the tragedy that was to follow, eyewitnesses saw the bomber bank to port and as it levelled out, its nose pitched up. Within seconds, it had stalled and dived into the ground. All were laid to rest by private arrangements, their funerals being held as far apart as Lancashire, in the case of F/S Dexter, and St. Helier in the Channel Islands, in respect of Sgt Valler. Sgt Bone's elder brother, F/L John Bone, was killed in the final stages of the war when his 3 Squadron Tempest crashed in north-west Germany; he is buried in Kiel War Cemetery. For further details, please refer to Fighter Command Losses, Volume 3, page 179.

21 Jun
1946

1653 HCU   **Lancaster III**   **PB681**   **Training**

F/O K Wood   T/o 1155 North Luffenham for a cross-country, eight crew being carried. Not long after its departure, the Lancaster passed between two layers of cloud and then entered a thick bank of cu. nimbus. The effect on the airframe was sudden and dramatic; within seconds it was subjected to very severe icing and the turbulence was such that it was propelled into a rapid climb and while trying to bring his aircraft back under control, F/O Wood found himself in a stalled situation, before diving at high speed. Eventually, at 3,500 feet, he was able to arrest the descent and at 1220 he landed , safely, at base. A technical examination revealed extensive wrinkling on both the upper and lower surfaces of the mainplanes, while a large number of rivets had either "popped" or sheared off. Not surprisingly, the bomber was deemed to be beyond economical repair.

12 Jul
1946

1653 HCU   **Mosquito XIX**   **TA306**   **Air Test**

W/O C M Ward   T/o 1443 North Luffenham for a night flying test, during which it was necessary to feather the port engine. Thus, at 1500, W/O Ward landed on one engine, finishing up in sideways skid that removed the wheels before stopping some fifty yards beyond the main runway.

15 Aug
1945

1653 HCU   **Lancaster III**   **LM524**   **Training**

F/L H K Baker   T/o 0910 North Luffenham to demonstrate three-
W/O J R Murfin   inj   engined landings. From one such landing, the
W/O Belson   Lancaster bounced but the pilot caught the air-
Sgt Warren   craft on the throttles and attempted to go round
F/S Barrow   again. However, the starboard tyre struck the
Sgt J A Wollaston   inj   top of a Nissen hut, the impact ripping the
F/S G S Thomas   inj   wheel from its axle. This left F/L Baker little option but to forced-land, which he did at 1046, coming down straight ahead and ending up near some trees, some of which were hit by the bomber in its last moments of flight.

2 Sep
1946

1660 HCU   **Lancaster III**   **PA966 TV-E**   **Training**

F/L J A Abbot   inj   T/o 1450 Swinderby for circuits and landings,
F/O L A Wildin   +   with F/O Wildin, the pupil pilot, at the controls.
F/S J A Stace   inj   Having reached a safe height, F/L Abbot shut down
F/L J W Wilkinson DFC   inj   the outer port engine and immediately the bomber
W/O C Mellstrom   inj   began to yaw and, at the same time, went into a shallow dive. At this point, F/L Abbot assumed full command, but was unable to recover the situation and at 1452 the Lancaster flew into some trees, near the airfield, and caught fire. F/O Wilden is buried in Willesden New Cemetery. Three of the four survivors were not too seriously hurt but F/L Abbot had to be admitted to RAF Hospital Rauceby.

Note. On 11 November 1946, 1660 Heavy Conversion Unit was absorbed by 1653 Heavy Conversion Unit at Lindholme, the latter having moved here from North Luffenham towards the end of October.

3 Dec
1946

1653 HCU   **Mosquito XIX**   **TA296**   **Training**

F/O D H Cox   T/o Lindholme for fighter affiliation training, at night. During the detail, the Mosquito's starboard engine began to run rough and on regaining Lindholme, F/O Cox made his approach faster than normal. Then, having touched down, he decided it would be prudent to overshoot but he was a shade too late in opening up and as the Mosquito began to climb, it flew into a totem pole and crash-landed. The time was 2351 and, as events were to prove, this was the last accident reported from a Bomber Command heavy conversion unit that resulted in the write off of the aircraft involved. As for "1653", it continued to provide the Command with a heavy bomber training capability and on 15 March 1947, was redesignated 230 Operational Conversion Unit, an establishment outside the remit of this series.

Note. During the preparation of this section, two serious accidents were overlooked, one through the misreporting of a date and the other through an oversight on the part of the compiler. Fortunately, these errors are now rectified and the two aircraft in question are summarised on the next page, thus, at least, keeping them in their appropriate section.

| 19 Dec | 1664 HCU | **Halifax V** | **EB180** | **Training** |
| 1943 | Sgt C J Stewart RCAF | | | |

T/o 1107 Dishforth but failed to become airborne as a consequence of the flaps dropping to their maximum travel. Still travelling at high speed, the Halifax ran through the overshoot area, crossed a public road, and finished up, wrecked, in a field. A shaken, but otherwise unharmed, crew trudged back towards the airfield.

2 Feb	1656 HCU	**Lancaster I**	**W4132**	**Training**
1944	P/O A W Rudge			
	WO2 R A Rember RCAF			

T/o Elsham Wolds with a crew complement of eight, briefed to practice night circuits and with WO2 Rember RCAF at the controls. Wrecked at 1910, after running beyond the end of the runway, the wheels having folded as the Lancaster encountered rough ground. Although fifty degrees of flap had been selected, the units only travelled to between twenty and twenty-five degrees before "sticking" (a figure of thirty degrees is mentioned elsewhere in the accident report). WO2 Rember RCAF later became a Path Finder pilot and was killed during operations to Kiel during July 1944 (see Bomber Command Losses, Volume 5, page 347). At the time of his death, he was serving with 582 Squadron at Little Staughton.

Section 3

Lancaster Finishing Schools

In early October 1942, the term "Heavy" was added to the title of the existing Conversion Units, this being a logical step which fully mirrored the task of these establishments. Thus, equipped with Halifax, Stirling and Lancaster types (plus some twin-engined Manchesters in the case of "1654", "1656", "1660" and 1661 Heavy Conversion Units), the steady process of upgrading crews arriving fresh from the Operational Training Units continued apace. Then, in the early winter of 1943 (and for reasons that I am not qualified to explain), a seed change took place, in that three Lancaster Finishing Schools (LFS) were formed, their titles reflecting their parent groups. At Lindholme, the operating base for 1656 Heavy Conversion Unit, the Lancaster element became A Flight of 1 LFS, while "1662" at Blyton and "1667" at Faldingworth supplied B and C Flights respectively for the same LFS.

At Feltwell, meanwhile, 3 LFS was formed to provide Lancaster experience for the re-equipping of 3 Group squadrons, presently operating Stirlings and which were soon to be withdrawn from Main Force operations, but unlike with the formation of 1 LFS, 3 LFS did not draw its initial equipment from existing heavy conversion units. As events were to prove, Feltwell, with its grass runways was far from ideal and detachments to better suited airfields became common place.

The third of the new establishments, 5 LFS formed at Syerston, taking up the Lancasters from 1668 Heavy Conversion Unit, which had moved here from Balderton on 17 November 1943, four days ahead of the formation of the new unit.

For a year in regard of 1 LFS and slightly longer for 3 LFS and 5 LFS, the status quo existed until the task of Lancaster training was handed back to the heavy conversion units. As remarked above, why this change should have been felt necessary, I am at a loss to say, but it does seem that the role of these units could quite easily have been continued under the existing umbrella of the heavy conversion units.

13 Mar 1944	5 LFS		Lancaster I	R5851		Training

F/L K Ruskell — inj
F/S E F Champness RAAF — inj
Sgt J P C Johnstone
Sgt V S J Zucker RAAF — inj
Sgt N C Scullard — inj
Sgt E Adair
Sgt L Jones
Sgt A L Pickering

T/o Syerston for dual. Shortly before 1805, the port outer failed and was feathered. It seems likely that the engine failure happened as the aircraft approached the runway, for it is reported that the instructor was at the controls and banking steeply to avoid a building when a gust of wind lifted the starboard wing and a crash-landing followed, almost straight away. Three of the four injured were treated in station sick quarters, but Sgt Scullard was quite badly hurt and he was taken to RAF Hospital Rauceby. Soon after this incident, F/S Champness RAAF (less his injured air bomber and F/L Ruskell) and the others here mentioned went to East Kirkby and joined 630 Squadron. On 22-23 May 1944, their Lancaster was part of a Main Force of 235 aircraft, drawn from 1 Group and 5 Group squadrons, ordered to attack the industrial town of Braunschweig. Falling victim to a night-fighter, F/S Champness, Sgt Johnstone and Sgt Pickering perished, while Sgt Zucker RAAF, Sgt Adair and Sgt Jones survived to sit out the rest of the war in captivity. For further details, please refer to Bomber Command Losses, Volume 5, page 235. Sgt Scullard meanwhile, is thought to have survived the war.

Note. Quite amazingly, the Lancaster Finishing Schools had operated for the better part of four months without a major incident. As the following summaries will show, this run of good fortunate had come to an end.

3 Apr 1944	5 LFS	Lancaster I	L7540 RC-U		Unknown

Reported to have been damaged beyond repair in a landing accident at Waddington, subsequently being allocated the maintenance serial 4092M. No accident card has been traced, but the aircraft's movement record shows its acceptance by 44 Squadron on 9 January 1942, followed by a host of squadron and conversion flight movements before being transferred to 1654 HCU on 4 September 1942 and, ultimately, to 5 LFS via 1661 HCU on 2 February 1944.

4 Apr	5 LFS	Lancaster I	R5726	Training

4 Apr 1944 — **5 LFS** — **Lancaster I** — **R5726** — **Training**

F/O J D Murray RAAF   +   T/o 1455 Syerston for general flying practice.
Sgt S Chappell   +   Dived out of low cloud, at an angle of forty-
F/S W H Keeble RAAF   +   five degrees, shedding its fins, elevators and
F/O W L Towers RAAF   +   wing tips before crashing at 1545 about half-a-
F/O F L Grimwood RAAF   +   mile from Brenston in Nottinghamshire. Funeral
F/S R G Williams RAAF   +   services for the five RAAF members of crew were
Sgt R E J Sisley   +   held at Oxford (Botley) Cemetery, while the
flight engineer, Sgt Chappell, and the tail
gunner, Sgt Sisley, were buried in South Kelsey (St. Nicholas) Churchyard and
Dover (Charlton) Cemetery, respectively.

8 Apr 1944 — **1 LFS** — **Lancaster I** — **R5672** — **Air Test**

W/C E F K Campling DSO DFC   +   T/o Hemswell and crashed at approximately 1700,
2nd Officer T Whittall ATA   +   having been seen diving steeply from a height,
Sgt L T D Regan   +   estimated, at 1,000 feet, the impact occurring
LAC R P Freer   +   near Caistor, Lincolnshire. Such was the total
AC1 T King   +   destruction of the bomber, accident investigators
AC1 H Quinton   +   were unable to determine the cause of the tragedy.
AC1 A H Spiller   +   W/C Campling of Clapham, London, is buried in
AC1 E R Steventon   +   Denbighshire at St. George Churchyard; Taniya
AC2 G V F Killick   +   Whittall of the Air Transport Auxiliary was taken
to West Hoathly (St. Margaret) Churchyard, while
their Welsh born flight engineer, Sgt Regan, received a military funeral at Cambridge City Cemetery. All six non-aircrew members were claimed by their next of
kin. W/C Campling was an outstanding bomber pilot with 1,672 solo flying hours
to his credit. On 12 February 1942, while flying Wellingtons with 142 Squadron,
he participated in the heroic, but, ultimately, futile attempt to sink the German
battle-cruisers, Scharnhorst and Gneisnau, accompanied by the light cruiser, Prinz
Eugen charging at speed through the North Sea on their way to ports in Germany
(see pages 234 and 235 of The Bomber Command War Diaries by Martin Middlebrook
and Chris Everitt for further details). Flying at 700 feet, his aircraft was hit
by enemy fire in the port wing, elevator trim tabs and fuselage, the hydraulics
being rendered unserviceable as a consequence. Then, having dropped to three
hundred feet, two fighters from the air umbrella covering the battle-cruisers
pounced on the Wellington and it was only the amazing flying skills of Campling
that saved the crew as they jinked and weaved at wave top height, eventually
escaping their adversaries and returning to base. For this action, he was
awarded an immediate DFC, Gazetted on 3 March 1942. Continuing with operations,
he won a DSO with 460 Squadron, this being promulgated on 27 July 1943. At the
time of his death, he was aged twenty-three.

14 Apr 1944 — **5 LFS** — **Lancaster I** — **W4103 RC-E** — **Training**

F/O H H Richardson DFM RCAF   +   T/o 1550 Syerston for general flying practice.
P/O P W Laidler RAAF   +   Destroyed circa 1630 in a midair collision, at
Sgt H E Herbert   +   one thousand feet, with a 1521 Flight Oxford
F/O P W R Holes   +   trainer, both aircraft coming down one and-a-
F/O D W McRuer   +   half miles S of the airfield (see 1521 Flight
Sgt G R B Aspinall   +   in Section 5 for details of this aircraft, and
Sgt F W Edwards   +   its crew). The first three named were taken to
AC2 S Stokoe   +   Oxford (Botley) Cemetery, but F/O McRuer of
Edinburgh was buried in Newark-upon-Trent
Cemetery. The others were claimed by their relatives. AC2 Stokoe is described
as an "under training pilot". F/O Richardson had flown with 50 Squadron, his
award being published on 13 August 1943.

17 Apr 1944 — **5 LFS** — **Lancaster I** — **W4232 RC-Y** — **Training**

P/O B L Humphreys RAAF   +   T/o 1601 Syerston for general flying training.
Sgt A Townsley   +   Four minutes later, and possibly while still
F/S A H Farrell   +   climbing (eyewitnesses assessed the Lancaster's
Sgt N H Cutler   +   height as at 1,000 feet), a stall occurred and
Sgt R J Brown   +   as the bomber fell, the port mainplane and the
Sgt J A Davies   +   tip of the starboard wing came off. Only five
Sgt A D Bale   +   bodies could be positively identified, thus,
the names of Sgt Townsley and Sgt Davies are
perpetuated on panels 239 and 228 respectively of the Runnymede Memorial. Four
were taken to their home towns, but twenty year old P/O Humphreys RAAF of Kew,
Victoria, rests with just over a one hundred-and-fifty of his fellow countrymen
in Oxford (Botley) Cemetery at North Hinksey.

29 Apr	5 LFS	Lancaster I W4797 RC-B	Training

1944 F/O L M Pedersen RCAF — T/o 0515 Syerston for circuit training, at dawn, but while taking off the starboard tyre burst and Flying Control advised the crew, eight in number, to divert to Woodbridge. This they did, arriving at the emergency strip at around 0720. On touch down, the starboard oleo gave way and as the Lancaster veered off towards the left hand side of the runway, the port undercarriage folded, effectively bringing to an end the Lancaster's active service.

1 May	5 LFS	Lancaster I W4794	Training

1944 F/O G F Maule — T/o Syerston for a flying exercise, during which the port tyre exploded as the Lancaster departed the runway. This time, Flying Control ordered the crew to make for Carnaby in Yorkshire and, once again, their arrival at 1945 resulted in the damaged unit breaking, damaging their aircraft beyond repair.

Note. I strongly suspect that F/O Maule had been attached to 5 Lancaster Flying School from 9 Squadron following a serious take off crash on 22 April (see Bomber Command Losses, Volume 5, page 178), the occasion of his fifth operational sortie (Braunschweig). His name next appears in squadron records on 3 May, when he participated in the costly raid on Mailly-le-Camp. Serving with him at the time was S/L H R Pooley, whose death, while flying with 1660 Heavy Conversion Unit, is summarised on page 171.

6 May	1 LFS	Lancaster I W4793	Transit

1944 P/O F H Swinger RAAF — T/o 1005 Sturgate with the intention of returning to Hemswell but went of control and crashed through a hedge, finishing up on Christmas Farm, Heapham. In his report, P/O Swinger RAAF stated that the rudder adjustment slipped and his feet came off the pedals. He then cut the throttles, but could not prevent the crash that followed.

16 May	1 LFS	Lancaster I W4965	Transit

1944 F/O J Archibold RNZAF — T/o 0110 Sturgate with the intention of returning to Hemswell but lost control, at high speed, and ended up on land belonging to Laburnham Farm where it caught fire.

17 May	1 LFS	Lancaster I ED567	Training

1944 P/O F Collett — T/o 0213 Hemswell for a night exercise, during which the port outer failed. With the airscrew feathered, P/O Collett attempted to land at Riccall but on landing at 0246, he lost control and after swinging off to the left side of the runway, the bomber ran over an obstruction and lost its wheels. With only six hours of solo on type, he was not experienced enough to deal with the situation in which he found himself.

19 May	5 LFS	Lancaster I DV368	Training

1944 F/L W H Kellaway — T/o 1750 Syerston for circuit practice but
F/S J H G South — just as the aircraft was about to become airborne, the port tyre deflated. F/L Kellaway closed the throttles but could not stabilise the swing that had developed. Consequently, the undercarriage collapsed and the port inner caught light.

26 May	5 LFS	Lancaster I L7578 RC-L	Training

1944
P/O G B Sanderson RCAF + T/o 1850 Syerston for a combined exercise, at
Sgt J G Middlemas + night, in navigation and practice bombing. From
Sgt A D Clark + a height, estimated as 8,000 feet, the aircraft
P/O A T Noble RCAF + dived and crashed 2215 at Glebe Farm, Gonalston
Sgt B Broe + some 9 miles NE from the centre of Nottingham.
F/S D Wright RCAF + All rest in a collective grave at Newark-upon-
Sgt D Nicholls + Trent Cemetery, a relatively unusual occurrence.
A memorial has, in recent years, been set on farmland, roughly thirty yards east of the impact area. On official papers, Mooton Park, Gonalston, is also given as the crash site.

Note. I am indebted to Brian Walker of Arnold, Nottingham, and to his good friend, Bill Baguley, for their cheerful and willing help over many years, and in particular for their input in respect of aircraft accidents in their area of Nottinghamshire.

26–27 May	5 LFS	Lancaster I	W4383	Training

1944

F/O K W Brown CGM RCAF	inj	T/o 2311 Syerston for dual circuit practice,
Sgt W C Freestone		at night. Landed 0136 atop another of the
Sgt Post		unit's aircraft that had moved onto the runway
Sgt D A Gage	inj	and was not seen until it was too late to avoid
F/O Woolam		this most unfortunate accident. F/O Brown RCAF,
Sgt Taylor		had taken part in the famous "Dams" raid, flown
Sgt Bullivant		the previous May, in which he operated as part
Sgt E E Henders	inj	of the reserve force, taking off from Scampton

in Lancaster III ED918 AJ-F at 0012 hours on the
seventeenth and, eventually, after a most adventuresome sortie, attacked the
Sorpe. For a full description of the raid, from which he was subsequently
decorated with the Conspicuous Gallantry Medal (London Gazette 28 May 1943),
please refer to Alan W Cooper's, "The Men who Breached the Dams", published
by William Kimber, 1982. The demise of his 617 Squadron Lancaster is recorded
in Bomber Command Losses, Volume 5, page 36. Sgt Gage and Sgt Henders were
taken to RAF Hospital Rauceby; Sgt Gage is presumed to have made a good recovery
but Sgt Henders died on 11 August 1946. Whether this was as a direct consequence
of the injuries he received in the accident, or from other causes, is not known.
Aged twenty-three, he is buried in Liverpool (Allerton) Cemetery.

27 May	5 LFS	Lancaster I	W4258	Ground

1944

F/O J Forsyth DFC RAAF	inj	At 0136, while on the Syerston runway and running
WO1 W M Blaine RCAF	inj	up engines in readiness for take off, hit by the
Sgt Jordan		aircraft described previously. The two Canadians
Sgt J F Reid RCAF	inj	were buried in Harrogate (Stonefall) Cemetery,
F/O W D Lewis RCAF	+	while Sgt Coldwell rests, not too far distant, in
Sgt W Coldwell	+	Barnsley Cemetery. Of the four who were injured,
Sgt R R Lynch RCAF	+	three were admitted to RAF Hospital Rauceby,
Sgt D E Reesor RCAF	inj	while WO1 Blaine RCAF joined F/O Brown RCAF, from

the other Lancaster, in station sick quarters.
F/O Forsyth RAAF had flown with 106 Squadron, details of his DFC being Gazetted
in England on 15 February and in Australia on 24 February 1944.

17 Jun	3 LFS	Lancaster I	W4851 A5–R2	Training

1944

W/O R Newman RNZAF	+	T/o Feltwell for a night cross-country. Crashed
Sgt J W Argent	+	circa 0200 at Stalloch Farm, in the vicinity of
Sgt A R Thomson	+	Lakenheath, the Lancaster diving almost verti-
Sgt J Greenan	+	cally into the ground and exploding in a ball
Sgt F A Still	+	of fire. W/O Newman RNZAF and Sgt Still, who
Sgt R L Ganderton	+	came from London, were afforded military funerals
Sgt J McD Chambers	+	at Cambridge City Cemetery, while the others were

buried by private arrangements.

	3 LFS	Lancaster I	ED376	Training

F/O R R F Whitby RCAF	+	T/o Feltwell similarly tasked. Came down, on
Sgt C Quanborough	+	farmland, near Southery, 5 miles SSE of Downham
F/O D R Gilchrist RCAF	+	Market, Norfolk, more or less at the same time
F/O P H Duval RCAF	+	as the aircraft described above. The bodies of
Sgt T W Bettridge	+	the five Canadians were conveyed to Brookwood
Sgt A K Hrychenko RCAF	+	Military Cemetery. Sgt Quanborough was laid to
Sgt O W Libby RCAF	+	rest in Grantham Cemetery, while Sgt Bettridge

lies in Radford (St. Nicholas) Cemetery.

Note. Accident investigators were unable to determine the cause of either
crash, though the close proximity of the two crash sites and similar time
factors suggest that a midair collision might have taken place.

3 Aug	3 LFS	Lancaster I	W4271	Training

944

P/O J S Mankey RAAF		T/o Swannington for P/O Mankey's first night
Sgt Stanley		solo, on type. On touch down at 2357, the
F/O Robertson		Lancaster swung first to starboard and then,
Sgt Musgrove		after being brought back onto the centre line,
Sgt Trenbath		veered sharply to port. Neither the application
Sgt Albiston		of the brakes or manipulation of the throttles
Sgt T F Worthington	inj	could remedy the situation and moments later

the undercarriage collapsed. On coming to a
halt, a fire broke out. Sgt Worthington's injuries were not too serious and
he was treated in station sick quarters.

28 Aug **1 LFS** Lancaster I W4790 3C-O **Training**
1944 F/O D O Dickie T/o 0245 Hemswell for night circuit practice.
Thirteen minutes into the detail, F/O Dickie
landed off a fairly fast approach, with thirty degrees of flap selected. After
touching down, he applied the brakes but with the end of the runway fast looming
into view he raised the wheels in order to stop, thereby wrecking his aircraft.
In his report, F/O Dickie stated that after taking off and retracting the flaps,
the left wing felt "heavy" and his suspicions were aroused as to a possible fault
in the starboard flap mechanism. He, therefore, elected to keep his speed up on
the approach in order to avoid stalling. His actions, it seems, were fully vin-
dicated as his commanding officer added a comment that the pilot "had handled his
aircraft coolly and skillfully".

25 Sep **1 LFS** Lancaster I R5866 **Ground**
1944 F/L W F Caldow While starting engines at 0845, at Hemswell,
ahead of his pupil and crew coming aboard,
F/L Caldow inadvertently raised the undercarriage with unfortunate consequences.

1 Oct **5 LFS** Lancaster I W4941 RC-M **Ground**
1944 F/O E McM Lawson RAAF T/o Syerston for night circuit training, during
which the wheels failed to lock down when lowered
normally. The emergency system was then operated and the aircraft landed safely.
Approximately eight hours later, at 0838, with the Lancaster parked on its dispersal pan, the undercarriage folded, damaging the bomber beyond repair, though
it appears to have been salvaged for ground training purposes with the serial
4791M allotted. F/O Lawson RAAF was posted to 207 Squadron and was killed in
a midair collision with a 57 Squadron aircraft on 2 March 1945 (see Bomber
Command Losses, Volume 6, page 99).

5 Nov **5 LFS** Lancaster I LL778 **Training**
1944 F/L J G Claridge RNZAF T/o 1559 Syerston to practise three-engined
P/O J Daring RAAF flying procedures. At around 1730, the pupil
pilot overshot his approach and allowed his
air speed to drop to a near critical level. F/L Claridge RNZAF assumed control
but was unable to retrieve the situation and the bomber crash-landed, without
injury to the crew, on the airfield.

18 Dec **3 LFS** Lancaster I R5674 A5-K **Training**
1944 P/O H W Harler RAAF + T/o 1851 Feltwell for general night training.
Sgt P A Gledhill + On return to base, and having joined the circuit,
F/S D S Harris + collided with another of the unit's aircraft,
F/O D E Parsons + both machines crashing 2151 into soft ground at
F/S P A Ewins RAAF + Hockwold cum Wilton, 10 miles WNW from Thetford
Sgt C F Farley + in Norfolk. The two Australians were laid to
Sgt J Foster + rest in Cambridge City Cemetery; their five
companions were taken to their home towns for
private burial.

3 LFS Lancaster I R5846 A5-H **Training**
F/S T G Jacobs RNZAF + T/o 1856 Feltwell similarly tasked and lost in
Sgt L A R Potter + the manner described previously. Two, the New
F/S G R T Taylor + Zealand born pilot and Sgt Potter of South
Sgt J Duffin + Norwood in Surrey, were buried by service
Sgt J W Hutton + arrangements in Cambridge City Cemetery, while
Sgt F A Oxlade + the others were claimed by their next of kin.
Sgt C Symonds + Both crews were attending No. 63 Course, and
their demise features on page 238 of "Final
Flights", by Ian McLachlan and published by Patrick Stephens Limited, 1989.

12 Jan **5 LFS** Lancaster III JB125 **Training**
1945 P/O G R Dunlop RNZAF + T/o 1845 Syerston for a night detail. On return
Sgt P J V Browne + encountered failing visibility, the cloud base
F/S P J Hill RNZAF + being down to between 500 and 600 feet, with a
Sgt A J Evans BEM + persistent drizzle. Flew beyond the airfield,
F/S R L Staples RNZAF + and while banking flew into the ground at 2150,
Sgt R H Sedgley + half-a-mile N of the Tree Hotel at Hoveringham,
Sgt W F Cairns + a villager on the E side of the main Nottingham
to Newark-upon-Trent road. The three RNZAF air-
men and Sgt Evans lie in Oxford (Botley) Cemetery, the rest in their home towns.

Note. In respect of the accident, reported at the base of the previous page, Errol Martyn notes that F/S Hill's elder brother, P/O Howard Perry Hill, died during the Battle of Britain, when his Spitfire I X4417 of 92 Squadron was shot down on 20 September 1940. He is buried in Folkestone New Cemetery. Norman Franks, in the first volume of his "Royal Air Force Fighter Command Losses of the Second World War", published in 1997 by Midland Publishing, states on page eighty-five that P/O Hill RNZAF fell victim to Oberst Werner Mölders, of JG51 and flying a Bf 109, the time of the action being given as 1135 over Dungeness.

29 Jan	3 LFS	Lancaster III	ND958	Training

1945

W/O T D Lloyd RNZAF	+	T/o 1720 Feltwell for a night cross-country,
Sgt W R Jackson	+	in the course of which the weather conditions
F/O R B Robinson RNZAF	+	deteriorated to such an extent that a recall
Sgt E G W Smart	+	message was broadcast. This call was ack-
Sgt L F Cook	+	nowledged, though the signal strength was very
Sgt R C Bailey	+	weak. At approximately 2100, now flying through
Sgt A J Crittenden	+	intermittent light snow and occasional rain,

the Lancaster was observed to pull up in order to avoid some trees and in doing so W/O Lloyd RNZAF lost control and crashed about a mile S of Barnham, Suffolk and roughly 4 miles S of Thetford in the neighbouring county of Norfolk. The two New Zealand airmen were buried in Cambridge City Cemetery (Errol Martyn has discovered that F/O Robinson's true age was 35 and not 33 as reported in the cemetery register. He had, apparently, understated his age when enlisting in 1942). The others were laid to rest by private arrangements.

5 LFS	Lancaster III	LM308	Training

WO2 R B Rathbone RCAF	+	T/o 0001 Syerston for a cross-country sortie.
Sgt A Mercer	+	Returned to base and acknowledged the landing
F/S H M MacKenzie RCAF	+	instructions from Flying Control. Two minutes
F/S J A Emerson RCAF	+	later, at 0216, the Lancaster crashed, at high
F/S J H Reid RCAF	+	speed, exploding on impact. Eyewitnesses say
Sgt J Martin	+	the aircraft was on fire, in the air. Five
Sgt J F Fitzgibbon RCAF	+	were buried in Harrogate (Stonefall) Cemetery,

while Sgt Mercer and Sgt Martin rest in South-
port (Duke Street) Cemetery and Castleford (Whitwood) Cemetery respectively.

4 Feb	5 LFS	Lancaster III	LM629	Training

1945

P/O H Hudson RAAF	T/o 1715 Syerston for night training. At

around 2030, while attempting to land on three-engines and having touched down from a fast approach, the Lancaster overran the runway and was wrecked on entering the overshoot area. Apparently, the flight engineer failed to hear, or misunderstood, P/O Hudson's instruction to close the throttles. A technical inspection of the port inner, which had been shut down as a precaution when the temperature gauge rose to give an above normal reading, revealed no obvious faults and, subsequently, it was discovered that the gauge itself was faulty.

Note. This was the last serious accident reported from 5 Lancaster Finishing School, prior to disbanding on 1 April 1945. Both sister establishments had ceased training, leaving the task of Lancaster conversion in the very capable hands of the heavy conversion units.

Section 4

1655 Mosquito Conversion/Training Unit

Originally known as 1655 Mosquito Conversion Unit and formed at Horsham St. Faith in No.2 Group, on 30 August 1942, this establishment whose "number plate" fell within the block of numbers allocated to heavy conversion units, had a relatively brief existence and was absorbed eight months later, at Bicester by 13 Operational Training Unit. Its absence was not, however, for long and when "13" was made a part of 2nd Tactical Air Force "1655" was reclaimed by Bomber Command, this time at Marham where it reformed on 1 July 1943, under the aegis of No.8 Group.

Its rôle was to provide trained crews for the increasing number of Mosquito squadrons forming in the Command, a task that it performed admirably for eighteen months before being merged on the last day of the year, 1944, with 16 Operational Training Unit at Upper Heyford.

Although regarded as one of the most versatile light-bombers of the Second World War, trainee pilots moving up from less potent twin-engined types found the power delivered by the Mosquitoes two Rolls-Royce Merlins to be quite daunting and, as the summaries that follow will show, more than a few aspiring Mosquito captains paid the ultimate price before fully mastering the complexities of De Havilland's "Wooden Wonder".

31 Oct 1942	1655 MCU	Mosquito IV	DZ346		Training
	Sgt W L Rhys		+	T/o Marham for a low-level flying exercise, in	
	F/O D H Hornby		+	the course of which the Mosquito flew into an elm	

tree and hurtled into a field less than a mile south of Norton Church, Norton, 6 miles E of Bury St. Edmunds, Suffolk. Twenty year old Sgt Rhys is buried in Carmarthenshire at Pembrey (St. Illtyd) Churchyard; his navigator, F/O Hornby, was taken to the City of London Cemetery at Manor Park, East Ham. At the time of the accident, weather conditions in the area were extremely poor. Unit records suggest the crew were either attached from, or were about to be posted to 139 Squadron.

26 Jan 1943	1655 MCU	Blenheim V	AZ961 S	Training
	F/L E A Costello-Bowen		T/o Marham but an engine cut, obliging the crew	
	Lt Moe		to forced-land, wheels up, at Parke Farm. In	
			addition to the two officers identified, the	

aircraft had three ground crew aboard. F/L Costello-Bowen had reported to "1655" for flying instructor duties on 31 October 1942, soon after returning to the United Kingdom from his adventures as an evader (see Bomber Command Losses, Volume 3, pages 191 and 301).

28 Feb 1943	1655 MCU	Mosquito IV	DZ347 N	Air Test
	F/L E A Costello-Bowen		T/o Marham with the bomb doors open and this	
	AC1 Burton		was followed by engine failure. Forced-landed,	
			without injury, on the airfield.	

Note. This was the last incident, involving the loss of an aircraft, before its absorption by 13 Operational Training Unit. Although "1655" had formed at Horsham St. Faith, the headquarters moved to Marham in late September 1942 and it would reform here on 1 July 1943, as 1655 Mosquito Training Unit.

18 Jul 1943	1655 MTU	Mosquito IV	DZ495		Training
	Capt O B Stene RNAF		+	T/o Marham and crashed after flying into high	
	Lt K Lochen RNAF		+	tension cables near Cranfield. Both officers	
				had been with the unit since mid-May 1943, and	

were nearing the end of their training. Representing "1655" at their funerals were F/L A A Mellor and F/O E A F Jackman.

25 Jul 1943	1655 MTU	Mosquito IV	DZ318		Training
	P/O C Prentice RNZAF		inj	T/o Marham for night flying. Crashed 2359 on	
	P/O J L Warner		inj	approach to land. P/O Warner was taken to RAF	
				Hospital Ely following local medical attention.	

11 Aug	1655 MTU	Mosquito III	HJ962	Training

F/O I G Broom DFC   inj   T/o Marham for night dual, during the course of
F/L B A MacDonald RCAF   inj   which the port engine failed at a critical stage
                                       of the approach. Crashed, heavily, at 0200 and
when aid reached the trapped crew, it was quite obvious that both were in a very
serious condition. F/O Broom was destined to spend the next few months in
RAF Hospital Ely, having fractured his spine, but his pupil, sadly, died soon
after his admittance to station sick quarters. He was buried in Marham Cemetery
on 16 August, his brother, Sgt A M MacDonald RCAF being the chief mourner at the
service conducted by the Revd O´Meara, the Roman Catholic Chaplin. Pall bearers
were drawn from No. 12 Course.

Note 1. F/O Broom became one of the outstanding Mosquito pilots of the Second
World War. Having made a full recovery from his terrible injuries, he continued to serve as a flying instructor until returning to operational duties
with 571 Squadron, where he teamed up with F/L Tony Broom (no relation) the
duo, not surprisingly, becoming known as the "Flying Brooms".   It was during
this time that he added a First Bar to his DFC (the original having being won
with 107 Squadron and Gazetted on 7 April 1942) and this was soon followed by
a Second Bar, the latter gained with 128 Squadron, these honours being published
on 3 October 1944 and 27 February 1945 respectively.   Remaining in the post-war
Royal Air Force, he converted to jet bombers, and, in 1955, was the captain of
"Aries IV", the Canberra that flew over the North Pole and set a new Ottawa to
London speed record. This was followed by a number of prestigious appointments,
including command of Royal Air Force Bruggen in West Germany and stints with the
Ministry of Defence and the Central Flying School before retiring in 1977 in the
rank of Air Marshal, by which time he had added a Distinguished Service Order
and an Air Force Cross to his many decorations. He had, in 1975, been further
honoured with a knighthood. He died on 24 January 2003, aged eighty-two.

Note 2. In the Daily Telegraph´s fine obituary to Air Marshal Sir Ivor Broom,
a personal account of the accident which came close to ending his flying career
(if not his life) reads as follows, "We had full flap down, and on a Mosquito
with full flap there is no way you can go round again.   I raised the undercarriage, and was going to let the aircraft settle on open countryside when the
pupil suddenly said, "We´re going to crash" - and fully opened the throttle on
the good engine."

8 Sep	1655 MTU	Mosquito IV	DK323	Training

F/O G D Forder   T/o 0925 Marham but swung to port and when the
                                       pilot over corrected, the Mosquito veered off
the runway, on the starboard side, and lost its undercarriage.

5 Nov	1655 MTU	Mosquito IV	DK285	Training

F/O P T L Hallett DFC RAAF   +   T/o 2205 Marham for a night cross-country.
F/O A W F Quick RAAF   +   Lost without trace. The two Australians are
                                       commemorated on panels 188 and 189 respectively
of the Runnymede Memorial. F/O Hallett had served previously with 460 Squadron
and his DFC was published in the London Gazette on 22 September 1942.

7 Jan	1655 MTU	Mosquito IV	DZ356	Training

F/L K F Jolly   +   T/o 1445 Marham for a standard day training
F/O W D Langworthy DFC RAAF   +   exercise. Forty-five minutes later, with the
                                       Mosquito near the Welsh border, an explosion
rent the air and debris was scattered around the village of Llangarron, some
thirteen miles SSW from Hereford. Accident investigators determined that the
pilot was blown from the aircraft, less his parachute. He was laid to rest on
12 January in St. Albans Cemetery, his funeral service being well attended by
officers and airmen from No. 1519 Beam Approach Training Flight which, until
recently, had been commanded by F/L Jolly. The day previous, F/O Langworthy
was buried in Bath (Haycombe) Cemetery with Padre Sands from the RAAF Overseas
Headquarters attachment officiating. Previously, he had flown Lancasters with
97 Squadron and details of his award had been promulgated on 14 May 1943.

Note.   Further to my mention, above, of the investigation into the tragedy,
the primary cause of the crash was traced to a flame trap nut, or screw, becoming embedded between a valve and its seating.   This permitted hot gasses
to burn on the seating which, in turn, caused a series of violent backfires
and, soon afterwards, failure of the engine´s supercharger.

25-26 Feb   **1655 MTU**   **Mosquito IV**   DZ312   **Training**
1944   F/O M J Taylor RNZAF   +   T/o 2300 Marham for a night navigation detail.
           P/O G W Manders DFC   +   Returned to base circa 0130, in conditions of
                                             low cloud which, at times, was down to around
four hundred feet. Still travelling at high speed, the Mosquito broke through
the overcast and hit the ground at a stalled angle of attack near Stradsett,
three miles ENE of Downham Market, Norfolk and disintegrated. As Errol Martyn
indicates, F/O Taylor RNZAF had very little experience of flying in adverse
weather, the majority of his near on one thousand hours of experience being
logged in the Pacific theatre of operations. He is buried in Cambridge City
Cemetery. P/O Manders rests in Bingley Cemetery; his name appears in the
Supplement to the London Gazette for 19 October 1943, where notification of
his DFC, gained in the service of 100 Squadron, is promulgated.

13 Mar   **1655 MTU**   **Mosquito IV**   DK288   **Transit**
1944   F/L I G Broom DFC   T/o Bury St. Edmunds (not confirmed) intending
                                             to fly to Warboys but three minutes into the
flight, the aircraft's dinghy sprang from its stowage and became entangled in
the tail surfaces. Despite having no elevator control, F/L Broom skilfully
forced-landed in a field near Bury St. Edmunds, Suffolk. As the Mosquito slid
to a halt, the airframe broke up but neither occupant (the navigator is not
named) sustained injury. It is suspected an electrical fault was the root
cause of this accident which for F/O Broom, recently being declared fit to
fly following the awful crash summarised at the top of the previous page,
must have been a most alarming experience.

26 Mar   **1655 MTU**   **Mosquito IV**   DZ388   **Training**
1944   S/L V Allport DFC RNZAF   +   T/o 1908 Warboys for an operational training
           F/L T W Matthews   +   sortie. Twenty-two minutes later, the bomber
                                             spun into the ground at Aslackby Farm, 5 miles
east-south-east of the Lincolnshire airfield of Folkingham and no great distance
from the village of Billingborough. A reasonably experienced pilot (he had completed a tour of operations flying Blenheims with 18 Squadron both in the United
Kingdom and in the Middle East and for which his DFC was awarded, Gazetted on
11 August 1942) with nearly 750 hours to his credit, S/L Allport RNZAF had only
logged a dozen on Mosquitoes and it was considered that in conditions, bordering
on instrument flying rules, he flew into a situation that proved to be his un-
doing. He is buried in Cambridge City Cemetery, while F/L Matthews was laid
to rest at 1430 hours on 3 April in Abney Park Cemetery, his funeral being
attended by F/O N E Litchfield and F/O A M McDonald.

20 Apr   **1655 MTU**   **Mosquito IV**   DZ439   **Training**
1944   F/O R Davison   +   T/o 1111 Warboys but came down two minutes later
           F/O J T Agnew DFC   +   at Little Raveley, 5 miles NNE of Huntingdon.
                                             F/O Davison is buried in Newcastle-upon-Tyne
(St. Andrew's and Jesmond) Cemetery, while F/O Agnew was taken home to Northern
Ireland and interred in Belfast (Dundonald) Cemetery. He is twice mentioned in
the London Gazette; the first on 28 September 1943, promulgating his commission
and the second on 10 December 1943, notifying the DFC gained with 100 Squadron.
The cause of the crash was traced to a failed rear inlet valve in the port Merli
which cut as the Mosquito climbed.

Note. Unit records show that their funerals were held on 25 and 27 April
with F/L F W Walton and F/L P S Davies travelling to Newcastle while the
Belfast service was attended by F/L J A Mahood and F/O W K McGregor.

22 Apr   **1655 MTU**   **Mosquito IV**   DZ603   **Training**
1944   P/O W Aston   inj   T/o Warboys for a night exercise. Crashed 2225
           W/O P Bond DFM   inj   in Marley Gap field, Hill Farm, near St. Ives,
                                             Huntingdonshire, after overshooting from an
approach with the starboard engine feathered. Both airmen were very seriously
hurt and were taken to RAF Hospital Ely. In his report, P/O Aston said that he
had observed excessive amounts of flame emitting from the exhaust shrouds and
believing the unit was on fire he took the precaution to close the motor down.
A technical inspection showed, however, that a blown exhaust gasket was the
culprit and there was no evidence of burning from within the Merlin itself.
W/O Bond's award had been published on 9 July 1943, following a tour of duty
in the Middle East with 142 Squadron.

25 Apr	1655 MTU	Mosquito III	LR525		Training

25 Apr
1944 1655 MTU   Mosquito III LR525   Training
F/O M G Henderson RCAF   + T/o 0132 Warboys for a night solo exercise.
                             A mere eight minutes had past, when Flying
Control staff observed the Mosquito flying overhead at 700 feet with its port
propeller feathered. Moments later, the Mosquito appeared to stall before
spinning in at Rectory Farm, just beyond the western boundary and a mile NW
of the village of Broughton on the SW side of the airfield. F/O Henderson
was taken to Cambridge City Cemetery and buried at 1130 hours on 27 April,
the service being led by Padre Roberts RCAF and assisted by S/L J W Bullen.

13 May
1944 1655 MTU   Oxford I DF517   Training
F/L A E H Cattle   + T/o Warboys for a cross-country sortie, during
F/O G H Bowen   + which the crew encountered turbulence of such
F/L M McIver DFC RCAF   + severity that the trainer broke up and crashed
F/O G G Halestrap DFC   + at 1615, debris falling some 2 to 3 miles W of
                             Melton Mowbray, Leicestershire. F/O Halestrap
of Tadworth in Surrey was buried locally in Melton Mowbray Cemetery; his skipper
rests in Southend-on-Sea (Leigh-on-Sea) Cemetery; F/L McIver RCAF was taken to
Brookwood Military Cemetery and F/O Bowen lies at Swansea (Oystermouth) Cemetery.
The two decorated officers had served with 106 Squadron and 192 Squadron respectively and their awards had been Gazetted on 15 October and 7 December 1943.

21 May
1944 1655 MTU   Mosquito IV DZ528   Training
F/L S C Holbrow   + T/o 1631 Warboys and climbed into cloud. Two
F/O G M Rea   + minutes later, the Mosquito emerged from the
                             overcast, spinning, and smashed into the ground
near Broughton on the SW side of the airfield and 5 miles NE of Huntingdon. On
impact, the aircraft burst into flames. F/L Holbrow is buried in Worcestershire
at Wick (St. Mary) Churchyard and F/O Rea lies in Cheadle and Gatley Cemetery.

27 Jun
1944 1655 MTU   Mosquito IV DZ550   Training
F/O W S Donovan DFM   + T/o 1448 Warboys briefed for a cross-country
Sgt G Royall   + and instructed to land at Wyton. Dived and
                             crashed at approximately 1740 at Chesterton
Farm, Benwick, 4 miles NW from Chatteris, Cambridgeshire. A pre-war trained
volunteer reserve pilot, F/O Donovan gained his DFM while flying Hampdens with
61 Squadron, the London Gazette for 23 December 1941, carrying the details.
He is buried in Sheffield (Burngreave) Cemetery, while Sgt Royall was taken
to Horninglow (St. John) Churchyard, Burton-upon-Trent.

2 Jul
1944 1655 MTU   Mosquito IV DZ442   Training
P/O R F Pate   T/o 1201 Wyton for local flying. An hour later,
                             the Mosquito landed only for the port oleo to
fold as the aircraft ran along the runway. Veering to starboard, the rest of
the undercarriage collapsed.

22 Jul
1944 1655 MTU   Mosquito IV DK300   Training
F/L J Wilmer   + T/o 1306 Warboys for an operational training
F/O A C H McConnell-Jones + exercise. Broke up and crashed 1326 near the
                             village of Pidley, 7 miles NE from Huntingdon.
F/L Wilmer was cremated at Golders Green Crematorium while his navigator, who
hailed from Glasgow, was buried in Cambridge City Cemetery.

25 Jul
1944 1655 MTU   Mosquito IV DZ421   Training
W/O C E Cook RNZAF   inj T/o Warboys for a night exercise in navigation.
Sgt W G Ashley   + Disintegrated and crashed 0130 at Woodhouse Farm,
                             close to Acklam, 14 miles NE of York. W/O Cook,
who was blown out of the aircraft as it fell, was taken to station sick quarters
at Full Sutton; he was not too badly hurt. His less fortunate navigator rests in
Birmingham (Yardley) Cemetery.

8 Aug
1944 1655 MTU   Mosquito XX KB262   Training
F/O H C Kimpton RNZAF   T/o 1615 Wyton but swung as a consequence of
                             advancing the throttles too quickly, As the
Mosquito left the runway, so its undercarriage collapsed.

Note. The Mosquito XX, featured above, had been built by de Havilland Aircraft
of Canada and was part of the production batch, KB180 to KB299 which had been
fitted with Merlin 33s.

13–14 Aug   **1655 MTU**   **Mosquito XX**   **KB269**   **Training**
1944   F/L H C Kimpton RNZAF   inj   T/o 2230 Warboys for a high-level night cross-
        F/O M Watkins   inj   country. While flying at 25,000 feet, flicked
                                         over and within seconds the Mosquito had gone
into a flat spin, with the control locked hard back. Abandoned circa 0100 and
left to crash at Egton, 6 miles SW of Whitby, Yorkshire, where the crew were
treated in the local hospital. Neither were seriously hurt but F/L Kimpton was
posted on 27 September 1944, to 31 Base at Stradishall, without completing his
course.

14–15 Aug   **1655 MTU**   **Mosquito IV**   **DZ477**   **Training**
1944   W/O C E Cook RNZAF   inj   T/o Warboys for a night cross-country. Lost
        Sgt J L Hartley   inj   control and, having been abandoned, crashed
                                         at 0059 near Madley, 6 miles WSW from Hereford.
Both airmen were treated at Madley's station sick quarters, W/O Cook RNZAF later
being transferred to RAF Hospital Credenhill. Soon after his release, Sgt Hartley
went to 128 Squadron, teaming up with F/O H J Bartley RCAF; sadly, he was killed
during operations to Braunschweig on 16–17 September 1944 (see Bomber Command
Losses, Volume 5, page 427). W/O Cook RNZAF, who had been injured in a serious
crash on 25 July (see the previous page for details), made a good recovery and,
eventually, returned to New Zealand.

19 Aug   **1655 MTU**   **Mosquito XX**   **KB224**   **Training**
1944   F/L J M Pearce   +   T/o 1005 Wyton for a cross-country, during
        P/O A A Young   +   which the crew were instructed to climb to
                                         28,000 feet, the order being given at around
midday. Little else is known, except it is believed the Mosquito performed
a bunt before shedding one of its wings and crashing 1255 at Downs Farm,
Longnor, 8 miles SSW of Shrewsbury, wreckage being spread over a wide area.
F/L Pearce was cremated at Cheltenham Crematorium, while P/O Young was taken
for burial at Newburn (Lemington) Cemetery in Northumberland. Accident investigators were unable to determine the precise cause of the crash but it
was thought that the oxygen supply may have failed.

21 Aug   **1655 MTU**   **Mosquito IV**   **DZ433**   **Training**
1944   F/O R B Bingham   +   T/o 1717 Wyton for a cross-country which ended
        W/O M Crowe   +   with the Mosquito spinning out of cloud and
                                         crashing 1802 at Everton, 5 miles SSE from
Finngley, Nottinghamshire. F/O Bingham of Nottingham received a military
funeral in the extension to Finningley (St. Oswald) Churchyard, but W/O Crowe
was buried by private arrangement at Paisley (Hawkhead) Cemetery.

       Note. Although the airfield at Finningley comes within the boundaries of York-
shire, the local village and churchyard is across the border in Nottinghamshire.

23 Aug   **1655 MTU**   **Mosquito IV**   **DK321**   **Training**
1944   F/L N E Lilley   T/o 1844 Warboys for night training. Approached
                                         on one engine but while attempting to overshoot,
lost control and crash-landed 2109 some 600 yards from the end of the runway.

30 Aug   **1655 MTU**   **Mosquito XX**   **KB207**   **Training**
1944   F/L I Alcuin-Jones   +   T/o 2211 Warboys for a night navigation sortie.
        F/L D A W Clarke   +   Encountered severe turbulence and disintegrated
                                         at 2315 near Lindean, 4 miles SSE of Galashiels
in Selkirk. The two officers were claimed by their next of kin.

5 Sep   **1655 MTU**   **Mosquito III**   **LR570**   **Training**
1944   F/L E W F Wall   inj   T/o 1354 Warboys to practice overshooting.
        S/L R C Alabaster   inj   Following one such attempt, the Mosquito swung
          DSO DFC & Bar   to port and lost both speed and height. To
                                         avoid flying into trees, the crew forced-landed
at 1429, coming down near the station's WAAF site. Both were treated in station
sick quarters and after his release, S/L Alabaster was posted on 27 September to
Wyton, where he joined 128 Squadron. His name appears five times in the London
Gazette; the first occasion, on 16 July 1940, notifying his commission, the
second would have published details of his DFC, while the third, on 30 July 1943
notes his First Bar and this was followed later in the year with the announcement
of his DSO, both awards being gained with 97 Squadron. A First Bar to his DSO
was Gazetted on 15 June 1945, following his command of 608 Squadron.

Note. Concerning the last entry on the page previous, S/L Alabaster was one of Bomber Command's outstanding pilots, the citation on 30 November 1943, reading, "Since being awarded a Bar to the Distinguished Flying Cross, this officer has participated in many sorties, including two attacks on Berlin. His fearlessness and skill have been an important factor in the many successes obtained. He is a most efficient flight commander and his example both in the air and on the ground has proved an inspiration to all." Equally impressive is his entry for 15 June 1945, "This officer has a splendid operational record, having partici-pated in a hundred bombing sorties. In these operations he has attacked a wide range of strongly defended targets and throughout has set the highest standard of devotion to duty. Highly skilled, brave and resolute at all times, Wing Commander Alabaster has set an example which has been well reflected in the op-erational efficiency of the squadron he commands." Interestingly, although the records for 1655 Mosquito Training Unit show his rank as squadron leader, the three Supplements of the London Gazette, reporting his decorations, describe him as an acting wing commander.

13 Sep 1944   **1655 MTU**   **Mosquito XX**   KB219   **Training**
F/L D C Wallington   inj   T/o 2115 Warboys for a navigation detail, at
P/O T A Armstrong DFM   +   night. Partially abandoned, after loss of control in cloud, and crashed 2250 at Low Milton Farm near Maybole, Ayrshire. F/L Wallington was taken to nearby Prestwick and received attention in station sick quarters. P/O Armstrong, whose DFM was won with 49 Squadron and Gazetted on 18 May 1943, is buried in Carlisle (Dalston Road) Cemetery.

13-14 Sep 1944   **1655 MTU**   **Mosquito XX**   KB270   **Training**
F/O J P Morgan RNZAF   T/o 2115 Warboys for a night cross-country. On completion of the detail, F/O Morgan RNZAF had the misfortune, on touch down, to damage the Mosquito's undercarriage and though he was able to climb away, discovered that the unit would no longer lock in the down position. Diverted to Woodbridge, he forced-landed here at 0150, without injury to himself, or his navigator (who is not named).

16 Sep 1944   **1655 MTU**   **Mosquito XX**   KB211   **Training**
F/L A W Rutledge   +   T/o 1725 Warboys for practice bombing but
P/O J K Evans   +   broke up, fifteen minutes later, and came down at Woodgate Farm, Moulton Chapel, 5 miles north-east of Spalding in Lincolnshire. F/L Rutledge was laid to rest in Middleton St. George (St. George) Churchyard, while his navigator, P/O Evans, who came from St. Johns in Newfoundland was taken to Cambridge City Cemetery.

Note. Unit records next report the loss of Mosquito XX KB210 but, as far as I am aware, this aircraft belonged to 128 Squadron and its loss is described in Bomber Command Losses, Volume 5, page 427, (see also my remarks on the previous page in respect of Sgt Hartley).

11 Oct 1944   **1655 MTU**   **Mosquito XX**   KB203   **Training**
F/L R J Beckley   +   T/o Wyton for a cross-country. Thought to
F/S W T Borrowman RCAF   +   have flown into cloud, lost control, and dived into the waters of Caernarfon Bay. Both bodies were recovered; F/L Beckley rests in Bandon Hill Cemetery, Surrey, while his New Westminster born navigator, F/S Borrowman RCAF, was taken to Scotland and buried in Carnwath New Cemetery. He had married Eva May Borrowman, presumably of Carnwath, Lanarkshire.

27 Oct 1944   **1655 MTU**   **Mosquito XX**   KB240   **Training**
F/L R McLean   T/o 0949 Warboys for a navigation detail. On
F/L Hunting   return to base an hydraulic failure prevented the wheels from locking down. Diverted to Woodbridge and written off in the subsequent emergency landing.

2 Nov 1944   **1655 MTU**   **Mosquito IV**   DZ436   **Training**
F/O D G Hannigan RNZAF   T/o 1450 Wyton but swung to starboard and in trying to bring his aircraft back onto the centre line, F/O Hannigan RNZAF over compensated and as a consequence he over stressed the undercarriage attachment points, thereby damaging the Mosquito beyond worthwhile repair.

8 Nov	1655 MTU	Mosquito IV	DZ632	Training

8 Nov
1944

1655 MTU   **Mosquito IV** DZ632   **Training**
F/L R W Clancey   + T/o 2120 Wyton for a night cross-country. Dived
F/O R W Alford MID   + and crashed 2150 between Hopton and Lound, two
             villages roughly 4 miles N and 4 miles NNW from
Lowestoft, Suffolk. F/L Clancey is buried in Enfield (Lavender Hill) Cemetery,
while F/O Alford was taken home to Devon and Bovey Tracey Cemetery. For the
parents of F/L Clancey, this was their second terrible blow of the war for his
brother, Sgt Douglas Allen Clancey of the 3rd County of London Yeomanry (Sharp-
shooters), Royal Armoured Corps, had been posted missing in North Africa on
27 November 1941. Then, during the bitter fighting that marked the Rhineland
offensive in March 1945, a third son, Lt Kenneth Cooper Clancey fell on the 11th
while serving with the 6th Battalion Cameronians (Scottish Rifles).

23 Nov
1944

1655 MTU   **Mosquito XX** KB232   **Training**
W/O N H Prior   T/o Warboys for a high-level navigation detail,
             climbing to 25,000 feet. And it was while
cruising at this altitude that the starboard engine failed. Although W/O Prior
was able to feather the unit, he found it impossible to maintain height and
while trying to reach the nearest airfield, he was obliged to forced-land in
a field, at 1548, on Turnbury Farm, Shirdley Hill near Birkdale, Lancashire.

24 Nov
1944

1655 MTU   **Mosquito IV** DZ429   **Training**
F/O R M Jones RCAF   + T/o 0118 Warboys heading off into the night
F/O D G MacKenzie   + intent on flying a high-level cross-country.
             At 0142, the Mosquito spun (presumably from
its briefed height of 28,000 feet) and crashed at Alrewas, 5 miles SW from
the centre of Burton Upon Trent, Staffordshire and not far from Lichfield
airfield. F/O Jones RCAF was buried, with full military honours, at Chester
(Blacon) Cemetery, while F/O MacKenzie rests in Glasgow (Cardonald) Cemetery.

8 Dec
1944

1655 MTU   **Mosquito B.25** KB440   **Air Test**
F/L D F White   T/o 1126 Wyton but swung and lost its under-
             carriage. This was the unit's last serious
accident prior to being absorbed by 16 Operational Training Unit at Upper
Heyford, though a good deal of flying would take place from Barford St. John.

Note. The records for 1655 Mosquito Training Unit allude, from time to time,
to events that, strictly, do not come under the umbrella of the unit itself,
an example of this being reported in the form of a note on page 187. However,
I believe it will not be out of place if I record the following accident as
it claimed the life of the unit's Chief Flying Instructor, S/L E A Costello-
Bowen, though the aircraft in which he died belonged to 487 Squadron. It is
not featured in any previous volume as "487", by this time, had transferred
from Bomber Command to 2nd Tactical Air Force.

9 Aug
1943

487 Sqn   **Ventura II** AJ454   **Air Test**
S/L E A Costello-Bowen AFC + T/o Marham and crashed near the airfield at
F/O S C B Abbott DFC RAAF + approximately 1530. All three members of crew
Cpl F R Magson   + were buried in Marham Cemetery, their funerals
             being held four days after the tragedy. In
order to allow as many personnel as possible to attend, the entire unit was
stood down and to accommodate the various religious denominations, the service
was conducted by the Revd D'Arcy-Hutton and the Revd O'Meara, Church of
England and Roman Catholic padres respectively. Also present was the widow
and closest relatives of Cpl Magson. F/O Abbott RAAF had flown the Ventura
with 464 Squadron, his DFC having been Gazetted on 15 June 1943, though he
had been "screened" since the March. Since then, he had flown as a staff
pilot in the unit's Oxford trainers.

Section 5

Flights

The units so far reported all had a common purpose within the training structure of the Command, the titles in themselves being pointers as to the form of instruction being conducted. Thus, the prime function of the heavy conversion units was to prepare crews fresh from an operational training unit, where they had mastered twin-engined flying, to the more exacting task of becoming proficient in the four-engined types that by late 1943 formed the backbone of Bomber Command's Main Force squadrons.

The flights, next to be summarised, were far more diverse and it is for this reason that I am reporting their losses by individual unit, rather than in chronological sequence. By adopting this approach, I am able to present some insight into the work of each flight, some of which passed to the control of other commands, while retaining their original titles, the beam approach training flights being a good example.

No. 3 Blind Approach Training Flight

Formed at Mildenhall, within No. 3 Group on 27 January 1941, 3 Blind Approach Training Flight, as its title implies, was tasked to train pilots in the art of approaching the runway in marginal weather conditions. To this end, simple ground radio transmitters were configured to send a series of dots and dashes, the reception of the signal in the pilot's earphones indicating whether he was to the left or to the right of the runway's centre line. A merged signal, giving a continuous note informed him he was on the centre line and with this knowledge, he could at least continue his approach to the point where the runway came into view, or if the weather conditions were too adverse he could over-shoot with a reasonable degree of confidence that the way ahead was not obstructed.

During October 1941, the term "Blind" was dropped in favour of "Beam" and, at the same time, its number plate was preceded by "150", thus becoming 1503 Beam Approach Training Flight. As such, the Flight continued to use Mildenhall until 5 September 1942, when it transferred to Holme-on-Spalding Moor and joined No. 1 Group. On 3 January 1943, the headquarters moved to Lindholme, where it disbanded on 6 August 1943. Throughout its existence, "3/1503" experienced its fair share of detachments and it was whilst using Newmarket that its sole flying accident occurred.

It is unlikely that the Wellingtons were employed much beyond the autumn of 1941, and in keeping with similar flights, twin-engined Oxford trainers became the principal type, though it is unlikely that more than half-a-dozen were on charge at any one time.

28 Aug	3 Flt	Wellington I	L4274	Training
1941	F/L R J Raphael			

T/o Newmarket for Blind Approach Training, beam flying. Whilst airborne, the crew discovered a fire behind an electrical fuse box mounted inside the fuselage on the starboard side. To their dismay, the fire extinguisher was not in its stowage and though F/L Raphael was able to land safely, the Wellington continued to burn and was destroyed.

No. 6 Blind Approach Training Flight

Formed at Waddington on 6 January 1941, 6 Blind Approach Training Flight was the first of two such flights to provide training for No. 5 Group. Its initial equipment was a hotchpotch of types; Anson, Blenheim and Hampden of which, in 1941, only the Hampden represented the principal type of bomber being operated by the Group's squadrons.

Similar to 3 Blind Approach Training Flight, its number plate and title were changed in the autumn of 1941, thus becoming 1506 Beam Approach Training Flight. Its main base remained at Waddington, but a move to Fulbeck took place on 9 February 1943, while on 23 August of that same year, the headquarters transferred to Skellingthorpe, disbanding here on 2 October 1943. By this time, "1506" was equipped with Oxford trainers, with at least a Boston or two on the unit's strength at one time or the other.

23 Sep	6 Flt	Oxford I V4041	Training
1941	F/O J H Leland		

T/o Waddington (not confirmed). Forced-landed at approximately 1835 at Old Surrey Hall, East Grinstead, Sussex, and while trying to avoid running into a hedge, turned down the slope of the field and cartwheeled. F/O Leland had nine hours on type and is not thought to have been hurt.

7 Oct	6 Flt	Oxford I V4033	Training
1941	F/L S C R Bell		

T/o Waddington for beam approach training, at night, but the weather closed in and the aircraft was abandoned, on the orders of the Regional Control Officer, and left to crash near Leadenham, 12 miles SSW of Lincoln.

	6 Flt	Oxford I V4034	Training
	P/O H V King		

T/o Waddington similarly tasked and lost in the manner described above. The remains of this Oxford were removed from fields near Fenton-by-Stubton, roughly 5 miles west-south-west from where F/L Bell's aircraft came down.

No. 7 Blind Approach Training Flight

The second of the two Blind Approach Training Flights to form within No. 5 Group, "7" came into existence, at Finningley, on 18 January 1941. Similar to "6", its initial equipment comprised of Anson, Blenheim and Hampden types, but by the late summer had received the usual complement of half-a-dozen twin-engined Oxfords. And, as with the two flights, previously mentioned, it became 1507 Beam Approach Training Flight.
  During its close on four years of service, it lost only two aircraft, one of which will be summarised under its then title of "1507". During September and October 1942, the Flight was detached to Cottesmore and this was followed by transfer of its head-quarters, first to Warboys and then to Gransden Lodge on 13 March and 17 June 1943, respectively. Disbanded on 27 November 1943.

21 Sep	7 Flt	Oxford I V4036		Training
1941	P/O R F Keighley		+	
	S/L A J F Churchill		+	
	F/S E Growes		inj	

T/o 0910 Finningley on instruments only to lose control and fly into a hangar. It is believed the Oxford took off along the beam, from a point near the inner marker. At the time visibility was assessed as down to one hundred-and-fifty yards. From Brixham in Devon, and a pre-war regular officer, S/L Churchill was buried in Finningley (Holy Trinity and St. Oswald) Churchyard extension, while his fellow pilot, P/O Keighley, was taken to Hornsea Cemetery. F/S Growes was very badly shocked but is not thought to have been seriously injured.

No. 419 (Special Duties) Flight

With the fall of France in June 1940, the Secret Intelligence Service was most anxious to establish a network of agents that would liaise with, and assist where necessary, the burgeoning resistance groups forming across occupied Europe. Thus, on 21 August 1940, No. 419 (Special Duties) Flight came into being at North Weald. The following month, "419" moved to Stapleford Tawney but its operating base, for clandestine flights to the occupied countries (principally France), would be at Tangmere in Sussex. The head-quarters, meanwhile, moved to Stradishall on 9 October 1940, coming under the control of No. 3 Group. Newmarket, too, was used by the Flight which, on 1 March 1941, was re-designated 1419 (Special Duties) Flight. For an insight into the work of these units, which in turn formed the nucleus of 138 Squadron, I can thoroughly recommend the late Hugh Verity's masterpiece, "We Landed by Moonlight", published by Airdata Publications and for a continuance of Special Operations Executive missions an equally enthralling tome, "Agents By Moonlight" by Freddie Clark (Tempus, 1999). M R D Foot and J M Langley's scholarly epic, "MI 9, Escape and Evasion 1939-1945", first issued through The Bodley Head, is also recommended.

11 Oct	419 Flt	Whitley V P5025	Training
1940	P/O Shreenhill		

T/o Stradishall. Approached the runway but opened the throttles to go round again, only to stall and finish up, at 1843, across the airfield's boundary road.

19–20 Oct	419 Flt	Lysander III	R9027	Op: France

1940   F/L W R Farley   T/o Tangmere and set course for France in order
P/O Philip Schneidau   to pick up "Felix" (Philip Schneidau). Landed, by prearranged signal, at 0117 in a field S of Fontainebleau. The return flight was made in atrocious weather, as a consequence of which F/L Farley could not be certain of his course. Eventually, with the dawn beginning to break, he forced-landed at 0650/0655, out of fuel, in a field near Connel, 4 miles NNE from Oban in Argyllshire. On touch down, the Lysander ran into some stout anti-invasion poles, and was wrecked.

Note. For a fuller account of this epic flight, please refer to "We Landed by Moonlight" by Hugh Verity, pages 34 to 36. F/L Farley was promoted to squadron leader on 1 December 1940 (London Gazette, 10 December 1940) and at the time of his death in late April 1942 (see Bomber Command Losses, Volume 3, page 74), he had risen to wing commander rank and had been decorated with a well deserved Distinguished Flying Cross, Gazetted on 7 March 1941, by which time "419" had become "1419" (see the previous page for details). In concluding this note, I cannot over emphasise the skilled airmanship and outstanding courage of pilots such as the late Walter Ronald Farley who map read their way over the occupied countries to deliver and recover agents who, in themselves, were the most courageous men and women that served their countries in the Second World War.

No. 1323 Automatic Gun Laying Turret Flight

Established on 29 November 1944, in No. 8 Group, and based, initially, at Bourn, "1323" was equipped with Lancasters and tasked to train and develop crews in the skills of radar gun laying. On New Year's Day, 1945, the Flight moved across to Warboys, where it continued its work alongside 1696 Bomber (Defence) Flight and Pathfinder Force Navigation Training Unit. The latter disbanded on 18 June 1945, while the former closed down on 28 September of that same year. Two days later, "1323" also disbanded. It seems that it held, at its peak, an establishment of ten Lancasters, plus a handful of twin-engined Oxfords which were used as support aircraft.

11 Sep	1323 Flt	Lancaster III	PB285	Training

1945   F/L R I Varney   T/o 1438 Warboys for an automatic gun laying test. Landed at 1608, only for the brakes to fail and in order to avoid running into some dispersed Mosquitoes, F/L Varney retracted the wheels. He was a pilot of some experience, having logged some eight hundred-and-two hours solo, of which one hundred and-twenty-eight were at the controls of Lancasters.

No. 1409 Meteorological Flight

From its formation on 1 April 1943, at Oakington from the Mosquito flight of 521 Squadron, "1409" was to play a key part in the operational success of Bomber Command's relentless night bombing campaign. Furthermore, the weather reconnaissance data that it gathered on its frequent sorties over Germany and occupied Europe was shared with the Americans, thus ensuring that its bomber groups had to hand the best weather reports possible ahead of their hazardous daylight operations to targets in the Third Reich. Coming under the authority of No. 8 Group, "1409" set the highest standards in operational efficiency and considering the dangers of their rôle, finished the war with remarkably few losses (during 1944, only three of their aircraft were lost under operational circumstances). By the end of hostilities, "1409" was based at Wyton, moving to Upwood in early July and thence to Lyneham on 10 October 1945, at which stage it severed its connections with Bomber Command.

16 Apr	1409 Flt	Mosquito IV	DZ406 W	Op: Pampa

1943   P/O G Griffiths   +   T/o 1125 Oakington for a long-range meteor-
Sgt R Brown   +   ological reconnaissance to Stuttgart. Presumed to have crashed in Belgium, as both airmen are now buried in Schoonselhof Cemetery, Antwerpen. P/O Griffiths had been employed on "Pampa" operations since August 1942, flying his first operational sortie on 8 August 1942 in a 1401 Meteorological Flight photographic reconnaissance D Type Spitfire (officially, "1401" had combined with "1403" to form 521 Squadron, at Bircham Newton, seven days previous).

9 May
1943

1409 Flt   **Mosquito IV**   **DZ316 M**   **Op: Pampa**

F/L P F Hall   pow   T/o 1845 Oakington for a long-range sortie to

F/L W C Woodruff   pow   Malines and Aalmaar. At approximately 2030, a
radio direction finding plot picked up returns
that indicated the presence of enemy aircraft patrolling along the intended
route of the Mosquito. Subsequently, it is believed the light-bomber was shot
down as it flew at 25,000 feet, S of Den Helder, by Fw 190s (unit records,
while agreeing on Holland, place the interception in the Eindhoven area).

14 Jun
1943

1409 Flt   **Mosquito IX**   **LR501**   **Op: Pampa**

W/O D Durrant   pow   T/o 1125 Oakington for a long-range meteor-

P/O R Taylor   pow   ological reconnaissance to Mayenne and thence
to St-Quentin, north-north-east of Paris. Re-
ported to have been intercepted at 28,000 feet, over or near Mayenne, by Fw 190s
and shot down. This was the first Mosquito IX reported missing from a sortie
in support of Bomber Command operations. Allotted, ex-works, to 109 Squadron on
25 May 1943, the Mosquito was transferred almost immediately to "1409" and when
reported missing had flown for a total of 10.45 hours.

18 Jul
1943

1409 Flt   **Mosquito IX**   **LR502**   **Op: Pampa**

S/L The Hon. P I Cunliffe- pow   T/o 0105 Oakington for a long-range sortie to
     Lister   Osnabrück on behalf of "Pinetree" (headquarters

F/L A P Kernon   pow   of the United States Army Air Corps, housed in
the requisitioned Wycombe Abbey School for Girls
and within a stones throw of Sir Arthur Harris´s own headquarters at High Wycombe)
At around 0350, very feint signals from this aircraft were picked up, requesting a
bearing. Although the radio frequency was being swamped by heavy static, a signal
was transmitted and this was duly acknowledged. However, nothing further was heard
until news filtered through, via the International Red Cross Committee, that both
officers were prisoners of war.

14 Nov
1943

1409 Flt   **Mosquito IX**   **ML912**   **Op: Pampa**

P/O F Clayton DFM   +   T/o 0740 Oakington for a long-range mission to

F/O W F John DFC   +   the Stuttgart area. Crashed near Merville in the
Department of Nord, France, both officers being
buried in the extension to the local communal cemetery. P/O Clayton was a most
experienced pilot, his operational career having begun on 31 May 1942, when he
took off from Bircham Newton in a Spitfire belonging to 1401 (Meteorological)
Flight. At the time of his death, he had amassed fifty-three sorties and his
Distinguished Flying Medal had been Gazetted as recently as 10 September; the
Distinguished Flying Cross, awarded to his navigator, was not published until
20 April 1945.

3 Dec
1943

1409 Flt   **Mosquito IX**   **ML918**   **Op: Pampa**

F/S H W Addis   inj   T/o 1525 Oakington for a long-range sortie to

Sgt J H Sharpe   inj   Nürnberg. Monitoring stations heard distress
calls from the aircraft which, at the time, was
flying in the vicinity of Dieppe. Homed to Exeter, the Mosquito crashed at
about 2000 some 600 yards S of Exeter´s runway and burst into flames. Both
airmen were still alive when dragged clear but they died very soon after being
admitted to hospital. F/S Addis now rests in Cinderford (St. John) Churchyard,
while Sgt Sharpe was taken to Norwich Cemetery. Six months later, the parents
of F/S Addis received news that his younger brother, Sgt Robert Edwin Addis,
was missing from air operations over the Mediterranean (he was flying Marauders
out from Alghero, Sardinia, with 14 Squadron). He is commemorated on the Malta
Memorial, the presumed date of his death being 7 May 1944.

5 Dec
1943

1409 Flt   **Mosquito IX**   **MM238**   **Op: Pampa**

F/O H F M Taylor CGM DFC   +   T/o 0750 Oakington intent on reconnoitring the

P/O J Burgess   +   Paris and Bordeaux areas but shortly after becoming airborne, F/O Taylor called Flying Control
to say his aircraft was damaged and he wished priority clearance for landing. As
the local weather conditions were poor, he was advised to divert to Manston and
on his arrival here he circled the airfield several times on one engine before
settling in for his approach. Tragically, he seems to have elected to overshoot
but as he opened up to go round again, he lost control and spun in at 0840, near
the runway. Both officers died instantly; F/O Taylor was taken home to Scotland
and interred in Falkirk Cemetery, while P/O Burgess is buried in Stockton Heath
(St. Thomas) Churchyard in Cheshire.

20 Dec	**1409 Flt**	**Mosquito IX**	**ML903**	**Air Test**

1943

F/S V S Moore DFM RNZAF
W/O V J C Miles

T/o 1630 Kenley but the throttles slipped back and the Mosquito swung, heading off towards some parked aircraft. F/S Moore RNZAF managed to avoid a collision, but while doing so the port wheel clattered into some petrol cans, causing the oleo to break. As the aircraft skidded, a fire broke out 'twixt the port Merlin and the cockpit, but both airmen managed to make good their escape before the flames took hold. In the summer of 1942, while flying Wellingtons with 57 Squadron, F/S Moore RNZAF was briefed to attack Bremen, in the course of which he was obliged to ditch in the North Sea, following a brave attack on German E-boats after the Wellington's starboard wing had been set on fire by these vessels. Three of his crew, subsequently, perished but Moore and two others were able to scramble aboard their dinghy and were rescued thirty-seven hours later. For his outstanding courage, and fortitude, he was awarded an immediate DFM, Gazetted on 7 August 1942 (see Bomber Command Losses, Volume Three, page 143 for details of the aircraft and crew, though at the time of preparing this volume, I was not aware of the facts, here summarised).

21 Jan	**1409 Flt**	**Mosquito IX**	**ML917**	**Op: Pampa**

1944

P/O H J Izatt
F/S A W Baines

T/o 1110 Wyton on a "Pampa" sortie, taking in Den Helder and Arnhem before entering the Ruhr. While cruising some 32 km SSW of Paderborn, the constant speed unit on the port engine failed and the motor began to over speed. P/O Izatt was unable to feather the propeller and not long afterwards, the spinner sheared as a result of severe vibration, the airscrew blades being damaged as it fell away. Unable to maintain height, the Mosquito eventually came down in the sea, at 1506, off Lowestoft in Suffolk and both occupants set off towards the shore. After fifteen minutes of swimming, they were sighted by a rescue craft and hauled aboard. Their aircraft, meanwhile, had remained afloat and it is rumoured that it was later towed into Lowestoft harbour. F/S Baines was decorated with the DFM, promulgated on 19 May 1944.

16 Feb	**1409 Flt**	**Mosquito XVI**	**ML928**	**Op: Pampa**

1944

F/O A W Powell-Wiffen   inj
  Twice MID
P/O H Ashworth DFM   inj

T/o 1145 Wyton for a sortie to 5330N 0200W and 5500N 0200E, but twenty minutes into the detail, the pilot came up on the radio to say he was returning to base. At around 1215, the aircraft entered the circuit, at low-level, and made two circuits of the airfield before crashing, heavily, and bursting into flames. Personnel from 83 Squadron dashed to the scene and managed to pull both airmen from the burning cockpit; sadly, neither survived, despite the best medical attention that RAF Hospital Ely was able to administer. F/O Powell-Whiffen rests in East Hendred Church Cemetery, while P/O Ashworth was cremated in Manchester Crematorium. His DFM had been published on 18 January 1944, and, according to unit records, he was nearing the end of his operational tour. His skipper came from Wellington, New Zealand and had married Violet Powell-Wiffen (née Powell) of East Hendred in Berkshire.

27 Mar	**1409 Flt**	**Mosquito IX**	**LR509**	**Training**

1944

F/S G W Roberts   +
F/S D S Sabine   +

T/o 1459 Wyton for a practice flight. Sixteen minutes later the Mosquito went out of control at 300 feet and smashed into the ground some 400 yards from houses at Bluntisham, 4 miles NE of St. Ives, Huntingdonshire. The pilot was buried, privately, in Bebington (St. Andrew) Churchyard, while his navigator, who came from Dawlish Warren in Devon, was provided with a service funeral at Cambridge City Cemetery. Accident investigators found parts of a wing flap, and fuselage debris, 500 yards from the impact point and these are thought to have burned off as the bomber came down. The main seat of the in flight blaze was pinpointed in the region of the starboard engine, inboard of the fuel tanks. For Christopher Cooper, then but an infant, the crash remains indelibly etched in his memory, for he was playing in the garden of a house just yards from where the two airmen passed from life into eternity.

27 Nov	**1409 Flt**	**Mosquito XVI**	**ML930**	**Op: Snooper**

1944

F/L J M W Briggs
F/O J C Baker

T/o 2020 Wyton armed with 3 x 500lb general purpose bombs and 1 x target indicator flash bomb and tasked to observe the Bomber Command attack on Neuss. Three runs were made over the target and fires appeared to be fairly strong. Experienced control problems and crash-landed 2305 on the runway, following several unsuccessful attempts to land.

Note. Regarding the last entry on the previous page, unit records note that the Mosquito had been flown back earlier in the day from Manston, crewed by F/O R H Youngman and F/O J E Gibbs. Subsequently, both F/L Briggs and his navigator, F/O Baker completed their tours of duty only to die, still together, in Canada on 10 May 1945. They are buried in Calgary (Burnsland) Cemetery, Alberta. At the time of their deaths, F/L Briggs had a DSO and F/O Baker had been decorated with a DFC and First Bar.

27 Feb	1409 Flt	Mosquito XVI	NS731 H		Op: Snooper
1945	S/L R D McLaren DFC		+	T/o 1524 Wyton and headed for Mainz where it
	F/L J A L Lymburner DFC		pow	was seen by F/L Lowther, operating in Mosquito
	RCAF			NS734 F, flying above the "heavies" in the
				target area.

S/L McLaren, a Canadian from Toronto, but serving with the Royal Air Force, is buried in Rheinberg War Cemetery. He had married Joyce Catherine McLaren from Hildenborough in Kent and his DFC, gained with "1409" had been published as recently as 2 January. F/L Lymburner RCAF had flown previously with 425 Squadron, and his award was announced the same day as that for his skipper.

27 Aug	1409 Flt	Mosquito XVI	NS733 C		Cook's Tour
1945	F/L A G Hughes		inj	T/o 1035 Upwood but swung from the runway after
	F/O A R Wray		inj	accelerating for 200 yards, lost its wheels and
	LAC J F Lloyd		inj	caught fire. All were taken to RAF Hospital Ely,
				where surgeons amputated one of LAC Lloyd's arms.

No. 1419 (Special Duties) Flight

Continuing the work of 419 (Special Duties) Flight (see page 190), "1419" had a brief existence of less than six months before being redesignated 138 Squadron. Apart from the usual posting in, or out, of personnel, few changes took place 'twixt the old "419" and the new "1419", while its equipment remained a mix of single-engined Lysanders and twin-engined Whitleys. For a while, a twin-engined Martin Maryland was assigned for experimental work.

17–18 Feb	1419 Flt	Whitley V	T4264		Op: SIS
1941	S/L F J B Keast DFC		pow	T/o Stradishall tasked to parachute a Belgian
	F/L E N Baker		pow	Secret Intelligence Service agent near Namur.
	W/O D H Bernard		pow	The drop was successful, but soon afterwards,
	Cpl A J Cameron		pow	while flying at 200 feet, flak hit an engine,
	W/O D W Davies		pow	causing a catastrophic loss of coolant. Crash-
	F/L K S McMurdie		pow	landed near a wood at Cognelee. W/O Bernard
				was a radio specialist and while in captivity

he "manufactured" several clandestine radios. By May 1945, he was incarcerated in the infamous Ravensbruck Concentration Camp and it was not until August 1945 that the Russian authorities sanctioned his release. On regaining his health, he remained in the air force and when eventually retired, he held the rank of wing commander and had been honoured with two Polish decorations as well as being made a Member of the Order of the British Empire. For much of the information pertaining to his prisoner of war time, I am indebted to a fellow prisoner of war and Bomber Command pilot, Harold Emery Batchelder DFM. The Distinguished Flying Cross awarded to S/L Keast was Gazetted on 17 June 1941, by which time he was languishing in a prisoner of war camp. Lastly, the Allied Air Forces Prisoner of War file, shows the rank for Cameron as "corporal"; I much suspect, however, that by the time of his release he had been elevated to the rank of warrant officer.

Note. All available evidence points to this aircraft and crew belonging to "1419", but observant readers will note that this title was not officially adopted until 1 March 1941. Secondly, in respect of the summary to follow, this corrects some of the information reported in Bomber Command Losses, Volume 2, page 41, while regarding the additional data concerning the names of the Polish saboteurs, I am indebted to Mr Kajetan Bieniecki of Montreal; Mr Krzysztof A Tochman, whose "Biographical Dictionary of Parachutists" (dropped over Poland) has been consulted; Mrs Irena Hrynkiewicz, secretary to the 1st (Independent) Polish Parachute Brigade Association and to Mrs Betty Clements for translating and collating the information so very kindly supplied by the aforementioned trio.

10–11 Apr	1419 Flt	Whitley V	T4165	Op: Adjudicate

1941	P/O J E Willson	inj

T/o 2000 Tangmere with the intention of dropping six Polish army saboteurs, tasked to destroy the Pessac power station in the western suburbs of Bordeaux. While flying over the Loire, the weapons container suddenly fell from the aircraft, an electrical fault being suspected. Having aborted the operation, P/O Willson returned to Tangmere but overshot his approach, and while trying to go round again, crashed at 0320 and caught fire. The survivors owe their lives to the Polish officers who, apart from cuts and abrasions, were unhurt. In the days that followed, Sgt Cowan was cremated at Golders Green Crematorium, while Sgt Morris was taken for burial at Middleton-on-the-Wolds Church Cemetery. P/O Willson was an experienced pilot with 3,775 flying hours to his credit, but only fifty-seven had been logged on Whitleys. It seems that he had, inadvertently, wound the tail trimmer too far back and on advancing the throttles he had insufficient time to retrim before the bomber stalled at one hundred feet. Subsequently, he went on to serve in the Middle East and was posted missing in action on 27 August 1943, while flying a Beaufighter from Reghaia, Algeria. He is commemorated on the Malta Memorial and, at the time of his presumed death, he held the DFC. F/O Oettle returned to flying duties on 28 October 1941, and was killed less than forty-eight hours later when his 138 Squadron Whitley crashed at Stradishall. Earlier in the war, he had survived a serious crash whilst operating with 51 Squadron (see Bomber Command Losses, Volumes 1 and 2, pages 43 and 169 respectively).

The crew of T4165:
- P/O J E Willson — inj
- F/O A J Oettle DFC — inj
- Sgt P E Pacy — inj
- Sgt A J Cowan — +
- Sgt L G Morris — +
- Sgt R T Briscoe — inj
- Capt M Kalicinski
- Lt K Bogdziewicz
- Lt K Dendor
- Lt S Kruszewski
- 2Lt W Miciek
- 2Lt L Zwolanski

25 Jul	1419 Flt	Whitley V	Z6727	Air Test

1941

The crew of Z6727:
- F/L A D Jackson — inj
- Sgt A Hughes — inj
- Sgt L R Burgin — inj
- Sgt R J Bramley — inj
- Sgt Lavender
- Lt Stewart
- Lt Baessonas FFAF — inj
- 2Lt Helat FFAF

T/o Newmarket to test, what is officially described as, "secret equipment". During the flight, both engines failed and in the ensuing emergency landing, the bomber hit a telegraph pole and crashed 1525, heavily. The four injured airmen were taken to White Lodge Hospital, F/L Jackson, at least, later being transferred to RAF Hospital Ely. He had joined "1419" in the April. By early 1944, he was seconded to 207 Squadron Spilsby, prior to taking command of an operational squadron. On 5-6 January, he joined F/L G H Ebert's crew, tasked to raid Stettin; their Lancaster failed to return. Sgt Hughes, meanwhile, had been posted missing from a Special Operations Executive sortie, with 138 Squadron, the previous September (see Bomber Command Losses, Volumes 4 and 5, pages 323 for Sgt Hughes and 27 for F/L Jackson).

No. 1427 (Ferry Training) Flight

Technically, "1427" was not a part of Bomber Command, having formed in No. 41 Group, at Thruxton, on 13 December 1941, for the purpose of providing Air Transport Auxiliary pilots with four-engined flying experience. On 18 May 1942, the flight moved to Hull-avington, and thence to Marham on 5 September, before settling on Stradishall early in October 1942. Here, it merged with the resident 1657 Heavy Conversion Unit on 1 April 1943. Ahead of this merger, "1657" borrowed aircraft from the flight, as will be seen from the summary that follows.

10 Feb	1427 Flt	Stirling I	N6008 XT-W2	Training

1943

The crew of N6008:
- P/O S C Rogers — +
- Sgt G T Pierce — +
- Sgt P S O'Carroll RNZAF — +
- Sgt B S Smith — inj
- Sgt R W Smith — +
- Sgt H J Howells RNZAF — inj
- Mr G Smith — +

T/o 0939 Stradishall borrowed by 1657 Heavy Conversion Unit, but almost immediately two engines failed. Flying on a south-easterly heading, its wheels still locked down, the Stirling failed to climb and at around 0940, the bomber flew into high tension cables before hitting some buildings at 8 Mill Hill, Kedington, 2 miles ENE of Haverhill, Suffolk. Twenty year old George Smith, who bravely ran to the scene to render aid, died, possibly electrocuted from the cables tangled in the wreckage. Sgt Pierce was taken to his home; the others rest locally.

No. 1428 (Ferry Training) Flight

Provisionally earmarked to form at Horsham St. Faith, 1428 (Ferry Training) Flight was established at Oulton on 29 December 1941, coming under the authority of No. 2 Group and tasked with converting crews to twin-engined Hudson aircraft. Disbanded 6 June 1942.

28 Jan 1942	1428 Flt F/S S J M Smith	Hudson III	V9098	Training

T/o 1805 Oulton but failed to become airborne due to ice accumulation on the wings.

1 Apr 1942	1428 Flt	Hudson III	AE558	Training
	P/O J H Ellis	+	
	Sgt H Clarke	+	
	Sgt W Luney	+	
	Sgt G Horton	+	

T/o Oulton tasked for a night cross-country, the route to be flown totalling 624 miles. Crashed 2235 at Beeston Fields, Biggleswade, Bedfordshire, some 7 miles S of track. Eye-witnesses to the crash say the Hudson appeared to be flying normally, between five hundred and a thousand feet, when the engines began "popping" (thus suggesting fuel starvation). P/O Ellis, who came from Ringmer in Sussex, rests in Cardington (St. Mary) Church Cemetery, Sgt Clarke is buried at Potters Bar (St. Mary) Church Cemetery, Sgt Luney was taken back to Northern Ireland and interred in Belfast City Cemetery, while Sgt Horton rests in Billingham (St. Cuthbert) Churchyard, Durham.

3- 4 Jun 1942	1428 Flt	Hudson III	AE515	Training
	Sgt B E Evanson	+	
	Sgt K Hall	inj	
	Sgt Bowyer		

T/o 2255 Oulton for a night navigation detail. Terminated the sortie, due to hydraulic failure, and returned to base at 0315, but while in the circuit, lost height and crashed at Leaselands, less than a mile E of the runway. Prior to the crash, Sgt Evanson baled his crew out from a thousand feet. From Sutton, Surrey, he was buried with full military honours in Norwich Cemetery.

No. 1429 (Czech Operational Training) Flight

Formed on New Year's Day, 1942, in No. 3 Group, at East Wretham and equipped with ten Wellingtons, "1429" trained crews in readiness for service with 311 Squadron. In late June 1942, the flight transferred to Woolfox Lodge, coming under the authority of No. 92 Group but two months later it settled at Church Broughton, where it was administered by No. 93 Group. Meanwhile, 311 Squadron had left Bomber Command (see Bomber Command Losses, Volume 3, Appendix 2), and "1429" was to do likewise when it went to Thornaby on 8 November 1942, joining No. 17 (Training) Group, Coastal Command.

24 Feb 1942	1429 Flt P/O J Capka	Wellington IC	L7841	Training

T/o East Wretham for night flying practice. At approximately 2220, P/O Capka attempted to overshoot the runway, having got into difficulties on his approach, but hit an obstruction on the up wind side of the airfield and crashed. A fire broke out and before the flames could be brought under control, the Wellington was com-letely destroyed. It is thought he may have mishandled the pitch controls.

6 Apr 1942	1429 Flt	Wellington IC	P9299	Training
	Sgt A Keda	+	
	Sgt R Vokurka	+	
	Sgt R Grimm	+	
	Sgt J Horinek	+	
	F/S J Stanovsky	+	
	P/O J Stefek	+	

T/o East Wretham for a cross-country exercise. Flying below hill tops in rough weather, and in limited visibility, Sgt Keda entered a valley and was suddenly confronted with rising ground ahead. Unable to climb, or turn safely, he crashed at 1312 on Bryn Uchat, 2 miles NW of Llanymawddwy on the River Dovey in Merioneth. All were brought back to Norfolk and laid to rest in East Wretham (St. Ethelbert) Churchyard.

Note. On 13 October 1942, an all Czechoslovakian crew perished while flying in Wellington IC Z8854 of 27 OTU Church Broughton (see Bomber Command Losses, Volume 7, page 168 for details). Interestingly, the Air-Britain (Historians) Z1000 to Z9999 serial listings, shows that Z8854 had been assigned to "1429", prior to its acceptance by 27 Operational Training Unit.

No. 1443 (Ferry Training) Flight

Although assigned to Bomber Command, many of the aircraft lost 'twixt 21 January 1942, and 30 April 1943, when it was retitled No. 310 Ferry Training Unit, came down while en route to the Middle East and, therefore, are beyond the remit of this book. For the sixteen months of its existence within the Command, "1443" was based at Harwell and came very much under the influence of the resident operational training unit, namely "15", whose many losses are described in Volume 7.

26 Apr	1443 Flt	Wellington IC	HF855		Training
1942	P/O J S Lindsay		+	T/o Harwell for a cross-country exercise and	

	Sgt W F G Hughes	+	fuel consumption test. At about 1720, the
	Sgt W J A Smart	+	crew returned to base but overshot their
	Sgt A E Payne	+	landing. Climbing to approximately 200 feet,
	Sgt C C McAllister	+	P/O Lindsay turned onto the downwind leg,
	Cdt W A Hughes ATC	+	only to stall and crash into a field. Three,
	Cdt RJ Ayres ATC	+	Sgt Hughes, Sgt Smart and Sgt McAllister, lie

in Harwell Cemetery, the others being taken to their home towns. The two Air Training Corps cadets, who had joined the crew for air experience flying, belonged to 966 (Wallingford Grammar School) Squadron; 18 year old Cdt Hughes rests in Didcot (All Saints) Churchyard, while sixteen year old Cdt Ayres is buried at Wallingford Cemetery.

30 Apr	1443 Flt	Wellington IC	DV442	Training
1942	Sgt A L Hayers		T/o 1100 Harwell for a cross-country sortie,	

combined with a fuel consumption test. While over the sea at around 1350, an engine failed and Sgt Hayers could not maintain height. Skilfully, he set his aircraft down in the water half-a-mile N of the South Stack (Ynys Law) Lighthouse, 3 miles W of Holyhead Harbour on Anglesey.

28 May	1443 Flt	Wellington IC	HX433		Training
1942	F/S W J P Grant RCAF		+	T/o Harwell for a cross-country flight and fuel	

	F/S H L Davis RCAF	+	consumption test, preparatory for delivery to
	Sgt G D Graham	+	the Middle East. It appears that the aircraft
	Sgt H N Williams RCAF	+	was flying in cloud and approximately thirty
	Sgt J I McDowell	+	degrees off course, when it smashed into the
	Sgt C J Thomas	+	top of a hill, 2,500 feet above sea level, at

Mynydd Moel (near Dolgellau), Merioneth. The first four named were interred in Towyn Cemetery, while Sgt McDowell rests in Ballyroney Presbyterian Churchyard, Co. Down and Sgt Thomas is buried in Wales at Mountain Ash (Maesyrarian) Cemetery, Glamorgan.

5 Jun	1443 Flt	Wellington VIII	HF907		Training
1942	Sgt N V Lloyd		+	T/o Harwell tasked for a six-hour fuel con-	

	Sgt L J Grove	+	sumption test and map reading. Failed to
	Sgt E A Bailey RAAF	+	return and is believed to have crashed in
	Sgt J W B Cockburn	+	the Irish Sea off Anglesey. Sgt Lloyd of
	Sgt W Hurley	+	Minting, Lincolnshire, is buried in Hoylake
	Sgt J W Ashby	+	(Grange) Cemetery, as is Sgt Ashby of Southern
	LAC R D J Macdonald RCAF	+	Rhodesia. Meanwhile, the body of Sgt Cockburn,

who came from Farnborough in Kent, was also recovered from the sea and laid to rest on the Isle of Man at Kirk Malew (St. Malew) Churchyard extension. The others are commemorated on the Runnymede Memorial. LAC Macdonald RCAF was a radio mechanic.

26 Jul	1443 Flt	Wellington II	Z8489	Training
1942	Sgt N R Millson		T/o Harwell for a cross-country exercise, in	

the course of which the port engine caught fire, necessitating an emergency ditching, at approximately 1600, just short of a mile S of Whitby Harbour, Yorkshire. Sgt Millson subsequently became a prisoner of war.

31 Aug	1443 Flt	Wellington IC	R1232	Unknown
1942			Reported to have come to grief at Moreton-	

in-Marsh. No accident details have been traced, but the aircraft's movement card indicates that it was once held at Moreton-in-Marsh and operated by the resident operational training unit before being passed to "1443". I suspect, however, that the Wellington belonged to "1446", a Moreton based flight.

30 Dec	**1443 Flt**	**Wellington VIII**	**HX745**		**Training**

1942 P/O A Waters RCAF

P/O Bullock

Sgt G A Duffy RCAF   inj

Sgt J P Hicks RCAF   inj

P/O C G Prest   inj

T/o 1130 Harwell for a cross-country. Shortly before 1400, one of the engines sustained a fracture to one of the internal drivers which, in turn, caused the drive on the unit's magneto to fail. Unable to maintain height, or locate an airfield, P/O Waters RCAF forced-landed on Charmy Down, colliding with a tree as he did so (he had overshot his intended spot and lost control when the Wellington swung as the airspeed decayed). Two, Sgt Duffy RCAF and Sgt Hicks RCAF, were treated in No. 152 Station Hospital, an American staffed military hospital at Bath, while P/O Prest was admitted to St. Martin's Hospital, Bath, where he died from his injuries. His grave is in Liverpool (Allerton) Cemetery.

8 Jan	**1443 Flt**	**Wellington III**	**BJ836**		**Training**

1943 Sgt F E W Clarke   inj

Sgt D H Neelin RCAF   inj

F/S J A Reynolds RCAF   inj

WO2 R V Bridgeman RCAF   +

Sgt C M J Murphy RCAF   inj

T/o Harwell to practice night circuits and landings. At approximately 2105, Sgt Clarke flew into high ground, 250 feet above the airfield level, downwind, and roughly 2 miles SSE from Harwell. WO2 Bridgeman RCAF was buried with full military honours in Harwell Cemetery. No firm cause could be established, but it would seem that Sgt Clarke had been posted to "1443" without having first attended a Wellington operational training unit as his solo flying on type is recorded as no more than ten hours.

No. 1444 (Ferry Training) Flight

The second of the Hudson-equipped Ferry Training Flights to form in No. 2 Group, "1444" came into being on 21 January 1942, at Horsham St. Faith but moved to Lyneham in Wiltshire five months later where it came under the control of No. 44 Group, thus passing out of the hands of Bomber Command.

9 Feb	**1444 Flt**	**Hudson III**	**AE516**		**Ferry**

1942 P/O P H Lowther   inj

P/O J M Macdonald   inj

T/o 1720 Horsham St. Faith intent on flying the first leg of their journey to the Far East, but both engines cut and the Hudson forced-landed two minutes later near the Cock Inn, Lakenham, on the southern outskirts of Norwich. P/O Lowther sustained second degree burns to his hands, while his navigator received a broken nose. Both were taken to the Norfolk and Norwich Hospital, from where, on 16 February, they were transferred to RAF Hospital Ely. It is noted that both officers had been attached from 139 Squadron which was in the throes of leaving No. 2 Group (where it had flown Blenheims both from the United Kingdom and in Malta) for India where, on 30 April 1942, it was absorbed by 62 Squadron. As readers of this series will be aware, "139" reformed as a light-bomber unit in June 1942, finishing the war as part of the Light Night Striking Force. P/O Lowther, meanwhile, made a good recovery and was posted to 18 Squadron. Sadly, he was killed in a flying accident on 18 July 1942 (see Bomber Command Losses, Volume 3, page 152).

25 Apr	**1444 Flt**	**Hudson III**	**V9059**		**Training**

1942 P/O J G Cowan-Hunt

T/o Kemble but swung out of control and lost its undercarriage.

	1444 Flt	**Hudson III**	**AE549**		**Transit**

Sgt D M Boon   inj

Sgt J D Ackerman RNZAF   inj

Sgt A R Keech   inj

P/O Bailey

T/o 1130 Horsham St. Faith intending to fly to Bircham Newton to collect aircraft spares, but an engine cut and as the Hudson veered off the runway, its wheels folded. On coming to a stop, a fierce fire broke out from which only P/O Bailey escaped unscathed. His three colleagues were taken to RAF Hospital Ely where the pilot was placed on the dangerously ill list. Sgt Boon made a good recovery, however, but was killed in action while flying Beauforts on anti-shipping operations with 39 Squadron on 10 January 1943. His name is commemorated on the Alamein Memorial. The Hudson crash is believed to have been caused by too lean a mixture setting for the twin-Wasps.

No. 1446 (Ferry Training) Flight

Similar to the flight at Harwell, described on page 197, "1446" was charged with the very important task of preparing aircraft for delivery to the overseas theatres of operations. Formed at Bassingbourn on 23 March 1942, and affiliated to 11 Operational Training Unit, "1446" transferred to Moreton-in-Marsh and settled in alongside the station's resident Wellington training unit, namely 21 Operational Training Unit. On 1 May 1943, "1446" was redesignated No. 311 Ferry Training Unit.

26 May 1942	1446 Flt P/O J Clark RAAF F/S L C Laver RAAF	Wellington IC	DV657 inj inj	Training T/o 2332 Moreton-in-Marsh for night circuit training but swung out of control, as a con- sequence of a tyre bursting, and collided with

Wellington IC X9934 belonging to 21 Operational Training Unit (see Bomber Command Losses, Volume 7, page 116). The parked aircraft had been loaded with 2 x 500lb general purpose bombs and four canisters of incendiaries and in the blaze that ensued, the ordnance exploded, completely destroying both machines. It is believed F/S Laver RAAF joined 69 Squadron and lost his life, while flying in twin-engined Baltimores, on 8 January 1943.

2 Jun 1942	1446 Flt P/O K Moore RAAF Sgt A B Dean RAAF	Wellington IC	DV658 inj inj	Training T/o Moreton-in-Marsh to practice circuits and landings. At around 1630, the Wellington came into land but the pilot at the controls levelled

out too high and then tried to ease the aircraft down onto the runway by using the throttles. On making contact, the bomber swung to the left at which point power was applied in an attempt to go round again. Moments later, having left the ground at an unusual angle of attack, the Wellington stalled and crashed, seriously injuring both pilots. On 4-5 April 1943, P/O Moore RAAF (now a recipient of the DFC) failed to return from Kiel (see Bomber Command Losses, Volume 4, page 94). At the time of his death, he was serving with 460 Squadron.

29 Nov 1942	1446 Flt F/O A Thompson F/O D Y McIntosh RCAF F/O E Martin RCAF Sgt C R Kippen Sgt W Fowler	Wellington IC	LB120 + + + +	Training T/o Moreton-in-Marsh for a fuel consumption test. At approximately 1535, the Wellington was seen on what appeared to be a normal approach when the nose pitched up and before the pilot could re- cover the situation, the bomber was on the ground and totally wrecked. Amazingly, Sgt Fowler es-

caped unharmed. F/O Thompson was buried in Sunderland (Bishopwearmouth) Cemetery and the others who perished were laid to rest in Moreton-in-Marsh New Cemetery. Sgt Kippen came from Durban in the Natal.

5 Dec 1942	1446 Flt Sgt S F Gardner Sgt C A Butt Sgt K G Gleave Sgt P C Shipman Sgt R C Simmons	Wellington IC	HD948 inj inj inj + +	Transit T/o 2108 North Front but having climbed to one hundred feet, slowly lost height and at 2109 it flew into the sea. Failure of the starboard engine's constant speed unit was deemed to have been a contributory factor. Sgt Shipman is commemorated on panel 93 of

the Runnymede Memorial, while Sgt Simmons is perpetuated on the Gibraltar Memorial, his body, having been recovered from the water and identified, being committed back to the sea. Sgt Gleave was subsequently commissioned, the details of this appearing in the London Gazette on 19 December 1944. Then, with just weeks of the war in Europe remaining, he lost his life while serving with 70 Squadron on 4 April 1945; he is buried in Italy at Bari War Cemetery.

Note. Normally when an aircraft left the United Kingdom for delivery to one of the overseas theatres, it severed its connection with any command that it may once have been assigned. However, in the case above, the Wellington was officially written off, still on charge of 1446 Flight, while the casualty details for the crew indicate they were from 21 Operational Training Unit. As a rider, the Station Commander at North Front (Gibraltar) recommended that pilots be given more training in taking off, at night, with heavily laden aircraft.

22 Dec	1446 Flt	Wellington II	W5494	Training

1942   F/O R L Grayson   + T/o Moreton-in-Marsh borrowed by 21 Operational
    F/O R Stables   + Training Unit and set off towards the Welsh
    F/O D W Hogg   + borders for a map reading exercise. Shortly
    Sgt R N Braithwaite   + before 1130, the Wellington, now flying very
    F/O E F Chatterton   + low, entered a valley and crashed into a hill-
side near Gertan and less than a mile E of the
small Caernarvonshire town of Bethesda, 5 miles SE from Bangor, a sheet of flame
lighting up the gloom as it impacted. All were claimed by their next of kin. It
is believed that F/O Grayson was desperately trying to turn and climb in those
last few moments of flight.

No. 1474 (Special Duties) Flight
No. 1474 Wireless Interception Flight

Formed at Stradishall from B Flight and C Flight of 109 Squadron, "1474" existed for just
six months between 4 July 1942 and 4 January 1943, when it was redesignated 192 Squadron,
and by which time it was operating from Gransden Lodge. Initially equipped with half-a-
dozen Wellingtons, a trio of Mosquitoes were added at the beginning of December. Its task
was to detect the wavelengths of enemy radars and though for its short life it carried
out this work under the authority of No. 3 Group, "1474" (and its sister flight "1473")
were the forerunners of squadrons (and flights) formed to provide Bomber Command with an
effective radio and electronic countermeasures arm. If possible, readers should acquaint
themselves with Martin Streetly's account of No. 100 Group, written under the apt title,
"Confound and Destroy" and published in 1978 by Macdonald and Jane's.

17 Aug	1474 Flt	Wellington IC	Z1104	Op: RCM

1942   Sgt H R Osborne   T/o 0050 Gransden Lodge but the undercarriage
    was retracted prematurely and the Wellington
sank back onto the runway before managing to climb away. Returning to base,
four hours later, the bomber was damaged beyond repair when the weakened unit
folded up on touch down.

3 Dec	1474 Flt	Wellington IC	DV819	Op: RCM

1942   Sgt E Paulton RCAF   T/o Gransden Lodge and during the course of
    the sortie, came under attack from a Ju 88
night-fighter. Badly damaged, Sgt Paulton RCAF was obliged to ditch his aircraft at 0824 off Walmer beach on the S side of Deal, Kent.

18 Dec	1474 Flt	Wellington IC	DV892 D	Op: RCM

1942   P/O F A Couper RAAF   + T/o 1421 Gransden Lodge for a special wireless
    F/O J Williams   + investigation sortie in the Yarmouth area, and
    F/S E F McKenna FNZAF   + up to thirty miles off the coast. At 1500, or
    P/O P R Ackernley   + thereabouts, eyewitnesses report the Wellington
    P/O W T Pickles   + orbiting Hopton and was last sighted at 1622 on
    P/O S C McLellan   + a south-easterly heading, making towards the
    F/S A Taylor   + sea. Despite an extensive search, no trace of
    the aircraft was found, but two bodies were,
eventually, recovered; P/O Couper RAAF was found at Vejers Strand and he now
rests in Denmark at Esbjerg (Fourfelt) Cemetery, while P/O Pickles was taken
from the water at 5216N 0149E and he is buried in Batley Cemetery, Yorkshire.
The others are commemorated on the Runnymede Memorial. F/O Williams held a
Bachelor of Science degree.

No. 1481 (Target Towing) Flight
No. 1481 Target Towing and Gunnery Flight
No. 1481 (Bombing) Gunnery Flight

Formed from No. 1 Group Target Towing Flight on 14 November 1941, at Binbrook, "1481"
amended its title several times before assuming its final designation in December 1942.
Initially equipped with Westland Lysander aircraft, modified for target towing duties,
twin-engined Whitleys and Wellingtons were added to the establishment, these being used
on several occasions during the summer of 1942 on bombing operations. During 1943, the
Whitleys were phased out of service, and the Lysanders gave way to Martinets, which, in
turn were replaced in late 1944 by Hurricanes. Eventually, on 4 December 1944, "1481"
was absorbed by 1687 Flight, by which time the headquarters had been settled on Ingham.

25–26 Jun 1942	1481 Flt	Wellington IC	X9812 Z		Op: Bremen

S/L M R Atkinson   +   T/o 2310 Binbrook tasked to participate in the
Sgt J G O'Sullivan RAAF   +   third "Thousand Plan" attack of 1942. Crashed
Sgt A N Blackley RAAF   +   in the sea off the north coast of Holland. Two,
Sgt D H McIntosh RAAF   +   Sgt O'Sullivan RAAF and Sgt McIntosh RAAF, are
Sgt W Waller   +   buried in Vlieland General Cemetery and Ter-
schelling (West-Terschelling) General Cemetery
respectively, while their three companions are commemorated on the Runnymede
Memorial.

22 Sep 1942	1481 Flt	Whitley V	Z9149	Training

F/O H R Astbury   T/o 1445 Binbrook but while climbing away, the
ailerons jammed and F/O Astbury was obliged to
forced-land, five minutes into the sortie, close to the airfield.

12 Sep 1943	1481 Flt	Wellington X	HE925	Air Test

F/S A Orr   T/o 1451 Binbrook only for the starboard engine
F/S T C Smith   to fail. At 1500, the Wellington was set down,
without injury, wheels up at Rothwell Top 'twixt
three and four miles WNW from the airfield.

26 Oct 1943	1481 Flt	Martinet TTI	HP322		Meteorological

F/S R J Wright DFM RNZAF   +   T/o 1037 Binbrook to report on weather conditions
F/O N H Knight-Brown RAAF   +   over the ranges off the Lincolnshire coast. The
crew were briefed to fly by way of the resorts of
Mablethorpe and Skegness, but failed to return. Subsequently, aircraft sent to
search the range areas reported seeing an aircraft's wing floating on the surface
and this is believed to have come from the Martinet. Weather conditions are described as foggy. Both airmen are commemorated on the Runnymede Memorial. In
November 1942, and at an early stage of his operational tour (flying Wellingtons
with 142 Squadron), F/S Wright RNZAF had been very severely wounded about the
body when his aircraft came under sustained enemy fire whilst laying mines.
Enemy fighters, attracted no doubt by the searchlights and flak, arrived on
the scene but despite the agonising pain from his wounds (he passed out several
times) and ably assisted by his air bomber, Sgt W Scarlett, F/S Wright RNZAF
succeeded in flying his bomber home for a safe landing. Both were decorated
with immediate DFMs, Gazetted 4 December 1942. F/O Knight-Brown RAAF had
married Henrietta Gordon Knight-Brown of Hamilton in Lanarkshire. It is
further noted that for F/S Wright his posting to "1481" was the first since
being declared fit to resume flying duties, his operational tour being terminated (in view of his dreadful injuries) after five sorties.

15 Apr 1944	1481 Flt	Wellington X	HE804		Training

F/S P Holt DFM   inj   T/o 1445 Ingham for a cine camera gun exercise,
F/O D A Black RCAF   inj   the crew comprising of pilot, wireless operator
F/O G Mann RCAF   inj   and seven air gunners of which three, Sgt Rout,
Sgt F H Rout   inj   Sgt Field and F/S Sparks had been attached from
Sgt E R Matthews RCAF   inj   No. 1 Lancaster Finishing School. Crashed 1515,
Sgt R L Holmgren RCAF   inj   into a small wood near Ollerton on the southern
Sgt W R Field   inj   outskirts of Broughton, Nottinghamshire and some
Sgt E Smith RCAF   inj   two hundred yards E of the Worksop to Ollerton
F/S F A Sparks   inj   road. Four, the first two named, Sgt Rout and
F/S Sparks were taken to the Victoria Hospital
in Worksop; F/O Mann RCAF and Sgt Field were admitted RAF Hospital Rauceby,
while Sgt Holmgren RCAF was treated at the Fulwood Head Centre in Sheffield.
It is assumed the remainder were not too seriously hurt. F/S Holt had gained
his award with 199 Squadron, the details being promulgated on 15 June 1943.
Sgt E Smith RCAF went on to fly with 626 Squadron and was killed in action
on 4 November 1944 (see Bomber Command Losses, Volume 5, page 477).

12 Aug 1944	1481 Flt	Wellington X	HF452		Training

F/O K B Smitheringale   T/o 1000 Ingham for a cine camera gun exercise.
Sgt Poulter   Lost power and forced-landed, at 1007, near the
Sgt A D Kall RCAF   inj   hamlet of Thorpe le Falkous, 4 miles SW of the
Sgt D Smith   inj   airfield. The three injured airmen were taken
Sgt D A Hookham RCAF   inj   to station sick quarters at Hemswell.
F/S Watson
Sgt Hambrook
Sgt Wilmot

No. 1482 (Target Towing) Flight
No. 1482 Target Towing and Gunnery Flight
No. 1482 (Bombing) Gunnery Flight

1482 (Target Towing) Flight began its service in similar manner to that of "1481" in that it was formed from a group target towing flight, namely No. 2 based at West Raynham in Norfolk. Although not specifically stated, I very much suspect that when No. 2 Group became a part of 2nd Tactical Air Force on 1 June 1943, 1482 (Bombing) Gunnery Flight, as it was now known, was taken under the control of the new formation.

17 Feb	1482 Flt	Martinet I	HN949	Training
1943	F/S N E Kilvert		+	T/o 1225 West Raynham for a drogue towing
	LAC M D Thomas		+	detail. Lost flying speed, while banking,

and spun in at 1315 near Burnham Norton, a Norfolk coastal village about midway between Hunstanton and Wells-next-the-Sea. F/S Kilvert was buried in Manchester Southern Cemetery, while his drogue operator, LAC Thomas, was taken to Glanamman (Tabernacle) Presbyterian Chapelyard in Carmarthen. Accident investigators could find no evidence of a technical defect and it is thought that F/S Kilvert may have lost control while looking back over his shoulder to check if the drogue had been recovered.

No. 1483 (Target Towing) Flight
No. 1483 Target Towing and Gunnery Flight
No. 1483 (Bombing) Gunnery Flight

Formed on 18 November 1941, from No. 3 Group Training Flight, at Newmarket, "1483" had a history similar to the two preceding flights. And, similar to "1481" its Wellingtons were used in the summer of 1942, to support Bomber Command operations. On 13 July 1942, the headquarters moved to Marham but returned to Newmarket on 29 June 1943, disbanding here on 11 March 1944, with the establishing of 1688 Flight. In just over two years of flying, its aircraft were involved in three accidents, all of them fatal.

24 May	1483 Flt	Wellington IC	T2802	Training
1942	F/O M A Coote MID		+	T/o Newmarket for fighter affiliation training
	Sgt R S Holden		+	using cine camera gun, the crew comprising of
	F/S J G Y Boyle MID		+	pilot, wireless operator (attached from 138
	F/S A Adderly DFM		+	Squadron), wireless operator air gunner, an
	LAC A W Hughes		+	air gunner, three ground staff, an Air Training
	AC1 W G Boyce		+	Corps cadet and an army artillery expert who was
	AC1 J Capp		+	attached to 109 Squadron. At around 1600, the
	F/S B V Long ATC		+	Wellington's main spar assembly failed outboard
	Capt D R White RA		+	of the starboard engine. With a large portion of

its wing missing, the bomber spun in near Stanton some 6 miles NE of Bury St. Edmunds, Suffolk. Three were buried in Newmarket Cemetery, while Capt White was taken to Brookwood Military Cemetery. The others were claimed by their next of kin. F/S Adderly had flown a tour of operations with 115 Squadron; his DFM had been published on 2 September 1941. It is also noted that F/S Boyle's third Christian name was Ypres.

30 Mar	1483 Flt	Wellington III	Z1747	Training
1943	F/L D B Greenup		+	T/o 1000 Marham for a cine camera gun sortie,
	F/S K M Newland RNZAF		+	the crew complement being pilot, observer,
	AC1 R J Chitty		+	wireless operator and six air gunners. By
	F/O B Neal RNZAF		+	a terrible coincidence, the Wellington's fate
	F/S B C Harvey RCAF		+	was the same as that reported above, its remains
	Sgt A L Laycock		+	being recovered from fields N of Barton Bendish,
	Sgt W H Lowey		+	seven miles WSW from Swaffham, Norfolk. The
	Sgt J Macneall		+	four Commonwealth members of crew were buried
	Sgt M R Langdale-Hunt RNZAF		+	in Marham Cemetery, while the rest were taken

to their home towns. F/S Harvey RCAF was an American from Medford in Massachusetts. Along with Sgt Laycock, Sgt Lowey, Sgt Macneill and Sgt Langdale-Hunt RNZAF, he had been attached from 1651 Heavy Conversion Unit.

Note. The precise cause of failure was traced to the lower rear bolts in the starboard main wing.

30 Aug 1943	1483 Flt	Defiant I	N1634	Training
	W/C J D Stephens DFC	+	T/o 1500 Mildenhall for local flying. Stalled	
	LAC J W Cole	+	and crashed 1540 near the airfield. An exam-	

T/o 1500 Mildenhall for local flying. Stalled and crashed 1540 near the airfield. An examination of the engine revealed a serious coolant leakage and it believed that W/C Stephens had been overcome by fumes seeping into the cockpit. His DFC had been Gazetted on 9 July 1943, following a tour with 149 Squadron, though his entry in the Friern Barnet (St. James The Great) Churchyard register shows him as belonging to 15 Squadron. Nine months later, his brother, S/L Harry Bernard Stephens DFC, died while flying with 109 Squadron (see Bomber Command Losses, Volume 5, page 212). LAC Cole, an engine fitter by trade, is buried at Kensington (Gunnersbury) Cemetery.

No. 1484 (Target Towing) Flight
No. 1484 Target Towing and Gunnery Flight
No. 1484 (Bombing) Gunnery Flight

Formed from No. 4 Group Target Towing Flight on 14 November 1941, "1484" was based at Driffield for most of its operating life, though when replaced by 1689 Flight, in mid-February 1944, the headquarters was at Leconfield, though much of its flying was, by now, taking place from Lissett. At first equipped with Lysanders and Battles, these types were augmented by Whitleys and by February 1943, Defiants and Martinets had replaced the Battles and Lysanders. In addition, a number of Oxfords were issued for supporting duties and, as the summaries to follow will show, two of their number came to grief with serious consequences for their crews.

26 Nov 1941	1484 Flt	Lysander TTI	V9777	Training
	Sgt I J Phillips			

T/o Driffield for target towing duties. While over the sea, the engine's oil pressure dropped and this was followed by loss of the propeller as the motor seized. Unable to make landfall, Sgt Phillips, a prewar volunteer reserve pilot with 278 solo flying hours to his credit (thirty-four of these on type) very skillfully put the Lysander down into the water 5 miles E of Flamborough Head.

10 Aug 1942	1484 Flt	Oxford II	BM821	Training
	Sgt H Walmsley DFM	inj	T/o 0102 Driffield for night bombing practice	
	Sgt A A Payne	inj	but having risen to a mere nine to twelve feet	
	Sgt G Wildig	inj	above the runway, the starboard engine cut.	

Sgt Walmsley closed the throttles and crash-landed, a fire breaking out as the trainer slid to a halt. At the subsequent Court of Inquiry, it was revealed that the Oxford had been held on the ground for fifteen minutes, due to the presence of enemy aircraft, and this delay very likely led to the starboard engine becoming oiled. A veteran of Halifax operations with 10 Squadron, Sgt Walmsley's immediate award had been Gazetted on 16 June 1942 (jointly with the Distinguished Service Order awarded to his squadron commander, W/C D C T Bennett) in recognition of his successful evasion from Norway (see Bomber Command Losses, Volume 3, page 81).

13 Aug 1942	1484 Flt	Defiant I	L6981	Training
	F/S D R Lord	+	T/o Driffield for air-to-air gunnery. Lost	
	Sgt A O Potts	+	control, while carrying out a mock attack on	

the drogue towing aircraft, spun and crashed at Scurfdike Farm, on the north bank of Scurf Dike, some two-and-a-half miles east-south-east from Hutton Cranswick airfield and between 4 and 5 miles SSE of Great Driffield, Yorkshire. F/S Lord rests at Burpham (St. Luke) Churchyard, while Sgt Potts was taken to Haltemprice (Anlaby, Tranby Lane) Cemetery on the west side of nearby Hull. Both were aged twenty.

15 Sep 1942	1484 Flt	Defiant I	N3501	Training
	W/O D F P Jannings RNZAF	+	T/o 1000 Driffield for a gunnery training sortie.	

On return to base, the undercarriage jammed and it is believed the pilot was attempting to free the unit by engaging in a series of aerobatic manoeuvres when he lost control. The air gunner (who is not named) managed to bale out, but W/O Jannings RNZAF was not so fortunate and he died in the crash at 1137 just to the NW of Suffield a hamlet in Hackness Park, roughly five miles W of Scarborough, Yorkshire. Prior to arriving with "1484", he had served with 40 Squadron, completing fourteen operational sorties. He is buried in Driffield Cemetery. The Defiant had flown a total of 122.25 hours.

3 Nov	1484 Flt	Oxford I	DF536	Training

1942   WO2 J J W Forster RCAF   + T/o 1959 Driffield for a night bombing exercise
Sgt H W Carter   + but almost immediately dived into the ground,
Sgt F J Faye   + eyewitnesses judging the height to be between
one hundred-and-fifty and two hundred feet.
On impact, the Oxford burst into flames. Accident investigations were unable
to say what had caused the crash, but it was possible an explosion had occurred
in the starboard engine, or in the wing itself. WO2 Forster RCAF was buried in
Driffield Cemetery; Sgt Carter was taken to Talbot Village (St. Mark) churchyard
and Sgt Faye was laid to rest in Skelton and Brotton (Brotton) Cemetery. He had
been attached from 408 Squadron.

29 Mar	1484 Flt	Whitley V	Z6490	Training

1943   F/S R L Evans   T/o 1550 Driffield for a gunnery detail. Iced up
and became impossible to control; abandoned and
left to crash circa 1740 at Callis High Wold Farm on Bishop Wilton Wold, Garrowby
Hill, Yorkshire. Some of the crew landed near the local searchlight battery at
Bishop Wilton. The Derwent District Civil Defence report shows the map reference
as 273682 Manor Green, Kirby Underdale, this being a hamlet north of the main
York to Great Driffield road and NNE of Bishop Wilton.

18 Oct	1484 Flt	Whitley V	Z9292	Training

1943   W/O J W J Butler   T/o 1355 Leconfield for gunnery training. Forced-
landed at approximately 1540, in a field, near
Mapperton, a village on the Yorkshire coast 3 miles SSE of Hornsea and roughly
thirteen miles due E of the airfield from whence it had departed. By the summer
of 1944, W/O Butler was serving with 30 Operational Training Unit and, sadly, was
killed in a flying accident on 12 August (see Bomber Command Losses, Volume 7,
page 309). He is buried in the City of London Cemetery, Manor Park, East Ham.

	1484 Flt	Whitley V	Z9430	Training

F/S E W Haines   T/o 1358 Leconfield similarly tasked and heading
towards the south-east. Just minutes into the
flight, the port engine cut and, in the words of his station commander, "the
pilot discharged commendable skill and coolness throughout" as he forced-landed
near Beverley, Yorkshire.

No. 1485 (Target Towing) Flight
No. 1485 Target Towing and Gunnery Flight
No. 1485 (Bombing) Gunnery Flight

The last of the target towing flights to form from a nucleus of aircraft and crews provided
by their parent group, in this instance No. 5 Group, "1485" was established at Coningsby on
30 October 1941. Its task, like the four flights already dealt with, was to provide air
gunnery refresher training for the parent group's units. The usual mix of Lysanders, plus
twin-engined Whitleys and Wellingtons were issued, but soon after moving to Dunholme Lodge
at the beginning of August 1942, the Whitleys were given up in favour of Manchesters (which
might have been regarded by some of the staff pilots as a retrograde step). Late in October
the Flight occupied Fulbeck where, in 1943, it boasted an establishment of eight Manchester
half-a-dozen Martinets, a quartet each of Lysanders and Defiants, plus eight Oxfords (a few
Wellingtons still remaining on charge). In August 1943, "1485" settled on Skellingthorpe,
but on 22 November of that same year, the headquarters went to Syerston where disbandment
took place on 26 February 1944, the remaining aircraft and crews coming under the aegis of
1690 Flight. Why it was felt necessary to disband the four bombing and gunnery flights that
were serving the Command well, only to re-establish them with a new series of numbers, I am
not qualified to say.

28 Mar	1485 Flt	Lysander III	T1687	Air Test

1942   W/O E L Tiley   + T/o Coningsby and, subsequently, crashed at
AC1 A Whitlock   inj approximately 1600, cartwheeling into a tree
at Sutton Farm, half-a-mile N of Cold Hanworth,
six miles SW from Market Rasen, Lincolnshire. Amazingly, AC1 Whitlock was not
too seriously hurt and his injuries were attended to by the medical staff at
Scampton's station sick quarters. W/O Tiley, however, was beyond help and he
is buried in Wandsworth (Putney Vale) Cemetery. It is thought he may have
been rendered unconscious before the Lysander hit the ground. Twenty-four
years of age, he was a product of the prewar volunteer reserve training scheme.

6 Oct 1942	1485 Flt F/S H H Taylor	**Manchester I**	L7473	**Training**

T/o 1440 Dunholme Lodge but after climbing to fifty feet, an engine failed. With remarkable skill, F/S Taylor (his service number shows that he enlisted in Rhodesia) flew a short circuit and crash-landed, on the airfield, without injury to the crew. The Manchester had accumulated a total of 213.00 flying hours.

11 Feb 1943	1485 Flt F/S R Eyres	**Manchester I**	L7391	**Training**

T/o Fulbeck for an air firing detail, during which the starboard engine cut at 1,200 feet. Unable to keep the Manchester in the air, long enough to find an airfield, F/S Eyres forced-landed 1540 at Fishtoft Drove, some 2 miles SE from the centre of Boston, Lincolnshire. Total flying hours; 160.00.

18 Jul 1943	1485 Flt	**Wellington III**	BK235	**Training**
	W/O J W Heard	+		
	F/S D Breslin DFM	+		
	G/C B E Lowe	+		
	G/C R V M Odbert	+		
	W/C A W S Matheson	+		
	S/L P Brandon-Trye	+		

T/o Fulbeck with four officers from Course 11 of the Senior Officers Assessment Course for a gunnery and fighter affiliation demonstration. While engaged on the second part of the detail, north of Brigg, structural failure of the main planes occurred and the Wellington crashed 1625 just over a mile SE of Appleby, 4 miles NE from Scunthorpe, Lincolnshire. Four were laid to rest in Brigg Cemetery; G/C Odbert of Monkstown, Co. Dublin in the Republic of Ireland lies in Newark-upon-Trent Cemetery, while F/S Breslin was taken home to Northern Ireland and interred at Strabane Cemetery, Co. Tyrone. He had recently completed a tour of duty with 106 Squadron, and details of his award had been published as recently as 15 June. I am indebted to Barry Moores of Lincoln for furnishing me with details of this awful tragedy, the subject of which he has had published in the Lincolnshire Aviation Society's magazine.

6 Aug 1943	1485 Flt W/O K Felus PAF	**Martinet I** +	HP318	**Training**

T/o 1621 Fulbeck for a fighter affiliation detail. Spun and crashed 1645 at Eagle, some seven miles SW from the centre of Lincoln. The funeral service for W/O Felus was held at 1530 hours on 10 August in Newark-upon-Trent Cemetery.

20 Sep 1943	1485 Flt	**Wellington X**	HE350	**Training**
	P/O W G Baker	inj		
	Sgt J Pemberton	inj		
	Sgt A Kirkman	inj		
	P/O R A Baker DFC	+		
	Sgt T C Newton	inj		
	Sgt A Bracey	+		
	Sgt T Baker	+		

T/o 1537 Skellingthorpe for air gunnery training but as the Wellington gained height, both motors cut. Unable to turn back, P/O Baker crash-landed at 1540, two to three miles NW of the runway. At least three were admitted to RAF Hospital Rauceby. Sgts Pemberton, Kirkman and Newton had been attached from 1654 Heavy Conversion Unit, while P/O Baker was serving with 50 Squadron. Details of his commission had been Gazetted on 15 June 1943, and promulgation of his DFC appeared, in the London Gazette, on 16 November of that same year. From Ferriby in Yorkshire, he lies in Cleethorpes Cemetery. His namesake, Sgt Baker, was taken to Corby Cemetery, while Sgt Bracey rests at Burton-upon-Trent Cemetery.

No. 1502 Beam Approach Training Flight

Retitled from No. 2 Blind Approach Training Flight, in October 1941, while based at Driffield, the unit's Whitleys participated in two of Bomber Command's "Thousand Plan" raids in 1942, losing an aircraft of the first. On 23 July 1943, the Flight moved to Leconfield and disbanded, here, on 15 August 1943.

30-31 May 1942	1502 Flt	**Whitley V**	Z9307 H	**Op: Köln**
	S/L J A S Russell DFC	pow		
	P/O D G Box RNZAF	+		
	F/S J H Godbehere RCAF	+		
	F/L D W Foster DFM	pow		
	Sgt W H Orman	+		

T/o 2310 Driffield tasked to support the first "Thousand Plan" raid. Homebound, shot down by Hptm Werner Streib, I./NJG1 and crashed near Hoboken in Antwerpen's SW suburbs. Shortly before the impact, the Whitley's port wing came off. Those who died lie in Schoonselhof Cemetery. F/L Foster had served with 58 Squadron; his award was Gazetted on 26 May 1942.

No. 1507 Beam Approach Training Flight

Please refer to page 190 for a summary of this unit's activities.

28 Sep	1507 Flt		Oxford I	V4035	Training

1942   P/O B G Tree   inj   T/o 0825 Finningley for dual beam flying. An
         Sgt H G R Cosker RAAF   inj   hour and ten minutes later (in weather that is
         F/S E Chamberlain   inj   described as "marginal") while following a
track two hundred-and-fifty yards to the left
of the beam, hit a tree and then stalled while trying to avoid other obstacles
in its path. All were taken to Doncaster Royal Infirmary, where two succumbed
to their injuries. P/O Tree rests in Cottingham Cemetery, while Sgt Cosker RAAF
was buried in the extension to Finningley (Holy Trinity and St. Oswald) Churchyard. F/S Chamberlain duly recovered from a broken left tibia and fibula. As
a consequence of this accident, it was recommended that the beam be moved away
from the NE boundary of the airfield and in the meanwhile, in poor weather, a
line of sodium flares should be lit to alert pilots of the present dangers.

No. 1508 Beam Approach Training Flight

The origins of this Flight lay with 8 Blind Approach Training Flight, which had formed
at Wattisham on 18 January 1941, in No. 2 Group. Retitled "1508" in the October of that
year, and operating from Horsham St. Faith, its sole accident occurred shortly after its
arrival at Attlebridge on 4 April 1943. Although not formally stated, it is very likely
"1508" came under the authority of 2nd Tactical Air Force on 1 June 1943.

29 Apr	1508 Flt		Oxford I	AT797	Training

1943   F/O R H Powell   inj   T/o 1420 Attlebridge to practice beam flying.
         Sgt R J Bird   inj   At approximately 1600, the Oxford flew into a
line of cables, near Swannington (at the time
an airfield still under construction), 9 miles NW of Norwich. Both pilots were
admitted to the Norfolk and Norwich Hospital where, at 1700 hours, five minutes
after his admission, F/O Powell died from his wounds. He is buried in the
extension to Edenbridge Cemetery, Kent.

No. 1513 Beam Approach Training Flight

First established in No. 3 Group, at Honington, on 22 September 1941, "1513" arrived at
Bramcote on 31 October 1942, where it came under the authority of No. 93 Group. Although
11 May 1944, is shown as its date of transfer to No. 44 Group, accident record cards in
respect of "1513" indicate it was part of Flying Training Command from as early as November 1943.

30 Jun	1513 Flt		Oxford I	V4134	Training

1943   Sgt N Bosworth   +   T/o 0930 Bramcote for beam approach practice.
         Sgt H G Sanders   +   At 1025, emerged from the cloud base, in a dive,
and failed to recover before crashing onto a
slag heap at Exhall Colliery near Black Bank, Bedworth, Warwickshire. From
Clarendon Park in Leicestershire, Sgt Bosworth was buried in Nuneaton (Oaston
Road) Cemetery, while Sgt Sanders rests at Rushden Cemetery.

No. 1515 Beam Approach Training Flight

Formed as 15 Blind Approach Training Flight on 22 September 1941, it was retitled "1515"
within a few weeks of its formation. Throughout its service, in No. 2 Group, "1515" operated from Swanton Morley before coming under the wing of Flying Training Command circa
May 1942, at which time it became affiliated to 3 (Pilots) Advanced Flying Unit.

24 Mar	1515 Flt		Oxford I	V4063	Training

1942   F/O D McL Craik   +   T/o Swanton Morley and destroyed in a midair
         Sgt E H Hawken RNZAF   +   collision with another of the unit's aircraft.
F/O Craik lies in Great Bedwyn Churchyard.

24 Mar	1515 Flt	Oxford I	V4137	Training

1942 F/S B Johnson DFM   + T/o Swanton Morley and lost in the manner des-
       Sgt S H Robinson RNZAF   + cribed at the foot of the previous page, debris
                                      from the two aircraft being recovered from
Foxley Wood, about a mile NE of Bawdeswell, 14 miles NW from Norwich (the time
of the tragedy being reported as 1600). F/S Johnson was taken to Cottingham
Cemetery; he had recently completed a tour of operations flying Hampdens with
144 Squadron and details of his award had been published on 23 December 1941.
Sgt Robinson RNZAF rests alongside his fellow countryman, killed in the other
Oxford, in Swanton Morley (All Saints) Churchyard. Both had been attached
from 15 (Pilots) Advanced Flying Unit at Leconfield.

No. 1516 Beam Approach Training Flight

1516 Beam Approach Training Flight was one of several similar establishments that helped
to train pilots in the art of beam flying, on behalf of No. 4 Group squadrons. Formed at
Topclife on 22 September 1941, as 16 Blind Approach Training Flight, its headquarters
moved to Middleton St. George, quite soon after being redesignated "1516". A year later,
the Flight moved to Croft, but after less than a month at its new home, "1516" returned
to Middleton St. George on 14 October 1942, and immediately became involved in the task
of instructing the newly established 420 Squadron (Wellingtons). However, in December
1942, "1516" went south to Hampstead Norris, where it came under the authority of No. 91
Group, only to be attached to 6 (Pilots) Advanced Flying Unit and by mid-April 1943, it
was affiliated to No. 44 Group and out of the hands of Bomber Command control.

12 Mar	1516 Flt	Oxford I	V4139	Training

1942 S/L I R Macpherson   inj T/o Middleton St. George for dual beam flying.
      P/O D K Hulme   inj Lost power (at 600 feet) while coming in to
      P/O A E Holt   inj land and crashed, quite heavily, at 1155 at
                                 High Goosepool Farm. It is noted, on the
accident form, that the Regional Control Officer had kept the crew waiting
for forty-five minutes while three Halifaxes were removed from No. 3 runway.

24 Jun	1516 Flt	Oxford I	V4140	Training

1942 Sgt F R Magson   + T/o Middleton St. George for dual practice, on
      Sgt J C W Sealey   + the beam. While flying at 2,000 feet and just
                               below the cloud base, collided with a Halifax
belonging to the resident 76 Squadron, and flown by Sgt J H G Bingham. Both
machines went down, out of control, and crashed at 1118 near the airfield (see
Bomber Command Losses, Volume 3, page 131 for details of the Halifax crew).
Sgt Magson is buried in Huntington (All Saints) Churchyard, while Sgt Sealey
was taken to Swindon (Radnor Street) Cemetery.

No. 1518 Beam Approach Training Flight

Formed at Scampton on 3 November 1941, in No. 5 Group, "1518" was equipped throughout
with Oxford trainers. On 14 June 1943, the Flight transferred its allegiance to No. 21
Group and Flying Training Command, having moved to Edzell in Kincardineshire. It will
be noted that the Flight operated, in 1942, from Dunholme Lodge.

23 Mar	1518 Flt	Oxford I	AT659	Training

1942 F/O H M McGuffie   + T/o Dunholme Lodge, the entire crew being
      Sgt T D Dakin RCAF   + attached from 49 Squadron. At 1440, the Oxford
      Sgt L D J Crozier RCAF + flew into high-tension wires and crashed near
                                 Pickerings Farm, lying to the south of the air-
field. F/O McGuffie rests in Taxal (St. James) Churchyard, while his two
squadron companions lie in Scampton (St. John The Baptist) Churchyard.

4 Nov	1518 Flt	Oxford I	AT663	Meteorological

1942 F/L C H Butt RNZAF   + T/o Scampton to carry out a weather test, using
      F/O R S Shaw RCAF   + the beam as an aid. During the test, F/L Butt
                                reported he was having difficulties with the
beam set, and he later acknowledged an instruction to head for North Luffenham.
However, at 1430 he hit some trees and crashed at The Grange Farm, Brattleby,
six miles NNW of Lincoln. Both rest in Scampton (St. John The Baptist) Churchyard.

No. 1519 Beam Approach Training Flight

Although formed during November 1941, at South Cerney, "1519" was assigned to No. 2 Group but appears to have done most of its work with 3 (Pilots) Advanced Flying Unit, which was based at South Cerney. However, the two accidents, summarised below, both occurred with the Flight operating under Bomber Command authority. On 15 April 1943, "1519" came under the authority No. 3 Group, at Feltwell (to whence it had moved in December 1941), but was affiliated to 20 (Pilots) Advanced Flying Unit at Kidlington.

4 Jun 1942	1519 Flt	Oxford I	AT724	Training
	Sgt A N Yeaman RAAF	+	T/o 1515 Mildenhall for beam flying practice.	
	Sgt R J Brewer	+	Lost power and crashed 1645 on the downwind	
	Sgt E G Cook	inj	side of the airfield and burst into flames.	

Sgt Cook had a miraculous escape and he was treated in the local station sick quarters. Sgt Yeaman RAAF is buried in Feltwell (St. Nicholas) Churchyard; Sgt Brewer rests in the City of London Cemetery at Manor Park, East Ham.

10 Nov 1942	1519 Flt	Oxford I	DF334	Training
	F/S T Stabler	inj	T/o 1315 Feltwell for standard beam approach	
	Sgt A Rankin	inj	training. After losing engine power, and	

fearful that the motor might catch fire, the pilot at the controls decided to land as quickly as possible. However, before he could reach his intended destination of Mildenhall, the Oxford clipped a tree and crashed at 1430. F/S Stabler was taken to RAF Hospital Ely, but it is thought that Sgt Rankin was treated locally, his injuries being described as slight - though he was badly shocked. Commissioned on 13 July 1943, he went on to serve with 75 Squadron and was killed in action on 24 August 1943 (see Bomber Command Losses, Volume 4, page 281).

1520 Beam Approach Training Flight

After commencing life in No. 1 Group, at Breighton on 10 October 1941, "1520" moved its headquarters to Holme-on-Spalding Moor and, later, to Leconfield where it came under the control of No. 4 Group. A move to Sturgate on 18 September 1944, after a little over four months of operations at Leconfield, saw "1520" back in the folds of No. 1 Group, but almost immediately left Bomber Command service and settled in Training Command.

3 Jun 1942	1520 Flt	Oxford I	AT621	Training
	Sgt E A Hooker		T/o Holme-on-Spalding Moor for beam training	
	Sgt W C Herr RCAF		but came to grief at 0900 following a mis-	

judged landing, during which the Oxford ran into a trench and turned over. On 28 August 1942, Sgt Hooker took off from Bicester in a Blenheim IV belonging to 13 Operational Training Unit and failed to return (see Bomber Command Losses, Volume 7, page 148).

20 Nov 1943	1520 Flt	Oxford I	AT619	Training
	S/L H C Langford	inj	T/o 0920 Holme-on-Spalding Moor for training	
	Sgt J R Coulter RAAF	inj	in beam approach procedures. At 1100, with	

the weather quite foggy and the beam approach equipment unserviceable, the Oxford touched down, bounced and flipped onto its back. Both airmen were treated in the local station sick quarters.

No. 1521 Beam Approach Training Flight

Initially formed during October 1941, at Stradishall, "1521" set to work to help in the training of No. 3 Group squadron crews to become competent in landing their aircraft in weather conditions that, without the aid of the beam, would prove hazardous to the extreme. This task was carried out for over a year before, on 15 March 1943, the Flight moved north to Finningley, where it came under the wing of No. 93 Group and was affiliated to 11 (Pilots) Advanced Flying Unit at Shawbury. From this point on, "1521" seems to have crossed back and forth between Training Command and Bomber Command authority, its headquarters being centred on Wymeswold, Castle Donnington and, for a second time, Wymeswold until leaving Bomber Command for good on 15 October 1944.

2 Nov	**1521 Flt**	**Oxford I AT765**	**Training**
1942	F/S E H Barrett RCAF	inj	T/o 0900 Stradishall for beam approach
	Sgt C C P Thaughland RNZAF	inj	training. Lost power and forced-landed
	Sgt A H Jeeves	inj	at 1025 near Glemsford, 10 miles SSW of

Bury St. Edmunds, Suffolk. All were taken
to St. Leonard's Hospital at Sudbury, where F/S Barrett RCAF died some thirty
minutes before midnight. He is buried in Haverhill Cemetery.

24 Nov	**1521 Flt**	**Oxford I AT788**	**Training**
1942	Sgt S R Bolick RCAF		T/o Stradishall to practise flying by aid
	Sgt S J Knox		of the beam. During the detail, the weather
	Sgt G A Kirkham		closed down totally and following two ab-

ortive attempts to land, Flying Control
ordered the crew to climb to a safe altitude and bale out. This they did,
safely, and their Oxford fell to earth at 1815 at Sible Hedingham, 3 miles
north-west from Halstead, Essex. Sgt Bolick RCAF came from the United States.

11 Feb	**1521 Flt**	**Oxford I AT786**	**Training**
1943	Sgt A Snell		T/o 1107 Stradishall for beam approach
	Sgt R Brunt		practice. While overshooting, lost power

from the starboard engine and forced-landed
at 1222 at Great Lodge Farm, Hundon, 5 miles NE of Haverhill, Suffolk. Neither
pilot survived the war. Sgt Brunt joined 49 Squadron and had risen to warrant
officer rank when his Lancaster failed to make it home from Berlin on 27 November 1943, while Sgt Snell was lost in late May 1944, while attacking Aachen
with 166 Squadron (see Bomber Command Losses, Volumes 4 and 5, pages 400 and
245 respectively). At the time of his death, Sgt Snell had recently been
commissioned, details of this being published in the Supplement to the London
Gazette on 12 May 1944, his seniority being backdated to 10 April 1944.

14 Apr	**1521 Flt**	**Oxford I LB415**	**Training**
1944	F/L J A Hawkins	+	T/o 1535 Wymeswold for beam approach training
	P/O B H Dennis	+	and destroyed in a midair collision, south of

Syerston, with a Lancaster from 5 Lancaster
Finishing School (see page 177). F/L Hawkins of Edinburgh is buried in Burton-
on-the-Wolds Church Cemetery, while P/O Dennis lies in St. Albans Cemetery.

No. 1681 Bomber (Defence) Training Flight

In total, ten Bomber (Defence) Training Flights were formed, four, including "1681" coming
into existence on the same day, 1 July 1943. However, these were not the leaders of the
pack, this honour falling to "1683" (which will be summarised, in due course). Setting up
home at Pershore, in No. 91 Group, "1681" was equipped with Curtiss-built Tomahawk fighters
and home-built Hawker Hurricanes, though the latter did not appear on the scene until 1944
by which time most of the Tomahawks were nearing the end of their useful life. Disbanded
on 21 August 1944, "1681" played a useful rôle in providing the Command's air gunners with
a useful fighter affiliation trainer on which to hone their gunnery skills. When finally
stood down, the Flight's headquarters was at Long Marston, having been domicile here since
8 March 1944.

31 Jul	**1681 Flt**	**Tomahawk I AH746**	**Training**
1943	Sgt D Leslie RCAF		T/o Pershore and when Sgt Leslie RCAF in-
			advertently failed to switch to the wing tanks,

having exhausted the fuel supply from the reserve tank, he was obliged to crash-
land at 1200, wheels up, with a "dead" engine near Worcester.

15 Aug	**1681 Flt**	**Tomahawk I AH776**	**Training**
1943	Sgt P West		T/o 1138 Pershore and on return to base at 1253,
			swung on touch down and lost the undercarriage.

In mitigation, it was reported that a strong crosswind was blowing at the time.

4 Apr	**1681 Flt**	**Tomahawk IIA AH885**	**Training**
1944	F/L J E Gilden		T/o 1530 Long Marston and on return to base
			at 1605, overshot its landing run and tipped

onto its nose. Although only slightly damaged, no repair work was authorised.
F/L Gilden had 460 solo hours of flying to his credit, eighty of these on type.

No. 1682 Bomber (Defence) Training Flight

Formed within No. 91 Group at Abingdon on 1 July 1943, "1682" moved its headquarters within twenty-four hours to Stanton Harcourt, and again on 26 February 1944, this time to Enstone. Disbanded 1 August 1944, having operated various Mks of Tomahawk and Hurricane IIc.

17 Aug	1682 Flt	Tomahawk I	AH822	Training

1943   Sgt G M Cameron   T/o 0955 Abingdon but soon afterwards its Allison engine burst into flames (due to the breakage of No. 2 conrod). With only 700 feet in hand, Sgt Cameron skilfully put the crippled fighter down in a field near Oxford, the Tomahawk's port wing snagging against a gate post as it skidded to a stop.

24 Feb	1682 Flt	Tomahawk I	AH860	Training

1944   Sgt P West   T/o 0940 Stanton Harcourt for fighter affiliation duties, during which the engine failed. Sighting nearby Abingdon, Sgt West arrived on the runway at 0952 but bounced very badly and it seems likely he tried to go round again, for it is reported that the Allison cut at 150 feet, obliging the pilot to forced-land at map reference sheet 105 827206. It will be recalled that Sgt West had already written off one Tomahawk, while serving with "1681" (see the previous page).

28 Feb	1682 Flt	Tomahawk I	AH852	Training

1944   WO1 J H Thompson RCAF   T/o 0920 Enstone for fighter affiliation but landed ten minutes later at Moreton-in-Marsh. However, on touch down the port brake jammed, causing the tyre to burst which, in turn, swung the fighter to starboard. The strain proved too great for the oleo, which promptly snapped.

31 Mar	1682 Flt	Tomahawk IIA	AH896	Training

1944   F/S J H Holden   T/o 1510 Enstone tasked for a fighter affiliation detail. On completion of the exercise, and as he was about to touch down, F/S Holden heard the undercarriage warning horn sounding and he immediately decided to overshoot. However, on his second approach, he discovered that he could not get the wheels to lower, while his flaps, also, remained stuck in their "up" position. For several minutes he tried to rectify the situation by using the hand pump, but when this proved ineffective, he forced-landed at 1645, wheels up. Subsequently, the airframe was salvaged and issued as a training aid to the Navigation Training Unit, Pathfinder Force, at Warboys with the serial 4315M applied.

12 May	1682 Flt	Tomahawk IIA	AH995	Training

1944   P/O J H Thompson RCAF   T/o 1036 Enstone for a fighter affiliation sortie. Landed, at base, at 1106 only for the port oleo to collapse, thus damaging the fighter beyond reasonable repair. This was P/O Thomspon's second Tomahawk mishap.

No. 1683 Bomber (Defence) Training Flight

This was the first of the ten Bomber (Defence) Training Flights to form, the occasion being 5 June 1943, at Bruntingthorpe in No. 92 Group. Various Mks of Tomahwak were issued, but soon after transferring to Market Harborough in February 1944, "1683" re-equipped with Hurricanes. Disbanded 1 August 1944.

23 Jul	1683 Flt	Tomahawk I	AH864	Training

1943   F/S W K F Merrett RAAF   inj   T/o 1755 Bruntingthorpe for fighter affiliation duties. Abandoned, following an uncontrollable engine fire, and left to crash at 1810 near Arnesby, 8 miles SSE from the centre of Leicester, to whose Royal Infirmary F/S Merrett RAAF was taken for treatment.

1 Oct	1683 Flt	Tomahawk IIA	AH941	Training

1943   Sgt D H M Nicholas   T/o 1250 Bruntingthorpe but a conrod failed and the Tomahawk was put down, in a field, at 1300, on Bygrove Farm, Grandborough, 11 miles E of Royal Leamington Spa, Warwickshire. At the subsequent Court of Inquiry, Sgt Nicholas's station commander said, that in the circumstances, he had coped well.

18 Dec	1683 Flt	Tomahawk IIA	AH884	Training

18 Dec **1683 Flt** **Tomahawk IIA AH884** **Training**
1943 F/S E Hughes inj T/o Bruntingthorpe for fighter affiliation
duties, during which the weather deteriorated.
Unable to find his way back to base, or find an alternative airfield, F/S Hughes
forced-landed circa 1500, out of petrol, a mile W of Conisborough, Yorkshire. On
being released from his cockpit, he was taken to Doncaster Infirmary.

5 Jan **1683 Flt** **Tomahawk I AH842** **Ground**
1944 F/S P A Kerr RAAF While taxying 1445 at Desborough, failed to see
a tractor and as a consequence of the collision
that followed, the Tomahawk was written off charge.

4 Feb **1683 Flt** **Tomahawk IIA AH899** **Training**
1944 Sgt T G Lewin T/o 1140 Market Harborough intending to link up
with a flight of Wellingtons. However, within
a few minutes of departure, the Allison emitted plumes of white smoke, tinged
with flames. Wisely, Sgt Lewin cut the switches and forced-landed, wheels up,
near the airfield. His sortie had lasted a mere ten minutes.

26 Mar **1683 Flt** **Tomahawk IIA AH882** **Training**
1944 F/S P A Kerr RAAF T/o 0903 Market Harborough but landed within
ten minutes at Bruntingthorpe, swinging to
starboard and breaking the undercarriage. It is remarked that this was his
third accident on type (see above for one; the other must have been a repairable
case) and it was recommended that he be posted to more "docile and easier to
handle types".

28 Mar **1683 Flt** **Tomahawk I AH853** **Unknown**
1944 Reported as damaged beyond repair on this date
but no accident card traced. First delivered to a Cunliffe Owen facility on
10 April 1941, this particular aircraft had brief spells of service with 400
and 231 Squadrons before being issued to "1683" on 2 September 1943. For most
of its life, however, it languished at various maintenance units, plus a very
lengthy spell with Short Brothers & Harland undergoing repairs (3 July 1942
to 27 April 1943). Its flying hours have not been appended.

No. 1684 Bomber (Defence) Training Flight

Formed on 29 June 1943, at Little Horwood, in No. 92 Group, moving to nearby Wing in mid-
July 1943, where it acquired some Hurricanes in March 1944. Disbanded on 1 August 1944.
It is believed "1684" might have pooled its Tomahawks with 26 Operational Training Unit,
which used Little Horwood and Wing and held the type on charge as a support aircraft.

4 Oct **1684 Flt** **Tomahawk IIA AH895** **Training**
1943 Sgt W Tuck T/o 1358 Wing for fighter affiliation, in the
course of which the Allision failed (suspected
conrod failure) and this led to a forced-landing at 1425 on Stake Gate Farm,
near Roade, 6 miles S of Northampton. Sgt Tuck had only seven hours on type,
though he had logged 415 hours of solo flying.

11 Oct **1684 Flt** **Tomahawk I AH781** **Training**
1943 F/S H Shephard + T/o 1343 Wing for fighter affiliation but came
down two minutes later, a mere mile from the
airfield. Eyewitnesses told the Court of Inquiry that the Tomahawk was flying
at 700 feet, in the circuit, and its speed seemed to be markedly low. It then
rolled onto its back and spiralled into a ploughed field. F/S Shephard, whose
experience on type was a useful sixty-four hours, was taken to Urmston Cemetery.

Note. The two aircraft, summarised above, may have been borrowed from 26 OTU.

30 Mar **1684 Flt** **Tomahawk I AH801** **Ground**
1944 F/S E C Foster T/o 1455 Wing for a fighter affiliation sortie,
which was successfully completed. After landing.
and while taxying at 1640, F/S Foster collided with an obstruction and his aircraft promptly tipped onto its nose. Very little damage was caused, but it was
decided, nonetheless, to write the airframe off charge.

No. 1685 Bomber (Defence) Training Flight

Formed on 1 July 1943, at Ossington in No. 93 Group, "1685" maintained a detachment at Finningley from 12 July 1944 until the unit's disbandment on 21 August 1944.

20 Jul	1685 Flt	Tomahawk I	AH795	Training

1943   Sgt R L Gawn RAAF   T/o 1333 Ossington tasked for fighter affiliation duties but as the Tomahawk cleared the runway, flames were seen streaming from the engine. Displaying remarkable calm, the young Australian pilot forced-landed at Papplewick, a village on the SW side of Sherwood Forest and 3 miles or so NE of Hucknall, Nottinghamshire. His flight had lasted for two very alarming minutes.

3 Aug	1685 Flt	Tomahawk I	AH777	Training

1943   Sgt E J Golley   T/o 1310 Ossington for fighter affiliation. On return to base, Sgt Golley was unable to get the wheels to lock down (due to the cover not being properly locked, the hydraulic reserve fluid tank had emptied) and, thus, a wheels up landing, at 1420, was carried out.

10 Nov	1685 Flt	Tomahawk IIA	AH986	Training

1943   Sgt R B T Adams   T/o Ossington for fighter affiliation practice. At the completion of the detail, Sgt Adams found himself flying in rather poor visibility and had the misfortune to lose contact with the Wellington which was leading him towards base. Uncertain of his position, he let down through the murk and at 0945 flew into some high-tension wires and forced-landed, near the airfield.

13 Dec	1685 Flt	Tomahawk I	AH825	Training

1943   W/O F Bidewell   T/o Ossington to gain flying experience on type. Forced-landed 1110, in a field not far from the runway, following engine failure. No injuries reported.

1 Apr	1685 Flt	Tomahawk I	AH764	Ground

1944   W/O F Bidewell   Taxying 1210, at Ossington, in preparation to take off for a fighter affiliation exercise, collided with a small motor transport vehicle. Despite being only slightly damaged, the Tomahawk was written off charge. In his report, W/O Bidewell stated that he had noticed the engine temperature gauge rising and was reaching down to open the radiator flap, when he felt the impact of a collision. Since his mishap, the previous December, he had logged around eighty-five hours on type, bringing his solo experience to 410 hours.

No. 1686 Bomber (Defence) Training Flight

Formed at Hixon on 1 July 1943, in No. 93 Group, and equipped with six Tomahawks, "1686" eventually received some Hurricanes before disbanding on 21 August 1944.

23 Dec	1686 Flt	Tomahawk IIB	AK128	Ground

1943   F/L L M Ralph RNZAF   Taxied into a fuel bowser at Hixon and damaged beyond repair, the accident being timed at 1710.

11 Mar	1686 Flt	Tomahawk I	AH832	Air Test

1944   F/O C S Chapman   T/o 1143 Hixon but the prevailing crosswind carried the fighter onto an embankment, damaging the airframe beyond repair. Attached to the accident card is a photograph of the Tomahawk, submitted to the authorities by F/O Chapman, on which he has penned, "My second prang". From the angle that the photograph was taken, it is impossible to see any unit markings, but a severely damaged nose section provides good evidence as to the severity of the accident.

14 Apr	1686 Flt	Tomahawk IIA	AH926	Training

1944   F/S J Cleece   T/o 1036 Hixon for fighter affiliation training. Landed thirty minutes later at Peplow, whereupon the starboard oleo snapped and when the Tomahawk veered off to the left, the port undercarriage leg folded.

No. 1687 Bomber (Defence) Training Flight

The principal equipment, supplied to the last of the four Bomber (Defence) Training Flights was a mixture of Hurricane and Spitfire types. Formed on 15 February 1944, "1687" appears to have operated throughout its thirty-three months of service in No. 1 Group, first from Ingham, followed by five months at Scampton before settling its headquarters at Hemswell on 2 April 1945. Disbanded on 30 October 1946.

12 Oct 1944	**1687 Flt**	**Hurricane IIC** LF390	**Training**
	W/O N L Pretlove	+ T/o Ingham for a fighter affiliation exercise	

with a Lancaster from 166 Squadron. At approx-imately 1240, while flying about a mile E of Hemswell, a midair collision 'twixt fighter and bomber (Lancaster I PD227) occurred and both machines plunged out of control. W/O Pretlove rests in Northampton General Cemetery. For details of the Lancaster's crew, please refer to Bomber Command Losses, Volume 5, page 448.

16 Mar 1945	**1687 Flt**	**Hurricane IIC** PG586	**Training**
	F/O Gumbrell	T/o 2140 Scampton for fighter affiliation, at night. Lost engine power and while trying to	

reach Ludford Magna, forced-landed 2230 just short of the runway.

19 Jul 1945	**1687 Flt**	**Spitfire VB** W3231	**Training**
	W/O C Hughes	T/o 1349 Hemswell for a fighter affiliation sortie. On return to base, W/O Hughes could	

not get the wheels to lower, despite using the aircraft's emergency system and, thus, he was obliged to forced-land at 1521. Subsequently, it was found that the hydraulic pump drive had fractured and the shuttle valve in the emergency system had also failed, caused by "foreign matter" on the valve seating. W/O Hughes had twenty-seven hours on Spitfires and 987 solo hours in total.

11 Jan 1946	**1687 Flt**	**Spitfire VB** AD413	**Training**
	F/O J Harris DFC	+ T/o 0954 Hemswell and set course for Leeming. Became lost, due to inclement weather along the	

flight path. At around 1010, F/O Harris decided to make a wheels down landing, in a wheat field, but in the gloom he failed to see a line of telegraph wires and, consequently, his wheels snagged the lines and sent the fighter out of control. He was down some 3 miles E of Howden and about 5 miles or so SW from Selby in Yorkshire, six miles off his intended track. Commissioned with effect from 4 June 1944, he went on to fly Lancasters with 550 Squadron, the London Gazette of 22 May 1945, carrying the details of his award. He is buried in Liverpool (Anfield) Cemetery.

27 Mar 1946	**1687 Flt**	**Hurricane IIC** PZ737	**Training**
	F/O A J Maxwell	inj T/o 1200 Hemswell to practice homing and area flying. Forced-landed 1245, wheels retracted,	

following a serious coolant leakage, at Bassingham, 8 miles SSW from Lincoln. This was the last Hurricane to be written off from a Bomber Command unit.

6 Apr 1946	**1687 Flt**	**Spitfire VB** AB194	**Ground**
	F/O G H Markes	T/o 0925 Hemswell for fighter affiliation. Landed 0945, safely, at Binbrook but while	

taxying the Spitfire's port wing struck a motor transport vehicle. Little damage resulted, but no repair work was sanctioned.

1 Jul 946	**1687 Flt**	**Spitfire VB** W3439	**Training**
	F/L W Hutchinson	T/o 1249 Hemswell for a fighter affiliation detail. At 1315, F/L Hutchinson approached	

Binbrook and was ordered by Air Traffic Control to land on light aircraft landing strip, as a strong crosswind was blowing across the main runway. How-ever, on touch down, the Spitfire swung and when he applied the brakes, the fighter promptly stood on its nose. Similar to the accident reported above, very little damage was caused but possibly due to the age of the airframe, no authority for repairs was forthcoming. F/L Hutchinson had logged in the region of 632 solo flying hours, eighty-nine of these on type.

No. 1688 Bomber (Defence) Training Flight

Formed within No. 3 Group, at Newmarket, on 11 March 1944, "1688" remained near the famous racecourse for close on a year before de-camping to Feltwell in Norfolk. From here, on 19 March 1946, its headquarters was established at Wyton, remaining in situ until disbandment on 30 September 1946.

11 Mar	1688 Flt	Hurricane IIC	LF426		Air Test

1944   W/O J M Tew RAAF   + T/o Newmarket and shortly before 1430, it was
                                      seen formating on an Oxford trainer. It seems
that W/O Tew RAAF broke off, banked steeply, lost control and failed to recover
before his Hurricane hit the ground and burst into flames near Weltmore Farm in
Norfolk. From Toowoomba in Queensland, he was buried at 1430 hours on 16 March
in Cambridge City Cemetery. An inauspicious start for the unit, which had
formed earlier in the day.

9 Aug	1688 Flt	Tiger Moth II	T7351		Training

1944   F/O G H Sizer   inj T/o 1524 Newmarket for local flying, during
                                     which F/O Sizer decided to pay a visit to
Stradishall. On touch down, here, at 1539, he lost control and collided with
a steamroller. According to the accident card, he had a mere ninety-eight
hours of solo flying, twenty-nine of these, apparently, on Tiger Moths.

19 Jan	1688 Flt	Spitfire VB	BM134		Training

1946   F/O B Pengilley   T/o Feltwell for a practice flight. Crossed
                                     the boundary hedge at 1015 but F/O Pengilley
held off too high and thumped onto the runway with such force that the wheels
folded. Despite having over nine hundred hours of solo flying experience, he
had flown the Spitfire for less than an hour.

No. 1689 Bomber (Defence) Training Flight

Formed from No. 1484 (Bombing) Gunnery Flight (see pages 203 and 204) on 15 February 1944, at Holme-on-Spalding Moor, "1689" was affiliated to No. 4 Group throughout its fifteen months of existence.

8 Nov	1689 Flt	Hurricane IID	HW684		Training

1944   F/O J Etchells   T/o Holme-on-Spalding Moor tasked to practice
                                     fighter affiliation with a 1663 Heavy Conversion
Unit Halifax and lost in the manner described on page 145, F/O Etchells para-
chuting safely. His Hurricane is reported to have fallen into fields near
Harrendale Farm.

3 Feb	1689 Flt	Spitfire VB	BL848		Training

1945   W/O J N Willoughby   inj T/o 1020 Holme-on-Spalding Moor for fighter
                                     affiliation. Landed 1035, at high speed, touching
down at least six hundred yards along the main runway at Elvington. Unable to
stop in the length of runway remaining, the Spitfire ran onto soft ground and
when the pilot stamped on the brakes, it flipped over. W/O Willoughby sustained
slight concussion but, after local treatment, he was returned to his unit.

10 Apr	1689 Flt	Spitfire VB	EN796		Training

1945   F/O J Charlesworth   T/o 0939 Holme-on-Spalding Moor for fighter
                                     affiliation duties. Landed 0954 at Pocklington,
only to be damaged beyond repair as a result of the undercarriage giving way.

No. 1690 Bomber (Defence) Training Flight

Formed from the remnants of No. 1485 (Bombing) Gunnery Flight, at Syerston, on 15 February 1944, "1690" maintained detachments at most of No. 5 Group's operational airfields. In mid-September 1944, the headquarters moved to Scampton but almost immediately transferred to Metheringham before, on 4 June 1945, returning to its original home of Syerston, where it disbanded on 12 October 1945. Equipped with Spitfire IIs (which it operated without loss) and Hurricanes, "1690" employed a variety of support aircraft, ranging in diversity between a Tiger Moth and a Wellington.

11 Sep	1690 Flt	Hurricane IIC	LF382	Training

11 Sep   **1690 Flt**   **Hurricane IIC**   **LF382**   **Training**
1944   F/S H W E Ramsay   +   T/o 1520 Fiskerton with the intention of carrying out a training sortie with a Lancaster. However, on arriving in the practice area, F/S Ramsay sighted a Master trainer, which seemed reluctant to depart. Thus, at 1550, the Hurricane dived towards the Master in, what is officially described as "a mock attack", but, tragically, a collision occurred and both aircraft spun in at Carleton-le-Moorland, 9 miles south-south-west of Lincoln. F/S Ramsay, who had enlisted on 24 August 1937 as an aircraft apprentice, was cremated in Bristol (Arnos Vale) Crematorium. It is reported that he managed to extract himself from the cockpit of his doomed fighter, but with insufficient height left for his parachute to fully deploy.

17 SFTS   **Master II**   **W9033**   **Training**
Lt S T Koroglu   inj   T/o Cranwell for solo flying by its Turkish Air Force student and destroyed in the circumstances described above. Lt Koroglu managed to bale out, safely and was not too badly hurt.

15 Jan   **1690 Flt**   **Hurricane IIC**   **LF395**   **Training**
1945   F/S F P Bratley   T/o 1541 Metheringham for fighter affiliation. Landed 1631, ran for fifty yards quite normally, and then the port undercarriage leg folded.

10 Feb   **1690 Flt**   **Hurricane IIC**   **PZ744**   **Training**
1945   F/L I H Hanlon RNZAF   inj   T/o 1016 Metheringham for a fighter affiliation sortie with Lancaster III PB146 of 189 Squadron. Shortly before 1100, the Hurricane formated on the Lancaster to indicate the detail had been completed, radio contact not being possible due to unserviceable equipment. Believing that the Lancaster pilot was aware that the exercise was over, F/L Hanlon RNZAF passed beneath the bomber and had just started to bank to starboard when his aircraft was struck by the Lancaster which appears to have followed him in the turn. F/L Hanlon managed to parachute (he was later admitted to RAF Hospital Rauceby), leaving his fighter to crash at 1101 near the railway station at Seacroft, a village on the Lincolnshire coast immediately below Skegness. The bomber, meanwhile, landed safely but with the navigator fatally injured:

Sgt W T Gothard   +   He is buried in Surrey at Addlestone Burial Ground. His service number indicates he was called up in July 1939, under the terms of the Royal Air Force (Volunteer Reserve) Military Training Act.

11 Mar   **1690 Flt**   **Hurricane IIC**   **PZ740**   **Training**
1945   F/O S F Parlato DFC RNZAF   +   T/o 2043 Metheringham for a night fighter affiliation sortie, involving Lancaster I LM130 of 463 Squadron. Both aircraft were destroyed, circa 2100, following a midair collision, debris and bodies being recovered from the fields around Blankney, some 9 miles N of Sleaford, Lincolnshire. Posted to the Flight in October 1944, F/O Parlato RNZAF had previously flown with 139 Squadron and 627 Squadron, his award being gained with the latter and Gazetted on 19 September 1944. He rests in Cambridge City Cemetery. For details pertaining to the Lancaster's crew, please refer to Bomber Command Losses, Volume 6, page 124.

19 Jun   **1690 Flt**   **Hurricane IIC**   **LF374**   **Training**
1945   F/O F H A Watts   T/o 0010 Syerston for a fighter affiliation detail, at night. Forced-landed 0055, just short of the runway after the engine failed at 4,500 feet.

9 Aug   **1690 Flt**   **Hurricane IIC**   **LF161**   **Training**
1945   F/O J A Sanders DFC & Bar   inj   T/o 0115 Syerston for a night exercise, during which the weather deteriorated. On return to base, F/O Sanders landed at 0226 but well down the runway and upon entering the overshoot area and encountering uneven ground, the Hurricane turned over. It is not thought that F/O Sanders was badly hurt, his injuries being attended to in station sick quarters. At the time of his accident, he had logged 688 hours of solo flying, 134 of these on type. He had proven to be a very resolute heavy bomber pilot as the footnote, heading the next page, will show.

Note. As remarked upon in the last summary, F/O Sanders had shown great re-
solution and devotion to duty during two tours of bombing operations. His
Distinguished Flying Cross, an immediate award, had been won with 49 Squadron
and the citation, published in the London Gazette on 25 April 1944, reads:
   "In February 1944, the officer piloted an aircraft detailed to attack Augs-
burg. When approaching the target the aircraft was attacked by a fighter and
sustained severe damage. Large holes were torn in the fuselage, while the
starboard rudder and elevator were almost shot away. The aircraft dived
steeply out of control. At this stage, the rear gunner reported that the
bomber was on fire near his turret. Nevertheless, Pilot Officer Sanders,
with the assistance of the flight engineer, managed to regain control. Meanwhile, other members of the crew fought the fire and although bullets were
exploding in the fuselage they succeeded in putting out the flames. The
inter-communication system was now out of action as the wiring had been burned
through. The rear gunner lay unconscious through lack of oxygen. In spite of
these trying circumstances perfect discipline prevailed. Course was set for
home and, displaying great skill, Pilot Officer Sanders, succeeded in flying
the badly damaged aircraft to base. He displayed courage, coolness and determination of a high order". A second tour of operations followed, this time
with 617 Squadron and the Fifth Supplement to The London Gazette on 1 December
1944, reports as follows "In October 1944, this officer piloted one of a formation of aircraft detailed to bomb the sluice gates of the Kembs Barrage. In
the face of much light anti-aircraft fire, Flying Officer Sanders pressed home
his attack with great determination. His heavy bomb fell very close to the required position. This officer has completed many sorties since being awarded
the Distinguished Flying Cross and has displayed the highest standard of skill
and captaincy."

No. 1691 (Bombing) (Gunnery) Flight

In certain respects, the duties of 1691 (Bombing) (Gunnery) Flight were not dissimilar to
those of the Bomber (Defence) Training Flights that have just been summarised. Formed on
1 August 1943, at Dalton, the majority of its personnel were drawn from No. 6 (RCAF) Group
units and during its relatively brief existence was equipped with Martinet and Oxford aircraft, the former being used to assist in gunnery training and the latter to aid bombing
practice. For reasons best known to the authorities, it was decided to disband "1691" on
15 February 1944, only to establish a new flight with the number plate "1695" in its place,
and with a slightly amended title.

3 Dec	1691 Flt	Martinet I	MS554	Meteorological
1943	F/S J A C Kemmett	+	T/o Dalton for a weather reconnaissance, failing	
	LAC A T Barnson RCAF	+	to return at its appointed time. Subsequently,	

the burnt remains of the Martinet, and its crew,
were found on 18 December in the bleak hills around Askrigg, Yorkshire. Both
airmen were buried privately; F/S Kemmett at Gloucester (Coney Hill) Cemetery
and LAC Barnson RCAF at Harrow Cemetery in Middlesex. Presumably, the arrangements for his funeral were carried out by family relatives.

No. 1692 (Radio Development) Flight
No. 1692 (Bomber Support Training) Flight

Initially formed at Drem in early July 1943, "1692" came into prominence within Bomber
Command when its headquarters settled at Little Snoring on 10 December 1943, and came
under the authority of No. 100 (Bomber Support) Group. Principally devoted to training
Mosquito crews in "Serrate", the Flight operated a wide variety of types, ranging from
single-engined Defiants and Hurricanes through to twin-engined Ansons, Oxfords, Beaufighters, Mosquitoes and Wellingtons. On 21 May 1944, "1692" moved to Great Massingham
and disbanded here on 16 June 1945.

31 Mar	1692 Flt	Beaufighter VI	X8147	Training
1944	F/O A B A Smith		T/o 1620 Little Snoring for Airborne Inter-	

ception training but swung out of control and
after crashing through a hedge, the aircraft caught fire and was destroyed.
F/O Smith, an experienced Beaufighter pilot with nearly two hundred hours on
type, escaped relatively unscathed.

21 Jul	1692 Flt	Beaufighter VI	EL156	Training

21 Jul 1944 | **1692 Flt** | **Beaufighter VI EL156** | **Training**

F/L J C Fletcher   inj   T/o 1000 Great Massingham but as the fighter
F/L L J S Spicer   inj   accelerated one of its engines began to splutter
and F/L Fletcher aborted the sortie. He could
not, however, prevent his aircraft from crashing out of control and he was
quite badly hurt as a consequence. Both officers were treated in station sick
quarters, F/L Fletcher latter being transferred to RAF Hospital Ely.

23 Nov 1944 | **1692 Flt** | **Mosquito II DD736** | **Air Test**

F/O C J Preece RCAF   +   T/o 1435 Great Massingham and reported to have
F/O F H Ruffle DFC   +   spun out of cloud and crashed 1520 near King's
Lynn, Norfolk (the official map reference is
quoted as 65/104361). From Hardisty in Alberta, F/O Preece RCAF was probably
claimed by his United Kingdom relatives as he lies in Bedfordshire at Clapham
(St. Thomas of Canterbury) Churchyard. His navigator, F/O Ruffle, was laid to
rest in High Hurstwood (Holy Trinity) Churchyard, Buxted. His DFC, gained
during service with 515 Squadron, was Gazetted on 1 December 1944.

29 Nov 1944 | **1692 Flt** | **Mosquito II DZ265** | **Training**

F/L Stathes   T/o 1010 Great Massingham for local flying
practice. Landed 1025, whereupon the under-
carriage collapsed, this being brought about by seizure of the hydraulic pump
on the port engine, which had prevented the unit from locking.

13 Dec 1944 | **1692 Flt** | **Oxford II V3535** | **Training**

S/L M W O'Brien DFC   inj   T/o 1435 Great Massingham and set forth on a
southerly heading. At 1540, S/L O'Brien
tried to land at Croydon Airport, having encountered failing visibility.
Unfortunately, he overshot his approach but while trying to go round again,
he saw some houses looming into view through the fog. Realising that he had
insufficient height and that a collision was imminent, he cut the throttles
and forced-landed. Seconds later, the Oxford lay, inverted, having crashed
through a fence and run up against a three to four foot high earth bank. A
survivor of a tour of operations with 192 Squadron (his DFC had been published
on 13 October 1944), S/L O'Brien escaped with minor injuries.

13 Mar 1945 | **1692 Flt** | **Mosquito IV PZ231** | **Training**

Sgt T Day   T/o 1000 Great Massingham but lost power and in
order to stop the Mosquito within the confines
of the airfield, Sgt Day raised the undercarriage. No injuries reported.

19 Apr 1945 | **1692 Flt** | **Mosquito IV HR216** | **Training**

F/O T W Jasper   +   T/o 0950 Great Massingham for air-to-air firing
practice. Shortly before 1035, the Mosquito was
sighted in a steep dive from which it failed to recover before breaking apart
and crashing near Walpole St. Andrew, 8 miles WSW from King's Lynn, Norfolk.
F/O Jasper of Wallington in Surrey was buried in Cambridge City Cemetery.

25 May 1945 | **1692 Flt** | **Mosquito XIX MM634** | **Training**

W/O Smythe   T/o 1515 Great Massingham but when the air speed
indicator failed to give a reading, W/O Smythe
throttled back and tried to stop his aircraft on the runway. In this he was unsuccessful and the Mosquito was wrecked on reaching the overshoot area.

No. 1694 (Target Towing) Flight
No. 1694 Bomber (Defence) Training Flight

Formed within No. 100 Group, at West Raynham, on 24 January 1944, "1694" was redesignated
to its second title on 1 November 1944, by which time it was based at Great Massingham.
Initially equipped with Martinets, the change of rôle necessitated the issue of half-a-
dozen Spitfire Vs. Disbanded on 30 July 1945.

22 Jan 1945 | **1694 Flt** | **Martinet I NR418** | **Meteorological**

W/O T Appleby   inj   T/o 1105 Great Massingham only to run into a snow
storm. Turned back, lost height and at 1115 hit
Mosquito XIX MM644 belonging to 169 Squadron a glancing blow before crashing onto
a radar hut, the casualties from this building being reported on the next page.

Cpl C R Mason RCAF	+	1692 Flight, of Oakville, Ontario, buried in Southall Cemetery, Middlesex.
LAC H L Brend RCAF	inj	1692 Flight, treated in station sick quarters.
Cpl J Looker	+	1694 Flight, buried in Alva Cemetery, Clackman.
Cpl H Parkinson	inj	1694 Flight, treated in station sick quarters.
LAC E W Cannings	inj	1694 Flight, treated in station sick quarters.
LAC L D Lewis	inj	1694 Flight, treated in station sick quarters.
ACW2 P J Carey WAAF	inj	1684 Flight, treated in station sick quarters.

Cpl Mason RCAF, Cpl Parkinson, LAC Brend RCAF and LAC Lewis are reported as radar mechanics, Cpl Looker is identified as a wireless operator, while LAC Cannings and ACW2 Carey are described as a mechanic assistant and aircraft hand general duties respectively. The Mosquito was not too badly damaged and following repairs, carried out locally, it was returned to service with 169 Squadron on 3 March 1945.

No. 1695 (Bomber) Target Towing Flight

It will be recalled that "1695" had its origins in 1691 (Bombing) (Gunnery) Flight (see page 216). The Flight, equipped initially with Martinets, but gaining Hurricanes and Spitfires as the year progressed, remained at Dalton in No. 6 (RCAF) Group until transferring its headquarters to Dishforth on 23 April 1945. Disbanded 28 July 1945.

3 Feb	1695 Flt	Spitfire VB	EP558	Training
1945	S/L M S Strange RCAF		T/o 1010 Dalton for the pilot's first solo on	

type. Landed twenty minutes later but swerved violently to starboard and as the fighter left the runway, it flipped onto its back. S/L Strange RCAF appears to have emerged from the wreck, unharmed.

9 Feb	1695 Flt	Hurricane IIC	LF535	Air Test
1945	F/L A B Summer RCAF	+	T/o 1520 Dalton for a night flying test. Turned	

finals at 300 feet but lost control and spun in at 1543, crashing at Eldmire Hill Farm on the SE side of the airfield. Rather surprisingly, F/L Summer RCAF was taken to Chester (Blacon) Cemetery and not to Harrogate (Stonefall) Cemetery as might have been expected. He was an experienced pilot with over 400 hours of Hurricane flying in his log book, forty of these at night.

5 May	1695 Flt	Spitfire VB	AD571	Air Test
1945	F/O W Kasper RCAF		T/o 0955 Dishforth. Lost power, while nearing	

the runway, and crash-landed 1035 in the under-shoot area, both oleos collapsing as the port tyre blew out on impact.

No. 1699 (Fortress) Training Flight

Formed on 24 April 1944, at Sculthorpe and equipped with three Fortresses, the Flight, as its titles implies, was responsible for training replacement crews, destined to serve with 214 Squadron. On 16 May 1944, the headquarters relocated to Oulton where, in the August, three Liberators were added and the Flight's title was amended to read (Training) Conversion Unit. Throughout its life, "1699" was assigned to No. 100 Group and although no details have been recorded of its disbandment, it can be assumed to be sometime after, or during May 1945.

12 Sep	1699 Flt	Fortress II	SR380	Training
1944	F/O Stainier		T/o 2050 Oulton for a night cross-country.	
	Sgt W Walsh	inj	Returned to base early, having experienced excessive airframe vibration (this ceased as	

the wheels were lowered in readiness for landing), and on touch down at 2240, the Fortress swung and tipped onto its nose. Sgt Walsh, an air gunner, was slightly hurt and was admitted to station sick quarters.

12 May	1699 Flt	Fortress II	SR386	Training
1945	F/O Theaker		T/o Oulton for night training during which the crew broke cloud, while approaching Sculthorpe,	

and clipped a tree. Diverted to Great Massingham, where it crash-landed at 0015, the pilot having being temporarily "blinded" by a flare fired from Flying Control.

Section 6

Ferry Training Units

In total, four of the thirteen Ferry Training Units established between late September 1942 and March 1944, have connections with Bomber Command and, thus, are eligible for inclusion in this volume.

That said, however, the principal task of these units had little relevance in the day to day activities of the Command and their casualties can only be regarded as being on the periphery of the Command's responsibilities. Of the four, only three lost aircraft and in view of these small numbers, I have decided to summarise them in chronological order, with a footnote showing additional data that may be of interest; bases, types, and disbandment details.

28 May 1943	307 FTU	Boston III	AL750		Training
	F/S H E Tyas		+		T/o Finmere for a cross-country exercise. Lost
	Sgt E F J Oliver		+		power from one engine and F/S Tyas attempted to
	F/S M N Williams		inj		land at Talbenny airfield but something went
	F/S G J Rankmore RCAF		+		tragically wrong and the Boston spun and came

down at 1345 near Little Haven, a small coastal village on the Pembrokeshire coast, 6 miles WSW from Haverfordwest. F/S Williams was dreadfully injured and he died the following day while undergoing treatment in the Pembroke County Hospital. F/S Rankmore RCAF was buried in Haverfordwest (City Road) Cemetery, while his three companions were claimed by their relatives.

Note. Formed at Bicester on 24 December 1942, in No. 92 Group, "307" was tasked to train ferry crews and as such it was equipped, initially, with Blenheims. On 18 February 1943, the headquarters was relocated at Finmere, where Bostons and Havocs supplemented the Blenheims. On 1 May 1943, the unit was transferred to Turweston, but returned eighteen days later to Finmere where, on 1 June 1943, the unit was given up to No. 70 Group.

7 Jul 1943	310 FTU	Wellington X	LN265		Training
	Sgt D C Joel		+		T/o Harwell for a fuel consumption test, the
	Sgt J Driver		+		crew being assigned from 15 Operational Training
	Sgt W R Wooding		+		Unit. Crashed at approximately 1105 at Duston on
	Sgt C Elvidge		+		the western outskirts of Northampton. Sgt Joel,
	Sgt O Holey		+		known to his family and friends as "Bill", was

buried in Oxford (Botley) Cemetery, as was thirty-four year old Sgt Wooding, while the others were laid to rest in their home towns. Sgt Wooding's younger brother, Sgt Alan Asquith Wooding, had been posted missing in action on 7 December 1940, while serving with 214 Squadron (see Bomber Command Losses, Volume 1, page 137).

Note. The origins of "310" can be traced to 1443 (Ferry Training) Flight (see page 197) and similar to its forebearer, "310" lost a number of aircraft whilst in transit to the Middle East, these losses coming outside the parameters of this volume. Basically, an all Wellington unit, an Anson or two were added, probably in a supporting rôle. Disbanded on 17 December 1943.

18 Dec 1943	311 FTU	Wellington III	BK132		Training
	F/S N C Ross RAAF		+		T/o Moreton-in-Marsh for a cross-country detail
	Sgt E R Phillips		+		which ended at 1408, when the bomber dived
	Sgt E J W Semmens RAAF		+		into the ground at Atcham, 3 miles SE from
	Sgt K R Halliday		+		Shrewsbury. The two Australians were taken to
	Sgt D H Wright		+		Chester (Blacon) Cemetery, the others being

laid to rest by private arrangements.

Note. Formed at Moreton-in-Marsh from 1446 (Ferry Training) Flight (see page 199), "311" was responsible for ferrying Wellingtons out to the Middle East, a task that it carried out until disbanded on 1 May 1944. In addition to the large numbers of Wellingtons issued, Anson and Oxfords assisted the training.

24 Jan **311 FTU** **Wellington X** **JA473** **Training**
1944   F/S E J Waller RNZAF   T/o 1025 Gaydon but swung to starboard, this
being corrected by manipulating the throttles.
Then, having travelled about six hundred yards, it swerved off to the right and
before F/S Waller RNZAF could remedy the situation, the Wellington crashed into
the station's bomb dump. No one was hurt, and this fortunate escape, by the
crew, from serious injury is attributed to the pilot's skill in managing to
partially lift the starboard wing and by doing so, lessen the impact.

Note. Gaydon had been used as a satellite by 312 Ferry Training Unit (the
fourth of the Ferry Training Units that had been assigned to Bomber Command),
and I think it likely that F/S Waller RNZAF had been tasked to collect the
Wellington for transfer to Moreton-in-Marsh, though records suggest "312" had
been reduced to a "number plate" basis with effect from 26 July 1943. And it
is by no means certain that the unit was issued with aircraft.

Section 7

Group Communications/Training Flights

This section is concerned with the handful of losses sustained by the myriad of minor units that operated under the protection of their parent Group, thus casualties from the communications flights, Group Servicing Unit (of which there was but one), target towing flights and training flights will now be reported in the order outlined.

The functions of these units will be readily apparent and, if the need arises, suitable footnotes will be appended.

Apart from the Group Servicing Unit, whose establishment and disbandment is not known, most (less the communications flights) were redesignated as hostilities progressed, even though their basic task remained the same.

25 Jul 1945	**BCComFlt** F/O Highton	**Anson I**	**MG553**	**Communications**

T/o 1205 from an unrecorded airfield, calling at various places before landing, 1830, at Buckeburg (B.151) in Germany. On touch down, the starboard tyre burst causing the Anson to swing and lose its undercarriage. It is believed that the tyre had been damaged whilst taxying at B.56 (Evere, Belgium).

23 Nov 1945	**BCComFlt** W/C R D Speare DSO DFC & Bar +	**Anson I**	**NL185**	**Communications**

T/o 1050 from an unrecorded airfield. At approximately 1145, the Anson struck The Cloughs in the southern part of the High Peak area of Derbyshire, near Edale. It was twenty-four hours before the wreckage of the aircraft was located and the body of the pilot was recovered by a search team sent out from the Royal Air Force station at Harpur Hill. In the official report, it is stated that W/C Speare had drifted some seventy degrees off his intended track and with no radio aids fitted to the Anson, it is assumed he descended through the clouds, in order to establish his position, believing he was over the east coast. The report quotes the crash site as map reference 37/558073. This much decorated officer (he had flown Lancasters with 460 Squadron) is buried in Bournemouth North Cemetery.

19 Jul 1942	**4 GComFlt** G/C J Bradbury	**B A Eagle II**	**HM506**	**Communications**

T/o 1150 Linton-on-Ouse but on landing, 1230 at Marston Moor, swung sharply to port. G/C Bradbury applied full opposite rudder and when this seemed to have little effect, he braked. Moments later, the undercarriage collapsed.

Note. In 1962, Peter W Moss produced a slim four volume series of registers, for Air Britain, devoted to the histories of British and Foreign aircraft impressed from the civil registers into military service. Thus, it is noted that the Eagle, described above, originally carried the civilian markings, G-AEGO, and was impressed on 6 August 1941, for use by 24 Squadron. In mid-November 1941, it was placed in storage at Kemble, but was released to Northolt in March 1942 and thence, twenty-four hours later, to Leeming arriving here on the 14th.
Three days later, the Eagle was flown over to Marston Moor for use by No. 4 Group. It then seems to have had a quite chequered career; on 3 May it landed, wheels up, at Clifton and following repairs was damaged for a second time when the wheels folded as it was being pushed into a hangar, at Marston Moor, on 17 June. Then came the incident, summarised above, to which the compiler added, "Thoroughly peeved by these antics, No. 4 Group had HM506 heaved into No. 60 Maintenance Unit (Shipton) where it was struck off charge on 27 July 1942. Total flying hours; 257.10.

31 Jul 1942	**4 GComFlt** S/L D A Willis	**Tiger Moth II**	**T7685**	**Communications**

T/o 0950 Middleton St. George to return to No. 4 Group headquarters. Became lost in haze and at 1030, or thereabouts, forced-landed a mile W of Shipton, Yorkshire. On touch down, the Tiger's port wing made contact with a hedge, causing the aircraft to slew sideways into a field.

24 Aug　**4 GComFlt**　　　**Tiger Moth II**　**DE405**　　　　　　　　　**Unknown**
1942　　　　　　　　　　　　　　　Reported as damaged beyond repair on this date.
The movement card shows that this Tiger Moth was delivered to 46 Maintenance Unit
at Lossiemouth on 1 April 1942, and taken on charge by the Group's communications
flight on 15 July. Its flying hours have not been recorded.

27 Dec　**3 ComFlt**　　　　　　**Mentor I**　**L4409**　　　　　　**Communications**
1942　　S/L I P Grant DFC AFC　　inj　T/o Haldon and set course for Exning, only to
　　　　S/O O Turnbull WAAF　　　inj　encounter adverse weather. At roughly 1240, the
　　　　　　　　　　　　　　　　　　　Mentor crash-landed at map reference 112/618838.
Both persons were badly injured; S/L Grant sustained a puncture to the base of
his skull, while Octavie Turnbull fractured her left tibia and fibula, and together they were admitted to RAF Hospital Wroughton. S/L Grant had gained his
Distinguished Flying Cross with 115 Squadron, Gazetted 22 September 1942, and
he also holds the distinction of participating in Bomber Command's first bombing
attack of the war, a strike by Wellingtons drawn from 9 Squadron and 149 Squadron
on enemy shipping at Brunsbüttel (see Bomber Command Losses, Volume 1, pages 11
12 and 14) on 4 September 1939.

19 Oct　**6 GComFlt**　　　　　**B A Eagle**　**DP847**　　　　　　　　**Air Test**
1943　　F/L T M Kneale RCAF　　　　　T/o Linton-on-Ouse. Landed at 1510, and damaged
　　　　　　　　　　　　　　　　　　beyond repair as a consequence of the wheels
folding. Soon after this incident, F/L Kneale was promoted to squadron leader
and joined 426 Squadron. Sadly, on 16 December 1943, he was killed, along with
most of his crew, when his Lancaster crashed whilst returning from Berlin. He
is buried Harrogate (Stonefall) Cemetery.

Note. Peter W Moss notes that this Eagle was impressed on 14 March 1941, from
the Marquess of Donegal (ex-G-ADVT) and served for most of the next twelve months
at White Waltham. It then spent a lengthy period, either in storage or undergoing repairs, before being released to No. 6 Group on 9 December 1942.

20 Sep　**4 GComFlt**　　　　　**Oxford II**　**P1070**　　　　　　　　**Unknown**
1944　　　　　　　　　　　　　　　Reported as crashed on this date, but with no
　　　　　　　　　　　　　　　　　supporting evidence.

18 Mar　**4 GComFlt**　　　**Leopard Moth**　**AX862**　　　　　　　　**Air Test**
1945　　W/C J M Viney DFC　　　　　　T/o 1330 Full Sutton. Landed 1350, at Carnaby
　　　　　　　　　　　　　　　　　　but after running for about fifty yards, the
port oleo collapsed. At the time of this mishap, W/C Viney had logged 1,970
hours of solo flying, but his Leopard Moth experience was limited to a single
hour. He was, however, an outstanding bomber pilot, gaining his award with
158 Squadron (Gazetted 9 July 1943) and some of his exploits are recorded in
my book, "In Brave Company", which traces the history of "158" between 1918
and 1945.

Note. Impressed on 15 June 1940, and flew for nearly a year in its civil
markings of G-ALCW. Accepted by the Group's communications flight on 20
June 1942, and appears to have a trouble free life until the accident reported above.

13 Nov　**91 GSU**　　　　　**Wellington X**　**HE750**　　　　　　　　**Ground**
1944　　　　　　　　　　　　　　　At approximately 1000, an airman working in
one of the hangars at Gamston accidentally slipped from some metal steps and
a spark ignited some petrol that had dripped onto the concrete. Although he
was able to make good his escape, the fire services were unable to save the
Wellington. As has been noted on the previous page, the origins and eventual
disbandment of 91 Group Servicing Unit is unknown.

26 Feb　**3 GTTFlt**　　　　　　**Battle I**　**P2260**　　　　　　　　**Training**
1940　　Sgt T Owens　　　　　　　+　T/o Mildenhall for a target towing detail.
　　　　AC2 W Mahon　　　　　　　+　Lost control in cloud, dived and crashed at
　　　　　　　　　　　　　　　　　　Gosberton, 5 miles N of Spalding, Lincoln-
shire. Sgt Owens was taken back to Wales and laid to rest at Merthyr Tydfil
(Aberfan Bryntaf) Cemetery, while eighteen year old AC2 Mahon is buried in
Moston (St. Joseph's) Roman Catholic Cemetery. Both airmen are recorded in
the Commonwealth War Graves Commission registers as belonging to 98 Squadron.

17 Sep	5 GTTFlt	Battle I L5715	Training

17 Sep **5 GTTFlt** **Battle I L5715**   **Training**
1940   Sgt J F Douglas   T/o Driffield for a target towing sortie.
  Lost power and ditched 1515, a mile to the
north of Hornsea on the Yorkshire coast. Subsequently, the wreck was salvaged
and, following basic attention, was released to No. 6 School of Technical
Training at Hednesford with the serial 2260M applied. Sgt Douglas was a prewar
volunteer reserve pilot who had gained his wings, at Prestwick, on 7 February
1940. In total, he had logged 413 solo flying hours, seven of these on Battles.

13 Oct **3 GTTFlt** **Battle I L5214**   **Training**
1940   P/O J Wizniewski PAF   T/o Marham for a target towing duty. Forced-
  landed 1535 some 3 miles from East Winch, itself
five miles ESE from King's Lynn, Norfolk. In the official report, it is stated
that P/O Wizniewski PAF experienced engine trouble and as he closed the throttle
he felt a severe vibration run through the airframe. At this point he should
have tried to apply power, but instead he retarded the throttle even further.
His error, noted as due to lack of experience, was further compounded by his
failure to pump down the flaps and on touch down his airspeed was too high for
the brakes to be effective.

21 Nov **3 GTrgFlt** **Wellington IC T2873**   **Unknown**
1940   Reported as missing on a ferry flight to Malta
  but nothing found to support this.

Note. The task assigned to No. 3 Group Training Flight was to reinforce the
Middle East Wellington squadrons with trained crews. Officially, the Flight
did not form (at Stradishall) until 1 February 1941, but from remarks on the
aircraft's movement card, there is little doubt that this Wellington was
issued to Stradishall, on 29 October 1940, for onward movement to the Middle
East theatre. Disbanded, and absorbed into 1483 (Target Towing) Flight on
7 February 1942 (see page 202).

6- 7 Apr **3 GTrgFlt** **Wellington IC N2818**   **Ferry**
1941   P/O G T Kimberley RNZAF + T/o Stradishall and set course for Malta. Lost
  Sgt K R Allen + way, in bad weather, and crashed 0300 some 5 km
  Sgt H L Williams + east of Ras el Akba and 4 km south from Ain Amora
  Sgt R W Fairlamb + in Algeria. All are buried in Bone War Cemetery,
  Sgt R C McCracken + Annaba.
  Sgt W A Watts RNZAF +

Note. This loss, and the three that follow, come within that "grey" area of
what should be included in this volume. In the case of the ferry flights,
the accident cards have been clearly annotated with remarks showing them to
be outside of the parameters set for this book, but the above, and the next
three losses, show the controlling command as bomber.

9 Apr **3 GTrgFlt** **Wellington IC W5677**   **Ferry**
1941   F/L R L Cox pow T/o Stradishall and, presumably, set course
  W/O D C B Jenkins RNZAF pow for Malta. No card has been raised in respect
  Sgt L Hudson pow of its loss, but the names of the crew, and
  Sgt J A Collett pow their very distinguished passenger, appear in
  W/O R J A Blackstock RNZAF pow records raised for 9 April 1941 and, apart from
  Maj Gen A Carton de Wiart pow Sgt Collett, four are identified in the Allied
   VC CB CMG DSO Air Forces prisoner of war file. Maj Gen (later
  Lt Gen) Carton de Wiart was of Belgian descent,
but had served with great distinction throughout the First World War, in which
he was wounded eight times, losing an eye and his left hand. He gained his DSO
as a captain in the 4th Dragoon Guards (Royal Irish), this being Gazetted on
15 May 1915. By the summer of the following year, he had been given command
of the 8th Battalion, The Gloucestershire Regiment, and in a series of desperate engagements on 2-3 July around La Boiselle in France, he won the Victoria
Cross, the opening line of the citation reading, "his dauntless courage and inspiration averted what could have been a serious reverse." It seems that he was
the sole senior officer left capable of taking command of the situation, three
other battalion commanders being severely wounded. On 21 April 1917, the
Supplement to the London Gazette carries the entry for awards bestowed on
officers by His Majesty King Of The Belgians, and in the case of Maj Adrian
Carton de Wiart VC DSO, His Majesty conferred the Ordre de la Couronne (Officier).
Credit: Victoria Cross Reference created by Mike Chapman and various Gazettes.

Note. Further to my reference, on the last line of the previous page, regarding various London Gazette entries, that for 8 April 1941 (and the day before he was reported missing) bears an entry stating the King had granted unrestricted permission for Maj Gen Carton de Wiart to wear the Krzyz Walecznych, conferred by the Polish Government in recognition of (his) distinguished services in Poland.

25 Apr 1941	3 GTrgFlt	Wellington IC	T2726		Ferry

F/L E F Nind

T/o St. Eval and set course for Gibraltar. Due to an error in the decoding of wireless messages, transmitted from Gibraltar, a bearing was misinterpreted as a course and, consequently, the Wellington turned away from its intended destination. When this error was discovered, the bomber was low on fuel and before it could reach the airfield at North Front, F/L Nind was obliged to ditch, injuring some of the crew. Later in the war, this officer flew with 97 Squadron, gaining a Distinguished Flying Cross, which was Gazetted on 15 October 1943.

27 Apr 1941	3 GTrgFlt	Wellington IC	W5652		Ferry

S/L G F Rodney   int
F/O E M Child-Villiers   int
Sgt C S Hunt   int
Sgt G H Burge   int
Sgt H E Harritey   int
Sgt N O Horrocks   int

T/o St. Eval and set forth across the Western Approaches and over the Bay of Biscay, making for Gibraltar. Crash-landed 0640 near Formentera in the Spanish Islas Baleares, S of Ibiza, and destroyed by its crew. Tragically, Sgt Hunt committed suicide on 30 April 1941, and he is buried in Palma Municipal Cemetery. The rest were held in Spain for just over a year, before being released into British custody at Gibraltar. S/L Rodney and F/L Child-Villiers returned to the United Kingdom on 8 May 1942, followed five days later by the three surviving non-commissioned officers.

30 Jun 1941	3 GTrgFlt	Wellington IC	R1321		Training

Sgt E A Nutt

T/o 1715 Langham becoming airborne after the pilot had corrected a severe swing. However, before he could commence climbing, the Wellington hit a fence and crashed, a fire breaking out soon afterwards. In retrospect, it was considered he should have stopped his take off run as he had sufficient runway length remaining in which to stop. On 25 May 1943, the London Gazette carried notification of his commission, seniority being backdated to 27 February 1943. Sadly, he was mortally injured on 23 September 1943, when his 1482 Flight Martinet I HP355 crashed at West Raynham during a mock attack on the airfield's Bofors guns. He is buried in Sunderland (Ryehope Road) Cemetery.

5 Jan 1942	5 GTrgFlt	Lysander TT	V9865		Training

Sgt J E Richards

T/o Swanton Morley for a target towing sortie. Encountered inclement weather, while returning to base, and written off in an emergency landing, at 1330, just to the NE of South Kyme, 10 miles WNW from Boston, Lincolnshire, the Lysander finishing up in a canal. Posted to 61 Squadron, Sgt Richards was killed during operations to Nürnberg on 28-29 August 1942 (see Bomber Command Losses, Volume 3, page 197).

6 Jan 1942	3 GTrgFlt	Wellington IC	L7863 B		Training

F/S F T Miniken   +
AC1 T Menzies   +
Sgt R A Butcher   +
Sgt M T Coon   inj
Sgt G G Cornes   +
Sgt R H W Lawrence   inj
Sgt J P Williams   +
Sgt A J Browne   +
Sgt A D Matthews   +
Sgt H Wolstenholme   +

T/o 1000 Newmarket for a gunnery detail, but on climb out the port engine cut and the Wellington crashed onto a railway embankment, from where it skidded into a building and burst into flames. Of those who died, Sgt Browne was buried in Newmarket Cemetery, while the others were taken to their home towns. The crew composition was made up from a pilot, flight mechanic (engines) five wireless operators and three air gunners.

Section 8

Miscellaneous Units

The penultimate part of this volume outlines the work carried out by a series of specialist establishments that were formed in the Command, mainly quite late on in the war and at a time when the technical developments of waging a sustained bombing campaign were becoming more complex.

Similar to my method of describing the functions of the myriad of flights that assisted Bomber Command, the task of each formation is explained, along with details pertaining to bases, equipment, etc, followed by the relevant summaries. As it will be seen, many of those identified were of senior rank.

Bomber Command Instructor's School

The Bomber Command Instructor's School, to give the unit its full title, was formed within No. 93 Group, at Finningley, on 5 December 1944. Staffed by very experienced instructors, the aim of the school was to ensure uniformity of instruction throughout the Command's many training establishments, and particularly in the area of the operational training units and heavy conversion units. For this important task, no less than twenty-two Wellingtons were issued, along with Halifaxes, Stirlings and Lancasters. On 14 February 1945, control was placed in the hands of No. 91 Group and, soon afterwards, the unit came under the umbrella of No. 7 Group, but returned to No. 91 Group on 21 December 1945, following disbandment, on this date, of the latter. Since coming into being, the Bombing Analysis School had become a separate entity, carrying out its work at Bruntingthorpe, but after six months of independence, it returned to the fold of the school. Meanwhile, the Engine Control Development Unit at Westcott was absorbed into the school though this section remained attached to 11 Operational Training Unit, at Westcott and, eventually, disbanded at the same time as its parent unit (18 September 1945). On 22 January 1947, the school transferred its headquarters to Scampton where, on 15 June 1947, it was redesignated Bomber Command Instrument Rating and Examination Flight. During its service, the school used Worksop as a satellite. Additional to the main types, the school was issued with a wide range of supporting aircraft, which included fighters, such as Hurricanes and Spitfires, and trainers. It is also observed that Mosquito T.IIIs and Lincolns were taken on as main types, ahead of the unit being retitled.

21 Mar 1945	BCIS	Wellington X	HF514	Training

S/L V Hughes
F/L W D Ervine DFC
F/S A E Barford DFM

T/o 1017 Worksop to practice single-engined landings. The exercise had not long begun when the instructor decided to un-feather the motor, which happened to be the starboard. His actions were carried out at 500 feet, but, unfortunately, the Hercules refused to pick up and a forced-landing ensued at 1032, S/L Hughes reporting that he could not lower the flaps beyond thirty degrees of travel. F/L Ervine had flown a tour of operations with 9 Squadron, commencing with the opening raid in the Battle of Hamburg, 24-25 July 1943 and appears to have ended over Stuttgart on 20-21 February 1944, by which time he had at least twenty-six sorties in his log book. On 20 March 1944, he was posted to 5 Lancaster Finishing School, his DFC being Gazetted four days later. F/S Barford's spell of operational duty had ended quite recently, his DFM being gained with 15 Squadron, the details being published on 16 February 1945.

30 Mar 1945	BCIS	Lancaster III	ND808	Training

F/O G A Cooper
F/L R W Mathers DFC
F/S D W Cole   inj

T/o 2110 Finningley for night circuit training. Approached on three engines, landed at 2135 and swung to starboard, ending up, on fire, near the fuel dump. F/S Cole was treated for his injuries in station sick quarters. F/L Mathers had won his award, with 9 Squadron, the Supplement to the London Gazette of 15 September 1944, carrying the news.

8 Apr 1945	BCIS	**Wellington X**	LN585	**Training**

F/L G A Clark   +

F/O W G Craig DFC RAAF   +

F/O G Lofthouse DFC   inj

F/S B F Griggs   +

T/o 1545 Finningley to practice overshooting on one engine and while doing so (with the starboard motor feathered) crashed off a slow turn to the right and burst into flames, the time of the tragedy being reported as 1600. F/L Clark was cremated in Sheffield Crematorium, F/O Craig RAAF, who had married Olive Mary Craig of Darlington, was buried here in the West Cemetery, while F/S Griggs was taken to Plymouth (Weston Mill) Cemetery. F/O Lofthouse was treated at Doncaster Royal Infirmary. His DFC had been gained with 626 Squadron, the London Gazette of 19 January 1945, announcing the details. Earlier, on 13 October 1944, this same paper had published the award won by F/O Craig RAAF in the service of 431 Squadron, while the Australia Gazette repeated this announcement thirteen days later.

3 May 1945	BCIS	**Spitfire VB**	BM474	**Air Test**

F/L Saunderson RCAF

T/o 1410 Finningley to test the flaps, following routine servicing. Landed at 1500, touching down three-quarters of the way along the runway after a very tight approach. Almost immediately the fighter swung sharply and lost its undercarriage. F/L Saunderson was an experienced pilot with nearly 300 hours on type and 1,814 solo flying in total.

26 Jun 1945	BCIS	**Master II**	W9015	**Training**

W/O W K Bale

T/o 1130 Finningley tasked to tow a glider. The sortie lasted for ninety minutes, during which time a number of landings were made. Then, at around 1300, W/O Bale touched down on some rough ground and smashed the tail wheel structure. Although the damage caused was only slight, no repair work was forthcoming.

6 Jul 1945	BCIS	**Wellington X**	MF556	**Training**

F/L R Burr DFC

F/L D R Aldridge DFC

T/o 1400 Finningley to practice single-engined flying. Unable to get the starboard Hercules to restart, the crew forced-landed at 1430, in a field, between Moorends and Thorne, Yorkshire. Both pilots had flown tours with 44 Squadron, their awards being Gazetted, respectively, on 14 December and 10 September 1943. It is noted in the citation for F/L Aldridge that he put up a magnificent performance during the Peenemünde raid (17-18 August 1943) in getting his Lancaster home after it had been very severely shot about by an enemy night-fighter.

19 Dec 1945	BCIS	**Mosquito III**	RR315	**Training**

W/C R S C Wood

T/o 1505 Finningley for flying practice, on type. Landed at 1530, but swung badly and the stress on the undercarriage mountings caused both oleos to collapse.

22 Jul 1946	BCIS	**Lancaster I**	PP757 WB-B	**Training**

F/L B F Russell

F/O W T Cake

T/o 2145 Finningley for night circuit practice. Flew into the ground at 2320, during a three-engined approach, finishing up on the left-hand side of the runway. F/L Russell had logged in the region of 1,840 hours, solo, and nearly 350 of these had been at the controls of Lancasters.

23 Oct 1946	BCIS	**Lancaster I**	HK762 WB-F	**Training**

F/L D Roberts DFC

F/L A R S Smith DFC

T/o 1200 Finningley for dual instruction and to practice landings without the aid of flaps. While carrying out one such landing, the Lancaster ran off the runway and into a ditch, the consequence of which caused the starboard wheel to fold. F/L Roberts had completed a tour, flying Lancasters, with 630 Squadron, while F/L Smith had flown Halifaxes with 102 Squadron, their DFCs being announced in the London Gazette on 30 June and 13 October 1944 respectively.

Bomber Support Development Unit

This unit formed in No. 100 Group, on 17 April 1944, and took over the tasks previously flown by the Special (Radar) Development Unit. First based at Foulsham, the headquarters transferred to Swanton Morley on 23 December 1944, where it was redesignated Radio Warfare Establishment on 21 July 1945. Principally equipped with Mosquitoes of various Mks.

2 Jan	BSDU	**Mosquito NF.30** MM797	**Training**

2 Jan BSDU **Mosquito NF.30** MM797 **Training**
1945 F/L H E White DFC & 2 Bars T/o 1739 Swanton Morley only for the port
engine to cut, the consequence of which led
to a wheels up landing, in a field, at map reference 425292. F/L White was
a very experienced Mosquito pilot, having spent much of his operational service
on night-fighter and bomber support duties with 141 Squadron, his awards being
Gazetted on 24 September 1943, 14 April and 13 October 1944 respectively. At
the time of this mishap, he had logged 1,310 solo flying hours, 340 of these
at the controls of Mosquitoes of various Marks.

5 Jul BSDU **Oxford I** HN372 **Transit**
1945 F/L A E Callard DFC T/o 1815 Jagel intending to fly to Swanton
Morley with equipment collected from Schleswig
Holstein and Jagel. At approximately 2000, F/L Callard landed at Twente in
Holland but swung to starboard and ran into an old bomb crater that had not
been firmed down after filling. Consequently, the Oxford's port undercarriage
snapped, damaging the aircraft beyond repair. His award had been published in
the London Gazette on 19 December 1944, following service with 515 Squadron.

8 Jul BSDU **Mosquito VI** PZ178 **Trials**
1945 S/L C J Merryfull MBE RAAF + T/o 1004 Swanton Morley for a "Window" trial.
LAC F Grady + At 1018, debris from the Mosquito fell near the
Norfolk village of Docking, some 14 miles NE of
King's Lynn. S/L Merryfull RAAF, who had been attached from 199 Squadron, was
buried in Cambridge City Cemetery, his MBE being Gazetted on 1 January 1946.
His passenger, LAC Grady, was taken to St. Helens Cemetery in Lancashire. A
detailed report of the tragedy was subsequently published, in which it is reported that the port "Window" tank had detached, due to failure of its attachment beam. As the tank fell away, it is believed it struck the tailplane and
caused the Mosquito to dive out of control. Instinctively, it is thought, the
pilot pulled back on the control column imposing severe "g" forces on the starboard wing, which then broke off.

Bombing Development Unit

This unit first came into existence on 20 July 1942, forming from 1418 Gee Development
Flight in No. 3 Group at Gransden Lodge. Its initial equipment consisted of a Proctor
(used for communications), six Wellingtons, two Halifaxes and single examples of Stirling and Lancaster bombers. During 1943, its headquarters moved twice, first to Felt=
well in the April and then on 13 September to Newmarket. Here it assumed the rôle of
Development and Radar Training, reorganising on a two flight basis. On 25 February
1945, the unit returned to Feltwell but headed north to Lindholme in the October, disbanding here on 27 November 1945.

17–18 Jul BDU **Halifax III** MZ369 **Training**
1945 F/L S A Clark DFC RNZAF T/o 2105 Feltwell with a crew complement of
nine, tasked for radar training. On return
to base, after midnight, F/L Clark RNZAF elected to go round again but as he
advanced the throttles, the Halifax yawed thirty degrees to starboard and,
moments later, the wheels made contact with the ground. The undercarriage
was then raised and the throttles cut, and after sliding for two hundred-
and-fifty yards, the bomber came to a stop, up against a building roughly
a hundred yards beyond the airfield. F/L Clark RNZAF had flown a tour of
operations with 75 Squadron, the London Gazette of 15 August 1944, carrying
details of his award.

Central Bomber Establishment

Formed 25 September 1945, at Marham, in No. 3 Group, possibly absorbing part, or all, of
the unit described previously. Operated a wide variety of types, ranging from single-
engined Spitfires to multi-engined Mosquitoes and Lancasters. Various Marks of Meteor
jet fighters also passed through the establishment, while Austers, Proctors and Ansons
were employed for communications duties. Transferred to Lindholme on 14 April 1949, and
disbanded on 21 December of that same year.

26 Mar	CBE	Mosquito XVI	PF503	Training

1946   F/L G Bates DFC   T/o 1420 Marham for familiarisation on type. Landed ten minutes later, but swung onto some rough ground, whereupon the undercarriage collapsed. F/L Bates had flown Lancasters on bombing operations with 218 Squadron, his DFC being promulgated on 22 May 1945. He had accumulated 1,132 solo flying hours.

18 Jun	CBE	Spitfire XVI	SL563	Training

1947   G/C J H T Simpson   T/o 1116 Marham for practice flying. Due, it is thought, to grit entering the undercarriage selector system, G/C Simpson was obliged to land at 1237 with the wheels firmly jammed in their bays. His service number suggests he entered the Royal Air Force in the 1920s, since when he had flown 3,393 hours solo, one hundred-and-fifty-four of these in Spitfires.

19 Jun	CBE	Mosquito XVI	PF556	Training

1947   S/L O J Wells   T/o 1451 Marham for a cross-country. Landed, at base, at 1526 and almost immediately the flaps retracted. Realising what had happened, S/L Wells lowered them, again, but moments later he sensed they were retracting for a second time. By this time he was rapidly running out of room to stop and, thus, he elected to pull up the wheels in order to remain on the airfield. Subsequently, a technical inspection traced the fault to a defective flap control valve.

Mosquito Servicing Section Upwood

Based at Upwood in Huntingdonshire, little is known about this unit, except for details of the accident summarised below.

29 Jun	MSS Upwood	Mosquito B.25	KB606	Transit

1945   F/L R L Bartley DFC & Bar   T/o 1035 Upwood for delivery to Wyton, landing ten minutes later at its destination. However, the starboard undercarriage failed to lock in its down position and on touchdown the entire unit gave way, wrecking the bomber. F/L Bartley flew his first operational tour with 50 Squadron (Hampdens) before converting to Mosquitoes and a second spell of duty, this time with 627 Squadron. His two well deserved decorations were published on 22 June 1942 and 8 December 1944.

Pathfinder Force Navigation Training Unit

Formed under the control of No. 8 Group, the Pathfinder Force Navigation Training Unit was established at Gransden Lodge on 10 April 1943. As its title implies, the task of the unit was to train crews, selected from Main Force squadrons, for pathfinder duties. On 17 June 1943, the unit moved to Upwood, an air party being established at Warboys with effect from the same date. Stirlings, Halifaxes and Lancasters were the main types used, though by late 1944, by which time the headquarters had long since been at Warboys, Mosquitoes were added along with a sizeable number of Oxfords, which were used for training as well as doubling up as communications aircraft. Disbanded 18 June 1945.

25 Jan	PFNTU	Halifax II	W7823	Training

1944   F/L B F McSorley DFC RCAF + T/o 2115 Upwood tasked for a target indicator
F/S F J P Jervis DFM + dropping exercise, but failed to gain height.
F/O G W C Candlin DFC DFM + Seconds later, having smashed through some
P/O L L Oram + trees, the Halifax was in a mass of flames
Sgt W G Stoneman + in Upwood village on the south side of the
Sgt W Ellenor + airfield. Terribly burned, LAC Preston, whose
AC2 A R Kavanagh + trade is described as "Air Gunner", was rushed
W/O H A W Jolly DFM + to Peterborough Memorial Hospital but despite
Sgt B K Mitra + the best efforts of the doctors and nursing
LAC A C Preston inj staff, he succumbed to his injuries the next day. F/O Candlin and W/O Jolly had been attached from 83 Squadron and 35 Squadron respectively. Apart from Sgt Mitra, whose parents, Haridas and Sudhanshu Bala Mitra, lived in Calcutta, all were buried under private arrangement. It is noted that Sgt Mitra was a graduate of the Royal Botanical Gardens, Edinburgh; he had enlisted on 3 March 1941.

Note. Continuing the observations on the crew, reported at the foot of the previous page, F/L McSorley RCAF was an American from Long Island, New York, though according to the Commonwealth War Graves Commission register for Shorn-cliffe Military Cemetery, he had married Marjorie McSorley of Vancouver. His Distinguished Flying Cross had been gained with 405 Squadron, details being published on 19 October 1943. F/O Candlin won both of his awards with 83 Squadron, the first being Gazetted on 9 July 1943 and the second appearing on 15 October of that same year. F/S Jervis and W/O Jolly were honoured in the London Gazette on 18 January 1944, and 12 January 1943, respectively, the former having flown with 156 Squadron and the latter with 35 Squadron. Lastly, AC2 Kavanagh, described as an under training air bomber, was taken back to the Irish Republic and buried in Rathnew Cemetery, Co. Wicklow.

| 9 Mar 1944 | **PFNTU** | **Lancaster III** | **EE120 QF-P** | **Training** |

S/L M Sattler DFC & Bar RCAF — T/o 2045 Warboys for dual night conversion, an
S/L E W Blenkinsop DFC RCAF — exercise which went well until 2130. Then, as
F/L Clarke — the Lancaster gathered speed for another circuit, its port tyre burst and moments later it lay, wrecked, alongside the runway with a smashed undercarriage. S/L Sattler RCAF gained his awards with 405 Squadron, the first being published on 15 October 1943, and the second appearing on 23 May 1944. S/L Blenkinsop RCAF won his DFC while attached to 425 Squadron; tragically, he would perish towards the end of the war while languishing in Belsen Concentration Camp (see Bomber Command Losses, Volume 5, page 199).

| 10 Apr 1944 | **PFNTU** | **Lancaster III** | **JB471** | **Training** |

F/L J L Sloper DFC & Bar + T/o Warboys for a cross-country exercise. At
W/C J D Green + approximately 1800, the bomber caught fire in
Sgt S J Warrenger + the air and crashed near Llanwrtyd Wells in
WO2 A P Malzan RCAF + Breckonshire, a small town of the A483 road
F/S G J B Shields RCAF + and roughly midway between Llandovery and Builth
Sgt H Johnstone + Wells. Five, including the two Canadians, are
Sgt W W Farmer + buried in Bath (Haycombe) Cemetery, while the
Sgt J H Cleminson-Passey + others rest in their home towns. F/L Sloper, one of the five lying at Bath, had recently completed a tour of pathfinder duties with 156 Squadron, his two awards being published on 19 October 1943, and 21 April 1944, respectively.

| 2 Sep 1944 | **PFNTU** | **Lancaster III** | **JB155** | **Training** |

S/L A O Price DFC — T/o 1109 Warboys for crew training, including
F/O J R Hartley RAAF — three-engined flying practice. Approaching the
P/O P E Cawthorne RAAF — runway at 1129, on three, the port outer cut. S/L Price tried to go round again, but stalled and crash-landed. Thirteen days after this incident, the London Gazette reported his DFC, won in the service of 7 Squadron. P/O Cawthorne RAAF went on to fly with 635 Squadron and lost his life during operations to Harburg on 4-5 April 1945 (see Bomber Command Losses, Volume 6, page 155). On 22 May 1945, the announcement of his Distinguished Flying Cross duly appeared in the London Gazette.

| 5 Oct 1944 | **PFNTU** | **Lancaster III** | **ED952** | **Transit** |

S/L J A Weber DFC — T/o 1130 Warboys with a crew complement of two and headed for Florennes in Belgium. Landed here at 1400, only to taxi into a loosely filled bomb crater and wrecked as a consequence. S/L Weber's DFC, gained with 405 Squadron, had been promulgated on 14 September 1943.

| 31 Dec 1944 | **PFNTU** | **Mosquito IV** | **DZ589** | **Training** |

F/O P Germaine RCAF — T/o 1207 Warboys for a high-level exercise. When the port engine caught fire at 12,000 feet, and being unable to feather the unit or quell the blaze, the crew baled out, leaving the Mosquito to crash at 1257, at Benwick on the Huntingdonshire and Cambridgeshire border, 6 miles SW of March.

| 3 Feb 1945 | **PFNTU** | **Mosquito IV** | **DZ437** | **Training** |

F/O A J Bodger DFC inj T/o 2008 Warboys and crashed almost immediately
F/L G H Hart inj some 800 yards SE of the airfield. Both officers were taken to RAF Hospital Ely. F/O Bodger had served with 576 Squadron, his DFC having been published on 22 February 1944.

19 Feb	**PFNTU**	**Mosquito IV**	**DK313**	**Training**

19 Feb
1945

PFNTU   **Mosquito IV**   **DK313**   **Training**

F/L V G Haley MM   +   T/o 2100 Warboys for a cross-country, at night.
F/L D V BIDDER MID   +   On return to base at 2331, the weather had deteriorated and while turning towards the outer
Drem lights, F/L Haley inadvertently allowed his speed to drop and, as a result,
he side slipped and crashed near Warboys railway station. Both are buried in
Sussex; F/L Haley at Bexhill Cemetery and F/L Bidder in West Thorney (St. Nicholas) Churchyard. F/L Haley (then a sergeant and serving with 218 Squadron)
features in Bomber Command Losses, Volume 2, page 157. Following his successful
evasion, he was awarded the Military Medal, Gazetted on 26 May 1942.

2 Mar
1945

PFNTU   **Mosquito XX**   **KB206**   **Training**

F/L A I Albertson AFC   +   T/o 1900 Warboys for a high-level night cross-
F/S R J Eaton RAAF   +   country, the crew being briefed to fly at
27,000 feet. At around 2100, the Mosquito
broke up at crashed at Yew Tree Farm, Basford Cheddleton, S of Leek, Stafford.
Both are buried in Cambridge City Cemetery, F/L Albertson hailing from Satooma
in Southern Rhodesia.

4 Mar
1945

PFNTU   **Oxford I**   **NM683**   **Training**

F/L F B Gipson DFC & Bar   inj   T/o 1120 Warboys for a day navigation sortie.
F/L D I Jones DFC   inj   While descending through cloud, flew into high
F/L W J Barclay DFC RAAF   inj   ground (1,000 feet above sea level) about a mile
F/O V P Skene-Rees   inj   south of Edale in the Derbyshire Peak District.
All were taken to RAF Hospital Wilmslow. The
three decorated members of crew had flown with 582 Squadron, 97 Squadron and
156 Squadron respectively, their awards being published on 14 November 1944 (his
First Bar being promulgated on 22 May 1945), 13 July 1943 and 15 September 1944.
The accident is reported to have taken place at roughly 1225, an hour and five
minutes or so after their departure.

11 Mar
1945

PFNTU   **Lancaster III**   **PB669**   **Training**

F/L A C Diemer MID   +   T/o Warboys for day training, the crew having
F/O K L Pile DFM   +   being attached from 156 Squadron. While cruising
F/L A M Stewart   +   over Northamptonshire, eyewitnesses report the
F/L B C Brooker DFC & Bar   +   Lancaster turning to port before its nose dipped
F/L J Robertson DFM   +   and without recovering it struck the ground, at
F/O C A Robson   +   high speed, at Old Weston, 1 mile E of Molesworth
F/S D W Kidd   +   airfield. Various times for the crash have been
W/O S Oldfield   +   quoted; 1230, 1310 and, as shown on page 124 of
Bomber Command Losses, Volume 6, 1430. The two
Distinguished Flying Medal holders had served, respectively, with 166 Squadron
and 97 Squadron, while F/L Brooker was a veteran of 35 Squadron. In crew order,
their awards were announced in the London Gazette on 19 September 1944, 11 June
1943, 19 May 1944 and 13 October 1944. W/O Oldfield enlisted on 7 July 1939, in
the regular air force; at the time of his death, the cemetery register indicates
his age as twenty-one.

28 Apr
1945

PFNTU   **Lancaster III**   **ND928**   **Training**

F/L Brown   T/o Warboys and written off in a landing mishap,
P/O H A B Brewington   inj   at base, after failing to gain height from an
F/O Fallow   overshoot.
F/O J C Boadway RCAF   inj
F/O Reynolds
F/S Graham
F/S Stoddard

6- 7 May
1945

PFNTU   **Mosquito XX**   **KB233**   **Training**

S/L W H Corbet DFC   +   T/o Warboys for a night cross-country, the
Lt P E R Brievik RNAF   +   exercise to be conducted at high-level. Dived
at 0010 and disintegrated, the bulk of the
wreckage being recovered from the railway line between Lydney and Gloucester.
Both officers were taken to Royal Air Force Moreton Valance for formal identification. S/L Corbet, who gained his DFC with 142 Squadron as long ago as
31 May 1940, was laid to rest in Halton (St. Michael) Churchyard.

Section 9

Station Flights

Prior to, and throughout the Second World War and beyond, active flying stations of the Royal Air Force maintained a handful of aircraft for communications purposes, under the guise of Station Flights.

This final section of the volume summarises the losses from the flights, associated with Bomber Command stations.

The principal types involved were, as may be expected, light aircraft or trainers.

---

3 Nov **SFlt** **Blenheim I** **K7061** **Ground**
1939   S/L E A Springall   Station Flight Wyton. Taxied into the path of
    Blenheim IV N6144 of 114 Squadron, captained by
Sgt N S Brady (see Bomber Command Losses, Volume 1, page 21). Both machines caught fire and were burned out, despite the intervention of the station fire services. No serious injuries, though, are indicated.

---

19 Nov **SFlt** **Magister I** **L5979** **Communications**
1939   F/L C H Simpson   Station Flight Marham. T/o Marham for Newmarket
    where it stalled on landing, due partly to en-
    countering a strong, gusting, wind.

---

13 Feb **SFlt** **Battle I** **L5229** **Communications**
1940   P/O A G White   Station Flight Abingdon. T/o from an unknown air-
    field and alighted in the English Channel. The
Battle's pilot was experienced with one hundred-and-twenty-eight hours on type.

---

27 Oct **SFlt** **Magister I** **L5960** **Enemy Action**
1940   Station Flight Mildenhall. Struck off charge on
this date, believed to have been damaged beyond repair during an enemy air raid.

---

18 Sep **SFlt** **Tiger Moth** **AX788** **Communications**
1941   P/O N Holden   inj Station Flight Wyton. T/o from an unknown air-
    P/O J R M Thomson + field, crewed by two officers from 15 Squadron.
    Shortly before 1600, P/O Holden asked P/O Thomson
to take over the controls, while he (Holden) checked his map. At the time, the Tiger Moth was flying at 900 feet, thus, when it dived suddenly, P/O Holden had insufficient time to recover the situation and he was very seriously injured when the light trainer hit the ground at Caxton Gibbet. P/O Holden was first treated in station sick quarters, but it is possible he was transferred to RAF Hospital Ely to continue his recovery. P/O Thompson, who was forty years of age and who may have joined the volunteer reserve under the commissioned air gunner scheme, is buried in Wyton (St. Margaret and All Saints) Churchyard. He was a graduate of Pembroke College, Cambridge, holding a Bachelor of Arts degree.

Note. The Tiger Moth, summarised above, had been impressed on 22 July 1940, ex-G-AFJH of the Merseyside Aero & Sports Company Limited and was delivered four days later to 15 Maintenance Unit at Wroughton. From here, it was re-leased to Wyton for station flight duties on 17 June 1941. Credit: Peter W Moss and the second volume of his Impressments Log (Air Britain, 1963).

---

8 Apr **SFlt** **Tiger Moth II** **N6857** **Communications**
1942   P/O P C Jones + Station Flight Abingdon. T/o Abingdon and while
    P/O Johnson inj flying at low-level, crashed at Pound Copse,
    Gare Hill, on the Somerset/Wiltshire border,
some 3 miles NE of Bruton, Somerset and about the same distance WSW from War-minster in Wiltshire. P/O Jones is buried in Newcastle-under-Lyme (St. George) Churchyard, where his is the sole service grave from either of the two World Wars. He was twenty-seven years of age, and married.

| 5 Oct | SFlt | Oxford I | N4574 | Unknown |

1942

Station Flight Moreton-in-Marsh. Reported as destroyed, on this date, but no accident card has been found to support this statement.

| 10 Mar | SFlt | Lysander II | N1302 | Communications |

1943 S/L P Johnson

Station Flight Wyton. T/o 1100 Wyton and set course for Speke. On his arrival, at 1215, the pilot was confronted with the surface wind gusting between fifteen and twenty knots, and coming from forty-five degrees off the runway. Thus, on touch down the Lysander swung and broke its undercarriage. Relegated for ground instruction, the airframe later received the serial 3889M.

| 14 Aug | SFlt | Oxford I | DF348 | Training |

1944 G/C Jefferson

Station Flight Skellingthorpe. T/o 1215 Skelling-thorpe for practice flying. Fifteen minutes later the Oxford approached the runway, but yawed slightly and G/C Jefferson tried to go round again, only to find himself flying directly towards a hangar and it was while he was taking action to avoid this obstruction that he stalled and crashed. It is indicated that he had 1,900 solo flying hours, twenty of these of Oxfords.

| 24 Aug | SFlt | Oxford II | W6571 | Unknown |

1944

Station Flight East Kirkby. Reported as crashed on this date, but no accident card has been found which might support this state-ment.

| 14 Nov | SFlt | Oxford I | R6273 | Unknown |

1944

Station Flight Tempsford. Reported as damaged beyond repair on this date, but, so far, no accident card has been located that lends weight to this assertion.

| 17 Jan | SFlt | Oxford I | T1338 | Training |

1945 F/L P G Cavanagh

Station Flight Elsham Wolds. T/o Elsham Wolds, with a crew of three, for a navigation exercise during which the starboard engine failed. Sighting the small grass airfield of St. Mary's on the Isles of Scilly, F/L Cavanagh decided to land but he arrived on the ground, at 1650, before the wheels had time to lock.

| 6 Feb | SFlt | Oxford II | V3787 | Ground |

1945 P/O B Pollard   inj

F/L F P G Alcock   inj

Station Flight Upwood. T/o 1535 Upwood with a crew of two, tasked to carry out beam approach training. Landed at 1605, but while taxying was struck by Mosquito XVI ML973 of the Mosquito Servicing Section Upwood. Neither pilot was seriously hurt, and damage to the Mosquito was only slight. It was stated that slight rain was falling and, in the late afternoon gloom, this might have impaired the vision of both crews.

| 7 Feb | SFlt | Oxford I | NJ292 | Communications |

1945 F/O D N Shefler RCAF

Station Flight North Creake. T/o 1445 North Creake and set course for the Handley Page air-field at Radlett. Landed at 1545, but in a strong crosswind and on a very wet runway. As the Oxford began to swing, F/O Shefler RCAF applied the brakes and when he realised these were having no effect, he opened up and tried to go round again. At that moment his aircraft was caught by a particularly strong gust which sent it to starboard and down a bank, where it finally came to rest up against a fence. No one was hurt, but the trainer was damaged beyond repair.

| 6 Mar | SFlt | Oxford I | PH518 | Training |

1945 F/L P G Cavanagh

Station Flight Elsham Wolds. T/o 1750 Elsham Wolds, with a crew of two, for a night cross-country. Shortly before 1900, F/L Cavanagh complained of feeling "dizzy" and he decided to land, as soon as possible. Being in the vicinity of Fairoaks, he made his approach but overshot the landing strip and hit a blast wall. No serious injuries reported.

| 28 May | SFlt | Tiger Moth II | T5631 | Training |

1945 F/L J Bradford

Station Flight Oulton. T/o 1439 Oulton but the undercarriage snagged in the long grass and the trainer flipped onto its back. F/L Bradford was shaken, but otherwise unharmed.

12 Jun   **SFlt**   **Oxford II**   **V3528**   **Communications**
1945   F/L D C James   Station Flight Bourn. T/o 1125 Bourn and set
                                                  forth for Fairford. Arrived in the Fairford
circuit at 1210, but the port Cheetah cut at 400 feet and unable to maintain
height, F/L James forced-landed some 2 miles SE of the runway. He was very
experienced on Oxfords, having 1,800 of his 2,400 solo flying hours logged on
type.

18 Mar   **SFlt**   **Oxford II**   **AB754**   **Training**
1946   G/C P G Chichester   inj   Station Flight Methwold. T/o 1225 Exeter to
     F/L N E J Linnett   inj   return to Methwold but immediately flew into
                                            such poor visibility that the pilot failed to
see rising ground until it was too late. Thus, five minutes after departure,
the Oxford crashed near Newton Poppleford, 2 miles NW of Sidmouth, Devon. Both
officers were admitted to the Royal Devon and Exeter Hospital. Forty-five year
old G/C Chichester (it was his birthday) had accumulated 3,432 solo flying
hours, forty-seven of these at the controls of Oxfords.

Note. During the initial research, in respect of the entries for this section,
published information led me to believe that the following aircraft had been
assigned to the station flight at Syerston. This proved not to be the case and
it should have been entered in the section concerned with the losses from the
training flights.

12 Sep   **1690 Flt**   **Martinet I**   **HP321**   **Training**
1944   W/O A A Graham   +   T/o Syerston presumably for a training detail.
     LAC V E Lewis   inj   Crashed 1345 at Hucknall airfield. LAC Lewis
                                            was critically injured and he died at 1630,
while being treated in the station's sick quarters. He is buried in Ilford
(Barkingside) Cemetery. His pilot, W/O Graham, rests in Hucknall Cemetery, his
home being Bpasso Piedpa, Trinidad.

Royal Air Force
BOMBER COMMAND LOSSES

Appendices

Appendix 1

Bases

Due to the plethora of units covered within this volume, ranging in diversity from squadron conversion flights, through to the specialist establishment, summarised in section eight, I have chosen to show the bases by order of section, in numerical sequence of formation, and restricting the data to those units that sustained aircraft losses.

15 CFlt	Wyton, Huntingdonshire	21 Jan 42 - 21 Jan 42	Affiliated to
	Alconbury, Huntingdonshire	21 Jan 42 - 5 May 42	15 Squadron
	Waterbeach, Cambridgeshire	5 May 42 - 7 Oct 42	Headquarters
		7 Oct 42	Disbanded into 1657 HCU
26 CFlt	Waterbeach, Cambridgeshire	5 Oct 41 - 2 Jan 42	Headquarters
		2 Jan 42	Disbanded into 1651 CU
28 CFlt	Linton-on-Ouse, Yorkshire	29 Aug 41 - 4 Nov 41	Headquarters
	Leconfield, Yorkshire	4 Nov 41 - 30 Dec 41	Headquarters
	Marston Moor, Yorkshire	30 Dec 41 - 2 Jan 42	Headquarters
		2 Jan 42	Disbanded into 1652 CU
35 CFlt	Linton-on-Ouse, Yorkshire	20 Jan 42 - 12 Jun 42	Affiliated to
	Dalton, Yorkshire	12 Jun 42 - 5 Sep 42	35 Squadron
	Marston Moor, Yorkshire	5 Sep 42 - 21 Sep 42	Headquarters
	Rufforth, Yorkshire	21 Sep 42 - 7 Oct 42	Headquarters
		7 Oct 42	Disbanded into 1652 HCU
49 CFlt	Scampton, Lincolnshire	16 Jan 42 - 9 Nov 42	Affiliated to 49 Squadron
		9 Nov 42	Disbanded into 1661 HCU
50 CFlt	Skellingthorpe, Lincolnshire	16 May 42 - 17 Jun 42	Affiliated to
	Swinderby, Lincolnshire	17 Jun 42 - 21 Aug 42	50 Squadron
	Wigsley, Nottinghamshire	21 Aug 42 - 22 Aug 42	Headquarters
		22 Aug 42	Disbanded into 1654 CU
76 CFlt	Middleton St. George, Durham	20 Jan 42 - 8 Jun 42	Affiliated to
	Dalton, Yorkshire	8 Jun 42 - 16 Sep 42	76 Squadron
	Riccall, Yorkshire	16 Sep 42 - 7 Oct 42	Headquarters
		7 Oct 42	Disbanded into 1658 HCU
78 CFlt	Croft, Yorkshire	20 Jan 42 - 12 Jun 42	Affiliated to
	Dalton, Yorkshire	12 Jun 42 - 30 Jun 42	78 Squadron
	Middleton St. George, Durham	30 Jun 42 - 15 Sep 42	Headquarters
	Riccall, Yorkshire	15 Sep 42 - 7 Oct 42	Headquarters
		7 Oct 42	Disbanded into 1658 HCU
97 CFlt	Coningsby, Lincolnshire	20 Jan 42 - 23 Sep 42	Affiliated to
	Skellingthorpe, Lincolnshire	23 Sep 42 - 16 Oct 42	97 Squadron
		16 Oct 42	Disbanded into 1660 HCU
101 CFlt	Oakington, Cambridgeshire	6 May 42 - 7 Oct 42	Affiliated to 101 Squadron
		7 Oct 42	Disbanded into 1657 HCU
102 CFlt	Dalton, Yorkshire	20 Jan 42 - 10 Jun 42	Affiliated to
	Topcliffe, Yorkshire	10 Jun 42 - 7 Aug 42	102 Squadron
	Pocklington, Yorkshire	7 Aug 42 - 31 Oct 42	Headquarters
		31 Oct 42	Disbanded into 1652 HCU

103 CFlt	Elsham Wold, Lincolnshire	3 May 42 - 31 Oct 42	Affiliated to 103 Squadron
		31 Oct 42	Disbanded into 1656 HCU
149 CFlt	Mildenhall, Suffolk	20 Jan 42 - 13 Feb 42	Affiliated to
	Lakenheath, Suffolk	13 Feb 42 - 2 Oct 42	149 Squadron
	Stradishall, Suffolk	2 Oct 42 - 7 Oct 42	Headquarters
		7 Oct 42	Disbanded into 1657 HCU
158 CFlt	Driffield, Yorkshire	6 May 42 - 7 May 42	Affiliated to
	Linton-on-Ouse, Yorkshire	7 May 42 - 5 Jun 42	158 Squadron
	East Moor, Yorkshire	5 Jun 42 - 25 Sep 42	Headquarters
	Rufforth, Yorkshire	25 Sep 42 - 1 Nov 42	Headquarters
		1 Nov 42	Disbanded into 1658 HCU
214 CFlt	Waterbeach, Cambridgeshire	10 Apr 42 - 1 May 42	Affiliated to
	Stradishall, Suffolk	1 May 42 - 9 Aug 42	214 Squadron
	Waterbeach, Cambridgeshire	9 Aug 42 - 1 Oct 42	Headquarters
		1 Oct 42	Disbanded into 1651 CU
218 CFlt	Marham, Norfolk	20 Jan 42 - 3 Mar 42	Affiliated to
	Lakenheath, Suffolk	3 Mar 42 - 2 Oct 42	218 Squadron
	Stradishall, Suffolk	2 Oct 42 - 7 Oct 42	Headquarters
		7 Oct 42	Disbanded into 1657 HCU
460 CFlt	Breighton, Yorkshire	22 May 42 - 15 Aug 42	Affiliated to
	Holme-on-Spalding Moor, Yorkshire	15 Aug 42 - 26 Sep 42	460 Squadron
	Breighton, Yorkshire	26 Sep 42 - 10 Nov 42	Headquarters
		10 Nov 42	Disbanded into 1656 HCU
1678 HCFlt	East Wretham, Norfolk	18 May 43 - 6 Aug 43	Headquarters
	Little Snoring, Norfolk	6 Aug 43 - 16 Sep 43	Headquarters
		16 Sep 43	Redesignated 1678 HCU
1679 HCFlt	East Moor, Yorkshire	18 May 43 - 13 Dec 43	Headquarters
	Wombleton, Yorkshire	13 Dec 43 - 27 Jan 44	Headquarters
		27 Jan 44	Absorbed by 1666 HCU
1651 HCU	Waterbeach, Cambridgeshire	2 Jan 42 - 20 Nov 43	Headquarters
	Wratting Common, Cambridgeshire	20 Nov 43 - 9 Nov 44	Headquarters
	Woolfox Lodge, Rutland	9 Nov 44 - 13 Jul 45	Headquarters
		13 Jul 45	Disbanded
1652 HCU	Marston Moor, Yorkshire	2 Jan 42 - 25 Jun 45	Headquarters
	Leconfield, Yorkshire	2 Jan 42 - 22 Jan 42	Detachment
	Dalton, Yorkshire	2 Jan 42 -	Detachment
	Rufforth, Yorkshire	7 Jul 42 - 13 Jul 42	Detachment
	Dalton, Yorkshire	13 Jul 42 - 22 Aug 42	Detachment
	Burn, Yorkshire	Nov 43 - Jan 44	Detachment
	Acaster Malbis, Yorkshire	44 -	Detachment
		25 Jun 45	Disbanded
1653 HCU	Polebrook, Northamptonshire	9 Jan 42 - 2 Jun 42	Headquarters
	Burn, Yorkshire	2 Jun 42 - 31 Oct 42	Headquarters
		31 Oct 42	Disbanded
		21 Nov 43	Reformed
	Chedburgh, Suffolk	21 Nov 43 - 27 Nov 44	Headquarters
	North Luffenham, Rutland	27 Nov 44 - 28 Oct 46	Headquarters
	Lindholme, Yorkshire	28 Oct 46 - 15 Mar 47	Headquarters
		15 Mar 47	Redesignated 230 OCU
1654 HCU	Swinderby, Lincolnshire	19 May 42 - 15 Jun 42	Headquarters
	Wigsley, Nottinghamshire	15 Jun 42 - 1 Sep 45	Headquarters
		1 Sep 45	Disbanded
1656 HCU	Lindholme, Yorkshire	10 Oct 42 - 10 Nov 45	Headquarters
	Breighton, Yorkshire	10 Oct 42 - 10 Nov 42	A Flight
	Elsham Wolds, Lincolnshire	10 Oct 42 - 3 Nov 42	B Flight
	Sandtoft, Lincolnshire	Aug 45 - 10 Nov 45	Detachment
		10 Nov 45	Disbanded

1657 HCU	Stradishall, Suffolk	7 Oct 42 - 14 May 44	Headquarters
	East Wretham, Norfolk	22 Mar 43 - 18 May 43	Detachment
	Woolfox Lodge, Rutland	8 Nov 43 - Nov 43	Detachment
	Shepherds Grove, Suffolk	14 May 44 - 5 Oct 44	Headquarters
	Stradishall, Suffolk	5 Oct 44 - 15 Dec 44	Headquarters
		15 Dec 44	Disbanded
1658 HCU	Riccall, Yorkshire	7 Oct 42 - 13 Apr 45	Headquarters
	Melbourne, Yorkshire	1 Nov 42 - Jan 43	Detachment
	Acaster Malbis, Yorkshire	44 -	Detachment
		13 Apr 45	Disbanded
1659 HCU	Leeming, Yorkshire	7 Oct 42 - 14 May 43	Headquarters
	Topcliffe, Yorkshire	14 May 43 - 10 Sep 45	Headquarters
	Dalton, Yorkshire	Nay 43 - Jun 43	Detachment
		10 Sep 45	Disbanded
1660 HCU	Swinderby, Lincolnshire	22 Oct 42 - 11 Nov 46	Headquarters
		11 Nov 46	Absorbed by 1653 HCU
1661 HCU	Waddington, Lincolnshire	9 Nov 42 - 1 Jan 43	Headquarters
	Winthorpe, Northamptonshire	1 Jan 43 - 24 Aug 45	Headquarters
		24 Aug 45	Disbanded
1662 HCU	Blyton, Lincolnshire	26 Jan 43 - 6 Apr 45	Headquarters
		6 Apr 45	Disbanded
1663 HCU	Rufforth, Yorkshire	2 Mar 43 - 28 May 45	Headquarters
	Acaster Malbis, Yorkshire	44 -	Detachment
		28 May 45	Disbanded
1664 HCU	Croft, Yorkshire	10 May 43 - 7 Dec 43	Headquarters
	Dishforth, Yorkshire	7 Dec 43 - 6 Apr 45	Headquarters
		6 Apr 45	Disbanded
1665 HCU	Mepal, Cambridgeshire	23 Apr 43 - 5 Jun 43	Headquarters
	Waterbeach, Cambridgeshire	1 May 43 -	Detachment
	Stradishall, Suffolk	1 May 43 - 9 Nov 43	Detachment
	Great Ashfield, Suffolk	1 May 43 - 6 Jun 43	Detachment
	Woolfox Lodge, Rutland	5 Jun 43 - 1 Dec 43	Headquarters
		1 Dec 43	Transferred 38 Group
1666 HCU	Dalton, Yorkshire	5 Jun 43 - 21 Oct 43	Headquarters
	Wombleton, Yorkshire	21 Oct 43 - 3 Aug 45	Headquarters
		3 Aug 45	Disbanded
1667 HCU	Lindholme, Yorkshire	1 Jun 43 - 8 Oct 43	Headquarters
	Faldingworth, Lincolnshire	8 Aug 43 - 8 Oct 43	Detachment
	Faldingworth, Lincolnshire	8 Oct 43 - 17 Feb 44	Headquarters
	Sandtoft, Lincolnshire	17 Feb 44 - 9 Nov 45	Headquarters
		9 Nov 45	Disbanded
1668 HCU	Balderton, Nottinghamshire	15 Aug 43 - 17 Nov 43	Headquarters
	Syerston, Nottinghamshire	17 Nov 43 - 21 Nov 43	Headquarters
		21 Nov 43	Disbanded into 5 LFS
		28 Jul 44	Reformed
	Bottesford, Leicestershire	28 Jul 44 - 17 Sep 45	Headquarters
	Cottesmore, Rutland	17 Sep 45 - 7 Mar 46	Headquarters
		7 Mar 46	Disbanded
1669 HCU	Langar, Nottinghamshire	7 Oct 44 - 16 Mar 45	Headquarters
		16 Mar 45	Disbanded
1678 HCU	Foulsham, Norfolk	16 Sep 43 - 12 Jun 44	Headquarters
		12 Jun 44	Disbanded

Note. The term "heavy conversion unit" came into use on 7 October 1942, prior to this the establishments were known, merely, as "conversion units". Until 3 November 1944, all (except for "1678" which had disbanded) were administered by their respective operational bomber groups, but on this date their administration came under the aegis of No. 7 Group, with its headquarters at St. Vincents, Grantham. Just over a year later, on 21 December 1945, the three remaining heavy conversion units, "1653", "1660" and "1668" transferred to the authority of No. 91 Group at Abingdon.

1 LFS	Lindholme, Yorkshire	21 Nov 43 - 20 Jan 44	Headquarters
	Lindholme, Yorkshire	21 Nov 43 - 5 Apr 44	A Flight
	Blyton, Lincolnshire	21 Nov 43 - 12 Feb 44	B Flight
	Faldingworth, Lincolnshire	21 Nov 43 - 24 Jan 44	C Flight

1 LFS	Hemswell, Lincolnshire	20 Jan 44 - 25 Nov 44	Headquarters
Contd	Sturgate, Lincolnshire	Apr 44 - Nov 44	Detachment
		25 Nov 44	Disbanded
3 LFS	Feltwell, Norfolk	21 Nov 43 - 31 Jan 45	Headquarters
	Lakenheath, Suffolk	Jan 44 - May 44	Detachment
	Mildenhall, Suffolk	Jan 44 - May 44	Detachment
	Snetterton Heath, Norfolk	Jan 44 - May 44	Detachment
	Woolfox Lodge, Rutland	7 Aug 44 - 28 Aug 44	C Flight
	Newmarket, Suffolk	5 Jan 45 - 29 Jan 45	A Flight
	Tuddenham, Suffolk	7 Jan 45 - 31 Jan 45	C Flight
	Methwold, Norfolk	8 Jan 45 - 31 Jan 45	B Flight
		31 Jan 45	Disbanded
5 LFS	Syerston, Nottinghamshire	21 Nov 43 - 1 Apr 45	Headquarters
		1 Apr 45	Disbanded

Note. In respect of 3 Lancaster Finishing School, due to the poor state of the grass surfaces at Feltwell, frequent detachments took place (as the table above shows). In addition to the airfields listed, Tempsford in Bedfordshire and the United States Army Air Force bases at Bury St. Edmunds and Lavenham, both in Suffolk, were used from time to time.

1655 MCU	Horsham St. Faith, Norfolk	30 Aug 42 - 28 Sep 42	Headquarters
	Marham, Norfolk	28 Sep 42 - 1 May 43	Headquarters
		1 May 43	Absorbed by 13 OTU
1655 MTU	Marham, Norfolk	1 Jul 43 - 7 Mar 44	Headquarters
	Warboys, Huntingdonshire	7 Mar 44 - 27 Jun 44	Headquarters
	Wyton, Huntingdonshire	27 Jun 44 - 30 Dec 44	Detachment
	Upper Heyford, Oxfordshire	30 Dec 44 - 31 Dec 44	Headquarters
		31 Dec 44	Absorbed by 16 OTU
3 Flt	Mildenhall, Suffolk	27 Jan 41 - Oct 41	Headquarters
		Oct 41	Redesignated 1503 Flight
6 Flt	Waddington, Lincolnshire	6 Jan 41 - Oct 41	Headquarters
		Oct 41	Redesignated 1506 Flight
7 Flt	Finningley, Yorkshire	18 Jan 41 - Oct 41	Headquarters
		Oct 41	Redesignated 1507 Flight
419 Flt	Stradishall, Suffolk	9 Oct 40 - 1 Mar 41	Headquarters
		1 Mar 41	Redesignated 1419 Flight
1323 Flt	Bourn, Cambridgeshire	29 Nov 44 - 1 Jan 45	Headquarters
	Warboys, Huntingdonshire	1 Jan 45 - 30 Sep 45	Headquarters
		30 Sep 45	Disbanded
1409 Flt	Oakington, Cambridgeshire	1 Apr 43 - Nov 43	Headquarters
	Bourn, Cambridgeshire	Nov 43 - 8 Jan 44	Headquarters
	Wyton, Huntingdonshire	8 Jan 44 - 5 Jul 45	Headquarters
	Upwood, Huntingdonshire	5 Jul 45 - 10 Oct 45	Headquarters
		10 Oct 45	Transferred 47 Group
1419 Flt	Stradishall, Suffolk	1 Mar 41 - 25 Aug 41	Headquarters
	Newmarket, Suffolk	Mar 41 - Jul 41	Detachment
		25 Aug 41	Redesignated 138 Squadron
1427 Flt	Stradishall, Suffolk	2 Oct 42 - 1 Apr 43	Headquarters
		1 Apr 43	Absorbed by 1657 HCU
1428 Flt	Oulton, Norfolk	29 Dec 41 - 6 Jun 42	Headquarters
		6 Jun 42	Disbanded
1429 Flt	East Wretham, Norfolk	1 Jan 42 - 26 Jun 42	Headquarters
	Woolfox Lodge, Rutland	26 Jun 42 - 26 Aug 42	Headquarters
	Church Broughton, Derbyshire	26 Aug 42 - 8 Nov 42	Headquarters
		8 Nov 42	Transferred 17 Group

1443 Flt	Harwell, Berkshire	21 Jan 42 - 30 Apr 43	Headquarters
		30 Apr 43	Redesignated 310 FTU
1444 Flt	Horsham St. Faith, Norfolk	21 Jan 42 - 20 Jun 42	Headquarters
		20 Jun 42	Transferred 44 Group
1446 Flt	Bassingbourn, Cambridgeshire	23 Mar 42 - 18 May 42	Headquarters
	Moreton-in-Marsh, Gloucestershire	18 May 42 - 1 May 43	Headquarters
		1 May 43	Redesignated 311 FTU
1474 Flt	Stradishall, Suffolk	4 Jul 42 - 10 Jul 42	Headquarters
	Gransden Lodge, Bedfordshire	10 Jul 42 - 4 Jan 43	Headquarters
		4 Jan 43	Redesignated 192 Squadron
1481 Flt	Binbrook, Lincolnshire	14 Nov 41 - 26 Sep 42	Headquarters
	Blyton, Yorkshire	26 Sep 42 - 2 Nov 42	Headquarters
	Lindholme, Yorkshire	2 Nov 42 - 7 May 43	Headquarters
	Binbrook, Lincolnshire	7 May 43 - 7 Mar 44	Headquarters
	Ingham, Lincolnshire	7 Mar 44 - 4 Dec 44	Headquarters
		4 Dec 44	Redesignated 1687 Flight
1482 Flt	West Raynham, Norfolk	Nov 41 - 29 May 43	Headquarters
	Great Massingham, Norfolk	29 May 43 - 1 Jun 43	Headquarters
		1 Jun 43	Transferred 2 TAF
1483 Flt	Newmarket, Suffolk	18 Nov 41 - 13 Jul 42	Headquarters
	Marham, Norfolk	13 Jul 42 - 29 Jun 43	Headquarters
	Newmarket, Suffolk	29 Jun 43 - 11 Mar 44	Headquarters
		11 Mar 44	Redesignated 1688 Flight
1484 Flt	Driffield, Yorkshire	14 Nov 41 - 23 Jul 43	Headquarters
	Leconfield, Yorkshire	23 Jul 43 - 15 Feb 44	Headquarters
	Lissett, Yorkshire	3 Jan 44 - 15 Feb 44	Detachment
		15 Feb 44	Redesignated 1689 Flight
1485 Flt	Coningsby, Lincolnshire	30 Oct 41 - 1 Aug 42	Headquarters
	Dunholme Lodge, Lincolnshire	1 Aug 42 - 27 Oct 42	Headquarters
	Coningsby, Lincolnshire	1 Aug 42 - 8 Mar 43	Detachment
	Fulbeck, Lincolnshire	27 Oct 42 - 23 Aug 43	Headquarters
	Skellingthorpe, Lincolnshire	23 Aug 43 - 12 Nov 43	Headquarters
	Syerston, Nottinghamshire	12 Nov 43 - 26 Feb 44	Headquarters
		26 Feb 44	Redesignated 1690 Flight
1502 Flt	Driffield, Yorkshire	Oct 41 - 23 Jul 43	Headquarters
	Melbourne, Yorkshire	Nov 42 -	Detachment
	Leconfield, Yorkshire	23 Jul 43 - 15 Aug 43	Headquarters
		15 Aug 43	Disbanded
1507 Flt	Finningley, Yorkshire	Oct 41 - 13 Mar 43	Headquarters
	Cottesmore, Rutland	Sep 42 - Oct 42	Detachment
	Warboys, Huntingdonshire	13 Mar 43 - 17 Jun 43	Headquarters
	Gransden Lodge, Bedfordshire	17 Jun 43 - 27 Nov 43	Headquarters
		27 Nov 43	Disbanded
1508 Flt	Horsham St. Faith, Norfolk	Oct 41 - 20 Dec 41	Headquarters
	Watton, Norfolk	20 Dec 41 - 19 Jan 42	Headquarters
	Horsham St. Faith, Norfolk	19 Jan 42 - 4 Apr 43	Headquarters
	Attlebridge, Norfolk	4 Apr 43 - 1 Jun 43	Headquarters
		1 Jun 43	Transferred 2 TAF
1513 Flt	Honington, Suffolk	Oct 41 - 31 Oct 42	Headquarters
	Bramcote, Warwickshire	31 Oct 42 - 11 May 44	Headquarters
		11 May 44	Transferred 44 Group
1515 Flt	Swanton Morley, Norfolk	Oct 41 - 1 Jun 43	Headquarters
		1 Jun 43	Transferred 2 TAF
1516 Flt	Topcliffe, Yorkshire	Oct 41 - 17 Nov 41	Headquarters
	Middleton St. George, Durham	17 Nov 41 - 16 Sep 42	Headquarters
	Croft, Yorkshire	16 Sep 42 - 14 Oct 42	Headquarters
	Middleton St. George, Durham	14 Oct 42 - 12 Dec 42	Headquarters
	Hampstead Norris, Berkshire	12 Dec 42 - Dec 42	Headquarters

1516 Flt	Harwell, Berkshire	Dec 42 - 13 Apr 43	Headquarters
Contd		13 Apr 43	Transferred
			44 Group
1518 Flt	Scampton, Lincolnshire	3 Nov 41 -	Headquarters
	Dunholme Lodge, Lincolnshire	- 14 Jun 43	Headquarters
		14 Jun 43	Transferred
			21 Group
1519 Flt	South Cerney, Gloucestershire	Nov 41 - Dec 41	Headquarters
	Feltwell, Norfolk	Dec 41 - 22 May 45	Headquarters
		22 May 45	Transferred
			23 Group
1520 Flt	Holme-on-Spalding Moor, Yorkshire	Oct 41 - 6 Jun 44	Headquarters
	Leconfield, Yorkshire	6 Jun 44 - 18 Sep 44	Headquarters
	Sturgate, Lincolnshire	18 Sep 44 - 29 May 45	Headquarters
		29 May 45	Disbanded
1521 Flt	Stradishall, Suffolk	Oct 41 - 15 Mar 43	Headquarters
	Finningley, Yorkshire	15 Mar 43 - 23 Apr 43	Headquarters
	Wymeswold, Leicestershire	23 Apr 43 - 30 May 43	Headquarters
	Castle Donnington, Leicestershire	30 May 43 - 21 Jun 43	Headquarters
	Wymeswold, Leicestershire	21 Jun 43 - 15 Oct 44	Headquarters
		15 Oct 44	Transferred
			44 Group
1681 Flt	Pershore, Worcestershire	1 Jul 43 - 8 Mar 44	Headquarters
	Kinloss, Moray	1 Jul 43 - 8 Mar 44	Detachment
	Long Marston, Gloucestershire	9 Mar 44 - 21 Aug 44	Headquarters
		21 Aug 44	Disbanded
1682 Flt	Abingdon, Berkshire	1 Jul 43 - 2 Jul 43	Headquarters
	Stanton Harcourt, Oxfordshire	2 Jul 43 - 26 Feb 44	Headquarters
	Enstone, Oxfordshire	26 Feb 44 - 1 Aug 44	Headquarters
		1 Aug 44	Disbanded
1683 Flt	Bruntingthorpe, Leicestershire	5 Jun 43 - 3 Feb 44	Headquarters
	Market Harborough, Leicestershire	3 Feb 44 - 1 Aug 44	Headquarters
		1 Aug 44	Disbanded
1684 Flt	Little Horwood, Buckinghamshire	29 Jun 43 - 17 Jul 43	Headquarters
	Wing, Buckinghamshire	17 Jul 43 - 1 Aug 44	Headquarters
		1 Aug 44	Disbanded
1685 Flt	Ossington, Nottinghamshire	1 Jul 43 - 21 Aug 44	Headquarters
	Finningley, Yorkshire	12 Jul 44 - 21 Aug 44	Detachment
		21 Aug 44	Disbanded
1686 Flt	Hixon, Staffordshire	1 Jul 43 - 21 Aug 44	Headquarters
		21 Aug 44	Disbanded
1687 Flt	Ingham, Lincolnshire	15 Feb 44 - 4 Dec 44	Headquarters
	Scampton, Lincolnshire	4 Dec 44 - 2 Apr 45	Headquarters
	Hemswell, Lincolnshire	2 Apr 45 - 30 Oct 46	Headquarters
		30 Oct 46	Disbanded
1688 Flt	Newmarket, Suffolk	11 Mar 44 - 25 Feb 45	Headquarters
	Feltwell, Norfolk	25 Feb 45 - 19 Mar 46	Headquarters
	Wyton, Huntingdonshire	19 Mar 46 - 30 Sep 46	Headquarters
		30 Sep 46	Disbanded
1689 Flt	Holme-on-Spalding Moor, Yorkshire	15 Feb 44 - 7 May 45	Headquarters
	Riccall, Yorkshire	Nov 44 -	Detachment
		7 May 45	Disbanded
1690 Flt	Syerston, Nottinghamshire	15 Feb 44 - 13 Jul 44	Headquarters
	Scampton, Lincolnshire	13 Jul 44 - 27 Sep 44	Headquarters
	Fiskerton, Lincolnshire	11 Aug 44 - 21 Sep 44	Detachment
	Metheringham, Lincolnshire	27 Sep 44 - 4 Jun 45	Headquarters
	Syerston, Nottinghamshire	4 Jun 45 - 21 Oct 45	Headquarters
		21 Oct 45	Disbanded
1691 Flt	Dalton, Yorkshire	1 Aug 43 - 15 Feb 44	Headquarters
		15 Feb 44	Redesignated
			1695 Flight
1692 Flt	Little Snoring, Norfolk	10 Dec 43 - 21 May 44	Headquarters
	Great Massingham, Norfolk	21 May 44 - 16 Jun 45	Headquarters
		16 Jun 45	Disbanded
1694 Flt	West Raynham, Norfolk	24 Jan 44 - 21 May 44	Headquarters
	Great Massingham, Norfolk	21 May 44 - 30 Jul 45	Headquarters
		30 Jul 45	Disbanded
1695 Flt	Dalton, Yorkshire	15 Feb 44 - 23 Apr 45	Headquarters
	Dishforth, Yorkshire	23 Apr 45 - 28 Jul 45	Headquarters
		28 Jul 45	Disbanded

```
1699 Flt  Sculthorpe, Norfolk                      24 Apr 44 - 16 May 44  Headquarters
          Oulton, Norfolk                          16 May 44 - 29 Jun 45  Headquarters
                                                               29 Jun 45  Disbanded


307 FTU   Bicester, Oxfordshire                    24 Dec 42 - 18 Feb 43  Headquarters
          Finmere, Buckinghamshire                 18 Feb 43 -  1 May 43  Headquarters
          Turweston, Buckinghamshire                1 May 43 - 18 May 43  Headquarters
          Finmere, Buckinghamshire                 18 May 43 -  1 Jun 43  Headquarters
                                                                1 Jun 43  Transferred
                                                                          70 Group
310 FTU   Harwell, Berkshire                       30 Apr 43 - 17 Dec 43  Headquarters
                                                               17 Dec 43  Disbanded
311 FTU   Moreton-in-Marsh, Gloucestershire         1 May 43 -  1 May 44  Headquarters
                                                                1 May 44  Disbanded


BCComFlt  Halton, Buckinghamshire                  12 May 42 -    Oct 46  Headquarters
          Booker, Buckinghamshire                     Oct 46 - 31 Dec 47  Headquarters
3 GComFlt Newmarket, Suffolk                        25 Jul 41 - 26 Feb 45  Headquarters
4 GComFlt Linton-on-Ouse, Yorkshire                       42 - 18 Jun 43  Headquarters
          Elvington, Yorkshire                     18 Jun 43 -  3 Jul 45  Headquarters
6 GComFlt Linton-on-Ouse, Yorkshire                18 Jun 43 -  5 Jun 44  Headquarters
91 GSU    Gamston, Nottinghamshire                 Not known  Not known  Headquarters
3 GTTFlt  Marham, Norfolk                          14 Feb 40 - 18 Nov 41  Headquarters
                                                               18 Nov 41  Redesignated
                                                                          1483 Flight
5 GTTFlt  Driffield, Yorkshire                     14 Feb 40 - 29 Dec 40  Headquarters
                                                               29 Dec 40  Absorbed by
                                                                          4 GTTFlight
3 GTrgFlt Stradishall, Suffolk                      1 Feb 41 - 21 May 41  Headquarters
          Newmarket, Suffolk                       21 May 41 -  7 Feb 42  Headquarters
                                                                7 Feb 42  Absorbed by
                                                                          1483 Flight
5 GTrgFlt Coningsby, Lincolnshire                   2 Oct 41 - 30 Oct 41  Headquarters
                                                               30 Oct 41  Absorbed by
                                                                          1485 Flight


BCIS      Finningley, Yorkshire                     5 Dec 44 - 22 Jan 47  Headquarters
          Worksop, Nottinghamshire                  5 Dec 44 -        45  Satellite
          Scampton, Lincolnshire                   22 Jan 47 - 15 Jun 47  Headquarters
                                                               15 Jun 47  Redesignated
                                                                          BCIR & EFlt
BSDU      Foulsham, Norfolk                         17 Apr 44 - 23 Dec 44  Headquarters
          Swanton Morley, Norfolk                  23 Dec 44 - 21 Jul 45  Headquarters
                                                               21 Jul 45  Redesignated
                                                                          RWE
BDU       Gransden Lodge, Bedfordshire             20 Jul 42 -  6 Apr 43  Headquarters
          Feltwell, Norfolk                         6 Apr 43 - 13 Sep 43  Headquarters
          Newmarket, Suffolk                       13 Sep 43 - 25 Feb 45  Headquarters
          Feltwell, Norfolk                        25 Feb 45 -    Oct 45  Headquarters
          Lindholme, Yorkshire                        Oct 45 - 27 Nov 45  Headquarters
                                                               27 Nov 45  Disbanded
CBE       Marham, Norfolk                          25 Sep 45 - 14 Apr 49  Headquarters
                                                               21 Dec 49  Disbanded
MSSU      Upwood, Huntingdonshire                  Not known  Not known  Headquarters
PFNTU     Gransden Lodge, Bedfordshire             10 Apr 43 -  5 Mar 44  Headquarters
          Warboys, Huntingdonshire                 17 Jun 43 -  5 Mar 44  Satellite
          Warboys, Huntingdonshire                  5 Mar 44 - 18 Jun 45  Headquarters
                                                               18 Jun 45  Disbanded
```

Note. I am indebted to Ray Sturtivant, John Hamlin and James J Halley, co-authors of Air-Britain (Historians) acclaimed publication, "Royal Air Force Flying Training and Support Units", published in 1997. This magnificent book is quite indispensable for the serious student of non-operational units of the Royal Air Force and without it my task in compiling the foregoing information would have taken me many weeks of additional research.

Appendix 2

Losses

Unit	Type	Op	Trg	Ea	Grnd	Misc	Unkn	Total
Section 1								
15 CFlt	Stirling I		1					1
26 CFlt	Stirling I		2			1		3
28 CFlt	Halifax I					1		1
35 CFlt	Halifax I				1			1
	Halifax II		1					1
49 CFlt	Manchester I	1						1
50 CFlt	Manchester I		1					1
76 CFlt	Halifax II	1						1
78 CFlt	Halifax I		2					2
	Halifax II		2					2
97 CFlt	Lancaster I					1		1
101 CFlt	Stirling I	1						1
102 CFlt	Halifax I		1					1
	Halifax II		3					3
103 CFlt	Halifax II		2					2
149 CFlt	Stirling I	1	3					4
158 CFlt	Halifax II		1					1
214 CFlt	Stirling I		1					1
218 CFlt	Stirling I	1	1					2
460 CFlt	Halifax II		1					1
	Total	5	23		1	3		32

Unit	Type	Op	Trg	Ea	Grnd	Misc	Unkn	Total
Section 1; sub-section								
1678 HCFlt	Lancaster II		2					2
1679 HCFlt	Lancaster II		4		1			5
	Total		6		1			7

Type	Op	Trg	Ea	Grnd	Misc	Unkn	Total
Losses, by type, for Section 1 and Section 1; sub-section							
Halifax I		3		1	1		5
Halifax II	1	10					11
Lancaster I					1		1
Lancaster II		6		1			7
Manchester I	1	1					2
Stirling I	3	9			1		13
Total	5	29		2	3		39

Unit	Type	Op	Trg	Ea	Grnd	Misc	Unkn	Total
Section 2								
1651 HCU	Lancaster I	1	5					6
	Lancaster III	2	2					4
	Stirling I	6	45		1	4		56
	Stirling III		7		2			9
	Tiger Moth II					1		1
1652 HCU	Halifax I	1	10					11
	Halifax II	3	43		1	5	1	53
	Halifax III		6		1			7
	Halifax V		2					2
	Spitfire VB		1					1
1653 HCU	Hurricane IIC		1					1
	Lancaster I		5					5
	Lancaster III		6					6
	Liberator II		2		1			3
	Mosquito XIX		1			1		2
	Spitfire VB		1					1
	Stirling I		13					13
	Stirling III		12			1		13
1654 HCU	Hurricane IIC		1					1
	Lancaster I	4	15					19
	Lancaster III	2	2					4
	Manchester I		5		1		1	7
	Manchester IA		3					3
	Oxford I		1					1
	Stirling III		23					23
1656 HCU	Halifax II		32					32
	Lancaster I	1	16		2			19
	Lancaster III		2		1			3
	Manchester I		1					1
1657 HCU	Lancaster II		1					1
	Stirling I		39	2		1		42
	Stirling III		11	1		1		13
1658 HCU	Halifax I		2					2
	Halifax II	1	63		2			66
	Halifax III		9				2	11
1659 HCU	Halifax II		42		1	3	1	47
	Halifax III		12		2			14
	Halifax V		11					11
1660 HCU	Halifax V		3					3
	Lancaster I		15					15
	Lancaster III		4					4
	Manchester I		4			1	1	6
	Stirling III		20					20
1661 HCU	Lancaster I		17					17
	Lancaster III		4					4
	Manchester I		5					5
	Stirling III		25			2		27
1662 HCU	Halifax II		23		1	2	1	27
	Halifax V		6			1		7
	Lancaster I		8					8
	Lancaster III		2					2
1663 HCU	Halifax II		5					5
	Halifax III	1	9		2			12
	Halifax V		53		2	1		56
1664 HCU	Halifax II	1	3					4
	Halifax III	1	4					5
	Halifax V		43			1		44
1665 HCU	Stirling I		6			1		7
1666 HCU	Halifax II		25		1	1	2	29
	Halifax V		2		1			3
	Lancaster I	1	1			1		3
	Lancaster II		2					2
	Lancaster III				1			1

Unit	Type	Op	Trg	Ea	Grnd	Misc	Unkn	Total
1667 HCU	Halifax V		40		5	1		46
	Hurricane IIC		1					1
	Lancaster I		5					5
	Lancaster III		4					4
1668 HCU	Beaufighter VIF					1		1
	Lancaster I		2					2
	Lancaster II		1		1			2
	Lancaster III		5					5
1669 HCU	Halifax II		3					3
	Halifax V		1					1
	Hurricane IIC		1					1
	Lancaster I		2					2
	Lancaster III		2					2
1678 HCU	Lancaster II		1					1
	Total	25	808	3	29	30	9	904

Type	Op	Trg	Ea	Grnd	Misc	Unkn	Total
Beaufighter VIF					1		1
Halifax I	1	12					13
Halifax II	5	239		6	11	5	266
Halifax III	2	40		5		2	49
Halifax V		161		8	4		173
Hurricane IIC		4					4
Lancaster I	7	91		2	1		101
Lancaster II		5		1			6
Lancaster III	4	31		2			37
Liberator II		2		1			3
Manchester I		15		1	1	2	19
Manchester IA		3					3
Mosquito XIX		1			1		2
Oxford I		1					1
Spitfire VB		2					2
Stirling I	6	103	2	1	6		118
Stirling III		98	1	2	4		105
Tiger Moth II					1		1
Total	25	808	3	29	30	9	904

Unit	Total	Op	Trg	Ea	Grnd	Misc	Unkn	Total

Section 3

Unit	Type	Op	Trg	Ea	Grnd	Misc	Unkn	Total
1 LFS	Lancaster I		2		1	3		6
3 LFS	Lancaster I		5					5
	Lancaster III		1					1
5 LFS	Lancaster I		10		2		1	13
	Lancaster III		3					3
	Total		21		3	3	1	28

Type	Op	Trg	Ea	Grnd	Misc	Unkn	Total
Lancaster I		17		3	3	1	24
Lancaster III		4					4
Total		21		3	3	1	28

Unit	Total	Op	Trg	Ea	Grnd	Misc	Unkn	Total

Section 4

Unit	Total	Op	Trg	Ea	Grnd	Misc	Unkn	Total
1655 MCU	Blenheim V		1					1
	Mosquito IV		1			1		2
	Total		2			1		3

Unit	Type	Op	Trg	Ea	Grnd	Misc	Unkn	Total
1655 MTU	Mosquito III		3					3
	Mosquito IV		20			1		21
	Mosquito XX		10					10
	Mosquito B.25					1		1
	Oxford I		1					1
	Total		34			2		36

Unit	Type	Op	Trg	Ea	Grnd	Misc	Unkn	Total

Section 5

Unit	Type	Op	Trg	Ea	Grnd	Misc	Unkn	Total
3 Flt	Wellington I		1					1
6 Flt	Oxford I		3					3
7 Flt	Oxford I		1					1
419 Flt	Lysander III	1						1
	Whitley V		1					1
1323 Flt	Lancaster III		1					1
1409 Flt	Mosquito IV	2						2
	Mosquito IX	6	1			1		8
	Mosquito XVI	3				1		4
1419 Flt	Whitley V	2				1		3
1427 Flt	Stirling I		1					1
1428 Flt	Hudson III		3					3
1429 Flt	Wellington IC		2					2
1443 Flt	Wellington IC		3				1	4
	Wellington II		1					1
	Wellington III		1					1
	Wellington VIII		2					2
1444 Flt	Hudson III		1			2		3
1446 Flt	Wellington IC		3			1		4
	Wellington II		1					1
1474 Flt	Wellington IC	3						3
1481 Flt	Martinet TTI					1		1
	Wellington IC	1						1
	Wellington X		2			1		3
	Whitley V		1					1
1482 Flt	Martinet I		1					1
1483 Flt	Defiant I		1					1
	Wellington IC		1					1
	Wellington III		1					1
1484 Flt	Defiant I		2					2
	Lysander TTI		1					1
	Oxford I		1					1
	Oxford II		1					1
	Whitley V		3					3
1485 Flt	Lysander III					1		1
	Manchester I		2					2
	Martinet I		1					1
	Wellington III		1					1
	Wellington X		1					1
1502 Flt	Whitley V	1						1
1507 Flt	Oxford I		1					1

Unit	Type	Op	Trg	Ea	Grnd	Misc	Unkn	Total

Section 5 Contd.

Unit	Type	Op	Trg	Ea	Grnd	Misc	Unkn	Total
1508 Flt	Oxford I		1					1
1513 Flt	Oxford I		1					1
1515 Flt	Oxford I		2					2
1516 Flt	Oxford I		2					2
1518 Flt	Oxford I		1			1		2
1519 Flt	Oxford I		2					2
1520 Flt	Oxford I		2					2
1521 Flt	Oxford I		4					4
1681 Flt	Tomahawk I		2					2
	Tomahawk IIA		1					1
1682 Flt	Tomahawk I		3					3
	Tomahawk IIA		2					2
1683 Flt	Tomahawk I		1		1		1	3
	Tomahawk IIA		4					4
1684 Flt	Tomahawk I		1		1			2
	Tomahawk IIA		1					1
1685 Flt	Tomahawk I		3		1			4
	Tomahawk IIA		1					1
1686 Flt	Tomahawk I					1		1
	Tomahawk IIA		1					1
	Tomahawk IIB				1			1
1687 Flt	Hurricane IIC		3					3
	Spitfire VB		3		1			4
1688 Flt	Hurricane IIC					1		1
	Spitfire VB		1					1
	Tiger Moth II		1					1
1689 Flt	Hurricane IID		1					1
	Spitfire VB		2					2
1690 Flt	Martinet I		1					1
	Hurricane IIC		6					6
1691 Flt	Martinet I					1		1
1692 Flt	Beaufighter VI		2					2
	Mosquito II		1			1		2
	Mosquito IV		2					2
	Mosquito XIX		1					1
	Oxford II		1					1
1694 Flt	Martinet I					1		1
1695 Flt	Hurricane IIC					1		1
	Spitfire VB		1			1		2
1699 Flt	Fortress II		2					2
	Total	19	110		5	17	2	153

Type	Op	Trg	Ea	Grnd	Misc	Unkn	Total
Beaufighter VI		2					2
Defiant I		3					3
Fortress II		2					2
Hudson III		4			2		6
Hurricane IIC		9			2		11
Hurricane IID		1					1
Lancaster III		1					1
Lysander TTI		1					1
Lysander III	1				1		2
Manchester I		2					2
Martinet TTI					1		1
Martinet I		3			2		5
Mosquito II		1			1		2
Mosquito IV	2	2					4
Mosquito IX	6	1			1		8
Mosquito XVI	3				1		4
Mosquito XIX		1					1
Oxford I		21			1		22
Oxford II		2					2

	Type	Op	Trg	Ea	Grnd	Misc	Unkn	Total

Section 5 Contd.

	Type	Op	Trg	Ea	Grnd	Misc	Unkn	Total
	Spitfire VB		7		1	1		9
	Stirling I		1					1
	Tiger Moth II		1					1
	Tomahawk I		10		3	1	1	15
	Tomahawk IIA		10					10
	Tomahawk IIB				1			1
	Wellington I		1					1
	Wellington IC	4	9			1	1	15
	Wellington II		2					2
	Wellington III		3					3
	Wellington VIII		2					2
	Wellington X		3			1		4
	Whitley V	3	5			1		9
	Total	19	110		5	17	2	153

Unit	Type	Op	Trg	Ea	Grnd	Misc	Unkn	Total

Section 6

Unit	Type	Op	Trg	Ea	Grnd	Misc	Unkn	Total
307 FTU	Boston III		1					1
310 FTU	Wellington X		1					1
311 FTU	Wellington III		1					1
	Wellington X		1					1
	Total		4					4

	Type	Op	Trg	Ea	Grnd	Misc	Unkn	Total
	Boston III		1					1
	Wellington III		1					1
	Wellington X		2					2
	Total		4					4

Unit	Type	Op	Trg	Ea	Grnd	Misc	Unkn	Total

Section 7

Unit	Type	Op	Trg	Ea	Grnd	Misc	Unkn	Total
BCComFlt	Anson					2		2
3 GComFlt	Mentor					1		1
4 GComFlt	B A Eagle II					1		1
	Leopard Moth					1		1
	Oxford II						1	1
	Tiger Moth II					1	1	2
6 GComFlt	B A Eagle					1		1
91 GSU	Wellington X				1			1
3 GTTFlt	Battle I		2					2
5 GTTFlt	Battle I		1					1
3 GTrgFlt	Wellington IC		2			4	1	7
5 GTrgFlt	Lysander TT		1					1
	Total		6		1	11	3	21

	Type	Op	Trg	Ea	Grnd	Misc	Unkn	Total

Section 7 Contd.

	Type	Op	Trg	Ea	Grnd	Misc	Unkn	Total
	Anson I					2		2
	B A Eagle					1		1
	B A Eagle II					1		1
	Battle I		3					3
	Leopard Moth					1		1
	Lysander TT		1					1
	Mentor I					1		1
	Oxford II						1	1
	Tiger Moth II					1	1	2
	Wellington IC		2			4	1	7
	Wellington X				1			1
	Total		6		1	11	3	21

Unit	Type	Op	Trg	Ea	Grnd	Misc	Unkn	Total

Section 8

Unit	Type	Op	Trg	Ea	Grnd	Misc	Unkn	Total
BCIS	Lancaster I		2					2
	Lancaster III		1					1
	Master I		1					1
	Mosquito III		1					1
	Spitfire VB					1		1
	Wellington X		3					3
BSDU	Mosquito VI					1		1
	Mosquito NF.30		1					1
	Oxford I					1		1
BDU	Halifax III		1					1
CBE	Mosquito XVI		2					2
	Spitfire XVI		1					1
MSS Upwood	Mosquito B.25					1		1
PFNTU	Halifax II		1					1
	Lancaster III		5			1		6
	Mosquito IV		3					3
	Mosquito XX		2					2
	Oxford I		1					1
	Total		25			5		30

Type	Op	Trg	Ea	Grnd	Misc	Unkn	Total
Halifax II		1					1
Halifax III		1					1
Lancaster I		2					2
Lancaster III		6			1		7
Master I		1					1
Mosquito III		1					1
Mosquito IV		3					3
Mosquito VI					1		1
Mosquito XVI		2					2
Mosquito XX		2					2
Mosquito B.25					1		1
Mosquito NF.30		1					1
Oxford I		1			1		2
Spitfire VB					1		1
Spitfire XVI		1					1
Wellington X		3					3
Total		25			5		30

Type	Op	Trg	Ea	Grnd	Misc	Unkn	Total

Section 9; losses from station flights

Type	Op	Trg	Ea	Grnd	Misc	Unkn	Total
Battle I					1		1
Blenheim I				1			1
Lysander II					1		1
Magister I			1		1		2
Oxford I	3				1	2	6
Oxford II	1			1	1	1	4
Tiger Moth					1		1
Tiger Moth II	1				1		2
Total	5	1		2	7	3	18

Section 1 to Section 9; totals

Type	Total	Type	Total
Anson I	2	Martinet I	5
B A Eagle	1	Master I	1
B A Eagle II	1	Mentor I	1
Battle I	4	Mosquito II	2
Beaufighter VI	2	Mosquito III	4
Beaufighter VIF	1	Mosquito IV	30
Blenheim I	1	Mosquito VI	1
Blenheim V	1	Mosquito IX	8
Boston III	1	Mosquito XVI	6
Defiant I	3	Mosquito XIX	3
Fortress II	2	Mosquito XX	12
Halifax I	18	Mosquito B.25	2
Halifax II	278	Mosquito NF.30	1
Halifax III	50	Oxford I	32
Halifax V	173	Oxford II	7
Hudson III	6	Spitfire VB	12
Hurricane IIC	15	Spitfire XVI	1
Hurricane IID	1	Stirling I	132
Lancaster I	128	Stirling III	105
Lancaster II	13	Tiger Moth	1
Lancaster III	49	Tiger Moth II	6
Leopard Moth	1	Tomahawk I	15
Liberator II	3	Tomahawk IIA	10
Lysander TT	1	Tomahawk IIB	1
Lysander TTI	1	Wellington I	1
Lysander II	1	Wellington IC	22
Lysander III	2	Wellington II	2
Manchester I	23	Wellington III	4
Manchester IA	3	Wellington VIII	2
Magister I	2	Wellington X	10
Martinet TTI	1	Whitley V	9
Total; columns 1 and 2			1236

Note.   Additional to the Bomber Command losses summarised, five aircraft from other commands are featured as they were written off in circumstances directly concerned with incidents described in this volume. They have not, however, been included in the statistics reported within this appendix.

Appendix 3

Prisoners of War & Internees

As with the previous volume, details in re-spect of airmen taken prisoners of war are shown in alphabetical sequence, regardless of rank. This information has been gleaned from AIR20 2336, the original being held at the National Archives Public Record Office, Kew. I am also mindful of the help given by Oliver Clutton-Brock, an acknowledged expert in all matters pertaining to airmen from the Allied air forces that found themselves in captivity. Identification of the camp codes appear at the end of this appendix.

Royal Air Force

Name	Date	Unit	Serial	Target/Duty	Camp	Number
F/L E N Baker	17-18 Feb 1941	1419 Flt	T4264	SIS	L3	463
W/O D H Bernard	17-18 Feb 1941	1419 Flt	T4264	SIS	L3	481
F/L D E Breed	28-29 Jul 1941	1651 CU	W7509	Hamburg	L3	567
W/O E J Butt	26-27 Jul 1942	76 CFlt	R9485	Hamburg	L6	39734
Cpl A J Cameron	17-18 Feb 1941	1419 Flt	T4264	SIS	L3	488
F/L R L Cox	9 Apr 1941	3 GTrgFlt	W5677	Ferry	L3	2677
W/O R L Cox	28-29 Jul 1942	1651 CU	W7509	Hamburg	344	25040
S/L The Hon. P I Cunliffe-Lister	18 Jul 1943	1409 Flt	LR502	Pampa	L3	1811
W/O D W Davies	17-18 Feb 1941	1419 Flt	T4264	SIS	L3	493
W/O D Durrant	14 Jul 1943	1409 Flt	LR501	Pampa	L6	310
F/L D W Foster DFM	30-31 May 1942	1502 Flt	Z9307	Köln	L3	548
F/S F E Gostling	1- 2 Jun 1942	1652 CU	R9372	Essen	357	568
F/L P F Hall	9 May 1943	1409 Flt	DZ316	Pampa	L3	1327
Sgt L Hudson	9 Apr 1941	3 GTrgFlt	W5677	Ferry	357	3771
W/O H Jackson	1- 2 Jun 1942	1652 CU	R9372	Essen	357	424
S/L F J B Keast DFC	17-18 Feb 1941	1419 Flt	T4264	SIS	L3	468
F/L A P Kernon	18 Jul 1943	1409 Flt	LR502	Pampa	L3	1715
F/L K S McMurdie	17-18 Feb 1941	1419 Flt	T4264	SIS	L3	474
F/S V A Martin	25-26 Jun 1942	1652 CU	V9993	Bremen	L4	338
W/O R Morrow	28-29 Jul 1942	1651 CU	W7509	Hamburg	344	25629
W/O C M Muir	26-27 Jul 1942	76 CFlt	R9485	Hamburg	344	25145
W/O C R Read	1- 2 Jun 1942	1652 CU	R9372	Essen	357	439
S/L J A S Russell DFC	30-31 May 1942	1502 Flt	Z9307	Köln	L3	39664
W/O R J Tavener	30-31 May 1942	1652 CU	L9605	Köln	357	447
W/O J L Warren	28-29 Jul 1942	1651 CU	W7509	Hamburg	L6	25047
F/L H A Williams	1- 2 Jun 1942	1652 CU	R9372	Essen	L3	386
W/O J Williams	1- 2 Jun 1942	1652 CU	R9372	Essen	357	457
F/L W C Woodruff	9 May 1943	1409 Flt	DZ316	Pampa	L3	1340
W/O R G W Woollard	26-27 Jul 1942	76 CFlt	R9485	Hamburg	344	25133
F/L S G Wright	30-31 May 1942	1652 CU	L9605	Köln	L3	387

Royal Canadian Air Force

WO2 H J W Daly	1- 2 Jun 1942	1652 CU	R9372	Essen	357	403
WO2 H V Dufour	28-29 Jul 1942	1651 CU	W7509	Hamburg	344	25046
WO2 H F Spratt	25-26 Jun 1942	1652 CU	V9993	Bremen	344	24944
WO2 R W Wagstaff	25-26 Jun 1942	1652 CU	V9993	Bremen	L3	24946

Royal New Zealand Air Force

W/O R J A Blackstock	9 Apr 1941	3 GTrgFlt	W5677	Ferry	344	32411
F/L D G Cookson	30-31 May 1942	1652 CU	L9605	Köln	L3	401

Royal New Zealand Air Force; Contd.

Name	Date	Unit	Serial	Target/Duty	Camp	Number
W/O D C B Jenkins	9 Apr 1941	3 GTrgFlt	W5677	Ferry	344	33658

The following are reported in unit records, or on casualty returns, as becoming prisoners of war, but for whom no details, as yet, have been traced.

Royal Air Force

Sgt J A Collett	9 Apr 1941	3 GTrgFlt	W5677	Ferry	
Sgt E C Sudbury	26-27 Jul 1942	76 CFlt	R9485	Hamburg	
P/O R Taylor	14 Jun 1943	1409 Flt	LR501	Pampa	

Royal Canadian Air Force

F/L J A L Lymburner DFC	27 Feb 1945	1409 Flt	NS731	Snooper	
F/O D B E McKenzie	25-26 Jun 1942	1652 CU	V9993	Bremen	

Camp	Location	Camp	Location
L3	Stalag Luft Sagan and Beleria	344	Stalag Lamsdorf
L4	Stalag Luft Sagan and Beleria	357	Stalag Thorn
L6	Stalag Luft Heydekrug		

Note 1. In the aftermath of the loss of Wellington IC W5677 of No. 3 Group Training Flight, its distinguished passenger, Maj Gen Adrian Carton de Wiart became a prisoner of war. At the time of his capture, he had been on his way to take up an appointment as head of the Military Mission to Yugoslavia. In the closing days of Italy´s exit from the war, he was released from captivity in order to assist in the surrender negotiations. Born in Brussels on 5 May 1880, this gallant soldier retired to Ireland and died on 5 June 1963, aged eighty-three, at Killinardrish, Co. Cork. His Victoria Cross had been Gazetted on 9 September 1916.

Note 2. Only one crew from the training formations, examined in this volume experienced a spell of internment and their names are shown below, along with the relevant WO208 class references.

Sgt G H Burge	27 Apr 1941	3 GTrgFlt	W5652	Ferry	3308 (-)725
F/O E M Child-Villiers	27 Apr 1941	3 GTrgFlt	W5652	Ferry	3308 (-)719
Sgt H E Herritey	27 Apr 1941	3 GTrgFlt	W5652	Ferry	3308 (-)723
Sgt N O Horrocks	27 Apr 1941	3 GTrgFlt	W5652	Ferry	3308 (-)724
S/L G F Rodney	27 Apr 1941	3 GTrgFlt	W5652	Ferry	3308 (-)718

Appendix 4

Captain Stanislaw Kruszewski

During the night of 10-11 April 1941, a team of Polish saboteurs boarded a Whitley bomber, belonging to No. 1419 Flight, taking off from Tangmere with the intention of destroying an electricity power station in the western suburbs of Bordeaux. The fate of this Whitley and its crew are reported on page 195 of this volume, but since learning the names of the six Polish officers involved in this abortive mission and summarising the events, I have been given permission to quote from a series of three articles written for "Spadochron", the periodical of the 1st Polish Independent Parachute Brigade Association, by Lieutenant (later Captain) Stanislaw Kruszewski, and first published in 1989. Some of the locations, and purpose of the operation, differ from what I report on page 195 but the basic features remain the same.

"For me the story began in January 1941, when I was stationed in Unit 118, Elie, Fifeshire. It was either in mid-January, or end January, when my commanding officer told me to report to Headquarters Leven, Fife, the following day. Lieutenants K Dendor and K Bogdziewicz from my unit got the same message. Next day, we sat on a bench in the headquarters waiting room and patiently waited. The number slowly increased as Captain Kalicinski and Second Lieutenants Miciek and Zwolanski from other units joined us. Soon we were summoned before the colonel (Colonel Sosabowski) who announced, "Gentlemen, you are under orders from the C-in-C and are to be moved. I cannot tell you the details, as I have no information. You will take these instructions with you and your units will be told that you are posted to British authorities for special training. Any questions? Right, well good luck!"

We were sent to British Diversionary Station No. 17, about fifty miles north of London, near Hertford, where we began intensive training in explosives, ambushes, traps, detonators, fuses, pistols, tommy-guns, hand-to-hand combat, etc. After a few days we were told details of the mission. We were to attack an airfield used by four-engined Focke-Wulf aircraft in the Bordeaux region. These aircraft were successfully co-operating with U-boats and greatly endangering Allied convoys. Our group had been selected on an ad hoc basis; we were strangers to each other and seemed ill assorted (one was not physically fit and one was nervous of the drop). This was rather worrying as for a job of this kind we needed full mutual confidence. However, Zwolanski and I understood each other well; he was a fine shot and had a hard head for drink (they called him the "Black Bandit"). We decided when it came to it we two would stick together.

We began our preparations. Based on aerial photographs, a plastic layout model had been made. We memorised every feature. We were given fictitious identities, and false names and committed every detail of our "legends" to memory. From the British cadre I specially remember Lieutenant Hotchkis-Fretchkis, known as Tommy. He was an expert instructor and knew every detail of the weapons, made his own mines and traps. He badgered his superiors to send him on an operation. They were reluctant to lose such a good instructor but at last in 1943 he was dispatched on a mission to Czechoslovakia but not a word of him was ever heard again. After the end of hostilities, Major Perkins set off to search for him but, sadly, came back with no result.

We returned to Ringway for four days of parachute practice. After all of us completed a number of day and night drops we went back to Hertford to hear very surprising news. Like a bolt from the blue we were told that the object of our attack had been changed. They had found a better target. We were stunned. All the previous effort seemed wasted. The Focke-Wulf airport was "out". The new object of our attention also played a vital rôle in the Battle of the Atlantic; it was a transformer station in Meriniao, north of Bordeaux, where twenty-four hours a day and seven days a week, U-boat batteries were being charged after every cruise. Our job was to destroy the transformers.

After considering all the pros and cons, we came to the conclusion that this new operation offered much greater chance of success and from our point of view would be easier to achieve. To attack aircraft spaced two hundred metres apart, with a guard by each, would have been a difficult job for our small group. The new target would be more compact in structure and easier to tackle.

Work now started again from the beginning; new aerial photos, new model, new maps, plans and intelligence reports. The transformer station was surrounded by a wall about three-and-a-half metres high with barbed wire along the top. We would have to cross this wall, laden with all our equipment, arms and ammunition, iron rations, etc. This would not be easy. After many ideas (someone suggested pole vaulting!) we chose double rope ladders with hooks that had to be fastened on the summit. We would climb up the ladders, fix the hooks and pull up the second half of the ladders and descend on the other side. The ladders would be left in position and used for the getaway. Transformer personnel on duty (according to the reports) would be about twelve German soldiers. Zwolanski and I would go first with the job of eliminating these men. Meantime, the rest of our team would carry the bombs over the wall and as quickly as possible place them on the transformers. The bombs would be time fused for twenty-five minutes so there would not be much time for the job. The getaway would be either via the rope ladders, or by forcing the entrance gates. Surprise was, of course, essential. Also required was fast action in complete silence. This was the most difficult thing. Fixing the hooks always made a certain amount of noise, especially at night and though we reached perfection in throwing the ropes over we could not completely avoid the metallic note of the hooks. The only way was to rely on our speed and all the rest of our practice was devoted to this end. Faster, faster! Zwolanski and I practised to the point where we could get over in twenty-five seconds. Of course, as soon as we began to eliminate the guards, silence would not be so important.

We still had to plan the getaway. France was now divided into two regions; our way led south in two groups and, after crossing the demarcation line, we had to make for Perpignan, where at a certain day and time we would rendezvous with a British submarine which would take us to Great Britain. The most dangerous part of the getaway was the first phase after planting the bombs. "Liquidating" the defending soldiers would, inevitably, involve shooting and would alert the guards. We had no information where they were stationed and how quickly they could arrive and join the fight. Being young and keen we did not think too much about it, for us the most important part was to destroy those transformers. I remember that Lieutenant Dendor, who had amazing powers of memory, committed to mind all the various road routes and distances we would have to cover. We spent a few more days on a systematic study of our identity "legends".

Another great surprise was the arrival of a second complete group; a Reserve! Four were from my unit at Elie and one of my friends was a sapper, Genio Jakubowski. The fact that they sent a sapper was a wonderful move. The bombs were to be dropped in containers and in the event of any unforeseen crisis with the bombs a sapper would be an enormous asset. However, we were firmly told that the second group was not intended as an addition, purely a reserve. We pleaded, but were firmly told NO. A great pity, but we could not change it. Members of the second group were told nothing at all of the mission; we were not allowed to discuss it - even between our own group, except in the operations room. We continued memorising the details. Although we still handled the explosives with due respect, with time we felt more confident that they were there to help us.

After a final check we were transported to an airfield somewhere in the south of England. With great interest we watched fighter aircraft returning from action, many performed "victory rolls" and we felt that the balance of war was slowly turning in favour of the Allies. However, the Atlantic still belonged to the lurking U-boats. Our containers had been packed in our No. 17 Unit at Hertford. As extras I took with me a Colt 38 pistol with ammunition, four magazines, two grenades, two rations, concentrated chocolate, a pipe containing a magnetic needle, sterilised dressings, ampoules of morphia, money, personal papers and chewing gum.

As far as I can remember, take off time was twenty hundred hours. We had our last meal before take off. It was a substantial and tasty meal; we ate well, not knowing when we would eat again, except from iron rations. Next we prepared for departure, collected and strapped on our parachutes. After a final scrupulous inspection we were loaded on to a 15 cwt van and went to the dispersal where our Whitley awaited. We climbed the aircraft steps slowly, due to the heavy equipment we carried and sat on the floor which was covered with some thick material. We were to fly at 13,000 feet. I was to jump first. Major Perkins had assured us that the crew of the aircraft was one of the best at this kind of operation. The British dispatcher entered the aircraft last and closed and secured the doors. The engines gathered speed and we were off.

On the way I dozed until I heard the pilot say on the intercom, "Twenty minutes to the Drop Zone". We began to get ready. The English instructor opened an exit in the floor and pulled our static lines through and hooked them up to the aircraft. We all waited for the red light and Action Stations. Suddenly, the door to the cabin opened and the navigator entered, lay down on the floor and peered through a crack at the bomb bay. We were rather amazed but thought it was nothing to do with us. Then, through the intercom came the awful news, "We have lost the containers", and the silly question, "do you want to drop without them?". How could we do the job without explosives, bite the transformers with our teeth? We would have to go back.

As I later discovered, it was the tail gunner who reported that he had seen two parachutes floating down to the Atlantic. At once the navigator had checked the bomb bay, confirmed it was empty and reported to the pilot.

Among us in the aircraft as we returned there was a feeling of a kind of relief; only Zwolanski was heard steadily cursing under his breath. I slept the whole way back as there was nothing better to do. I awoke as the engines changed their revs and we were losing speed. I guessed we were landing when, suddenly, the aircraft fell and hit the ground heavily and I briefly lost consciousness. When I opened my eyes, the pilot's cockpit was on fire. Zwolanski was by the doors and shouting at the English instructor to open them, but this was not easy as in the impact with the ground the locks had jammed.

Finally Zwolanski and the Englishman kicking and heaving with all their strength managed to force the doors open. We began to tumble out and someone started shooting. For a moment I thought we had come down in Europe, but no, Royal Air Force airmen were running to and fro. I realised later it was the machine gun ammunition exploding in the fire. I jumped out of the fuselage. A voice called, "Come on, come on, hurry up you will all be hurt." I looked back at our Whitley rapidly burning away to nothing. Suddenly I noticed the shape of a person in the fuselage with his hair on fire, lying on the floor. Without thinking, I pushed back into the fuselage, seized the chap under his armpits and dragged him outside. His hair was still burning and I tried to extinguish it by rolling him on the ground. At first I thought he was one of our lot, but it was one of the British crew. Soon orderlies ran up and laid him on a stretcher. They wanted to do the same for me but I said, "No, I am OK." They ordered me to get clear of the aircraft because the petrol tanks would explode at any moment. It was still dark and I did not know where our group was but they soon called me and I joined them. Major Perkins was with us, we were alive and well.

The English instructor, who was standing when the aircraft hit the ground, had broken his leg. They took us by ambulance to the sick bay and gave us a quick going over. We were not in the worst condition; we had come through the disaster whole, though some had cuts and bruises, three had strained necks and backs. Zwolanski and I had no injuries at all.

The British crew came out of it far worse. The wireless operator, and the tail gunner were killed. The second pilot had head injuries, the front gunner had serious burns to his head, face and hands. I was particularly sorry about the death of the tail gunner. His alertness in noticing the loss of the containers prompted the cancellation of the whole operation in the air at about ten miles from the Drop Zone. Had it not been for him, we would have jumped without the containers; the job would have been impossible to achieve, we would have wandered about France and God knows how many of us would have made it back to England. We were prepared for all eventualities of fighting, wounds, capture, even death would have been of small account if we could have finished the job and done something to hurt the Huns. Without the containers, there would have been only disappointment and anger. That is why we had so much to thank the tail gunner for. It has always seemed to me so unfair that he had to pay with his life.

When we were alone and the excitement gradually faded we began to question Major Perkins. How was it we lost the containers? Sabotage. How and when? Not known. Enquiries would be very difficult as the bomb release mechanism was destroyed in the crash. What caused the crash? Fog (blind navigation aids were in their infancy at the time).

We went back to the No. 17 station at Hertford where they greeted us warmly and with sympathy. Two days later we lined up before our colonel; we looked a sorry sight after the accident and he invited us to come and sit down and tell him all about it. We let him know our opinion of the inefficient way we had been selected and other aspects. We returned to Scotland and were ordered to tell friends nothing of our escapade. We were given two weeks leave, which I spent at Ringway. On return from leave I was posted to the Polish parachute school at Ringway (together with Zwolanski). To my great surprise, I was decorated with the Polish gallantry award, the Cross of Valour. I remained as an instructor at Ringway for the next three-and-a-half years."

Note. First and foremost, I thank Irene Hrynkiiewicz, general secretary of The Polish Airborne Forces Association, for allowing me permission to quote from Stanislaw Kruszewski's article. Equally, I am indebted to Betty Clements for her excellent translation of the original and also to Kajetan Bieniecki of Montreal whose detective work in tracing the names of the six paratroopers was aided by Krzysztof A Tochman's book, "Stownik Biograficzny Cichociemnych", published in 1996. At the time of preparing his article, Stanislaw Kruszewski (and his stalwart friend, Zwolanski) was living in Australia. Fate prevented Stanislaw Kruszewski from participating in the Arnhem operation but his friend Zwolanski was present and his bravery was justly recognised in the form of the Virtuti Militari Class V.

Addenda

Since preparing, and printing, the pages of this volume, my attention has been drawn to additional material that enhances some of the summaries recorded. Thus, readers may find the following notes to be helpful in their appreciation of the significant losses sustained by the various establishments that feature in this book. In the way of a general observation, I offer an insight into the solemn matters of funeral arrangements made in the aftermath of the tragic accident suffered by 1660 Heavy Conversion Unit on 31 January 1944 (see page 86). The crew comprised of a Canadian staff pilot, Flying Officer James Hubert Mason, heading a standard trainee bomber crew. As commented upon in the summary, Flying Officer Mason was probably buried under private arrangements. However, at least three funerals were, I suggest, handled by the services; namely those for Warrant Officer McKnight of Cheltenham, Flying Officer Trueman RCAF and Sergeant Duke of Paddington. I would, therefore, have expected to find all three buried in the same cemetery, but one, namely Warrant Officer McKnight, was interred at nearby Newark-upon-Trent Cemetery, while his two companions were taken to Thurlby (St. Germain) Churchyard, a burial ground used by "1660" and other units in the Thurlby area between 1941 and late 1944.

Page 16   158 CFlt   Halifax II BB203 Two brothers, George and Arthur Pearson of
                                         Castle Hill, Sheriff Hutton, were commended
for their courage in attempting to rescue the bomber's crew. Subsequently,
their actions were officially recognised in the London Gazette on 4 January
1943. See National Archives Public Record Office, AIR2 16972.

Page 27   1653 CU   Liberator II AL588 For a fascinating insight into the complexities
                                           surrounding the awards to civilians who assisted
at the scene of military air accidents, readers should consult AIR2 16971 and
the official correspondence in respect of Gilbert Gingell, George Hewick and
Alan Snowden, all of whom made valiant efforts to extract the crew from the
burning Liberator. In the case of Gilbert Gingell, a George Medal was the
recommendation from Air Marshal Sir Arthur Harris, but following a lengthy
period of discussion, the Civilian Gallantry Awards Committee decided that
a British Empire Medal, or perhaps a mere commendation, would suffice. In
the event, a British Empire Medal was approved for both Gilbert Gingell and
George Hewick, while Alan Snowden received a commendation, details appearing
in the London Gazette on 26 February 1943.

Page 32   1651 HCU   Stirling I BF314 In respect of the note that follows the summary,
                                         Bryce Gomersall has looked into the matter and
has located the London Gazette entry for Squadron Leader Lofthouse's award; this
being 29 January 1943. Also honoured with British Empire Medals (Military Division)
were Aircraftman First Class John Edward Taylor and Aircraftman Second Class Albert
Henry Martin.

Page 36   1660 HCU   Manchester I L7482 Apart from Flying Officer Goodyear RCAF, all were
                                           killed in action on 9-10 April 1943, while flying
with 9 Squadron on operations to Duisburg. See Bomber Command Losses, Volume 4,
page 99 for further details.

Page 37   1659 HCU   Halifax II W1146 The funerals for those who died were held on
                                         1 February 1943. Sergeant Drago's father,
accompanied by Mr. Gilbert, a family friend, attended. Two Canadian padres
officiated; Flight Lieutenant H F D Smeaton conducted the Roman Catholic service,
while Flight Lieutenant H E D Ashford oversaw the Church of England interments.
Also in attendance was a firing party, drawn from personnel stationed at Leeming.
At 1000 hours, on the day following the crash, a Court of Enquiry was convened to
try and determine the cause of the accident. The President appointed was Wing
Commander A Earle of 428 Squadron, with Squadron Leader H Hill DFC and Pilot
Officer J E Garlick, both of 1659 Heavy Conversion Unit, attending as members.

Page 47   1663 HCU   Halifax V   DG408   At the time of the accident, it is believed this
                                           aircraft carried the individual letter "M".

Page 53   1665 HCU   Stirling I BF339   Following his recovery, and completion of his
                                           training, Flying Officer Kennett joined 620
Squadron at Chedburgh. As was so common in the turbulent months of 1943 and
1944, his tour was not destined to last for long. Detailed to accompany Squadron
Leader A D Lambert DFC to Peenemünde on 17-18 August 1943, he died when their
Stirling was shot down by a night-fighter; see Bomber Command Losses, Volume 4,
page 276 for further information.

Page 69   1662 HCU   Halifax II HR930   Although the circumstances surrounding the demise
                                           of this Halifax are not known, it is believed that
it carried "A2" on its fuselage, but as to which of the two unit code combinations
(KF or PE) was displayed remains a mystery.

Page 74   1652 HCU   Halifax II DG230   Reported to have been carrying the letter "J" at
                                           the time of the crash.

Page 75   1658 HCU   Halifax II DT578   Sergeant Thomas Noel Chadwick, elder brother to
                                           the pilot, was killed in action on 28 March 1943,
while flying Mosquitoes with 105 Squadron (see Bomber Command Losses, Volume 4,
page 82). He is buried in France at Lille Southern Cemetery.

           1678 HCU   Lancaster II DS653 From their entries in the Haycombe cemetery
                                           register, published by the Commonwealth War
Graves Commission, it is noted that Warrant Officer Second Class Johnston was
a Bachelor of Arts graduate from the University of Saskatchewan. It is further
observed that Sergeant Batterham had a stepmother, while Flight Sergeant Burton
had a stepfather. The three English members of crew all came from the London
area. It was the unit's sole fatal flying accident in ten months of existence.

Page 76   1658 HCU   Halifax II DT490   Sergeant Jenkins was a Member of the Typo-
                                           graphical Association. He was aged thirty-
                                           three, and married.

Page 78   1661 HCU   Lancaster I LM307   Sergeant Austin was a Member of the Pharma-
                                           ceutical Society. He was aged twenty-nine,
                                           and married.

Page 81   1656 HCU   Halifax II W7772   Pilot Officer Jenkins, after attending a Lancaster
                                           conversion course, was posted to 100 Squadron at
Grimsby, only to fail to return from Bomber Command's last major raid on Berlin;
see Bomber Command Losses, Volume 5, page 131 for additional details.

Page 85   1660 HCU   Stirling III EH933 A mere four weeks previous to the loss of this
                                           Stirling, a Martinet trainer belonging to No.
18 Operational Training Unit crashed during the course of a fighter affiliation
exercise (see Bomber Command Losses, Volume 7, page 268). Its pilot was Flying
Officer Peter Robert Street, brother to the Sergeant Street who perished in the
Stirling accident.

Page 87   1662 HCU   Halifax II V9983   Sergeant Freeman's brother, Petty Officer John
                                           Herbert Freeman, lost his life while serving
aboard the aircraft carrier, HMS Indomitable on 15 August 1942. He is commemorated on the Lee-on-Solent Memorial, Bay 3, panel 3.

Page 88   1663 HCU   Halifax V   EB195   Believed to have been carrying the letter "O".

Page 89   1652 HCU   Halifax II W1005   Believed to have been displaying the combination
                                           GV-L at the time of its demise.

Page 97   1653 HCU   Stirling I R9280   In respect of Bomber Command Losses, Volume 5,
                                           page 183, it will be observed that the name of
the tail gunner was Sergeant S Glaister RCAF, whose service number was R/200002.
Referring to the station records for Chedburgh, the appendices clearly indicate
Sergeant J D Glaister RCAF, quoting his service number as R/200001. Consequently
Bryce Gomersall has looked into the matter and he confirms that there were two
Glaisters and that they were brothers. Both enlisted on 10 November 1942, and
with Stanley Glaister being the younger, at eighteen years of age, his father's

Page 97   1653 HCU   Stirling I R9280 Contd. permission was necessary; this was duly
                              forthcoming on 10 December 1942. It is almost
certain that the initial training paths of the two brothers followed parallel
paths and they both arrived in the United Kingdom on 19 September 1943. Following
a few days spent at a reception centre, they joined No. 12 Operational Training
Unit and completed this stage of their training on 28 January 1944. Their ways
now appear to separate; the elder of the two attended 1651 Heavy Conversion Unit
while Stanley arrived at Chedburgh. Thus, it appears likely that while he was
undergoing his heavy conversion training, his elder brother paid him a visit
and was "invited" to fly with Sergeant Dobson on 22 March 1944, and, as no one
was hurt, no questions were asked. What is certain, of course, is that Stanley
Glaister lost his life while serving with 90 Squadron, while his brother, James
Douglas Glaister, went on to complete twenty-nine sorties with 115 Squadron,
finishing his tour of duty on 13 August 1944.

Page 98   1659 HCU   Halifax II JD317 Both Flying Officer Beresford and Sergeant Cowan
                              lost their lives on bombing operations, the former
on 9 August 1944, whilst serving with 427 Squadron and the latter on 29 July 1944,
failing to return from a sortie to Hamburg with 434 Squadron; please refer to
Bomber Command Losses, Volume 5, pages 376 and 358 respectively.

Page 126   1661 HCU   Stirling III LK591 Pilot Officer Allan Ernest Bullock went on to
                              fly with 467 Squadron, gaining a Distinguished
Flying Cross. Details of his decoration were published in the London Gazette
on 21 September 1945, and were repeated in the Australia Gazette on 4 October
1945.

Page 157   1653 HCU Lancaster III DV161 Insert "DFM" after the name of Pilot Officer
                              Marritt. He was a "screened" flight engineer
who gained his award while serving with 7 Squadron, the details in the London
Gazette on 21 April 1944.

Page 158   1660 HCU   Stirling III LK400 It is believed this aircraft came down, not as
                              reported but at Morton Hall, on the north side
of Swinderby, slightly injuring the wireless operator, Flight Sergeant Shimmons.

Page 172   1656 HCU Lancaster III W4994 Reported to have been carrying the combination
                              EK-N at the time of its write off.

Page 182   1655 MCU   Blenheim V AZ961 Hans de Haan of Almere in Holland suggests
                              that the navigator, identified as "Lt Moe"
might well be Lieutenant Tycho Didrik Castberg Moe of the Royal Norwegian
Air Force, missing in action on 26 February 1943, while flying in Mosquito IV
DZ481 of 139 Squadron (see Bomber Command Losses, Volume 4, page 50). He has
no known grave.

           1655 MCU   Mosquito IV DZ495 Hans de Haan of Almere in Holland advises that
                              the bodies of both officers were exhumed, soon
after the war, and reinterred in Norwegian soil. Thus, on 18 October 1945, at
Oslo Vestre Aker Cemetery, Captain Olav Bakke Stene was laid to rest, while on
5 October 1945, just thirteen days earlier, his navigator, Lieutenant Kjell
Lochen, was buried in Oslo Ullern Cemetery. Although I cannot be certain, I
much suspect that their original burials took place at Marham.

Page 197   1443 Flt Wellington IC HF855 It is almost certain that Cadet Hughes had a
                              twin-brother, namely Aircraftman Second Class
Vivien Stanley Hughes. He died, aged twenty-one, on 12 February 1945, and is
buried with Cadet Hughes in a joint grave at Didcot (All Saints) Churchyard.

Page 206   1507 Flt   Oxford I V4035 Pilot Officer Tree had trained, as a pilot,
                              with the prewar volunteer reserve. Prior to
joining No. 1507 Beam Approach Training Flight, he had served with 49 Squadron,
gaining a Distinguished Flying Medal (Gazetted 29 November 1941).

Page 207   1518 Flt   Oxford I AT663 Flight Lieutenant Butt had been mentioned in
                              despatches, but the date of his award is, as
                              yet, untraced.

Amendments to Volume 7

In respect of the amendments to Volume 7, invariably all entries that refer to airmen who hailed from New Zealand, whether they were serving with the Royal New Zealand Air Force, or on short service commission with the Royal Air Force, have their origins in material kindly supplied by Errol Martyn. Thus, instead of presenting the amendments in as brief a form as possible, I have taken advantage of Errol's fulsome notes and report the amendments in as much detail as possible. Similarly, David Gunby's excellent account of the history of 40 Squadron, published by Pentland Press in 1995, under the title, "Sweeping The Skies" has been the source for material mentioning this famous Royal Flying Corps/Royal Air Force squadron. I am, of course, extremely grateful to everyone who has sent me additional material; without your support, these amendments would be much the poorer.

Page 12   12/P2273   Add: P/O Barnett was the younger brother of Wing Commander Denis Barnett (later Air Chief Marshal), who commanded 40 Squadron between 4 June and 23 December 1940.

Page 16   12/K9481   Add: T/o 1000 Benson.
           12/L4977   Add: T/o 0945 Benson. Crashed at around 1120. Both crews had been instructed to avoid rainstorms and areas where visibility was poor. The two crashes occurred as the aircraft were flying on the Exeter to Lyme Regis leg. Weather conditions in the Exeter area are reported as good, with the cloud base assessed as between 1,500 and 2,000 feet, but, according to Squadron Leader Hawkins, who was based at Exeter and who attended the accident sites, low cloud in the Sidmouth region undoubtedly covered the tops of local high ground.

Page 17   12/P2269   Delete: RNZAF after the pilot's name, both in the crew matrix and in the text. Also, take out the last sentence and replace with, "He completed his ab-initio training in New Zealand, having being accepted for a short service commission in the Royal Air Force."

           12/L5282   Amend: P/O N C Pettit. He was killed on 26 August 1941, in Nigeria, while flying with the Fighter Defence Flight or the Takoradi Despatch Flight. He is buried at Ikoyi No. 2 Cemetery. Aged twenty, and from New Zealand, he was serving with the Royal Air Force on a short service commission.

Page 18   16/L4138   Add: P/O Rowe hailed from New Zealand, but was serving with the Royal Air Force on a short service commission.

Page 21   17/L9171   Amend: Hawerna (in Note) to read Hawera.

Page 22   20/R9583   Amend: Sgt C B G Knight DFM RNZAF. He was the first Royal New Zealand Air Force airman to be injured at an Operational Training Unit, administered by Bomber Command. He was also the first RNZAF airmen to win a Distinguished Flying Medal (Gazetted 20 February 1940). His death was reported in 1998.

Page 23   12/P2271   Add: P/O Parry came from New Zealand and, following his initial training, he joined the Royal Air Force on a short service commission in June 1940.

Page 24   10/K9015   Add: P/O Miller came from New Zealand and had joined the Royal Air Force on a short service commission just prior to the outbreak of the Second World War.

           12/L4943   Insert: "his first" between "for" and "solo".

Page 27   12/L9419   Delete: RNZAF after the pilot's name. Similar to P/O McIntyre (page 17), he had trained in New Zealand and then joined the Royal Air Force, in July 1940, on a short service commission.

Page 27   12/L5283   Add: P/O Paterson, a New Zealander who, in the May, had joined the
                       Royal Air Force on a short service commission, was posted missing
           from operation in May 1942 (see Bomber Command Losses, Volume 3, page 89). At
           the time he was flying with 115 Squadron and risen in rank to flight lieutenant.

Page 28   17/L8682   Add: P/O Rockel had been accepted for a short service commission
                       in May 1940. From New Zealand, he survived the war.

Page 31   13/L4883   Add: His Distinguished Flying Cross had been promulgated in the
                       London Gazette on 9 July 1940.

Page 32   20/L7778   Add: P/O Gilmour was very serious injured and he was admitted to
                       Kingseat Naval Hospital at Dyce. While convalescing he was promoted
           to flying officer, and on being declared fit to resume flying duties, he rejoined
           his unit. Soon afterwards, however, on 6 May 1941, he was posted to 24 Squadron.

Page 35   12/L5432   Add: P/O Topp had trained in New Zealand and was accepted into the
                       Royal Air Force on a short service commission during May 1940. He
           was killed during operations to Hamburg on 16-17 July 1941 (see Bomber Command
           Losses, Volume 2, page 93). Note. It now seems that "Bethridge" was his second
           Christian name, and not the first of a hyphenated surname.

Page 37   17/L4868   Insert: Sgt J M Poole (the injured member of the crew).

Page 53   20/N2885   Add: P/O Fitch subsequently flew with 40 Squadron and died during
                       the night of 2-3 September 1941 (see Bomber Command Losses, Volume 2,
           page 135) when his Wellington came down in the sea off Harwich.

Page 55   20/R1664   Amend: Sgt J F Barron RNZAF
                       Add: Rose to the rank of wing commander and when killed in action
           on his seventy-ninth sortie, 19-20 May 1944, marking the railway yards at le Mans
           in France, he had been richly decorated with a Distinguished Service Order and
           First Bar, a Distinguished Flying Cross and a Distinguished Flying Medal, the
           latter being gained with 15 Squadron and Gazetted on 26 May 1942. At the time
           of his death, aged twenty-three, he had logged 1,264 flying hours. See, also,
           Bomber Command Losses, Volume 5, page 227.

           11/R3178   Amend: F/S Sayer (in the summary).

Page 60   19/K9036   Amend: P/O W B Mackley DFC RNAF
                       Add: P/O Mackley's award was published three days later.

Page 62   19/K9033   Amend: Sgt G Carman RNZAF
                       Add: Not long after this incident, he joined 78 Squadron and
           failed to return from Hüls on 6-7 September 1941 (see Bomber Command Losses,
           Volume 2, page 139).

Page 66   23/X9659   Amend: 13 Aug 1943 to read 13 Aug 1941.

Page 73   25/P4302   Amend: Sgt R G Henderson
                       Add: In a letter, July 2002, Sergeant Henderson, then aged eighty-
           seven, stated that he believes the Hampden's starboard engine caught fire. Para-
           chuting at low-level, the canopy wrapped about him and when found he was deeply
           unconscious. For eleven days he remained in a coma and when, eventually, dis-
           charged from RAF Hospital Rauceby, he was downgraded to ground duties. Service
           at Kinloss heralded a posting to Sierra Leone and prior to his release from the
           service in November 1945, he was a signals instructor at Cranwell.

Page 74   20/Z8809   Amend crew matrix to read:
                       F/S F C N Kiteley   + Lossiemouth Burial Ground
                       Sgt D H Budden RCAF   + Lossiemouth Burial Ground
                       P/O R D Anderson RCAF   + Lossiemouth Burial Ground
                       Sgt W G Chant   + Tottenham and Wood Green Cemetery
                       F/S H J H Kitson DFM   + Rhondda (Treorchy) Cemetery
                       Sgt J D Hogden   + Pelton Cemetery
                       Sgt H S Dunbar   inj This accident happened at 0225, the
           stationary aircraft being identified as 20 OTU's Wellington IC N2824, which was
           damaged beyond repair and, therefore, should be entered ahead of Z8809. F/S Kitson
           had served with 75 Squadron and his award had been Gazetted on 22 October 1940.
           Sgt Dunbar died in a flying accident on 4 August 1942 (see Bomber Command Losses,
           Volume 7, page 142), while continuing his training at Lossiemouth.

Page 75   18/R3216   Delete: T/o Bramcote and insert T/o Bitteswell.
    Add: Sgt Zietkiewicz PAF was rescued by a motor transport driver, S W J Green, whose bravery was subsequently recognised through the award of the George Medal.

    10/P4942   Delete: 15 December 1942 and insert 9-10 December 1942 (Please be advised that the data recorded on page 277 of Volume 3 should be amended for, as Errol Martyne advises, all fifteen passengers and crew lost their lives, somewhere between Cairo and Malta, and their names are recorded on the Alamein Memorial).

Page 79   12/R1037   Amend: Sgt C H Brumby RNZAF
    Add: By the spring of 1943, Sgt Brumby was serving at 5 Operational Training Unit, a Coastal Command training establishment operating from Long Kesh in Northern Ireland with a satellite station at Maghaberry, Co. Antrim. On 23 May 1943, the Beaufort I in which he was flying (DW995) failed to return from a training exercise and his name is now perpetuated on panel 198 of the Runnymede Memorial. As a measure of the severity of his injuries, suffered at Chipping Warden, he was to spend fourteen months undergoing recovery.

Page 80   23/Z8786   Amend: F/L R J Newton RNZAF
    Add: Having attained the rank of wing commander, and command of 75 Squadron, W/C Newton died, with his crew, on 1-2 January 1945, while attacking the railway yards at Vohwinkel (see Bomber Command Losses, Volume 6, page 26). At the time of his death, he had been decorated with the Distinguished Flying Cross, and had been mentioned in despatches.

Page 81   11/T2705   Amend: P/O E C Ball RNZAF
    Add: After completing two tours of bombing operations (flying with 103 Squadron and 75 Squadron), F/L Ball, as he had now become, switched to Fighter Command and joined 488 Squadron at Bradwell Bay in Essex. Late in the evening of 9 October 1943, his Mosquito NF.XII HK204 crashed some six miles north-west of base, killing both members of crew. Remarkably, F/L Ball remained undecorated, despite flying fifty-seven operational sorties and logging in excess of a thousand hours of flying.

Page 84   25/N2783   Amend: Sgt Coe's injuries were far more severe than, perhaps, indicated for as Errol Martyn writes, "he was admitted to Doncaster Infirmary and (later) transferred to the RAF Hospital Rauceby on 19 November. As a result of the accident he had two fingers amputated, a fractured right leg, and his ears and face burnt. He was discharged from hospital in January 1942. On 10 May 1942, he embarked for New Zealand on repatriation for ground duties. However, he embarked for the United Kingdom in October 1943, arriving in the December, and was accepted for flying duties. Commissioned and on his thirtieth sortie, he died, with his skipper S/L Ian George Medwin RNZAF, on 6 April 1945, when their 487 Squadron Mosquito FB.VI SZ990/E crashed shortly after take off from Rosieres-en-Santerre. Both officers were buried on 11 April at the Anzac Cemetery at Villers Bretonneux, theirs being the first interments here since the end of the First World War." For further details, please refer to Errol Martyn's second volume of "For Your Tomorrow", published by Volplane Press in 1999.

Page 85   25/L7248   Delete: L7248 and T/o Finningley for night navigation, crashing at 2245 and replace with: L7428 T/o Bircotes for a night flying test, crashing at 1632.

Page 99   20/T2707   Add: Although unproven, it is possible (as Errol Martyn suggests) that the observer was Sgt (or F/S) D W Cross RNZAF. Posted to 20 Operational Training Unit on 7 January 1942, his biography mentions that while undergoing training, he baled out from an aircraft that had been stricken with engine trouble (the date, however, is not specified). On 7 March 1942, he was posted to the Middle East and joined 148 Squadron. His tour, sadly, was brief and he was killed during operations to Benghazi on 21-22 June 1942, while flying in Wellington IC ES990, captained by W/C D A Kerr DSO. Five of the six-man crew perished and their names are commemorated on the Alamein Memorial.

Page 102   21/R1329   Add: Sgt Hickman went out to the Middle East, where he joined 40 Squadron. On 11-12 August 1942, his Wellington IC HX377/A was shot down during operations to Tobruk. For the next eight days and nights, the crew managed to evade capture, but having walked for at least ninety miles towards the Allied lines, they were picked up and made prisoners of war.

Page 111   15/   Add: P/O Jenner RNZAF had flown with 40 Squadron in 1941. Post war, he became an airline pilot, flying with British Overseas Airways Corporation and, later, with British Airways.

Page 115   25/DV841   Add in the form of a note to the summary: In 2002, I was contacted by Mr. L Henderson who, with others, has carried out a detailed investigation into the loss of this Wellington and its crew. His letter reads, "A Wellington bomber was seen by eyewitnesses from Peases West, flying from the direction of Stanley. It passed over Billy Row, smoke trailing behind it from an engine fire and it gradually lost height as it skimmed over Roddymoor, before finally crashing in a ploughed field near the ponds. A main witness was a farmer's son, who was narrowly missed as the aircraft crashed in an adjacent field. The port wing first hit the ground and the fuselage cleaned out the fence before the aircraft finally came to rest, tilted on its starboard side. The farmer (I presume the father of the witness referred to above) ran to the aircraft, where he saw one airman inside and another lying on the ground nearby. As he attempted to pull the airman from the aircraft, there was an explosion and a fire resulting in bullets exploding all around as people ran towards the aircraft. The landing wheels and the gun turret, still with the gunner inside, were thrown about two hundred yards by the explosion. All the various services eventually arrived but the aircraft was burnt out, due to its difficult position. An hour later, the geodetic construction was still smouldering and there was a strong smell of burning perspex in the air. The army then took over from the home guard until the site was cleared."

Page 119   11/R1065   Amend: W/O K A Dunkley RNZAF

Page 129   12/Z8800   Amend: Sgt J W Keane RNZAF
                      Add: Sgt Keane RNZAF was killed when his 103 Conversion Flight Halifax crashed on 1 August 1942 (see page 17 of this volume for details).

Page 132   22/R1036   Delete (in the summary): Fedirchyk and replace with Fedigan.

Page 133   22/R1465   Add: after "cairn" constructed in 1980 by pupils and staff of Tredegar Comprehensive School.

Page 135   14/X2974   Add: P/O Lyons RAAF was posted to 408 Squadron and was killed in action on 29 August 1942 (see Bomber Command Losses, Volume 3, page 200).

               23/R1414   Delete: "Along with his skipper, who hailed from Manefield, Ohio, he was posted to 425 Squadron and both became casualties during operations to Hamburg on 9 November 1942" and replace with, "Sgt Foltz was posted to 425 Squadron and was lost on operations to Hamburg on 9 November 1942, as was Sgt Burke RCAF (see Bomber Command Losses, Volume 3, page 259)." Prior to the deletion, and in the fourth line of the summary, correct "mine" to read "minor".

Page 138   25/T2707   Amend: T2701

Page 147   10/N1443   Amend: Sgt J R A Hodgson
                      Add: F/S S R Farley
                                P/O F L E Dupre RCAF
                                Sgt D Keenan
                                Sgt R A Weese RCAF
Unusually, this crew did not progress to a No. 4 Group squadron but found themselves flying Wellingtons under the authority of No. 1 Group and 166 Squadron. All were killed during the course of operations to Bochum on 29-30 March 1943 (see Bomber Command Losses, Volume 4, page 85).

Page 148   24/BD380   Insert: P/O Taffs RCAF (after P/O Graham)

Page 153   16/R1346   Add: Sgt Leng, too, died alongside his skipper who, had been involved in a crash, on 28 February-1 March 1943, during operations to St. Nazaire.

Page 158   12/BJ728   Add: Sgt Ferguson was born in New Zealand and had enlisted in his native country with the intention of flying with the Fleet Air Arm but in March 1941, having departed New Zealand the previous August, he joined the Royal Air Force (Volunteer Reserve) and trained as an observer.

Page 164   10/Z6485   Amend: P/O J G Duffill RNZAF
                      Amend: Sgt T R D Shirley
                      Add: P/O Duffill RNZAF, Sgt Bakewell and Sgt Shirley proceeded to
                      101 Squadron and were posted missing in action on 17-18 January 1943
            whilst operating to Berlin (see Bomber Command Losses, Volume 4, page 22).

Page 169   22/DV789   Add: Sgt A T E McCormack RCAF   inj
                            Sgt D F Heybourne   inj
                            Sgt K A Reed RCAF   inj
                      Insert between: "in a field" and "near Salford Priors" "at Abbots
                      Salford".

Page 173   13/T1991   Amend: Sgt J F Hanna RNZAF (also in summary)
                      Note: Errol Martyn advises that it was coincidence that Hanna's
                      service number was 412682 and that Hannah's was 412683.

Page 178   12/BK250   Amend: F/O M L Gaudin

Page 179   14/DV929   Amend: P/O W F Rielly (amend his name in the summary, as well).

Page 182   10/Z9437   Amend: P/O F L Perrers RNZAF
                      Amend: "on the beach" to read "off the beach"

Page 183   26/X9622   Delete: Sgt Lennox +

Page 187   11/R1174   Amend: Sgt F W R Cumpsty RNZAF

Page 188   16/Z1665   Amend: P/O D F S Clark

Page 190   11/X9953   Amend: "Of the four survivors, three were destined to lose their
                              lives; Sgt Hoey, who was posted to 75 Squadron was killed on 23-24
                      September 1943, while four nights later his colleague, Sgt Sharp RNZAF, serving
                      with 90 Squadron, died in a crash near Cambridge. Sgt Tvrdeich RNZAF lost his
                      life while flying with 15 Squadron (see Bomber Command Losses, Volumes 4 and 5,
                      pages 330, 336 and 128 respectively)."

Page 191   14/DV449   Delete: Cottesmore and insert Saltby.
                      Add: This accident was witnessed by F/L S (Steve) Stevens DFC AFC
                      who, in 1943, served with distinction with 57 Squadron.

Page 192   81/LA766   Add: WO1 Roberts RCAF had recently served in the Middle East with
                            70 Squadron and had been involved in a non-fatal accident on 21 July
                      1942, when Wellington IC DV504 (repaired) crashed on take off from Abu Sueir.

Page 194   11/X9616   Add: Flying with Sgt Gavin was Sgt Robinson RNZAF and his fellow
                      countryman, Sgt Cooksley. Both survived, albeit as prisoners of war.

Page 195   29/BJ779   Amend: Sgt J Amos
                      Amend: "Verey" (in summary) to read "Very"

Page 199   26/DV725   Add as a footnote: In a letter to the author, in 2002, Mr B J Tooke
                      added that the Wellington finished up near the gate keeper's cottage
                      at the local railway level-crossing, the cottage being lived in by his parents.
                      Either Sgt Belcher, or a member of the crew, was found by by Mr Tooke's elder
                      brother (who worked on the railway) and taken into the cottage and cared for by
                      their mother, until the arrival of the authorities.

           11/N2761   Delete the last sentence in the summary and replace it with, "Sgt
                      Noble RNZAF went to the Middle East, where he joined 37 Squadron.
                      On 19 September 1943, his aircraft was shot down and, subsequently, he became a
                      prisoner of war. He was on his twenty-fifth operational sortie."

Page 202   24/BD285   Amend: F/S M A Peterson RNZAF

Page 203   10/Z6812   Errol Martyn writes, "Hatchard's biography offers a different
                      version of events. From his fourth patrol, after spending twenty-
                      nine hours in a rubber dinghy, he was picked up by the steamship "Northern Foam"
                      and returned safely to England." Although Errol (and I concur) thinks it un-
                      likely, it is possible that Sgt Hatchard became separated from his crew and,
                      thus, they were picked up within the four hours indicated in the summary.

Page 212   81/EB346   Add: F/O Page had served in the Middle East with 104 Squadron.
At Kabrit, on 23 October 1942, he had the misfortune to write off
Wellington II W5359.

Page 214   15/DV936   Add: Twenty year old F/S Boyes RAAF of Hobart, Tasmania, had
married Joan Boyes and was the father of Lynne. In view of his
age, it is possible he never saw his baby daughter.

Page 217   24/BD219   Add: Sgt L G Davies RCAF (one of the two injured airmen).

Page 218   19/BD381   Delete: West Lothian and replace with Lanarkshire, followed by,
"north of the village of Shotts and west of Harthill. It is bel-
ieved the pilot was trying to ditch in, or forced-land alongside, the Roughrigg
Reservoir.

           20/DV949   Insert: JM-K
                      Add to crew and text:
           Sgt E H Burgess   with a crew of seven for a combined exercise
           Sgt T McKenzie   in bombing and night navigation. Nearly two
           Sgt R Harrington   hours into the detail, and while flying at
           Sgt A Woodward RCAF 8,000 feet, the starboard engine began to give
                               so much trouble that Sgt Watson, fearing for
the safety of his crew, ordered everyone to bale out, height having been lost to
around 2,000 feet. He then forced-landed the ailing bomber on the beach, close
to an unlit airfield on the island of Benbecula. Meanwhile, the navigator, air
bomber and wireless operator had landed safely on North Uist, while from South
Uist came the good news that the tail gunner, Sgt Woodward and two other members
of the crew were safe. Sgt Harrington informs me that those who have been identified went, eventually, to 78 Squadron and, subsequently, gained Distinguished
Flying Crosses (Gazetted on various dates in 1944).

Page 219   22/HE218   Add: WO1 Kerby RCAF had served in the Middle East with 108 Squadron
                      where, on 16 November 1942, his Wellington IC HX380 had crashed
during the course of bombing operations. His co-pilot, P/O H A B Baker, later
returned to the United Kingdom and was posted missing in action on 30 July 1944,
while serving with 97 Squadron (see Bomber Command Losses, Volume 5, page 365).

Page 220   21/T2562   Amend: F/S K B Rogers RNZAF

Page 223   23/X3704   Delete: Star Hotel and replace with the Brandy Cask public house,
                      Bridge Street. Remove the statement in parenthesis and replace
with, (a propeller blade from a Wellington is displayed at the rear of the Star
Hotel, next door to the Brandy Cask). Mrs Berry was the wife of the licensee of
the Brandy Cask. I am indebted to Brian Keward, author of "Angry Skies across
the Vale" for the corrections pertaining to the summary, and for various amendments reported in respect of 23 and 24 Operational Training Units.

Page 224   20/R1701   Delete: R1701 and replace with R1707.

           24/Z6639   Delete: 200 yards and replace with 250 yards west from, while in
                      the footnote, delete "all five airmen clear" and replace with "Sgt
Elkins clear". Brian Keward points out that the Observer Post was roughly 250
yards east of Broadway Tower which, at the time, was home to Mr Ernest Hollington,
his wife and children. The area is now a country park. In 2000, Brian purchased,
and presented, a plaque to the memory of the crew.

Page 230   23/BK408   Delete: Sgt R A Harris and replace with Sgt R A Hanks.

Page 237   24/N1390   Amend: P/O K O Law DFM RNZAF
                      Add: P/O Law RNZAF had served with 150 Squadron; details of his
                      award had been Gazetted on 11 August 1942.

Page 239   26/X3790   Add: After "T/o Little Horwood" (crew No. 7), while at the end of
                      the summary, on page 240, add, "I am indebted to Jeff Harrison, the
aircraft´s sole survivor, for much of the information here summarised."

Page 242   11/R1337   Amend the last sentence to read, "F/S Harries RNZAF was born in
                      Blackpool but emigrated to Australia at an early age. He arrived
in New Zealand at sometime in 1938, probably from East Perth in Western Australia."

Page 243   82/BK399   Errol Martyn has not been able to trace any airman by the name of "F/O O L Macfarlane RNZAF" serving with the Royal New Zealand Air Force.

Page 245   22/HE556   Delete: "at Honeybourne airfield" and replace with "near Honey-bourne railway station".

Page 246   30/X3564   Add: WO2 Chester RCAF had been obliged to forced-land Wellington IC HX775 on Lasipalmas Island while staging from Portreath to Gibraltar on 23 October 1942. His crew, on that occasion, were:
Sgt M N Walker RNZAF
Sgt H E M Howell RAAF
Sgt J H Wilkinson RAAF
Sgt D D Gardner RAAF
All had been attached to 1446 (Ferry Training) Flight and all under-went a brief spell of internment, before being returned to the United Kingdom. Their reports are held at the National Archives Public Record Office under WO208 3312, file references (-)1120 (Sgt Chester RCAF) to (-)1124 inclusive.

Page 248   14/DV479   Delete: Welford in Berkshire and replace with Home Farm, Sulby, two miles NNE from Welford, Leicestershire. I am, indeed, most grateful to John H Collier, an acknowledged expert on aviation incidents that occurred in the county of Leicestershire.

Page 249   11/DV608   Amend: Sgt A L Dickison RNZAF (also in summary)

Page 259   24/AD675   Amend: Sgt F W Forster RCAF pow 4B 269844 (this data should be inserted, also, on page 365).

Page 260   27/X3637   Add: P/O McGiggan RAAF had served with 40 Squadron, in the Middle East, and, on 5-6 October 1942, had been involved in a minor flying accident whilst piloting Wellington IC BB516 (repaired).

Page 263   14/DV435   Errol Martyn has traced the following information, in respect of F/O Clark RNZAF, "On the night of 24 November 1943, F/O Clark was a member of crew of a Wellington bomber aircraft which was involved in a flying accident at Shuttlegate, Derbyshire. Information received from the Air Ministry stated that F/O Clark baled out, and as a result of this action received a leg injury. He was admitted to station sick quarters at Finningley, Yorkshire. From the time he became a casualty, up to the time of his return to No. 14 OTU on 2 May 1944, he was admitted to various hospitals for the treatment of his injury. These included the Doncaster Royal Infirmary, and the RAF Hospital, Ely, Cambridgeshire. During this period he was granted a considerable amount of sick leave. In July 1944, F/O Clark proceeded from No. 14 OTU to Headquarters No. 51 Base." He was subsequently killed on air operations, while serving with 207 Squadron, to Duren in November 1944 (see Bomber Command Losses, Volume 5, page 486).

Page 268   17/X3344   Errol Martyn informs me that F/O Gilmore RNZAF and S/L Gilmour RNZAF were not in anyway related, despite the closeness of their service numbers and my implied remarks in the note that accompanies the summary.

Page 270   11/Z8793   Amend: Sgt C W Estcourt RNZAF

Page 273   84/HZ474   Add: Sgt J D Kennedy + Streatham Park Cemetery, Mitcham.
Delete: Nottingham and replace with Northampton.

Page 277   24/N1375   Add: Sgt Tate

           24/Z6673   Add: F/O Spearin

Page 280   11/HE229   Amend: F/L A B Smith DFC RNZAF
Add: F/L Smith had previously served in the Middle East, flying Wellingtons with 40 Squadron. On 23-24 February 1942, whilst piloting IC BB478/C he had been obliged to ditch, spending the next eighty-two hours in a dinghy.

Page 281   11/HF480   Amend the last sentence to read, "F/S Jamieson RNZAF rest....".

Page 285   11/LN482   Either the time of take off has been incorrectly entered, or the timing of the crash has been wrongly given. To be investigated.

Page 287   17/HZ412   Amend (in note): F/O John Hawarth Heath RNZAF

Page 288   28/Z1621   Amend: F/O M D Muggeridge DFM RNZAF
                                 F/S P J McVerry RNZAF
                         Add: F/O Muggeridge RNZAF had won his DFM while flying in the
                         Middle East with 104 Squadron, the details appearing in the London
Gazette on 25 May 1943. F/S (later F/O) McVerry RNZAF became a Pathfinder pilot
and flew with 582 Squadron (see Bomber Command Losses, Volume 6, page 52).

Page 295   30/DF641   Delete: "about 5 miles SW of Ingham" and replace with "near
                         Thorpe in the Fallows, 6 miles NW of Lincoln".

Page 299   16/BK258   Amend: F/S J H C Molloy RNZAF

Page 317   24/LP499   Add: P/O Kennedy RCAF had been involved in a distressing incident,
                         whilst flying Wellington X NC650 on 16 September 1944, when, after
losing control off St. Catherine´s Point on the Isle of Wight, three members of
the crew baled out. Two were rescued from the water, but Sgt W R Mattless RCAF
was drowned. Subsequently, P/O Kennedy, and the two remaining members of crew,
landed safely at Odiham.

Page 321   19/AD625   Delete: "the harbour at Seaham" and replace with "a triangular
                         field on Slingy Hill Farm, Murton, two and-a-half miles WSW of
                         Seaham".

Page 323   12/HE806   Amend: F/L L T V Dudding RNZAF

Page 327   11/LN845   Amend: F/S C R Wagstaff RNZAF

Page 330   11/HE740   Amend in summary: North Marston

Page 335   20/LN453   Add: F/O Last, who had flown in the Middle East with 40 Squadron,
                         had baled out from Wellington IC HE107/C on 2-3 January 1943.

Page 342   27/PG259   Amend: F/O D R Britton DFC RNZAF
                                 W/O D M Fimmell

           20/NC594   Add: F/O Rickard had served with 40 Squadron in the Middle East.
                         On 9-10 March 1943, he had crashed while piloting Wellington IC
                         AD651/D.

Page 363   Delete Sgt D Dunkley and all detail.

Page 365   Insert (where appropriate) under Royal New Zealand Air Force
                         W/O K A Dunkley 30-31 May 1942 11 OTU R1065 Köln 357 406

Page 367   P/O F L Perrers was RNZAF and, therefore, his name, and details,
                         should be removed from the Royal Air Force section and reinserted
                         beneath a new sub-heading, Royal New Zealand Air Force.

It is inevitable that some aircraft, relevant to a particular year or series, are overlooked, either through misreporting of their units, or through an oversight on my part,
while trawling through the serial registers.   Thus, the following aircraft have been
identified as requiring further inspection:

7 Aug 1942   15 OTU   Wellington IC   DV445
7 Mar 1943   16 OTU   Defiant I   AA325
19 Feb 1944   14 OTU   Tomahawk IIA   AH929
11 Mar 1944   26 OTU   Tomahawk I   AH855
4 Jun 1944   26 OTU   Tomahawk IIB   AK116
5 Jul 1944   26 OTU   Tomahawk IIA   AH918
1 Feb 1945   16 OTU   Oxford II   AB688
17 Jun 1945   16 OTU   Mosquito XX   KB272

Addendum addition:

Page 200   19/Z9156   Amend: Sgt S Bellis   + Bebington Cemetery

Conclusion

As is not so uncommon, with the structure of the book laid out and printed, additional information comes my way which, from a close perusal, indicates that the data is worth committing to print. Thus, from Errol Martyn in New Zealand came two weighty packages of material, garnered from various official sources, both in the United Kingdom, and from files held in New Zealand, from which a selection will now be reported. Some has a bearing on the present volume, while the rest is appropriate to Volume 7. First, however, a summary pertaining to a Tiger Moth which has been reported as belonging to Abingdon Station Flight but which, I strongly believe, came to grief while on charge with No. 10 Operational Training Unit:

13 Jun	10 OTU	Tiger Moth II N6673	Training
1941	P/O F H J Ashley	T/o Abingdon to practice aerobatics. At around	

1145, P/O Ashley failed to recover from a loop and hit the top of a tree in Nuneham Park, a mile or so SW from Nuneham Courtney in Oxfordshire and a little over 2 miles E of the Berkshire town of Abingdon.

Next, a precis of the evidence that came to light during the enquiry into the fatal flying accident involving two Wellingtons from No. 25 Operational Training Unit, and summarised in Volume 7, on page 138. As there are no amendments, or additions, to the crews, I will dispense with this detail and merely copy the relevant observations (I am reporting the times, as quoted, and leave it to you, the reader, to draw your own conclusions):

"Short account of accident. The two aircraft collided in midair and crashed approximately one mile northwest of Finningley Aerodrome at 0335 hours on 24 July 1942. Wellington DV476 (P/O Beck) had taken off at 0320 hours for the purpose of carrying out high-level night practice bombing at Mission (sic) bombing range. This flight was to be of approximately two hours duration. Wellington T2701 (W/O Smith) had taken off at 0330 hours for the purpose of carrying out night circuits and landings. After having been airborne for about five minutes, Wellington T2701 requested, and was given permission to land, but the aircraft overshot and the pilot decided to go round again. He then called again and was given "pancake", which he acknowledged. It was almost immediately after this that the collision occurred. It was later found that Wellington DV476 had not dropped any of its bombs. This aircraft had only been airborne for thirty minutes at the time of the accident and was not due back for at least another hour. Weather conditions throughout were fairly good. There was no low cloud but 10/10ths medium cloud at about 8,000 feet. Visibility was four miles. The evidence is that the accident occurred at a height of between 800 and 1,000 feet; the two aircraft having converged until they collided."

"Finding of the Investigating Officer. Due to accidental collision, although the evidence shows that the navigation lights of both aircraft were lit, and the visibility good. The moon had set. The collision occurred approximately half-a-mile to the west of Finningley Aerodrome in circumstances which indicate that Wellington DV467 was returning from an abortive high-level bombing practice, when it collided with T2701, the pilot of which was in the act of making a circuit of the aerodrome, following an overshoot when attempting a night landing. There is no evidence to prove why DV467 passed the aerodrome at so low an altitude after only thirty minutes flying, when it had been scheduled for a two hour flight. As no bombs had been released, it may be assumed that the captain returned through some fault. Alterations had to be made in the night flying programme because of interference by enemy aircraft and change of aircraft serviceability, but there was no enemy interference at the time of the accident. There is no evidence of any omissions or delinquencies on the part of the personnel responsible for night flying organization."

The extract that follows on the next page has been obtained from the National Archives Public Record Office Kew, the original being held in WO208 3312 (-)1046 and 1047. The relevant summary is on page 182 of Volume 7.

M.I.9/S/P.G.(-) 1046
         (-) 1047

The information contained in this report is to be treated as
MOST SECRET

———

STATEMENT BY

1345587 Sgt CLAPPERTON, John, R.A.F.V.R. 10 O.T.U. No. 91 Group, Bomber Command

1384274 Sgt WALPOLE, William, R.A.F.V.R. Stn. H.Q. St.Eval. (Special Duties)
                                         Coastal Command

Left: GIBRALTAR 20 Jan 43
Arrived: GOUROCK 26 Jan 43

	Sgt CLAPPERTON	Sgt WALPOLE
R.A.F. Service:	1 year 6 months	1 year 10 months
Peacetime Profession:	Police Officer	Journalist
Private Address:	1 George Street	80 Cecil Avenue
	DUNBLANE	ENFIELD
	Perthshire	Middlesex
Post in aircraft:	Navigator	Second Pilot

1942	We were members of the crew of a WHITLEY aircraft which took off from ST. EVAL at 1000 hours on 10 Dec 42, (11 Dec 1942, as summarised, is correct) on an anti-submarine patrol in the BAY OF BISCAY. The other members of the crew, who are interned at ALHAMA DE ARAGON, were:

P/O PERRERS R.N.Z.A.F., Captain and Pilot;
Sgt WHITE, Bomb-aimer;
Sgt MUTUM (sic), Wireless operator; and
Sgt CROWE, Rear-gunner.

10 Dec Forced-landing at CAPE PENAS, NORTH SPAIN AVILES 13 Dec VALLADOLID 14 Dec ALHAMA DE ARAGON 1943 Jan MADRID GIBRALTAR	Owing to engine trouble, we made a forced-landing in the sea at 1520 hours, off CAPE PENAS, in North SPAIN. No one was injured. We destroyed secret equipment and maps, but not the aircraft, though we were later told that it blew up next day. We waded ashore. Civil guards took us to the Customs House, and we were later taken to AVILES. Here we stayed in a hotel, where we were met by two SPANISH Air Force officers. On 13 Dec we were taken by bus to VALLADOLID, where we stayed in a hotel. Here WALPOLE and some others, (but not CLAPPERTON) were interrogated by a Spanish Air Force officer. Questions asked were type of aircraft, duties, bomb load, crew carried, and why were we over SPAIN. We answered ambiguously. On 14 Dec 42 we were taken to a hotel at ALHAMA DE ARAGON. We stayed here till 3 Jan 43, when we went to MADRID. We stayed with British people here for about eight days, when we went to GIBRALTAR.

Note. The remaining members of crew returned a little while later and, as will be noted from Appendix 5, in Volume 7, their reports are filed under WO208 3312 (-) 1095 to 1098 inclusive, the last being an account given by Sgt Newton, reported above as "MUTUM".

Although sent by Errol Martyn, the following notes have their origins in material, secured from Kew, by Pel Temple and forwarded, in the first instance, to David Gunby in New Zealand for examination in respect of David's Middle East bomber losses project. To place this material in context, it will be necessary to refer to pages 223 and 224, concentrating on those summaries pertaining to No. 3 Group Training Flight and, in particular, the summary in respect of Wellington IC T2873. According to the casualty signal, sent from Stradishall to Air Ministry and various addressees, including Headquarters Bomber Command, the aircraft belonged to 214 Squadron Middle East Flight, though an extract taken from another document refers to the Wellington as belonging to the "Reserve Squadron", which, later, became No. 3 Group Training Flight. This notwithstanding, the text of the message is most interesting in that the crew, and its two passengers, are identified and, thus, a revised summary follows.

21-22 Nov	3 GTrgFlt	Wellington IC	T2873		Ferry
1940	S/L N P Samuels DFC		pow	T/o 2331 Stradishall and set course for Malta.	
	F/L A J Payn		pow	At 0710 Greenwich Mean Time, this aircraft was	
	P/O J C Watson		pow	heard by Butser Long Range Direction Finding	
	W/O C W Evans		pow	to be calling Malta, but it did not land there.	
	Sgt W Wynn		pow	Air Marshal Boyd had been appointed to the post	
	AM O T Boyd CB OBE MC AFC		pow	of Deputy Air Officer Commanding-in-Chief at	
	F/L Leeming		pow	air headquarters Middle East and, it is assumed,	

his fellow passenger, F/L Leeming, was also expecting to take up an appointment in the Mediterranean theatre. Three of the seven named have been identified in the Allied Air Forces prisoner of war file, their details being as follows: S/L Samuels at Stalag Luft 1, Barth Vogelsang with the number 2325; F/L Payn (on the casualty signal he is reported as "Payne") is listed, but without any supporting information; W/O Evans at 7A, Moosburg (Isar) with the number 173.

Note. Oliver Clutton-Brock confirms that the number allocated to S/L Samuels does not fall into any known block for numbers issued in 1940, and, therefore, it appears most likely that he was first held at a camp, or camps, in Italy and only arrived in Germany post September 1943. Air Marshal Boyd, it is assumed, fell victim to ill health and he must have been repatriated prior to his death on 5 August 1944. Aged 54, he is buried in Paddington (Mill Hill) Cemetery, Hendon, Middlesex. A trawl of various web sites on the internet reveals:

Clan Boyd Society, International: Indian Army Quarterly List for 1 January 1912: Boyd, Owen Tudor, date of birth 30 August 1889, commissioned 20 January 1909, appointed Lieutenant 20 April 1911, unit 5th Cavalry.

Supplements to the London Gazette:

28 July 1916:   Lieutenants to be temporary Captains, dated 1 September 1915: Owen Tudor Boyd, 5th Cavalry.

19 August 1916:   His Majesty the KING has been graciously pleased to confer the Military Cross on the undermentioned Officers and Warrant Officers, in recognition of their gallantry and devotion to duty in the field:- Lt Owen Tudor Boyd, Ind. Army, and R.F.C. For conspicuous gallantry when on a bombing raid in unfavourable weather. He descended to less than 1,000 feet and bombed a train, which he afterwards attacked with his machine gun though heavily attacked by rifle and machine gun fire.

8 June 1939:   The KING has been graciously pleased, on the occasion of the Celebration of His Majesty's Birthday, to give orders for the following promotion in, and appointments to, the Most Honourable Order of the Bath:- To be Ordinary Members of the Military Division of the Third-Class, or Companions, of the said Most Honourable Order:- Air Vice-Marshal Owen Tudor Boyd, O,B.E., M.C., A.F.C., Royal Air Force.

19 November 1940: Air Vice-Marshal Owen Tudor Boyd C.B., O.B.E., M.C., A.F.C., is granted the acting rank of Air Marshal. 8th Nov. 1940.

In respect of this summary, it will be necessary to amend data in the relevant preceding appendices.

Included with the papers dealing with the loss of Wellington IC T2873, were a number of documents that originated from Headquarters No. 3 Group, many of which concerned the movement of Wellingtons to the Middle East. Cross-checking the serials quoted in these papers with information published in the Air-Britain (Historians) serial registers, it seems most likely that the following ought to be included under the general mantle of No. 3 Group Training Flight:

11 Dec 1940	3 GTrgFlt F/O Collins	Wellington IC	R1246	Ferry T/o 0013 Stradishall and set course for Malta. Failed to arrive.

	3 GTrgFlt F/O Brain	Wellington IC	R1250	Ferry T/o 0027 Stradishall and set course for Malta. Failed to arrive. This Wellington, and the one

above are shown in the registers as; "Middle East; missing".

4 Feb 1941	3 GTrgFlt P/O A L T Todd	Wellington IC	R1385 +	Ferry T/o 2325-2340 Stradishall and set course for Malta. Failed to arrive. P/O Todd is commem-

orated on the Runnymede Memorial, panel 35, with his presumed date of death given as 4 February 1941. The document from which his name, and the identity of his aircraft, has been taken is annotated; "14/2/41?", while the serial register for R1385 shows; "Middle East; struck off charge 13.2.41".

14-15 Mar 1941	3 GTrgFlt Sgt R H Alington RNZAF	Wellington IC	W5644 +	Ferry T/o 2022-2039 Stradishall and set course for Gibraltar. From the first volume of Errol

Martyn´s "For Your Tomorrow", it seems that the crew reached their first des- tination safely, continuing their flight from Gibraltar in the company of three other Wellingtons and an escorting Maryland. Fifteen minutes prior to their estimated time of arrival at Malta, a wireless message was intercepted stating that the aircraft was under attack from enemy fighters. Their position, at the time, was estimated to be some seventy miles short of the island. All seven members of crew are commemorated on the Runnymede Memorial. Referring first to the serial register, this shows; "Middle East; missing", while the document prepared by No. 3 Group identifies the remaining Wellingtons as; "W5622 and W5646", captained by Sgt Goodall and Sgt Anderson respectively. This same paper also quotes in respect of W5644; "The last signal received from this machine was "Am being attacked", which was received at 0545 Greenwich Mean Time from the direction of 300 degrees."

18 Mar 1941	3 GTrgFlt Sgt Mackay	Wellington IC	W5630	Ferry T/o 1948 Stradishall to proceed to Benina. Failed to arrive. According to the serial

register, this Wellington was assigned to the Middle East and is shown as missing with effect from 26 March 1941.

Note. In the light of the evidence presented above, it seems most likely that these Wellingtons were on charge of the Training Flight and, therefore, the necessary adjustments should be made to the appropriate appendix.

BRITISH SECRET PROJECTS – JET FIGHTERS SINCE 1950

Tony Buttler

BRITISH SECRET PROJECTS JET BOMBERS SINCE 1949

Tony Buttler

We hope you enjoyed this book . . .

Midland Publishing titles are edited and designed by an experienced and enthusiastic team of specialists.

Further titles are in preparation and we always welcome ideas from authors or readers for books they would like to see published.

In addition, our associate company, Midland Counties Publications, offers an exceptionally wide range of aviation, military, naval and transport books and videos for sale by mail-order around the world.

For a copy of the appropriate catalogue, or to order further copies of this book, and any of the titles mentioned on this or the following page, please write, telephone, fax or e-mail to:

Midland Counties Publications
4 Watling Drive,
Hinckley, Leics,
LE10 3EY,
England

Tel: (+44) 01455 254 450
Fax: (+44) 01455 233 737
e-mail: midlandbooks@compuserve.com
www.midlandcountiessuperstore.com

A huge number of fighter projects have been drawn by British companies over the last 50 years, in particular prior to the 1957 White Paper, but with few turned into hardware, little has been published about these fascinating 'might-have-beens'. One reason was that all military brochures remained classified once a competition winner had been chosen. This work makes extensive use of previously unpublished primary source material, much recently declassified. It gives an insight into a secret world where the public had little idea of what was going on, while at the same time presenting a coherent nationwide picture of fighter development and evolution. Particular emphasis is placed on tender design competitions and some of the events which led to certain aircraft either being cancelled or produced. Some of the many and varied types included are the Hawker P.1103/P.1136/P.1121 series, and the Fairey 'Delta III' (shown in the Keith Woodcock cover painting). The book includes many illustrations plus specially commissioned renditions of 'might-have-been' types in contemporary markings.

Hbk, 282 x 213 mm, 176 pages
130 b/w photos; 140 three-views,
and an 8-page colour section
1 85780 095 8 **£24.95**

This long-awaited title forms a natural successor to the author's successful volume on fighters. The design and development of the British bomber since World War Two is covered in similar depth and again the emphasis is placed on the tender design competitions between projects from different companies. Extensive reference has been made to recently declassified archives in national and industry collections which allows many little-known projects to be brought together within a full narrative of bomber development. The design backgrounds to the V-Bomber programme, Canberra, Buccaneer, Avro 730, TSR.2, Harrier, Jaguar and Tornado are revealed in more detail than has probably ever been published before, but attention is also given to anti-submarine types and stillborn programmes such as the RAF's first requirement for a low-level bomber and the AFVG. Includes many previously unpublished illustrations plus specially commissioned renditions of 'might-have-been' types in contemporary markings. Keith Woodcock's cover painting shows how the Avro 698 might have looked in service had it not become the Vulcan.

Hbk, 282 x 213 mm, 224 pages
160 b/w photos; many three-views,
and 9 pages of colour
1 85780 130 X **£24.99**

RAF COASTAL COMMAND LOSSES Volume 1
Aircraft and Crew Losses 1939-1941

Ross McNeill

RAF FIGHTER COMMAND LOSSES OF THE SECOND WORLD WAR

Norman Franks

ROYAL AIR FORCE BOMBER COMMAND LOSSES of the SECOND WORLD WAR

W R Chorley

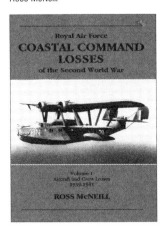

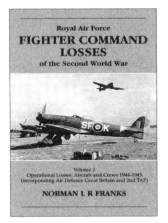

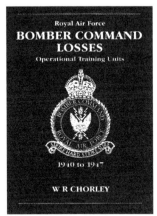

This first in a new companion series to the acclaimed *Fighter Command* and *Bomber Command Losses* series details the aircraft and crew losses suffered by the Royal Air Force coastal squadrons operating from United Kingdom bases under the control of Coastal Command as either full units or as detachments from other RAF commands.

Each chapter is introduced by a brief description of the coastal campaign for the period under review. As with the companion series this book records Coastal Command's losses on a day-by-day basis, listing the units, the crews, aircraft types and service serial numbers, the unit code letters, and the circumstances behind each loss, where known. Appendices include summaries of losses by type, group and squadron, as well as details of unit bases, PoWs, escapers, evaders, and internees.

This first volume covers the period from the formation of Coastal Command on 13th July 1936 to the end of 1941 by which time its constituent units had lost 1,006 aircraft and suffered 2,026 fatal casualties.

Softback
234 x 156 mm, 208 pages
32 b/w photographs
1 85780 128 8   **£16.99**

Following the Battle of France and the retreat through Dunkirk, Britain stood alone awaiting the inevitable onslaught from Germany. At the forefront of the UK's defence was Fighter Command and it was their Hurricanes, Spitfires, Blenheims and Defiants that became the world-famed 'Few' that managed to repulse the Luftwaffe in 'The Battle of Britain' during the summer of 1940.

Germany's failure to overcome the RAF and lthe decision to attack Russia, allowed Britain to consolidate, rebuild, go on the offensive, and after D-day, battle across Europe to the bitter end..

Between 1939-45 Fighter Command, ADGB and 2nd TAF lost over 5,000 aircrew. This work examines on a day-to-day basis the sacrifices made by these men during the desperate years of the war. The reasons and circumstances for the losses are given as crucial campaigns are enacted.

Available in 234 x 156mm sbk format:

Volume 1: 1939-41
Details 1,000 aircraft losses; 168pp
40 b/w pics 1 85780 055 9   **£12.95**

Volume 2: 1942-43
Details 1,800+ aircraft losses; 156pp
53 b/w pics 1 85780 075 3   **£12.95**

Volume 3: 1944-45
Details c.2,450 acft losses; 200pp
83 b/w pics 1 85780 093 1   **£14.95**

This highly acclaimed series identifies, on a day-by-day basis, the individual aircraft, crews and circumstances of each of the 10,000+ aircraft lost in the European Theatre of operations during the Second World War.

Appendices include loss totals by squadron and aircraft type each year; Group loss totals; Squadron bases, bomber OTU losses by unit and type, PoWs, escapers and evaders etc.

Available in 234 x 156mm sbk format:

Volume 2: 1941
Details 1,515 aircraft losses; 224pp
0 904597 87 3   **£12.95**

Volume 3: 1942
Details 2,035 aircraft losses; 318pp
0 904597 89 X   **£15.95**

Volume 7: Operational Training Units 1940-1947
Details 2,400 aircraft losses; 384pp
1 85780 132 6   **£18.99**

Please note that volumes 1, 4, 5 and 6 are currently out of print.